Handbook of Motivation and Cognition

HANDBOOK OF
MOTIVATION AND COGNITION
Foundations of Social Behavior

Edited by

Richard M. Sorrentino
University of Western Ontario

E. Tory Higgins
New York University

THE GUILFORD PRESS
New York • London

Library of Congress Cataloging in Publication Data

Sorrentino, Richard M., 1943–
    Handbook of motivation and cognition; Foundations of social behavior.

    Includes bibliographies and index.
    1. Motivation (Psychology) 2. Cognition.
I. Higgins, E. Tory (Edward Tory), 1946–
II. Title.
BF503.S66   1986   153.8   85-24916
ISBN 0-89862-667-6

Contributors

Steven J. Breckler, Department of Psychology, Johns Hopkins University, Baltimore, Maryland

Nancy Cantor, Institute for Social Research, University of Michigan, Ann Arbor, Michigan

Michael Conway, Department of Psychology, University of Waterloo, Waterloo, Ontario

Russell H. Fazio, Department of Psychology, Indiana University, Bloomington, Indiana

Susan T. Fiske, Department of Psychology, Carnegie-Mellon University, Pittsburgh, Pennsylvania

Anthony G. Greenwald, Department of Psychology, Ohio State University, Columbus, Ohio

E. Tory Higgins, Department of Psychology, New York University, New York, New York

Martin L. Hoffman, Department of Psychology, New York University, New York, New York

Ruth Klein, Department of Psychology, New York University, New York, New York

Julius Kuhl, Max Planck Institute for Psychological Research, Munich, Federal Republic of Germany

Dean B. McFarlin, Department of Psychology, State University of New York at Buffalo, Buffalo, New York

Hazel Markus, Institute for Social Research, University of Michigan, Ann Arbor, Michigan

Paula Niedenthal, Institute for Social Research, University of Michigan, Ann Arbor, Michigan

Paula Nurius, Institute for Social Research, University of Michigan, Ann Arbor, Michigan

Mark A. Pavelchak, Department of Psychology, University of Pittsburgh, Pittsburgh, Pennsylvania

Joel O. Raynor, Department of Psychology, State University of New York at Buffalo, Buffalo, New York

Michael Ross, Department of Psychology, University of Waterloo, Waterloo, Ontario

Judith-Ann C. Short, St. Thomas Psychiatric Hospital, London, Ontario

Richard M. Sorrentino, Department of Psychology, University of Western Ontario, London, Ontario

Thomas K. Srull, Department of Psychology, University of Illinois at Urbana-Champaign, Champaign, Illinois

Timothy Strauman, Department of Psychology, New York University, New York, New York

Abraham Tesser, Institute for Behavioral Research, University of Georgia, Athens, Georgia

Yaacov Trope, Department of Psychology, Hebrew University, Jerusalem, Israel

Robin R. Vallacher, Department of Psychology, Florida Atlantic University, Boca Raton, Florida

Daniel M. Wegner, Department of Psychology, Trinity University, San Antonio, Texas

Bernard Weiner, Department of Psychology, University of California at Los Angeles, Los Angeles, California

Robert A. Wicklund, Department of Psychology, Universität Bielefeld, Bielefeld, Federal Republic of Germany

Henri Zukier, Department of Psychology, New School for Social Research, New York, New York

Preface

The jacket of this book is based on a Mobius strip. If you trace the figure with a stylus or finger, you will note an interesting phenomenon—although there appear to be two sides to the figure, there is no point at which one side ends and the other begins. You simply return to the place you began without ever actually crossing over from one side to the other. We have chosen this figure to represent the interface between *motivation* and *cognition* (see Chapter 1). The red side represents "hot" motivational processes, the blue side represents "cold" cognitions. There is no point at which motivation ends and cognition begins. The two are synergistic. This synergism is what we call the Warm Look.

This book includes a number of articles representing the main body of evidence supporting a synergistic approach to the study of motivation and cognition. It is not merely a collection of papers from other sources, nor is it based on talks at a loosely organized symposium. Rather, the chapters were written specifically for this *Handbook*. Each contributor was charged with the task of discussing the interface between motivation and cognition within his or her specific domain. Indeed, several of our contributors were *nudged* to think of the importance of the Warm Look for their own research. This has led to a number of new and exciting ideas. In discussing these ideas with others, we have learned that there are many more investigators who have much to say concerning the interface between motivation and cognition. Consequently, this book may be the first in a series devoted to that interface.

This book contains an "Overview," in which we state our case for the Warm Look. Following that the book is divided into three parts. The first two parts are devoted to important mechanisms relating human motivation to cognition, the self, and affect. In the Self section, motivation is related to the self-concept (Nancy Cantor, Hazel Markus, Paula Niedenthal, and Paula Nurius); facets of the self (Steven J. Breckler and Anthony Greenwald); and memory reconstruction of one's own past (Michael Ross and Michael Conway). In addition, Robert Wicklund discusses the role of static versus dynamic fit with the environment on self-attribution; E. Tory Higgins, Timothy Strauman, and Ruth Klein discuss the role of standards on the self-evaluation process, relating such standards to affect.

In their separate chapters in the Affect section, Martin Hoffman and Bernard Weiner discuss the role of affect in the attribution process and relate it to empathy, cognition, and action. Russell H. Fazio presents his case that attitude is affect and demonstrates how attitudes guide behavior. Finally, Susan T. Fiske and Mark A. Pavelchak present their schema-triggered affective model, which distinguishes between category-based and piecemeal-based affective responses.

The Goals and Orientations section has three chapters devoted to affective and informational theories of social behavior. The first chapter is by Joel O. Raynor and Dean B. McFarlin, on motivation and the self system. The second chapter is by Yaacov Trope, on self-enhancement and self-assessment; the third is by Richard M. Sorrentino and Judith-Ann C. Short, on uncertainty orientation, motivation, and cognition. In the remainder of the section, Julius Kuhl presents a new look at decision making, dynamic conflict, and action control, in relating motivation to information processing; Abraham Tesser discusses the effects of self-evaluation maintenance on cognition and action, Henri Zukier notes the importance of goal orientation for social inference, as do Thomas K. Srull and Robert Wyer, Jr. for social information processing. Daniel M. Wegner and Robin R. Vallacher finish this section with their chapter on action identification.

In publishing this book, we wish to express our sincere appreciation to many people. Foremost, we must thank the contributors, whose book this really is. Their initial and persistent enthusiasm not only can be readily seen in their respective chapters, but has encouraged us to continue this effort in the future. No small amount of appreciation goes to our publisher, The Guilford Press, particularly its representative, Seymour Weingarten. His remarkable knowledge of psychology (not to mention delightful restaurants) and his support for this endeavor were of great value. Although this book is intended primarily for graduate students and professional researchers, we did try out an advanced copy on a senior-level undergraduate class. It was a resounding success! The students were extremely excited and interested in the subject matter, and our thanks go to them as well. Linda Tupholme, our major typist, came through for us once again when we needed her. Thanks also to Arie Kruglanski, who related our ideas to the Möbius strip, and to Jim Olson, who suggested we color the strip red and blue. There are three people who served as an inspiration for this book: John W. Atkinson, Milton Rokeach, Stanley Schachter. They are the roots of the Warm Look. Finally, to our wives, sons, lovers, dogs (Judy, Robin, Eric, and Jamie—order varies), mothers, and fathers—thanks.

Contents

Overview   **1**

CHAPTER 1   **Motivation and Cognition: Warming Up to Synergism**   *Richard M. Sorrentino* and *E. Tory Higgins*   **3**

PART I   **The Self**   **21**

CHAPTER 2   **Standards and the Process of Self-Evaluation: Multiple Affects from Multiple Stages** *E. Tory Higgins, Timothy Strauman,* and *Ruth Klein*   **23**

CHAPTER 3   **Orientation to the Environment versus Preoccupation with Human Potential** *Robert A. Wicklund*   **64**

CHAPTER 4   **On Motivation and the Self-Concept** *Nancy Cantor, Hazel Markus, Paula Niedenthal,* and *Paula Nurius*   **96**

CHAPTER 5   **Remembering One's Own Past: The Construction of Personal Histories**   *Michael Ross* and *Michael Conway*   **122**

CHAPTER 6   **Motivational Facets of the Self** *Steven J. Breckler* and *Anthony G. Greenwald*   **145**

PART II   **Affect**   **165**

CHAPTER 7   **Category-Based versus Piecemeal-Based Affective Responses: Developments in Schema-Triggered Affect**   *Susan T. Fiske* and *Mark A. Pavelchak*   **167**

CHAPTER 8   **How Do Attitudes Guide Behavior?** *Russell H. Fazio*   **204**

CHAPTER 9   **Affect, Cognition, and Motivation**
Martin L. Hoffman   **244**

CHAPTER 10   **Attribution, Emotion, and Action**
Bernard Weiner   **281**

PART III   *Goals and Orientations*   *313*

CHAPTER 11   **Motivation and the Self-System**   *Joel O. Raynor*
and *Dean B. McFarlin*   **315**

CHAPTER 12   **Self-Enhancement and Self-Assessment in Achievement Behavior**   *Yaacov Trope*   **350**

CHAPTER 13   **Uncertainty Orientation, Motivation, and
Cognition**   *Richard M. Sorrentino* and
Judith-Ann C. Short   **379**

CHAPTER 14   **Motivation and Information Processing: A New
Look at Decision Making, Dynamic Change, and
Action Control**   *Julius Kuhl*   **404**

CHAPTER 15   **Some Effects of Self-Evaluation Maintenance on
Cognition and Action**   *Abraham Tesser*   **435**

CHAPTER 16   **The Paradigmatic and Narrative Modes in Goal-
Guided Inference**   *Henri Zukier*   **465**

CHAPTER 17   **The Role of Chronic and Temporary Goals in
Social Information Processing**   *Thomas K. Srull*
and *Robert S. Wyer, Jr.*   **503**

CHAPTER 18   **Action Identification**   *Daniel M. Wegner* and
Robin R. Vallacher   **550**

Author Index   **583**

Subject Index   **595**

Handbook of Motivation and Cognition

Overview

CHAPTER 1

Motivation and Cognition
Warming Up to Synergism

RICHARD M. SORRENTINO
University of Western Ontario

E. TORY HIGGINS
New York University

There is a classic area of research in psychology that dates back to the late 1940s. It deals primarily with momentary and chronic individual differences in construct accessibility (see Higgins, King, & Mavin, 1982). It has shown, consistently, that one can heighten the accessibility in memory of various constructs and study the effects of increased accessibility on subsequent covert (cognitive) *and* overt (behavioral) responses. In addition, this classic area has long been able to demonstrate not only that one can measure individual differences in construct accessibility but that one can predict long-term effects on such overt responses as performance on various tasks, college attendance, course grades, and success in business.

Yet not too many cognitive theorists appear cognizant of this area, which has successfully predicted covert and overt behavior for almost 40 years. Indeed, self-criticism has been expressed, such as, "We simply acknowledge that we share our field's inability to bridge the gap between cognition and behavior, a gap that in our opinion is the most serious failing of modern cognitive psychology" (Nisbett & Ross, 1980, p. 11). The area of which we speak is the development and use of *n*-achievement to infer the achievement motive. This projective device, much maligned and criticized (see Weinstein, 1969), continues to this day to predict reliably choice, persistence, and performance in achievement-oriented activity (see Atkinson & Raynor, 1974; Sorrentino, Short, & Raynor, 1984). But why, you may ask, are we choosing to call it an individual difference in construct accessibility? The answer to that is simple—it is.

The fact that, as far as we are aware, this point has not been made in the literature is indicative of the almost total exclusion of motivation in research on cognition. We will return later to our argument that *n*-achievement is an individual difference variable in construct accessibility. First, let us see how this historical accident may have occurred.

3

MOTIVATION, COGNITION, AND SOCIAL BEHAVIOR: AN HISTORICAL PERSPECTIVE

As one follows the development of any science, it is expected, to use a Hegelian analysis, that one proceeds from thesis to antithesis to synthesis. Although one might expect that motivation and cognition would be at the final stage by now, this is not the case. Indeed, for social behavior, it appears that synthesis has at least temporarily been usurped by antithesis (Hegel, 1801/1977).

The reason for this paradox can perhaps be traced back to the rise of behaviorism in North American psychology. Until that point, various views relating motivation and/or cognition to behavior were flourishing. Darwin (1872) carried considerable weight, as did Freud (1917/1955) and McDougall (1908), in putting forth instinct as the underlying motivational force accounting for behavior. On the other hand, others were putting forth a primarily cognitive and/ or rational viewpoint as the basis for behavior. William James (1890), for example, stressed the importance of will and the self in determining what he called voluntary behavior. By the structuralists and functionalists (e.g., Galton, 1883, the phrenologist; and Titchener, 1899), we were told that the mind and various streams of consciousness were all that were worthy of study. There was, however, a third and ultimately overwhelming viewpoint that won the day—behaviorism. This school of thought rejected all other approaches—or any approach that focused on the internal machinations of the individual. Consider, for example, the following statement from James B. Watson (1930), the "father of behaviorism":

> The Behaviorist began his own formulation of the problem of psychology by sweeping aside all medieval conceptions. He dropped from his scientific vocabulary all subjective terms such as sensation, perception, image, desire, purpose, and even thinking, and emotion as they were subjectively defined. (p. 5)

This statement, which reflected the predominant feeling among North American psychologists at the time, obviously did little to promote the fields of motivation, cognition, and social psychology. It is interesting that cognition was the last of the three areas to fully recover from the attack of the behaviorists:

> The behaviorist program and the issues it spawned all but eliminated any serious research in cognitive psychology for 40 years. The rat supplanted the human as the principal laboratory subject, and psychology turned to finding out what could be learned by studying animal learning and motivation. (Anderson, 1980, p. 9)

Motivation and social psychology were a bit more fortunate. It soon became apparent that motivation could not be swept aside as a by-product of learning principles, as Hull (1943) had hoped (was driven?) to do. Tolman's (1932, 1959) empirical demonstrations of purposive behavior in animals met the rat behaviorists head on, until they were forced to embrace the concept of motivation as something other than a learning phenomenon. Social psychology was also soon to reemerge, largely thorugh the influence of Kurt Lewin (1935, 1951), whose field theory had concepts that were strikingly similar to those of Tolman (see Atkinson, 1964).

It is important to note that these theories were not motivational or cognitive, but *both*. The expectancy-value theories of Tolman and Lewin took account of both motivational and cognitive factors when attempting to predict behavior. Tolman, in predicting maze behavior, spoke of the expectancy of the goal and the demand for the goal. Lewin, in research on level of aspiration and decision making, spoke in terms of potency and valence. When a rate moves through a maze or a human moves through his or her life space, it is done purposively, and both motivation and cognition are important elements in accounting for this behavior. Although Tolman's points were well taken, prompting Hull and the neo-Hullians (e.g., Miller, 1948; Spence, 1956) to modify their viewpoint, the influence of B. F. Skinner, a staunch atheoretical behaviorist, continued to dominate in that area. Within social psychology, however, models involving the interactive effects of motivation and cognition flourished well into the early 1970s. This was a direct consequence of Lewin's charismatic appeal, which enabled him to pass many of his theoretical ideas to his students and associates and to their students (e.g., Festinger, Cartwright, Zander, Back, Atkinson, Deutsch, Kelley, Schachter, Zajonc). Indeed, much of social psychology up to that point could be traced to Lewin and others (e.g., Bruner, Heider, Newcomb) who saw the importance of both motivation and cognition in their theories. In the 1970s, a major shift in emphasis began occurring in social psychology; cognition emerged as the dominant force, and motivation declined to a secondary, mostly implicit element.

This reversal (antisynthesis?) may be directly attributable to the rejection of motivational concepts in the study of cognition and perceptual processes in general psychology. As Anderson (1980) pointed out, cognitive psychology did not begin to emerge from the attack of the behaviorists until quite recently. He cited three areas that account for the information-processing approach that emerged in the late 1960s and early 1970s: human factors research in World War II (see Atkinson & Schiffrin, 1968; Broadbent, 1958), interest in artificial intelligence (e.g., Newell & Simon, 1972), and psycholinguistics (e.g., Chomsky, 1957). Anderson cited Neisser's (1967) *Cognitive Psychology* as the book that gave "a new legitimacy to the field." Motivation had little place in these three areas. These nonmotivation information-processing concepts began to influence research and theory in social psychology in the late 1970s, with the premise that cognition can account for many behaviors that others claimed to be motivated. In an earlier period, the premise had been quite the opposite. The "New Look" argued that motivation could account for many responses that others claimed to be strictly perceptual.

HOT COGNITIONS: THE NEW LOOK

In his article "On Perceptual Readiness," Jerome Bruner (1957) began with the following statement:

> About ten years ago I was party to the publication of an innocent enough paper entitled, "Value and Need as Organizing Factors in Perception." It was concerned

with what at that time was the rather obscure problem of how extra-stimulus factors influenced perception, a subject then of interest to only a small band of us—Gardner Murphy, Nevitt Sanford, Muzafer Sherif, and a few others. Obviously, Professor Boring is quite right about the mischievousness of the *Zeitgeist*, for the appearance of this paper seemed to coincide with all sorts of spirit-like rumbling within the world of psychology that were soon to erupt in a most unspirit-like torrent of research on this very topic—perhaps three hundred research reports and theoretical explications in the ten years since then. (p. 123)

Bruner then went on to present, in this classic article, his views on perceptual readiness, in which the New Look plays an important role. His notion regarding category accessibility, for example, was that it was determined by learning and by "the requirements of search dictated by need states and the need to carry out habitual enterprises such as walking, reading, or whatever it is that makes up the round of daily, habitual life" (Bruner, 1957, pp. 148–149). He concluded his article with the following statement:

In conclusion, it seems appropriate to say that the ten years of the so-called New Look in perception research seem to be coming to a close with much empirical work accomplished—a great deal of it demonstrational, to be sure, but with a promise of a second ten years in which hypotheses will be more rigorously formulated and, conceivably, neural mechanisms postulated, if not discovered. The prospects are anything but discouraging. (p. 149)

COLD COGNITIONS: THE FAULTY COMPUTER

The New Look is gone. Bruner was correct in that the New Look carried on for 10 years and, indeed, might have had its heyday in the 1960s. The notion of motivational influences on perception and cognition was highly discussed, though always controversial in perception (e.g., Dember, 1960) and cognition (e.g., Harper, Anderson, Christensen, & Hunka, 1964). In the Harper *et al.* (1964) book, there is a section of particular relevance to the present volume. It is entitled, "Cognition, Motivation and Personality," and it includes articles that deal with effects of motivational processes on cognition (Henle, 1964) and cognitive aspects of motivation (Prentice, 1964) as well as some very interesting contributions by investigators of social behavior. Here we have Schachter and Singer's (1962) classic article on cognitive, social, and physiological determinants of emotional state; Festinger's articles on the motivating effects of cognitive dissonance (Festinger, 1958) and the psychological effects of insufficient rewards (Festinger, 1961); and many others (e.g., Berkowitz, 1960; Pettigrew, 1958; Secord and Backman, 1960). Hence, as a consequence of the New Look, there was a very rich sense of the interplay among motivation, cognition, and social behavior.

All of that is gone now. In books on sensation and perception (e.g., Coren, Porac, & Ward, 1984; Levine & Shefner, 1981), the New Look and motivation are mentioned rarely if at all. Similarly, no mention of the New Look or motivation is made in Anderson's (1980) cognitive psychology book, *Cognitive*

Psychology and Its Implications. When it comes to social behavior, the situation is similar. For example, in a highly influential book by Nisbett and Ross (1980), the New Look is discussed, as is motivation, but both are treated as peripheral to central human inference processes.

In much of psychology, then, the New Look and its impact are no longer felt. Indeed, in some areas of social cognition, there is evidence of hostility toward anyone who would dare use the term "motivation" in anything other than a pejorative manner. One of our undergraduate students, for example, upon arriving at a graduate center well known for social cognition, proudly presented the results of his honors thesis (subsequently published in the *Journal of Personality and Social Psychology*) at a conference. The student was cautioned by his new advisor not to mention the study "around here"—the reason being that since the study involved a motivational construct, the student might jeopardize his standing with the faculty.

What appears to account for the demise of the New Look is the fact that motivation was seen as an alternative explanation for a cognitive process. Rather than studying the interaction of motivational and cognitive processes, a battle developed regarding which of the two, motivation or cognition, was a better explanation of the phenomenon. Dember (1960), for example, pointed out that in the classic experiment by Bruner and Goodman (1947), in which children overestimated the size of coins compared to neutral discs, the results might not be due to motivation, as was originally proposed, "but more simply by a culturally acquired association between value and size" (Dember, 1960, p. 340). Research on perceptual defense (e.g., Blum, 1954; Postman, Bruner, & McGinnis, 1948) also fell under heavy criticism, mostly because of methodological shortcomings.

In the 1970s and early 1980s, social psychologists were quick to jump on the bandwagon. Social-cognitive theorists also attempted to put motivational theories to rest with alternative explanations. Thus, for Nisbett and Ross (1980), biases and problems in inference or behavior are often due to information-processing errors and cognitive limitations—the notion of "people as faulty computers." Self-serving biases in attribution and prejudice, for example, may not be at all motivational:

> In both cases nonmotivational factors seem sufficient to account for most of the phenomena. In the case of so-called ego-defensive biases in attribution, it is clear that actors usually hold preconceptions and possess evidence that on purely intellectual grounds would seem to justify, if not demand, asymmetric responses to success and failure. In the case of prejudice, it seems clear that stereotypes of ethnic or racial groups are similar to the schemas or theories that encapsulate socially based knowledge of many other categories of people, objects, or events. (p. 247)

A similar "faulty computer" perspective on judgmental errors and biases may be found in the works of Cantor and Mischel (1977), Dawes (1976), Markus (1977), Hamilton (1979), and Miller and Ross (1975).

Contrary to the history of research and theory in social psychology, and in spite of the teachings of many current practitioners' advisers whose lineage could be traced back to Heider and Lewin, the "cold" approach became the predominant theme in the study of social behavior. Indeed, even motivational theories of achievement behavior have been under attack from cognitive theorists. Trope (1975) argued that differences in behavior as a function of achievement-related motives are primarily due to differences in cognitive information seeking, not affective arousal. He and Weiner (1972) argued that preferences for tasks of intermediate difficulty on the part of success-oriented persons (see Atkinson, 1964; Atkinson & Raynor, 1974) are due to the fact that such tasks are most diagnostic of the person's ability, rather than being due to the interaction of motivational and situational components that the affective theory specifies.

In the area of social behavior, then, cognitive theories have become the *Weltanschaung*, whereas motivation may best be described as "flat on its back."

Given the previous history of social behavior, the present cold approach is, in a sense, a step backward. It is hoped that this volume will help reverse the direction. Just as "hot" cognitions are insufficient explanations of information processing and perceptual processes, so, too, is the "cold" approach an inadequate explanation of social phenomena.

THE WARM LOOK

In the television and film series *Star Trek*, there is an all-too-familiar scene of the typical confrontation between Mr. Spock (the Vulcan first officer), Dr. McCoy (the ship's surgeon) and Captain Kirk (the ship's commander). The confrontation is usually initiated by Spock or McCoy, with the former commenting on the passionate, irrational nature of humans and the latter being appalled and disgusted by Mr. Spock's lack of feelings and sensitivity. The cold, rational character of Spock and the affectively motivated Dr. McCoy are terrific foils for Captain Kirk. Although he is rarely perfectly balanced, Captain Kirk is the ideal person, who will come forward at the right time with the necessary interplay between motivation and cognition—saving the day and/or the lives of the crew.

This example came to us as we attempted to imagine a person with one but not the other system. Spock and McCoy could not exist, at least in a human world, without both cognitive and motivational systems. Spock would be the proverbial person "buried in thought," unable to act. McCoy, of course, would act too rapidly and irrationally. Hence, we put forth the notion of the "Warm Look," reflecting the blending of "cold" cognitive and "hot" motivational processes. We have come to the conclusion that motivation and cognition are, in fact, inseparable. Behavior is not a product of hot cognitions, as suggested by the New Look perspective, nor of cold cognitions, as suggested by the "faulty computer" perspective. In addition, it is not simply that cognition leads to motivation and motivation leads to cognition. Rather, each is a property or facet of the other. They are *synergistic* in that they operate together to produce combined effects.

What we are saying, then, is that whatever determines behavior is neither hot nor cold—it is warm. Our conception is much like Hofstedter's (1979) eternal braid, the Möbius Strip (see Figure 1.1), which appears to have either a black

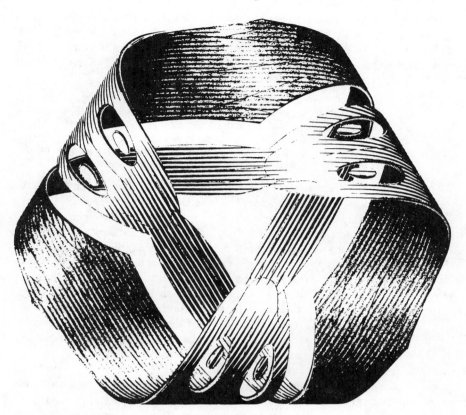

FIGURE 1.1 The Möbius strip. © M. C. Escher heirs care of Cordon Art–Baarn–Holland.

surface (with a white underside) or a white surface (with a black underside), depending on which end of the object one focuses on, whereas, in fact, the object is a one-sided combination of black and white. Similarly, we would argue that although one can focus on one behavioral determinant or the other, motivation and cognition are not truly separable factors.

Although not all of the contributors to this volume necessarily agree with this position, most of the arguments are at least generally compatible. From the cognitive side, for example, Weiner (Ch. 10) states as his fourth principle: "A theory of motivation must be concerned with conscious experience." He says:

> Motivation has been inseparably linked with the study of overt behavior. Throughout the history of this field, well-known books have had behaviorally oriented titles. . . . But we experience, feel, and think, as well as act. All these processes have a place within the study of motivation. A theory of motivation is responsible for examining the experiential state of the organism and the meaning of an action. Hence, the theory must embrace phenomenology and accept the position so clearly articulated by Lewin (1935) that organisms act on a perceived, rather than an objective world.

On the motivational side, Zukier (Ch. 16) argues that although social-cognitive approaches that relegated social and motivational dimensions of cognition to the background may have produced a beneficial shift away from an earlier overemphasis on affective factors (e.g., Hamilton, 1981; Nisbett & Ross, 1980):

> ... it again has become evident from these studies that non-cognitive personal and motivational factors such as goals and values, or attitudes and needs, are not merely adjuncts to cognition that color judgments and either interfere with or impel cognitive activity. Rather, these factors emerge as a constitutive part of cognition, and their neglect often results in very partial descriptions of the cognitive processes themselves.

In Chapter 10, Weiner goes on to describe the wide range of emotions and conscious experiences surrounding achievement-oriented activity (see also Higgins, Strauman, and Klein, Ch. 2). Zukier (Ch. 16) also examines how personal and sociocultural roles and goals modulate social inference. His distinction between two kinds of cognition—categorical and narrative understanding—is consistent with our synergistic viewpoint in that the two types are inherently a motivational distinction as well. The interplay between thought and planned action is heavily stressed in Wegner and Vallacher's chapter on action identification and action emergence (Ch. 18). Indeed, their model's major concern is with the information-processing properties that determine where in the hierarchical level one selects a plan and the information-processing factors that change a plan. Moreover, carrying out any particular plan can redirect information processing. Hence, it is a synergistic model in that it emphasizes the interface of motivation and cognition. Wicklund (Ch. 3) makes some intriguing comments concerning two kinds of orientations that vary in the extent to which they involve attributional concerns—a static orientation that does versus a dynamic orientation that does not. When a person is in perfect harmony with the environment, attention is focused not on understanding the act but on performing the act. Ironically, because of this, expert practitioners in a given area are the least likely to describe what it takes to perform in that area. The variable of "attributional concerns"—motivation for understanding—is itself an excellent example of a synergistic factor. Hoffman (Ch. 9) convincingly argues that a change in one's affective state can cause a change in one's interpretation of an event (and vice versa). For him, a property of affect is its causal interpretation (and vice versa). Hence, in his theory, affect and attribution are explicitly synergistic.

Many of the chapters do not explicitly describe synergistic variables but do discuss various ways that motivation and cognition are interrelated. Srull and Wyer (Ch. 17), for example, make a convincing case for the influence of subjective goal states on information processing:

> Goals often determine what we attend to, how we perceive objects and events, how we use reasoning processes to make inferences about causal connections, how these events are organized and represented in memory, how they affect both the long-term storage and retrieval of relevant information, how they influence the integration of information (or lack thereof) to make higher order judgments, and how they enter into possible affective reactions.

In a complementary fashion, Kuhl (Ch. 14), presents an elegant model that relates information processing to motivation. His evidence suggests that informatio-processing mechanisms operating on motivational states differ in some respects from cognitive information processing. However, consistent with the Warm Look, he argues, "Even those few cognitive models that do not leave man 'buried in thought' (Guthrie, 1935) provide a simplistic shortcut from cognition to action that ignores most questions regarding the functional relationship between cognitive processes and motivational processes." His model directly addresses these issues.

Ross and Conway (Ch. 5) describe how changes in attitude (the motivational construct) induce cognitions (i.e., episodic memory reconstruction) that make sense of the attitude. Similarly, Tesser (Ch. 15) stipulates that whether we will choose the cognitive mode of social comparison or the cognitive mode of balance (basking in reflected glory) depends on our motivational state (see also Raynor and McFarlin's hypothesis concerning this phenomenon in Chapter 11). For Fiske and Pavelchak (Ch. 7), people's motivational orientation to a target depends on a cognitive property—the nature of the information processing (category-based or piecemeal) that yielded their affective response to the target.

In the area of self-evaluation, Higgins, Strauman, and Klein (Ch. 2), propose that there is a cognitive facet of motivation in the sense that people have mental representations (cognitions) of their goals and rules for behavior, and that the relation between these mental representations and the mental representation of their actual self, as well as the cognitive accessibility of these relations, influences their motivational/affective states. Similarly, Cantor, Markus, Niedenthal, and Nurius (Ch. 4) propose that mental representations of life tasks and imagined possibilities determine the course of motivation. More generally, Sorrentino and Short (Ch. 13) argue that to predict behavior, one must take into account both people's cognitive schemata (e.g., uncertainty orientation) and appropriate sources of motivation (e.g., achievement-related motives).

It is clear from the theories and proposals of most of our contributors that motivation and cognition cannot be treated as separate entities; rather, their synergistic nature must be considered.

THEMES OF THE WARM LOOK

In this section, we will briefly describe the major themes that emerge in this volume and provide the focus for future research. These focal themes concern the self, affect, and goals and orientations.

The Self

Five chapters are devoted to the self mechanisms, and many others refer to some aspect of the self. Higgins, Strauman, and Klein (Ch. 2) present a model of self-evaluation that distinguishes between factual reference points as evaluative standards (e.g., social category, meaningful other, and autobiographical reference points) and acquired guides as evaluative standards (e.g., ideal/own and ought/ other guides). From this, in combination with distinguishing among different stages of evaluation (e.g., stimulus encoding, interpretation), they are able to predict the affective states induced by self-evaluation. An important implication of this model is that minor changes in context can change which self-relevant standard is most accessible and thus utilized, hence completely changing the individual's affective state from one moment to the next. This implication highlights the dynamic interplay between cognitive and affective/motivational processes as they unfold in natural situations.

As discussed earlier, Wicklund (Ch. 3) raises the general issue of when and why self-evaluation is operating. He proposes that when the organism is in a dynamic fit with the environment (e.g., the person is highly competent in the task at hand), the person has no need to make attributions about the self and, indeed, may be unable to tell anyone exactly how he or she operated during that period. It is only the relatively incompetent person who engages in self-evaluation—a person with a static orientation toward the environment. (This may be akin to Raynor and McFarlin's behavioral system versus self-system, discussed later in this section and in Chapter 11.)

In Chapter 4, Cantor, Markus, Niedenthal, and Nurius point out how notions of the self may, indeed, direct motivational processes. By imagining a number of future possible selves, we decide on a course of action. Thus, motivation may reside within the self-concept. Ross and Conway (Ch. 5) also present some intriguing data that demonstrate how we reconstruct our past memories to be consistent with our current self-evaluation. In one study, for example, although subjects did not improve in their course work as a function of a remedial studying program, they viewed their pre-course work as much worse than it actually was. Breckler and Greenwald (Ch. 6) distinguish among the diffuse self, the public self, the private self, and the collective self—each of which forms a different motivational basis for behavior.

Several other contributors allude to the self-concept as being critical for motivation. Tesser (Ch. 15) discusses the importance of self-evaluation mainten- ance on cognition and action. He describes two major processes of self-evaluation: the comparison process and the reflective process, and he presents a number of fascinating studies that support his proposed model for interrelating these processes. A note of caution regarding the self stems, however, from the chapter by Raynor and McFarlin (Ch. 11), who point out that a clearly defined self-system is not necessary for behavioral functioning. These authors distinguish between the self-system and the behavioral system and claim that only those who partake in a "psychological career" may have an articulate self-system. Finally, Sorrentino and Short (Ch. 13) present a new individual difference variable—uncertainty orientation. As a result of some data that they cite, consistent with Raynor and McFarlin (Ch. 11), they warn that many theories of the self may have to be re- evaluated:

> We wish to draw to the attention of many cognitive theorists, as well as proponents of the Warm Look, the fact that there are many people who simply are not interested in finding out information about themselves or the world, who

do not conduct causal searches, who couldn't care less about comparing themselves with others, and who don't "give a hoot" for resolving discrepancies or inconsistencies about the self.

Our contributors thus expand the importance of the self to many domains of motivation and cognition. They also attempt to specify when and where it is or is not important.

Affect

A major theme in many of the chapters is the central role played by affect in the relationship between motivation and cognition. Kuhl (Ch. 14) proposes the following distinction among affect, motivation, and cognition:

> It is assumed that cognitive, emotional, and motivational subsystems relate to the world in three different ways. The term *cognition* is reserved for those processes that mediate the acquisition and representation of knowledge about the world, i.e., processes that have a *representative* relation to the world of objects and facts. *Emotional* (affective) processes evaluate the personal significance of those objects and facts. *Motivational* processes relate to the world in an actional way, e.g., they relate to goal states of the organism in its attempt to produce desired changes in its environment.

Kuhl goes on to discuss some interesting interactions among the three subsystems in terms of three motivational phenomena: choice, persistence, and effort. His discussion is a *tour de force* that shows why each of these subsystems must be taken into account in any theory of human behavior.

In a similar fashion, Fiske and Pavelchak (Ch. 7) present a model and supportive research describing the relationship between affect and mode of impression formation (i.e., category-based versus piecemeal-based) and indicating how affect is inextricably embedded in information processing in general. Although these authors do not discuss the relevance of their model to motivation *per se*, Sorrentino and Short (Ch. 13) discuss how such a model could be expanded to incorporate motivation as well. In his attempt to relate affect, cognition, and behavior, Fazio (Ch. 8) states that attitude essentially *is* affect. He then presents a model characterizing the attitude-to-behavior process. Fazio considers "the influence of attitude (affect) upon subsequent behavior through mediating cognitive processes involving one's perceptions of and cognitions about the attitude object in the immediate situation in which the attitude object is encountered." In perhaps the strongest statement regarding affect, Hoffman (Ch. 9) states: "It may not be an exaggeration to suggest that psychology is in the early stages of a paradigm shift in which affect no longer takes a back seat." He points out that things are already changing, especially among cognitive psychologists (e.g., Bower, 1981; Norman, 1980; Piaget, 1981; Simon, 1982) and social psychologists (see Clark & Fiske, 1982). In his view, and in Weiner's (Ch. 10) view as well, affect plays a key role in determining the interaction of motivational and cognitive processes. Other chapters describe the relationship between affect and cognitive structures and processes (e.g., Higgins, Strauman, and Klein, Ch. 2; Srull & Wyer, Ch. 17).

Goals and Orientations: Informational Versus Affective Value

One major theme has emerged that transcends many single contributions to this Handbook. It has to do with the critical distinction between informational versus affective value. In the section of the "cold" approach, we pointed out that cognitive theorists have gone so far as to reinterpret affective theories of motivation in terms of cognitive information seeking. This came initially from Weiner's (1972) suggestion that although affect is important in achievement-oriented activity, information relevant to one's ability is another important dimension. Trope (1975) carried this one step further, arguing that, indeed, the primary goal of achievement situations is to remove uncertainty regarding one's ability. In his view, differences in performance due to achievement-related motives could simply be due to differences in self-assessment, not affect (pride in accomplishment, shame over failure; see Sorrentino and Short, Ch. 13).

In Chapter 10 of this Handbook, Weiner develops his current ideas concerning the importance of attributional theory to motivation and emotion. Although some issues concerning individual differences remain (see Sorrentino and Short, Ch. 13), he presents a worthwhile framework for considering what is required for a theory of motivation. Both affect and self-attributions now play central roles. Trope (Ch. 12) presents the reader with two diverse, well-formalized theories of achievement behavior—one based on the premise that self-enhancement is the primary goal of achievement behavior, the other on the premise that self-assessment is the primary goal. Although one would expect that he thinks it is the latter, Trope maintains a relatively neutral stance regarding which of these goals predominates.

Further valuable insights on the self-assessment versus self-enhancement controversy are provided in the chapter by Raynor and McFarlin (Ch. 11). From their expectancy-value origins, these authors argue that all behavior is a function of the value of that activity to the organism. What is interesting and perhaps crucial to many contributors of this volume is that value is composed of two types—information value and affective value, finding out versus feeling good. Both self-assessment and self-enhancement are important. (Similar conclusions may be derived from Trope's Chapter 12 and Kuhl's Chapter 14.) Taking this as their basic assumption, these authors proceed to reinterpret many areas related to the self (i.e., assessing self-esteem, self-enhancement, self-evaluation maintenance theory, self-consistency theory, self-confirmation theory). For example, they suggest a resolution to the long-standing issue of precisely when someone will actually fail at a task to maintain a negative image of the self (see Aronson & Carlsmith, 1962; Swann, 1983). If there are no affective consequences to success or failure at the activity (i.e., the situation has low affective value), and if failure will reduce confusion about the person's self image (i.e., the situation has high information value), then the person will work to fail at the activity.

Their model also sheds light on earlier issues through its use of the previously cited distinction between the self-system and the behavioral system for self-evaluation maintenance (see Tesser, Ch. 15). Raynor and McFarlin point out that the reflective process of BIRGing ("basking in reflected glory" over the success of another) is high in affective value related to the behavioral system; it is simply feeling good. Conversely, people who are trying to hinder another person's performance on tasks related to self-relevant attributes are probably trying to avoid negative affect in the self-system. Thus, affective value and information value in both the self-system and the behavioral system must be considered in research related to the Warm Look.

This point is taken very seriously by Sorrentino and Short in Chapter 13. These authors show that previous research and theory on achievement behavior may have confused information value with affective value. They introduce their views on uncertainty orientation with the notion that uncertainty orientation is primarily an informational variable, whereas achievement-related motives are primarily affective variables. Thus, all those aspects of achievement situations that are informational in nature (e.g., information about the self or the environment) are related to individual differences in uncertainty orientation. All those aspects that are related to affective arousal (feeling good or bad about the self or the environment) are due to achievement-related motives (as well as to any other source of motivation aroused by the situation). Thus, finding out about one's ability (Trope, 1975; Weiner, 1972) and feeling good or bad (Atkinson & Raynor, 1974) are all important elements that must be integrated in a unified theory of motivation and cognition. Sorrentino and Short (Ch. 13) also distinguish between two ways of obtaining information value. The first is to *attain* clarity about the self or environment—that is, to find out. The second is to *maintain* clarity—that is, to adhere to what is already known and not engage in confusing situations. They argue that most investigators of social behavior assume that all people seek to attain clarity but that this is not the case. Only uncertainty-oriented persons seek to find out new information about the self or the environment. Certainty-oriented persons find such situations irrelevant.

Having stated our arguments and perused some (but by no means all) of the contributions made by the Warm Look, let us conclude with the prototypical synergistic construct with which we began.

n-ACHIEVEMENT: A PROTOTYPICAL SYNERGISTIC CONSTRUCT

From the very inception of motivation theory, McClelland, Atkinson, and their colleagues (McClelland & Atkinson, 1948; McClelland, Atkinson, Clark, & Lowell, 1953) assumed that motives involve, in our terms, highly accessible constructs. The basic notion behind the Thematic Apperception Test, developed by Murray (1938) and used extensively by the McClelland and Atkinson group, is (using our jargon) that if a person is motivated to achieve a particular state, then thoughts concerning that motive should be readily accessible in memory. It was thought that the Thematic Apperception Test would be an ideal method for measuring those cognitions because it is a semiambiguous projective technique. That is, it presents a picture or sentence to the subject with a cue that should elicit comments related to a motive if the person is high in that motive (temporarily or relatively permanently). Thus, when a person is presented with a picture or a sentence lead of a boy playing a violin, thoughts should be elicited about playing at Carnegie Hall, being detained from playing with friends, or perceiving the playing as a way to influence one's parents, depending on the relative strength (or accessibility) of the person's achievement, affiliation, and power motivation, respectively. Similarly, the sentence, "Two persons are working in a laboratory on a piece of equipment," might elicit thoughts about Banting and Best discovering insulin (at least in Canadian students), two lovers desiring each other, or best friends enjoying each other's company, depending on the relative strength of a person's achievement, sex, and affiliation motivation, respectively.

Indeed, their research program was initially designed to demonstrate that motivational constructs are accessible and can be assessed. This was first done by directly manipulating hunger (via food deprivation; Atkinson & McClelland, 1948), fear (proximity to an atomic bomb blast; Walker & Atkinson, 1958), and sexual arousal (which worked correctly only when subjects were "under the influence"; Clark, 1952, 1955). After demonstrating that one can accurately assess basic drives via projective techniques, this research group moved on to show that conceptually similar methods could be used to "prime" achievement-oriented constructs in memory (e.g., telling subjects that they were taking a test of important abilities; McClelland *et al.*, 1953). One could similarly prime affiliation constructs (e.g., having subjects perform sociometric ratings of their fraternity brothers prior to administration of the TAT; Atkinson, Heyns, & Veroff, 1954).

If one were to assess the true baseline level of achievement or other sources of motivation, however, one would administer the test under neutral conditions so that there would be no exogenous priming influences. In other words, if the relevant source of motivation is strong, it should have high chronic accessibility in memory, so that a neutral testing condition (e.g., not telling the subject why he or she is being tested) will elicit the motivational construct and related categories (see Atkinson, 1958).

The assumption, then, was that one could either prime in memory or measure an already accessible construct associated with a particular source of motivation. It is interesting that in spite of all the criticisms directed at it (see Atkinson, Bongort, & Price, 1977, for attack and retaliation), the projective measure of *n*-achievement continues to be the single best predictor of actual performance in achievement-oriented activity—as anyone working in the area will tell you.

The fact that one can conceive of individual differences in construct accessibility as a key property of motives and of motives as a key property of some accessible constructs is the bridge that united the two coeditors of this volume. It may be that whatever lack of success cognitive theorists have had in predicting overt behavior can be directly attributable to the failure to incorporate motivational phenomena into the equation. Hence, a readily accessible construct that has motivational ties (such as achievement, success, approval, friendship, power) can predict overt behavior (such as performance, grades, social relationships, leadership emergence).

We have belabored this example because we hope that it will demonstrate the synergistic nature of the influence of motivation and cognition on behavior. The fact that the study of motivational aspects of cognition (i.e., the New Look) and the study of cognitive aspects of motivation (i.e., *n*-achievement) generally went their own ways for the last quarter-century was highly unfortunate for psychology. We hope that this volume will serve as the start of something that should have been old.

References

Anderson, J. R. (1980). *Cognitive psychology and its implications*. San Francisco: Freeman.

Aronson, E., & Carlsmith, S. M. (1962). Performance expectancy as a determinant of actual performance. *Journal of Abnormal and Social Psychology, 65*, 178–182.

Atkinson, J. W. (Ed.). (1958). *Motives in fantasy, action, and society*. Princeton, NJ: Van Nostrand.

Atkinson, J. W. (1964). *An introduction to motivation*. Princeton, NJ: Van Nostrand.

Atkinson, J. W., Bongort, M., & Price, L. H. (1977). Explorations using computer simulation to comprehend TAT measurement of motivation. *Motivation and Emotion, 1*, 1–27.

Atkinson, J. W., Heyns, R. W., & Veroff, J. (1954). The effect of experimental arousal of the affiliation motive on thematic apperception. *Journal of Abnormal and Social Psychology, 49*, 405–410.

Atkinson, J. W., & McClelland, D. C. (1948). The projective expression of needs: II. The effect of different intensities of the hunger drive on thematic apperception. *Journal of Experimental Psychology, 38*, 643–658.

Atkinson, J. W., & Raynor, J. O. (1974). *Motivation and achievement*. Washington, DC: Winston.

Atkinson, R. C., & Shiffrin, R. M. (1968). Human memory: A proposed system and its control processes. In K. Spence & J. Spence (Eds.), *The psychology of learning and motivation* (Vol. 2, pp. 90–195). New York: Academic Press.

Berkowitz, L. (1960). The judgmental processes in personality functioning. *Psychological Review, 67*, 130–142.

Blum, G. S. (1954). An experimental reunion of psychoanalytic theory with perceptual vigilance and defense. *Journal of Abnormal and Social Psychology, 49*, 94–98.

Bower, G. H. (1981). Mood and memory. *American Psychologist, 36*, 148–199.

Broadbent, A. E. (1958). *Perception and communication*. New York: Pergamon Press.

Bruner, J. S. (1957). On perceptual readiness. *Psychological Review, 64*, 123–152.

Bruner, J. S., & Goodman, C. C. (1947). Value and need as organizing factors in perception. *Journal of Abnormal and Social Psychology, 42*, 33–44.

Cantor, N., & Mischel, W. (1977). Traits as prototypes: Effects on recognition memory. *Journal of Personality and Social Psychology, 35*, 38–49.

Chomsky, N. (1957). *Syntactic structures*. The Hague: Morton.

Clark, M. S., & Fiske, S. T. (1982). *Affect and cognition: The Seventeenth Annual Carnegie Symposium on Cognition*. Hillsdale, NJ: Erlbaum.

Clark, R. A. (1952). The projective measurement of experimentally induced levels of sexual motivation. *Journal of Experimental Psychology, 44*, 391–399.

Clark, R. A. (1955). The effects of sexual motivation on phantasy. In A. C. McClelland (Ed.), *Studies in motivation* (pp. 44–57). New York: Appleton-Century-Crofts.

Coren, S., Porac, C., & Ward, L. M. (1984). *Sensation and perception* (2d ed.). Orlando, FL: Academic Press.

Darwin, C. (1872). *The expression of emotions in man and animals*. New York: Appleton.

Dawes, R. M. (1976). Shallow psychology. In J. S. Carroll & J. W. Payne (Eds.), *Cognition and social behavior* (pp. 3–11). Hillsdale, NJ: Erlbaum.

Dember, W. N. (1960). *The psychology of perception*. New York: Holt, Rinehart and Winston.

Festinger, L. (1958). The motivating effect of cognitive dissonance. In G. Lindzey (Ed.), *Assessment of human motives* (pp. 65–86). New York: Holt, Rinehart and Winston.

Festinger, L. (1961). The psychological effects of insufficient reward. *American Psychologist, 16*, 1–11.

Freud, S. (1955). A childhood recollection from "Dichtung and Wahrheit." In J. Strachey & A. Freud (Eds.), *The Standard edition of the complete psychological works of Sigmund Freud* (Vol. 17). London: Hogarth Press. (Original work published 1917)

Galton, F. (1883). *Inquiries into human faculty and its development*. London: Macmillan.

Guthrie, E. R. (1935). *The psychology of learning*. New York: Harper & Row.

Hamilton, D. L. (1979). A cognitive attributional analysis of stereotyping. In L. Berkowitz (Ed.), *Advances in experimental social psychology* (Vol. 12, pp. 53–84). New York: Academic Press.

Hamilton, D. L. (1981). *Cognitive processes in stereotyping and intergroup behavior*. Hillsdale, NJ: Erlbaum.

Harper, R. J. C., Anderson, C. C., Christensen, C. M., & Hunka, S. M. (Eds.). (1964). *The cognitive processes: Readings*. Englewood Cliffs, NJ: Prentice-Hall.

Hegel, G. W. F. (1977). *Difference between the systems of Fichte and Schelling* (H. S. Harris & W. Cerf, Trans.). Albany: State University of New York Press. (Original work published 1801)

Henle, M. (1964). Some motivational processes on cognition. In R. J. C. Harper, C. C. Anderson, C. M. Christensen, & S. M. Hunka (Eds.), *The cognitive processes: Readings* (pp. 389–399). Englewood Cliffs, NJ: Prentice-Hall.

Higgins, E. T., King, G. A., & Mavin, G. H. (1982). Individual construct accessibility and subjective impressions and recall. *Journal of Personality and Social Psychology, 43*, 35–47.

Hofstadter, D. R. (1979). *Godel, Escher, Bach: An eternal golden braid*. New York: Vintage.

Hull, C. L. (1943). *Principles of behaviour*. New York: Appleton-Century.

James, W. (1890). *The principles of psychology* (Vols. 1 & 2). New York: Holt.

Levine, M. V., & Shefner, J. M. (1981). *Fundamentals of sensation and perception*. Reading, MA: Addison-Wesley.

Lewin, K. (1935). *A dynamic theory of personality*. New York: McGraw-Hill.

Lewin, K. (1951). *Field theory in social science*. New York: Harper & Brothers.

Markus, H. (1977). Self-schema and processing information about the self. *Journal of Personality and Social Psychology, 35*, 63–78.

McClelland, D. C., & Atkinson, J. W. (1948). The projective expression of needs: I. The effect of different intensities of the hunger drive on perception. *Journal of Psychology, 25*, 205–232.

McClelland, D. C., Atkinson, J. W., Clark, R. A., & Lowell, E. (1953). *The achievement motive*. New York: Appleton-Century-Crofts.

McDougall, W. (1908). *Introduction to social psychology*. London: Methuen.

Miller, A. T., & Ross, M. (1975). Self-serving biases in the attribution of causality: Fact or fiction? *Psychological Bulletin, 82*, 213–225.

Miller, N. E. (1948). Studies of fear as an acquirable drive: I. Fear as motivation and fear-reduction as reinforcement in the learning of new responses. *Journal of Experimental Psychology, 38*, 89–101.

Murray, H. A. (1938). *Explorations in personality*. New York: Oxford University Press.

Neisser, U. (1967). *Cognitive psychology*. New York: Appleton-Century-Crofts.

Newell, A., & Simon, H. A. (1972). *Human problem solving*. Englewood Cliffs, NJ: Prentice-Hall.

Nisbett, R., & Ross, L. (1980). *Human inferences: Strategies and shortcomings of social judgment*. Englewood Cliffs, NJ: Prentice-Hall.

Norman, D. A. (1980). Twelve issues for cognitive science. In D. A. Norman (Ed.), *Perspectives on cognitive science: Talks from the La Jolla conference* (pp. 265–295). Hillsdale, NJ: Erlbaum.

Pettigrew, T. F. (1958). The measurement and correlates of category width as a cognitive variable. *Journal of Personality, 26*, 532–544.

Piaget, J. (1981). Intelligence and affectivity: Their relationship during child development (T. A. Brown & C. E. Kaegi, Eds. and Trans.). *Annual Reviews, 14*, 77.

Postman, L., Bruner, J. S., & McGinnis, E. (1948). Personal values as selective factors in perception. *Journal of Abnormal and Social Psychology, 43*, 142–154.

Prentice, W. C. H. (1964). Some cognitive aspects of motivation. In R. J. C. Harper, C. C. Anderson,

C. M. Christensen, & S. M. Hunka (Eds.), *The cognitive processes: Readings* (pp. 400–411). Englewood Cliffs, NJ: Prentice-Hall.

Schachter, S., & Singer, J. E. (1962). Cognitive, social, and physiological determinants of emotional state. *Psychological Review, 69*, 379–399.

Secord, P. F., & Backman, C. W. (1960). Personality theory and the problem of stability and change in individual behaviour: An interpersonal approach. *Psychological Review, 68*, 21–32.

Simon, H. A. (1982). Comments on affective underpinnings of cognition. In M. S. Clark & S. T. Fiske (Eds.), *Affect and cognition: The Seventeenth Annual Carnegie Symposium on Cognition* (pp. 333–342). Hillsdale, NJ: Erlbaum.

Sorrentino, R. M., Short, J. C., & Raynor, J. O. (1984). Uncertainty orientation: Implications for affective and cognitive views of achievement behaviour. *Journal of Personality and Social Psychology, 46*, 189–206.

Spence, K. W. (1956). *Behavior theory and conditioning.* New Haven: Yale University Press.

Swann, W. B. (1983). Self-verification: Bringing social reality into harmony with the self. In J. Suls & A. G. Greenwald (Eds.), *Social psychological perspectives on the self* (Vol. 2, pp. 33–66). Hillsdale, NJ: Erlbaum.

Titchener, E. B. (1899). Structural and functional psychology. *Philosophical Review, 8*, 290–299.

Tolman, E. C. (1932). *Purposive behavior in animals and men.* New York: Century.

Tolman, E. C. (1959). Principles of purposive behaviour. In S. Koch (Ed.), *Psychology: A study of a science* (Vol. 2, pp. 92–157). New York: McGraw-Hill.

Trope, Y. (1975). Seeking information about one's own ability as a determinant of choice among tasks. *Journal of Personality and Social Psychology, 32*, 1004–1013.

Walker, E. L., & Atkinson, J. W., with the collaboration of Veroff, J., Birney, R., Dember, W., & Moulton, R. (1958). The expression of fear-related motivation in thematiac apperception as a function of proximity to an atomic explosion. In J. W. Atkinson (Ed.), *Motives in fantasy, action, and society* (pp. 143–159). Princeton, NJ: VAn Nostrand.

Watson, J. B. (1930). *Behaviourism.* New York: Norton.

Weiner, B. (1972). *Theories of motivation: From mechanism to cognition.* Chicago: Markham.

Weinstein, M. S. (1969). Achievement motivation and risk preference. *Journal of Personality and Social Psychology, 13*, 153–172.

PART I
The Self

CHAPTER 2

Standards and the Process of Self-Evaluation
Multiple Affects from Multiple Stages

E. TORY HIGGINS
TIMOTHY STRAUMAN
RUTH KLEIN
New York University

Psychologists have been concerned with the emotional consequences of self-evaluation for many years. James (1890/1948), for example, suggested that people feel disappointed when their attributes do not match their aims or pretensions, and Cooley (1902/1964) stated that people feel ashamed and unworthy when they believe their attributes do not fulfill the hopes or aspirations of others for them. According to Freud (1923/1961), people feel guilty when their performance is discrepant from their own prescriptions and sense of duty and feel anxious when their performance doesn't conform to the prescriptions and normative expectations of significant others (see also Horney, 1937; Sullivan, 1953). Adler (1929/1964) suggested that people who believe they are incapable of ever changing their attributes or performance sufficiently to achieve their goals feel hopeless. Lewin (1951) argued that feelings of success and failure depend on one's level of performance relative to a particular frame of reference, and Atkinson (1964) distinguished between the capacity to experience pride in accomplishment (associated with the hope of success) and the capacity to experience shame given nonattainment of a goal (associated with the fear of failure). More recently, Weiner (1982) has described the interrelations among people's causal attributions for their performance (e.g., ability), the causal features reflected in such attributions (e.g., stable, internal locus of control), and their emotional reactions to their performance (e.g., pride).

This literature suggests that the same performance can produce different emotions in different individuals, depending on how it is causally interpreted and on which standard or frame of reference is used to evaluate it. The emotional consequences of self-evaluation, however, are typically described as if a single judgment of a stimulus property (i.e., a performance or attribute) produces a single emotion. But is this always the case? Imagine a situation in which three different students each receive 80% on an exam when the average mark was 70%. One of the students might simply feel proud, another might feel proud but dissatisfied, and the third might feel ashamed and dissatisfied but hopeful. If a single performance or attribute can produce multiple emotional responses, as seems intuitively to be the case, then models of motivation and behavior that focus only on single emotional responses limit their predictive power and range of applicability. At present, however, there is not even a general model for understanding how multiple and disparate emotional responses would be produced in an individual by a single stimulus property. The purpose of this chapter is to address this initial need in an admittedly preliminary manner. In doing so, we will address the following questions: How could the same stimulus property produce different kinds of emotions and a different number of emotions in different people? How could a particular stimulus property produce both positive and negative emotions in the same person?

The model of self-evaluation presented here is based on a more general theory of social evaluation (i.e., evaluation of self and others) that involves the following basic postulates:

1. There are different kinds of standards that individuals use to evaluate the stimulus properties of self and others.
2. Social evaluation is a process that involves multiple stages of information processing and judgments.
3. Different standards can be utilized at the different stages in the process of social evaluation.
4. Utilizing different standards at different stages of social evaluation can produce different emotions.
5. Both personality variables and contextual variables can influence which standards are used at which stage of social evaluation.

Each of these postulates will be considered in turn. Although our discussion will focus on self-evaluation, evidence from the literature on evaluating others will be described as well to provide support for the postulates. At the end of the chapter, we will briefly discuss possible differences between self-evaluation and evaluation of others.

STANDARDS OF SELF-EVALUATION

A wide variety of standards of self-evaluation have been described in the literature. Sherif (1936) and Lewin (1951) stated that judgments and experiences of success and failure take place within some frame of reference, where the frame of reference can be the interiorization of the norms and values of one's culture, the achievements of others, one's own level of aspiration (i.e., one's personal goals), or one's own past performance. The literature on reference groups, where judgments are anchored to membership and nonmembership groups, describes two basic kinds of social group influence on people's self-judgments (Hyman, 1942; Kelley, 1952; Merton & Kitt, 1952; Newcomb, 1952; Sherif, 1948). First, there are social groups that serve as a comparison point against which a person can evaluate himself or herself (considered to be a "perceptual" standard). Second, there are norm-setting and norm-enforcing social groups whose code defines the acceptability or propriety of a person's behavior (considered to be a "motivational" standard). In addition to social groups, it has also been suggested that particular individuals can serve as standards for self-evaluation (Festinger, 1954; Freud, 1923/1961; Mead, 1934; Merton & Kitt, 1952), either because the individual is salient or emotionally significant in one's life or because the individual's attributes permit a valid assessment of one's ability (Goethals & Darley, 1977).

It has also been proposed that different self-concepts or ego states function as standards for self-evaluation, such as James's (1890/1948) "ideal social" self and "spiritual" self, Freud's (1923/1961) "superego," and Rogers's (1961) "ideal" self (see Higgins, 1983, for a review of these kinds of standards). Bandura (1982) distinguished between such "personal standards" and the "social referential comparison" standards described earlier. Most recently, it has been suggested that self-evaluation can even involve comparisons to constructed or imaginary standards, such as mental simulations (Kahneman & Tversky, 1982) or "possible" selves (Markus & Nurius, 1983), which can consist of dreams and fantasies as well as logical possibilities (see also Freud's [1923/1961] discussion of the "ego-ideal").

Even from this brief review, it is evident that many different kinds of standards for self-evaluation have been identified in the literature. What is missing, however, is a general framework that systematically organizes and distinguishes among these and other varieties of standard. Such a framework is necessary to appreciate the complex role of standards in the process of self-evaluation and the full extent of possible individual differences in their use. Our proposed classification scheme, shown in Table 2.1, distinguishes among three major types of standards: *factual points of reference, acquired guides,* and *imagined possibilities.* In the present chapter, we will concentrate on the first two general types of standards. Our discussion will also focus on the use of standards in the process of self-evaluation, but we will briefly note when the different kinds of standards to be described can be used to evaluate others as well.

Factual Points of Reference

One major type of standard involves the evaluator's beliefs about the actual performance or attributes of one or more persons, which are used as points of reference for judging his or her own attributes or performance. It must be noted

TABLE 2.1   Classification Scheme for Standards of Self-Evaluation

Factual Points of Reference
Social category reference points
Meaningful other reference points
  Relevant other reference points
  Significant other reference points
Autobiographical reference points
Social context reference points

Acquired Guides
Ideal/own guide
Ideal/other guide
Ought/own guide
Ought/other guide

Imagined Possibilities

that although such a point of reference is subjectively or phenomenologically factual, it may or may not be objectively accurate. There are four basic kinds of factual reference points: social category, meaningful other, autobiographical, and social context reference points. Before beginning our discussion of these reference points, it should be noted that although we discuss them as if there were a particular point underlying an individual's standards, there is often a distribution of points. Various theories have been proposed concerning which point in the distribution is used as the standard of reference—the mean attribute or performance, the midpoint of the range of attributes or performances, the median of the frequency of attributes or performances, or the extreme end points or anchors of the distribution (Eiser & Stroebe, 1972; Helson, 1964; Ostrom & Upshaw, 1968; Parducci, 1965; Volkmann, 1951). For the purposes of this chapter, it is not crucial to decide which of these possible distribution points is actually used. Indeed, which distribution point is used may vary for different individuals and different contexts.

Social Category Reference Points

A social category reference point is a factual standard defined by the "average" performance or attributes (e.g., mean, median, modal, prototypical) of the members of some social category or group. The evaluator may or may not be a member of the group and may or may not have any direct social interaction with the group members (see Merton & Kitt, 1952; Newcomb, 1952). Moreover, the size of the social category or group can vary greatly, from "people in general" to "closest friends." Changes in the social category to which an individual compares his or her performance have been shown to influence the individual's self evaluation. For example, Hyman (1942) found changes in people's judgments of their own status when they were asked to judge their economic status first in comparison to "all adults in the U.S." and then in comparison to "adults in your occupation." Social category standards can also influence how information about others' performance is processed. Higgins and Lurie's (1983) study, for example, found that subjects recalled a target trial judge's sentencing behavior differently, depending on what social category norm for trial judges' sentencing behavior had been established for subjects prior to recall (i.e., a relatively lenient, moderate, or harsh social category reference point).

Meaningful Other Reference Points

A meaningful other reference point is a factual standard defined by the performance or attributes of another individual who is meaningful to the evaluator, either because of the *relevance* or appropriateness of the individual's attributes for social comparison (Bernstein & Crosby, 1980; Festinger, 1954; Goethals & Darley, 1977) or because of his or her emotional *significance* or importance to the evaluator. The meaningful other may or may not be a personal acquaintance of the evaluator (e.g., a movie star) and may or may not be currently alive (e.g. a deceased father). Merton & Kitt (1952) describe such meaningful others to whom soldiers in World War II may have idiosyncratically compared their lot—a civilian friend in a "cushy" job back home, a cousin enjoying life as a war correspondent, an undrafted movie star about whom a soldier had read in a magazine. Reference to a meaningful other can also influence judgments of others (Higgins & King, 1981; Nisbett & Ross, 1980; Sarbin, Taft, & Bailey, 1960).

Autobiographical Reference Points

An autobiographical reference point is a factual standard defined by the evaluator's own past performance or attributes. It can represent a single instance or a distribution of instances, and the performance or attribute can be recent or remote. According to Suls and Mullen (1982), a common orientation to self-evaluation of children 3–5 years old is to compare their present performance with their past performance, which leads to relatively positive self-evaluation given that children show rapid advancement in their skills during this period (see also Ruble, 1983; Veroff, 1969). There is also considerable evidence that young children frequently judge others' performance in terms of their own performance (Higgins, 1981b; Shantz, 1983) and that under certain circumstances, adults do so as well (Ross, 1977).

Different self-evaluations can occur, depending on whether an individual uses a recent or a remote autobiographical reference point. In fact, a change from using a remote to using a recent autobiographical reference point could account for why lottery winners' and accident victims' ratings of their present happiness (a few months, on the average, after the event) were considerably less discrepant than one might expect (Brickman, Coates, Janoff-Bulman, 1978). If the individuals in each group had compared their current lives to their lives prior to the event (i.e., prior to winning the lottery or having the accident), their self-evaluated happiness would have been extremely different. But if they had compared their current lives to their recent lives since the event, the difference between the groups would be considerably reduced, which would explain Brickman et al.'s (1978) findings.

There is another distinction among autobiographical reference points that may underlie other results in the Brickman et al. (1978) study. That is, there is a distinction between an individual comparing the level of a current attribute to his or her previous level on that attribute versus an individual comparing the change in the level of an attribute to the change in the level of one of his or her other attributes. When the subjects in Brickman et al.'s (1978) study were asked to rate the pleasure they currently derived from everyday, mundane activities (e.g., watching television, reading a magazine, talking to a friend), the accident victims and the lottery winners expressed the *same level* of enjoyment in these activities, which was lower than the level expressed by a control group of subjects. These intriguing results can be understood if one assumes that the accident victims and lottery winners used different autobiographical reference points. The accident victims (given their current difficulty in performing even simple tasks) would derive less pleasure from these activities than they had prior to the accident, and the lottery winners would have experienced less change in these mundane activities since winning the lottery than in other activities that were more dependent on wealth (e.g., travel, buying gifts). Another example of this latter type of autobiographical reference point would be an individual who negatively evaluates his or her performance in one activity because the rate of improvement has been less than what he or she has achieved in other activities (e.g., a gymnast or a swimmer comparing his or her rate of improvement in different events).

Social Context Reference Points

A social context reference point is a factual standard defined by the performance or attributes of the immediate context of people to whom the evaluator is currently exposed (and notices). The social context can be one or more people. Morse and Gergen (1970), for example, found that people will evaluate themselves more highly after exposure to a person with undesirable characteristics than after exposure to a person with desirable characteristics. The developmental literature has shown that children in the early elementary school years begin to evaluate their performance on the basis of how other children in their immediate context have performed and even earlier evaluate others' performance in terms of the immediate social context (Dweck & Elliot, 1983; Ruble, 1983).

In fact, when a social context is available and salient, the reference point is often given by the context, which can be linguistic or extralinguistic. A common case in which the reference point is provided by the linguistic context is comprehension of comparative statements. For example, in the comparative statement, "Tom is more friendly than Sam," the standard of friendliness is given as Sam (see Higgins, 1977; Huttenlocher & Higgins, 1971; Lyons, 1968). With respect to extralinguistic contexts, many studies have found that people will vary their evaluations of a stimulus as a function of the context in which it appears, where the stimulus is evaluated in terms of its position along some dimension relative to the position of the context along that dimension (Glucksberg, Krauss, & Higgins, 1975; Olson, 1970; Rosenberg & Cohen, 1966). Manis and Armstrong (1971), for example, found that subjects evaluated neutral faces more positively when they appeared within a context of unpleasant faces than when they appeared within a context of pleasant faces. Higgins and Lurie's (1983) Study 2 found that subjects' evaluations of a target trial judge's sentencing decisions varied depending on the harshness or leniency of the sentencing decisions of other trial judges about whom they read at the same time (i.e., the social context reference point) and demonstrated that this variation was due to the context's functioning as a judgmental comparison point (*not* to its causing perceptual, adaptation-level effects). Moreover, Higgins and Lurie's (1983) Study 1 found that this social context–induced evaluation, in combination with the social category norm for trial judges that had been previously established for subjects (described earlier), determined subjects' subsequent recall of the target judge's sentencing decisions.

When the reference point is defined by an immediate context of people to whom the evaluator is exposed, one might wish to argue that this is simply another kind of social category reference point. The immediate social context, however, is a momentary stimulus event. It is not a preestablished or predefined social construct that is represented in, and retrieved from, conceptual memory, as is the case for social category reference points. Of course, when people are still forming a social category, the information about category instances in the immediate context (which is currently used as a social context reference point) will be represented as part of the established social category that is later retrieved from conceptual memory (i.e., to be used as part of a social category reference point).

It is also important to distinguish social context reference points from general "context effects" on the evaluation process. The context of the evaluator must be distinguished from the context surrounding the presentation of the target (i.e., the social context reference point). Admittedly, this distinction blurs in the case of self-evaluation. But even in the case of self-evaluation, a context effect refers to the impact of the context on *which* standard is selected and utilized, as when conceptual priming increases the relative accessibility of a particular standard (see Higgins & King, 1981), rather than itself being a type of standard. Of course, if a contextual prime, such as exposure to information about the "friendly" behaviors of others (Srull & Wyer, 1979), is considered together with the target person (self or other), it could end up functioning as a social context reference point. This might happen if the prime is sufficiently salient and occurs in close enough proximity to the target so that the target is considered in conjunction with (i.e., relative to) the prime. When this happens, the prime might produce a "contrast" effect on the target judgment, rather than the usual "assimilation" effect (see also Herr, Sherman, & Fazio [1983] for another case in which a prime can become a context standard). Most priming studies have avoided this problem by using either subconscious priming or an unobtrusive priming context that is phenomenologically unrelated to the context in which the target is judged (Bargh, 1984; Higgins & King, 1981).

Acquired Guides

Another major type of standard involves *criteria of excellence or acceptability*— guides for behavior. The basic distinction between factual reference points and acquired guides is similar to Kelley's (1952) classic distinction between comparison and normative reference groups (see also Bandura's [1982] distinction between personal standards and social referential comparison points). As we have seen, however, comparison reference groups are only one kind of factual reference point. Likewise, normative reference groups are only one kind of acquired guide— a prescriptive obligation demanded by others. The traditional self and psychodynamic literatures suggest a variety of other guides as well.

James (1890/1948) distinguished between the "spiritual" self, which resembles Kelley's (1952) normative reference group in its reference to moral and religious (i.e., normative) social expectations, and the "ideal social" self, which refers to others' beliefs about a person's potential (i.e, their hopes and aspirations for the person). Cooley (1902/1964) also described a social "ideal" self, built up by imagining how a "better I" of aspiration would appear in the minds of people to whom we look up. The literature has also described a standard defined by what an individual would personally like to be (Allport, 1955; Colby, 1968; Lewin, 1935; Rogers, 1961). Thus, Rogers (1961) distinguished between what others believe a person should or ought to be (i.e., the normative standard) and the person's own belief about what he or she would ideally like to be. In discussing "level of aspiration," Lewin (1935) also distinguished between the expectations of adult authority figures that can raise a child's level of aspiration and the child's own hopes and personal goals. This same basic distinction can be found in Freud's conception of the "superego" (see Cameron, 1963; Freud, 1923/1961). The most emphasized aspect of the superego is the conscience, which involves a person's conceptions of his or her parents' moral and ethical standards (i.e., the normative standard). But there is also the "ego-ideal," which includes what a person would ideally like to be (or imagines is possible to be).

Once again, the literature provides a rich source of descriptions of different kinds of guides for behavior. But once again, different theorists emphasize different standards without providing a general framework or set of parameters for organizing and distinguishing among these standards. Recently, we have developed a theory of discrepant selves (Higgins, 1983; Higgins et al., 1985; Higgins et al., 1984) that proposes two dimensions as underlying the different kinds of acquired guides: *domains of the self* and *standpoints on the self*.

Self-discrepancy theory first distinguishes between the "ideal" self and the "ought" self (as well as the "actual" self). The "ideal" self is a person's representation of the attributes that someone (self or other) would ideally like the person to possess—someone's hopes, aspirations, or goals for the person. The "ought" self is a person's representation of the attributes that someone (self or other) believes the person should or ought to possess—someone's rules, injunctions, or prescriptions for the person. The "ought" domain differs from the "ideal" domain in that it involves a sense of duty, moral responsibility, and obligation, rather than desires, wishes, and wants.

In addition to different domains of the self, there are also different standpoints on the self, where a "standpoint" is a point of view or position from which a person is judged, reflecting a set of attitudes or values. Each of the domains of the self can involve different standpoints. Turner (1956) distinguished between self-attitudes or self-viewpoint (i.e., own standpoint) and the attitudes or viewpoints of others (e.g., mother's standpoint, friends' standpoint). Self-discrepancy theory (Higgins, 1983) combines these two dimensions to propose four basic kinds of guides for behavior: *ideal/own, ideal/other, ought/own,* and *ought/ other*. Each individual can, and often does, have multiple "other" standpoints on his or her self that are meaningful or relevant (e.g., mother, father, older brother, best friend, spouse, boss, colleagues). Thus, each individual can have multiple "ideal" and "ought" guides for behavior, which may vary in accessibility in different contexts or circumstances.

The previous literature on self standards has described the emotional consequences of discrepancies between people's attributes or performance and one of their acquired guides. Using our framework, one can discover considerable agreement in the literature concerning which discrepancies produce which negative emotions. The literature suggests that a discrepancy between an individual's attributes or performance and his or her *ideal/own* standard produces dissatis-faction and disappointment (Adler, 1929/1964; Allport, 1955; Duval & Wicklund, 1972; Horney, 1950; James, 1890/1948; Rogers, 1961), whereas a discrepancy between an individual's attributes or performance and his or her *ideal/ other* standard produces shame (Cooley, 1902/1964; Erikson, 1950/1963; James, 1890/1948; Lewin, 1935; Lewis, 1979). The literature also suggests that a discrepancy between an individual's attributes or performance and his or her *ought/own* standard produces guilt and feelings of worthlessness (Erikson, 1950/ 1963; Freud, 1923/1961; Horney, 1950; James, 1890/1948; Lewis, 1979), whereas a discrepancy between an individual's attributes or performance and his or her *ought/other* standard produces apprehension, panic, and insecurity (Erikson, 1950/1963; Freud, 1923/1961; Sullivan, 1953).

Thus, across a variety of sources, one can discriminate a pattern of relations between particular actual self versus guide discrepancies and particular emotional consequences. No previous research, however, has identified or directly compared each of the different actual self versus guide discrepancies and their emotional consequences. Higgins, Klein, and Strauman (1985) and Higgins, Strauman, and Klein (1984) have examined this issue in a recent study, in which nondepressed, slightly depressed, and moderately depressed undergraduates were asked to fill out a variety of questionnaires: the Selves Questionnaire, the Beck Depression Inventory, the Blatt Depressive Experiences Questionnaire, the Emotions Questionnaire (measuring chronic rather than momentary affect), and the Hopkins Symptom Checklist (Depression, Anxiety, Hostility, and Somatization subscales). The Selves Questionnaire asked the subjects to list up to ten attributes associated with each of six different self states where each self state (actual or potential) involved a particular domain of the self (i.e., the "actual" self, the "ideal" self, or the "ought" self) combined with a particular standpoint on that self (i.e., the subject's "own" standpoint or the standpoint of a significant "other"). To calculate the magnitude of discrepancy between any two self states, the attributes in each self state were compared to the attributes in the other self state, and the total number of attribute pairs that matched (i.e., synonyms) was subtracted from the total number of attribute pairs that mismatched (i.e., antonyms). To examine the relations between the different kinds of discrepancies and various emotions and symptoms associated with depression and anxiety, zero-order correlations and partial correlations (where the relation between a particular kind of discrepancy and a particular emotion or symptom was calculated with the contribution to this relation from associations to other kinds of discrepancies being partialled out) were then performed.

The results of this study suggest that discrepancies between people's beliefs about their chronic performances (i.e., their actual/own self-concept) and different guides for their behavior are associated with different chronic negative emotions. Actual/own versus ideal/own discrepancy was associated with chronic feelings of dissatisfaction. Actual/own versus ideal/other discrepancy was associated with the chronic absence of pride. Actual/own versus ought/own discrepancy was associated with chronic feelings of worthlessness and guilt. Finally, actual/own versus ought/other discrepancy was associated with chronic spells of terror or panic.

These results are quite consistent with the observations in the previous literature and, together with those observations, suggest that chronic performance discrepancies with people's different guides for behavior are associated with different negative emotions. Thus, the previous literature and our own results suggest that the emotional consequences of self-evaluation vary according to which kind of guide for behavior is used as the standard of evaluation.

THE PROCESS OF SELF-EVALUATION AND ITS EMOTIONAL CONSEQUENCES

Many models of social evaluation—especially models of self-evaluation—describe the evaluative process as if it involves a particular critical judgment that has some emotional consequence. In Festinger's (1954) theory of social comparison, for example, people evaluate an ability or opinion in some area by judging it in relation to some "similar" other's ability or opinion in the same area. As a result of such comparisons, a person may feel "adequate" or "inadequate" (for abilities) or may feel "proper" or "improper" (for opinions). Thus, in this model, self-evaluation involves a judgment relative to a meaningful other reference point. Although reference group theory (Hyman, 1942; Kelley, 1952; Merton & Kitt, 1952; Sherif, 1948) proposes two different kinds of self-evaluative standards—social category reference points and "other" standpoint acquired guides—any particular self-evaluative judgment is described as involving only a single standard and producing a single emotion, such as dissatisfaction with one's lot because it is worse than that of some reference group.

More recently, Weiner and his associates (Weiner, 1982; Weiner, Russel, & Lerman, 1978) have proposed an impressive, well-formulated model of self-evaluation that systematically relates specific kinds of causal attributions for one's performance to specific emotional consequences. For example, the model predicts that people will feel pride and positive self-esteem when they attribute the locus of causality of a positive outcome to themselves and that they will feel guilty when they attribute the locus of causality of a negative outcome to themselves and believe that the outcome was personally controllable (e.g., effort-related). Like the other models already discussed, this model clearly identifies an important factor in the self-evaluative process. Once again, however, the model focuses on a critical judgmental stage (in this case, the stage of causal attribution) that produces a particular emotion, with the specific emotion depending on the specific judgment made. Although there is some discussion of how other factors can independently influence affect, such as Weiner *et al.*'s (1978) discussion of outcome-dependent affects, the emotional consequences of a particular kind of judgment are emphasized.

The foregoing models of self-evaluation do make it clear why the *same* performance can make one person feel "inadequate" (performance less than that of

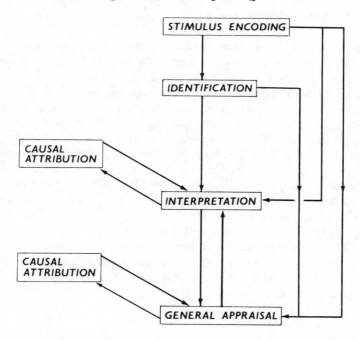

FIGURE 2.1 Illustration of the process of social evaluation.

a meaningful other), another person feel "dissatisfied" (performance less than that of some reference group), and a third person feel "guilty" (causal attribution of negative performance to controllable aspect of self). But these models provide less help in understanding why individuals can have multiple, distinct emotional reactions to a single performance and sometimes can have both positive and negative emotions. Returning to our opening example, what processes of self-evaluation could cause a person to feel ashamed, dissatisfied, and hopeful from the same performance?

To answer this question, it is necessary to consider more fully the process of self-evaluation and the role of both standard utilization and causal attribution in this process. We propose that social evaluation, whether of self or of others, is a multistage process in which there are a number of judgmental stages that can have emotional consequences. As illustrated in Figure 2.1, we propose that there are four basic stages in the process of social evaluation—*stimulus representation, identification, interpretation,* and *general appraisal*—plus causal attributions that can have a variety of possible effects once the stimulus is identified (i.e., "Why did this kind of stimulus occur?"). We will first describe each of the stages and its possible emotional consequences in relation to self-evaluation. Then we will discuss how these stages are interrelated and the emotional implications of these interrelations.

Stages of the Self-Evaluative Process

Because the emotional consequences of causal attribution as an independent stage have already received considerable attention in the literature (Storms & McCaul, 1976; Weiner *et al.*, 1978), we will consider the role of causal attribution in the self-evaluative process only with respect to its interrelations with the later stages. Thus, in this section, we will restrict our attention to the stages of stimulus representation, identification, interpretation, and general appraisal. To provide some initial sense of the differences among these stages, consider the examples of self-evaluation shown in Table 2.2. Example 1 concerns a teenage girl from a small town who is visiting New York City for the first time; Example 2 concerns a freshman seeing his final course grade on a posted list; Example 3 concerns a wife arguing with her husband on a political issue about which she cares deeply; and Example 4 concerns a 9-year-old boy who is learning to skip rope. These examples reflect the utilization of a variety of different standards of evaluation. Each example involves different standards being utilized at different stages in the evaluative process, thus producing both positive and negative emotions in the same person. Let us now consider the distinctions among the different stages of self-evaluation reflected in these examples.

Stimulus Representation

The stimulus representation stage involves the registration and representation of the details and features of the attribute- or performance-related stimulus (action,

TABLE 2.2 Examples of Stimulus Representation, Identification, Interpretation, and General Appraisal

Example	Stimulus Representation	Identification	Interpretation	General Appraisal
1	I said "Hello" and smiled to stranger on street	Greeting	Friendly (most people don't greet strangers on street)	Bad (I should not be friendly to strangers on street)
2	I received 80% on test	Pass	Success (I noticed more lower scores than higher scores on the part of the list I saw)	Bad (I wanted to get over 90%)
3	I said "That was a stupid thing to say" to husband	Insult	Hostile (I have never been so antagonistic before)	Good (I want to be able to express anger)
4	I continuously stepped on skipping rope	Not getting the hang of it	Failure (my sister learned to skip in much less time)	Good (I ought to be poor at girlish games)

event, performance outcome, etc.). As exemplified in Table 2.2, this stage is restricted to describing or encoding the salient aspects of the stimulus information. Although inferential processes can be involved even at this stage (e.g., inferring that turned-up corners of the mouth is a smile, not a grimace) and the judgment can be influenced by concomitant circumstances (e.g., perceptual contrast or assimilation effects), neither the evaluative standards described earlier nor causal attribution are utilized in this stage. In addition, this judgmental stage is the least likely to produce an emotion. This is not to say that the attribute- or performance-related stimulus is unlikely to produce an emotion. In fact, the actions involved in Example 3 (yelling) and Example 4 (tripping) in Table 2.2 are likely to arouse feelings. (See also Lader & Marks [1972] for a discussion of "unconditioned emotional responses" to events). But this does not mean that the stage of stimulus representation itself produces an emotion. Nevertheless, even this stage can have emotional consequences if aspects of the representation have emotional associations (e.g., positive associations to "smiled" in Example 1).

Identification

The identification stage involves designating the attribute- or performance-related stimulus as being a particular type of entity or event. As exemplified in Table 2.2, this stage involves recognizing that the attribute or performance is an instance of some previously established action class or event class (e.g., an instance of "greeting" behavior). If the stimulus is not an instance of some previously established stimulus class, this stage of the self-evaluative process will not occur. As shown in Figure 2.1, the evaluator can go directly from the stimulus-representation stage to the interpretation stage (or even to the general appraisal stage). In fact, when the attribute or performance is truly novel, an interpretation of it may be necessary to create or establish a new stimulus class for future identification.

Like the stimulus representation stage, neither the evaluative standards described earlier nor causal attributions are involved at this stage of the self-evaluative process. Of course, this is not to say that inferences or comparison processes are not involved at this stage, as the process of identification involves comparing the degree of match or similarity between the stimulus and alternative stimulus classes of which it could be an instance (see Rosch, 1978; Tversky & Gati, 1978). This stage is more likely to produce emotions than the stimulus representation stage because the stimulus classes themselves can have emotions associated with them that are aroused when the construct is activated by a new instance of the class (see Fiske, 1982; Higgins, 1981a). For example, "pass" may be a performance construct whose utilization in the past has typically co-occurred with positive emotions, so that it can arouse a positive emotion even without further interpretation (Karabenick, 1972). Similarly, because instances of the construct "insult" typically occur in unpleasant circumstances, the construct could become associated with a negative emotion, so that activating the construct by identifying a new instance could induce a negative emotion.[1] This stage can also produce emotions as a function of whether performance matches some absolute standard. Recognizing that one's performance has failed to meet an experimenter-provided task criterion, for example, can lead to negative self-evaluation and discomfort (see Carver & Scheier, 1982; Wicklund, 1975).

Interpretation

The interpretation stage involves inferring or construing the personal meaning or implications of an attribute- or performance-related stimulus. In contrast to stimulus representation and identification, interpretation necessarily involves the utilization of some standard of evaluation. We propose that the standards utilized in the interpretation stage are typically factual points of reference. This is exemplified in Table 2.2, where Example 1 involves the use of a social category reference point, Example 2 involves the use of a social context reference point, Example 3 involves the use of a autobiographical reference point, and Example 4 involves the use of a meaningful other reference point. As we will discuss in a later section, however, some individuals may use acquired guides to interpret their attribute or performance, so that even their evaluation of actual "success" or "failure" may be determined by what they hoped for, wanted, or believed ought to happen, rather than by the factual level of the stimulus. And almost everyone, on occasion, will judge his or her own performance, or another's performance, in terms of what he or she wanted to occur, rather than what he or she factually should have expected to occur. Imagined possibilities may also be used in interpretation, as when individuals interpret their performance as a success or a failure depending on the level of performance they imagine a significant other would have achieved on the same task or they themselves would have achieved if they had tried harder.

Because of the ambiguity of many trait-related judgments, it is often difficult to distinguish between judgments reflecting identification and judgments reflecting interpretation. For example, the statement "I was friendly" could mean "I behaved in a friendly manner," "I behaved in a more friendly manner than the others did in that situation," or "I displayed a more friendly disposition than the others did." The first assertion need not involve more than recognizing the act as an instance of the "friendly" performance class, without any use of standards (i.e., identification), whereas the second and third assertions both involve interpretation and the use of standards (the standards being others' behavior in the situation and others' dispositions, respectively).

With trait-related judgments, it is also often difficult to know whether the judgment did or did not involve a causal attribution. The current person perception literature seems to assume that judgments such as "I was friendly" necessarily reflect some causal attribution. This assumption may derive, in part, from a common (though by no means universal) failure to distinguish explicitly between the use of attributionally relevant information (i.e., sources of information that *could* be used to make attributions) and the actual process of causal reasoning. Consider Example 2 in Table 2.2, for instance. The freshman interprets his test score as a "success" because it was generally higher than the other scores he noticed on the list. In our model, this judgment reflects the use of a social context reference point to interpret the score. From an attributional perspective (e.g., Heider, 1958; Kelley, 1967), however, one could describe this judgment as involving the use of social "consensus" information (or "task difficulty" information).

Similarly, the use of social category reference points (and, to a lesser extent, meaningful other reference points) could be described as involving the use of "consensus" information, and the use of autobiographical reference points could be described as involving the use of "consistency" information. In such cases, therefore, interpretation involves the use of attributionally relevant information sources. But this does not imply that a process of causal reasoning, such as Kelley's (1967) ANOVA process, is necessarily involved. A comparative judgment relating the performance to some standard is sufficient to interpret the performance. In fact, the evaluator may be interested not in a causal explanation for the performance (i.e., "Why did I get 80% on the test?") but simply in whether he did better or worse than others did. Furthermore, interpretation need not even involve attributionally relevant information sources. For example, the utilization of an ideal/own acquired guide need not involve the use of consensus, consistency, or any other attributionally relevant information source. Thus, interpretation of one's performance can occur without the involvement of either causal reasoning or the use of attributionally relevant information. This possibility is reflected in Weiner *et al.*'s (1978) discussion of outcome-dependent affects, in which people's initial judgments of their performance as a success or failure are described as influencing their emotions independently of their explanations for the success or failure.

More than either the stimulus representation stage or the identification stage, the interpretation stage is likely to have emotional consequences, because the interpretation of one's performance necessarily has personal, self-evaluative significance. Of course, the degree of emotional impact depends on both the subjective connotations of the performance class judged to be involved and the extremity of the judgment. For example, being "friendly" may have different emotional connotations for different people, or different people may judge the degree of their "friendliness" differently (e.g., "considerably," "very," "extremely"). One important source of the emotional connotations of a performance class is people's acquired guides; thus, the general appraisal stage can influence the emotional consequences of the interpretation stage. But there are also other sources of the emotional connotations of a performance class (e.g., linguistic associations, associations within implicit personality structures, formal ethical education). For this reason, the emotional connotations and emotional consequences of a particular performance class cannot be predicted or understood solely in terms of its absence or presence in a person's acquired guides.

Finally, in the examples shown in Table 2.2, the identification and interpretation judgments were selected to have similar evaluative tone, but this need not be the case. For instance, if the freshman in Example 2 had used his best friend as the standard for interpretation (i.e., a meaningful other reference point) and his friend had received 90% on the exam, he would have interpreted his performance as a "failure," which has an emotional significance that is opposite to the emotion associated with identifying the performance as a "pass."

General Appraisal

The general appraisal stage involves an overall estimation of the worth or value of the attribute- or performance-related stimulus. When general appraisal occurs early in the process of self-evaluation, it resembles Lazarus's notion of primary appraisal (Coyne & Lazarus, 1980), although in our model it necessarily involves the utilization of some standard of evaluation. We propose that the standards used in the general appraisal stage typically are acquired guides (and, to a lesser extent, imagined possibilities). This is exemplified in Table 2.2, where Example 1 involves the use of an ought/parents guide, Example 2 involves the use of an ideal/own guide, Example 3 involves the use of an ideal/therapist guide, and Example 4 involves the use of an ought/own guide. Even more than the interpretation stage, the general appraisal stage is inherently evaluative, with direct emotional impact. Although we will describe the general appraisal stage as if it involves the application of a single standard, frequently more than one standard is applied in this stage. For example, Austin, McGinn, and Susmilch (1980) found that subjects' satisfaction with their reward for performing a task was influenced in an additive manner by both the level of reward received by another person for performing the same task (i.e., a social context reference point) and the level of reward they had previously received (i.e., an autobiographical reference point). Similarly, it is possible for multiple acquired guides, as well as a combination of factual reference points and required guides, to be used to appraise the same performance.

As discussed earlier, self discrepancy theory (Higgins, 1983; Higgins *et al.*, 1985) predicts which specific emotions are most likely to be associated with which kinds of discrepancies between a person's attributes and his or her acquired guides. Previous observations in the literature, as well as our own recent studies, support the theory's predictions that a discrepancy between a person's attributes (i.e., actual/own self-concept) and his or her ideal/own guide is associated with dissatisfaction and disappointment, a discrepancy between performance and ought/own guide is associated with feelings of guilt (which may not be expressed), a discrepancy between a person's attributes and his or her ideal/other guide is associated with shame or loss of pride, and a discrepancy between a person's attributes and his or her ought/other guide is associated with fear of punishment and panic. The theory also predicts that a match between a person's attributes and one of these kinds of guides is associated with an emotion that is opposite to the emotion associated with a discrepancy (Higgins, 1983). For example, a match between a person's attributes and his or her ideal/other guide is associated with feeling proud.

As exemplified in Table 2.2, the interpretation stage and the general appraisal stage can produce different emotions of opposite valence. In Example 1, the girl may first feel pleased to have been friendly to a stranger but then feel anxious because she broke one of her parents' rules. In Example 2, the freshman may first feel proud to have succeeded relative to the other students whose grades he noticed but then feel disappointed and dissatisfied to have missed the grade he wanted. In Example 3, the wife may first feel nervous or alarmed to have been so uncharacteristically hostile but then feel proud to have accomplished the goal her therapist had set for her. And in Example 4, the 9-year-old boy may first feel ashamed of having performed worse than his sister but then feel content or at ease for having performed the way he ought to perform as a *real* male (i.e., not a sissy). The switch in this example, as well as in Example 3, from a negative to a positive emotion as the evaluator moves from the interpretation stage to the general appraisal stage nicely exemplifies the old saw, "Every cloud has a silver lining."

Not only is the general appraisal stage more inherently emotional than the interpretation stage, but it can also produce more than one emotion for a single attribute or performance. The interpretation stage involves the utilization of a single standard—typically, a factual reference point—to make a specific judgment that can have an emotional consequence. In the general appraisal stage, however, it is possible for a person to use multiple acquired guides to evaluate his or her attributes or performance, with each resultant judgment potentially having its own emotional consequence. For example, a person's performance could match his or her ideal/own guide but be discrepant from his or her ought/other guide, thus producing both satisfaction and apprehension. This possibility of multiple emotions from multiple standard use during a *single* stage of processing is one of the most interesting features of the general appraisal stage. Moreover, as the foregoing example demonstrates, this feature alone can account for multiple emotions of opposite valence during the self-evaluation process.[2]

Judgmental Processes

These distinctions among stimulus representation, identification, interpretation, general appraisal, and causal attribution could, perhaps, clarify some issues in the literature concerning the processes underlying people's responses to their own and other's behavior. For example, consider the provocative question raised by Zajonc (1980): *"Do preferences need no inferences?"* (emphasis added). From the perspective of our model, there would be no single answer to this question. One would first have to decide whether "preferences" refers simply to emotional reactions or to evaluative judgments, since emotional reactions can occur as early as the stimulus representation stage whereas evaluative judgments occur only after identification has occurred. One would also have to decide whether "inferences" refers simply to going beyond the information given, which can occur even in the stimulus representation stage (i.e., the utilization of previously stored information that supplements the information available in the stimulus), or to drawing a conclusion on the basis of inductive or deductive reasoning, which occurs only at the interpretation, causal attribution, and general appraisal stages. Thus, depending on what one chose to mean by "preferences" and "inferences," one could safely conclude either that preferences need no inferences (e.g., emotional responses to a stimulus need no interpretations of or attributions to the stimulus) or that preferences do need inferences (e.g., evaluative judgments need to go beyond just the information given).

Even the evidence on frequency of exposure effects on stimulus preference without stimulus discrimination (reviewed in Zajonc, 1980) can lead to different conclusions, depending on what one means by "preference" and "discrimination." If subjects prefer stimulus A, which has appeared ten times, more than stimulus B, which has appeared only once, then subjects' mental records of A and B must be different in some way as a function of their different exposure histories. Moreover, when new instances of A and B appears later duruing testing (i.e., A_{11} and B_2), each instance must activate the correct imprint. Otherwise, the recorded difference between A and B would have no effect on the preference judgments. That is, if A_{11} were as likely to activate B as A, and if B_2 were as likely to activate A as B, then there would be no mean difference in preference judgments for A_{11} and B_2. The issue then becomes how to conceptualize this activation process.

This activation process would not require interpretation, general appraisal, or causal attribution; thus, to this extent at least, preferences need no such "inferences." On the other hand, this activation process would require stimulus representation; thus, to this extent at least, preferences need such "inferences." The only real controversy, then, revolves around whether identification of the stimulus is or is not necessary for preference judgment. Given that the activation process described here involves recognizing A_{11} as an instance of A or B_2 as an instance of B, our model suggests that identification would have to be involved. This does not imply, of course, that the stimulus could or would be verbally categorized.

But if preferences involve identification, why did the studies reviewed by Zajonc (1980) find that subjects' recognition performance was little better than chance? In these studies, the different instances of a frequently occurring stimulus were repetitions of the same stimulus. Given the novelty and complexity of the stimuli used, however, it is quite possible that subjects perceived these repetitions as different instances of the same stimulus class. In fact, if subjects had already recognized the instances as repetitions of the identical stimulus, they should have performed better on the recognition measure. As stated earlier, the preference judgment simply requires that each new instance be correctly recognized as a member of an established stimulus class (i.e., be identified) for the frequency difference between stimuli to have an effect. But the "recognition" measure used in these studies requires that a new instance be recognized as *identical* to a previously occurring instance (i.e., recognized as a repetition), which is a much finer and more difficult discrimination. Thus, correct performance on this "recognition" measure requires more than just identification.[3]

Interrelations Among the Self-Evaluative Stages

To consider the interrelationships among the different stages of the self-evaluation process, we begin by describing the interrelationships among stimulus representation, identification, interpretation, and general appraisal and then discuss the complex interrelationships between causal attribution and the later stages. As shown in Figure 2.1, we propose that the process of self-evaluation begins with stimulus representation and that the identification stage, when it occurs, appears before either interpretation or general appraisal. Otherwise, the order of the stages and the presence or absence of any stage is quite variable. We do expect, however, that interpretation precedes general appraisal more than the reverse, as reflected in the ordering of stages in Figure 2.1 and Table 2.2.

Figure 2.1 reflects our proposal that people do not always proceed through all the stages. They can move from the stimulus representation stage directly to the interpretation stage or even directly to the general appraisal stage (Lazarus, 1966) or from the identification stage directly to the general appraisal stage. For instance, the freshman in Example 2 of Table 2.2 could have encoded the information that he received 80% on the test (the stimulus representation stage) and then immediately appraised this as being discrepant from the 90% he wanted to obtain (the general appraisal stage), without going through either the identification or interpretation stages. Figure 2.1 also reflects our proposal that although interpretation may typically precede general appraisal (as exemplified in Table 2.2), general appraisal can precede interpretation. For an instance of the latter possibility, let us elaborate on the preceding example. The freshman begins with stimulus representation and then immediately appraises it as discrepant from his ideal/own guide, producing disappointment. At this point, the student could compare his grade to some other posted scores, decide that his score was higher than those of most of the other students, and feel some pride in being relatively successful (yet another way of finding the silver lining in the cloud).

The interrelationship between causal attribution and the later stages of self-evaluation is especially complex. The attribution literature has emphasized the impact of causal attribution on general appraisal and, especially, on interpretation (Bem, 1972; Heider, 1958; Kelley, 1967; Weiner *et al.*, 1971). Attributional processes do not occur prior to identification, because people must know what the stimulus is before they can ask why it occurred. As an example of how attribution following identification can influence interpretation, consider the girl in Example 1 of Table 2.2. If she had attributed her "greeting" to situational constraints or pressure, she would not have subsequently interpreted it as "friendly." As an example of how attribution following interpretation can influence general appraisal, consider the 9-year-old boy in Example 4 of Table 2.2. If he had attributed his "failure" in getting the hang of skipping to others' disruptive efforts (e.g., being jeered at by his sister's girlfriends), he would not have subsequently appraised his performance as "good" (cf. Weiner *et al.*, 1978).

As shown in Figure 2.1, it is also possible for general appraisal to be followed by a causal attribution. In such cases, the causal attribution could function to intensify or diminish the emotion produced by the general appraisal or could even produce a new emotion. For instance, the freshman in Example 2 of Table 2.2 could feel dissatisfied and disappointed after appraising his score as falling short of his personal goal, but if he then attributed his performance to insufficient preparation for the test, he could convince himself that he would do better next time, thus reducing his dissatisfaction with his performance and creating hope for the future. At the same time, this attribution could increase his disappointment, because he would believe that he could have achieved his goal if only he had worked harder.

In all of these cases, the impact of causal attribution on the stages of the self-evaluation process is momentary. But causal attribution could also have a chronic impact by influencing the formation and accessibility of alternative self-evaluation standards. For example, the attributional process could play a role in establishing which meaningful other is considered most relevant as a factual reference point (Goethals & Darley, 1977).

The attribution literature has paid little attention to the alternative relationship between causal attribution and other self-evaluation stages—the impact of identification, interpretation, or general appraisal on causal attribution. This is surprising, because causal attributions are obviously influenced by how the performance is identified and interpreted. Different attributions are made depending on whether the performance is judged to be a success or failure (cf. Hieder, 1958; Weiner *et al.*, 1971), but what determines this judgment? Storms and McCaul (1976) state that attribution of unwanted behavior to the self leads to "anxiety," but what determines whether the behavior is judged as wanted or unwanted? Thus, prior to the causal attribution, the performance must be identified, interpreted, or appraised sufficiently to determine whether it is a success or a failure, whether it is wanted or unwanted. Only then can the causal explanation for the performance be initiated. Moreover, this evaluation could influence which emotion is produced by the attribution. For example, if the performance is appraised as unwanted because it violates some rule of a significant other (i.e., a performance versus ought/other discrepancy), then an attribution to self may lead to anxiety, as Storms and McCaul (1976) suggest. But if the performance is unwanted because it fails to meet one's personal hopes or goals (i.e., a performance versus ideal/own discrepancy), then an attribution to self may produce dissatisfaction or disappointment, rather than anxiety.

If a person's judgments of success or failure were chronically influenced by his or her standards, the impact on causal attribution would be even greater. For instance, consider what would happen if the standard of interpretation used chronically by the student in Example 2 of Table 2.2 were his very high ideal/own guide (or some highly skilled significant other). This would produce a history of "failure" interpretations, which would tend to make him attribute any subsequent "failure" to a stable, internal cause and the rare "success" to an unstable, external cause (Feather & Simon, 1971).

It is also possible for a causal attribution to be influenced by the *emotion* produced by a preceding self-evaluation stage. (For a general discussion of the impact of emotions on social information processing, see Higgins, Kuiper, & Olson, 1981.) For example, if the freshman's performance in Example 2 of Table 2.2 is discrepant with his personal goals or hopes (i.e., a performance versus ideal/own discrepancy), he is likely to feel dissatisfied or disappointed. But he may also feel frustrated and angry at failing to obtain his needs (Higgins *et al.*, 1985). When he subsequently attempts to find an explanation for his performance, he may feel a need for the causal attribution to be consistent with his feeling of frustration and anger, such as "I was lazy and careless" or "The test was unfair" (see Weiner, 1982). Such cases are interesting because the attribution need not be based on either a comparative judgment or a causal analysis of the performance *per se*. Rather, it could simply involve the person's selecting the most accessible alternative among the set of possible interpretations for frustration and anger. (See Hoffman, Chapter 9 of this volume, for other cases of attribution being influenced by a prior affect.)

Finally, the emotions produced by causal attribution can also be influenced by the other self-evaluation stages, especially the general appraisal stage. Although it may be generally true that a particular kind of causal attribution tends to produce a particular kind of emotion (Weiner *et al.*, 1978), the particular emotion produced can also be influenced by *how the attribution itself is evaluated*. Consider, for example, the freshman in Example 2 of Table 2.2. What would happen if he attributed his "success" to the helpful effects of others? Weiner *et al.* (1978) suggest that he would feel grateful and appreciative. However, his emotions may also depend on how he interprets this help (e.g., "ashamed" because the other students didn't need any help) or on how he appraises it (e.g., "anxious" because his parents believe that one should not accept help from others). Even attributions such as "lack of effort" (as an explanation for failure) or "high ability" (as an explanation for success) can produce different emotions depending on how they are appraised. For example, despite his failure to win, a man may feel good that he has finally accomplished his goal of competing without the need to "go all out," or a woman may feel bad that she once again succeeded without being challenged.

Thus, the other self-evaluation stages can influence both the causal attribution itself and the emotion that is produced by it.[4]

INDIVIDUAL AND CONTEXTUAL VARIABILITY IN STANDARD UTILIZATION

It is evident from our description of the various kinds of standards that can be utilized in the different stages of the self-evaluation process, as well as the complex interrelations among these stages, that the self-evaluation process has the potential for considerable variability across individuals and contexts. This section explores some of the possible kinds of variability and their implications.

Individual Differences in Standard Utilization

In considering potential individual differences in standard utilization, there are a number of logical possibilities. One major way in which people could differ is with respect to which *type of standard* they typically utilize at different self-evaluation stages. As mentioned earlier, we expect that most people use factual reference points at the interpretation stage, but some people may use acquired guides. In fact, some evidence from the Higgins *et al.* (1985) study suggests that low self-esteem individuals, especially, may be prone to using acquired guides as a standard for interpretation. Item 1 on the Blatt Depressive Experiences Questionnaire asks respondents to agree or disagree with the statement "I set my personal goals and standards as high as possible." We found a *negative* relation between scores on this item and self-discrepancy, which was greatest for subjects with an actual/own versus ideal/own discrepancy. Thus, individuals who believe they are not the kind of person they would like to be—individuals with low self-esteem—apparently do not believe that their goals and standards (i.e., acquired guides) are especially or artificially high, whereas high self-esteem individuals are more likely to consider their personal goals and standards to be purposely exaggerated. This difference could reflect the extent to which acquired guides are considered to be reasonable standards for interpreting one's performance, with low self-esteem individuals being more likely than high self-esteem individuals to consider it reasonable to use an acquired guide as a standard for interpretation. This, in turn, would contribute to chronic individual differences in self-evaluation.

If low self-esteem individuals use an acquired guide (e.g., their ideal/own standard) as a basis for self-evaluation, they are likely to interpret many of their attributes and performances as a "failure," since they are likely to fall short of their standard. This is particularly true if their personal guide is higher than normal. There is some evidence, in fact, that depressed individuals have a higher level of aspiration in skill tasks and somewhat higher standards of self-evaluation than nondepressed individuals (Carver & Ganellen, 1983; Golin & Terrell, 1977). High self-esteem individuals, on the other hand, would be less likely to use an acquired guide as a basis of interpretation, because they recognize that this standard is not reasonable given that it was purposely set "as high as possible." Thus, they are more likely to use factual comparison points to interpret their attributes and performance. This would increase the likelihood of judging most of their attributes and performances as a "success" (see Miller & Ross, 1975). It should be emphasized that the critical difference we are proposing between low versus high self-esteem individuals (or between depressed versus nondepressed individuals) is not that low self-esteem individuals necessarily have higher factual standards or acquired guide standards but that they use an acquired guide at the interpretation stage, whereas high self-esteem individuals use a factual reference point. Thus, a general measure of level of standards, as used by Carver and Ganellen (1983), would not be expected to differentiate strongly between low and high self-esteem individuals (or between depressed and nondepressed individuals) unless the stage of application is also taken into account.

Low self-esteem individuals, according to our proposal, would tend to have a history of self-interpreted "failure," whereas high self-esteem individuals would tend to have a history of self-interpreted "success." This, in turn, would create differences in their attributions for subsequent performance. A history of self-interpreted "failure" would tend to make low self-esteem individuals attribute their subsequent successes to unstable, external factors and attribute their subsequent failures to stable, internal factors. In contrast, a history of self-interpreted "success" would tend to make high self-esteem individuals attribute their successes to stable, internal factors and attribute their subsequent failures to unstable, external factors (see Feather & Simon, 1971; Heider, 1958; Kelley, 1967). This hypothesized difference in attributional bias parallels the difference in attributional bias between depressed and nondepressed individuals that has been noted in the literature (Abramson & Martin, 1981; Seligman, Abramson, Semmel, & Von Baeyer, 1979; Sweeney, Shaeffer, & Golin, 1982). It is also consistent with Beck's (1967) description of depressed individuals' tendency to "maximize" failure and "minimize" success. Finally, although low self-esteem individuals may use an acquired guide to interpret their own performance, one would not expect them to use it when interpreting others' performance. Thus, one would expect their attributions and evaluations of others to be less negative than their attributions and evaluations of themselves and to be more similar to how people in general evaluate others. Such a pattern of differential evaluation of self and others would parallel the pattern found in the depressive literature (Beck, 1967; Kuiper, Derry, & MacDonald, 1982; Sweeney *et al.*, 1982) and potentially provides an explanation for this pattern.

Even when the same type of standard is used at a particular self-evaluation stage, there can be individual differences with respect to which particular standard subtype is used most frequently. With regard to factual reference points, there may be individual differences in the tendency to use either social category, meaningful other, autobiographical, or social context reference points as standards of evaluation. As mentioned earlier, for example, there may be a developmental shift during the juvenile period from using autobiographical reference points to using social category and social context reference points to evaluate self and others

(Ruble, 1983; Suls & Mullen, 1982; Veroff, 1969). Personality variables might also be related to the use of different reference points. For example, people who are chronically high in objective self-awareness (Duval & Wicklund, 1972) may be more likely to use autobiographical reference points than people who are chronically low in objective self-awareness; high self-monitors (Snyder, 1979) may be more likely to use social context reference points than low self-monitors; and high authoritarians (Adorno, Frenkel-Brunswik, Levinson, & Sanford, 1950) may be more likely to use positive reference groups and significant other reference points than low authoritarians.

For acquired guides as well, there may be individual differences in the tendency to use ideal/own, ideal/other, ought/own, or ought/other as standards of evaluation. For example, one would expect high authoritarians to use ought/own and ought/other as standards of evaluation more than low authoritarians (see Adorno *et al.*, 1950). And individual differences in the tendency for self-esteem maintenance could influence the extent to which particular standards are selected to maximize positive self-evaluation and positive emotional consequences (see Bandura, 1982; Kaplan, 1975).

It is also possible that even when people utilize the same standard subtype, there could be individual differences with respect to the specific content of the particular standard subtype that is used. With regard to factual reference points, individuals are especially likely to differ in the specific reference point they have in mind when they use autobiographical and significant other reference points, since the level of their own performance and that of the significant people in their lives is likely to differ. Also, to the extent that people chronically live in different social and/or cultural worlds, as children do in different phases of life (Higgins & Parsons, 1983), individual differences in specific social category and social context reference points will occur. Given the varied socialization backgrounds of different people, it is even more obvious that there will be individual differences in the specific nature of their ideal/own, ideal/other, ought/own, and ought/other acquired guides.

Additional factors can cause individual differences in the emotional consequences of utilizing the same guide. For example, individual differences in the extent to which a person believes that his or her chronic performance is discrepant from a particular guide (e.g., ought/other) are likely to cause individual differences in the emotional impact of evaluating a new performance in terms of that guide.

An especially important individual difference variable is the extent to which people feel a need to meet their acquired guides and are resistant to changing them—especially the extent to which they believe that the love and approval of others are contingent upon meeting these standards. There is some evidence in the clinical literature that depressed individuals tend to grow up in families in which the children are made to feel that care, affection, and approval are dependent on living up to and pursuing their parents' high expectations for them (Arieti & Bemporad, 1978; Beck, 1967). This suggests that there are individual differences in the interpersonal significance of standards. Indeed, in a recent study (see Higgins, Klein, & Strauman, in press) we found that there was a relation between depression and both individuals feeling unloved when they didn't live up to their parents' ideals for them and believing that their parents would reject them if they didn't live up to those ideals.

The importance of the interpersonal significance of standards for the emotional consequences of standard utilization is suggested by a further finding in this study. Mild depressive emotions and symptoms in our sample were generally associated only with those individuals whose actual versus ideal discrepancies were high *and* whose ideal standards had high interpersonal significance (as measured by items such as those just described). Individuals who had either a high actual versus ideal discrepancy or ideal standards of high interpersonal significance but *not* both were generally no more likely to have depressive emotions and symptoms than individuals who were low in both.

Individual differences in tolerance for discrepancy could also cause individual differences in the emotional consequences of standard utilization. In our most recent study (Higgins *et al.*, 1984), we discovered that the relation between people's self-discrepancies and their emotional problems varies as a function of their level of authoritarianism. Using Byrne and Kelley's (1981) measure of authoritarianism, we divided our undergraduate sample into three levels of authoritarianism (low, moderate, and high, with 15 subjects in each group). The relation between authoritarianism and emotional problems was then calculated for the low authoritarians and high authoritarians separately, using partial correlations, where total self-discrepancy was partialled out to control for any possible contribution to the correlation from any additional relation between authoritarianism and the amount of self-discrepancy. In this way, we could address the question of how authoritarianism influences the impact of performance versus guide discrepancy on emotional problems while controlling for the amount of discrepancy. (It should also be noted that there was no significant relation between authoritarianism and self-discrepancy.) For low authoritarians, the correlations between authoritarianism and our six general measures of emotional problems were all positive, with four of these positive correlations being significant or borderline significant. In direct contrast, for high authoritarians, the correlations between authoritarianism and our six general measures of emotional problems were all negative, with three of these negative correlations being significant or borderline significant. For low authoritarians, the greater a subject's authoritarianism, the greater is the negative impact of any performance versus guide discrepancy that he or she has. This result is consistent with authoritarianism being associated with an intolerance for conflict (see Adorno *et al.*, 1950). For high authoritarians, on the other hand, the greater a subject's authoritarianism, the *less* evidence there is of a negative impact from any performance versus guide discrepancy that he or she has. This paradoxical finding is, in fact, consistent with a key difference between high and low authoritarians described by Adorno *et al.* (1950). Whereas low authoritarians are considered to be relatively objective in their self-appraisal, high authoritarians are described as self-glorifying, unwilling to admit fallability or weaknesses, and lacking in insight or self-criticism, and as rejecting tendencies that they are not ready to face, denying negative traits, distorting "reality," and expressing "official optimism." Thus, for high authoritarians, there are two factors working in opposite directions. Like low authoritarians, the more authoritarian they are, the more conflict or discrepancy bothers them. But, in addition, the more authoritarian they are, the less likely they are to notice, admit, or express that they have conflict or conflict-induced emotional problems.[5]

According to Sorrentino and Short (Chapter 13 of this volume), the low authoritarian group would tend to be uncertainty-oriented and thus would be primarily concerned with maintaining clarity about the self, whereas the high authoritarian group would tend to be certainty-oriented and thus would be primarily concerned with avoiding confusion about the self. For the low authoritarian group, then, the more authoritarian an individual is, the more he or she will be bothered by a discrepant self-concept that prevents clear self-definition, whereas for the high authoritarian group, the more authoritarian an individual is, the more he or she will be motivated to avoid the confusion engendered by self-concept discrepancy (by denying it, ignoring it, etc.).

Implications of Individual Differences in Standard Utilization for Achievement Motivation

Some of the individual differences in standard utilization described here suggest an alternative way of conceptualizing individual differences in resultant achievement motivation. High resultant achievers have been described as deriving a great deal of pleasure from success but relatively little displeasure from failure (Atkinson, 1964), as attributing success to effort and ability and attributing failure to lack of effort (Weiner, 1972), and as having high expectations for success (Kukla, 1978). In contrast, low resultant achievers have been described as anticipating little pleasure from success and much displeasure from failure (Atkinson, 1964), as attributing failure to lack of ability (Weiner, 1972), and as having low expectations for success (Kukla, 1978). How might our model conceptualize individual differences in resultant achievement motivation to explain these relations?

We propose the following basic hypothesis: The standards utilized by low (resultant) achievers to interpret their performance are different from the standards utilized by high (resultant) achievers. In particular, low achievers may utilize high-standard, interpersonally significant acquired guides to interpret their performance (similar to our earlier hypothesis about low self-esteem individuals), whereas high achievers may utilize lower standard, factual reference points of less interpersonal significance (e.g., the "average" person, their own previous performance). If low and high achievers do differ in this way, a number of implications follow.

First, low achievers would be likely to have a self-interpreted history of "failure," whereas high achievers would be likely to have a self-interpreted history of "success." This difference, in turn, would cause low achievers to have low expectations for future success and a tendency to attribute any new "failure" to a lack of ability, and it would cause high achievers to have high expectations for future success and a tendency to attribute any new "success" to ability, which is consistent with the differences between low and high achievers reported in the literature. Moreover, in our model, the amount of pleasure produced by success or the amount of displeasure produced by failure would depend on the extent to which the performance decreased or increased, respectively, a person's self-concept discrepancies (as well as the interpersonal significance of failing to meet the standard). For a performance to do so, it must be interpreted as reflecting on the person's actual/own self-concept, which means that the performance must be attributed to a stable trait. Low achievers perceive failure but not success as stable, whereas high achievers perceive success but not failure as stable. Therefore, as the literature suggests, low achievers should anticipate much displeasure from failure but little pleasure from success, whereas high achievers should anticipate much pleasure from success but little displeasure from failure. Given this difference between low and high achievers, as well as the difference in their expectations for future success and failure, described earlier, it would not be surprising if low achievers tended to avoid task performance and high achievers tended to approach task performance, as has also been reported in the achievement literature (e.g., McClelland, 1961).

The implications of our hypothesis with respect to the anticipation of pleasure or displeasure raise another issue. What, exactly, is the nature of the pleasure or displeasure to which Atkinson (1964) refers? The traditional literature on achievement motivation typically refers to the "shame" of failure and the "pride" of success (Weiner, 1972). On the other hand, the motive to avoid failure (associated with low achievers) has usually been measured in terms of anxiety and described as "fear" of failure, and the motive for success (associated with high achievers) has usually been measured in terms of competition with a standard of excellence (as reflected in subjects' TAT responses) and described as "hope" of success.

Thus, the pleasure (i.e., pride) and displeasure (i.e., shame) that has been proposed as accompanying success and failure, respectively, reflect the utilization of the ideal/other standard, whereas the operational measures used to identify low achievers and high achievers reflect the utilization of the ought/other standard and the ideal/own standard, respectively. From the perspective of self-concept discrepancy theory, these particular operational measures may have optimized the distinction between low and high achievers and may have increased the likelihood of finding motivational differences. After all, failure relative to an ideal/own guide (used to identify high achievers) produces dissatisfaction that could spur the individual to try harder, whereas failure relative to an ought/other guide (used to identify low achievers) produces fear of punishment and anxiety that could paralyze the individual.

It would be useful, however, to distinguish among different kinds of low achievers and high achievers in terms of the acquired guides they utilize for interpretation or general appraisal. In this way, one could predict what kind of pleasure and displeasure they would experience from success and failure, respectively. For example, low achievers who interpret their performance in terms of an ideal/own guide would be predicted to have a different emotional reaction to "failure" and thus a different motivation for subsequent performance from those of low achievers who interpret their performance in terms of an ought/other guide. Also, if an individual had an extreme and chronic performance versus ideal/own guide discrepancy, he or she would feel hopelessness and despair and would likely behave like a low achiever. In any case, the area of achievement motivation needs to address the current confounding of need achievement with guide utilization. Of course, if our original hypothesis is correct, it may be that some differences between low and high achievers actually reflect a difference in which type of standard is utilized to interpret performance (e.g., acquired guides versus factual reference points). And it may also be that this difference is especially pronounced when low achievers utilize the ought/other guide and it has high interpersonal significance.

If these hypotheses are correct, it would indicate that the classic low achiever is not someone with a low performance standard or a low desire to perform well but, rather, someone who has a high ought/other standard of high interpersonal significance that is used at the interpretation stage to judge whether a performance is a success or failure. The classic high achiever would also have a high standard, but it would be an ideal/own standard that is used only at the appraisal stage. At the interpretation stage, a moderate, factual reference point would be used. Thus, high achievers could have both the confidence that comes from feeling successful (relative to others or to their own past performance) and the motivation to do better next time that comes from feeling dissatisfied (relative to their goals or aspirations). The notion that high and low achievers may have different standards of self-evaluation is generally consistent with Kuhl's (1978) proposal that there are individual differences in personal standards of excellence. In fact, Kuhl (1978) suggests that both classic high fear-of-failure individuals (who especially avoid difficult tasks) and high motive-to-succeed individuals (who especially approach difficult tasks) have high or difficult personal standards. From our perspective, however, the critical individual differences are not simply a function of differences in the level of standard but are also a function of *which* standards are used and *when* they are used in the process of self-evaluation. For example, a high ought/other standard is more likely to lead to an avoidance orientation than a high ideal/own standard, and any acquired guide is more likely to be motivationally debilitating if it is used at the interpretation stage than if it is used at the appraisal stage. In fact, we would predict that if an individual used a high ideal/own standard at the interpretation stage, he or she would tend to interpret his or her performance as a "failure" and thus would not be motivated to approach difficult tasks.

Contextual Variability in Standard Utilization

Context can influence standard utilization in a variety of ways. Different factual reference points tend to be used in different situations and for different activities, such as for different tasks (Bandura, 1982). Festinger (1954) suggests that it is the meaningful others in one's environment who are most likely to be selected for social comparison purposes. Moreover, the significant others that are available in a person's environment change as he or she goes through life, in part because of systematic changes as a person moves from one social life phase to another (see Higgins & Parsons, 1983; Morse & Gergen, 1970). Changes in acquired guides are also likely to occur as a person moves from one social life phase to another, such as the formation of an ought/teacher guide or an ideal/peers guide during the elementary school years (cf. Higgins & Parsons, 1983) or an ought/boss guide later in life. Which acquired guide is most emphasized or salient may also vary as a function of momentary changes in setting or activity, as when situational cues bolster adherence to a particular guide (see Bandura, 1982; Charters & Newcomb, 1952).

In general, two variables that influence the utilization of standards are their *accessibility* and their *goal-relevance*. As discussed earlier, the accessibility and goal-relevance of standards can vary as a function of individuals' personality. They can also vary as a function of *contextual priming* and *contextual adaptation*. With respect to contextual priming, there is considerable evidence that momentarily increasing the relative accessibility of a social construct increases the likelihood that it will be utilized subsequently to identify or categorize a social stimulus (for reviews, see Higgins & King, 1981; Wyer & Srull, 1981). For example, Higgins, Rholes, and Jones (1977) found that subjects' characterizations of an ambiguous description of a stimulus person's behavior were strongly influenced by which alternative label for the behavior had been primed or activated in a previous, "unrelated" study (e.g., "adventurous" versus "reckless," "persistent" versus "stubborn"). There is also substantial evidence that people will utilize different social constructs in describing and evaluating a stimulus person to suit their immediate social context (for a review, see Higgins, 1981a). For example, in a study involving an interaction between personality and contextual adaptation, Higgins and McCann (1984) found that subjects' evaluative descriptions of a stimulus person were influenced in goal-relevant directions by both the audience's ostensible attitude toward the stimulus person and the relative status of the audience.

Contextual priming and contextual adaptation could have both direct and indirect effects on standard utilization. The indirect effects include influencing the stages of stimulus encoding and identification, as the foregoing examples demonstrate. Although standard utilization in the interpretation and general appraisal stages is not determined by the judgments made during stimulus representation and identification, it is certainly influenced by these judgments. Diener, Dineen, Endresen, Beaman, and Fraser (1975), for example, have shown that when an activity involving aggressive behavior toward others has been previously described as a "game," subjects perform more aggressively than when it has been previously described as an "aggressive" activity. Presumably, the prior labeling of the activity as a "game" increased the likelihood that subjects would identify their own subsequent performance as game-related, which in turn increased the likelihood that they would interpret and appraise their performance in a more positive manner than if they had identified it as "aggressive." But contextual priming and contextual adaptation also directly affect standard utilization by influencing the accessibility and goal-relevance of alternative standards.

Varying the accessibility of alternative factual reference points has been shown to influence individuals' self-interpretation and self-appraisal. As mentioned earlier, Morse and Gergen (1970) found that making a meaningful other with desirable characteristics accessible decreased subjects' self-esteem, whereas making a meaningful other with undesirable characteristics accessible increased subjects' self-esteem. Similarly, Clark and Clark (1939) found in a field study that black children who attended integrated schools had more self-hatred than those who attended segregated schools. Although this finding was probably multiply determined, one possible cause was the greater accessibility in the integrated schools of the relatively high reference points introduced by white students. As mentioned earlier, even elementary school children interpret their performance differently depending on which reference point is accessible when the judgment is made (Ruble, 1983). For example, Rogers, Smith, and Coleman (1978) found that the reference point defined by the achievements of a student's classmates (i.e., made accessible by the context) was a major determinant of his or her self-evaluation, rather than just the actual level of his or her performance.

The accessibility of acquired guides can also vary as a function of the context. For example, if the accessibility of individuals' "personal standards of correctness" is increased, such as by having them listen to a recording of their own voice or perform in front of a mirror, their self-evaluation will decrease because of an increased actual self versus guide discrepancy (Duval & Wicklund, 1972; Ickes, Wicklund, & Ferris, 1973). In a field study, Rosenberg (1962) found that people have more emotional problems when they live in a neighborhood where the predominant religion is different from their own than when they live in a neighborhood where their own religion is the predominant one, especially when the other religion values different personal qualities from those valued by their own religion. Rosenberg (1962) suggests that people's behavior is more likely to be discrepant from the values or guides of dissimilar religions than from those of their own religion, and living in a neighborhood where a dissimilar religion predominates is likely to make that religion's values or guides more accessible.

There is also evidence that momentary group composition can influence self-evaluation and self-description (Higgins & King, 1981; McGuire & Padawer-Singer, 1976). For example, Higgins and Smith (described in Ruble & Higgins, 1976, and Higgins & King, 1981) found that undergraduate males and females who were asked to "tell us about youself" in small groups of three or four people were more likely to describe themselves as having positive, stereotypical traits of the opposite sex when they were the sole member of their sex in the group than when their sex predominated or neither sex predominated. Solo females, for instance, were more likely to describe themselves as "ambitious," and solo males were more likely to describe themselves as "sensitive." These results suggest that group sex composition can influence the relative accessibility of traditional versus modern guides regarding which traits are desirable for males and females to possess (Higgins & King, 1981).

If the accessibility of an individual's guides varies with changes in context, as the foregoing results suggest, then the emotions produced by performance versus guide discrepancies should also vary as the context changes. Moreover, the greater an individual's chronic performance versus guide discrepancies, the more his or her emotions should change as a function of changes in context. Some support for this prediction was found in our recent study (Higgins *et al.*, 1984). Two of the items on the Blatt Depressive Experiences Questionnaire are concerned with the extent to which changes in context are associated with changes in emotions: Item 4, "Sometimes I feel very big, and other times I feel very small," and Item 36, "The way I feel about myself frequently varies: there are times when I feel extremely good about myself and other times when I see only the bad in me and feel like a total failure." The correlation between the magnitude of individuals' total self-discrepancy and the extent to which they agreed with the statement was positive and significant for both of these items.

One important way in which an individual's immediate contexts can vary is the presence or absence in the context of his or her significant others, particularly those significant others represented in his or her "other"-standpoint guides. In contrast, the individual is always present in his or her own immediate context (although, as described earlier, there can be contextual variability in the degree of objective self-awareness). Thus, changes in context should generally have a greater impact on the accessibility of "other"-standpoint guides than on the accessibility of "own"-standpoint guides. This, in turn, should result in greater emotional change as a function of changes in context for discrepancies involving "other"-standpoint guides than for discrepancies involving "own"-standpoint guides. If so, the correlations between "other"-standpoint discrepancies and Blatt Items 4 and 36 should be greater than the correlations between "own"-standpoint discrepancies and Blatt Items 4 and 36. This was, indeed, the case. The correlations between the combined "other"-standpoint discrepancies (i.e., ideal/other and ought/other) and Items 4 and 36 were both higher than the correlations between the combined "own"-standpoint discrepancies (i.e., ideal/own and ought/own) and these items. These results, as well as those described previously, are consistent with the hypothesis that the emotions produced by performance versus guide discrepancies will vary as a function of contextually induced changes in the accessibility of alternative guides.

Other kinds of contextually induced changes in standard utilization can also occur. Higgins and Lurie (1983), for example, have described various ways in which standard utilization can change over time for the *same* performance-related stimulus. People must have some standard in mind both when they initially evaluate a stimulus and when they subsequently use this evaluation to make additional inferences or to recall the properties of the stimulus. Higgins and Lurie's (1983) Study 1 considered what happens when a person's performance is initially evaluated in terms of a social context reference point but this context standard is no longer accessible when the person's performance is later recalled. Subjects read about the sentencing decisions of a target trial judge in the context of other trial judges who consistently gave either higher sentences or lower sentences than the target judge. As predicted, subjects tended to evaluate the target judge as "lenient" in the former, harsh context condition and as "harsh" in the latter, lenient context condition (i.e., they used the social context reference point as the standard). A week later, subjects read about the sentencing decisions of some additional judges and then recalled the sentencing decisions of the target judge they had read about the week before. Across the two sessions, either a harsh, moderate, or lenient social category reference point for judges' sentencing decisions was established by having subjects read about decisions that involved either high, medium, or low sentences, respectively. The results indicated that subjects recalled the target judge's decisions by interpreting their prior evaluation of his behavior in terms of the social category reference point established across the two sessions, rather than in terms of the original social context reference point. Thus, subjects who were exposed to the same target in the same circumstances, and who initially evaluated the target in the same way, nevertheless remembered his behavior differently if their social category reference point was different at the moment of recall.

The "change of standard" in this study involved a change from using a social context reference point when the target's performance was originally evaluated to using a social category reference point when the evaluation was subsequently used to reconstruct the target's performance. This unrecognized change of standard caused serious errors in memory. It could also cause serious inferential errors and inappropriate emotional responses (Higgins & Lurie, 1983). And this is not the only type of change of standard. Higgins and Lurie (1983) describe three other major types. There could be a change from using the encoding context as a social context reference point when the target's performance is originally evaluated to using the recall context as a new social context reference point when the evaluation is subsequently reinterpreted. There could also be a change from using a social category reference point when the target's performance is originally evaluated to using the recall context as a social context reference point when the evaluation is subsequently reinterpreted. Finally, there could be a change from using one social category reference point when the target's performance is originally evaluated to using a different social category reference point when the evaluation is subsequently reinterpreted.

Other possible types of change of standard were not described by Higgins and Lurie (1983), such as a change from using an acquired guide (or imagined possibility) when the target's performance is originally evaluated to using a factual reference point when the evaluation is subsequently reinterpreted. Consider what would happen, for example, if the freshman in Example 2 of Table 2.2 originally interpreted his test score (80%) using his high, ideal/own guide (90%) but later reinterpreted his evaluation using a moderate, social category reference point (e.g., the class average, which was 70%). Given that his test score was less than his guide standard, he would originally evaluate his performance as a "failure." Much later, he would remember that his performance was a "failure" but would forget his exact test score and which standard was used in making his prior evaluation. If he reinterpreted his previous evaluation in terms of the currently most accessible reference point, he would mistakenly infer that his performance must have been less than the class average, which would cause him, inappropriately, to feel ashamed and humiliated. It would also cause him to misremember his test score.

As another example, consider what would happen if a girl who was better than her classmates at one school then moved to another school where the students' average performance was higher and at both schools used her classmates' performance as the standard for self-evaluation. If she failed to recognize the change of standard, she would mistakenly believe that her performance had dropped, and she might attribute the "change" in her performance (i.e., from "success" at the first school to "failure" at the second school) to a change in her academic ability or effort. Thus, even though her actual performance had not changed, the unrecognized change of standard could produce disappointment in and anger at herself. Other kinds of change of standard could cause a person to misremember his or her performance as having been better or worse than it actually was. If the misremembered prior performance is then used as an autobiographical reference point, this false judgment of having previously performed better or worse could itself produce negative or positive self-evaluations and emotions, respectively.

Failing to recognize a change of standard can also influence a person's behavior. There is evidence suggesting that people will attempt to behave in a manner consistent with a previous evaluative judgment, even though this judgment was based on a standard that is irrelevant to the current behavioral context. For example, Ostrom (1970) has shown that people will behave in a manner consistent with their previous judgment of themselves as being a "harsh" or "lenient" person, even though the category standard on which this judgment was based is different from the current category standard (i.e., the norm of "leniency" or "harshness" has changed because of the introduction of new, extreme instances of the category). Also, Sherman, Ahlm, Berman, and Lynn (1978) have demonstrated that people will use their prior attitude judgment to guide their current behavior, even though this judgment was biased by the particular context reference point that happened to be salient when the judgment was made. The "self-fulfilling" nature of self-labels could also derive, at least in part, from this factor. For example, a teenage boy who was called "bad" by his parents for naughty behavior as a child could continue to believe that he was "bad" but reinterpret this label in terms of his currently accessible standards. If he felt a need to behave in a manner consistent with this reinterpretation, his behavior might now be delinquent rather than just naughty. Thus, in a variety of ways, context-induced changes of standard could have a significant impact on people's self-evaluations, emotions, memory, and behavior.

SUMMARY AND CONCLUSIONS

This chapter began with an interest in understanding how people who perform at the same objective level could have markedly different emotional reactions to their performance and how the same performance by a single individual can produce multiple emotions and even emotions of opposite valence. A social evaluation model focusing on the process of self-evaluation was proposed to provide a preliminary answer to these questions. We first identified different kinds of standards for evaluating performance and attributes: factual reference points (including social category reference points, meaningful other reference points, autobiographical reference points, and social context reference points), acquired guides (including ideal/own guides, ideal/other guides, ought/own guides, and ought/other guides), and imagined possibilities. Then we described different stages in the process of social evaluation—the stimulus representation stage, the identification stage, the interpretation stage, the general appraisal stage, and causal attribution stages—and their interrelations. We discussed how each of these stages could produce an emotion during self-evaluation (or more than one emotion in the case of the general appraisal stage) and which standards were most likely to be utilized at each stage. The various ways in which different stages can influence the judgment and emotion produced at another stage were also described, including cases in which causal attribution can be influenced by judgments and emotions occurring at an earlier stage. The stages were also described as being sufficiently independent to produce emotions of opposite valence, as when a freshman feels proud because he did better than others in his class (an interpretation relative to a factual reference point) but also feels disappointed because he failed to accomplish his goal (a general appraisal relative to an acquired guide).

On the basis of this model, we proposed various kinds of individual differences in the utilization of standards and their interpersonal significance that could lead to striking differences in how people evaluate and respond emotionally to their attributes and performance. The model was also used to reinterpret and elaborate on well-known personality dimensions related to self-evaluation, such as achievement motivation, authoritarianism, and self-esteem. In addition, the impact of context on standard utilization was explored, including the self-evaluative and emotional consequences of different types of "change of standard."

This model also has implications for other issues concerning evaluative judgments. First, the *meaningfulness* of an evaluation could be reconceptualized in terms of the number of stages that were included in the process of evaluation. The more stages that were included, the more likely it is that multiple, distinct judgments and emotions would be produced by the process, which would increase one's sense of its richness and depth (i.e., meaningfulness). Individual differences in *emotionality* could be related to the number of stages a person typically includes in his or her evaluation, the kinds of standards a person typically uses at different stages, and the interpersonal significance of the standards used. Greater emotionality would be associated with the inclusion of more stages, greater use of acquired guides that have interpersonal significance, and the use of acquired guides at earlier stages in the process. *Developmental change* would also be related to the number of stages included in the evaluative process, as well as which stages, and to the kinds of standards used. For example, the number of stages included in the process would increase developmentally, identification would appear earlier in development than interpretation, and factual reference points (especially autobiographical reference points) would be used earlier in development than acquired guides (with imagined possibilities being used even later).

The model also raises questions concerning the determinants of people's evaluative judgments. Much of the literature on this issue has focused on people's conflicting motivations for informative self-evaluations versus positive self-evaluations (see Raynor and McFarlin, Chapter 11 of this volume). But the utilization of an acquired guide need not provide self-definitional information (e.g., "I am disappointed," *not* "I am good" or "I am bad"), and the use of any factual reference point can lead to informative judgments (e.g., autobiographical—"My running has improved"—versus social category—"I am a below-average runner"). Thus, the choice of standard cannot be based solely on informational considerations. As suggested in the literature, an alternative possibility is that people select whichever standard maximizes positive self-evaluation (or minimizes negative self-evaluation). But it is not uncommon for individuals to evaluate themselves less positively than the facts require. Therefore, there must be other determinants of standard selection. One possibility is standard selection so as to maintain self-consistency (see Raynor and McFarlin, Chapter 11 of this volume). Another possibility is that people select whichever standard is most predictive of the payoff consequences of the performance (i.e., whichever standard will lead to the self-evaluation that is most predictive of how others are likely to respond to the performance). Elementary schoolchildren, for example, might learn to use social category or social context reference points rather than autobiographical reference points because authority figures begin to punish and reward them in terms of their performance relative to other children, whereas previously the payoffs were contingent only on their own improvement. Another example of this motivational factor would be low self-esteem individuals using an unrealistically high "ideal" standard to interpret their performance because it has high interpersonal significance to them—even though it leads to both inaccurate and negative self-evaluations. An alternative nonmotivational determinant of standard selection would be momentary and chronic differences in the accessibility of different standards, as discussed earlier.

Finally, the standards and stages described in this model can be involved in the evaluation of others as well as in self-evaluation. Throughout the chapter, we have provided examples of the model's applicability to social evaluation in general. However, the process of evaluating others would differ in interesting ways from the process of self-evaluation. First, acquired guides are less likely to be used as standards for evaluating others than for self-evaluation, which could explain why depressed individuals do not differ from nondepressed individuals in evaluating others, even though they differ greatly in self-evaluation (Beck, 1967; Kuiper *et al.*, 1982; Sweeny *et al.*, 1982). Moreover, to the extent that acquired guides are utilized in evaluating others, discrepancies between another person's performance and an individual's guides may produce different emotions from the individual's own performance versus guide discrepancies. For example, if an individual used his or her ought/own guide to evaluate another person's performance (i.e., hedonic relevance) and the other person's performance was discrepant from the individual's ought/own guide, this would be more likely to produce anger than guilt.

Self-evaluation and evaluation of others can also differ with respect to the kinds of factual reference points used in evaluation. For example, when judging the performance of another person (e.g., a teacher evaluating a pupil), it is often more reasonable to use the target's past performance as the standard—a biographical reference point—rather than one's own past performance (i.e., an autobiographical reference point). Nevertheless, it is quite common for people to use their own past performance (i.e., "What did I do in the same situation?") and even their imagined performance (i.e., "What would I have done in the same situation?") to evaluate the performance of others (see Higgins, 1981b; Markus & Smith, 1981; Ross, 1977; Shrauger & Patterson, 1974; Tagiuri, 1969). In fact, there are individual differences, including developmental differences (see Higgins, 1981b), in the extent to which evaluators use themselves or others as the standard of comparison. There are also likely to be individual differences in the extent to which people use different standards to evaluate themselves versus others, which in turn is likely to have interpersonal consequences.

There are other central issues that a general theory of social evaluation should address in the future. First, when a performance produces multiple emotions, does the relative influence of the different emotions on motivation and behavior change over time? Can one emotion dominate initially and another emotion dominate later? What is the role of personality and context in this time course? Second, do the different emotions always remain distinct, or can they become integrated or blended? If they can become integrated, how are they integrated? More generally, how independent are the emotions, and does this change over time? Finally, what are the motivational and behavioral consequences of multiple rather than single emotional responses to a performance? We would expect—indeed, we are obliged to predict—that exploring these complex and challenging issues will produce multiple and conflicting emotions.

Notes

1. Not only can "identification *as* an X" (i.e., categorization) produce emotions, but "identification *with* an X" (i.e., perceived resemblance) also can produce emotions. (See Higgins & King [1981] for discussion of these two kinds of identification). Gilovich (1981), for example, has demonstrated that people will respond to a college football player more positively if his attributes are comparable to those of some professional football player than if they are not (even when the attributes are not actually correlated with performance level).

2. The notion of multiple standards to which performance may be compared raises problems for applying Mandler's (1982) general theory of emotion to self-evaluation, because the same performance can induce *both* positive and negative emotions when multiple standards are used. Moreover, the standard used may be an acquired guide rather than the factual standards emphasized in Mandler's theory. In addition, one needs to know which specific standard is used at which stage of processing to be able to predict which specific emotion will be induced.

3. It is interesting to note that Marcel's (1983) well-known finding of better recognition performance for semantically similar probe words than for graphically similar probe words is probably due to the same factor. Each target word and its semantically similar probe word were members of the same preestablished construct (e.g., alarm/warning, gay/happy, moral/ethical), whereas this was not true of the target words and their graphically similar probe words, which would make the graphic recognition task more demanding than the semantic recognition task.

4. To the extent that these cases involve multiple emotions that are preceded by cognitive shifts, they would be consistent with Weiner's (1982) general position that cognitive shifts induce affective shifts. The cognitive shifts, however, need not be attributional in nature.

5. This pattern of correlations also could have occurred if moderate authoritarians had greater emotional problems than either high or low authoritarians, which was possible, given that moderates on a personality dimension often have greater or lesser scores on some other variable than either highs or lows (see Sorrentino & Short, 1977). However, the low, moderate, and high authoritarian groups in this study did not differ in their level of emotional problems.

References

Abramson, L. Y., & Martin, D. J. (1981). Depression and the causal inference process. In J. H. Harvey, W. Ickes, & R. F. Kidd (Eds.), *New directions in attribution research* (Vol. 3, pp. 117–168). Hillsdale, NJ: Erlbaum.

Adler, A. (1964). *Problems of neurosis.* New York: Harper & Row. (Original work published 1929)

Adorno, T. W., Frenkel-Brunswik, E., Levinson, D. J., & Sanford, R. N. (1950). *The authoritarian personality.* New York: Harper.

Allport, G. W. (1955). *Becoming.* New Haven: Yale University Press.

Arieti, S., & Bemporad, J. (1978). *Severe and mild depression: The psychotherapeutic approach.* New York: Basic Books.

Atkinson, J. W. (1964). *An introduction to motivation.* Princeton, NJ: Van Nostrand.

Austin, W., McGinn, N. C., & Susmilch, C. (1980). Internal standards revisited: Effects of social comparisons and expectancies on judgments of fairness and satisfaction. *Journal of Experimental Social Psychology, 16,* 426–441.

Bandura, A. (1982). The self and mechanisms of agency. In J. Suls (Ed.), *Psychological perspectives on the self* (Vol. 1, pp. 38–49). Hillsdale, NJ: Erlbaum.

Bargh, J. A. (1984). Automatic and conscious processing of social information. In R. S. Wyer, Jr., & T. Srull (Eds.), *Handbook of social cognition* (pp. 1–43). Hillsdale, NJ: Erlbaum.

Beck, A. T. (1967). *Depression: Causes and treatment.* Philadelphia: University of Pennsylvania Press.

Bem, D. J. (1972). Self-perception theory. In L. Berkowitz (Ed.), *Advances in experimental social psychology* (Vol. 6, pp. 1–62). New York: Academic Press.

Bernstein, M., & Crosby, F. (1980). An empirical examination of relative deprivation theory. *Journal of Experimental Social Psychology, 16,* 442–456.

Brickman, P., Coates, D., & Janoff-Bulman, R. (1978). Lottery winners and accident victims: Is happiness relative? *Journal of Personality and Social Psychology, 36,* 917–927.

Byrne, D., & Kelley, K. (1981). *An introduction to personality.* Englewood Cliffs, NJ: Prentice-Hall.

Cameron, N. (1963). *Personality development and psychopathology.* Boston: Houghton Mifflin.

Carver, C. S. & Ganellen, R. J. (1983). Depression and components of self-punitiveness: High standards, self-criticism, and overgeneralization. *Journal of Abnormal Psychology, 92,* 330–337.

Carver, C. S., & Scheier, M. F. (1982). Outcome expectancy, locus of attribution for expectancy, and self-directed attention as determinants of evaluative and performance. *Journal of Experimental Social Psychology, 18,* 184–200.

Charters, W. W., & Newcomb, T. M. (1952). Some attitudinal effects of experimentally increased salience of a membership group. In G. E. Swanson, T. M. Newcomb, & E. L. Hartley (Eds.), *Readings in social psychology* (2d ed., pp. 415–420). New York: Holt, Rinehart and Winston.

Clark, K. B. & Clark, M. P. (1939). The development of consciousness of self and the emergence of racial identification in Negro preschool children. *Journal of Social Psychology, 10,* 591–599.

Colby, K. M. (1968). A programmable theory of cognition and affect in individual personal belief systems. In R. P. Abelson, E. Aronson, W. J. McGuire, T. M. Newcomb, M. J. Rosenberg, & P. H. Tannenbaum (Eds.), *Theories of cognitive consistency: A source book* (pp. 520–525). Chicago: Rand McNally.

Cooley, C. H. (1964). *Human nature and the social order.* New York: Schocken Books. (Original work published 1902).

Coyne, J. C., & Lazarus, R. S. (1980). Cognitive style, stress perception, and coping. In I. Kutash & L. Schlesinger (Eds.), *Handbook on stress and anxiety: Contemporary knowledge, theory and treatment* (pp. 182–224). San Francisco: Jossey-Bass.

Diener, E., Dineen, J., Endresen, K., Beaman, A. L., & Fraser, S. C. (1975). Effects of altered responsibility, cognitive set, and modeling on physical aggression and deindividuation. *Journal of Personality and Social Psychology, 31*, 328–337.

Duval, S., & Wicklund, R. A. (1972). *A theory of objective self-awareness.* New York: Academic Press.

Dweck, C. S., & Elliot, E. S. (1983). Achievement motivation. In P. H. Mussen (Ed.), *Handbook of child psychology* (Vol. 4, pp. 643–691). New York: Wiley.

Eiser, J. R., & Stroebe, W. (1972). *Categorization and social judgment.* New York: Academic Press.

Erikson, E. H. (1963). *Childhood and society* (2d ed.). New York: Norton. (Original work published 1950).

Feather, N. T., & Simon, J. G. (1971). Attribution of responsibility and valence of outcome in relation to initial confidence and success and failure of self and other. *Journal of Personality and Social Psychology, 18*, 173–188.

Festinger, L. (1954). A theory of social processes. *Human Relations, 7*, 117–140.

Fiske, S. T. (1982). Schema-triggered affect: Applications to social perception. In M. S. Clark & S. T. Fiske (Eds.), *Cognition and affect: The 17th Annual Carnegie Symposium on Cognition* (pp. 55–78). Hillsdale, NJ: Erlbaum.

Freud, S. (1961). The ego and the id. In J. Strachey (Ed. and Trans.), *Standard edition of the complete psychological works of Sigmund Freud* (Vol. 19, pp. 3–66). London: Hogarth Press. (Original work published 1923).

Gilovich, T. (1981). Seeing the past in the present: The effect of associations to familiar events on judgments and decisions. *Journal of Personality and Social Psychology, 40*, 797–808.

Glucksberg, S., Krauss, R. M., & Higgins, E. T. (1975). The development of referential communication skills. In F. Horowitz, E. Hetherington, S. Scarr-Salapatek, & G. Siegel (Eds.), *Review of child development research* (Vol. 4, pp. 305–345). Chicago: University of Chicago Press.

Goethals, G. R., & Darley, J. M. (1977). Social comparison theory: An attributional approach. In J. M. Suls & R. L. Miller (Eds.), *Social comparison processes: Theoretical and empirical perspectives* (pp. 259–278). Washington, DC: Hemisphere.

Golin, S., & Terrell, F. (1977). Motivational and associative aspects of mild depression in skill and chance tasks. *Journal of Abnormal Psychology, 86*, 389–401.

Heider, F. (1958). *The psychology of interpersonal relations.* New York: Wiley.

Helson, H. (1964). *Adaptation-level theory.* New York: Harper & Row.

Herr, P. M., Sherman, S. J., & Fazio, R. H. (1983). On the consequences of priming: Assimilation and contrast effects. *Journal of Experimental Social Psychology, 19*, 323–340.

Higgins, E. T. (1977). Communication development as related to channel, incentive, and social class. *Genetic Psychology Monographs, 96*, 75–141.

Higgins, E. T. (1981a). The "communication game": Implications for social cognition and persuasion. In E. T. Higgins, C. P. Herman, & M. P. Zanna (Eds.), *Social cognition: The Ontario Symposium* (Vol. 1, pp. 343–92). Hillsdale, NJ: Erlbaum.

Higgins, E. T. (1981b). Role taking and social judgment: Alternative developmental perspectives and processes. In J. H. Flavell & L. Ross (Eds.), *Social cognitive development: Frontiers and possible futures* (pp. 119–153). New York: Cambridge University Press.

Higgins, E. T. (1983). *A theory of discrepant self-concepts.* Unpublished manuscript, New York University.

Higgins, E. T., & King, G. (1981). Accessibility of social constructs: Information processing consequences of individual and contextual variability. In N. Cantor & J. Kihlstrom (Eds.), *Personality, cognition, and social interaction* (pp. 69–121). Hillsdale, NJ: Erlbaum.

Higgins, E. T., Klein, R., & Strauman, T. (1985). Self-concept discrepancy theory: A psychological model for distinguishing among different aspects of depression and anxiety. *Social Cognition, 3*, 51–76.

Higgins, E. T., Klein, R., & Strauman, T. (in press). Self-discrepancies: Distinguishing among self-states, self-state conflicts, and emotional vulnerabilities. In K. M. Yardley & T. M. Honess (Eds.), *Self and identity: Psychosocial perspectives.* New York: Wiley.

Higgins, E. T., Kuiper, N. A., & Olson, J. (1981). Social cognition: A need to get personal. In E. T. Higgins, C. P. Herman, & M. P. Zanna (Eds.), *Social cognition: The Ontario Symposium* (Vol. 1, pp. 395–420). Hillsdale, NJ: Erlbaum.

Higgins, E. T., & Lurie, L. (1983). Context, categorization, and memory: The "change-of-standard" effect. *Cognitive Psychology, 15,* 525–547.

Higgins, E. T., & McCann, C. D. (1984). Social encoding and subsequent attitudes, impressions, and memory: "Context-driven" and motivational aspects of processing. *Journal of Personality and Social Psychology, 47,* 26–39.

Higgins, E. T., & Parsons, J. E. (1983). Social cognition and the social life of the child: Stages as subcultures. In E. T. Higgins, D. N. Ruble, & W. W. Hartup (Eds.), *Social cognition and social development: A socio-cultural perspective* (pp. 15–62). New York: Cambridge University Press.

Higgins, E. T., Rholes, W. S., & Jones, C. R. (1977). Category accessibility and impression formation. *Journal of Experimental Social Psychology, 13,* 141–154.

Higgins, E. T., Strauman, T., & Klein, R. (1984). *Self-discrepancy and emotional problems.* Unpublished manuscript, New York University.

Horney, K. (1939). *The neurotic personality of our time.* London: Routledge & Kegan Paul.

Horney, K. (1950). *Neurosis and human growth.* New York: Norton.

Huttenlocher, J., & Higgins, E. T. (1971). Adjectives, comparatives, and syllogisms. *Psychological Review, 78,* 487–504.

Hyman, H. H. (1942). The psychology of status. *Archives of Psychology,* No. 269.

Ickes, W. J., Wicklund, R. A., & Ferris, C. B. (1973). Objective self awareness and self-esteem. *Journal of Experimental Social Psychology, 9,* 202–219.

James, W. (1948). *The principles of psychology.* New York: World. (Original work published 1890).

Kahneman, D., & Tversky, A. (1982). The simulation heuristic. In D. Kahneman, P. Slovic, & A. Tversky (Eds.), *Judgment under uncertainty: Heuristics and biases* (pp. 201–208). New York: Cambridge University Press.

Kaplan, H. B. (1975). Prevalence of the self-esteem motive. In H. B. Kaplan (Ed.), *Self-attitudes and deviant behavior* (pp. 16–27). Pacific Palisades, CA: Goodyear.

Karabenick, S. A. (1972). Valence of success and failure as a function of achievement motives and locus of control. *Journal of Personality and Social Psychology, 21,* 101–110.

Kelley, H. H. (1952). Two functions of reference groups. In G. E. Swanson, T. M. Newcomb, & E. L. Hartley (Eds.), *Readings in social psychology* (2d ed., pp. 410–430). New York: Holt, Rinehart and Winston.

Kelley, H. H. (1967). Attribution theory in social psychology. In D. Levine (Ed.), *Nebraska Symposium on Motivation* (Vol. 15, pp. 192–238). Lincoln: University of Nebraska Press.

Kuhl, J. (1978). Standard setting and risk preference: An elaboration of the theory of achievement motivation and an empirical test. *Psychological Review, 85,* 239–248.

Kuiper, N. A., Derry, P. A., & MacDonald, M. R. (1982). Self-reference and person perception in depression: A social cognition perspective. In G. Weary & H. Mirels (Eds.), *Integrations of clinical and social psychology* (pp. 79–103). New York: Oxford University Press.

Kukla, A. (1978). An attributional theory of choice. In L. Berkowitz (Ed.), *Advances in experimental social psychology* (Vol. 11, pp. 113–144). New York: Academic Press.

Lader, M., & Marks, I. (1972). *Clinical anxiety.* New York: Grune and Stratton.

Lazarus, R. S. (1966). *Psychological stress and the coping process.* New York: McGraw-Hill.

Lewin, K. (1935). *A dynamic theory of personality.* New York: McGraw-Hill.

Lewin, K. (1951). *Field theory in social science.* New York: Harper.

Lewis, H. B. (1979). Shame in depression and hysteria. In C. E. Izard (Ed.), *Emotions in personality and psychopathology* (pp. 371–396). New York: Plenum.

Lyons, J. (1968). *Introduction to theoretical linguistics.* London: Cambridge University Press.

Mandler, G. (1982). The structure of value: Accounting for taste. In M. S. Clark & S. T. Fiske (Eds.), *Affect and cognition* (pp. 3–36). Hillsdale, NJ: Erlbaum.

Manis, M., & Armstrong, G. W. (1971). Contrast effects in verbal output. *Journal of Experimental Social Psychology, 7,* 381–388.

Marcel, A. J. (1983). Conscious and unconscious perception: Experiments on visual masking and word recognition. *Cognitive Psychology, 15*, 197–237.

Markus, H., & Nurius, P. (1983). *Possible selves.* Unpublished manuscript, University of Michigan.

Markus, H., & Smith, J. (1981). The influence of self-schema on the perception of others. In N. Cantor & J. F. Kihlstrom (Eds.), *Personality, cognition and social interaction* (pp. 233–262). Hillsdale, NJ: Erlbaum.

McClelland, D. C. (1961). *The achieving society.* Princeton, NJ: Van Nostrand.

McGuire, W. J., & Padawer-Singer, A. (1976). Trait salience in the spontaneous self-concept. *Journal of Personality and Social Psychology, 33*, 743–754.

Mead, G. H. (1934). *Mind, self, and society.* Chicago: University of Chicago Press.

Merton, R. K. & Kitt, A. S. (1952). Contributions to the theory of reference-group behavior. In G. E. Swanson, T. M. Newcomb, & E. L. Hartley (Eds.), *Readings in social psychology* (2d ed., pp. 430–444). New York: Holt, Rinehart and Winston.

Miller, D. T., & Ross, M. (1975). Self-serving biases in the attribution of causality: Fact or fiction? *Psychological Bulletin, 82*, 213–225.

Morse, S. J. & Gergen, K. J. (1970). Social comparison, self-consistency, and the concept of self. *Journal of Personality and Social Psychology, 16*, 148–156.

Newcomb, T. M. (1952). Attitude development as a function of reference groups: The Bennington study. In G. E. Swanson, T. M. Newcomb, & E. L. Hartley (Eds.), *Readings in social psychology* (2d ed., pp. 420–430). New York: Holt, Rinehart and Winston.

Nisbett, R. E., & Ross, L. D. (1980). *Human inference: Strategies and shortcomings of informal judgment* (Century Series in Psychology). Englewood Cliffs, NJ: Prentice-Hall.

Olson, D. R. (1970). Language and thought: Aspects of a cognitive theory of semantics. *Psychological Review, 77*, 257–273.

Ostrom, T. M. (1970). Perspective as a determinant of attitude change. *Journal of Experimental Social Psychology, 6*, 280–292.

Ostrom, T. M., & Upshaw, H. S. (1968). Psychological perspective and attitude change. In A. G. Greenwald, T. C. Brock, & T. M. Ostrom (Eds.), *Psychological foundations of attitudes* (pp. 217–242). New York: Academic Press.

Parducci, A. (1965). Category judgment: A range-frequency model. *Psychological Review, 72*, 407–418.

Rogers, C. M., Smith, M. D., & Coleman, J. M. (1978). Social comparison in the classroom: The relationship between academic achievement and self-concept. *Journal of Educational Psychology, 70*, 50–57.

Rogers, C. R. (1961). *On becoming a person.* Boston: Houghton Mifflin.

Rosch, E. (1978). Principles of categorization. In E. Rosch & B. B. Lloyd (Eds.), *Cognition and categorization* (pp. 27–48). Hillsdale, NJ: Erlbaum.

Rosenberg, M. (1962). The dissonant religious context and emotional disturbance. *American Journal of Sociology, 68*, 1–10.

Rosenberg, M. (1979). *Conceiving the self.* New York: Basic Books.

Rosenberg, S., & Cohen, B. D. (1966). Referential processes of speakers and listeners. *Psychological Review, 73*, 208–231.

Ross, L. (1977). The intuitive psychologist and his shortcomings: Distortions in the attribution process. In L. Berkowitz (Ed.), *Advances in Experimental Social Psychology* (Vol. 10, pp. 173–220). New York: Academic Press.

Ruble, D. N. (1983). The development of social comparison processes and their role in achievement-related self-socialization. In E. T. Higgins, D. N. Ruble, & W. W. Hartup (Eds.), *Social cognition and social development: A socio-cultural perspective* (pp. 134–157). New York: Cambridge University Press.

Ruble, D. N., & Higgins, E. T. (1976). Effects of group sex composition on self-presentation and sex-typing. *Journal of Social Issues, 32*, 125–132.

Sarbin, T. R., Taft, R., & Bailey, D. E. (1960). *Clinical inference and cognitive theory.* New York: Holt, Rinehart and Winston.

Seligman, M. E. P., Abramson, L. Y., Semmel, A., & Von Baeyer, C. (1979). Depressive attributional style. *Journal of Abnormal Psychology, 88*, 242–247.

Shantz, C. U. (1983). Social cognition. In J. H. Flavell & E. M. Markman (Eds.), *Cognitive*

Development, Vol. 3 in P. H. Mussen (Ed.), *Carmichael's manual of child psychology* (4th ed., pp. 495–555). New York: Wiley.

Sherif, M. (1936). *The psychology of social norms*. New York: Harper & Brothers.

Sherif, M. (1948). *An outline of social psychology*. New York: Harper.

Sherman, S. J., Ahlm, K., Berman, L., & Lynn, S. (1978). Contrast effects and their relationship to subsequent behaivor. *Journal of Experimental Social Psychology, 14*, 340–350.

Shrauger, J. S., & Patterson, M. B. (1974). Self-evaluation and the selection of dimensions for evaluating others. *Journal of Personality, 42*, 569–585.

Snyder, M. (1979). Self-monitoring processes. In L. Berkowitz (Ed.), *Advances in experimental social psychology* (Vol. 12, pp. 85–128). New York: Academic Press.

Sorrentino, R. M., & Short, J. A. C. (1977). The case of the mysterious moderates: Why motives sometimes fail to predict behavior. *Journal of Personality and Social Psychology, 35*, 478–484.

Srull, T. K., & Wyer, R. S. (1979). The role of category accessibility in the interpretation of information about persons: Some determinants and implications. *Journal of Personality and Social Psychology, 37*, 1660–1672.

Storms, M. D. & McCaul, K. D. (1976). Attribution processes and emotional exacerbation of dysfunctional behavior. In J. H. Harvey, W. J. Ickes, & R. F. Kidd (Eds.), *New directions in attribution research* (Vol. 1, pp. 143–164). Hillsdale, NJ: Erlbaum.

Sullivan, H. S. (1953). *The collected works of Harvey Stack Sullivan* (Vol. 1, H. S. Perry & M. L. Gawel, Eds.). New York: Norton.

Suls, J., & Mullen, B. (1982). From the cradle to the grave: Comparison and self-evaluation across the life-span. In J. Suls (Ed.), *Psychological perspectives on the self* (Vol. 1, pp. 97–125). Hillsdale, NJ: Erlbaum.

Sweeney, P. D., Shaeffer, D., & Golin, S. (1982). Attributions about self and others in depression. *Personality and Social Psychology Bulletin, 8*, 37–42.

Tagiuri, R. (1969). Person perception. In G. Lindzey & E. Aronson (Eds.), *The handbook of social psychology* (2d ed., Vol. 3, pp. 395–449). Reading, MA: Addison-Wesley.

Turner, R. H. (1956). Role-taking, role standpoint, and reference-group behavior. *American Journal of Sociology, 61*, 316–328.

Tversky, A., & Gati, I. (1978). Studies of similarity. In E. Rosch & B. B. Lloyd (Eds.), *Cognition and categorization* (pp. 79–98). Hillsdale, NJ: Erlbaum.

Veroff, J. (1969). Social comparison and the development of achievement motivation. In C. P. Smith (Ed.), *Achievement-related motives in children* (pp. 46–101). New York: Russell Sage Foundation.

Volkmann, J. (1951). Scales of judgment and their implications for social psychology. In J. H. Rohrer & M. Sherif (Eds.), *Social psychology at the crossroads* (pp. 273–294). New York: Harper & Row.

Weiner, B. (1972). *Theories of motivation: From mechanism to cognition*. Chicago: Rand McNally.

Weiner, B. (1982). The emotional consequences of causal attributions. In M. S. Clark & S. T. Fiske (Eds.), *Affect and cognition* (pp. 185–209). Hillsdale, NJ: Erlbaum.

Weiner, B., Frieze, I., Kukla, A., Reed, L., Rest, S., & Rosenbaum, R. M. (1971). Perceiving the causes of success and failure. In E. E. Jones, D. E. Kanouse, H. H. Kelley, R. E. Nisbett, S. Valins, & B. Weiner (Eds.), *Attribution: Perceiving the causes of behavior* (pp. 95–120). Morristown, NJ: General Learning Press.

Weiner, B., Russel, D., & Lerman, D. (1978). Affective consequences of causal ascriptions. In J. H. Harvey, W. Ickes, & R. F. Kidd (Eds.), *New directions in attribution research* (Vol. 2, pp. 59–90). Hillsdale, NJ: Erlbaum.

Wicklund, R. A. (1975). Objective self-awareness. In L. Berkowitz (Ed.), *Advances in experimental social psychology* (Vol. 8, pp. 233–275). New York: Academic Press.

Wyer, R. S. & Srull, T. K. (1981). Category accessibility: Some theoretical and empirical issues concerning the processing of social stimulus information. In E. T. Higgins, C. P. Herman, & M. P. Zanna (Eds.), *Social cognition: The Ontario Symposium* (Vol. 1, pp. 161–197). Hillsdale, NJ: Erlbaum.

Zajonc, R. B. (1980). Feeling and thinking: Preferences need no inferences. *American Psychologist, 35*, 151–175.

CHAPTER 3

Orientation to the Environment versus Preoccupation with Human Potential

ROBERT A. WICKLUND
Universität Bielefeld

This chapter will advance some conceptual distinctions that imply a certain psychological basis for the human preoccupation with the ascribing of dispositions. It is proposed that people whose ongoing relation with the salient or immediate environment is characterized by incompetence, or by a poor fit, are thereby inclined to think of themselves and others in terms of dispositions. Conversely, people who meet the challenges of the immediate, pressing environment—that is, maintain a good fit between their cognitive or behavioral repertoire and the environment—will be less likely to dwell on and use the societally given language of dispositions. Thus, the preoccupation with and ascribing of dispositions (personality traits, potentials, abilities, attitudes) are considered a result of a failure to come to terms directly with the perceived call of the environment.

SOCIETAL ORIGINS OF DISPOSITION NAMES

The psychology of individual differences (Anastasi, 1958) recognizes that trait names, disposition names, ability names, and related concepts are necessary only because people manifest different behavioral potentials. In a highly simplified, rudimentary society in which each person is capable of drawing all possible necessary distinctions and in which each person is competent to perform all necessary functions, the institution of trait names would serve little function. People would go about their business, describing and dealing with the environments confronting them, and every person would be able to describe the others' environment and to enact the others' behaviors. Although there is no logically necessary reason to think that people in such a rudimentary society would not use

64

such terms as "athletic" or "creative," one would most certainly wonder about the functional worth of such terms. Since everyone in such a society would discern everyone else's environment with the same degree of perspicacity, and everyone would be able to perform all functions, the trait names would apply to all individuals—thus serving only the most superficial of functions.

Accordingly, it becomes more sensible to return to the main thesis of personologists, that dispositional names ("concepts") have their origin in behavioral differences—differences that we can come to terms with only with the help of such concepts. It is not too difficult to imagine how some of these concepts might have arisen. Let us suppose that some small proportion of the people in a given society is confronted with an aspect of the environment—food gathering—with much greater regularity than others and that by some accidental circumstances (perhaps even genetic selection), they come to develop a repertoire of *perceptiveness* for determining the kinds of game available, when and where the animals are to be found, what they eat, and related animal habits and instincts. This same minority of the society then develops *behavioral repertoires* that match these sophisticated animal environments. They learn how to stalk the animals and how to construct various weapons and traps.

The Dynamic Orientation

As these "hunter" members of the society are going about their business of procuring game, there would be no functional value in their being anything other than task-oriented. They have to think continuously about the habits of the game they are pursuing, about the construction and functioning of their weapons or traps, and, perhaps more generally, about bringing their behavioral repertoires to bear on this multifaceted environment. One could say that there is, at this point, a *dynamic fit* between the demands of the environment and the individual's perceptual and behavioral readiness. For each complexity of the environment, there is a corresponding perceptual or behavioral reaction; the actions of the game gatherers are continually being brought into line with the environment.

This dynamic orientation to the environment is very similar to Csikszent-mihalyi's (1975) description of the "flow experience." The experience of "flow"—that is, "flowing" along with the environment—is viewed as an ideal condition midway between boredom and anxiety. This ideal fit with the environment carries with it a loss of ego and also entails a control over one's actions. Further, for the flow experience to be engaged, the demands for action must be clear and relatively free of potential conflict (Csikszentmihalyi & Rochberg-Halton, 1981, p. 8).

In the course of a dynamic fit between person and environment, it would serve no function for any one of these game pursuers to engage in the self-ascribing or other-ascribing of dispositions. Each person is actively—dynamically—focusing on the relation between act and environment. To turn one's thoughts to membership in such categories as "aggressive," "creative," "sportsmanlike," or anything of the kind would constitute moving one's thoughts away from task-relevant preoccupations. Thus, for the actively involved person who is exercising a dynamic fit with the environment, the ascribing of dispositions would play no functional role.

As Csikszentmihalyi (1975) noted:

> Self-forgetfulness does not mean losing touch with internal or external processes, however. On the contrary, these may be registered more intensely and vividly than at other times. What is lost is not the awareness of one's body or of one's functions, but only the self *construct*. (p. 43)

Although Csikszentmihalyi has gone a long way toward characterizing the psychological or experiential qualities of the human's moving, fitting relation to the immediate environment, it remains unclear how the human arrives at a dynamic fit with respect to any given aspect of the environment. The problem has been recognized by Eckblad (1981): "A match between competence and challenge as defined by Csikszentmihalyi is not enough to ensure flow" (p. 55). Eckblad's answer to the problem is the suggestion that there must be a "scheme"—a backlog of personal capabilities and/or experiences—that would enable the person to undertake spontaneous activity in the environment in question and that the researcher would thereby be led in the direction of hereditary dispositions and the individual's experiential history. Her point is well taken. To be sure, Csikszentmihalyi's conceptualizations have not dealt with the personal backgrounds of individuals—heredity, particular learning experiences, or patterns of socialization—that would be conducive to the person's fitting to the environment. On the other hand, one might contend in defense of Csikszentmihalyi that his purpose was not to chart out a developmental psychology of the person's behavioral fit with the environment. Rather, the goal has been to begin with the person whose capabilities enable a good fit with the environment and then proceed from there to capture the phenomenology of the person caught up in the task.

However, there is a further dimension that seems psychologically central in a causal analysis of the dynamic orientation to the environment. This dimension takes us back to the work of Murray (1938).

Environmental Press

Murray's (1938) concept of "press" is extremely useful in the present context, although we shall be using it in a more general manner than Murray did. The reason for drawing on his term is that it stood for a kind of relationship between the person and an environment that was variously demanding, as illustrated in the following:

> The organism and its milieu must be considered together, a single creature–environment interaction being a convenient short unit for psychology.
> A *long unit*—an individual life—can be most clearly formulated as a succession of related *short units*, or *episodes*. . . . In crudely formulating an episode it is dynamically pertinent and convenient to classify the SS [stimulus situation]

according to the kind of effect—facilitating or obstructing—it is exerting or could exert upon the organism. Such a tendency of "potency" in the environment may be called a *press*. (Murray, 1938, p. 40)

Rather than being as specific as Murray, who imbued "press" with such qualities as "nourishing," "coercing," "injuring," or "amusing," (p. 40), I use the term here to depict the condition whereby a person feels a subjective pull (or push) from the immediate surroundings to "do something." The precise psychological antecedents of experienced psychological press can be manifold. A strong need in combination with an environment that can satisfy that need is a primal case of environmental press. Press may also result from conditioning, whereby a person simply feels impelled to act on the basis of associations or prior repetitions. Abelson's (1976) idea of "scripted" behavior, for instance, is similar to the idea of a highly conditioned response. Press may also arise for reasons quite independent of central "traditional" needs and conditioning. For instance, an entire school of thought is based on the idea that a challenging, unknown, or moderately difficult set of circumstances will create a motivational state entailing involvement with that environment (e.g., Hunt, 1965).

This chapter is not concerned with the precise psychological antecedents of psychological press; rather, press is treated as a general psychological variable that can vary in strength—sometimes as a function of factors associated with the organism together with a situation that is pertinent to those factors, and sometimes just as a function of the situation itself. More generally, the press factor can be looked at through the perspectives of a variety of motivational theories. The crucial point is that psychology has means at its disposal for analyzing the antecedents of the press of any particular environmental component on the individual. Some examples will illustrate that there is no dearth of such approaches.

Alper (1946), in her discussion of the concept of ego-involvement, directly addresses those conditions that cause the individual to be especially attuned to a performance context. Variations on that theme—called "importance", "relevance to self," and so forth—are seen in numerous investigations (e.g., Wicklund & Gollwitzer, 1982). A method for creating degrees of press within the world of social psychology stems from the work on helping by Darley & Latané (1968). The smaller the number of helpers available at the scene of an emergency (particularly when the number of helpers declines to one), the greater is the pressure on the individual.

The Darley & Latané approach uses rather subtle factors to create press; broadly conceived, it is one of many social influence notions with which psychology has dealt. Another notion, which deals in part with blatant attempts to influence others, was formulated by Brehm (1966) in a theory of psychological reactance. One implication of reactance theory is that the perception a communicator intends to influence will set up psychological forces within the person and that the response to such felt pressure will be resistance, to the extent that the person already feels the freedom to agree or disagree.

The important point stemming from such analyses is that they are, in part, theories of *salience*; the person's attention is assumed to turn to the particular feature of environment in question, and motivations and thoughts are presumed to be similarly directed.

A high degree of press means that the person feels called upon subjectively to "do something" with respect to that context. The exact nature of this "doing something" can vary considerably, of course, but if the person has the antecedent hereditary equipment and appropriate training and socialization, then the emergence of a fit—a dynamic relation—with that aspect of the environment should follow. Thus, the psychological factors antecedent to the dynamic condition are (1) the *possibility* of a fit between one's potentials and the environment and, importantly, (2) the degree of press the person experiences with respect to that environment.

Returning to the example of the hunters, let us suppose that their behavioral repertoires equip them to match the demands of the environment and that the fit is ideal. They proceed about their business, and their hunting activities appear to capture the spirit of the dynamic orientation. Now a crucial question enters the picture.

The Attempt to Capture Dynamic Functioning with Trait Terms

What about the remainder of the hunters' society? The end results of the activities of the minority—the hunters—are highly relevant for the rest of society; at the same time, however, the rest of the society is not equipped perceptually or behaviorally to deal with the same environment directly. The intricacies and regularities of animal behavior are unknown to them; so is the myriad of behavioral routines. Nonetheless, the environment consisting of animals, and the end products of the hunting activities are central to their existence. It therefore becomes functional to identify those individuals who can cope successfully with that environment. The remainder of the society needs to know who these individuals are—these "experts" who can react to the environment in a unique, not quite describable way. Hence, it is necessary to categorize these individuals:

> Among the earliest records of human activity there is evidence that individual differences were recognized and utilized. In pre-literate cultures, the artist, the medicine man, and the tribal chief are examples of persons who displayed special talents or personality characteristics. (Anastasi, 1958, p. 1)

The categorization can take many forms. "Hunter," "woodsman," or "nature expert" are labels that might be called "roles" in a sociological context. However, the larger society might also refer to certain of these hunters as "brave," "aggressive," "cunning," "creative," "persistent," "cruel," and other terms. Quite independent of whether the ascription corresponds to the modern social science terms "role," "trait," "personality," "disposition," or "ability," the point here is that the ascription of such terms begins in society's need to identify those who can cope directly with an environment that is difficult to comprehend:

Concepts of personality are among the most common and widespread cultural devices for "making sense" of interpersonal behavior. . . . One of their most important [uses] is in the interpretation of social behavior. Personality descriptors, however, may symbolize complex actions and mental states. They most often cannot be linked easily with observable referents. (White, 1980, p. 760)

Personality psychology and anthropology may well go further than merely stating that the attribution of dispositions serves to "identify." We might also say that the purpose is to "understand" or "make sense of" or "create a context for interpretation." The exact language used to describe the functions of the dispositions does not really matter. The underlying issue is simply that a language of dispositions arises out of the necessity to react to those who behave and react to environments in ways that are not completely comprehensible to the remainder of society.

Our examples do not have to be confined to societal good deeds, such as "industrious," "visually creative," or "athletically gifted." "Paranoid," "hyper-aggressive," "lethargic," and other terms—although they do not characterize individuals who are societally valued—serve a similar function. The remainder of society spots individuals whose modes of responding are not easily replicated by others and who appear to be reacting to an environment that others do not perceive fully. To "label," "understand," or "predict" these individuals, a dispositional term is applied to them; that is, they are put into a category.

The attempt to understand other humans by placing them into categories that serve predictability is a phenomenon addressed thoroughly by Lewin (1931), under the label "Galileian and Aristotelian modes of thought." It was Lewin's view that science remains at the level of primitive cultures insofar as the placement of individuals into categories substitutes for a comprehension of the various psychological forces acting on an organism. Although Lewin elaborated in great detail on the character and consequences of an Aristotelian mode of thinking, he did not delve into its psychological roots.

The thesis here would pick up where Lewin left off, in the sense that coming to understand the world (and oneself) by means of placement into categories is something that develops out of societal necessity. As will become progressively clearer, the point here is that one's comprehension of all of the forces acting on a person has to do with one's perceptiveness in regard to that event and also with one's relevant behavioral capacities. Thus, the kind of understanding that Lewin advocated—the Galileian mode of thinking, with its emphasis on examining the multitude of forces acting on an organism—is associated with the neglect of categories and comes from a close familiarity and expertise with regard to the object being studied.

What Goes into the Dynamic Fit?

Before moving to a consideration of the antecedents of two orientations—one toward the environment, the other toward the category—it is necessary to spell out in more detail exactly what is entailed in the dynamic fit to the environment.

Perceptiveness and *performance* seem to be integral aspects of the dynamic orientation. This is not meant to imply, however, that every instance of a dynamic fit with the environment carries with it the maximal and most detailed perception of the intricacies of the environment and the highest level of performance. Rather, the psychological character of the dynamic orientation can better be viewed in the following manner.

If a certain aspect of the environment becomes focal for the person and the person experiences the press to do something vis-à-vis that environment, the process may proceed on the level of perception and recognition, whereby the individual becomes engaged in identifying the different components of that environment. When someone is confronted with a "What's wrong here?" picture, with an unfamiliar, abstract work of art or piece of music, or with an unfamiliar person, the course of "getting into" that environment can consist of the perceptual response—the process of identifying, comparing, and discriminating. It is perhaps the task of a teacher to attempt to break down the elements of whatever is being analyzed—the art work, athletic performance, or any type of problem with which a student might be confronted—and to recognize or identify those elements.

Although being perceptive and discriminating with regard to a specific environment is obviously a kind of performance, one can also deal with the more motor-related or overt kinds of performances that are often highly prized by society. Someone who is confronted with an unfamiliar picture might not only analyze it but also proceed to paint something similar, or the person who is confronted with an occasion for athletics might join in directly. Thus, "fitting" one's repertoires to the environment can take place on numerous different levels, and it would be incorrect to limit the notion of a dynamic orientation to any one of those levels. The important point is that, in the dynamic orientation, the person's reaction to the press is to *approach* the environment, to allow one's reactions to be guided by the perceived details of the environment.

QUESTIONING SOME ASSUMPTIONS ABOUT DISPOSITIONS

Within the context of the psychology of dispositions or traits, it would be fair to allow for the following assumptions: (1) trait terms—or, more generally, terms referring to the behavioral potential of the person—have embedded within them direct, objective behavioral referents; the occurrence of those behaviors is antecedent to the attribution to the person of dispositional terms; (2) these trait terms serve a useful communication function; and (3) knowing oneself with respect to such terms facilitates a dynamic orientation to the environment.

1. That trait terms have a direct origin in behaviors is a common thesis in modern personality and social psychology. For example, Bem (1983), Locksley and Lenauer (1981), and Markus (1977, 1983) treat traits as the end product of the self-perception (or other-perception) process, whereby an inference regarding attitudes, values, or personalities is derived solely from knowledge of the act and its environmental surroundings.

2. That trait terms serve a communicative function is an established and accepted principle (Kirk & Burton, 1977; Super, Harkness, & Baldwin, 1977). Super *et al.* (1977), for example, noted the relatively simple principle that the use of categories (including categories of humans) serves as a more efficient approach to communicating the nature of a given stimulus person. This point would appear to be obvious. Describing someone as psychopathic is obviously a more efficient means of communication than detailing all of the undesired behaviors that would point to that conclusion. Mehlhorn and Mehlhorn (1977) made a similar point in their examination of research on creativity, noting that creativity researchers are not about to become directly involved in the creativity process and thus must find categories with which they can come to terms with those individuals who can produce societally valued, "creative" works.

3. Self-knowledge is commonly regarded as the product of considering one's various potentials, such that one "knows" those potentials in terms of various human categories. Characteristically, we do not define self-knowledge as identical with past performances, nor with the details of what we perceive, but rather in terms of potentials—which are indicated by means of describing one's relative ability, tendency toward aggressiveness, honesty, consistency, and so forth. Although very few psychologists have drawn the explicit conclusion that self-knowledge furthers one's specific performances (Markus, 1983, is an exception), the assumption is treated quite broadly as a valid one—as, for example, in the context of psychotherapy.

How do these three assumptions appear if we view them in regard to a person who, in some particular context, characteristically manifests a dynamic orientation? For example, how do the assumptions apply when we are dealing with a highly active and proficient athlete, writer, painter, or mechanic?

First, what about the assumption that the involved individual desires, and can use to the benefit of performance, the self-knowledge that is composed of trait names? How would this assumption apply, for example, in the case of the artist? The trait names "capable, clever, confident, egotistical, humorous, individualistic, informal, insightful, intelligent, interests wide, inventive, original, reflective, resourceful, self-confident, sexy, snobbish, and unconventional"—some of the components of Gough's (1979) Creative Personality Scale—have been found to be positively associated with creative performances (Amabile, 1983). If such terms constitute the artist's or poet's or composer's self-knowledge, we then have to ask whether knowing oneself to be "humorous" or "individualistic" or "snobbish" would have a favorable impact on one's artistic or other creative performances. Does the self-knowledge "I am humorous, individualistic, and snobbish" help propel one into a dynamic relation with the environment? Perhaps not. As Alfred Brendel (1982), the renowned pianist, remarked in an interview: "The personality of composers does not explain their music" (p. 15).

One kind of "performance" that has been addressed increasingly in psychological research is the accuracy of self-reported behavioral expectations. Certainly it would be reasonable, within a model of the rational human, for high or strong self-knowledge to be related to the ability or willingness to give accurate reports about one's future behavior. This topic has been investigated by Warshaw and Davis (1984), who had the foresight to come to grips with self-knowledge in terms of an unequivocal operationalization. Their subjects were simply asked to respond to the following item, as a measure of general self-understanding: "I know myself well 0 1 2 3 4 5 6 7 8 9 10 don't understand myself at all" (p. 115). In a subsequent interview, the same subjects were asked to estimate the probabilities of their enacting each of several distinct behaviors (e.g., drinking alcohol) during the next 5 days. Then, in a final interview, the investigators established—via self-report—whether the subjects had indeed carried out those behaviors.

For the data analysis, the subjects were divided into three groups: high, medium, and low general self-understanding. The correlations between prediction of one's own behavior and actually carrying out the behavior were then calculated within each of the three groups, and, to be sure, the correlations were generally higher among the medium-self-understanding subjects than for the low-self-understanding subjects. The remarkable finding occurred with respect to the medium-versus-high differences: the mean correlation between prediction and enactment was .60 in the medium group and .53 in the high group. This overall difference is not statistically significant, although the comparisons are quite compelling for some of the behavioral areas. For example, for the criterion behavior "perform illegal behavior," the correlation between prediction and enactment was a considerable .76 for the medium-self-understanding group but dropped to .34 for the high-self-understanding group.

Thus, this timely study, which at least ostensibly addressed the self-knowledge issue head on, suggests that a claim to self knowledge does not necessarily relate positively to a societally valued performance—in this case, the performance being the prediction of one's own behaviors.

A second and closely related question has to do with the psychological basis of the ascription of such traits. From the artist's point of view, for example, how would the person move from the details of performance (brush strokes and detailed considerations of the object being painted) to the self-knowledge "I am individualistic"? Although certain traits that are more definitely related to behaviors may be ascribed in line with self-perception terms, it would be absurd to argue that the artist deduces the possession of such traits on the basis of a dynamic orientation to the environment. As is readily apparent by now, the same criticism applies to the observer. An observer of the artist who happens to be completely attuned to the refinements of the artist's behaviors and environment could hardly deduce such personality traits from those observations. As White (1980) noted:

> Personality descriptors, however, may symbolize complex actions and mental states. They most often cannot be linked easily with observable referents. Indeed, evidence which shows no direct parallel between the structure of trait attributions and actual consistencies in the behavior of individuals (D'Andrade, 1974;

Shweder, 1977) suggests that language creates as well as describes the phenomena it seeks to represent. (p. 760)

Given the foregoing objections, what about the communication function of trait terms? Do they not still serve a valuable function? If we look at the foregoing creativity example from the standpoint of the functional-communicative role of trait names, it becomes clear what that segment of the psychology of creativity is trying to do. If it is discovered that creatively performing people are "individual-istic" or "sexy," then society (psychology included) has better predictive control over knowing who will manifest creative actions in the future. Thus, the functional use of such category names is not to be disputed; they allow the identification of individuals who can perform within certain arenas and, therefore, the prediction of who will perform adequately on future occasions.

If the trait names—no matter how closely related they are to behavior or how distant—have such functional value, then who finds them to be functional? For our purposes in this chapter, this question cannot be dissociated from the variable *press*. A question about the relative engagement in the dynamic orientation or about the use of traits is not meaningful without this variable. Press enters in the following manner.

If a person has the requisite behavioral repertoire to develop a dynamic orientation to a given environment, then as the press increases, that person is increasingly likely to move into a one-to-one relationship with that environment. This means that one's own self is necessarily neglected (Csikszentmihalyi, 1975), and attention moves largely to the elements of the situation, to one's actions, and to the content of thoughts pertinent to involvement with the environment. As the press increases, and as the dynamic fit becomes better, there is progressively *less* room for the person to entertain cognitions (such as traits) that are not integral to the dynamic fit.

ACTORS VERSUS OBSERVERS: A DIFFERENT SET OF QUESTIONS

Approximately at this point, the reader is likely to find a certain parallel to the analysis of Jones and Nisbett (1971), whose seminal work dealt with the differences between actors' and observers' tendencies to employ dispositional terms in explaining behavior. According to Jones & Nisbett, the actors (those who are analyzing their own behaviors) are inclined to explain what they do in terms of situational factors, because (1) the actors are prone to focus attention on the relevant environment at hand, not on antecedent personal traits or dispositions, and (2) the actors are said to have relatively complete access to the situational antecedents and constraints relevant to that behavior. By comparison, the observer (someone who is analyzing the *actor's* behavior) (1) would turn attention more toward the actor as a person, hence toward dispositions, and (2) has less access to knowledge of situational constraints on the actor's behaviors and thus would fill in the gaps with presumed dispositions.

A crucial difference between that analysis and the present one resides in the meaning of the term "actor." The focus of analysis for Jones and Nisbett is differences in individuals in terms of whose behavior is being examined. Quite independent of how competent, interested, and so forth, the actor may be, the definition of "actor" resides in the fact that the actor's momentary attributions refer to his own actions. The observer is defined in terms of "analyzer of others' behaviors"—that is, the actor's behaviors.

In the present analysis, the precise role of the individual (i.e., self-observer or other-observer) is not the focal point. What is important is the person's momentary fit with the environment, which leads to the following implications: (1) whether people are analyzing their own actions or another's actions, the course of the analysis will be determined by the analyzer's fit with the environment, rather than solely by the nature of the person (self or other) who is being analyzed; and (2) the present formulation gives environmental press the power of determination of the individual's momentary set toward ascribing dispositions. If there is no press whatever, then neither a static nor a dynamic orientation will be present; thus, the possibility the individual will undertake a trait analysis will be minimal. In comparison, the Jones and Nisbett (1971) analysis followed the lead of attribution theory in not postulating a psychological mechanism whereby the attribution process would be set off. Within that framework, actors and observers make their respective kinds of attributions insofar as they are asked for attributions, and they are generally ready to do so. In any case, the psychological basis for the ascription of personalities or traits is not treated as a psychological variable within the actor–observer system.

It is clear that the psychological starting points for these two analyses can be sharply discriminated. The focus for Jones and Nisbett was on the variable of self-analysis versus other-analysis. This variable was treated as the primary independent variable—the determining factor. Within the present formulation, the deciding factor (among others to be discussed) is the person's ongoing fit with the environment. Actors, while analyzing their own behavior, could be experiencing a very strong (or weak) fit; correspondingly, an observer, in the moment of observing, may also be experiencing a very strong (or weak) fit. Thus, the present formulation homogenizes the actor and observer—necessarily so, because the object of the attribution is not seen as the deciding factor.

A PSYCHOLOGICAL ORIGIN OF THE STATIC ORIENTATION

We are still left with the crucial question of who makes use of trait names. One simple answer is that the person who is capable of the dynamic fit, and who is not momentarily subject to a great deal of press, would conceivably use trait names for the same reasons others use them—to identify others who can (or cannot) fit with the specified environment in a dynamic manner. Even though the language associated with the trait ("individualistic," and so forth) in no way captures the performer's own dynamic orientation to the environment, the performer in the moment of nonperformance would likely have some use for communicating about, or predicting, the performance potential of others as well as oneself.

A further issue brings us directly back to the relationship between the individual's fit with the environment and the degree of press. What happens when the environment exerts a strong press on the person, yet no dynamic orientation is possible? If the press is felt subjectively, the person feels an impulse to "do something," but the nature of that "something" cannot be the dynamic relationship. In terms of the explanatory repertoire of existing psychological conceptions, what other reaction possibility remains? Concepts such as "frustration" or "helplessness" come to mind, and, to be sure, these reactions seem likely so long as no other mode of responding exists. However, the central proposal here deals with another mode of responding.

Society socializes each individual into realizing that an acceptable mode of responding involves addressing oneself to the *potential* basic to the dynamic relationship that *could* or *should* be enacted. Rather than considering the details of the pressing environment, and rather than attempting to coordinate one's thoughts and actions with those environmental elements, the person can be socialized into reactions that involve thinking of the human categories that are *appropriate* to the environment in question.

Assuming that trait terms have functional value for society, the basis of the reasoning here should be evident. If any given individual, or society as a whole, cannot relate to a facet of the environment in a dynamic manner, then there is great functional worth in shifting the focus from that "frustration" to the issue of determining who can relate in that way. Those who do not have the behavioral repertoire to handle the environment stand to profit by knowing or identifying individuals who can perform; in this sense, the functional value of the trait terms seems clear.

Thus, it comes to be accepted (and ingrained) by society that one reacts by describing onself and others in terms of categories. The stronger the press, the greater the tendency to engage in this static mode of responding—*static* because the focus is on the human potential that would be relevant to a dynamic orientation, not on the actual elements intrinsic to the dynamic orientation.

The reasoning here leads to a seeming paradox. A rational psychology—one that advocates the idea that trait terms stem directly from observations of behavior—would have to argue that those who can see and discriminate a given environment and who know how to perform would be in the best position to draw detailed conclusions regarding traits. This conclusion seems direct in that the more concrete information available to the person, the more definite and the more accurate the derivation to trait terms can be.

On the other hand, it cannot work this way. As pointed out earlier, the nature of trait terms—their nonbehaviorally based abstractness—prevents the possibility that they are universally derived from behaviors. In short, those who can execute a dynamic mode of functioning within a certain context would not tend to be caught up in the process of concluding things about themselves and others (in trait language) on the basis of concrete actions, since the semantic relationship between behavioral or environmental elements and trait names is unclear. Rather, the person who can perform would be more inclined to remain within a highly concrete linguistic level that is appropriate to the dynamic relationship in question. Hence, we have the paradox that it is the person who *cannot* react dynamically and who is confronted with a great deal of press who must deal with situations in trait terms, for there is no other possible level of functioning.

If we were to draw the minimal implication from the foregoing, we would conclude that it is necessary to consider the relative competence of a person, within the context of the immediate environmental demand, to know the extent to which that person would focus on elements of the situation and necessary behaviors rather than on the human potential (i.e., the dispositions) that should be relevant in the situation. Suppose that two people are confronted with having to create an accurate sketch of a house. One of them, who has a great deal of experience in architecture and drawing, would proceed to think in terms of the elements that are to be represented on canvas. This person would size up the perspectives that are part of the task. The second person, who was never trained and is without experience in drawing or architecture, would be without the requisite rudimentary qualities for contemplating all of the necessary perspectives of the situation. Such a person would therefore be dependent on another way of reacting to the situation, and the only way left, other than a simple frustration or helplessness response, is the alternative provided by society. This alternative is the system of dispositions—that is, names for types of people who can function in situations calling for painting or sketching. Such dispositional names are the individual's only way to make contact with, or react to, the setting, since a more direct reaction—one not mediated by societally defined dispositions—is not even possible. Accordingly, the person will become preoccupied with thinking about relevant dispositions insofar as the situation remains salient or pressing.

This implication is a reasonable first step in conceptualizing the issue of the relationship between dynamic fit and the use of dispositional terms, but it does not go far enough. Some crucial factors need to be considered in this analysis in order to bring the analysis closer to what we already know about the functioning of the human. The following section will sketch out a more systematic treatment of this overly simple implication.

THE CHARACTERS OF TWO ORIENTATIONS

The Dynamic Orientation

Much of the character of the dynamic orientation has already been sketched out here, albeit not in a systematic fashion. This section attempts to characterize further the psychological state of the person who is in a dynamic fit with the environment.

The person's attention will be on the particulars of the relevant environment. Relative to someone who is not in a dynamic orientation, this person will be better able to attend to complexities, draw distinctions, and recall pertinent aspects. The person will also be attuned to the behavioral nuances necessary to create the perfect fit, although the amount of attention necessary will depend on the degree of automatization of behaviors that has already taken place.

Once the dynamic orientation is underway, the person will neglect facets of the situation that are not directly relevant to the ongoing behavior–environment fit (Csikszentmihalyi, 1975). For example, in the course of painting a whole landscape scene, an artist would at any given moment be focused only on a particular tree—or portion of a tree—and the remainder of what is to be done, as well as other environments, would be shut out. To the extent that the person does think of environments that are not immediately relevant, the dynamic fit between behavior and environment would be less than perfect, and using the definitions here, the dynamic orientation would thereby be weaker.

As postulated by Csikszentmihalyi (1975), the person who is caught up in a blend of actions and environment can be presumed to have positive affect. Thus, a perfect fit between one's actions and the environment can be viewed as motivating in and of itself.

The person's momentary existence is defined solely by the pertinent environment as long as the person is in the dynamic orientation. This is because the character of the fit between one's own behaviors and the environment is defined largely by the character of the environment. If the environment consists of something unknown or unusual, and the person is thereby drawn to it, the degree of complexity associated with the environment will dictate how long, and in what manner, the person will be associated with that environment. If the context consists of a discrete task, a similar argument applies. If the dynamic orientation revolves around such goal-oriented activities as discovering a solution to a problem or working a puzzle, the theme is again the same: the person's efforts and skills fit to the requirements of the perceived situation; thus, the person's momentary existence as a psychologically experienced individual is defined by the character of the environment.

In this context, it is appropriate to remark on the semantic component of the dynamic orientation. The person who is actively caught up in a fit with the environment is, in one important sense, limited linguistically. There is no adequate terminology for the "character" or "state" of the person that would serve to communicate the person's essence at the time of active involvement. To be sure, one could argue that such a person would be capable of saying, "My ability for this part of the task is at the 90th percentile" or "What I am doing now requires a very high creativity." But such ascriptions—locating the individual in categories such that others might have some grasp of the person who is functioning—in no way characterize the relevant nature of the person who is behaving. This is because the psychologically pertinent components of the dynamic orientation are nothing more than the components of the environment and the person's behavioral repertoire. A static portion of the self (IQ, ingenuity, creativity) has no functional, psychological place in the dynamic fit.

The Static Orientation

By definition of the static orientation, the particulars of the press-exerting environment are excluded. Rather than attending to the complexities and behaviorally pertinent components of the environment, the person's thoughts are directed instead toward the societally defined categories that indicate the types of people who *would be* capable of responding directly to the environment in question. Thus, the person is indeed drawing distinctions, but the distinctions are among categories that stand for certain kinds of human potential.

To the extent that the person's attention is on the plane of behaviors, the behaviors will not be those that are coordinated to the relevant part of the environment. For instance, if the person's attention turns to "aggressiveness" as the kind of trait that would be especially useful (in the face of some given environmental press), the behaviors that the person associates with the trait would not necessarily be coordinated with the components of the immediate environment. Rather, the behaviors would be those that are stereotypically associated with the trait "aggressiveness."

Just as in the case of the dynamic orientation, there will be a certain neglect of the situation, but with one important difference: the individual in a static orientation will neglect the entire situation, not just those facets that would not be pertinent to potential action taking. This general neglect is necessitated by (1) the person's incapacity or unwillingness to form a behavioral link to the pressing environment and (2) the consequent attention placed on the static human potential that is relevant to the situation.

The implication is that avoidance, or *rejection*, should characterize and accompany the static orientation. As long as the person can reject or deny the existence of particulars or elements within the environment, then, psychologically, there is nothing to respond to in a detailed manner. It is as though a detailed mode of responding is occasioned only by the acute realization that there are details to which one could respond. By denying or not accepting the existence of these details, the person's static orientation is made free of conflict in the sense that if the material for a dynamic orientation is perceived not to be there, there is consequently no reason to try to undertake a dynamic relation to the situation.

There are two differences between the static and dynamic orientations in terms of affect. First, the greater focus on the person's own condition that is characteristic of the static orientation will necessarily make the person more likely to think about affect, satisfaction, frustration, ability, and related self-issues. Second, given that the static condition is likely to be associated with blocks or with incompetence, affect would be expected to be consistent with those kinds of events. Thus, in general, the static-oriented person will be more attuned to affect states and will experience them as more negative.

The psychological state of the person—that is, the momentary sense of existence of self—is not defined by the nature of the pressing environment. Rather, the person either has pulled away or has been driven away from a possible momentary fit with the environment and thinks, instead, of the human (including one's self) as fitting or not fitting into the myriad of possible societally defined categories that stand for human potential. As a result, the static state cannot be carried through to an end as the dynamic orientation can be. This point can be made more lucid if we think in more detailed terms of how the two orientations would work. Suppose that people are confronted with the challenge of having to design a bridge. Some of them—because of prior experience, training, and related factors—would jump into the task, fitting the components of their behavioral repertoires to the elements of the environment and eventually arriving at the solution. Arrival at the solution, as spelled out earlier, is determined by the nature of the task. Thus, for those with a dynamic orientation, there is a clear sense of moving through the task to a definite completion.

On the other hand, people who do not form a dynamic orientation to the environment—because of a lack of training or other factors—will come to dwell on the situation in terms of the kinds of human potentials that would be right for the situation. Regardless of whether they are thinking about themselves or about others, the focus will be on the *potential*, not on the elements of the relationship between environment and human being; and dwelling on this condition of potential does not bring the person to a closure or to an environmentally defined goal.

ORIGINS OF THE TWO ORIENTATIONS

The foregoing discussion has advanced the notion that the extent of environmental press brings a person into either a static or a dynamic orientation. Now it is necessary to spell out the precise circumstances that lead the person in one direction or another. These factors can be discussed in a way that parallels the development of the individual person in society, since developmentally, the dynamic orientation precedes the possibility of the static one.

Since much of the preceding discussion has focused on the idea of the dynamic fit between person and environment, not a great deal of further comment is necessary. One additional, central assumption is important, however. The dynamic orientation will be maximized as the press grows and as the individual's response repertoire is challenged approximately 100% by the perceived relevant environment. If the environment contains many subtleties or complexities and the person's possible response repertoire is exactly as complex as that environment, the person will then be maximally in the dynamic orientation. Quite clearly, the alternative cases are those in which the environment is overwhelming (or else not sufficiently challenging), so that the possibility of experiencing a fit with that environment is reduced. This assumption and the factor of environmental press are the two central considerations in anticipating whether an individual will move into a dynamic orientation.

Correspondingly, the higher the environmental press and the *worse* the fit between the person's response repertoire and the pressing environment, the more likely it is that the person will be found in a condition of static orientation.

However, being in the static orientation as we have described it assumes that the person has a familiarity with society's system of categories, and here is where two developmental or perhaps quasi-developmental variables become crucial.

On the assumption that a society has a substantial repertoire of trait, disposition, role, and aptitude names, and the like, the possibility of finding oneself in a static orientation depends on whether this cultural system has been incorporated personally. Accordingly, a young child who finds it impossible to fit with the environment may not have access to the alternative condition (the static orientation), since the relationship between certain classes of response to the environment and corresponding dispositional terms is a sophisticated body of knowledge that is learned slowly. Furthermore, the socialization process must impart to the child that reacting in terms of categories is an acceptable and/or desirable mode of response. The following remarks by Bromley (1977) are instructive in this regard:

> There is little evidence that children below the age of seven years can conceptualize psychological dispositions; although by that age the average child has a good vocabulary for describing on-going behaviour, including both overt action and covert mental processes. His lack of psychological conceptualization means that he cannot describe or understand covert *dispositional* characteristics like motives, traits, abilities and attitudes. . . . The structure of human behaviour—its organization and episodic nature—is not "given" in perception, but is learned through experience of actual behaviour *in the context of an accompanying lanugage.* . . . So the way we perceive behaviour is partly a function of the terms and concepts we have acquired through social learning and language learning. (p. 11)

Based on a number of studies (Flapan, 1968; Livesley & Bromley, 1973; Peevers & Secord, 1973), Miller (1984) has concluded: "References to general dispositions of the agent, it has been observed, increases significantly over development among Western populations." In short, adults are more inclined to use dispositional explanations, whereas children depend more heavily on actions and other contextual factors.

The second variable relates to the stage of development of a society. In a rudimentary society in which there is no need for a richly developed set of dispositional terms, the likelihood of moving to the static orientation is low. As societies become increasingly complex, such that the functions to be performed multiply and virtually no one understands any of the behavioral functions, the catalogue of dispositional terms becomes infinite. At the same time, the chances that a person will move into the static orientation in such a society are that much greater. A possible case in point is the contrast between the Hindu culture and the American culture. Comparing subjects in Mysore, India, with respondents from Chicago, Miller (1984) demonstrated greater reference to dispositions as explanatory constructs among Americans.

This cultural-developmental factor allows some interesting implications concerning the place of socialization in the dynamic-versus-static orientation condition. If it were possible to document the ages at which children within a certain, circumscribed segment of a society have access to particular trait names, to disposition names, or, more generally, to the idea that behavioral potential can be signaled by category membership, we could predict the persistence of children of different ages in the face of a highly challenging environment. Suppose that children are confronted with a complex environment to which they can fit their behavioral repertoire to some extent; but suppose also that the degree of fit becomes progressively worse because of a changing environment. Given that the press of that environment remains high, the question now is whether the children can move into another mode of functioning—the static mode—and away from actual involvement with the elements of the task. The likelihood of this happening will depend on the children's familiarity with the meaning of the dispositional terms that are relevant to their situation. The less familiar they are with the system of categories that stands for behavioral potential, the more persistent they will be in trying to fit their skills to the task requirements.

This prediction can be carried still further. It is conceivable that within certain highly advanced segments of society, the system of categories has advanced to the point where the likelihood of stepping into the static mode of functioning is practically zero. In fact, this would be guaranteed, since one's working knowledge of the categories develops more rapidly than one's skills in fitting directly with the environment. On a more concrete level, this point could take the following form: A child is informed regarding the meaning of "intelligence," coming to understand that a high IQ is defined as a strong potential to do practically anything—whether verbal, mathematical, logical, or mechanical. The child has perhaps been socialized to think of a high IQ as a genuine response to the demands of a situation, as when adults read of scientific discoveries and exclaim, "That would take a great deal of *intelligence* or *creativity*." Thus, the child is easily socialized into thinking that the adaptive response to a challenge from the environment has to do with membership in a category. Depending on the sophistication of those around the child in regard to use of category terms, it would become an easy matter for the child to respond to demands in school simply by referring to his high IQ or by making reference to particular people who obviously have a great deal of "IQ." When such a mode of responding and thinking is supported by the adult social milieu, it would not be surprising if the child continued to behave in this mode.

It follows that such an orientation would prevent the formation of dynamic orientations to particulars in the environment. The child would be so well versed in all of the distinctions among categories of potential and so preoccupied with reacting to new situations in terms of which categories might be suitable that attention to the pertinent, behaviorally relevant components of the environment would suffer.

DRAWING A DISTINCTION: SELF-FOCUSED ATTENTION

The dichotomy explicated here—between an orientation toward the relevant environment (dynamic) and an orientation toward human potential (static)—is not intended to imply that the static orientation is synonymous with self-directed attention. Rather, self-directed attention, by definition, can be directed toward any facet of the self, and certain self-components could be directly pertinent to the demands of a certain situation. If we analyze this issue within the context of self-awareness theory (Duval & Wicklund, 1972; Wicklund, 1975), the pertinent self-awareness concepts are *focus of attention* and *personal standards*. If people find themselves in a situation in which they have the requisite competencies—hence, potentially, a good behavioral fit with the elements of the setting—it is not difficult to construe that person–environment fit as being composed, in part, of their standards in that setting. For instance, in a situation where certain moral judgments could be applied, there would be a variation in how much the people call up their own moral standards and apply them. Or in a performance setting, there may well be a variation in the degree to which personal performance standards come to the people's attention.

If the person becomes self-focused upon entering such situations, and if the salient aspect of the self is the situation-relevant standard (a moral, a performance standard), the induction of self-focused attention should have a motivating effect on the person. Provided that the self-focus does not stray to performance-irrelevant parts of the self, and provided that the person has the behavioral repertoire necessary for a dynamic fit, the induction of self-focus should enhance performance, as illustrated in research reported by Duval & Wicklund (1972).

If self-focused attention does not necessarily interfere with the dynamic orientation, then exactly what is the difference between the concepts of *self-focus* and *static orientation*? Static orientation is a condition in which the person retreats from the specific demands of the environment. Particulars of the situation, aspects of pertinent behaviors, *and* specific, personal performance standards are neglected, and instead of thinking of these elements, the person's thoughts move toward nonbehaviorally specific dispositional concepts. Accordingly, self-focused attention is theoretically independent of the dynamic/static distinction, in that thinking about certain facets of the self might well be a part of the static condition, whereas thinking about one's own performance-relevant standards can most certainly be a part of the dynamic orientation. Since the concepts of self-focus and static/dynamic functioning are, in theory, independent of one another, the relationship between them will not be spelled out in further detail in this chapter.

EMPIRICAL ILLUSTRATIONS

Variation in Fit with the Task

The respondents in a study by Heckhausen (1982) were university students who were in the process of taking an extremely important examination in their major area of study. Immediately after the exam, they were asked to recollect the kinds of thoughts they had during the exam. Heckhausen classified their thoughts according to different kinds of task-irrelevancy. The important finding was that virtually all kinds of self-related thoughts (such as own ability, anticipated outcome) were experienced by subjects as interfering with their performance. This was particularly so among subjects who tended to be failure-oriented. From the subjects' reports, it appeared that the only kinds of thoughts that did not interfere with performance were those that were directly pertinent to the elements of the examination material.

A modest conclusion to be drawn from this study is that concern with self—whether it is labeled failure anxiety, self-knowledge, focus on one's own abilities, or anything of the kind—stems from faltering performance and serves to disrupt performance further. In the language of this chapter, the finding implies an inverse relationship between the extent of dynamic and static functioning. Heckhausen's results and certainly the theoretical proposals of Wine (1971) point toward the mutual exclusivity of the two modes of functioning. The student who cannot pour his energies directly into the exam material—who stumbles and falters—is thereby forced into a static orientation, as reflected in the frequency of self-related thoughts.

Somewhat earlier, Diener and Dweck (1978) showed that children who try to solve problems, when the challenge is difficult, spend little of their time thinking about possible personal factors behind their failure. Such "mastery-oriented" children are more inclined to devote their attention to task-related details, whereas "helpless" children's minds wander toward questioning their ability and toward a variety of other solution-irrelevant thoughts.

Both of the foregoing studies illustrate the functioning of the static orientation in that the *frequency* of self-related (i.e., ability, personality, traits) thoughts increases to the degree that the person cannot deal directly—that is, dynamically—with the immediate task environment. However, there are other possible indicators of the presence of the static condition. If the press of the environment forces the person to react, and if a dynamic fit is impossible, then a reaction in the static mode will be revealed in terms of frequency of thoughts not just about membership in categories but also about definiteness of category membership. In short, when the person's attention is focused only on a single dispositional dimension, the static-functioning person should tend to see the object of judgment (self or others) as more extreme in the category in question. This assumes, of course, that membership in the category implies culturally that one *could* deal with the environment in question.

Once again, it is crucial to keep in mind that the conceptualization advanced here is not a blanket implication that incompetent performance leads to the imputation of a potential for competence. Rather, the critical mediator of the processes under study here is the extent of environmental press, such that the tendency to place oneself or another into a category of potential will be manifest only to the extent that the press is compelling.

Variation in Press

A useful introduction to the theme of press can be found in several studies on subjectively rated confidence. These cumulated studies make clear (1) that ratings of confidence are by no means predicted simply on demonstrated performance capacity and (2) that the tendency to impute confidence, when one cannot perform, depends on the extent of press.

Our analysis begins with some early research by Henmon (1911), who asked each of his subjects to make numerous discriminations between pairs of lines that differed only slightly in length. After each judgment, subjects gave an indication of their felt confidence in the preceding judgment on a 4-point answering continuum ranging from *perfectly confident* to *doubtful*. Although there was an overall tendency for correct answers to be followed by expressions of higher confidence, Henmon noted such profound variability in the performance–confidence relation that he concluded: "The relation of confidence to accuracy seems to be an individual matter without any well-defined general tendency" (p. 200).

Klein and Schoenfeld (1941) went a step further in their study of confidence ratings over a number of tasks as a function of subjects' ego-involvement. In the first session, run under relaxed conditions, subjects worked four different intellectual tasks; opposites, mental additions, definitions, and dot apprehension. After each problem, they indicated their confidence in the correctness of the solution on a 7-point scale. Rather than computing the absolute level of confidence, Klein and Schoenfeld correlated the confidence levels associated with each task with the confidence levels associated with every other task. They did this because their interest was in whether confidence was task-specific or a more general "personality trait." The data for the first session showed an average confidence level intercorrelation of +.22.

The same subjects were then run through a second, highly ego-involving session, in which the tasks were said to be a measure of intelligence. Unfortunately, the order of sessions was confounded with the ego-involvement variable, so the results must be viewed with some caution. In any case, the average intercorrelation of confidence ratings for the second session was +.45, a substantial increase from the non-ego-involving session. The authors concluded from this differential pattern of correlations:

> In our first period, the atmosphere was "neutral," that is, the subjects worked without strain, and with very little competitive spirit. Probably they relied much more upon their actual ability for their feelings of confidence, and less upon what they would have liked, or wished, to achieve. When on the second occasion the Ego-involvement created an active desire to do well on the tests, their confidence ratings may have reflected this desire as well as, or in addition to, the objective ability to perform. . . . This fact would mean that "confidence" would appear as a personality trait when the Ego is involved, but that it would be a function of the nature and difficulty of the tasks when the situation is "neutral." (Klein & Schoenfeld, 1941, p. 257)

The next step, to make clear how this experiment relates to the present formulation, is to show how the ego-involvement manipulation is pertinent. First, focusing subjects' thoughts on their intelligence would lead directly to a static orientation. Intelligence is a human potential; taken by itself, the concept has no bearing on any specific, dynamic orientation. Second, making the subjects' intelligence dependent on task performance would also increase the press of the immediate environment (cf. Alper, 1946); thus, no matter what the dominant orientation—dynamic or static—they would have tended more toward that orientation. Assuming that the ego-involving instructions were sufficient to push subjects in the direction of a static orientation and that the press experienced under these instructions was high, it would then follow that subjects would try to view themselves as generally capable; that is, they would imbue themselves with a sense of potential across the whole array of tasks.

Therefore, confidence would be determined less by their actual behavioral relation to individual tasks and more by the overriding tendency *to have a sense of potential*. The foregoing quotation from Klein and Schoenfeld (1941) expresses the idea succinctly: Confidence ratings within the ego-involvement condition have less to do with objective ability to perform the individual tasks and thus would not vary so much from task to task for a given subject. The higher the correlation, the less that differential performance on the tasks would guide the confidence ratings.

In summary, the data point toward the conclusion that the expressions of a person's own potential, in terms of confidence, are less likely to be predicated on the reality of objective performance if the person is in a static state of orientation— generated by ego-involving instructions.

A more recent study by Stephan, Fischer, and Stein (1983) comes still closer to illustrating the present theoretical idea. College students at the University of Trier, Germany, were in the process of taking an oral exam that was central to their progress in their studies. The press of the examining environment was clearly very high. Just after receiving feedback on their exams, they were asked a number of questions that formed a confidence index pertaining to their confidence in their exam-relevant abilities. As it turned out, the worse they did on the exam, the *more* confidence they manifested on the confidence index ($r = -.43$).

The result is a strong and simplistic illustration of the principle we are dealing with here. Subjects who faltered at the task came to view themselves as having particularly high potential (in this case, confidence) with respect to the material of the exam. Once again, numerous other measures could have been implemented to reflect the existence of a static orientation, such as a general concern with dispositions, a tendency to ascribe dispositions to others as well as to oneself, or an absence of attunement to details of the task at hand.

An External Source of Category Ascription

The ego-involvement study of Klein and Schoenfeld (1941) illustrated one way of instigating a high degree of press and the resultant static orientation. A still more direct manner of moving people into a static orientation would consist of foisting the category—the knowledge that they have, or could have, the potential— directly onto them. To the degree that they become surrounded by indications of their own membership in the particular category, the resultant dynamic orientation with respect to activities related to the category should be diminished.

A striking example comes from a well-known experiment by Lepper, Greene, and Nisbett (1973). When children were given the opportunity to play with an interesting task—that is, to draw freely with felt-tipped pens—a continued overt interest in the task waned when the children were supplied incentives for good performance. In particular, when they anticipated receiving "Good Player Awards" (including a big gold star and a bright red ribbon) for their performance, they showed less persistence on the free-drawing task.

According to the original theoretical point of Lepper et al., the external incentive undermines intrinsic motivation, in that the subjects could not be sure that they were truly interested in the tasks because external rewards had been promised. However, rather than viewing the experiment in terms of the subjects' confusion about exactly why they worked or not, another psychological meaning could be that the highly self-relevant rewards, signifying a definite potential ("Good Player Awards"), brought the subjects' attention to a consideration of their potential, and such preoccupation interfered with the more dynamic orientation toward drawing with the felt-tipped pens.

A Summary of Implications

The foregoing examples are an admittedly inadequate set of illustrations of the ideas proposed here. The range of applications of the dynamic/static notion is considerably broader, and a number of dimensions must be outlined to sketch out the full range. First, the notion applies whether the object of judgment is oneself or others. In the foregoing research illustrations, the focus was on evaluation of oneself, but the theoretical reasoning also applies when the person—whether in a dynamic or a static state—has to evaluate or consider another person. Furthermore, one force that is basic to the instigation of a static (or dynamic) orientation is the goodness of fit between the person's response repertoire and the nature of the environment confronting that person. As the challenge of the environment approaches 100% of the person's response repertoire, we can say that there is a fitting, one-to-one match between person and environment. If the challenge is insufficient, or if it is too great, the person will tend toward the static orientation. A second force, also examined in the foregoing research, is the antecedent tendency of the person to move toward the static state—quite independent of any possible fit between repertoire and environment. For instance, if the person, through prompting of society, comes to the situation with high ego-involvement (Klein & Schoenfeld, 1941), or if the person is prompted to think of the situation in terms of being a star or prize-winner (Lepper et al., 1973), then the chances of that person's entering a dynamic relationship with the environment are diminished. What is important here is not just the immediate social background of the person, as in the studies just cited, but also the general cultural background of the person and the extent to which that background has been assimilated or internalized. Thus, the extent of static orientation within the culture and the degree of internalization of that cultural orientation would be critical variables in this analysis. Finally, the extent of experienced press from the immediate environment is the crucial factor that heightens whichever orientation happens to predominate at the time. The preceding research examples reflect only a few of the kinds of effects that are pertinent to the ideas here. The several aspects of the dynamic orientation and the corresponding aspects of the static orientation provide the fundamental groundwork for measurable variables.

AN ILLUSTRATION FROM A CLASSIC DICHOTOMY: ACHIEVEMENT MOTIVATION VERSUS TASK ORIENTATION

It is commonly thought that people who are interested in achievement would also be adept at a variety of tasks, particularly when the tasks are personally important. Part of the reason for this belief is that a person's good intentions (intentions to achieve things) may easily be confused with what in fact transpires. A thesis by Atkinson (1974) corrects this faulty impression.

It is Atkinson's contention that, given a task of some complexity, high achievement motivation is detrimental to performance. His assertion may be seen as a specific application of the Yerkes-Dodson (1908) law, which was the original assertion of a nonmonotonic relationship between motivation and performance. Although it was not the basis of Atkinson's assertion, it is informative that at least one operationalization of achievement motivation is very much a case of people placing themselves into categories of potential, not a straightforward task orientation. The desires to attain a standard of excellence (characteristically a socially defined standard) or to accomplish something uniquely valued are tendencies bearing on the person's orientation toward a self-defining condition, not toward adapting oneself to the particulars of some given environment. The operationalization in question is that of McClelland, Clark, Roby, and Atkinson (1949), in which task-related responses to the Thematic Apperception Test (TAT) cards were explicitly ruled out and status-related, position-related, and competition-related responses were ruled in as the definition of achievement motivation (pp. 245–246). Such an operationalization was entirely congruent with Murray's (1938) notion of need for achievement ("power over things, people and ideas," p. 80). Highly achievement-motivated people, at least within the context of the McClelland *et al.* (1949) and Atkinson (1957) schools, try to view themselves as oriented toward a final position of conquering or superiority. Accordingly, the prediction by Atkinson (1974) makes perfect sense. If the task is at all complex, the highly achievement-motivated person, being less than optimally dynamically oriented, would falter at the task.

This point becomes clear if we look at the early research of McClelland *et al.* (1949), in which the authors set out to validate the TAT technique as a measure of achievement motivation. It was reasoned that the condition of achievement motivation would be set off under conditions of ego-involvement, particularly if subjects failed at the tasks. The crucial comparison was between subjects in such a failure condition and subjects in a relaxed condition.

McClelland *et al.* scored the TAT protocols following performance and

TABLE 3.1   Percentages of Task-Related, Achievement-Related, and Unrelated Stories Written Under Relaxed and Failure Conditions

	Relaxed condition	*Failure condition*
Type of imagery:		
Task-related	46.8	35.9
Achievement-related	16.7	48.1
Unrelated	36.5	16.0

Note. Adapted from McClelland, D. C., Clark, R. A., Roby, T. B., & Atkinson, J. W. (1949). The projective expression of needs. IV. The effect of the need for achievement on thematic apperception. *Journal of Experimental Psychology, 39*, 242–255.

feedback on the task and grouped the subjects' recorded thoughts into three categories: task-related imagery, general achievement motivation–related imagery, and unrelated imagery. Following failure on an ego-related task, subjects showed a slight decline in task-related imagery, as shown in Table 3.1. They also showed a considerable rise in achievement motivation–related imagery—from 16.7% to 48.1%. In short, the pattern of data fits readily with the interpretation of achievement motivation as a static orientation, in that subjects who were made ego-involved and who found that they could not fit their potentials to the task environment showed a slight decline in their focus on tasks and a strong increase in their focus on Murray's "power over things, people and ideas." It is instructive that the ego-involvement instructions of Klein and Schoenfeld (1941), described earlier, also led to a pattern of responses that appeared to reflect a static orientation.

The point can be made in a second way if we also consider another source of motivation stipulated by Atkinson (1974). Achievement motivation is not the only contributor to resultant motivation in a task situation; the task's personal importance to the individual also plays a role. According to the Atkinson formulation, the greater the personal importance, the higher the resultant motivation, with resulting losses in performance on complex activities. Again, it appears that Atkinson was suggesting that if such personal aspects as intelligence, creativity, or other human potential are brought into play (cf. Alper, 1946), orientation toward the details of the task will be lessened.

As a concluding thought, a limitation of this discussion of achievement motivation should be noted. The reasoning here is based entirely on the research of McClelland *et al.* (1949) and, of course, on the associated theoretical basis of their scoring system. Thus, the question remains open whether alternative operationalizations of achievement motivation are more likely to tap into the person's dynamic orientation toward certain environments.

A SEEMING CONTRADICTION WITH SELF-PERCEPTION THEORY

A common view of the development of conceptions of oneself and others is that consistent, overt behaviors are the starting point of conclusions regarding human dispositions. A clear case is found in Locksley and Lenauer (1981), who extend Bem's (1972) self-perception logic to the development of firm self-conceptions and firm other-conceptions.

Let us suppose (with the reasoning of Locksley & Lenauer, 1981) that several people are asking themselves whether they are creative. Their first step is said to be a scanning of past behaviors—but only behaviors that are pertinent to creativity. If there have been many instances of creative behavior and if there are not too many countercases, the people will conclude with a high subjective probability that they possess the trait "creativity." The same route would be taken in inferring such a trait in another person. First, the observer would gain access to the observed person's behavioral history—behaviors that are representative of the construct in question. If the observed person has shown many instances of creative efforts, that trait in that person is then inferred with certainty.

Bem's (1983) recent discussion of dispositions carries the same message:

> As laypersons, we are both idiographic and person centered. In fact, this is how our intuitions manage to finesse the consistency problem altogether . . . we first review the individual's behavior and then select a small subset of descriptions that strike us as pertinent precisely because they seem to conform to the patterning of the individual's behavior . . . we do not first impose a trait term . . . we attempt first to organize the person's behaviors into recognizable patterned sets and only then to label them; we search for a set of recognizable templates or prototypes to which the target person can be assimilated. (p. 569)

Perhaps a good description of this kind of formulation, which is also found in Markus (1977), is that the individual's ascribing of dispositions has a firm basis in behavioral realities. Thus, the process of ascribing dispositions is said to be a cautious one, in the sense that it is not thought to race ahead of the actual performance of behaviors that the dispositional names are intended to represent or summarize. For instance, Markus's (1977) view of self-knowledge, or "self-schemata," is that "self-schemata can be viewed as a reflection of the invariances people have discovered in their own social behavior (p. 64)." If a person has a variety of opportunities to manifest creativity—in art, music, literature, athletics, or any other endeavor—and apparently does not rise to the challenge, such a person would not begin to undertake a self-placement into the "creative" category.

However, there is some theoretical reason, and certainly reason in the empirical work just reported, to think that human category ascriptions are not necessarily based in behavioral reality. To the contrary, a flimsy behavioral fit with the environment can accelerate the focus on dispositions—including possession of valued dispositions. The most blatant case in point is the study of Stephan *et al.*

(1983), in which an *increment* in reported confidence stemmed from inadequate examination performance.

Thus we arrive at the question of whether the self-perception thesis must be completely incorrect. Raising the question may be ludicrous, since psychologists already know that there are clear instances of the self-perception process, in the sense of ascriptions to oneself and to others that are based directly on previously existing behavioral reality. For example, when a person is asked for a statement of attitude for the first time, in an unfamiliar domain, it can be demonstrated easily that immediately preceding, freely chosen behaviors are the determinants of one's strong conclusion about one's own attitudes (Pryor, Gibbons, Wicklund, Fazio, & Hood, 1977, Experiment 3). Thus, if we have no prior information about the taste of Greek food but eat a great deal of it the first time we try it, that particular relation to the environment can be shown to lead to a positive attitude. The more frequent or intense the behavior, the stronger the disposition (attitude) that would be ascribed.

The self-perception thesis and the variations on it have been implemented in research primarily in cases in which no special behavioral repertoires are required and the environment is not overwhelmingly complex. The objects of study have almost invariably been such internal states as pain, social attitudes, or a liking for concrete objects. Thus, the behavioral repertoires appropriate to these dispositions, and the environmental circumstances relevant to them, have been simple. This means that the Bemian tradition has dealt with dispositions that could be related easily to one of several highly discrete behaviors. Furthermore, and also important, none of the dispositions has stood for broad, sophisticated, or mysterious human potentials that would presumably be basic to high-performance behaviors, creative behaviors, highly unusual behaviors, or perhaps more generally, behaviors that would be executed in the face of complex environmental demands.

In other words, self-perception research characteristically has addressed itself to *attitudes*, which, in contradistinction to personality or trait dispositions, revolve around a particular object and are operationalized almost entirely in terms of beliefs or affect in regard to that object (Sherman & Fazio, 1983). In short, the attitudes that have been the topic of self-perception research are dispositional names whose meaning resides almost entirely in the environment. For instance, the conclusions (or attributions) "I feel pain when Stimulus X is present" or "I like Spanish desserts" are characterizations of the relationship between the person and a specific object. The conclusion drawn about the nature of the person does not separate the individual from the environment but, rather, describes a mode of responding. Thus, such self-perceptions (or other-perceptions) could well be part of a dynamic orientation to the environment.

Accordingly, we can surmise that the self-perception thesis—or, more generally, the thesis that dispositions are based in objective behaviors—applies singularly to those dispositions that are, in fact, defined in terms of the behavior–environment connection within some circumscribed setting. This implies not that the making of such attributions inevitably signals the person's presence in a dynamic orientation, but only that such attributional processes could well take place within the dynamic mode of functioning.

Once we move to dispositions that make no explicit reference to the environmental and behavioral facts, which are transsituational (intelligent, creative, patriotic) and necessarily vague with respect to behaviors or environments in question, we are then in the arena in which the functional value of the disposition can be clearly understood. Society has coined such terms because of a failure or unreadiness to comprehend directly the environment–behavior fit. Thus, by definition, such dispositional terms are not readily reduceable to specific elements of the environment. It is this feature that puts such terms in the realm we have referred to as the static orientation.

This discussion can be moved to a more theoretical plane by treating the attitude-versus-trait distinction on a much more general level. We can begin by stipulating that there is a large class of terms that serves to summarize, or characterize, the person's relation to the environment. Such terms, which can be called *dispositional* terms, can have various degrees of abstraction, or removal, from that environment–person fit. At the most concrete level, the terms merely restate precisely specific instances of the person's meeting with the environment, as is done in characteristic research on self-perception theory. For instance, "Harry loves pea soup" is easily reduceable to the observation that Harry devours pea soup. At the other extreme, when it is clear that the ascriber of dispositions is exposed to certain complex interactions between the person and the environment but that the terms used in making ascriptions do not have as their referents the details of those complex interactions, we then have abstract terms, which we refer to as trait terms—sociability, creativity, and so forth. These terms are well removed from the person–environment fit.

Thus, the critical dimension in determining whether self-perception processes might apply (and thus whether the proposals of Bem, Locksley and Lenauer, and Markus apply) is the degree to which the language associated with the ascription is removed, or abstracted, from the concrete details of the person–environment fit. If there is no abstraction whatever and the ascriptive term refers directly to the discrete parts of the person–environment fit ("Harry loves pea soup"), the "inference" of trait from behavior is scarcely an inference, in that it stays closely attuned to behavior. Under such conditions, it is clear that the self-perception thesis will function. On the other hand, the thesis advanced in this chapter—that the preoccupation with and use of dispositional terms stems from an absence of an ongoing behavior–environment fit—assumes some degree of abstraction, because the world of dispositions and traits provides an alternative response mode only insofar as it frees the person from the necessity to be attuned to environmental and behavioral details. In this regard, it does not help us make theoretical distinctions among attitudes, abilities, traits, dispositions, predilections, and so forth. Rather, the important point is to keep in mind the extent of abstraction from the person–environment fit.

Why Ascribe at All?

There is still another important difference between these two formulations that has not been addressed in earlier research. Independent of the *form* that ascriptions of dispositions take (e.g., positive or negative), the reality-based formulations (such as self-perception) do not deal with the *preoccupation* with ascribing permanent characteristics to humans. In other words, the frequency or likelihood that a person will even be concerned about ascribing dispositions is not treated as a psychological variable. An example comes from Locksley and Lenauer (1981):

> For example, suppose an individual is wondering whether or not he or she is an extravert. If he or she can retrieve a number of instances in which he or she behaved like an extravert . . . (p. 271)

The explicit starting point for the Locksley and Lenauer self-inference process is the individual's musing about what he or she might be like, but the psychological determinants of the person's arrival at that self-inquiring stance are not dealt with, nor is the issue even raised.

Similarly, attribution theory on a broader scale (e.g., Kelley, 1967) has no systematic variables that would indicate the propensity to make ascriptions other than the stipulation of a general need for control (Kelley, 1972). This absence of a theoretical concern with the frequency or intensity of ascribing characteristics to people is reflected generally in attribution research and more particularly in self-perception research. All subjects in such research are asked to ascribe, and the tendency to do so or not is not considered relevant. Thus, it is no surprise when all subjects perform some kind of self-inference (or inference about another person). This kind of methodology leaves open the possibility that—operating in the realm of easily comprehensible environments and with behaviors that are not at all unusual—there would be no special propensity to make ascriptions.

Particularly germane here is a small amount of neo-attribution-theory research that has taken up the issue of the frequency of making attributions. Notable is an analysis by Berscheid, Graziano, Monson, and Dermer (1976), in which Kelley's (1972) suggestions about the need for control were expanded into the postulate that situations threatening the individual's control will call forth tendencies to attribute dispositions to people in those situations. Berscheid *et al.* found, for example, that subjects who expected a date with a given stimulus person were more inclined to make extreme and highly confident trait attributions regarding that person, relative to a baseline that entailed a "nondate" stimulus person.

In a much different paradigm, Diener and Dweck (1978) engaged children in a procedure designed as a challenge to their persistence. They classified their subjects according to whether they continued to try to meet the challenge rather than giving up. A pronounced by-product of giving up—that is, removing oneself from the environment—was the frequency of self-related thoughts, such as a focus on abilities. Again, being confronted with an environment with which one cannot fit readily appears to trigger the tendency to impute dispositions—in this case to oneself. Another study within this general theoretical format was reported by Pittman and Pittman (1980), who showed that attributing activities are more common among people who are rendered helpless; that is, subjects who have faltered in cognitive problem-solving tasks are much more likely to take mand and tact information into account in making attributions of causality to a target person. Taking all of these studies together, it would appear that an overly challenging environment generates a readiness to undergo a causal analysis, in the sense of a preoccupation with sorting out the dispositions that are pertinent to the task or situation at hand.

Summary

The reality-based effects postulated by self-perception theory and its variants can be expected, provided that the inference to be made is with respect to a disposition that refers explicitly to concrete person–environment exchanges ("Harry hates pea soup," "Martha loves writing letters"). The issue of whether or not people are even interested in making such inferences has not been addressed formally within attribution theory, and neo-attribution-theory research has pointed toward the prior necessity of a faltering relation with the environment. That is, if the measure is whether or not to ascribe a disposition at all, the person whose response repertoire does not fit with the environment appears to be the most strongly oriented toward dealing in dispositions.

The static orientation with which we have been concerned assumes that the disposition in question does not have as its referent the components of the person–environment interaction. If it did, the orientation would not be a static orientation as it has been defined and operationalized here. The static orientation assumes the existence of and access to dispositional terms that do not have objective environmental components or objective behaviors as their referents.

Finally, the crucial issue of press of the environment must be taken into account in looking at the movement back and forth between dynamic and static orientations and at psychological states that are neither dynamic nor static. For the person to have *any* relation to an aspect of environment—whether dynamic or static—the environment in question must exert a psychological push, a subjective feeling of the need to respond to it.

Acknowledgments

The author would like to express thanks to Alois Angleitner, C. Daniel Batson, Ottmar Braun, Peter M. Gollwitzer, E. Tory Higgins, James L. Hilton, Michael Koller, Wulf-Uwe Meyer, Joan G. Miller, Richard M. Sorrentino, William B. Swann, Jr., Ulrich Wagner, and Daniel M. Wegner for their criticisms and suggestions.

References

Abelson, R. P. (1976). A script theory of understanding, attitude and behavior. In J. Carroll & T. Payne (Eds.), *Cognition and social behavior* (pp. 33–45). Hillsdale, NJ: Erlbaum.
Alper, T. G. (1946). Task-orientation vs. ego-orientation in learning and retention. *American Journal of Psychology, 59*, 236–248.
Amabile, T. M. (1983). *The social psychology of creativity*. New York: Springer-Verlag.
Anastasi, A. (1958). *Differential psychology*. New York: Macmillan.
Atkinson, J. W. (1957). Motivational determinants of risk-taking behavior. *Psychological Review, 64*, 359–372.
Atkinson, J. W. (1974). Strength of motivation and efficiency of performance. In J. W. Atkinson & J. O. Raynor (Eds.), *Motivation and achievement* (pp. 117–142). Washington, DC: Winston.

Bem, D. J. (1972). Self-perception theory. In L. Berkowitz (Ed.), *Advances in experimental social psychology* (Vol. 6, pp. 1–62). New York: Academic Press.

Bem, D. J. (1983). Constructing a theory of the triple typology: Some second thoughts on nomothetic and idiographic approaches to personality. *Journal of Personality, 51,* 566–577.

Berscheid, E., Graziano, W., Monson, T., & Dermer, M. (1976). Outcome dependency: Attention, attribution, and attraction. *Journal of Personality and Social Psychology, 34,* 978–989.

Brehm, J. W. (1966). *A theory of psychological reactance.* New York: Academic Press.

Brendel, A. (1982). Unterwegs mit Beethoven. [Underway with Beethoven] [Interview]. *Die Zeit.* No. 42, 14–15.

Bromley, D. B. (1977). *Personality description in ordinary language.* London: Wiley.

Csikszentmihalyi, M. (1975). *Beyond boredom and anxiety.* San Francisco: Jossey-Bass.

Csikszentmihalyi, M., & Rochberg-Halton, E. (1981). *The meaning of things.* New York: Cambridge University Press.

D'Andrade, R. G. (1974). Memory and the assessment of behavior. In T. Blalock (Ed.), *Measurement in the social sciences.* Chicago: Aldine.

Darley, J. M., & Latané, B. (1968). Bystander intervention in emergencies: Diffusion of responsibility. *Journal of Personality and Social Psychology, 8,* 377–383.

Diener, C. I., & Dweck, C. S. (1978). An analysis of learned helplessness: Continuous changes in performance, strategy, and achievement cognitions following failure. *Journal of Personality and Social Psychology, 36,* 451–462.

Duval, S., & Wicklund, R. A. (1972). *A theory of objective self-awareness.* New York: Academic Press.

Eckblad, G. (1981). *Scheme theory.* New York: Academic Press.

Flapan, D. (1968). *Children's understanding of social interaction.* New York: Teachers College Press.

Gough, H. G. (1979). A creative personality scale for the adjective check list. *Journal of Personality and Social Psychology, 37,* 1398–1405.

Heckhausen, H. (1982). Task-irrelevant cognitions during an exam: Incidence and effects. In H. W. Krohne & L. Laux (Eds.), *Achievement, stress, and anxiety* (pp. 247–274). Washington, DC: Hemisphere.

Henmon, V. A. C. (1911). The relation of the time of a judgment to its accuracy. *Psychological Review, 18,* 186–201.

Hunt, J. McV. (1965). Intrinsic motivation and its role in psychological development. In D. Levine (Ed.), *Nebraska Symposium on Motivation* (Vol. 13, pp. 189–282). Lincoln: University of Nebraska Press.

Jones, E. E., & Nisbett, R. E. (1971). *The actor and the observer: Divergent perceptions of the causes of behavior.* Morristown, NJ: General Learning Press.

Kelley, H. H. (1967). Attribution theory in social psychology. In D. Levine (Ed.), *Nebraska Symposium on Motivation* (Vol. 15, pp. 192–238). Lincoln: University of Nebraska Press.

Kelley, H. H. (1972). Attribution in social interaction. In E. E. Jones, D. E. Kanouse, H. H. Kelley, R. E. Nisbett, S. Valins, & B. Weiner (Eds.), *Attribution: Perceiving the causes of behavior* (pp. 1–26). Morristown, NJ: General Learning Press.

Kirk, L., & Burton, M. (1977). Meaning and context: A study of contextual shifts in meaning of Maasai personality descriptors. *American Ethnologist, 4,* 734–761.

Klein, G. S., & Schoenfeld, N. (1941). The influence of ego-involvement on confidence. *Journal of Abnormal and Social Psychology, 36,* 249–258.

Lepper, M. R., Greene, D., & Nisbett, R. E. (1973). Undermining children's intrinsic interest with extrinsic rewards: A test of the overjustification hypothesis. *Journal of Personality and Social Psychology, 28,* 129–137.

Lewin, K. (1931). The conflict between Aristotelian and Galileian modes of thought in contemporary psychology. *Journal of General Psychology, 5,* 141–177.

Livesley, W. J., & Bromley, D. B. (1973). *Person perception in childhood and adolescence.* London: Wiley.

Locksley, A., & Lenauer, M. (1981). Considerations for a theory of self-inference processes. In N. Cantor & J. F. Kihlstrom (Eds.), *Personality, cognition, and social interaction* (pp. 263–277). Hillsdale, NJ: Erlbaum.

Markus, H. (1977). Self-schemata and processing information about the self. *Journal of Personality and Social Psychology, 35*, 63–78.

Markus, H. (1983). Self-knowledge: An expanded view. *Journal of Personality, 51*, 543–565.

McClelland, D. C., Clark, R. A., Roby, T. B., & Atkinson, J. W. (1949). The projective expression of needs. IV. The effect of the need for achievement on thematic apperception. *Journal of Experimental Psychology, 39*, 242–255.

Mehlhorn, G., & Mehlhorn, H.-G. (1977). *Zur Kritik der bürgerlichen Kreativitätsforschung* [A critique of bourgeois creativity research]. Berlin: VEB Deutscher Verlag der Wissenschaften.

Miller, J. G. (1984). Culture and the development of everyday social explanation. *Journal of Personality and Social Psychology. 46*, 961–978.

Murray, H. A. (1938). *Explorations in personality*. New York: Oxford University Press.

Peevers, B., & Secord, P. (1973). Developmental changes in attribution of descriptive concepts to persons. *Journal of Personality and Social Psychology, 27*, 120–128.

Pittman, T. S., & Pittman, N. L. (1980). Deprivation of control and the attribution process. *Journal of Personality and Social Psychology, 39*, 377–389.

Pryor, J. B., Gibbons, F. X., Wicklund, R. A., Fazio, R. H., & Hood, R. (1977). Self-focused attention and self report validity. *Journal of Personality, 45*, 513–527.

Sherman, S. J., & Fazio, R. H. (1983). Parallels between attitudes and traits as predictors of behavior. *Journal of Personality, 51*, 308–345.

Shweder, R. A. (1977). Likeness and likelihood in everyday thought: Magical thinking in judgments about personality. *Current Anthropology, 18*, 637–658.

Stephan, E., Fischer, M., & Stein, F. (1983). Self-related cognitions in test anxiety research: An empirical study and critical conclusions. In H. M. van der Ploeg, R. Schwarzer, & C. D. Spielberger (Eds.), *Test anxiety research* (Vol. 2, pp. 45–66). Hillsdale, NJ: Erlbaum.

Super, C. M., Harkness, S., & Baldwin, L. M. (1977). Category behavior in natural ecologies and in cognitive tests. *Quarterly Newsletter of the Institute for Comparative Human Development, 1*, 4–7.

Warshaw, P. R., & Davis, F. D. (1984). Self-understanding and the accuracy of behavioral expectations. *Personality and Social Psychology Bulletin, 10*, 111–118.

White, G. M. (1980). Conceptual universals in interpersonal language. *American Anthropologist, 82*, 759–781.

Wicklund, R. A. (1975). Objective self awareness. In L. Berkowitz (Ed.), *Advances in experimental social psychology* (Vol. 8, pp. 233–275). New York: Academic Press.

Wicklund, R. A., & Gollwitzer, P. M. (1982). *Symbolic self-completion*. Hillsdale, NJ: Erlbaum.

Wine, J. (1971). Test anxiety and direction of attention. *Psychological Bulletin, 76*, 92–104.

Yerkes, R. M., & Dodson, J. D. (1908). The relation of strength of stimulus to rapidity of habit-formation. *Journal of Comparative and Neurological Psychology, 18*, 459–482.

CHAPTER 4

On Motivation and the Self-Concept

NANCY CANTOR
HAZEL MARKUS
PAULA NIEDENTHAL
PAULA NURIUS*
University of Michigan

An understanding of motivation and its connection to an individual's specific actions requires an investigation of the self-relevant cognitive instigators of goal-directed behavior. In the cognitive approach that has characterized the study of the self in recent years, the self-concept has been investigated as a system of knowledge structures about the self (Epstein, 1973; Greenwald & Pratkanis, 1984; Kihlstrom & Cantor, 1984; Markus & Sentis, 1982). In the present analysis, we will pursue this approach and focus on the knowledge structures associated with the individual's personally significant goals, plans, motives, values, hopes, fears, and threats. The emphasis here will be on those elements of self-knowledge that incite and direct people's self-relevant actions and thus are directly relevant to motivation.

Psychologists have continually grappled with the task of connecting motivation to observable behavior. Many instruments have been designed to measure the strength of an individual's power, achievement, and affiliation motives. Despite the success of much of this work in detecting the presence of such motives, the capacity to predict how motivation will be manifest in an individual's actions remains somewhat limited. Studies exploring the kinds of situations that motivate individuals to achieve, for example, report time after time that no single experimental condition will consistently elicit achievement motivation from individuals, even when only those with high need for achievement are considered (Atkinson, 1958; Atkinson & Feather, 1966; Heckhausen, Schmalt, & Schneider, in press). Similarly, cross-sectional studies of these motives demonstrate

*Order of authorship was determined alphabetically.

change, not stability, in the meaning of achievement or affiliation or power as individuals encounter different contextual demands (Veroff, 1983). Why should individual differences in global motives—so easy to observe in the stories that subjects produce in projective testing situations—tell us so much less than we desire to know about behavioral differences? What does it mean for our understanding of the nature of motivation that the *meaning* and *features* of motives as basic as the need for affiliation and achievement fluctuate markedly in response to variation in the cultural, interpersonal, or intrapersonal environment? To us, these findings suggest that motivation cannot be fully understood without reference to the self-concept; they suggest that motivation is largely manifest in people's understanding of themselves.

In the present analysis, knowledge structures about the self are assumed to be constructed creatively and selectively from past experience and to guide the processing of self-relevant information. New experiences and events are interpreted and absorbed within the context of these preexisting structures, and these knowledge structures, in turn, become further elaborated and differentiated as new information is integrated. Self-knowledge has several crucial functions. Most obviously, it provides a sense of individual identity and continuity—the content and organization reflecting the individual's efforts to achieve and maintain personal meaning. More important for the current purpose, however, self-knowledge is also viewed as a significant *regulator* of ongoing behavior. Self-knowledge provides a set of interpretive frameworks for making sense of past behavior, but it also provides the means–ends patterns for new behavior.

Self-concept researchers have become increasingly intrigued with the diversity and complexity of self-knowledge (Baumeister, 1982; Epstein, 1984; Gergen, 1971; Greenwald, 1982; Higgins, 1983; McGuire, in press; Nuttin, 1984). Most people reveal an extensive understanding of themselves. They know a great deal about their preferences, their abilities, their social roles, and their demographic and personality characteristics. Yet people also have a systematic and thorough knowledge of many of their values, their hopes and fears, their plans, their goals, their potential, and their future, and it is these components of the self-concept that serve to generate individual differences in motivated behavior.

LIFE TASKS AND POSSIBLE SELVES

Broadly, motivation concerns itself with changes in behavior and with the factors that direct this change (see Atkinson, 1958, 1964; Feather, 1981; Festinger, 1957; McClelland, 1951; Nuttin, 1976; Tolman, 1932). A study of what people know of their own potential, what they plan to accomplish, or, alternatively, what they fear for their future can reveal the meaning, the direction, and the boundaries of these behavioral changes. In examining these future-oriented elements of self-knowledge, we will focus on two conceptual elements that carry and give specific cognitive form to an individual's motivation: life tasks and possible selves.

Life tasks refer to the problems that people see themselves as working on and devoting energy to solving at a particular period in life. They are the basic units into which people lump their daily activities and by which they give specific and concrete meaning to their current goals. Most people in the same period of life are likely to be working at comparable life tasks. For example, almost all college students report being involved in a similar set of life tasks: academic tasks of getting good grades and establishing a direction for the future, social tasks of making friends and being independent without a family, and time-management tasks of setting priorities and balancing diverse interests (Brower & Cantor, 1984; Klinger, 1977). Levinson (1978) has argued that distinctive constellations of universal and genotypic life tasks are definitive of the "seasons of a man's life." According to this theory, adult male development follows a sequence of periods during which particular cognitive-emotional tasks (developing a sense of self as adult) and structural tasks (settling down) are encountered. The termination of each stage is marked by significant transitions in life structure and commitments as men complete or relinquish certain tasks and embrace new or modified ones.

In identifying and ordering the normative life tasks to which people commit themselves during various times in the life cycle, we gain some insight into the general goals or motives that are likely to at least delimit the thoughts and actions of "the average person." Still, any two individuals at a given life juncture are inevitably working on many tasks, and they may therefore differ significantly with respect to which of these tasks *predominates* in influencing their behavior.

Consider, as an example, two adolescents making the transition from home and high school to college. One may be preoccupied with all the trappings of academic life—grades, classes, gaining the professors' attention, and gathering and fine-tuning the all-important study skills. The other student, making the same transition, may also be concerned with grades but may be primarily absorbed in a very different set of life tasks—a set of social life tasks, which may include making friends, settling roommate disputes, and pursuing romance. Thus, two individuals facing the same situation may construe it very differently, depending on their predominant life tasks. Simply, people's predominant life tasks lend structure and organization to the social environment as it guides their interpretation of current events.

Most important, however, contemporaneous life tasks and the priorities they are accorded give concrete form to and reflect the order of importance of people's diffuse needs for achievement, power, and affiliation. An individual's set of life tasks gives meaning to a particular life period and colors the interpretation given to commonly experienced events and demands. Life tasks are those commitments that organize the individual's important activities over long periods of time and give these activities a long-term focus and direction. They are a form of goals, but they are goals that, when accomplished, represent a significant personal change for the individual.

The value of a systematic appraisal of how adults negotiate life tasks was a key element in the theory of Adler (1929, 1931). Adler proposed two universal organizing life goals (perfection and the more maladaptive, personal superiority) that he believed guided an individual's perception of and approach to three major life tasks: successful and cooperative interaction with his or her "fellow man," choice of and preparation for an occupation, and engagement in love and marriage. For Adler (1931), the "style of life" was manifest in the individual's personal management of life tasks, given a commitment to one or another of the primary life goals:

> If we could infer the individually comprehended goal from the ornaments and melodies of human life and, on this basis, develop the entire style of life (and the underlying individual law of movement), we could classify a person with almost natural science accuracy. We could predict how a person would act in a specific situation. (p. 296)

Although he moved toward an idiographic account of motivation, in which the self-concept played a key role, Adler accorded people inevitable rigidity in their "style of life" after early childhood. In contrast, the approach taken here stresses not only a narrower specification of current life tasks (with a interest in how they are articulated by the individual) but also attention to the flexibility in the meaning and value of these goals for people over time, given their unique configuration of self-knowledge.

In pursuing particular life tasks, people are likely to be guided by distinct representations of themselves in the future. Within the context of life tasks, we are suggesting that it is "possible selves" that give *personalized* meaning to global motives. Possible selves are the component of self-concept that reflect the individual's perceived potential. They include those selves that individuals *could* become, would *like* to become, or are *afraid* of becoming, including the selves that are hoped for—the successful and accomplished professional self, the witty, creative self, or the loved and admired self—and the selves that are dreaded—the blundering pseudointellectual self or the "bag lady" self.

People are assumed to have a diverse repertoire of possible selves that can be viewed as the cognitive manifestations of their enduring goals, aspirations, values, motives, and threats. In addition, the repertoire of possible selves may include some potentials for the individual that have been clearly specified by influential others (e.g., parents and teachers). These possible, or "ought," selves include the prescriptions and proscriptions for things the individual ought (or ought not) to be or to become (Higgins, Klein, & Strauman, 1985).

Possible selves systematically represent the potential for change in the self, for better or worse, from the present to the future. These *cognitive* representations include ideas about what is possible for the individual to be, to think, to feel, to experience, or to be perceived as, and as such, they provide end states to strive for or to avoid. In situations that facilitate a predominant life task, representations of possible selves reflect the opportunities people perceive to be afforded them by the environment as well as the expectations they have for themselves in those settings.

An individual's set of possible selves is likely to be a fairly idiosyncratic collection because it is through possible selves that needs and motives become personalized and thereby acquire the specific capacity to regulate behavior. Thus, an individual does not just have an abstract goal of "getting a BA." What this means cognitively for the individual is that she has a distinct representation of *herself getting a BA* or *herself having a BA*—that is, herself with a new job, new friends, admiration from parents and peers, herself as articulate and perhaps even better looking. The individual pursuing the academic life task may be striving to attain a cherished, well-elaborated, and salient "successful, high-achieving self." In contrast, the individual pursuing a social life task may be chiefly concerned with avoiding a feared but very vivid "lonely, homesick self."

Thus, possible selves do more than cognitively represent goals and motives within the accessible pool of self-knowledge. They vividly represent the potential of the *self* actually accomplishing hoped-for end states or avoiding feared or dreaded ones. They depict not only outcome expectancies (and feelings) but also personal *efficacy* expectations, images, and feelings (see Bandura, 1982, for a fuller discussion of this distinction). In short, we maintain that motivation does not reside outside the self-concept but, instead, derives from enduring self-knowledge that represents the individual's potentials, desires, and values. Thus, to understand more about motivation, we should look at representations of people's goals and motives and their affective valence *within* the self-concept in the form of possible selves.

These representations of selves in future states operate as positive or negative incentives for behavior and thus greatly influence the nature and direction of behavioral change. As traditionally posited, global motives take their form independent of personal history or current life demands. In fact, they are assumed to be most sensitively revealed in unstructured, ambiguous situations. In contrast, possible selves represent *specific* motives in domains of potential for a person in particular sets of circumstances. They provide distinct end states for the individual's predominant life tasks. In turn, the individual's life tasks determine which of the possible selves will be particularly salient and available for mediating ongoing behavior.

In the present analysis, we see both life tasks and possible selves as important elements of the self-concept, and we will argue that they are the representations that embody motivation and mediate action. An individual's predominant life tasks color the interpretation of life events by focusing attention on certain aspects of the situation relevant to a currently important self-concept. In specific contexts, certain possible selves become the directors of action; they represent potential end states and specify strategies for reaching the relevant life task goals. Representations such as life tasks and possible selves serve as cognitive bridges for the individual, spanning the distance between the present and the future. They illuminate the types of changes that can be expected and provide an indication of the likely paths of such change. Ideas about what the individual hopes to accomplish or notions about what it is possible for him or her to be, to think, to feel, or to experience thus provide a specific impetus and direction for action.

In the following discussion we will (1) expand the description of life tasks and possible selves and (2) present a variety of empirical work to demonstrate that these elements of self-knowledge are accessible, can be reported and reflected on by the individual, and are implicated in individuals' strategies of action. Implicit in our discussion will be an attempt to specify the path from global motives to specific behavior, with emphasis at each turn on the *self-relevant* cognitive components of this motivated activity.

A DYNAMIC VIEW OF SELF

Others have begun this cognitive formulation of motivation by focusing on the role of expectancies and on the mental representations of motives (Kagan, 1972; Kuhl, 1984; Nuttin, 1972, 1984; Schank & Abelson, 1977). Still others have pursued the relationship between the self and motivation (Lewin, Dembo, Festinger, & Sears, 1944). Yet these analyses have not been specific about the elements of self-knowledge that give shape to the relationships between the self and motivation. At least part of the difficulty in drawing out these connections rests in the traditional formulation of the self-concept.

Most theorizing about the self suggests that the self-concept is dynamic and capable of change; it reflects and regulates the actions of individuals who must adjust to and negotiate within a variety of social circumstances and environments. Still, the self-concept is typically approached as a monolithic core of self-knowledge that is stable over time and consistent across situations (cf. Allport, 1955, 1961; Festinger, 1957; Heider, 1958; Lecky, 1945; Newcomb, 1959, 1961; Osgood & Tannenbaum, 1955). In addition, many self theorists have posited self-consistency as a centrally important need (Epstein, 1973; Rogers, 1951; Snygg & Combs, 1949; for reviews, see Dipboye, 1977, and Shrauger, 1975). Relatively little empirical effort has been directed toward specifying the self-concept as a dynamic structure. In fact, the most pervasive finding from the recent surge of empirical work on the self is that structures of the self (e.g., self-schemata and self-relevant prototypes) are quite stable and are impressively resistant to change (see Greenwald & Pratkanis, 1984; Markus, 1977).

Findings that seem to suggest the mutability of the self are regarded as something of a paradox, if they are noted at all (e.g., Gergen, 1972; Martindale, 1980; Tedeschi & Lindskold, 1976; Zurcher, 1977). There is, however, a great deal of intuitive evidence that our self-conceptions can change quite dramatically according to the nature of the social situation—ranging in most people from self-confident thoughts and smug feelings of self-approval to equally strong stirrings of self-doubt and self-recrimination. Certainly, most research on behavioral and attitudinal consistency implies that stability is really the exception. Either there is very little involvement of the self-concept in the individual's extremely variable thoughts, feelings, behavior and self-concept, or researchers have yet to observe the features of the self-concept that are implicated in such changes and the mechanics whereby these changes occur.

Diverse Self-Conceptions

The problem of viewing the self-concept as both stable and malleable can be handled if the self-concept is not considered a single, generalized average of self-images. Rather, the self-concept includes within its scope a diverse collection of images and cognitions about the self—the good selves (the ones we remember fondly), the bad selves (the ones we would like to forget), the hoped-for selves, the feared selves, the not-me selves, the ideal selves, the ought selves. These various images and cognitions of the self are also often elaborated with plans and strategies for how to realize them or how to avoid them. (For more detailed descriptions of the nature of these selves, see Gergen, 1965; Greenwald & Pratkanis, 1984; Higgins, 1983; Jones & Pittman, 1982; Kihlstrom & Cantor, 1984; McGuire, in press; Sullivan, 1953; Tesser & Campbell, in press.) This notion of a multiplicity of selves has substantial intuitive appeal and is finding increasing empirical support (Gergen, 1965; Higgins, 1983; Nurius & Markus, 1984; McGuire, in press).

We assume that all conceptions of the self have the potential to exert an influence on individual functioning. Self-relevant images and cognitions comprise a variegated set, yet at least three important dimensions of variation can be specified (cf. Epstein, 1973). The self-concept can be imagined as a space of self-conceptions, each point representing a particular self-conception. These self-conceptions differ, first, with respect to their degree of affective, cognitive, or behavioral elaboration. Some self-conceptions are extremely well articulated and densely elaborated with behavioral data gathered by the individual during years of observing and organizing his or her reactions in a particular domain (the student self, the professor self, the brother or sister self, the jogger self, the anxious or worrying self, the procrastinator self). These selves may include what Gordon (1968) refers to as *factual* self-conceptions—those of maximum perceived "actuality" (e.g., some ascribed characteristics, major roles, and group member-ships)—or they may be very well substantiated self-conceptions of personal importance.

Other selves are probably tied to only a relatively small amount of actual social experience (e.g., the humiliated self, the dishonest self, the uncaring self) or are not linked to any actual social experience at all, but rather are the results of symbolizing feelings, hopes, and fears (e.g., the unloved self, the rich self, the unemployed self, the famous self). The degree of elaboration that characterizes a particular image of the self is doubtlessly influenced by how much importance or value has been attached to it in the individual's life. That is, those self-conceptions that are replete with defining detail and have involved considerable cognitive investment are likely to have achieved this status because of their significance to the individual. However, although it may be true that unimportant self-images are unlikely to be elaborated and that those that are elaborated are likely to be important, it need not be assumed that all important self-images are highly elaborated. Many hoped-for and feared outcomes are of great importance to us yet may, indeed, be quite simple and even ill-defined in their representation.

At least two other dimensions of the differences among self-conceptions can also be seen here. Self-images differ with respect to valence, and they vary with respect to the positivity or negativity they imply for the individual. The degree of elaboration of a particular self-conception and its positivity is likely to be highly correlated for most individuals. Yet important counterexamples can be imagined.

With depressive individuals, for example, affective and cognitive elaboration may be associated with negative aspects of self.

A third dimension of variation, already implicit in the examples given here, is what Schutz (1964) called the "tense" of the self, Nuttin (1984) called "temporal sign," and Raynor and McFarlin (Chapter 11 of this volume) call "time-linked sources of value." Where in time is a particular self-conception located? Many of an individual's self-conceptions are images of the *now* or current selves; they describe the self as it presently is. Other self-conceptions, however, refer to *past* selves—selves that no longer characterize the self but could again be relevant under some circumstances (e.g., the dependent self, the intolerant self). Still other self-conceptions are *future* selves—images of the self that have not yet been realized but that are hoped for or feared. These selves are not elaborated with much direct social experience, as some past selves are likely to be, yet they may be extremely well elaborated both affectively and cognitively if they are relevant to the individual's important life tasks.

From the standpoint of motivation, many of the most important self-conceptions are those that represent the individual at a time other than the present. They are self-conceptions that represent the individual's accomplishment or failure to accomplish life tasks. They are views of the individual as he or she will be after having actually attained or failed to attain particular goals. As a result of these images and cognitions, a goal is not abstract; rather, it takes a cognitive form that is specifically meaningful for a given individual in a given context.

These types of self-conceptions help people assess their progress, evaluate their instrumental acts, and revise their aspirations. They provide an overall consistency to the direction of people's strivings and integrate the life tasks being pursued with other life tasks. As central cognitive components of motivated behavior, these self-conceptions form the substance of the rich and complex internal life that is the basis of much overt behavioral change. They are likely to be importantly implicated, for example, in mood changes; in shifts in attributions, expectancies, and self-esteem; and in observable behavioral strategies and outcomes.

A Working Self-Concept

To incorporate these components of motivation within the self-concept, it is necessary not to think in terms of *the* self-concept but to think more specifically in terms of the *current* self-concept. Not all of the self-conceptions that together constitute the self-concept are available for thinking about the self at any one time. Only some *subset* will be salient. This approach involves hypothesizing a "working self-concept"—that is, the self-concept of a given moment, the subset of self-knowledge structures that is currently "on-line" in information processing. The current view of the self is thus derived from the particular collection of self-views that are made salient and dominant by the prevailing social context. It is this form of self-knowledge that the individual uses to receive, interpret, and act upon self-relevant incoming information in the immediate social environment.

Under most circumstances, the working self-concept is unlikely to include only a single image or a single cognitive structure of the self. Rather, it is likely to be composed of a variety of interrelated self-conceptions, including some images of the past self and some views of the now (in the situation) self, as well as some conception of future possibility, which includes those possible selves that come to be judged as more (or less) probable in a particular situation.

Consider, for example, a person who is pursuing the life task of winning a particular promotion. As a consequence of this task, a variety of past, now, and possible self-conceptions relevant to this concern are more likely to be primed and available for thinking about the self than are self-conceptions associated with less prominent life tasks. These self-conceptions, which are some subset of the total pool, are those that represent the individual as he or she was, is, and will be after having succeeded or failed in past or anticipated agentic tasks. Further, if this individual, at an important office social gathering, makes a particularly inappropriate remark to a colleague (perhaps one intended to be witty but emerging instead as cutting and sarcastic), the working self-concept of the individual at that particular time is distinct and quite different from other working self-concepts that are active on other occasions.

The resultant working self-concept certaintly includes some well-elaborated core conceptions that, because of their importance in identifying or defining the self (e.g., self-schemata), are chronically available (Higgins, Mavin, & King, 1982). More distinctively, however, it also consists of a variety of other conceptions that are likely to be associated with failure (the nervous or anxious self, the petty or jealous self, the disliked self). Many of these self-conceptions may be fairly impoverished or temporally remote. They are unlikely to show up in generalized, noncontextual assessments of self-concept and self-regard, yet they are likely to be quite salient and to have a substantial impact on mood, self-esteem, and subsequent behavior.

This particular working self-concept can be contrasted with one that might occur for the same individual at the same gathering after delighting his or her friends with a particularly well-executed new joke. The core self-conceptions that are shared by both of these working self-concepts are now likely to be embedded in a very different context of possibility, one that includes the conceptions of the self as successful—the self at ease, charming, popular, and in control of the situation. Thus, even those dimensions of self-knowledge that tend to generalize across contexts may well function differentially, depending on the prevailing nature of the working self-knowledge of which they are a part.

The working self-concept is thus a subset of the individual's total pool of self-knowledge, not a generalized average of this knowledge. The self can be characterized as stable in that the universe of self-conceptions is relatively stable. To be sure, some new self-conceptions will be added and revisions will occur as the individual grows and matures. Yet once a particular self-conception has been formed, it is unlikely to disappear from the pool, even if it is seldom activated or elicited. At the same time, however, the self-concept appears as mutable or flexible, because the contents of the working self-concept change. The subset of self-conceptions that is currently dominant in processing information and driving behavior changes as the life tasks and the salient features of the social environment change.

MOTIVES WITHIN THE DYNAMIC SELF-CONCEPT

This dynamic view of the self, with its diverse self-conceptions and a flexible working self-concept of the moment, provides a framework within which to specify the role of life tasks and possible selves in inciting and directing behavior. To see their function more clearly, we can imagine an individual at a point of life transition—perhaps the transition from high school to college or from college to the work place. At major transition points, such as entrance into a new job, relationship, or institution, many people feel highly "motivated" to respond to demands in the new environment (Hormuth, 1984; Veroff, 1983).

At such times, people see themselves as tackling new problems or learning to work on old problems in new ways. College students, for example, speak explicitly of "taking personal control" over their lives. Transitions to new social institutions also encourage some uniformity in the salient life tasks, because similar pressures are encountered by most of the participants. At college, for example, most first-year students face the demands of increased academic and social pressures and the need to define changing relationships with family and friends. Against this backdrop of uniformity, it becomes increasingly likely that there will be idiosyncratically defined cognitive representations of self that guide behavior in unique directions.

Figure 4.1 illustrates this implicit progression from an individual's life tasks in a particular period to his or her interpretation of an event as importantly self-relevant and on to the selection of behavior to match the then-salient possible selves. Our choice of one direction of flow along this path is not meant to preclude others, of course. It is best to imagine that we are tracing one path, as a person comes to interpret a life event or situation in progressively more specific ways, using self-knowledge to direct himself or herself toward actions. We turn now to various empirical efforts aimed at demonstrating that life tasks and possible selves could reasonably be assumed to help orchestrate such action. In these demonstrations, we have concentrated on the dynamic self-knowledge of college students.

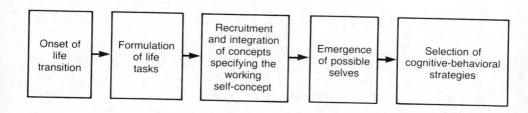

FIGURE 4.1 Progression from motives to action: conceptual structure.

A Brief Look at Life Tasks

The life tasks of first-year college students provided the focus of a recent investigation (Brower & Cantor, 1984). Forty-four first-year students at the University of Michigan were asked to describe their first-year experience in terms of "the areas to which you have been, and expect to be directing your energies; your thoughts about what will make this both a good and bad year for you; and the plans you may have for accomplishing some of your goals during your time here." As a first step, they provided a list of "*all* of the life tasks that come to mind for you as you think about the coming year . . . tasks ranging from the mundane to the monumental . . . those that you will actively seek out and those that you will simply stumble onto."

As it turned out, these students found it easy and interesting to consider their life tasks. They seemed to have little difficulty listing life tasks, listing, on average, eight or nine life tasks. They were then able to order these tasks according to the challenge or difficulty involved (for them at this time) and to select the two most important tasks (at this time in their life). Moreover, there was substantial agreement among the students regarding the domains from which they chose their two most important (predominant) life tasks; 27 of 44 students listed some form of academic life task in the top two tasks, and 32 of them chose a social task as "important."

The students also seemed to construe their academic and social life tasks similarly; the phrasings of the specific tasks were not highly idiosyncratic (two judges agreed in placing 85% of the 88 "important" life tasks into five specific categories). The general predominance of achievement and affiliation life tasks certainly coincides nicely with descriptions of this life period provided in the personality literature (see Erikson, 1950; Little, 1983; Murray, 1951).

As much as most of the students were preoccupied with their various academic and social life tasks, they were also quite concerned with time management. The students focused on the conflicts between life tasks and wanted to learn how to "put together various interests," or set new priorities. Many of these students had already found it easier to handle *either* academic *or* social tasks, as assessed by their ratings of "difficulty of this task for me" and by the emotional reactions that they endorsed as "typical of me" in specific task-relevant situations. Although very preliminary, these data suggest that there may be striking individual differences in the meaning and relative predominance of academic versus social life tasks for different students (see also Little's [1983] data on "personal projects" and Klinger's [1977] findings on "current concerns").

Aside from providing some confirmation that individuals can articulate their life tasks in the context of a new life period, these data are encouraging for the present analysis because they hint at both the cognitive elaboration of life tasks and their motivating function. These students did not simply possess diffuse needs for achievement, affiliation, and control. They had very detailed knowledge of the life situations and events that were relevant to each predominant life task. For each predominant life task, the students were able to list another set of more specific, and often uniquely defined, personal projects (Little, 1983) or target situations that tapped the predominant life task; they knew where and when and how these concerns were going to arise in their current life environment. Also, their task-relevant knowledge was quite personal; it delineated how *they* would appear in each situation.

When one student, for example, described his qualms about "how I am going to make my living," he had particular self-relevant hurdles and issues in mind: "being a senior and still not knowing what to do," "disagreeing with family over career choice," "liking my major, but not finding a job to go with it," and so forth. The configuration of task-relevant situations and events (subprojects associated with the broader life task) differed somewhat from student to student, even when the basic task was phrased similarly. It is as if the predominant life task took on a slightly different meaning for each student as it recruited different sets of life situations and projects for each one. Therefore, we see, already, that relatively global motives, encouraged to surface by common life circumstances, take on different cognitive forms from person to person.

However, these predominant life tasks do even more work for the individual. Not only do they seem to color the interpretation of the problems to be solved in different situations, but they also help define a pool of relevant self-knowledge with which to plan behavior. That is, these students were able to describe *themselves* in different situations associated with a particular life task. They knew a great deal about how they would feel in those situations and, more important, they could articulate "plans for handling" the situation. Most of the plans of these students were quite "simple," in that multiple courses of action were not considered. However, some of these novices at college life even listed "complex" plans in which at least one full iteration of action–consequences–reaction was delineated and multiple plausible outcomes were considered (Kahneman & Tversky, 1982; Schank & Abelson, 1977; Spivak, Platt, & Shure, 1976). The students described their plans for eight different situations; 31 of the 44 students listed at least one "complex" plan in their description.

For example, when some students anticipated "fights with roommates," they already had in mind different negotiating tactics and strategies for "cooling down the situation" (see also Klos, Loomis, & Ruhrold, 1983). When these students considered their different life tasks in the context of their ongoing lives, they imagined different end states for themselves and, in so doing, accessed a selective set of self-conceptions—a working self-concept composed of diverse conceptions of themselves in that context, *now* and in the *future*.

Feared and Desired Possible Selves

These data on life tasks are only suggestive of the variety and diversity of end states that students imagine for themselves in the different contexts of college life. For example, the student who fretted over a career decision clearly conceived of his "frustrated, jobless" possible self as well as his "disappointment to parents" possible self. In fact, from his descriptions of plans and activities, it seems reasonable to assume that these possible selves worked as powerful negative incentives for him. But these life task plans only hint at the richness of possible selves and their importance as incentives for action.

Markus and Nurius (1983) collected data on students' endorsements of different possibilities for the self; these self-reports speak directly to this element of dynamic self-knowledge. In one study, 344 students were asked to consider their possible selves—both those they anticipated positively and those they anticipated negatively. Next, they were asked to consider a large collection of self-descriptions. The items derived from six general categories: (1) general descriptors or adjectives typically found in self-concept inventories (e.g., creative, selfish, intelligent); (2) physical descriptors (e.g., good-looking, blind, wrinkled, athletic); (3) lifestyle descriptors (e.g., having an active social life or being health conscious, a cancer victim, or alcohol dependent); (4) general abilities (e.g., able to fix things, able to cook well, able to influence people, knowledgeable about art or music); (5) descriptors of various occupations; and finally, (6) descriptors focused on others' views (e.g., appreciated, loved, feared, unpopular). In each of the categories, one-third of the descriptors were consensually judged as positive, one-third as negative, and one-third as neutral. For each descriptor, the respondents were asked to consider whether it described them in the past, whether it characterized them now, whether it characterized a possible self, and how likely it was to characterize a possible self for them in the future.

The first and, for our purpose, most central finding involves the pervasiveness of possible self-conceptions. Whether the conceptions were elaborated from direct experience or in imagery work, the students endorsed almost as many conceptions of what they had been in the *past* and could be in the *future* as they did *present* selves. These possible selves varied considerably in affective valence, supporting their potential as either positive or negative incentives. Also, although there were certainly differences in the total number of possible selves endorsed by individual students and in the prevalence of negative and positive self-conceptions, all of the students appeared to have a diverse set of possibilities that they could imagine for themselves. Notably, these respondents were extremely confident of many of their judgments about their possible selves. Thus, it was not surprising that in predicting the individual's current affective and motivational state (as determined by a series of self-report instruments), the ratings of possible selves could explain variations beyond those that could be explained by the rating of only the now or current self.

Moreover, it appears that possible selves can be recruited into a working self-concept that is appropriately geared toward the life task goals that are most salient in a particular context. Nurius and Markus (1984) randomly assigned some students to one of two social context conditions—a role-playing context in which they imagined moving to a new city and facing either obstacles or successes at work and with friends. After imagining the context, these students performed the foregoing self-concept endorsement task. A third group of students did the self-concept endorsements without having their achievement and affiliation goals made salient by the context manipulation.

Students in the context conditions endorsed achievement- and affiliation-relevant self-conceptions as both more currently self-descriptive and more probable for them, as compared to the other self-descriptors in the list. In other words, it seems that life tasks, when primed, recruit semantically appropriate possible selves. Moreover, when students imagined a context in which things were going well on their life tasks—the facilitation context—they endorsed both more self-descriptors as *very probable* for themselves and more of the selves as *very improbable* for themselves than did students in the frustration context. The facilitating context seemed to help the students delineate a working self-concept of the moment.

These studies suggest that self-knowledge is dynamic—diverse in content and responsive to cues in the current environment. Knowledge of likely possible selves associated with different life contexts should provide a ready basis for the selection of behavior. These possible selves represent each person's unique potential for behavior change across time in different life contexts.

TRANSLATING MOTIVES INTO BEHAVIOR

Thus far, we have suggested that, as a first step toward action, the person's predominant life task in a particular context recruits appropriate possible selves and now selves into the working self-concept of the moment. Once recruited, the possible selves mark end states to be approached or avoided, while the now selves mark the distance to be traveled or highlight the current state to be protected in the service of the now-salient life task goal (Higgins, 1983; Markus, 1983; Markus & Nurius, 1983; see also Raynor & McFarlin, Chapter 11 of this volume). The possible and now selves do not simply mark potential outcomes. As cognitive representations of the self, they summarize feelings, thoughts, and behaviors characteristic of a self in a particular context and strategies for maintaining or achieving that self. But how does a particular combination of now and possible selves influence the plans, thoughts, and behaviors that an individual employs in the service of her or his life task goals?

However defined, motives are ultimately supposed to instigate specific action and to guide the selection of problem-solving and other task behaviors that are tied to the goals active at that time. Whether people are selectively avoiding or approaching a possible self, they draw on this dynamic self-knowledge to form the basis of a variety of self-protective, self-monitoring, and self-presentation *strategies* (Carver & Scheier, 1981; Greenwald, 1982; Jones & Pittman, 1982; for a review, see Showers & Cantor, 1985). The translation from general motives to specific action, therefore, follows a coherent and organized theme, which is illustrated in its structural form in Figure 4-1. At the broadest level of analysis, we have suggested, the theme begins with the articulation of life tasks at some period in an individual's life. Although many individuals in similar life periods may be working through the same life tasks, however, the influences of life tasks in a given setting specify *unique* configurations of now and possible selves. The actual and future states evoked in a life task setting, in turn, motivate behavior that is shaped by a particular cognitive strategy employed by the individual. It is to these cognitive-behavioral strategies that we turn next.

In general, it seems that most people are naturally inclined to work through cognitive simulations or play through a series of scenarios in which they imagine themselves in different plausible outcomes for the situation in question (Kahneman & Tversky, 1982). As Nuttin (1984) suggested:

> It is generally accepted that a state of need or motivation activates an individual's behavior.... Motivation activates not only a subject's overt behavior and movement but his cognitive functions as well. In other words, a state of need makes us think, as much as it makes us move. Thinking, now, is a kind of behavior in which symbolic substitutes of objects—say concepts—are "manipulated" and combined instead of the objects themselves. This cognitive manipulation of things has several important characteristics; it is much more flexible and quicker than the physical manipulation of material objects and situations. For instance, after trying out a combination, at the cognitive level, one can easily and quickly undo it and try out another one. Moreover, objects and situations that are not easily available in reality are always at our disposal at the level of symbolic representation and thinking: a storehouse of everything ever perceived, experienced or done is available for retrieval in memory . . . this superiority of cognitive operations is of major importance in the goal setting and planning process. (p. 12)

As yet, however, the literature provides only hints at the process by which individuals may adopt certain approaches to sketching out plans and considering potential end states (Showers & Cantor, 1985). Different people consider different types of outcomes as plausible, and the nature of these outcomes can guide the understanding and prediction of differences in motivated behavior. That is, people may not simulate all plausible outcomes. For instance, they may selectively focus on best- or worst-case outcomes for an event or situation (Norem & Cantor, 1984; Showers & Cantor, 1985). This distinction between playing through best- as opposed to worst-case outcomes seems to illustrate current strivings for a desired possible self. People who adopt the best-case perspective may be laboring to preserve a cherished now self in that task context, whereas those who concentrate on worst-case outcomes may be working to avoid a feared possible self. In either case, those current and possible selves that are relevant in light of the current predominant life task, especially the ones most elaborated by past experience or imagery, will direct the individual's motivated behavior; the action will be appropriate in light of the activated self-knowledge.

This analysis suggests that one avenue for exploration is the specification of factors, both chronic and transitory, that lead a person to adopt a best-case or a worst-case simulation focus in a specific context. In the case of depressed individuals, it appears that *chronic negative affect* is fueled by negative self-knowledge and negative experiences (Higgins *et al.*, 1984; Pietromonaco, 1985). Such people seem chronically to play through the worst-case outcomes across a variety of life events. For other people, a history of negative experiences in one domain may highlight a set of worst-case outcomes, but only in some contexts. Thus, the "underachiever" college student may have elaborated a large set of negative self-knowledge and experiences in the achievement domain, so that when he or she works on achievement tasks, the worst-case outcomes may surface quite routinely and persistently. The same student may be well versed, however, in a variety of social skills and, with this expertise in hand, may play through more positive scenarios regarding an upcoming date with an attractive person.

Of course, a transitory bad mood, elicited by one recent negative experience, can serve to activate the worst-case outcomes in even the most optimistic people (see Isen & Means, 1983). After all, even the optimistic "star student" is shaken by a poor grade and comes to fear the potential for further defeats. Also, some situations seem to be constructed so as to elicit relatively positive or negative outcome simulations from most participants. As mentioned earlier, Nurius and Markus (1984) demonstrated this point by asking college students to imagine specific contexts in which their achievement or affiliation goals were facilitated or thwarted. Students whose goals were facilitated endorsed significantly greater numbers of positive (and fewer negative) past, present, and future self-conceptions than did the students whose goals were thwarted. Moreover, their salient self-knowledge was different both in domains relevant to these achievement or affiliation goals and in other areas of life. For all of these students, a worst-case focus (in their working self-concepts) was positively related to affective measures of hopelessness and negatively related to indices of personal self-efficacy. It seems clear that contingencies in a situation, which may facilitate or impede important life task goals, can serve to initiate a best- or worst-case outcome simulation by recruiting a biased set of now and possible selves.

We have argued, then, that a variety of personal and situational factors—chronic and transitory mood states, positive or negative past experiences, facilitating or inhibiting contingencies—conspire to elicit a working self-concept that may give central focus to either best- or worst-case outcomes. People have such a variety of self-conceptions that it is not hard to imagine the same person appearing as the "essential optimist" in one context and the "gloomy pessimist" at another time and place. Regardless of pervasiveness or origin, once activated, the positive, hoped-for possible selves and the negative, feared possible selves will instigate very different strategies of action. According to our analysis, individual differences in motivated behavior will follow from the selective highlighting of particular possible selves. In support of this point, we will turn now to a brief look at individual differences in achievement performance and in decision making in an affiliation problem.

Performance Strategies: Protecting and Achieving Self

Specification of the cognitive bases of motivated behavior is likely to be most useful in cases in which several individuals appear to have equivalently intense prevalent motives and yet execute different behaviors. An examination of the literature on achievement motivation (e.g., Atkinson & Birch, 1978; Weiner, 1980) and performance strategies (Bandura, 1977; Jones & Berglas, 1978; Jones & Pittman, 1982; Sherman, Skov, Hervitz, & Stock, 1981) suggests that this is an appropriate beginning for such an analysis.

Consider, for example, three college students who have very good grade point averages, past base rates of success, and intense concerns about their performance in tasks that tap "native ability." Imagine all of them facing final examinations in courses that are of some importance to them. We will assume for this example that all three students have *construed* this task as an achievement task. This is important, because people will recruit different strategies to plan or cope with other types of tasks. How are we to explain the following individual differences in these students' reactions to the achievement demands. Student A, who has confidently assessed his analytic abilities in the past, surprisingly withdraws effort rather ostentatiously and overtly by staying out late with his friends the night before the exam. Student B, also happy with his past performances, responds by setting high expectations for himself and studying vigorously in an effort to "better" his "successful" prior record in an achievement setting. Student C, abashedly acknowledging a record of academic successes, focuses on the likelihood of failure in this task and sets very low expectations for himself; all the while, he prepares doggedly for the exam, never for a moment slowing his frantic pace (Norem & Cantor, 1984).

It is difficult to see a way to account for these individual differences in performance strategies simply by alluding to variations in need-for-achievement or fear-of-failure motives. All three students are highly involved in the achievement task and they admit to prior histories of success. In fact, Students A and C, the self-handicapper (Jones & Berglas, 1978) and the defensive pessimist, respectively (Showers & Cantor, 1985; Norem & Cantor, 1984), both evidence a fear-of-failure reaction. What accounts for the withdrawal of effort by one student and the intensification of effort for the other? After all, a person who *really* feared failure wouldn't risk the opportunity of failing, as does the self-handicapper who has slacked off after having established a "winning" impression. Conversely, why would the defensive pessimist, who embraces the likelihood of failure with the passion of a true depressive, work as hard as the cheery optimist at an achievement task?

Although a description of these individualized achievement strategies conjures images of need-for-achievement and fear-of-failure motives, to unpack the specifics of these students' behaviors in an achievement task, it would be better to look more to particular cognitions about the self—"I'll look like a fraud if I fail" or "I've done well before, why not go for the moon this time" or "I can't count on past glories to protect me in future tests"—than to these global motives. The strategies of these students are associated with and, we believe, are derived from very particular configurations of past, present, and future selves that are elaborated in each student's working self-concept in the achievement context. These possible combinations of specific *content* of the working self—the knowledge that might serve to tie together a global life task and momentary behavior in a current achievement situation—are illustrated in Figure 4.2.

From the present perspective, the behavior of these students can be understood in terms of variations in the contents of their working self-concepts in the exam setting. The self-handicapper, playing through a worst-case outcome, fears the "found out at last" possible self and withdraws effort to at least protect his past image as a person of high ability; if he doesn't study for the exam, no one can claim that his true ability has been tested. The cheery optimist, focusing on a best-case outcome, sets high expectations for himself and strives to reach an "even better" possible self, deriving security from his past successes. The defensive pessimist, obsessed with even the remote possibility of a worst-case outcome, uses the "careless failure" possible self as a prod to motivate vigilance, all the while

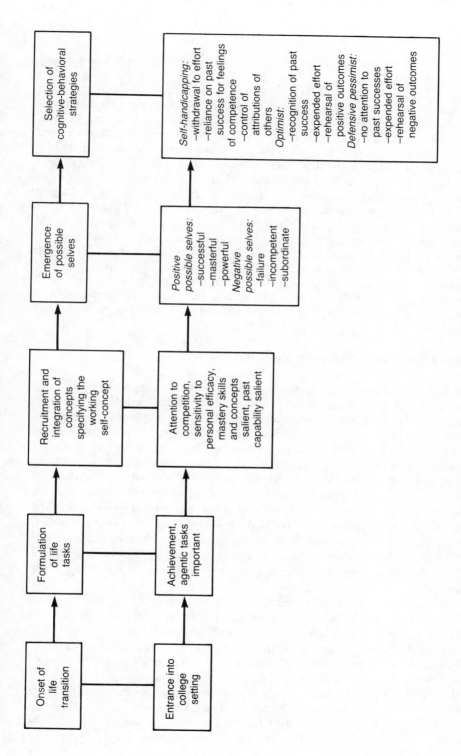

FIGURE 4.2 Progression from motives to action in an achievement setting.

cushioning the potential blow to self-esteem by predicting the worst and setting low expectations.

The self-handicapper and the defensive pessimist share a worst-case focus, but whereas one takes a chance at failing in the service of protecting a cherished now self, the other risks losing that successful now self by working very hard to avoid the failure outcome. The optimist and the defensive pessimist share "effort-intensification" strategies, but whereas one "copes" with the risk of failure in advance by predicting doom, the other repairs any tears in his "super ability" now self after the fact by embracing any available external attributions for his less-than-perfect, "by chance" mistakes. The individual differences in the verbalized expectations, the performance behavior, and the *post hoc* attributions of these students seem most appropriately linked to variations in the contents of the dyanmic self-knowledge upon which each one draws in an achievement task (see Baumeister, 1982; Greenwald, 1981, 1982; Jones & Pittman, 1982; McFarlin & Blascovich, 1981). The foregoing discussion leaves open, of course, the question of why different possible selves are activated by individuals with comparable goals in similar contexts. This is an important developmental problem that goes well beyond the scope of this chapter, and we hope to address it elsewhere.

Lifestyle Choices: Maintaining the Affiliative Self

Specification of dynamic self-knowledge has been useful in explicating individual differences within traditional achievement-motivation paradigms (Kuhl, 1984). It also may be useful to consider the role of the working self-concept in contexts in which the links between global motives and behavior are less obvious. For that purpose, we turn to studies that implicate self-knowledge in decision strategies about lifestyle choices (e.g., buying a car, choosing a college major). In one such study, Niedenthal, Cantor, and Kihlstrom (1985) assessed the goals, self-knowledge, and choice strategies of first-year college students faced with the task of choosing college housing. The housing-choice problem fits well within the rubric of important *affiliative life tasks* (living independently, exploring lifestyles, getting along with others) that first-year college students lay out for themselves. Also, students who construe this choice as part of their interpersonal, affiliative task should have access to a decision strategy well suited to fulfilling those goals.

Previous research has suggested that students can articulate the characteristics of the person who would be most comfortable in a variety of common life situations (Cantor, Mischel, & Schwartz, 1982) and, more important, that they have little difficulty assessing the degree of match between their own character-istics and those of the prototypical person-for-the-situation (Cantor, Mackie, & Lord, 1984). In fact, this self-prototype matching strategy provides a convenient decision rule for people intent on choosing to enter situations in which they can "be themselves" and thus maintain their working self-concept in the affiliative domain (Burke & Reitzes, 1981; Chassin, Presson, Sherman, Corty, & Ol-shavsky, 1981; Snyder, 1981; Snyder & Kendzierski, 1982). From the perspective of the present analysis, then, we might expect some students—those with affiliative goals in this choice domain and a desire to achieve a comfortable-at-home possible self—to utilize most systematically a self-prototype decision strategy in selecting college housing.

The Niedenthal *et al.* (1985) study provides some supportive evidence in that regard. In that study, 116 first-year college students at the University of Wisconsin responded to a series of questionnaires about their preferences in college housing, the factors most important to them in this decision, the type of information that would be most useful in making their selections, and so forth. They also described themselves at present by rating the self-descriptiveness of 100 trait adjectives (Kihlstrom & Chew, 1981).

In another section of the questionnaire packet, the students were asked to rate the descriptiveness of those same 100 trait adjectives for the person who would be "comfortable and happy" living in each of the seven available student housing options at the university. In this manner, each student generated a person-in-situation prototype for the following housing options: coed dormitory, single-sex dormitory, fraternity or sorority, room in a private residence, rented house, cooperative, and apartment. Accordingly, those students most motivated to reach their comfortable-at-home possible self (or avoid their uncomfortable-at-home self) should have indicated housing preferences that maximized the overlap between their self-descriptions and the prototype description for the housing selection. Who would such comfort-seeking students be?

As noted earlier, it seems likely that the housing choice problem would be construed as primarily an affiliative one by a sizable number of students. In fact, in their responses to open-ended questions, half of this student sample indicated that they had interpreted this task as one with important consequences for their affiliative self. That is, they saw the problem as one in which the potential outcomes were "I am (am not) happy living here with these kinds of people." They articulated affiliative goals by reporting that the most important factors in their decision were concerns about 'Who I will live with," "Where I will be most happy and comfortable," "Having people to rely on," "Where I will have fun."

The remainder of the students, however, interpreted the task as one with "economical" versus "uneconomical" outcomes and articulated more pragmatic goals by highlighting such considerations as the price of rent and utilities, location, convenience, and condition of facilities. (If the self-concept was implicated at all in the decision of the latter group of students, it seems that they were working from a "financially dependent" self-view in this decision.) Even with this cursory look at the construction of this decision problem by different students, it is clear that similar life events take on different specific meanings as a function of the individual's interpretation of the relevant motives or tasks (e.g., for affiliation, social acceptance, security, and so on).

We have narrowed our candidates for the students most motivated to use a self-prototype matching strategy in their selection of college housing to those with especially salient affiliative goals and interpersonally focused working self-concepts. However, a more stringent test of our central proposition—that the key to these students' choice behavior resides in the specific contents of their current self-knowledge—would be to demonstrate individual differences in comfort seeking *within* the sample of students with affiliative goals and then to link those differences to the contents of the students' available self-concepts. Such a test of the utility of a cognitive analysis of motivation and the self was provided by the present data.

The self-prototype matching choice strategy was conceptualized as an indicator of the motivation to find a living situation in which the student could be her or his "true self at home." It is interesting that the strategy was used significantly more systematically by students (within the affiliative-goals sample) who held especially well-delineated opinions about their *now* selves. Students who had rated an unusually large number of characteristics as *very untrue* of themselves—students with relatively distinctive now self-concepts—demonstrated a significantly stronger motivation to find a housing option in which they could be interpersonally comfortable than did other students with those same affiliative goals but less distinctive self-concepts. This is predictable if Sherif and Hovland's (1961) theory of social judgment is applied to self-judgment. Highly distinctive individuals can be seen as having strong feelings of resistance to change and a narrow "latitude of acceptance" to alternative definitions of self. Also, as we would predict in the present analysis, when the interpersonally oriented self-prototype matching strategy was not relevant to the goals of the students (i.e., in the practical-goals sample), the distinctiveness of the working self-concept did not have the same mediating impact on choice behavior.

How are we to interpret these data in the light of the present approach to motivation and the cognitive self? The following analysis seems in order. Students with affiliative goals in this domain focus on the self-as-comfortable or self-as-uncomfortable possible outcomes. Salient within their working self-concepts are current conceptions of self that emphasize affiliative attributes that are or are not characteristic of them in a living domain. For those students with many such characteristics that are *not true* of the now self, the specter of a possible "unhappy and incompatible with housemates" self looms large in their current thinking. The feared end state is made particularly plausible by the limits on social flexibility implied by the students' highly distinctive self-concepts. These students turn to a choice strategy designed to protect their distinctive now selves by maximizing the fit between their distinguishing characteristics and those commonly exhibited by people in the housing of choice.

Another strategy—one quite available to them—would be a "take a chance" strategy in which the present self-conceptions are purposely ignored to instantiate a "me-as-I-want-to-be" possible self. This strategy, however, would be most appropriate for individuals who do not particularly like their present "interpersonal" selves and see an opportunity for finding a new working self-concept in this domain (Wurf & Markus, 1983). It is important, in this regard, to note that the students with highly distinctive self-concepts in this study did not necessarily possess more negative views of self; these students were quite simply clear on *what sorts of attributes did not describe them*; accordingly, they worked hard to find a housing situation that did not "demand" such personality attributes.

What were the students with less distinctive self-concepts doing in this problem-solving situation? Remember, many of these students also had affiliative goals in this situation. Although the data do not directly address this question, we can speculate that it is these more flexible, interpersonally focused decision makers who might take a chance on striving for a new yet desired possible self in the housing domain. The working self-concepts in their cases may have included relatively positive desired potentials ("a wilder, partying" possible self, "an ascriber to alternative lifestyles" self-at-home). These students, inspired by a desired possible self, may have used a strategy in which they compared their concept of this *potential* self with their person-in-housing prototypes (cf. Chassin *et al.*, 1981; Snyder, 1981) and then may have selected the situation that would "pull out" the desired self. The students with less distinctive (or less rigid and limiting) self-concepts would be likely to feel further from the uncomfortable-at-home possible outcome and, perhaps, more optimistic about experimenting with a new and daring (given their current self-conceptions) lifestyle choice.

For these students, a better assessment of their working self-concepts in this task would be a checklist of "characteristics that I would like to change" and "characteristics that I would like to preserve" in the housing choice (see Higgins *et al.*, 1984, on students' ideal selves). Presumably, we might then find that the students with relatively flexible social self-concepts and affiliative goals in their housing choice problem were actually maximizing the potential for reaching some ideal social self in their housing selections. Again, we are faced with the case of different choice behaviors from those of individuals with very similar global motives in a task but seemingly divergent strategies for reaching the desired end states. Also, as in the case of individual differences in achievement behavior, these differing strategies for fulfilling affiliative goals appear to depend on variations in the precise content of the individual's dynamic self-knowledge.

One issue raised by this analysis concerns the extent to which people are able to regulate their use of different task-related strategies in different settings. Clark and Isen (1982) have discussed the *automatic* versus *controlled* use of mood-facilitating or mood-altering strategies. It may well be that many decisions are resolved through the use of strategies that come to be automatic over time, as increasing expertise and/or past success strengthen the probability of their being relied upon. Conversely, strategies may become more controlled as the individual seeks to avoid using maladaptive strategies relied on previously (e.g., "I made some disastrous mistakes by attempting to try out new and different fashions and friends in high school that I don't want to repeat in college") or as he or she learns to discern which goals in which contexts would be best served by a given strategy.

CONCLUDING REMARKS

We have presented a series of cognitive representations that seem to lend coherence and meaning and give concrete form to people's global motives. The analysis began with the designation and articulation of primary life tasks, narrowed to the definition of a working self-concept in response to that context, included the emergence of possible selves that mark the end states to be approached or avoided, and finally resolved at the cognitive-behavioral strategies with which people work to construct a reality that in some way serves their goals. Nowhere do we argue that all tasks or problem-solving settings engage people in a recruitment of self-concepts and related strategies. Nowhere do we assert that entrance into pertinent contexts is a necessary and sufficient condition for the evocation of a self-concept enriched with the kinds of knowledge and affect we suggest represent motivation. However, we do believe that dynamic self-knowledge of the sort described here plays an influential role in directing and inciting diverse forms of social behavior.

The strength of the cognitive approach to motivation and the self is twofold. Such a specification portrays the individual as one who is not simply pushed and shoved by an ominous motive. Nor is he or she entirely at the mercy of the structure of the social situation or context. As we see it, the individual attempts to behave in line with important life tasks and possible selves. Because of these conceptual elements, the individual can be said to have an agenda as he or she approaches some responses and avoids others. Finally, we have offered a picture of an individual who can plan action and use strategies that are responsive to both personal agendas and contingencies operative in the situation at the moment.

Life tasks and possible selves appear to do a great deal of work for the "motivated" actor. These conceptual elements may also help the observer make sense of individual differences in social behavior. Traditionally, it seems that much has been lost in the translation from global motives to specific action. It seems that what is needed is a middle-level analysis of people's thoughts about their goals, plans, and possible outcomes in different life contexts. Furthermore, it is this dynamic self-knowledge that often probably directs social behavior. Therefore, it is time to turn attention to uncovering people's conceptions of their most desired, feared, threatening, or inspiring selves as they work on currently important tasks and problems. In so doing, we will better see the interface between motivation and the self-concept.

References

Adler, A. (1929). *The science of living.* New York: Greenberg.

Adler, A. (1931). *What life should mean to you.* Boston: Little, Brown.

Allport, G. H. (1955). *Becoming: Basic considerations for a psychology of personality.* New Haven: Yale University Press.

Allport, G. W. (1961). *Pattern and growth in personality.* New York: Holt, Rinehart, and Winston.

Atkinson, J. W. (1958). *Motives in fantasy, action and society.* Princeton, NJ: Van Nostrand.

Atkinson, J. W. (1964). *An introduction to motivation.* Princeton, NJ: Van Nostrand.

Atkinson, J. W., & Birch, D. (1978). The dynamics of achievement-oriented activity. In J. W. Atkinson & J. O. Raynor (Eds.), *Personality, motivation and achievement.* Washington, DC: Hemisphere.

Atkinson, J. W., & Feather, N. T. (1966). *A theory of achievement motivation.* New York: Wiley.

Bandura, A. (1977). Self-efficacy: Toward a unifying theory of behavior change. *Psychological Review, 84,* 191–215.

Bandura, A. (1982). The self and mechanisms of agency. In J. Suls (Ed.), *Psychological perspectives on the self.* Hillsdale, NJ: Erlbaum.

Baumeister, R. F. (1982). Self-esteem, self-presentation, and future interaction: A dilemma of reputation. *Journal of Personality, 50*, 29–45.

Brower, A., & Cantor, N. (1984). *College students' life tasks.* Unpublished manuscript, University of Michigan.

Burke, P., & Reitzes, D. C. (1981). The link between identity and role performance. *Social Psychology Quarterly, 44*(2), 83–92.

Cantor, N., Mackie, D., & Lord, C. (1984). Choosing partners and activities: The social perceiver decides to mix it up. *Social Cognition, 2,*

Cantor, N., Mischel, W., & Schwartz, J. (1982). A prototype analysis of psychological situations. *Cognitive Psychology, 14*, 45–77.

Carver, C. S., & Scheier, M. F. (1981). *Attention and self-regulation: A control theory approach to human behavior.* New York: Springer-Verlag.

Chassin, L., Presson, C. C., Sherman, S. J., Corty, E., & Olshavsky, R. W. (1981). Self-images and cigarette smoking in adolescents. *Personality and Social Psychology Bulletin, 7*, 670–676.

Clark, M., & Isen, A. M. (1982). Toward understanding the relationship between feeling states and social behavior. In A. H. Hastorf & A. M. Isen (Eds.), *Cognitive social psychology.* New York: Elsevier North-Holland.

Dipboye, R. L. (1977). A critical review of Korman's self-consistency theory of work motivation and occupational choice. *Organizational Behavior and Human Performance, 18*, 108–126.

Epstein, S. (1973). The self-concept revisited, or a theory of a theory. *American Psychologist, 28*, 404–416.

Epstein, S. (1984). The self-concept: A review and the proposal of an integrated theory of personality. In E. Staub (Ed.), *Personality: Basic issue and current research.* Englewood Cliffs, NJ: Prentice-Hall.

Erikson, E. (1950). *Childhood and society.* New York: Norton.

Feather, N. T. (Ed.). (1981). *Expectations and actions.* Hillsdale, NJ: Erlbaum.

Festinger, L. A. (1957). *A theory of cognitive dissonance.* New York: Harper & Row.

Gergen, K. J. (1965). The effects of interaction goals and personalistic feedback on the presentation of self. *Journal of Personality and Social Psychology, 1*, 413–424.

Gergen, K. J. (1971). *The concept of self.* New York: Holt, Rinehart and Winston.

Gergen, K. J. (1972). Multiple identity: The healthy, happy human being wears many masks. *Psychology Today, 5*, 31–35, 64–66.

Gordon, C. (1968). Self-conceptions: Configuration of content. In C. Gordon & K. J. Gergen (Eds.), *The self in social interaction.* New York: Wiley.

Greenwald, A. G. (1981). The totalitarian ego: Fabrication and revision of personal history. *American Psychologist, 35*, 603–618.

Greenwald, A. G. (1982). Ego task analysis: An integration of research on ego-involvement and self-awareness. In A. H. Hastorf & A. M. Isen (Eds.), *Cognitive social psychology.* New York: Elsevier North-Holland.

Greenwald, A. G., & Pratkanis, A. R. (1984). The self. In R. S. Wyer & T. K. Srull (Eds.), *Handbook of social cognition.* Hillsdale, NJ: Erlbaum.

Heckhausen, H., Schmalt, H.-D., & Schneider, K. (in press). *Advances in achievement motivation research.* New York: Academic Press.

Heider, F. (1958). *The psychology of interpersonal relations.* New York: Wiley.

Higgins, E. T. (1983). *A theory of discrepant self-concepts.* Unpublished manuscript, New York University.

Higgins, E. T., Klein, R., & Strauman, T. (1985). Self-concept discrepancy theory: A psychological model for distinguishing among different aspects of depression and anxiety. *Social Cognition, 3*, 51–76.

Hormuth, S. E. (1984). Transitions in commitments to roles and self-concept change: Relocation as a paradigm. In V. Allen & E. van de Vliert (Eds.), *Role transitions.* New York: Plenum.

Isen, A. M., & Means, B. (1983). The influence of positive affect on decision-making strategy. *Social Cognition, 2*, 18–31.

Jones, E. E., & Berglas, S. (1978). Control of attributions about the self through self-handicapping strategies: The appeal of alcohol and the role of underachievement. *Personality and Social Psychology Bulletin, 4*, 200–206.

Jones, E. E., & Pittman, X. X. (1982). Toward a general theory of strategic self-presentation. In J. Suls (Ed.), *Psychological perspectives on the self* (Vol. 1). Hillsdale, NJ: Erlbaum.

Kagan, J. (1972). Motives and development. *Journal of Personality and Social Psychology, 22*, 51–66.

Kahneman, D., & Tversky, A. (1982). The simulation heuristic. In D. Kahneman, P. Slovic, & A. Tversky (Eds.), *Judgment under uncertainty*. Cambridge, England: Cambridge University Press.

Kihlstrom, J. F., & Cantor, N. (1984). Mental representations of the self. In L. Berkowitz (Ed.), *Advances in experimental social psychology* (Vol. 17). New York: Academic Press.

Kihlstrom, J. F., & Chew, B. (1981). *Adjective checklist*. Unpublished manuscript, University of Wisconsin–Madison.

Klinger, E. (1977). *Meaning and void*. Minneapolis: University of Minnesota Press.

Klos, D. S., Loomis, J. W., & Ruhrold, R. E. (1983). *Anger and strategic thinking during interpersonal conflict*. Unpublished manuscript, University of Michigan.

Kuhl, J. (1984). Volitional aspects of achievement motivation and learned helplessness: Toward a comprehensive theory of action control. *Personality Research, 13*, 99–171.

Kuhl, J., & Wassiljew, I. (1984). *Intrinsic task-motivation, coping with failure and problem-solving: Motivation and emotional determinants of the complexity of action plans*. Unpublished manuscript, Ruhr-University Bochum, West Germany.

Lecky, P. (1945). *Self-consistency: A theory of personality*. New York: Island Press.

Levinson, D. J. (1978). *The seasons of a man's life*. New York: Ballantine.

Lewin, K., Dembo, T., Festinger, L., & Sears, P. S. (1944). Level of aspiration. In J. McV. Hunt (Ed.), *Personality and the behavior disorders*. New York: Ronald Press.

Little, B. (1983). Personal projects: A rationale and method for investigation. *Environment and Behavior, 15*, 273–305.

Markus, H. (1977). Self-schemata and processing information about the self. *Journal of Personality and Social Psychology, 35*, 63–78.

Markus, H. (1983). Self knowledge: An expanded view. *Journal of Personality, 51*, 543–565.

Markus, H., & Nurius, P. (1983). *Possible selves*. Unpublished manuscript, University of Michigan.

Markus, H., & Sentis, K. (1982). The self in social information processing. In J. Suls (Ed.), *Psychological perspectives on the self*. Hillsdale, NJ: Erlbaum.

Martindale, C. (1980). Subselves: The internal representation of situational and personal dispositions. In L. Wheeler (Ed.), *Review of personality and social psychology* (Vol. 1). Beverly Hills, CA: Sage.

McClelland, D. C. (1951). *Personality*. New York: Holt, Rinehart and Winston.

McFarlin, D. B., & Blascovich, J. (1981). Effects of self-esteem and performance feedback on future affective preferences and cognitive expectations. *Journal of Personality and Social Psychology, 40*, 521–531.

McGuire, W. J. (in press). Search for the self: Going beyond self-esteem and the reactive self. In R. A. Zucker, J. Arnoff, & A. I. Rubin (Eds.), *Personality and the prediction of behavior*. New York: Academic Press.

Murray, H. A. (1951). Toward a classification of interaction. In T. Parsons & E. A. Shils (Eds.), *Toward a general theory of action*. Cambridge, MA: Harvard University Press.

Newcomb, T. M. (1959). Individual systems of orientation. In S. Koch (Ed.), *Psychology: A study of a science* (Vol. 3). New York: McGraw-Hill.

Newcomb, T. M. (1961). *The acquaintance process*. New York: Holt, Rinehart and Winston.

Niedenthal, P.M., Cantor, N., & Kihlstrom, J. F. (1985). Prototype-matching: A Strategy for social decision-making. *Journal of Personality and Social Psychology, 48*, 575–584.

Norem, J., & Cantor, N. (1984). *Pessimism as a cognitive cushion*. Paper presented at the meeting of the Midwestern Psychological Association, Chicago.

Nurius, P., & Markus, H. (1984). *The mutable self-concept: Social context as reflected in self-knowledge*. Unpublished manuscript, University of Michigan.

Nuttin, J. R. (1972). The outcome of a behavioral act: Its reinforcement and information functions in human learning and perception. *Abstract Guide of the 20th International Congress of Psychology*.

Nuttin, J. R. (1976). Motivation and reward in human learning: A cognitive approach. In W. K. Estes (Ed.), *Handbook of learning and cognitive process* (Vol. 5). Hillsdale, NJ: Erlbaum.

Nuttin, J. R. (1984). *Motivation, planning, and action: A relational theory of behavior dynamics.* Hillsdale, NJ: Erlbaum.

Osgood, C. E., & Tannenbaum, P. H. (1955). The principle of congruity in the prediction of attitude change. *Psychological Review, 62,* 42–55.

Pietromonaco, P. (1985). The influence of affect on self-perception in depression. *Social Cognition, 3,* 121–134.

Rogers, C. (1951). *Client-centered therapy.* Boston: Houghton Mifflin.

Schank, R., & Abelson, R. (1977). *Scripts, plans, goals and understanding: An inquiry into human knowledge structures.* Hillsdale, NJ: Erlbaum.

Schutz, A. (1964). On multiple realities. In M. Natanson (Ed.), *Collected papers of Alfred Schutz* (Vol. 1). The Hague: Martinus Nijhoff.

Sherif, M., & Hovland, C. I. (1961). *Social judgment,* New Haven: Yale University Press.

Sherman, S. J., Skov, R. B., Hervitz, F. E., & Stock, C. B. (1981). The effects of explaining hypothetical future events: From possibility to actuality and beyond. *Journal of Experimental Social Psychology, 17,* 142–158.

Showers, C., & Cantor, N. (1985). *The effects of best- and worst-case strategies: Making sense of judgment "bias."* Paper presented at the meeting of the Midwestern Psychological Association, Chicago.

Shrauger, J. S. (1975). Responses to evaluation as a function of initial self-perceptions. *Psychological Bulletin, 82,* 581–596.

Snyder, M. (1981). On the influence of individuals on situations. In N. Cantor & J. F. Kihlstrom (Eds.), *Personality, cognition and social interaction.* Hillsdale, NJ: Erlbaum.

Snyder, M., & Kendzierski, D. (1982). Choosing social situations: Investigating the origins of correspondence between attitudes and behavior. *Journal of Personality, 50,* 280–295.

Snygg, D., & Combs, A. W. (1949). *Individual behavior: A new frme of reference for psychology.* New York: Harper & Row.

Spivak, G., Platt, J. J., & Shure, M. B. (1976). *The problem-solving approach to adjustment.* San Francisco: Jossey-Bass.

Sullivan, H. S. (1953). *The interpersonal theory of psychiatry.* New York: Norton.

Tedeschi, J. T., & Lindskold, S. (1976). *Social psychology: Interdependence, interaction and influence.* New York: Wiley.

Tesser, A., & Campbell, J. (in press). Self-definition and self-evaluation maintenance. In J. Suls & A. Greenwald (Eds.), *Social psychological perspectives on the self* (Vol. 2). Hillsdale, NJ: Erlbaum.

Tolman, E. C. (1932). *Purposive behavior in animals and men.* New York: Appleton-Century.

Veroff, J. (1983). *Contextual determinants of personality.* Unpublished manuscript, University of Michigan.

Weiner, B. (1980). *Human motivation.* New York: Holt, Rinehart and Winston.

Wurf, E., & Markus, H. (1983). *Cognitive consequence of the negative self.* Paper presented at the annual meeting of the American Psychological Association, Anaheim, CA.

Zurcher, L. A. (1977). *The mutable self: A self-concept for social change.* Beverly Hills, CA: Sage.

CHAPTER 5

Remembering One's Own Past
The Construction of
Personal Histories

MICHAEL ROSS
MICHAEL CONWAY
University of Waterloo

It is making severe demands on the unity of the personality to try and make me identify myself with the author of the paper on the spinal ganglia of the petromyzon. Nevertheless, I must be he. . . .

Sigmund Freud to Karl Abraham, 21 September 1984 (Sulloway, 1979)

We are all personal historians. In most cases, our own pasts, like our children or pets, hold an interest for us that they hold for no others. The reasons to study the past include entertainment, curiosity, and, most important, the need to achieve self-understanding. We can examine the past to learn about our preferences, abilities, values, and so forth. A sense of personal identity involves, among other things, a view of oneself through time.

However, there may be constraints on what can be learned from considering the past. Much has been written about the biases and errors of trained historians when they reconstruct and interpret the events of preceding eras (Becker, 1935; Fischhoff, 1982; Gallie, 1964; Nowell-Smith, 1970). For example, historians are susceptible to the hindsight bias: They bestow an appearance of inevitability on known outcomes. Recently, the average person's rendering of his or her personal history has been the subject of similar scrutiny in social psychology (e.g., Fischhoff, 1975, 1982; Greenwald, 1980). Such recall is the focus of the present chapter.

The past can be probed in various ways. Two relevant considerations are the time period in question and the attribute being examined. Suppose that you are asked what you were like last week, last year, or 10 years ago: How did you feel about abortion or about your spouse? Have your attitudes become more favorable, less favorable, or have they remained the same? Or consider abilities: Has your intelligence or your aptitude for mathematics, spelling, writing, teaching, or formulating research improved, worsened, or remained the same? And what about your personality? Are you more or less shy, more or less sincere, more or less courageous, or more or less honest? Finally, consider physical characteristics: Has your stamina improved or worsened? Are you fatter? Are you better looking? Or have you remained the same?

Such questions go to the heart of our sense of personal identity; they have been posed in different forms by philosophers for centuries. When is the self I am today different from the self I was yesterday? William James (1890/1950) noted that our sense of personal identity is derived from the perception of temporal consistency or sameness. We see a constancy rather than a continual flux. In general, I say that I am the same self that I was yesterday, just as my bed is the same bed it was yesterday.

Of course, there is change. Even beds do not remain the same forever: Springs weaken, mattresses sag, and headboards become chipped and dented. We recognize alterations in ourselves, too. James had two major things to say about this. First, we see continuity as a past self blends into a more recent one; shifts are perceived to be gradual and smooth, rather than discontinuous. Second, James suggested a means by which we may decide whether a change has occurred, whether a past self is different from the present self. He argued that we feel a sense of warmth and intimacy when we contemplate our present self. If these same feelings are aroused when we consider a distant self, then no change is assumed. When distant selves fail to arouse these feelings or arouse them to a lesser extent, we then *feel* like a changed person.

To what extent does this analysis explain people's answers to queries concerning temporal stability or changes in their attitudes, abilities, and so forth? To answer such questions, people need to assess their present status and how they were back then (a week, a year, or 10 years ago). James doesn't indicate how we go about doing this. He seems to assume that memories of past selves are safely stored away in our heads and that we can retrieve these memories when needed. This implies the recovery of the same material that was originally stored.

Many philosophers, sociologists, and psychologists would propose a quite different view of long-term memory (e.g., Bartlett, 1932; Berger, 1963; Lindsay & Norman, 1972; Mead, 1934; Taylor & Crocker, 1981). First, recall can be selective; we tend to exhume only a subset of our experiences. Second, over time, we come to see things quite differently. We reinterpret and reexplain our pasts. Finally, we forget, and we fill in the gaps in memory by inferring what probably happened. Thus, long-term memory often involves a process of active reconstruction.

The question then becomes: What guides people's selection of particular memories, their interpretations, or their inferences? The present self is likely to be an important benchmark in this process. Our current status is most salient and available to us. Reconstruction of the past may consist, in large part, of characterizing the past as either different from or the same as the present. To determine my attitude toward abortion 5 years ago, I might ask myself: Is there any reason to believe that I felt differently than I do now?

How do individuals make such a judgment? One possible answer is that people make use of implicit theories about personal stability and change when they are attempting to reconstruct their pasts. These theories could have several origins. For example, they could reflect social-cultural ideas about development and change (e.g., people get more conservative as they get older or settle down when they marry). They could reflect theories about shifting trends in the population (e.g., everybody is more liberal on women's issues these days). They could reflect theories of personality (e.g., a person's level of honesty does not change). The nature of the theory may also be affected by the motivation to maintain a certain image of oneself; for instance, I may want to see myself as a person with stable opinions, rather than one who changes views on a whim.

The idea that people's self-perceptions or social perceptions may be guided by implicit theories is certainly not new. For example, people's theories about how various personality traits are related to one another are well documented (Schneider, 1973). Even more relevant to present concerns is Nisbett and Wilson's (1977) work on people's perceptions of the causes of their *current* behavior. The Nisbett and Wilson thesis is that people must rely on implicit causal theories to reconstruct recent cognitive processes. By the same token, we are suggesting that the retrieval of cognitions, feelings, and behaviors from the more distant past is guided by implicit theories of stability and change.

To provide a more general framework for how implicit theories may influence recall, we again follow James's lead by discussing three major aspects of the self: the material self, the social self, and the spiritual self. We then relate these facets of the self to recall. The material self refers primarily to our bodies, clothes, and possessions. The social self is the self we present to others. People show different sides of themselves to different individuals, and each is a social self. For example, the self we present to our lovers may be very different from the self we present to our bosses. This perspective antecedes many subsequent theories in which the self is viewed not as a stable entity that moves from one situation to the next, but as a process continuously recreated in each social situation (see Berger, 1963; Cooley, 1902/1970; Goffman, 1959; Mead, 1934). Finally, James described the spiritual self, which consists of our inward life, our sensations, our personalities, our attitudes, and so forth.

Now think of the likelihood of change with respect to each of these aspects of the self. Certainly, we expect change in the realm of the material self. We anticipate that as we age, our bodies first grow and strengthen and then soften and weaken. Also, throughout our working years, we expect our possessions to multiply. For the most part, we suppose such changes to be gradual (there are exceptions, such as debilitating diseases and lottery wins). These theories of physical and material development are likely to affect reconstructions of the past. If I am asked to recall the recent past, I should assume little difference from the present; if I am asked to recall the distant past, I may assume change. The nature of the perceived change will depend, in part, on my current stage in the life cycle. A 25-year-old may posit a past self physically weaker than the present self, whereas a 70-year-old may posit a stronger past self.

Next, consider the social self. To reconstruct a previous social self, I may need to know the group or person with whom I was interacting and whether our relationship has changed over time. Was the self I presented to my lover back then the same self I present to my lover now? Again, my reconstruction may be theoretically guided. If we have married in the interim, I may suspect that certain changes have occurred.

Finally, consider the inner core—the traits and dispositions that make up the spiritual self. In the absence of major changes in circumstance (e.g., illness, imprisonment, war, financial disaster, or divorce), we assume relatively little shift in abilities, attitudes, or personality. However, the time frame and nature of the disposition influence whether we adopt a theory of consistency or change. Over extended periods of time, dispositions such as ability can change. For example, I may not consider myself to be the same tennis player I was 10 or 15 years ago. Also, some dispositions seem more alterable than others. If I am an honest person, I am honest today and I was honest 10 years ago. In contrast, attitudes are seen as potentially changeable. I might have voted happily for a politician 10 years ago but detest him today. Moreover, shifts in traits and attitudes are anticipated as a person enters new life phases—such as mother, supervisor, or full professor.

Theories regarding elements of the spiritual self thus imply considerable stability but leave open the possibility of change over long periods of time or due to shifts in circumstance. Memories of traits and dispositions may reflect, in part, the particular theory we adopt in reconstructing the past.

Our characterization of the self to this juncture is undoubtedly too passive. People can try to shape their own destinies. They can work to reduce their weight, improve their abilities, change their personalities (e.g., become more assertive) or attitudes (e.g., become less prejudiced). People may then use evidence of their intent to change or of their efforts to achieve certain goals as a basis for assuming that change has occurred. That is, people have theories not only about the malleability of various aspects of the self but about how they might actively modify themselves.

In summary, sometimes we change; sometimes we don't. Sometimes we perceive change; sometimes we don't. Whether we infer change depends, in part, on the theory we invoke to guide our recall. Our reconstructions of the past are shaped by theories that dictate assumptions of either differences from the present or consistency. The accuracy of the reconstructions will depend on the validity of the theories. Suppose that 70-year-old possesses the theory that the ability to remember things decreases with age, whereas wisdom increases. He or she is then likely to assume that, relatively speaking, 30 years ago he or she was a fool with a good memory. If these theories of development are valid, this reconstruction of the past self will be generally accurate. If the theories are invalid, the reconstruction will be wrong.

In recent years, a number of social psychologists have examined people's memories of their past. These studies have been conducted from a variety of theoretical perspectives, and we shall acknowledge such heterogeneity later. Initially, though, we shall attempt to demonstrate that the research can be interpreted from the foregoing perspective—that people's reconstructions of the past are guided by implicit theories of stability and change. We preface this review and analysis with the following warning: Social psychologists tend to focus on people's foibles, rather than on their strengths. The research suggests that people are inadequate personal historians. At times, they deny change and variability that are manifestly present. At other times, they err in the opposite direction, exaggerating the degree to which they have changed over time. Our review does not imply, however, that such inaccuracies are necessarily the rule. Accuracy often involves applying the right theory at the right time. Thus, we will be describing situations in which people appear to invoke perfectly plausible theories but in the wrong context.

ATTITUDE CHANGE

The first set of studies we consider is drawn from research on attitude change. The paradigm in the earlier studies was as follows: Subjects were induced to change their attitudes and then were asked to recall what their attitudes were previously. The first experiment along these lines was conducted by Bem and McConnell in 1970; their results were replicated in 1973 by Ross and Shulman and by Goethals and Reckman. The Goethals and Reckman (1973) study is perhaps the most convincing of the lot in that it involved a salient, controversial attitude topic and massive attitude change. The subjects were Massachusetts high school students. At the initial experimental session, they completed an opinion questionnaire, indicating their attitudes on various political and social topics. They returned 4–14 days later for a group discussion of one of the attitude issues. All groups discussed the statement: "Busing should be widely used to achieve racial balance in U.S. schools." The discussion was supposedly being conducted to find out what high school students were thinking. Groups were composed of students who were either all probusing or all antibusing on the initial questionnaire, and a confederate of the experimenter. The confederate, a respected high school senior—had the task of changing the attitudes of group members. He was armed with persuasive arguments and dominated the conversation. After group discussion, attitudes toward busing were assessed privately. There were strong shifts; originally antibusing subjects were now more in favor of busing than originally probusing subjects. Subjects were then asked to recall as accurately as possible their initial attitudes on eight topics, including busing. They were asked to complete the scales exactly as they had in the initial experimental session.

Try to put youself in the place of these youngsters. They were required to reconstruct an attitude that they had expressed about a week earlier. Presumably, what was salient to them now was their current attitude. They had to decide whether their past attitude was different. A week is not a very long time, and we generally expect our attitudes to be stable over short periods. Moreover, the subjects did not come into the experiment wanting a change in attitude. Nor, as far as we know, did they consciously attempt to change their attitudes or think that the experiment was designed to change their attitudes (its true purpose was disguised). When people change their attitudes in such circumstances, are they likely to perceive that they have done so? Perhaps not, because many of the usual cues for change—such as a lengthy time period, a desire to change, or effort directed toward change—are presumably missing. Therefore, when asked to recall their attitudes, they may use the best available information—their current opinions—and assume that their past attitudes were similar. The data from this study support this interpretation. Despite a large shift in attitudes, the subjects recalled their initial opinions as being very similar to their postdiscussion views on the issue.

Note that, in many contexts, people would be correct in assuming temporal consistency in attitudes (Mischel & Peake, 1982). In the foregoing attitude change experiment, the theory happened to be invalid because, unbeknownst to the subjects, they had altered their opinions. We should note that Goethals and Reckman did not directly ask the subjects whether they had changed their opinions. However, other researchers using this paradigm have done so (Bem & McConnell, 1970; Ross & Shulman, 1973). Subjects typically answer no.

Attitudes and Behavior

Our implicit theories of the self suggest other consistencies as well. One that is of particular interest to social psychologists concerns the relationship between attitudes and behavior. Research has shown that attitudes and behavior are often inconsistent (Calder & Ross, 1973; Fishbein & Ajzen, 1975; Wicker, 1969). William James did not discuss behavior in this context, but the commonsense view of a unified self presumably includes a correspondence between attitudes and behaviors. This means that our behavior provides us with information about our attitudes, and our attitudes provide us with information about our behavior. Research has shown that people assume both of these links.

Salancik and Conway (1975) have provided convincing support for the idea that people infer their attitudes from their behavior. They manipulated whether people saw themselves as performing proreligious or antireligious behaviors in the past. Subjects were provided with a series of statements, such as "I attend church," followed by the adverbs "frequently" or "on occasion." People are more likely to endorse statements incorporating "on occasion" than ones incorporating "frequently". Therefore, to engender a proreligious behavioral history, Salancik and Conway inserted "on occasion" in proreligious statements and "frequently" in antireligious statements (e.g., "I *frequently* refuse to donate money to religious institutions"). They reversed this pattern to foster an antireligious behavioral history. They then asked subjects to report their attitudes toward religion. The subjects' attitudes shifted in the direction of their assigned behavioral histories.

The Salancik and Conway study shows that people may infer their current attitudes from their supposed past behaviors. This implies that people hold two theories of consistency: (1) that attitudes and behaviors correspond and (2) that past behaviors and attitudes are good predictors of current attitudes.

The reverse relationship has also been considered. Researchers have examined whether current attitudes may be used as bases for reconstructing past behaviors (Olson & Cal, 1984; Ross, McFarland, Conway, & Zanna, 1983; Ross, McFarland, & Fletcher, 1981). The hypothesis that attitudes influence behavior recall is most readily tested with new attitudes. With existing attitudes, a correspondence between behavior recall and attitudes may well be veridical. To demonstrate that attitudes *bias* behavior recall, it is necessary to alter the attitude and show an impact on behavior recall in the absence of a genuine shift in behavior. In the first study of this type (Ross *et al.*, 1981), subjects were asked to listen to and evaluate various health appeals that were known to have a significant impact on attitudes. Later, the subjects were asked, in a different context, to recall how often they had engaged in past behaviors relevant to their newly formed attitudes. The frequency estimates were biased in the direction of the new attitudes. For example, subjects who had heard an expert railing against the value of frequent toothbrushing (it causes erosion of the enamel and harms the gums, leading to infection and tooth loss) reported that they brushed their teeth less often in the previous two weeks than did subjects who had heard a message praising toothbrushing. This effect of attitudes on recall has been replicated several times with different attitude issues and with considerable effort directed at reducing any demands subjects may feel to bias their recall. For example, recall of the relevant behavior is typically obtained anonymously in a "second study" and is imbedded in a lengthy questionnaire that assesses memory for many other behaviors as well.

Clearly, there are limits to this phenomenon. Attitudes are not always going to affect behavior recall. If you ask me whether I ate potato chips yesterday while watching a televised football game, I don't have to think about my attitudes toward potato chips to reply. Many past behaviors are readily accessible in memory and can be retrieved without difficulty. When memory becomes hazy, though, and people have to reconstruct the past, then attitudes may serve as a basis for recall. Suppose that you ask me whether I have ever hit any of my children. I would respond by doing a quick memory check—I can't recall doing so—and this, together with my negative attitude toward spanking, would lead me to conclude that it is unlikely. Attitudes that are salient and are judged relevant to the behavior in question may guide reconstructive memory.

Note that behavior recall may be brought in line with current attitudes only when people assume that their attitudes have not changed. In the aforementioned research, the attitude-change aspect of the study was deliberately masked. Consequently, participants were likely to view their attitudes as stable. If people perceive a correspondence between their behaviors and attitudes, they can assume that they have already engaged in actions consistent with their present opinions. With a little selectivity and reinterpretation, they can identify such behaviors.

Implications of a False Perception of Temporal Consistency

The research suggests that people both infer their current attitudes from their recall of past behaviors and base their recall of past behaviors on current attitudes. A recent set of studies has demonstrated that this reciprocal relationship between behavior recall and current attitudes has implications for people's commitment to their attitudes (Lydon, Zanna, & Ross, 1983; Ross *et al.*, 1983). Subjects who were required to engage in behavior recall after attitude change were shown to be more committed to their newly formed attitudes than subjects who were not required to engage in recall. For example, behavior recall increased subjects' intentions to behave in line with their new attitudes in the future, increased their resistance to an attack on their new attitudes, and increased their tendency to selectively recall arguments in factor of their new attitude position.

Why would biased behavior recall increase commitment to an attitude? When attitudes influence the recall of past behaviors, a review of past actions appears to validate the attitudes. For instance, if someone persuades me that I like to eat turnips, I may then recall choosing to eat turnips more often in the past than if I had been persuaded that I dislike turnips. In short, past behavior appears to be consistent with current attitudes and thus provides support for the attitudes. In addition, past behavior is seen as irrevocable and seems to bind people to the attitudes (Kiesler, 1971). People have the sense that they cannot undo that which has been done. What is being posited, then, is a form of self-fulfilling prophecy: Attitudes alter recall, which, in turn, inappropriately bolsters a person's commitment to those attitudes.

This reciprocal relationship between attitudes and behavior recall may have implications for the durability of attitude change. When people do not recognize a shift in attitude, they may revise their pasts in a manner that permits the new opinion to become an integral part of the self. They see the attitude as representative of their past feelings and reconstruct a behavioral history around it. As a consequence, the attitude becomes firmly anchored within the self-concept and resistant to change. On the other hand, we hypothesize a very different sequence of events when individuals see themselves as adopting a new opinion. The perception of change should lead them to reconstruct past attitudes and behaviors that are at variance with their new views. The opinion change may then be less firmly anchored within the self-concept and, as a consequence, may be inherently unstable. Such opinion changes are unlikely to persist unless they can be supported by subsequent changes in the environment or in behavior (Cook & Flay, 1978; Festinger, 1964).

In summary, the picture in the attitude domain is one of consistency. In the aforementioned experiments, the subjects did not realize that they had experienced a change in attitudes—in part, because social psychologists have mastered the art of disguising the true purpose of their studies. When people have no reason to think that their attitudes have changed, they assume temporal consistency ("My attitude today is the same attitude I had yesterday") as well as a correspondence between present attitudes, past behaviors, and future behaviors.

External Validity of the Research

This reliance on experimental deception raises some important questions about the external validity of the results. Are the consistency findings generalizable to the real world, where events are possibly staged with less artifice than is used in the social psychology laboratory? In everyday life, opinions can change for a variety of reasons. Abrupt attitude shifts following a communication may be relatively rare. Many of our opinions probably shift gradually and almost imperceptibly over time. Who can say when the young liberal transforms himself or herself into the old conservative? Who can identify the moment when love or friendship blossoms or fades, or when talent dissipates, or when children become adults? Sometimes, these shifts are sudden and are identifiably linked with explicit events. More often, however, they simply emerge over time. To return to our major theme—when are people likely to observe that a change has occurred? The answer, we argue, depends on the theory that guides the person's recall of past selves.

As an initial attempt to examine this issue, McFarland and Ross (1984) had university undergraduates record their evaluations of themselves and their steady dating partners on a number of dimensions. For example, they reported on bipolar scales their impressions of their own and their partners' honesty, openmindedness, friendliness, kindness, and intelligence. They also indicated how much they liked and loved their partners. Two to three months later, they returned and were asked to record their current impressions on the same scales and to recall, as accurately as possible, their responses at the initial meeting.

Put yourself in the subjects' place. The trait judgments they were being asked to recall relate to what James referred to as the spiritual self. The dispositions associated with this component of the self are seen to be relatively enduring. Similarly, affection and liking for a partner may not be expected to alter significantly in such a short time span. On looking back, then, participants should generally assume that their current feelings are representative of the way they have felt for some time.

We thus predict, once again, a consistency effect, and that is exactly what McFarland and Ross (1984) obtained. Participants who become more positive about themselves or their partners recalled their initial evaluations as being more favorable than they were. Similarly, participants who became more negative recalled less favorable evaluations than they had provided. These data suggest that perceived consistency is not restricted to contexts in which naive participants are subjected to contrived and deceptive procedures.

Finally, the assumption of self-consistency has interesting implications for our evaluations of others who are at earlier stages in the life cycle than ourselves. We presume that our past selves are very much like our present selves. This may help explain why university professors complain that students don't seem as bright or as motivated as they were when they were students, or why each generation of parents bemoans the changing values and mores of children. We are not really able to evaluate the young against how we were at a comparable stage. Instead, we unknowingly evaluate them against a reflection of our present image—and they are found wanting.

This presumption of consistency need not always work to the disadvantage of the target. For example, full professors who have slowed up a bit may be amazed and impressed by the energy displayed by their younger colleagues. As a result of underestimating changes in ourselves, we see the behavior of younger others as more discrepant from our own, and hence more deviant, than the objective historical evidence probably warrants.

CONTRASTING THEORETICAL INTERPRETATIONS

We have rather imperialistically interpreted various findings from our own theoretical standpoint. We now discuss alternative interpretations of the research and compare them to our own. We consider three major theoretical orientations: cognitive dissonance theory, impression management theory, and Bem's self-perception theory.

Dissonance Theory

In the Goethals and Reckman (1973) study, high school students' attitudes toward busing changed dramatically, yet the students recalled their past attitudes as being consistent with their current opinions. Goethals and Reckman explained these results in terms of dissonance theory. People feel embarrassed or uncomfortable when they realize that their current attitudes clash with their prior beliefs. They can reduce this discomfort (dissonance) by forgetting their original positions and assuming that their opinions have not altered. Indeed, forgetting is one of the mechanisms that Festinger (1957, p. 271) originally posited as a means to reduce dissonance.

The cognitive dissonance explanation of these results seems to assume that subjects possess an implicit theory of temporal consistency of attitudes. People would not experience embarrassment over inconsistency unless they expected to be consistent. As we shall soon document, however, people do not always assume consistency; at times, they acknowledge and even exaggerate change. Clearly, then, the perception of inconsistency is not sufficient to induce dissonance. Dissonance occurs only when admitting to change represents a violation of a theory the person holds about himself or herself.

The suggested role of implicit theories in dissonance phenomena indicates that the two interpretations are not mutually incompatible. We have suggested that theories of self-consistency may underlie a dissonance explanation; however, the reverse is not true. We need not propose a motivated, dissonance-induced forgetting to explain the memory results. On the basis of existing data, it is not possible to tell how crucial dissonance is to the process.

Although this may sound like a call for further research to evaluate the validity of two competing theoretical perspectives, it isn't. A good deal of past research has been directed as pitting motivational against nonmotivational ("information processing") explanations of social and self-perception (for reviews, see Bradley, 1978; Miller & Ross, 1975; Nisbett & Ross, 1980; Ross & Fletcher, in press; Tetlock & Levi, 1982). For all the effort that has been exerted, the results are disappointing. In almost every case, one can, with a little ingenuity, dredge up another information-processing or motivational interpretation to account for allegedly recalcitrant data. The most reasonable conclusion is that each view may be correct. Motivated forgetting does occur, whether the motivation is dissonance, guilt, or whatever. However, not all forgetting has motivational components, and theories of the self can play an important role in reconstructions of the past.

Impression Management

Our culture values consistency. The dissonance interpretation implies that people are embarrassed by inconsistency because it violates their preferred self-concept. The impression management explanation suggests that people are not so much concerned with their own perceptions but with the impressions others, such as experimenters, have of them (Tedeschi, Schlenker, & Bonoma, 1971). Thus, we try to manage our impressions so that we appear consistent to others. We believe that the appearance of consistency will enhance our credibility, whereas inconsistency looks foolish.

The impression management interpretation can account for at least some of the research findings. Perhaps the subjects in the Salancik and Conway (1975) study feigned attitudes that were consonant with their assigned behavioral histories so that they would appear consistent to the experimenter. Similarly, perhaps the subjects in the Ross *et al.* (1981, 1983) studies altered their reports of past behaviors to convince the experimenter that their attitudes and behaviors were consistent. In all of these studies, procedures were adopted to reduce public demands for consistency (e.g., subjects' responses were confidential and anonymous), but the possibility cannot be totally eliminated.

Impression management is a plausible explanation when experimenters cannot test the veridicality of subjects' self-reports. In some studies, though, (e.g., Goethals & Reckman, 1973), subjects were asked to recall a response that they had provided at an earlier time. In such situations, the experimental demands are for accuracy, and there would appear to be no advantage to faking consistency when the experimenter can prove you wrong. Hence, the impression management interpretation does not provide a credible explanation for some of the major evidence for exaggeration of temporal consistency.

Bem's Self-Perception Theory

The self-perception interpretation of the attitude consistency finding starts from a different perspective from that of dissonance or impression management theory (Bem, 1972; Bem & McConnell, 1970; Salancik & Conway, 1975). Bem assumed that people often do not "know" even their current attitudes. Instead, they infer their present attitudes from their past behavior. As noted earlier, Bem and McConnell (1970) conducted a study in which recall of past attitudes was assessed. They found that subjects who freely chose to write a counterattitudinal essay shifted their attitudes in the direction of its contents. Yet the subjects incorrectly assumed that their prior attitudes were virtually identical to the opinions they adopted after writing the essay. According to Bem, this assumption of similarity is based not on a theory of attitude consistency over time but, rather, on a theory of human behavior. In effect, the subjects ask themselves: "Why would I freely choose to argue the position unless I believed it in the first place?" (The flaw in this logic, of course, is that they did not really have free choice. The experimental situation was carefully engineered to induce virtually everyone to write the essay.)

Bem reasoned that the self-perception processes he described occurred only when "internal cues are weak, ambiguous, or uninterpretable" (Bem, 1972, p. 2). Subsequent research has substantiated this limitation. When attitudes are well defined and salient, people do not infer them from previous behavior (Chaiken & Baldwin, 1981). From our perspective, however, an exaggeration of temporal consistency in attitudes could occur even when present attitudes (but not past ones) are salient and well defined. Indeed, current attitudes *must* be salient to serve as a cue for the reconstruction of past opinions.

In addition, the self-perception analysis posits that people hold a particular theory of consistency—namely, that attitudes are consonant with behaviors. People don't always assume, however, that behaviors reflect attitudes. For example, Bem pointed out that people are unlikely to infer their attitudes from behavior that is forced or "manded" by the situation. Yet we would still expect people to infer a consistency between present and past attitudes in such contexts. After manded behavior, people can use their current attitudes as a guide for reconstructing their prior opinions. The soldier who is forced by the enemy to make unpatriotic statements may nonetheless see himself as patriotic and infer that he was always patriotic.

In summary, not all of the current findings can be readily explained in terms of Bem's self-perception theory. The perception of temporal consistency in attitudes may occur in contexts in which, according to Bem, self-perception processes should not be invoked. Finally, in contrast to Bem, we assume that people generally do know their current feelings, beliefs and so forth. It is the past they have trouble with.

ADDITIONAL EVIDENCE OF FALSE PERCEPTIONS OF TEMPORAL CONSISTENCY

To this point, we have focused on attitudes. However, a false consistency in recall has been a major theme in other domains as well. A great deal of recent research has focused on the impact of current emotions on memory. The mood people happen to be in when they recall events in their own lives influences what past incidents or situations come to mind. When they are in a good mood, people tend to remember happy events; when they are in a bad mood, they remember sad events. Consistency between current mood and the affective quality of recall has been demonstrated with various types of mood manipulations, including hypnotic induction, success–failure experiences, and reading of depressing or elating self-referent statements (Bower, 1981; Isen, Shalker, Clark, & Karp, 1978; Mischel, Ebbesen, & Zeiss, 1976; Snyder & White, 1982; Wright & Mischel, 1982).

The dominant interpretation of these results is that mood acts as a retrieval cue for memories of corresponding affective quality. Past events are presumably encoded along with the affect with which they are associated, and current mood cues these affective associations (Bower, 1981). The results can thus be construed as demonstrating a state-dependent learning effect. When they are in a specific mood, people remember best the past events that occurred when they were in that same mood.

The data on recall of past life events can also be characterized as reflecting a tendency to exaggerate the consistency between past and present selves. People remember themselves as being more like their current selves than was actually the case. For example, in one study (Conway & Ross, 1984b), university students completed a brief questionnaire immediately before writing an examination. They were asked to indicate their current mood state by putting slashes through lines with endpoints labeled *tense–relaxed, anxious–calm*, and *unhappy–happy*. Two weeks later, they were given an identical questionnaire and asked to specify, as accurately as possible, where they had put their slashes on the initial questionnaire. The students remembered being significantly less tense and anxious and non-significantly less unhappy than they had been. They appeared to remember themselves as being more like their current, less stressed selves than was the case. Bower (1981) also reported that ratings of the affective quality of past events shift in the direction of current mood. These findings are reminiscent of the purported tendency of women to underestimate their labor pains retrospectively.

A possible interpretation of the impact of mood on memories of past life events is that people see themselves and others as possessing relatively stable traits and dispositions. When I am unhappy, I see this as an enduring state; that is, I am the kind of person to whom unfortunate things happen. This view of myself then guides my recall, and I tend to remember things that have gone wrong in my life. Similarly, if I am calm and relaxed now, I assume that I felt more or less the same way in the past. Thus, in their perception of a unified self, people may underestimate the extent to which moods and traits fluctuate with changes in age and situation.

Note that the operative word here is "underestimate." The assimilation is not total. For example, people realize that they are more anxious before an exam than during an ordinary class. Nonetheless, they underestimate how different these two selves really are.

A similar type of error has been demonstrated in research on parents' memories of their children. Although our focus in this chapter is on social-psychological efforts to understand personal recall, it is noteworthy that the validity of memories for past events has been of concern to developmental psychologists for some time. In early attempts to understand child development, researchers interviewed parents and asked them to recall their child-rearing practices and their children's achievements. Considerable doubt has been raised regarding the validity of such retrospective methodologies (e.g., Yarrow, Campbell, & Burton, 1970). Marion Yarrow and her associates attempted to evaluate these concerns empirically by assessing how accurately mothers recall the ages at which their children passed various developmental milestones (Yarrow *et al.*, 1970). The researchers had the actual ages available to them from nursery school records. Mothers tended to recall their children as being toilet trained, as having their first tooth, and so forth, at earlier ages than these events had actually occurred.

Obviously, many interpretations of such data are possible. Certainly, mothers are not known to underestimate the accomplishments of their offspring. Nevertheless, the finding again represents an exaggeration of temporal consistency. People are remembered as having been more similar to their current selves (e.g., the children are now toilet trained, have all their teeth, etc.) than was the case.

IMPLICIT THEORIES OF CHANGE

So far, we have provided evidence that people are cognitive conservatives who bias their memories so as to deny change and maintain temporal consistency and coherence. According to our analysis, this tendency to exaggerate consistency should occur primarily when people adhere to a theory that implies stability in the context of actual change. In contrast, if people hold a theory of change, they may acknowledge a transformation and may even exaggerate the degree to which they have altered. Thus, people are likely to overestimate change when they hold a theory of change in a situation of actual stability.

One setting in everyday life where this may occur is self-improvement programs. Many different kinds of improvement programs thrive, and there is no shortage of participants who testify to their merits. New diet books are often best-sellers. Pop therapies and so-called cults, such as Erhard Seminar Training (est) and Scientology, have attracted and apparently satisfied many. Yet most of these programs have been judged by informed professionals to be ineffective or even harmful (e.g., Polivy and Herman, 1983).

What is the basis of this difference of opinion between professional program evaluators and program participants? There are three obvious possibilities. The first is that the professionals are wrong—and it certainly wouldn't be the first time. The second is that the participants are unusually gullible—not a possibility to be sneered at. The third is that experts and participants are evaluating the program on the basis of very different criteria; again, this almost certainly occurs.

Let us consider another alternative, however. Suppose that a program appears valid but, in fact, promises more than it delivers. The participants may believe the promises, and they may then inadvertently manufacture evidence that supports the claims. One possibility is that they will overestimate their postprogram standing. This is not always feasible, though, as there frequently are reality constraints. For instance, obese people cannot persuade themselves, or a scale, that they are now thin. More often, participants may be able to claim improvement by revising how they were before the program began, since the past is more malleable than the present. In effect, they can say to themselves: "I may not be perfect now, but I was much worse before." Such revision is most likely if objective records of the past either were not taken or have become unavailable.

Thus, our hypothesis is that participants in a self-improvement program may attribute greater gain to themselves than seems warranted, by exaggerating in recall how poorly off they were before the program. A number of conditions seem likely to foster this tendency to rewrite the past as a consequence of participating in an intervention program. First, as suggested earlier, the program should be assumed valid by its participants. This assumption may be facilitated when the program demands the commitment of considerable energy, time, or money (Cooper, 1980). Otherwise, participants may discount the whole exercise and may adopt, with a vengeance, a theory of consistency. When participants accept the program's validity, they will anticipate change from the outset; and as they are going through the program, they may adopt a theory of change. Second, participants' theories should dictate a greater amount of change than actually occurs. Even if recall is theory driven, it can be accurate. An overestimation of change is most likely if participants expect change when actual improvement is minimal. Finally, participants should desire improvement. If they do, they would be most susceptible to adopting a theory of change.

We selected a context in which to test our hypothesis on the basis of ou. analysis of when exaggeration of change is likely to occur (Conway & Ross, 1984a). A study skills program seemed to meet our needs. First, as we planned to draw subjects from a university student population, such a program would address issues of concern to them. Second, the study skills programs commonly offered in many universities and colleges require a certain amount of effort, if only to attend program meetings. Third, formal evaluation, typically adopting academic performance as the criterion, suggests that study skills programs are of questionable worth, despite their prevalence and face validity. After a review of the study skills literature, Gibbs (1981) concluded that researchers have found "no difference in academic performance between those who had received guidance and a carefully chosen control group" (p. 69). Moreover, research on one of the most "highly developed and heavily sold courses in Britain" revealed "only *short-term* differences in study habits and even a deterioration in some habits" (Gibbs, 1981, p. 69, italics in original). In reflecting on these and other studies, Main (1980) drew a similar, albeit less extreme, conclusion: "There is already enough disquiet to suggest that courses in methods are not a universal answer to student study difficulties" (p. 65). Finally, in line with our major theme, it is noteworthy that study skills courses are judged beneficial by students who take them (see Chibnall, 1979; Hills & Potter, 1979).

We examined the impact of a standard study skills program on subjective and objective indicants of skills. Subjects evaluated their study skills and reported their study time at a first meeting and then were randomly assigned either to the skills program or to a waiting-list control group. After program participants had attended three weekly skills sessions, they and the waiting-list subjects returned for a final meeting. All subjects were asked to recall their initial responses, to rate their skills improvement, and to predict their grades at the end of the semester. Recall was examined to determine whether participants in the skills program, relative to waiting-list control subjects, belittled their prior study skills and amount of study time. In addition, we obtained subjects' final grades to compare participants' perceived improvement in study skills to their academic performance. This also allowed us to assess the program's impact on an objective measure of performance. Finally, 6 months after the last meeting, we assessed subjects' recall of their academic performance for the term during which the study was conducted. This recall was examined to determine whether participants might retrospectively exaggerate how well off they were *after* the program.

The results supported the hypotheses. Program participants recalled their original study skills evaluations as being worse than they had actually reported; waiting-list subjects exhibited no systematic bias in recall. In short, program participants belittled their prior study skills; waiting-list control subjects did not. However, all subjects were relatively accurate in their recall of study time. Besides derogating their prior skills, program participants reported significantly greater improvement in their study skills and expected better grades than waiting-list subjects did. The participants' expectations were unwarranted; their academic grades were not affected by the program. It is interesting, however, that this did not prevent program participants from subsequently recalling their performance as superior. When contacted 6 months later, the program participants remembered better grades than they had actually obtained in their majors for the term during which the program was conducted. In contrast, waiting-list subjects did not exhibit a systematic bias in recall.

The major finding in this study was that program participants retrospectively disparaged their initial study skills. A strong experimental imperative to be accurate argues against the possibility that self-presentation concerns and demand characteristics contributed to the results. Conceivably, to look good and to please the program leader, program participants could have intentionally derogated their past so as to glorify the present. But what is the point of purposely rewriting the past when the experimenters assert that they can and will assess the accuracy of the recall?

There is a more subtle alternative interpretation of these results. Perhaps the program participants' recall of their initial study skills evaluations reflected a *reassessment* of their past skills. Subjects might have been incapable of putting aside standards adopted as a consequence of taking the skills program and might have been unaware of the influence of these standards of their recall. Thus, even under demands for accuracy, the program participants might have reassessed their initial status. This adoption of new standards is probably an integral part of most improvement programs and may well contribute to the tendency of participants to belittle their past status.

The results are also consistent with a dissonance theory explanation (Aronson, 1969; Cooper, 1980). Individuals who voluntarily exert effort to improve their study skills can justify their labors by perceiving improvement even in its absence, and one way to perceive improvement would be to derogate the past. Of course, belittling one's previous abilities might itself produce dissonance, as it is not consistent with maintaining a positive view of self. But people may be able to shrug off their past failings so long as they see themselves as better off now.

There are several applied implications of the reconstructions obtained in the study skills research. First, the research reveals, once again, the potential invalidity of self-reports and the need for formal evaluation to assess improvement programs. This lesson is not new, but it is easy to forget. Even informed observers sometimes base their analyses of the effectiveness of therapeutic approaches on self-reports (e.g., Schachter, 1982).

Second, although those who conduct worthless programs are often criticized by the press and the public, these helpers may simply be too credulous. Any doubts they might have about their programs' effectiveness may be assuaged by participants' glowing reports. It is noteworthy that sophisticated observers have long questioned the value of clients' self-reports on the grounds that they might represent efforts at self-presentation. Health professionals, for example, often realize that patients may feel compelled to report that a treatment is helpful even when they know it is not (Ross & Olson, 1982). We are saying something different here, however: Patients may well believe their reports of self-improvement yet be wrong. The best reminder of this sort of error can be found in the history of medicine, which is replete with examples of "miracle cures" that turn out to be placebo effects (Ross & Olson, 1981, 1982). Many of these cures were evaluated solely on the basis of patients' self-reports. When self-reports are a primary indicant of improvement, a conspiracy of ignorance may emerge in which the helper and the helped both erroneously believe in the achievement of their common goal.

As opponents of cults, fad diets, and pop therapies have found, it is not easy to persuade participants that a program is ineffective (e.g., Conway & Siegelman, 1979). In our study skills experiment, we obtained anecdotal evidence of the tenacity with which participants adhered to a theory of improvement. At the end of the experiment, subjects were debriefed and were informed that study skills programs are generally ineffective. They reacted strongly to this information, emphasizing the potential benefits of the program. Some argued that even if their study skills weren't improved, they had acquired greater self-confidence, which would hold them in good stead at exam time. However, their reasoning did not seem to be supported by their exam results or those of participants in other programs.

Finally, we should emphasize that there are situations in which exaggeration of change is advantageous. In a self-improvement program that is effective but whose benefits take a relatively long time to accrue, participants may persist better in their efforts if they adopt a theory of short-term change and exaggerate their progress. Other instances of adaptive theories of change may be found in how people cope with personal crises. For example, a person's psychological reactions to breast cancer or spinal cord injury often include the perception that she or he is now a "better person." This perceived improvement gives meaning to the illness and contributes to psychological adjustment (Bulman & Wortman, 1977; Taylor, 1983). Conceivably, victims exaggerate their improvement by overestimating how petty, misguided, or maladjusted they were before their misfortune. In this way, theories of personal improvement contribute to the illusions that facilitate coping with undesirable life events.

THE NATURE OF RECONSTRUCTIVE MEMORY

We have not yet commented explicitly on the extensiveness or nature of the reconstructions in memory documented in this chapter. We are not suggesting that people rewrite their entire autobiographies with every passing mood state or with every shift in attitudes. People do not necessarily even consider their pasts. Although the subjects in the experiments reported in this chapter were asked to do so, we don't really know when or how often people engage in such recall in everyday life. For example, we suspect—but don't have empirical evidence—that people's participation in self-improvement programs is likely to prompt recall of their status prior to the programs.

In addition, the reconstructions we have described are limited to a fraction of the autobiography. We are positing relatively minor editorial revisions that bring the past more in line with the person's current self-image. We believe that such shifts are psychologically important and may have long-term, nonobvious implications—for example, their impact on commitment to current attitudes or on the perpetuation of current mood states (Bower, 1981; Ross et al., 1983). However, we also believe that analogies that have been drawn relating the reconstructions of autobiographies to the rewriting and fabrication of history that occurs in totalitarian political regimes (see Berger, 1963; Greenwald, 1980) are, perhaps, overly dramatic and misleading. Personal recall is malleable, but we have little evidence that people are totally out of touch with reality.

MOTIVATION AND COGNITION

This chapter appears in a book on motivation and cognition, and our explanations of the reconstructive memory data tend to reflect a tilt toward the cognitive end of the spectrum. It has not escaped our notice, however, that most of the reconstructions documented in this chapter probably confirm individuals' preferred images of themselves. People see consistency and stability where it is likely to be valued. Where change may be esteemed, however—as in the context of self-improvement programs—the reconstructions accommodate a perception of change. In short, the reconstructions are likely to foster feelings of positive self-regard.

This tendency is not universal. There is some evidence, for example, that people in negative mood states reconstruct a past that is not flattering; indeed, their recall is likely to maintain or increase their negative mood (Bower, 1981). There are also people, such as the depressed, who may chronically reinterpret the past to make it appear that they are always doing terrible things (Beck, 1967). Nonetheless, in the main, reconstructions of the past probably serve to enhance self-esteem. The focus on particular memories and the reconstruction and interpretation of the past may be prompted and biased, at times, by people's motives, hopes, and fears. In other words, people probably adopt theories of stability and change that are consistent with their preferred images of themselves.

CONCLUDING COMMENTS

In this chapter, we have examined personal recall from the standpoint of beliefs about consistency and change. This analysis links theory on the self with research on memory and attitudes. We readily acknowledge that there are plausible alternative interpretations for much of the research data. The research originated from a variety of theoretical perspectives and was not explicitly designed to test our views. As a result, we have had to rely on our own and our readers' intuitions regarding the personal beliefs that are presumed to mediate the memory effects. Although these beliefs were not assessed directly in the research, we consider our inferences to be defensible. For example, it seems entirely reasonable to assume that a study skills program invokes a theory of improvement in its participants. Yet there is a danger of circularity. Given evidence of a false consistency between past and present, we find ourselves assuming that subjects based their recall on a theory of consistency. It is obviously necessary to establish people's theories independently of the recall data.

There is also a need for a thorough analysis of dispositions. Attribution theorists have tended to treat the various kinds of dispositions (e.g., attitudes, feelings, abilities, habits, personality characteristics) as a largely homogenous class (Ross & Fletcher, in press). Yet people perceive differences among dispositions in terms of their stability over time. For instance, research on stereotyping of the elderly reveals that some dispositions are seen to shift with age, whereas others are seen as relatively stable over the life span (Rothbaum, 1983). We know little about the theoretical underpinnings of such distinctions, however, or about the details of the expected shifts. Are they sudden or gradual—and what is the age of their onset? When does a person stop being rash and become contemplative and wise? Nor do we know much about how perceiver characteristics, such as age, affect the adoption of such theories. To answer these questions, we need to investigate people's theories of the development of the self. Such theories may have an important impact on people's current self-perceptions and may provide a framework for their reconstructions of the past.

A consideration of implicit theories of life-span development raises the issue of how people regard their futures. We would argue that just as the assumption of a stable self often prompts people to extend their present selves into the past, it should also lead them to extend their present selves into the future. Along these lines, Simone de Beauvoir (1973) has written eloquently about our failure to prepare adequately for old age, in part because we don't anticipate becoming old and feeble. Stability does not always rule, however. Reconstructions of personal histories sometimes provide evidence of the adoption of theories of change. Similarly, in anticipating the future, people may perceive the possibility of radical change, of becoming a "new" person (Markus & Nurius, 1984). In this context, implicit theories may become quite personal, and expectations of how the future will unfold may be influenced by very specific motives and goals.

Finally, we should note that the relationships among the present, the past, and the future are more complex than we have allowed so far. We have reasoned that because the present is salient and available, people reconstruct the past or make future projections on the basis of their current status. Even the attitude-commitment studies that demonstrated a reciprocal relationship between attitudes and behavior recall were predicated on the assumption that the action begins with the present: Current attitudes affect behavior recall, which, in turn, affects current attitudes.

The causal flow need not start with the present, however. For example, people's perceptions of their current selves reflect their recall of past selves. Thus, middle-aged adults may maintain body images that are more consistent with their youthful physiques than with their current status. A 40-year-old man with a developing potbelly may still see himself as thin if he was thin for the first 25 years of his life. Moreover, our projections of the future may influence both our memories of past selves and our perceptions of present selves. For example, dwelling on desired outcomes may lead people to perceive the past and present in a manner that makes the outcomes seem more attainable. A person who hopes to obtain a particular job may focus on the abilities and experiences that make him or her seem tailor-made for the position and may ignore the areas in which the fit is less than perfect.

In conclusion, although most of this chapter has been devoted to an analysis of how the present guides reconstructions of the past, the present is not the only possible benchmark. We have merely begun to explore the relationships among people's perceptions of where they are, where they've been, and where they are going.

References

Aronson, E. (1969). The theory of cognitive dissonnace: A current perspective. In L. Berkowitz (Ed.), *Advances in experimental social psychology* (Vol. 4, pp. 1–34). New York: Academic Press.

Bartlett, F. C. (1932). *Remembering: A study in experimental and social psychology.* London: Cambridge University Press.

Beck, A. T. (1967). *Depression: clinical, experimental, and theoretical aspects.* New York: Harper & Row.

Becker, C. (1935). Everyman his own historian. *American Historical Review, 40,* 221–236.

Bem, D. J. (1972). Self-perception theory. In L. Berkowitz (Ed.), *Advances in experimental social psychology* (Vol. 6, pp. 1–62). New York: Academic Press.

Bem, D. J., & McConnell, H. K. (1970). Testing the self-perception explanation of dissonance phenomena: On the salience of premanipulation attitudes. *Journal of Personality and Social Psychology, 14*, 23–31.

Berger, P. L. (1963). *Invitation to sociology: A humanistic perspective.* Garden City, NY: Doubleday.

Bower, G. H. (1981). Mood and memory. *American Psychologist, 36*, 129–148.

Bradley, G. W. (1978). Self-serving biases in the attribution process: A re-examination of the fact or fiction question. *Journal of Personality and Social Psychology, 36*, 56–71.

Bulman, R. V., & Wortman, C. B. (1977). Attributions of blame and coping in the "real world": Severe accident victims react to their lot. *Journal of Personality and Social Psychology, 35*, 351–363.

Calder, B. J., & Ross, M. (1973). *Attitudes and behavior.* Morristown, NJ: General Learning Press.

Chaiken, S., & Baldwin, M. W. (1981). Affective-cognitive consistency and the effect of salient behavioral information on the self-perception of attitudes. *Journal of Personality and Social Psychology, 41*, 1–12.

Chibnall, B. (1979). The sussex experience. In P. J. Hills (Ed.), *Study courses and counselling: Problems and possibilities.* Surrey, England: Society for Research into Higher Education, Guilford.

Conway, F., & Siegelman, J. (1979). *Snapping.* New York: Delta.

Conway, M., & Ross, M. (1984a). Getting what you want by revising what you had. *Journal of Personality and Social Psychology, 47*, 738–748.

Conway, M., & Ross, M. (1984b). *Recall of affective states.* Unpublished manuscript, University of Waterloo.

Cook, T. D., & Flay, B. R. (1978). The persistence of experimentally induced attitude change. In L. Berkowitz (Ed.), *Advances in experimental social psychology* (Vol. 11, pp. 1–57). New York: Academic Press.

Cooley, C. H. (1970). *Human nature and the social order.* New York: Schocken. (Original work published 1902)

Cooper, J. (1980). Reducing fears and increasing assertiveness: The role of dissonnace reduction. *Journal of Experimental Social Psychology, 16*, 199–213.

de Beauvoir, S. (1973). *The coming of age.* New York: Warner.

Festinger, L. (1957). *A theory of cognitive dissonance.* Evanston, IL: Row, Peterson.

Festinger, L. (1964). Behavioral support for opinion change. *Public Opinion Quarterly, 28*, 404–417.

Fischhoff, B. (1975). Hindsight≠foresight: The effect of outcome knowledge on judgment under uncertainty. *Journal of Experimental Psychology: Human Perception and Performance, 1*, 288–299.

Fischhoff, B. (1982). For those condemned to study the past: Heuristics and biases in hindsight. In D. Kahneman, P. Slovic, & A. Tversky (Eds.), *Judgment under uncertainty: Heuristics and biases.* Cambridge: Cambridge University Press.

Fishbein, M., & Ajzen, I. (1975). *Belief, attitude, intention, and behavior: An introduction to theory and research.* Reading, MA: Addison-Wesley.

Gallie, W. B. (1964). *Philosophy and the historical understanding.* London: Chatto & Windus.

Gibbs, G. (1981). *Teaching students to learn.* Milton Keynes, England: Open University Press.

Goethals, G. R., & Reckman, R. F. (1973). The perception of consistency in attitudes. *Journal of Experimental Social Psychology, 9*, 491–501.

Goffman, E. (1959). *The presentation of self in everyday life.* Garden City, NY: Doubleday.

Greenwald, A. G. (1980). The totalitarian ego: Fabrication and revision of personal history. *American Psychologist, 35*, 603–618.

Hills, P. J., & Potter, F. W. (1979). Group counselling and study skills. In P. J. Hills (Ed.), *Study courses and counselling: Problems and possibilities.* Surrey, England: Society for Research into Higher Education, Guilford.

Isen, A. M., Shalker, T. E., Clark, M., & Karp, L. (1978). Affect, accessibility of material in memory, and behavior: A cognitive loop? *Journal of Personality and Social Psychology, 36*, 1–12.

James, W. (1950). *The principles of psychology.* New York: Holt. (Original work published 1890)

Kiesler, C. A. (1971). *The psychology of commitment: Experiments linking behavior to belief.* New York: Academic Press.

Lindsay, P. H., & Norman, D. A. (1972). *Human information processing: An introduction to psychology.* New York: Academic Press.

Lydon, J., Zanna, M. P., & Ross, M. (1983, June). *The effects of behavior recall on the persistence of attitude change.* Paper presented at the convention of the Canadian Psychological Association, Winnipeg.

Main, A. (1980). *Encouraging effective learning.* Edinburgh: Scottish Academic Press.

Markus, H., & Nurius, P. (1984). *Possible selves.* Unpublished manuscript, University of Michigan.

McFarland, C., & Ross, M. (1984). *The effect of changes in impressions of self and others on recollections of the past.* Unpublished manuscript, University of Waterloo.

Mead, G. H. (1934). *Mind, self and society.* Chicago: University of Chicago Press.

Miller, D. T., & Ross, M. (1975). Self-serving biases in the attribution of causality: Fact or fiction? *Psychological Bulletin, 82,* 213–225.

Mischel, W., Ebbesen, E. B., & Zeiss, A. M. (1976). Determinants of selective memory about the self. *Journal of Consulting and Clinical Psychology, 1,* 92–103.

Mischel, W., & Peake, P. K. (1982). Beyond déjà vu in the search for cross-situational consistency. *Psychological Review, 89,* 730–755.

Nisbett, R. E., & Ross, L. (1980). *Human inference: Strategies and shortcomings of social judgment.* Englewood Cliffs, NJ: Prentice-Hall.

Nisbett, R. E., & Wilson, T. D. (1977). Telling more than we can know: Verbal reports on mental processes. *Psychological Review, 84,* 231–259.

Nowell-Smith, P. H. (1970). Historical explanation. In H. E. Kiefer & M. K. Muritz (Eds.), *Mind, science and history.* Albany: State University of New York Press.

Olson, J. M., & Cal, A. V. (1984). Source credibility, attitude and the recall of past behaviours. *European Journal of Social Psychology, 14,* 203–210.

Polivy, J., & Herman, C. P. (1983). *Breaking the diet habit.* New York: Basic Books.

Ross, M., & Fletcher, G. J. O. (in press). Attribution and social perception. In G. Lindzey & E. Aronson (Eds.), *Handbook of social psychology* (3d ed.). Reading, MA: Addison-Wesley.

Ross, M., McFarland, C., Conway, M., & Zanna, M. P. (1983). Reciprocal relation between attitudes and behavior recall: Committing people to newly formed attitudes. *Journal of Personality and Social Psychology, 45,* 257–267.

Ross, M., McFarland, C., & Fletcher, G. J. O. (1981). The effect of attitude on the recall of personal histories. *Journal of Personality and Social Psychology, 10,* 627–634.

Ross, M., & Olson, J. M. (1981). An expectancy-attribution model of the effects of placebos. *Psychological Review, 88,* 408–437.

Ross, M., & Olson, J. M. (1982). Placebo effects in medical research and practice. In J. R. Eiser (Ed.), *Social psychology and behavioral medicine.* New York: Wiley.

Ross, M., & Shulman, R. F. (1973). Increasing the salience of initial attitudes: Dissonance versus self-perception theory. *Journal of Personality and Social Psychology, 28,* 138–144.

Rothbaum, F. (1983). Aging and age stereotypes. *Social Cognition, 2,* 171–184.

Salancik, G. R., & Conway, M. (1975). Attitude inferences from salient and relevant cognitive content about behavior. *Journal of Personality and Social Psychology, 32,* 829–840.

Schachter, S. (1982). Recidivism and self-cure of smoking and obesity. *American Psychologist, 37,* 436–444.

Schneider, D. J. (1973). Implicit personality theory: A review. *Psychological Bulletin, 79,* 294–309.

Snyder, M., & White, P. (1982). Moods and memories: Elation, depression, and the remembering of the events of one's life. *Journal of Personality, 50,* 149–167.

Sulloway, F. J. (1979). *Freud, biologist of the mind.* New York: Basic Books.

Taylor, S. E. (1983). Adjustment to threatening events: A theory of cognitive adaptation. *American Psychologist, 38,* 1161–1173.

Taylor, S. E., & Crocker, J. (1981). Schematic bases of social information processing. In E. T. Higgins, C. P. Herman, & M. P. Zanna (Eds.), *Social cognition: The Ontario Symposium* (Vol. 1). Hillsdale, NJ: Erlbaum.

Tedeschi, J. T., Schlenker, B. R., & Bonoma, T. V. (1971). Cognitive dissonance: Private ratiocination or public spectacle. *American Psychologist, 26,* 685–695.

Tetlock, P. E., & Levi, A. (1982). Attribution bias: On the inconclusiveness of the cognition-motivation debate. *Journal of Experimental Social Psychology, 18*, 68–88.

Wicker, A. W. (1969). Attitudes versus actions: The relationship of verbal and overt behavioral responses to attitude objects. *Journal of Social Issues, 25*, 41–78.

Wright, J., & Mischel, W. (1982). Influence of affect on cognitive social learning person variables. *Journal of Personality and Social Psychology, 5*, 901–914.

Yarrow, M., Campbell, J. D., & Burton, R. V. (1970). Recollections of childhood: A study of the retrospetive method. *Monographs of the Society for Research in Child Development, 35*, (5).

CHAPTER 6

Motivational Facets of the Self

STEVEN J. BRECKLER
Johns Hopkins University

ANTHONY G. GREENWALD
Ohio State University

Self-evaluation is a potent energizer of human activity. Behavior can be variably directed at pleasing other people, pleasing oneself, or satisfying the goals, norms, and expectations of important reference groups. In this chapter, we focus on this important, persisting task of achieving a significant audience's favorable evaluation. Central to this treatment is an approach called *ego-task analysis*, which offers a general framework for analyzing the interaction of situation and personality in determining behavior. A review of the literature on ego-involvement leads to the identification of three significant evaluative audiences: public, private, and collective. The associated motivational facets of the self are then related to research and theory on social influence, self-awareness/self-consciousness, self-presentation, and self-esteem.

EGO-TASK ANALYSIS: AN INTRODUCTION

Greenwald (1982a) introduced ego-task analysis to integrate the large literature on ego-involvement (Allport, 1943; Sherif & Cantril, 1947; Sherif, Sherif, & Nebergall, 1965) with more recent work on self-awareness theory (Buss, 1980; Duval & Wickland, 1972; Scheier & Carver, 1983). The difficulty of that task became apparent when the review led to the identification of three distinct meanings of ego-involvement, each deriving from a different theoretical tradition. The three meanings of ego-involvement nevertheless share a common theme—self-evaluation. They differ primarily in the source identified for the standard of evaluation—other people, oneself, or one's reference groups.

Three Conceptions of Ego-Involvement

In one sense, ego-involvement refers to a concern about one's public impression, or evaluation by others. This sense of ego-involvement is similar to evaluation apprehension (Rosenberg, 1969) and approval motivation (Crowne & Marlowe, 1964). It is the type of ego-involvement that becomes engaged when subjects in a psychology experiment are instructed that performance in the experimental task reflects a valued, socially desirable skill (e.g., intelligence).

In a second sense, ego-involvement refers to a concern about one's self-evaluation, or private self-image. This second sense is similar to self-esteem maintenance and achievement motivation (McClelland, Atkinson, Clark, & Lowell, 1953). This type of ego-involvement occurs when a subject compares task performance to a personal standard of achievement. In this second sense of ego-involvement, the evaluator is oneself rather than others.

A third usage of ego-involvement originated in the work of Sherif and Cantril (1947), who wrote that "all attitudes that define a person's status or that give him some relative role with respect to other individuals, groups, or institutions are ego-involved" (p. 96). Those other individuals and groups are reference groups, which include "those groups to which the individual relates himself as a part or to which he aspires to relate himself psychologically" (Sherif, 1956, p. 175).

The Concept of Ego Task

In day-to-day activity, people are faced with a variety of tasks to accomplish. These can range from the relatively mundane tasks of mailing a letter or opening a door to relatively important tasks, such as giving a public presentation or taking an exam. Among the most important tasks are the ones that become engaged under the various conditions of ego-involvement. These are the tasks of establishing one's self-worth by achieving a significant audience's favorable evaluation. We shall call these very important tasks *ego tasks*. Ego-task goals—that is, achieving favorable self-evaluations—take precedence over the goals of most other tasks. Unlike most other tasks, however, obtaining the goal does not end an ego task; the goal continues to be important.

Ego-Task Analysis

Ego tasks, like most tasks, have two components. One is a cognitive representation of what is to be accomplished—the task goal. The other includes strategies for achieving the goal. The goal component is determined jointly by incentives in the situation and by the person's goal preferences. Similarly, the strategy component is influenced both by the situation and by personal preferences among strategies. Thus, ego-task analysis offers a general framework for analyzing the interaction of situation and personality in determining behavior (Greenwald, 1982a; see also Magnusson & Endler, 1977).

Ego-task analysis can be illustrated by considering the task of achieving parental approval. Two goals may satisfy this task—gaining verbal praise or receiving a monetary reward. One *situational* determinant of the goal is the presence of another. For example, verbal praise may be the desired goal when a sibling has just been similarly complemented. Alternatively, one may have a *personal* preference for monetary rewards. Strategies can likewise be determined by situational influences, such as by modeling a sibling's successful approach.

TABLE 6.1 Interrelationships of Facets of the Self, Ego Tasks, Personality Measures, Experimental Procedures, and Performance Strategies

	Facets of the Self			
	Diffuse Self	*Public Self*	*Private Self*	*Collective Self*
Ego-task designation	Hedonic satisfaction	Social accreditation, self-definition	Individual achievement	Collective achievement
Basis for self-evaluation	Attainment of positive affect	Approval of others (outer audience)	Internal standards (inner audience)	Internalized goals of reference group
Individual-difference measures of task orientation		Public self-consciousness, need for approval, high self-monitoring	Private self-consciousness, need for achievement, low self-monitoring	
Situational inducers of task orientation	Anonymity in group; drug intoxication	Minority status in groups, solo before audience, camera, public failure	Privacy, exposure to performance replay, mirror, private failure	Reference group salience, cohesive group, superordinate goals
Strategies in service of task	Norm violation	Conformity, obedience, opinion moderation, basking in reflected glory	Independence, defiance, opinion resistance	Cooperation in group endeavors

Strategies can also be determined by personal preferences among the available alternatives (for example, getting praise by doing a favor rather than by asking for it).

FOUR MOTIVATIONAL FACETS OF THE SELF

The three ego tasks, as identified in the three meanings of ego-involvement, can be placed within a larger context that considers four motivational *facets* of the self (cf. Greenwald & Breckler, 1985; Greenwald & Pratkanis, 1984). Table 6.1 summarizes these facets of the self—the diffuse, public, private, and collective facets—within the ego-task analysis framework. The second, third, and fourth facets of the self each correspond to one of the meanings of ego-involvement described earlier. The first facet represents a more primitive aspect of the self.

The Diffuse Self

The diffuse facet of the self is a very primitive self. It is a condition of not distinguishing sharply between self and others. Behavior is simply guided toward positive affective states. The task of the diffuse self can be called hedonic satisfaction, which is not properly an ego task because it does not presuppose a sense of self. Identification of the diffuse self proves useful, however, in considering past analyses of ego development and in resolving a paradox in treatments of deindividuation (see later discussion).

The Public Self

The public facet of the self can be associated with the first of the three meanings of ego-involvement. The public self is sensitive to the evaluations of significant others (e.g., parents and authorities) and seeks to win their approval. The ego task of the public self can be described, in part, as social accreditation—that is, earning credit in exchange relationships with others. This facet of the self is the one most commonly identified in treatments of self-presentation (e.g., Goffman, 1959) and impression management (Schlenker, 1980). The public self was recognized by James (1890) in his description of the social self, which includes "an innate propensity to get ourselves noticed, and noticed favorably, by our kind" (p. 293).

The Private Self

The private facet of the self can be identified with the second meaning of ego-involvement. The private self's ego task is individual achievement. The term "achievement" is used, in the sense of McClelland *et al.* (1953), to indicate guidance by internal standards. By providing an inner audience for behavior, the private self permits self-evaluation to be effected in the absence of others.

The Collective Self

The collective self is the *we* facet of the self; it can be identified with the third meaning of ego-involvement. Its ego task is collective achievement—that is, achieving the goals of and fulfilling one's role in a reference group. Typical reference groups include co-workers, religious organizations, clubs, athletic teams, and family.

The relationship between the self and the other people who provide the basis for self-evaluation is central to the distinction between the public and collective facets of the self. The public self seeks to win the approval of specific others, especially those who control rewards and other reinforcements (e.g., parents or teachers). In satisfying this ego task, however, the public self cannot be assumed to adopt the values, norms, or attitudes of those others. The collective self, in contrast, does adopt the values of others; it seeks to achieve the goals of reference groups, as internalized by the person (cf. Sherif & Sherif, 1964).

Facets of the Self in Ego Development

The four motivational facets of the self are assumed to develop in the left-to-right order of Table 6.1. The diffuse self is best thought of as a preself. The public self depends on development of a cognitive discrimination between self and others and an ability to attend to those aspects of one's behavior that are also noticed by others. An important aspect of the public self's ego task is to internalize the evaluative standards of others, which leads to development of the private self. The collective self represents a further developmental step in which the goals of reference groups have become internalized. This proposed developmental sequence has support in several analyses by developmental theorists, which we review here very briefly.

The Diffuse Self

In summarizing the mental development of the child, Piaget (1964/1967) noted that "at the outset of mental evolution there is no definite differentiation between the self and the external world" (p. 12). The neonate's behavior is guided largely toward the satisfaction of certain hedonic impulses (e.g., to eat and to sleep). Loevinger (1976) similarly identified the initial stage of ego development (the "presocial" stage) as one in which the infant is unable to differentiate self from the outer world.

The Public Self

The first real sense of self begins to emerge when the child is able to distinguish self from others. As Piaget (1964/1967) noted, "the young child must cope not only with the physical universe . . . but also with two new and closely allied worlds: the social world and the world of inner representations" (p. 18). The public self also has a correspondence in what Loevinger (1976) has identified as the "conformist" stage in ego development. As the label implies, the conformist stage is marked by conformity to external rules, with conscious preoccupations centering on appearance and social acceptability.

The Private Self

As the self develops, an internalization of the evaluative standards of others begins to occur. Piaget (1964/1967) articulated this internalization process as "the general rule that one always ends by applying to oneself behavior acquired from others" (pp. 40–41). The private self is also seen in the "conscientious" stage of ego development (Loevinger, 1976). At this stage, "the major elements of an adult conscience are present [including] long-term, self-evaluated goals and ideals, differentiated self-criticism, and a sense of responsibility" (p. 20). The individual achievement orientation of the private self is especially evident at this stage, where "achievement . . . is measured primarily by [one's] own standards, rather than mainly by recognition or by competitive advantage, as at lower levels" (p. 21).

The Collective Self

Primarily the product of socialization experiences, the collective self represents an internalization of the goals, norms, and expectations of important reference groups. In discussing the socialization of behavior, Piaget (1964/1967) noted that "among the older children there is progress in two directions: individual concentration when the subject is working by himself and effective collaboration in the group" (p. 39). The former direction of progress reflects the developing private self, whereas the latter represents the emergence of a collective self. In Piaget's treatment, however, it is not until the further developmental stages that mark adolescence that the collective facet of the self fully develops (see also Piaget, 1932/1965). Analyses of altruism (a form of collective behavior) also support the proposition that the collective self represents a relatively mature stage of ego development (Cialdini, Baumann, & Kenrick, 1981; Froming, Allen, & Jensen, in press).

Facets of the Self in Social Influence

Three facets of the self (the public, private, and collective facets) have a direct correspondence to Kelman's (1961) analysis of social influence. Kelman identified three processes of social influence: compliance, internalization, and identification. *Compliance* occurs when another's influence is accepted "to achieve a favorable reaction from the other" (p. 62). *Internalization* occurs "because the induced behavior is congruent with [one's] value system" (p. 65). Finally, *identification* reflects behavior that is adopted because it satisfies "a role relationship that forms a part of the person's self-image" (p. 63).

The correspondence between Kelman's analysis and the present ego-task formulation is shown in Table 6.2, where parallels are drawn between compliance and the public facet, between internalization and the private facet, and between identification and the collective facet of self. It can be seen from Table 6.2 that the primary concern of the person being influenced corresponds directly to an ego task's basis for self-evaluation (see Table 6.1). Two important points follow from the Table 6.2 summary. First, it implies that no one of the three methods of social influence is generally most effective; rather, each can be effective with the appropriate combination of situation and influence target. Second, it suggests a

TABLE 6.2   Facets of the Self in Social Influence

	Compliance	*Internalization*	*Identification*
Facet of the self	Public	Private	Collective
Type of effective influencer	Powerful, uses rewards and punishments	Expert, trustworthy	Attractive, members of a reference group
Conditions under which influence is lost	Influencer is absent or loses power	Exposure to more expert influence	Influencer loses attractiveness or changes influence
Primary concern of influencee	Obtaining reward or approval, avoiding punishment	Justifying belief or action in terms of internalized principles, being correct	Maintaining identification with reference group (or person)

Note: This table is an application of the facets-of-the-self analysis to the theorization of Kelman (1961).

basis for describing individual differences in susceptibility to the three types of influence. For example, compliance may be most effective when one's primary concern is to win favorable evaluations from other persons. However, internalization may be the more effective type of social influence for those who dispositionally strive toward achieving private goals and standards.

The Paradox of Deindividuation

"Deindividuation" refers to a condition in which one's individual identifiability is decreased and internal constraints against various types of action are reduced. In summarizing previous reviews (Diener, 1977, 1980; Dipboye, 1977), Greenwald (1982b) noted the following paradoxical aspects of deindividuation:

> Deindividuation is sometimes associated with loss of identity but other times with acquisition of identity via a distinctive group (of which one is an indistinguishable member); it is sometimes sought but other times avoided; and it is sometimes associated with chaotic, norm-violating behavior but other times with conforming, uniform behavior. (p. 172)

The distinction between the diffuse and collective facets of the self can help resolve this paradox. All deindividuating conditions reduce the salience of internal standards. These conditions include anonymity in a group, alcohol or drug intoxication, and strong, unstructured stimulation. However, some situations can make the subject's participation in a reference group salient—for example, being amidst a shouting crowd of home-team supporters at a football game or wearing a uniform that hides one's individual features while making one's group affiliation apparent. Deindividuating procedures that make a reference group salient can engage the collective self, leading to coordinated or norm-adhering behavior. This is to be contrasted to nonsocial conditions that fail to engage any of the developed, or socialized, facets of the self and that can lead to social chaos or norm-violating behavior. Greenwald (1982b) suggested that the term "sociation" be applied to the former effects of social situations that elicit coordinated, norm-adhering behavior—ones that (in present terms) invoke the collective self. The term "deindividuation" should be restricted to the effects of nonsocial procedures that elicit norm-violating behavior—ones that, by suppressing the public, private, and collective selves, effectively invoke the diffuse self.

ACHIEVING EGO-TASK GOALS

Different strategies are specially suited for achieving the goals of different ego tasks. The goal of the public self's ego task is to win the approval of other persons. This is most often accomplished by conforming to the expectations, requests, or actions of high-status others or by affiliating with another's success. The goal of the private self's ego task is to meet one's personal standards of achievement. This can be done, for example, by acting on the basis of one's own perceptions rather than on the basis of what others desire. Finally, achieving the internalized goals of a reference group (the collective self's ego task) can be accomplished by cooperating in group endeavors or by behaving in accordance with a reference group's norms and expectations.

Of course, many everyday achievements serve two or more ego tasks simultaneously. For example, winning a job promotion, earning a college degree, and raising children are achievements that simultaneously earn the approval of others, achieve success by personal standards, and fulfill a reference group's goals. Indeed, these may be such strongly satisfying experiences precisely because they serve the interests of a public self, a private self, and a collective self, all at the same time.

An Illustration of Ego-Task Strategies: The Conformity Experiment

Asch's (1951, 1956) classic conformity experiment can help illustrate the various strategies used to achieve ego-task goals. The subject's explicit task in the conformity experiment is to judge line lengths. However, there are also some implicit tasks, such as completing requirements for a psychology course, learning about laboratory research in psychology, or trying to achieve a favorable evaluation by the experimenter.

Neither the explicit task nor any of the implicit tasks of the conformity experiment poses a problem to the subject until the first critical trial. It is at that point that each of the experimenter's confederates gives a blatantly incorrect response. It then becomes the subject's turn to respond. There are three important audiences present, and the subject cannot choose a strategy that will please all three. One audience is the experimenter. A second audience is the group of which the subject is a part; to achieve the goal of this group, there should be consensus among all group members. The remaining audience is the inner audience, which can be pleased only by independence (i.e., by the subject's rejecting the obviously incorrect majority judgment).

The power of the conformity experiment, in ego-task analysis terms, is its simultaneous evocation of at least two different ego tasks. That is, the ego task of pleasing other people is in direct conflict with the individual-achievement ego task of pleasing oneself. Deciding whether to conform or to act independently in the face of this conflict is left to the subject's relative predispositions to please one or another audience.

The Concept of Ego-Task Orientation

Almost every adolescent or adult should have some tendency to perform each of the four ego tasks. Nevertheless, for any given person or situation, some ego tasks may be more important than others. The relative importance of an ego task can be referred to as the strength of *orientation* toward that task. Consistent with the framework of ego-task analysis, ego-task orientations can vary as a function of both situational influences and personality differences.

Results from Asch's (1951, 1956) conformity experiment can help illustrate the concept of ego-task orientation. The conformity effect—that is, agreeing with an incorrect unanimous majority—is sensitive to several situational variables. The conformity effect depends, importantly, on the presence of incorrect and unanimous others. Control subjects, who make their judgments in the absence of others, are correct on virtually every trial. Asch also found that allowing subjects to record their judgments privately (compared to the public announcement of judgments in the original experiment) substantially increases independence (Asch, 1956). These effects demonstrate the extent to which subjects' judgments can be made to please different evaluative audiences under different situational constraints.

Asch (1956) also observed systematic individual differences in the conformity experiment: "There were completely independent subjects, and there were others who went over to the majority without exception" (p. 11). It is interesting to examine subjects' explanations for their behavior. One subject was "concerned over what his judgments might do to the experimenter's results" (p. 39). This subject said, "I wanted to conform. Was picturing in my mind the graph of results with a big dip in it—I wanted to make your results better" (p. 40). This subject appears to have been oriented toward the social-accreditation ego task of the public self. Independent subjects (those who yielded on two or fewer trials) seemed very much aware that they were going against a majority, but they also recognized "the importance of thinking for oneself and being an individual" (p. 36). Thus, independent subjects can be identified as those who were oriented toward the individual-achievement ego task of the private self. Finally, many yielders were characterized as "trying desperately to merge in the group in order not to appear peculiar" (p. 45). This strategy is consistent with the ego tasks of the public self and of the collective self.

Asch's (1956) qualitative analyses emphasize the point that people differ considerably in their orientations toward engaging in the ego tasks of the public, private, and collective selves as a function of both situational influences and personality differences. We now consider, in more detail, research demonstrating situational and dispositional sources of influence, especially for the ego-task orientations of the public and private selves.

Situational Determinants of Ego-Task Orientation

Situations vary in the opportunity they provide to evoke the various ego-task orientations. The diffuse self can be engaged by drug intoxication, by isolation, or by anonymity in a group. Concern over one's public self is likely to be engaged when admired or socially powerful others are present. The individual-achievement task (private self) may be engaged most readily when the subject is alone. In contrast, collective achievement should be engaged by the (actual or symbolic) presence of an important reference group, such as by suggesting to subjects that their performances will be compared with those of other racial, religious, or ethnic groups or with students from rival schools.

Mirrors and Cameras

Two general procedures for inducing the ego tasks of the public and private selves correspond to procedures suggested by Buss (1980) for inducing public and private self-awareness, respectively. A camera implies the existence of an audience of others and is therefore assumed to engage the public self's ego task. Consistent with this interpretation, the presence of a camera has been shown to increase susceptibility to conformity pressure (Duval, 1976), a strategy in the service of the public self's ego task. The presence of a mirror—especially a small one, according to Buss (1980)—calls one's actions to the attention of the inner audience, thereby evoking the private self's individual-achievement ego task. In support of this prediction, the presence of a small mirror has been shown to increase resistance to persuasion (Carver, 1977), which reflects an ego-task strategy of the private self.

Public and Private Responding

When an experimental task requires that a subject make public responses, the ego task of the public self is made salient. In contrast, private and anonymous reporting conditions should evoke the private self's ego task. A study of the effects of public versus private responding on anticipatory attitude change supports the ego-task analysis predictions (McFarland, Ross, & Conway, 1984). An anticipatory change in attitude occurs when an individual's attitude shifts in the direction of an anticipated, but not yet received, persuasive appeal. One explanation for this effect is that the change reflects a self-presentational effort to avoid appearing gullible or easily persuaded. Indeed, when subjects are informed that they will not be receiving the anticipated message, their attitudes "snap back" to the original position (Cialdini, Herman, Levy, Kozlowski, & Petty, 1976). McFarland *et al.* (1984) demonstrated, however, that this self-presentational tactic (an ego-task strategy of the public self) occurs only under *public* reporting conditions. Under *private* reporting conditions, anticipatory changes in attitude persist, suggesting some kind of self-persuasion process.

Personal Importance

Experimental tasks can be manipulated so that they are more or less personally relevant to a subject. For example, evaluating a proposal that advocates the adoption of senior comprehensive exams can be very "involving" if the exams are being proposed for immediate adoption at the subject's own school, but less involving if they are proposed for another school or for a later date. Brickner, Harkins, and Ostrom (in press) used this manipulation to study effort expenditure on a group task. Earlier research (Latané, Williams, & Harkins, 1979) had shown that subjects generally work harder at group tasks when their individual efforts are identifiable than when they are not. One interpretation of this "social loafing" effect is that the public self's ego task becomes engaged only when one's output can be identified. By making the task personally important, however, Brickner *et al.* (in press) were able to eliminate the social loafing effect (see also Harkins & Petty, 1982). The involvement manipulation presumably invoked the private self's ego task, effectively making private standards more salient than social ones.

Individual Differences in Ego-Task Orientation

Just as situations vary in their ability to evoke the various ego tasks, people vary in their relative predispositions to engage in each of the four ego tasks. Although no measures have yet been developed to assess individual differences in the four ego-task orientations, various existing measures may be useful for this purpose, at least in regard to the ego-task orientations of the public and private facets of the self. These existing, related measures are public and private self-consciousness, self-monitoring, achievement motivation, and approval motivation.

Public and Private Self-Consciousness

Fenigstein, Scheier, and Buss (1975) developed scales that measure consciousness of the public and private facets of the self. They define the public self as consisting of observable self-produced stimuli, such as physique, clothing, grooming, facial expression, and speech. The private self consists of self-produced stimuli that are not publicly observable, such as internal bodily sensations, feelings, thoughts, and self-evaluations (see also Buss, 1980). Fenigstein *et al.* (1975) interpreted public and private self-consciousness as a difference in *focus of attention*, which can be directed toward the public or private self. In contrast, ego-task analysis makes *evaluative orientation* toward outer versus inner audiences central to the public versus private distinction. Nevertheless, these two analyses overlap substantially in their empirical implications, because people concerned about evaluations of others should be attentive to the signals they transmit to those others. Likewise, people guided by internalized evaluative standards should be relatively attentive to their private thoughts and feelings.

Opinion moderation in anticipation of a discussion (i.e., anticipatory change in the direction of possible opposition) can be regarded as a self-presentational strategy of the public self's ego task. Consistent with this interpretation, Scheier (1980) found that such anticipatory change was greater for subjects high in public self-consciousness than for those low in public self-consciousness. Likewise, expression of opinion change in front of an experimenter who has just administered a counterattitudinal role-playing procedure can be interpreted as an impression-management strategy of maintaining consistency. It follows that such opinion change should be associated with high scores on public self-consciousness, as was found by Scheier and Carver (1980).

The private self should resist the opinion-change effects of a public counterattitudinal role-playing induction. In support of this prediction, opinion resistance to counterattitudinal role playing was associated with high scores on private self-consciousness (Scheier & Carver, 1980). Similarly, subjects high in private self-consciousness are more likely to resist group pressure than are those low in private self-consciousness (Froming & Carver, 1981).

Self-Monitoring

Snyder's (1974) self-monitoring scale provides a measure that relates to the motivational orientations of the public and private facets of the self. The person high in self-monitoring is one who is particularly sensitive to cues transmitted in social interaction, and who uses these cues to guide self-presentations (Snyder, 1979). This description is suggestive of the outer-audience orientation of the public self. In contrast, Snyder and Campbell (1982) describe the low self-monitor as a "principled self." The self-presentations of low self-monitors are "controlled from within by their affective states and attitudes . . . rather than molded and tailored to fit the situation" (Snyder, 1974, p. 89). This suggests that the low self-monitor's concern is primarily with the private facet of the self.

Achievement Motivation

The concept of achievement motivation was developed by McClelland *et al.* (1953) to describe individual variations in motivation to succeed in intellectual and social endeavors. Success in such endeavors was defined as the surpassing of *internal* standards of excellence. The concept of achievement motivation is therefore similar to the individual-achievement ego task of the private self. (Indeed, the ego task of the private self was given the "achievement" label in consideration of McClelland *et al.*'s definition of achievement motivation.) If achievement motivation is indicative of a general orientation toward an inner audience, then subjects high in achievement motivation should, like those high in private self-consciousness, be resistant to group pressure. McClelland *et al.* (1953) reanalyzed the data from a subset of subjects in Asch's (1956) conformity experiment. Of the subjects classified as high in achievement motivation, 87% were "independents." In contrast, 87% of the subjects low in achievement motivation were "yielders." McClelland *et al.* concluded that subjects who are high in achievement motivation "show courageous independence when under social pressure to conform" (p. 287).

Approval Motivation

The Social Desirability Scale was developed by Crowne and Marlowe (1964) as a measure of approval motivation, which was defined as concern about evaluation by others. This suggests that the Social Desirability Scale might serve as a measure of the ego-task orientation of the public self. Consistent with this interpretation, Strickland and Crowne (1962) reported that subjects scoring high on the Social Desirability Scale (that is, those classified as high in approval motivation) were most responsive to a social influence attempt.

FACETS OF THE SELF AND SELF-PRESENTATIONS

Identifying the public self's ego task with such concepts as approval motivation and social accreditation suggests that it is this facet of the self that is involved in self-presentation (Goffman, 1959) or impression-management (Schlenker, 1980) processes. Several theoretical treatments confirm that an outer audience is conceived as the target for self-presentations or managed impressions. For example, Goffman (1959) noted that "when an individual appears in the presence of others, there will usually be some reason for him to mobilize his activity so that it will convey an impression to others which it is in his interests to convey" (p. 4). Similarly, Jones and Pittman (1982) defined strategic self-presentation as "those features of behavior . . . designed to elicit or shape others' attributions of the actor's dispositions" (p. 233). Baumeister (1982) considered self-presentations to be "aimed at establishing . . . an image of the individual in the minds of others" (p. 3), and Arkin (1980) stated that "people often behave in ways that will create a certain impression on others; social psychologists refer to this phenomenon as *self-presentation*" (p. 158).

To Whom Is the Self Presented?

As the foregoing quotations indicate, the prevalent answer to this question has been that self-presentations are targeted at an audience of other persons. Ego-task analysis offers the alternative view, however, that the self can be presented to *multiple audiences*. These audiences include, in addition to the outer audience, an inner audience (oneself) and a reference group audience. Thus, one can "play to the audience within" just as one can "play to the audience without" (Snyder, Higgins, & Stucky, 1983; see also Schlenker, 1980; Weary & Arkin, 1981).

Are Favorable Self-Presentations Genuinely Believed?

Terms such as "self-presentation" and "impression management" carry with them at least an implicit assumption that people typically harbor, inwardly, a less worthy being that they hope to prevent others from discovering. The self-presenter is an actor whose part is to create the most favorable impression possible. In his dramaturgical approach, Goffman (1959) states that the presenter "must offer a show of intellectual and emotional involvement in the activity he is presenting, but must keep himself from actually being carried away by his own show" (p. 216). It would seem, then, that the self-presenter is really a *mis*presenter.

Even though the self may often be presented in ways that appear too good to be true, several lines of research evidence indicate that these favorable self-presentations are genuinely believed by their presenters. First, people *ordinarily* perceive themselves as being successful in achieving personal goals, including those of ego tasks (Greenwald, 1980; Greenwald & Breckler, 1985). Second, self-enhancement occurs under private reporting conditions in which subjects should have little reason to mispresent themselves (Arkin, Appleman, & Burger, 1980; Frey, 1978; Greenberg, Pyszczynski, & Solomon, 1982; Schlenker, Hallam, & McCown, 1983; Weary, Harvey, Schwieger, Olson, Perloff, & Pritchard, 1982). Third, subjects make self-enhancing judgments even when they are convinced that dishonest judgments can be detected (Riess, Rosenfeld, Melburg, & Tedeschi, 1981; Stults, Messé, & Kerr, 1984). Finally, favorable self-judgments are often made more quickly than unfavorable ones (Breckler & Greenwald, 1981), suggesting that favorable self-relevant judgments are faithful reports from self-knowledge (cf. Markus, 1977; Rogers, Kuiper, & Kirker, 1981).

SELF-ESTEEM: VARIATIONS IN EXPECTED SUCCESS AT EGO TASKS

A person may strongly wish to impress others but may nevertheless expect to make a poor impression. This person can be described as being oriented toward the social-accreditation ego task of the public self but as having a low expectation of success. Likewise, a person may expect to fall short in achieving reference group goals and expectations. Variations in expected success at the ego tasks of the public, private, and collective selves constitute important individual differences in the level of, and basis for, a sense of self-worth, or self-esteem.

Public Self-Esteem Versus Private Self-Esteem

Ego-task analysis indicates the desirability of having separate measures for public self-esteem (expected success at social accreditation) and private self-esteem (expected success at individual achievement). A recent analysis of socially desirable responding supports the utility of distinguishing between these two varieties of self-esteem. Paulhus (1984) has identified two components associated with favorable self-descriptions. One component reflects favorable self-evaluations that are genuinely believed (a "self-deception" factor), and the other component corresponds to favorable self-evaluations intended to impress others (an "impression-management" factor). It is interesting that scores on the self-deception factor (private self-esteem) do not vary under public and private reporting conditions, whereas scores on the impression-management factor (public self-esteem) do (Paulhus, 1984). These results are consistent with the expectations of ego-task analysis (see also Tesser & Paulhus, 1983).

Ambiguity of Self-Esteem Measures

There are many measures of self-esteem (see Wylie, 1974). Examination of the items in most self-esteem scales, however, suggests that they measure a global self-esteem that mixes expected success at the ego tasks of both the public self and the private self. Among these global measures is the Janis-Field scale (Hovland & Janis, 1959), which includes several items that refer to expected evaluation by outer audiences (e.g., "How often are you troubled with shyness?" and "Do you find it hard to make talk when you meet new people?") as well as items that refer to evaluation by the inner audience (e.g., "Do you ever feel so discouraged with yourself that you wonder whether anything is worthwhile?"). Among existing measures, Rosenberg's (1965) scale is one that appears to include almost exclusively items that measure private self-esteem (e.g., "I feel I have a number of good qualities"), and Fenigstein et al.'s (1975) measure of social anxiety appears to focus well on public self-esteem (e.g., "I don't find it hard to talk to strangers"). No existing measures of which we are aware focus on expected success in achieving reference group goals; that is, there are no measures of what might be called collective self-esteem.

CONCLUSION: REMAINING TASKS

The results reviewed in this chapter provide substantial support for the classification of ego tasks in Table 6.1. However, it is difficult to evaluate the extent to which our review has focused selectively on supportive evidence. Accordingly, the claim that ego-task analysis provides a successful framework for analyzing person–situation interactions must depend on its success in stimulating and explaining further research, which we can foresee in the following problems.

Motivating Subjects in Psychology Experiments

In her research on memory for finished and unfinished tasks, Zeigarnik (1938) provided a clear, if controversial, illustration of how ego-task analysis principles can be used to motivate subjects in psychology experiments:

> Three "types" of subjects could be distinguished. The first were those who sought to perform as instructed because they wished to please the experimenter. Another, the ambitious type, strove to excel as if in competition with others. The third type was interested in the task for its own sake and sought to solve each problem in the way the problem itself demanded. In keeping with these differences the experimenter did not preserve a fixed mien and method with all subjects. Those of the first type were allowed to see the experimenter's pleasure when a task was well done. Work done by the second group was inspected with the air of an examiner, while the third group was allowed to work unmolested, the experimenter in this case remaining passive. (p. 303)

Contemporary students of experimental social psychology are taught, of course, to avoid the techniques used by Zeigarnik to motivate her subjects. Nevertheless, it is generally desirable to get subjects "involved" in experimental tasks. Carlsmith, Ellsworth, and Aronson (1976) refer to this as *experimental realism*. Similarly, Weber and Cook (1972) suggest that treatments "should have enough impact that subjects become absorbed in them" (p. 292). If the goal of experimental realism is to motivate as many subjects as possible, then procedures that evoke multiple ego tasks should be used. Doing so will not ordinarily pose a threat to validity so long as the evoked ego task is not one that is postulated as mediating the effect (Weber & Cook, 1972).

Applications to Research on Persuasion and Social Influence

Three facets of the self were related (in Table 6.2) to the social-influence processes of compliance, internalization, and identification (Kelman, 1961). One implication of that analysis was its suggestion of individual differences in susceptibility to the three types of influence. Thus, social pressure (compliance) techniques may be most effective for people who have a relatively strong predisposition to engage in the social-accreditation ego task of the public self; rationally based (internalization) appeals may work best for those who are oriented toward the individual-achievement ego task; and modeling by an admired other or appeals based on reference group values (identification) may be optimal for collectively oriented persons. Likewise, as Kelman has already observed, situations should vary in supporting the three processes of social influence. For example, compliance will be effective only so long as socially powerful others are present. Influence that must persist during the absence of others, however, would better be achieved through internalization or identification.

Research on Collective-Achievement Ego Tasks

There is no doubt that collective efforts are important in political, industrial, scientific, and even recreational endeavors. It is therefore disheartening to observe that little recent effort has been directed to the study of collective performance. Social psychologists have largely failed to follow the lead of early reference group theorists (e.g., Merton, 1957; Newcomb, 1943; Sherif & Sherif, 1964; Sumner, 1906; Whyte, 1981) or of Sherif and Cantril (1947), who *defined* ego-involvement as concern with the goals of reference groups. One explanation for this recent lack of effort may be that few persons attach importance to collective endeavors (cf. Latané *et al.*, 1979). It may also be, as suggested by Sampson (1977), that concerns of the psychological establishment reflect an individualistic orientation of our contemporary culture.

Nevertheless, past research indicates the important role of the collective self in determining behavior. For example, the attitudes of the women at Bennington College (Newcomb, 1943) were influenced in no small way by reference groups, and that influence appears to have had a lasting impact (Newcomb, Koenig, Flacks, & Warwick, 1967). And the Robbers' Cave experiment (Sherif, Harvey, White, Hood, & Sherif, 1961) demonstrated how superordinate, collective goals can be used in overcoming intergroup hostility.

Self-Esteem Theory and Measurement

There is generally a lack of standardization among self-esteem measures—or what we have called expected success at ego tasks. There are many measures of self-esteem (Wylie, 1974), but it is apparent that these measures assess mixtures of expected favorable evaluation from outer and inner audiences, and none measures expected success at meeting reference group goals. Self-esteem has been identified as a possible mediator in a variety of psychological processes, including persuasion (Hovland & Janis, 1959), task persistence (McFarlin & Blascovich, 1982; Shrauger & Sorman, 1977), and prejudice (Allport, 1954; Wills, 1981). Because different facets of the self can be invoked, by both situational and personality variables, in processes like persuasion, persistence, and prejudice, it should prove useful to have separate measures of individual differences in the level and importance of public, private, and collective esteem in studying these phenomena.

Other Audiences, Other Objects of Evaluation

The present ego-task analysis identifies three evaluative audiences (public, private, and collective), all of which take the single person as the evaluated object. A possible extension of this analysis would be to include other classes of evaluative audiences. For example, the goal of being evaluated favorably by a sexual partner may be sufficiently different from the other goals in Table 6.1 to be worthy of separate treatment. Another extension would be to go beyond the single person to a collective entity as the evaluated object. Such an extension might help explain intentional acts of risk taking or self-sacrifice. It may also be useful to distinguish among the various groups of others toward whom social accreditation efforts are directed, or among different reference groups. These additional distinctions could be valuable to the extent that the favorable regards of different categories of others require different strategic approaches.

Acknowledgments

This chapter was written, in part, while the first author was an NIMH postdoctoral trainee in the Department of Psychology at Northwestern University. The authors thank Anthony R. Pratkanis for comments on an earlier draft.

References

Allport, G. W. (1943). The ego in contemporary psychology. *Psychological Review, 50*, 451–478.

Allport, G. W. (1954). *The nature of prejudice.* Reading, MA: Addison-Wesley.

Arkin, R. M. (1980). Self-presentation. In D. M. Wegner & R. R. Vallacher (Eds.), *The self in social psychology* (pp. 158–182). New York: Oxford University Press.

Arkin, R. M., Appelman, A. J., & Burger, J. M. (1980). Social anxiety, self-presentation, and the self-serving bias in causal attribution. *Journal of Personality and Social Psychology, 38*, 23–35.

Asch, S. E. (1951). Effects of group pressure on the modification and distortion of judgments. In H. Guetzkow (Ed.), *Groups, leadership, and men* (pp. 177–190). Pittsburgh: Carnegie Press.

Asch, S. E. (1956). Studies of independence and conformity: I. A minority of one against a unanimous majority. *Psychological Monographs, 9* (Whole No. 416).

Baumeister, R. F. (1982). A self-presentational view of social phenomena. *Psychological Bulletin, 91*, 3–26.

Breckler, S. J., & Greenwald, A. G. (1981, May). *Favorable self-referent judgments are made faster than nonfavorable ones.* Paper presented at the 53d meetings of the Midwestern Psychological Association, Detroit.

Brickner, M. A., Harkins, S. G., & Ostrom, T. M. (in press). The effects of personal involvement: Thought provoking implications for social loafing. *Journal of Personality and Social Psychology.*

Buss, A. H. (1980). *Self-consciousness and social anxiety.* San Francisco: Freeman.

Carlsmith, J. M., Ellsworth, P. C., & Aronson, E. (1976). *Methods of research in social psychology.* Reading, MA: Addison-Wesley.

Carver, C. S. (1977). Self-awareness, perception of threat, and the expression of reactance through attitude change. *Journal of Personality, 45*, 501–512.

Cialdini, R. B., Baumann, D. J., & Kenrick, D. T. (1981). Insights from sadness: A three-step model of the development of altruism as hedonism. *Developmental Review, 1*, 207–223.

Cialdini, R. B., Herman, C. P., Levy, A., Kozlowski, L. T., & Petty, R. E. (1976). Elastic shifts of opinion: Determinants of direction and durability. *Journal of Personality and Social Psychology, 34*, 663–672.

Crowne, D., & Marlowe, D. (1964). *The approval motive*. New York: Wiley.

Diener, E. (1977). Deindividuation: Causes and consequences. *Social Behavior and Personality, 5*, 143–155.

Diener, E. (1980). Deindividuation: The absence of self-awareness and self-regulation in group members. In P. Paulus (Ed.), *The psychology of group influences* (pp. 209–242). Hillsdale, NJ: Erlbaum.

Dipboye, R. L. (1977). Alternative approaches to deindividuation. *Psychological Bulletin, 84*, 1057–1075.

Duval, S. (1976). Conformity on a visual task as a function of personal novelty on attitudinal dimensions and being reminded of the object status of self. *Journal of Experimental Social Psychology, 12*, 87–98.

Duval, S., & Wickland, R. A. (1972). *A theory of objective self-awareness*. New York: Academic Press.

Fenigstein, A., Scheier, M. F., & Buss, A. H. (1975). Public and private self-consciousness: Assessment and theory. *Journal of Consulting and Clinical Psychology, 43*, 522–527.

Frey, D. (1978). Reactions to success and failure in public and private conditions. *Journal of Experimental Social Psychology, 14*, 172–1?9.

Froming, W. J., Allen, L., & Jensen, R. (in press). Altruism, role-taking and self-awareness: The acquisition of norms governing altruistic behavior. *Child Development*.

Froming, W. J., & Carver, C. S. (1981). Divergent influences of private and public self-consciousness in a compliance paradigm. *Journal of Research in Personality, 15*, 159–171.

Goffman, E. (195?). *The presentation of self in everyday life*. New York: Doubleday.

Greenberg, G., Pyszczynski, T., & Solomon, S. (1982). The self-serving attributional bias: Beyond self-presentation. *Journal of Experimental Social Psychology, 18*, 56–67.

Greenwald, A. G. (1980). The totalitarian ego: Fabrication and revision of personal history. *American Psychologist, 35*, 603–618.

Greenwald, A. G. (1982a). Ego task analysis: An integration of research on ego-involvement and self-awareness. In A. H. Hastorf & A. M. Isen (Eds.), *Cognitive social psychology* (pp. 109–147). New York: Elsevier North-Holland.

Greenwald, A. G. (1982b). Is anyone in charge: Personalysis versus the principle of personal unity. In J. Suls (Ed.), *Psychological perspectives on the self* (Vol. 1, pp. 151–181). Hillsdale, NJ: Erlbaum.

Greenwald, A. G., & Breckler, S. J. (1985). To whom is the self presented? In B. R. Schlenker (Ed.), *The self and social life* (pp. 126–145). New York: McGraw-Hill.

Greenwald, A. G., & Pratkanis, A. R. (1984). The self. In R. S. Wyer & T. K. Srull (Eds.), *Handbook of social cognition* (pp. 129–178). Hillsdale, NJ: Erlbaum.

Harkins, S. G., & Petty, R. E. (1982). Effects of task difficulty and task uniqueness on social loafing. *Journal of Personality and Social Psychology, 43*, 1214–1229.

Hovland, C. I., & Janis, I. (Eds.). (1959). *Personality and persuasibility*. New Haven: Yale University Press.

James, W. (1890). *The principles of psychology* (Vol. 1). New York: Holt.

Jones, E. E., & Pittman, T. S. (1982). Toward a general theory of strategic self-presentation. In J. Suls (Ed.), *Psychological perspectives on the self* (Vol. 1, pp. 231–262). Hillsdale, NJ: Erlbaum.

Kelman, H. C. (1961). Processes of opinion change. *Public Opinion Quarterly, 25*, 57–78.

Latané, B., Williams, K., & Harkins, S. (1979). Many hands make light the work: The causes and consequences of social loafing. *Journal of Personality and Social Psychology, 37*, 822–832.

Loevinger, J. (1976). *Ego development*. San Francisco: Jossey-Bass.

Magnusson, D., & Endler, N. S. (Eds.). (1977). *Personality at the crossroads: Current issues in interactional psychology*. Hillsdale, NJ: Erlbaum.

Markus, H. (1977). Self-schemata and processing information about the self. *Journal of Personality and Social Psychology, 35*, 63–78.

McClelland, D. C., Atkinson, J. W., Clark, R. A., & Lowell, E. L. (1953). *The approval motive*. New York: Appleton-Century-Crofts.

McFarland, C., Ross, M., & Conway, M. (1984). Self-persuasion and self-presentation as mediators of anticipatory attitude change. *Journal of Personality and Social Psychology, 46*, 529–540.

McFarlin, D. B., & Blascovich, J. (1982, August). *Affective, behavioral, and cognitive consequences of self-esteem*. Paper presented at the symposium Functioning and Measurement of Self-Esteem, 90th annual meetings of the American Psychological Association, Washington, DC.

Merton, R. K. (1957). *Social theory and social structure* (rev. ed.). Glencoe, IL: Free Press.

Newcomb, T. M. (1943). *Personality and social change*. New York: Holt, Rinehart and Winston.

Newcomb, T. M., Koenig, K. E., Flacks, R., & Warwick, D. P. (1967). *Persistence and change*. New York: Wiley.

Paulhus, D. (1984). Two-component models of socially desirable responding. *Journal of Personality and Social Psychology, 46*, 598–609.

Piaget, J. (1965). *The moral judgment of the child*. New York: Free Press. (Original work published 1932)

Piaget, J. (1967). *Six psychological studies*. New York: Vintage. (Original work published 1964)

Riess, M., Rosenfeld, P., Melburg, B., & Tedeschi, J. T. (1981). Self-serving attributions: Biased private perceptions and distorted public descriptions. *Journal of Personality and Social Psychology, 41*, 224–231.

Rogers, T. B., Kuiper, N. A., & Kirker, W. S. (1977). Self-reference and the encoding of personal information. *Journal of Personality and Social Psychology, 35*, 677–688.

Rosenberg, M. (1965). *Society and the adolescent self-image*. Princeton, NJ: Princeton University Press.

Rosenberg, M. J. (1969). The conditions and consequences of evaluation apprehension. In R. Rosenthal & R. L. Rosnow (Eds.), *Artifact in behavioral research* (pp. 279–349). New York: Academic Press.

Sampson, E. E. (1977). Psychology and the American ideal. *Journal of Personality and Social Psychology, 35*, 767–782.

Scheier, M. F. (1980). The effects of public and private self-consciousness on the public expression of personal beliefs. *Journal of Personality and Social Psychology, 39*, 514–521.

Scheier, M. F., & Carver, C. S. (1980). Private and public self-attention, resistance to change, and dissonance reduction. *Journal of Personality and Social Psychology, 39*, 390–405.

Scheier, M. F., & Carver, C. S. (1983). Two sides of the self: One for you and one for me. In J. Suls & A. G. Greenwald (Eds.), *Psychological perspectives on the self* (Vol. 2, pp. 123–157). Hillsdale, NJ: Erlbaum.

Schlenker, B. R. (1980). *Impression management*. Monterey, CA: Brooks/Cole.

Schlenker, B. R., Hallam, J. R., & McCown, N. E. (1983). Motives and social evaluation: Actor-observer differences in the delineation of motives for a beneficial act. *Journal of Experimental Social Psychology, 19*, 254–273.

Sherif, M. (1956). *An outline of social psychology* (rev. ed.). New York: Harper.

Sherif, M., & Cantril, H. (1947). *The psychology of ego-involvements*. New York: Wiley.

Sherif, M., Harvey, O. J., White, B. J., Hood, W. R., & Sherif, C. W. (1961). *Intergroup cooperation and competition: The Robbers' Cave experiment*. Norman, OK: University Book Exchange.

Sherif, M., & Sherif, C. W. (1964). *Reference groups*. New York: Harper & Row.

Sherif, M., Sherif, C. W., & Nebergall, R. (1965). *Attitude and attitude change: The social judgment-involvement approach*. Philadelphia: Saunders.

Shrauger, J. S., & Sorman, P. B. (1977). Self-evaluations, initial success and failure, and improvment as determinants of persistance. *Journal of Consulting and Clinical Psychology, 45*, 784–795.

Snyder, C. R., Higgins, R. L., & Stucky, R. J. (1983). *Excuses: Masquerades in search of grace*. New York: Wiley.

Snyder, M. (1974). Self-monitoring of expressive behavior. *Journal of Personality and Social Psychology, 30*, 526–537.

Snyder, M. (1979). Self-monitoring processes. In L. Berkowitz (Ed.), *Advances in experimental social psychology* (Vol. 12, pp. 85–128). New York: Academic Press.

Snyder, M., & Campbell, B. H. (1982). Self-monitoring: The self in action. In J. Suls (Eds.), *Psychological perspectives on the self* (Vol. 1, pp. 185–207). Hilldale, NJ: Erlbaum.

Strickland, B. R., & Crowne, D. P. (1962). Conformity under conditions of simulated group pressure as a function of the need for social approval. *Journal of Social Psychology, 58*, 171–181.

Stults, D. M., Messé, L. A., & Kerr, N. L. (1984). Belief discrepant behavior and the bogus pipeline: Impression management or arousal attribution. *Journal of Experimental Social Psychology, 20*, 47–54.

Sumner, W. G. (1906). *Folkways*. Boston: Ginn.

Tesser, A., & Paulhus, D. L. (1983). The definition of self: Private and public self-evaluation management strategies. *Journal of Personality and Social Psychology, 44*, 672–682.

Weary, G., & Arkin, R. M. (1981). Attributional self-presentation. In J. H. Harvey, W. Ickes, & R. F. Kidd (Eds.), *New directions in attribution research* (Vol. 3, pp. 223–246). Hillsdale, NJ: Erlbaum.

Weary, G., Harvey, J. H., Schwieger, P., Olson, C. T., Perloff, R., & Pritchard, S. (1982). Self-presentations and the moderation of self-serving attributional biases. *Social Cognition, 1*, 140–159.

Weber, S. J., & Cook, T. D. (1972). Subject effects in laboratory research: An examination of subject roles, demand characteristics, and valid inference. *Psychological Bulletin, 77*, 273–295.

Whyte, W. F. (1981). *Street corner society* (3d ed.). Chicago: University of Chicago Press.

Wills, T. A. (1981). Downward comparison principles in social psychology. *Psychological Bulletin, 90*, 245–271.

Wylie, R. C. (1974). *The self-concept* (Vol. 1). Lincoln: University of Nebraska Press.

Zeigarnik, B. (1938). On finished and unfinished tasks. In W. D. Ellis (Ed.), *A source book of gestalt psychology* (pp. 300–314). New York: Humanities Press.

PART II

Affect

CHAPTER 7

Category-Based versus Piecemeal-Based Affective Responses
Developments in Schema-Triggered Affect

SUSAN T. FISKE
Carnegie-Mellon University

MARK A. PAVELCHAK
University of Pittsburgh

BACKGROUND

This chapter is one step toward developing a model located at the intersection between social cognition and social affect. The model focuses on some ways that people's understanding of another person (i.e., their social cognition) contributes to their feelings about that person (i.e., their social affect). Recently, social cognition research has produced sophisticated models that typically neglect affect, whereas earlier person perception research developed models that included affect without the benefit of recent advances in social cognition research. Thus, one main theoretical effort is to integrate the earlier insights about social affect with the recent insights about social cognition. To anticipate our later discussion, the central premise is that social categories enable a rapid affective response to an instance of the category, a response that does not require an attribute-by-attribute affective response to the instance. There will be two classes of hypotheses: (1) how social categories and their associated affect might be represented and processed in memory and (2) the limiting conditions for the first class of hypotheses when applied to real-world settings. In a final section, we will describe some specific applications of our approach to stereotyping, consumer attitudes, political attitudes, and group decision making.

The proposed model builds on work in person perception (for a review, see Schneider, Hastorf, & Ellsworth, 1979) and social cognition (for a review, see Fiske & Taylor, 1984). In particular, we draw on person perception work for models of how people form evaluative impressions, and we draw on social cognition work for models of how people form an understanding of others. A brief look at person perception research will show that its models were necessarily imprecise about cognitive processes because that work predated the recent growth of interest in social cognition. Then, a brief look at social cognition research will show how its models of cognitive representation tend to neglect interpersonal affect. Both research traditions have crucial contributions to make to theories of interpersonal affect and cognition. Although they have not been thoroughly integrated before, the marriage of the two traditions within the proposed theory fits into a growing effort by other cognitive and social psychologists to integrate affect and cognition (examples are collected in Clark & Fiske, 1982).

Our particular effort focuses on specific components of affect and of cognition. With regard to affect, our current proposals are limited to evaluative judgments of likability, pleasantness, favorability, and the like. Although affect also can include complex arousal-based emotions, we view the simple version of affect (i.e., evaluation) as a useful starting point. That is, all taxonomies of affect that we have seen share the central dimension of pleasantness/unpleasantness or valence. Other dimensions often include arousal or intensity. At this stage, we do not expect our approach to be much altered when applied to more complex, arousal-based emotions. Similarly, we address only some limited aspects of cognition. As will be seen, we focus primarily on categorization processes and on memory retrieval (see Fiske [1981, 1982] for more details on both points). Although our current discussion is focused on the foregoing aspects of affect and cognition, the model described here has much wider potential applicability.

Person Perception Research

The proposed theory takes person perception research as the starting point for its analysis of affective–evaluative processes. In a classic paper, Asch (1946) suggested two competing models of evaluative impressions: the configural model and the elemental model. Neither is cognitively sophisticated by modern standards, but both are useful bases for more detailed theory.

The configural model, based on Gestalt principles, posits that impressions are holistic; the entire configuration of a person's attributes determines the perceived "root of the personality." The perceived unity of another's personality stems from the perceived *relationships* of traits to each other within an overall impression. One major factor that encourages a unified impression, according to Asch (1946), is the presence of central or important traits: "The whole system of relations determines which [traits] will become central. . . . And it is not until we have found the center that we experience the reassurance of having come near to an understanding of the person" (p. 284).

To illustrate, suppose that you were trying to make sense of a new colleague who frequently seemed fragmented and confused, whose behavior was quite unpredictable, whose ideas were bizarre, and who tended to be obsessional. The whole system of trait impressions might best be organized around the trait "bizarre," with its links to mental illness or even schizophrenia. Although such an example is somewhat extreme, it illustrates the process of puzzling about someone's personality until the entire configuration fits together as a unified whole organized around a central trait. Asch's configural model, with its emphasis on central traits, continues to make theoretical and intuitive sense today. However, the configural model is imprecise, in modern terms, about exactly how the attributes are brought into relationship to form a unified impression. In the current proposal, as described later, the configural model is developed in a more fine-grained fashion as one mode of affective processing.

In contrast to the configural model, Asch's elemental model assumes that evaluative impressions are elemental, or what we will call "piecemeal"; they are the combination (sum or average) of the evaluations of *isolated* attributes. The elemental model posits that the evaluative component of each attribute is determined independently of the others present, and then the isolated evaluations are combined into a summary judgment. For example, in forming an impression of a schizogenic colleague, the perceiver would combine the isolated evaluations of being fragmented, confused, unpredictable, bizarre, and obsessive to reach a summary judgment. Asch (1946) described the elemental model essentially as a foil to the configural model, which he clearly endorsed: "Few if any psychologists at the present time apply this [elemental] formulation strictly" (p. 259). Rather, Asch emphasized organization around a central core—that is, the configural model. Nevertheless, elemental theories of person perception have developed in considerable detail since Asch. Moreover, the elemental models of impression formation have generated considerable research (e.g., N. H. Anderson, 1974; Fishbein & Ajzen, 1975). However, they are insufficiently developed from a cognitive perspective (Fiske, 1982). In fact, they originally made no statements about internal processes. Recently, the work of Norman Anderson (1983) and Lola Lopes (1982) has begun to address this problem, but the effort is still preliminary at this point. In the current proposal, the elemental model is developed from a cognitive perspective, and it is retained as a second mode of affective response.

Previous research on the configural and elemental models of person perception failed to establish either one as preferable, for both theoretical and methodological reasons (Hamilton & Katz, 1975; Lingle, Geva, & Ostrom, 1975; Ostrom, 1977). We would suggest (1) that it is now possible to specify and to demonstrate the cognitive processes implied by each and (2) that both models are applicable under certain specifiable circumstances. In summary, person perception research has provided preliminary ideas about interpersonal evaluation, but the models were (necessarily) insufficiently developed with regard to cognitive processes because they predated such research.

Social Cognition Research

Recent research, including our own, relies on a principle that dates back to Allport (1954), Bartlett (1932), Bruner (1957), and Lippmann (1922), among others. In this view, people categorize other people, social roles, social events, and even themselves to simplify the complex task of interpersonal understanding. Categorization is the process of identifying a stimulus as a member of its class, similar to other members and dissimilar from nonmembers. Categories, then, are cognitive structures that contain instances of the class. Categorizing an instance allows the perceiver to apply to the instance general knowledge and expectations about the category, without having to ascertain that those features indeed apply to that instance. In short, categorization allows the perceiver to "go beyond the information given" (Bruner, 1957). The way categories are hypothesized to do this is by invoking organized prior knowledge, or what are often termed "schemata."

A "schema" is defined as a cognitive structure that contains knowledge about the attributes of a category and the links among those attributes (Rumelhart & Ortony, 1977). Thus, a social schema organizes knowledge and expectations about stimuli that fall into certain socially defined categories. It is conceptually useful to keep the terms "schema" and "category" separate; thus, a category contains instances of the class, whereas a schema contains the features typical of the category. In this chapter, we will attempt to use "category" when discussing classification and "schema" when discussing attribute knowledge (cf. J. Mandler, 1979).

Recent cognitively oriented social research has demonstrated that perception, memory, and inference are guided by categorization and social schemata in ways that simplify information processing (for exemplars, see Cantor & Mischel, 1979; Markus, 1977; for overviews, see Hastie, 1981; Taylor & Crocker, 1981; for comments, see Fiske & Linville, 1980). The cognitive functions of categorization and schemata complement person perception's configural model as we will apply it to interpersonal affective responses.

It is noteworthy that until recently, social cognition research generally has neglected affect (cf. Fiske, 1981; Higgins, Kuiper, & Olson, 1981; Zajonc, 1980). From a practical perspective, affect is often the reason social schemata matter so critically. For example, although much recent work suggests that categorized individuals will be perceived and remembered in biased ways, it neglects the evaluative implications of those biases.[1] In actual interpersonal interactions, affect (evaluation) is at least equal in importance to cognition (schemata).

THE BASIC MODEL

Drawing on the aforecited research traditions, our model describes a relatively fine-grained interface between social cognition and social affect. Our approach draws on the research traditions cited, and it is developed from earlier papers (Fiske, 1981, 1982). Consistent with these previous efforts, in the discussion that follows, we will describe the model as applied to the categorization of persons. At the end of the chapter, we will apply the model to other affect-laden social categorization processes.

In our view, people's reactions to a new person consist of an initial categorization stage and a second affect-generation stage. Social categorization is presumed to invoke schemata stored in memory, and the schemata may include the set of cognitions about certain social groups, personality types, social roles, and the like. The schemata are hypothesized to consist of a category label at the top level and the expected attributes at a lower level, as shown in Figure 7.1. According to the typical current models of memory, the label and attributes can be thought of as nodes in a memory network (J. R. Anderson, 1983; McClelland & Rumelhart, 1981; Rumelhart & McClelland, 1982; Wickelgren, 1981). Such models are commonly used by social psychologists theorizing about memory for information about people (e.g., Hastie *et al.*, 1980; and especially Lui & Brewer, 1983).

In this view, memory retrieval operates by activation spreading along the links from one node to another. Links can vary in their strength—that is, their potential for transmitting activation from node to node.[2] Within the schema structure, the attributes are presumed to have strong links to the category label and weaker links to each other. One implication of this is that a category label will have more impact than any single typical trait, because the label has more and stronger links to the attributes than the attributes do to each other. (We will return to this point.) Like most person memory models, ours assumes that recall of category-consistent attributes is facilitated by the presence of the category label. Recall of category-discrepant attributes will be poor if subjects do not have time to link the inconsistent attributes to the rest of the impression (Hastie, 1980; Srull, 1981). And recall of category-irrelevant attributes will be poor in any case.

We hypothesize that affect may be added to such a model as follows: Each attribute has an "affective tag" that indicates its evaluative value. Such affective tags result from prior experience with the relevant attributes. At the top level, the category label also has an affective tag that substitutes for the evaluations of all the attributes associated with the schema (see Figure 7.2). The category label's

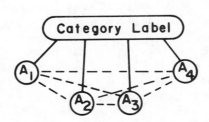

FIGURE 7.1 Hypothesized representation of a schema cued by categorization.

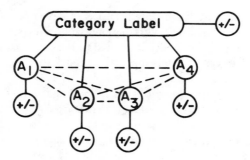

FIGURE 7.2 Hypothesized representation of affect in schema structure.

affective tag could stem from many sources. For example, the tag could come from an initial weighted averaging or summation of the lower-level affective tags when the category is first learned, before it develops any configural meaning. After the top-level affective tag is established, it becomes independent of access to the attributes' tags. Alternatively, the top-level affective tag could come from a conditioned response to the category label, or it could come from socialization— for example, someone else stating that a certain category is good or bad, exciting or annoying. In each of these cases, however, the top-level affective tag can be accessed without accessing the tags for the schema's lower-level attributes.

The entire affective–cognitive structure fits into a processing model with two major stages (see Figure 7.3). People first try to categorize others, using explicitly provided labels or using the individual's fit to the attributes of a category prototype or exemplar. The process of fitting an instance to a category is clearly important, but it is not our primary concern here. (For models of such processes, see Brooks, 1978; Cantor & Mischel, 1979; McCloskey & Glucksberg, 1979; Medin & Schaffer, 1978; Rosch, 1978; E. E. Smith, Shoben, & Rips, 1974; for a review, see E. E. Smith & Medin, 1981). People may be categorized in a variety of ways. For example, a person may be categorized as a schizophrenic on the basis of a label, on the basis of a set of prototypical attributes (e.g., unpredictable, confused, bizarre, obsessive, fragmented), or on the basis of resemblance to a specific exemplar (behavior similar to a specific schizophrenic whom the perceiver has encountered). In the strong form of the model, the affective tags are hypothesized to play no role in the initial categorization stage, which depends, instead, on the fit between the individual's and the category's attributes.

Given that people can be categorized in a variety of ways, some categories are more likely than others to be used by perceivers. Previous research in social cognition suggests that categories will dominate if any of the following are true: (1) they are cued early in the set of information received about the person (primacy effects: Asch, 1946; Schneider *et al.*, 1979); (2) they differentiate the person from others in context (salience and related effects: Higgins & Lurie, 1983; McGuire, McGuire, Child, & Fujioka, 1978; Taylor & Fiske, 1978); (3) the perceiver has used them recently or frequently in other, even unrelated, contexts (priming

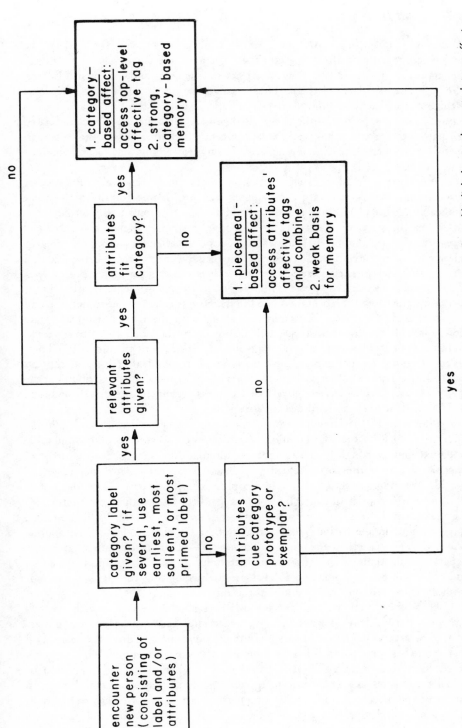

FIGURE 7.3 Processing of interpersonal affect. (The first major processing stage, categorization, is indicated by light boxes; the second stage, affect generation, is indicated by dark boxes.)

effects: Higgins, Rholes, & Jones, 1977; Srull & Wyer, 1980); or (4) The perceiver's concurrent affect matches the most available negatively or positively tagged categories (paralleling mood effects on memory and judgment: Bower, 1981; Clark & Isen, 1982). Thus, categorization according to the label "schizophrenic" will be more likely if the label is one of the first characteristics learned about the person, if the person is the only schizophrenic in the context of normals, if the perceiver has used the label recently or frequently in other contexts, or if the perceiver is experiencing negative feelings (assuming that "schizophrenic" is negatively tagged).

Whatever their basis, categorization attempts can be relatively successful or unsuccessful; that is, the target may show varying degrees of fit to the most applicable category. The outcome of the initial categorization stage determines the mode of the second major stage—affective response. Relatively successful categorization (i.e., good fit) allows one mode of affective response, whereas relative failure to categorize (i.e., poor fit) suggests another mode. If categorization is successful, the target can be evaluated in a *category-based mode*—that is, simply in terms of the affect linked to the top level of the schema. When categorization is successful, the category label is activated in memory (i.e., it "comes to mind"), and the associated affect is quickly activated along with the label because they are closely linked. Because the affect is linked directly to the label, access to it should be faster than access to the affective tags linked with each of the attributes. Thus, given successful categorization, the perceiver can respond affectively at the top level of the category, rather than on the basis of all the individual's attributes at the lower level. Consequently, category-based affect is presumed to be an efficient (i.e., rapid and effortless) mode of affective response.

Alternatively, the categorization attempt may fail, either because no applicable category is cued by the configuration of attributes or because the most applicable category implies some attributes that are dramatically inconsistent with (e.g., opposite to) those the target actually possesses. As an example of inconsistency, consider meeting someone labeled "schizophrenic" who is predictable and not at all obsessive (inconsistent traits) but is bizarre and confused (consistent traits). It is difficult to evaluate such a person quickly on the basis of the "schizophrenic" category, and an alternative category may not readily come to mind. Instead, one is forced to evaluate the person in a *piecemeal mode*—that is, attribute by attribute. Separate evaluations of the person's predictability, lack of obsession, bizarreness, and confusion can be combined to evaluate the person, but the attributes cannot easily be integrated into an overall impression.

Thus, there may be two modes of interpersonal resonse, which we call "category-based" and "piecemeal," given successful and unsuccessful categorization, respectively. Each mode bears on both affective and cognitive responses, and each mode has some parallels in classic models of person perception. The category-based mode builds on Asch's configural model, whereby the configuration of stimulus attributes cues a coherent, integrated impression based on central traits. In our view, the perceived configurality of a person's attributes often can be based on fit to a prior category. The central trait, in effect, cues a category that integrates the remaining set of traits. In addition, our category-based mode builds on current cognitive models of person memory. However, the current model adds affective tags to the schema at the top level (category label) and at the lower level (associated attributes). Similarly, the piecemeal mode builds on the elemental models suggested by Asch, by N. H. Anderson, and by Fishbein and Ajzen. In these views, affect generation is an attribute-by-attribute process that results from simply combining the evaluations of isolated attributes that do not influence each other. Thus, the piecemeal mode is an elemental process of social cognition and affect, in contrast to the configural category mode.

To review, our focus is on piecemeal versus category-based processing of affective tags at the levels, respectively, of attributes versus the category as a whole. Our basic premise is that person categories enable a rapid affective response based on merely categorizing someone as belonging to a social group. Our model, as stated, may be extended in several conceptual respects. After discussing the possible extensions, we will turn to the ways the model differs from previous models of category-based processing and previous models of affect. Then we will describe several specific hypotheses that derive from the model.

POSSIBLE CONCEPTUAL EXTENSIONS

The preliminary model, as stated, is a first approximation. Several conceptual issues require further explanation and development. First, it may appear initially that configural processing can take forms other than categorization. That is, perhaps the social perceiver can go beyond elemental, piecemeal processing by considering the relationships among traits without reference to an overarching schema. For example, Asch (1946) suggested: "The gaiety of an intelligent man is not more or less than the gaiety of a stupid man; it is different in quality" (p. 287). Similarly, people interpret the friendliness of an insincere person quite differently from that of a sincere person. One might argue that such noncategorical configural processing could take the form of relying on naive theories of personality structure; for example, people are not typically expected to be simultaneously cruel and generous.

In one study that might seem to typify such a noncategorical configural process, Higgins and Rholes (1976) discussed a role fulfillment approach to holistic (versus elemental) impression formation processes. For example, both a mature wine and an aged wine fulfill the wine "role," and both are evaluated positively, even though, in isolation, *mature* is evaluated positively and *aged* is evaluated negatively. A simple elemental model does not easily account for such results. We would interpret the specific Higgins and Rholes approach as an instance of category fit and subsequent category-based affect, not as an instance of noncategorical configural processing. Similar issues of the relationships among attributes have arisen in other studies, when person perception researchers debated the plausibility of individual traits showing a change in meaning depending on context (e.g., N. H. Anderson & Lampel, 1965; Hamilton & Zanna, 1974;

Zanna & Hamilton, 1977). We suggest that the configural processing debated in such contexts may be essentially an instance of categorization. If so, configural processing would not be possible without specific reference to a category, either implicit or explicit. This is ultimately an empirical question.

A second conceptual issue is that piecemeal processing may take two forms, which we will call "algebraic processing" and "thoughtful processing." Algebraic processing can occur when a set of unlabeled attributes simply does not fit an obvious prior category or when a set of labeled attributes does not fit the category given. In both cases, people may average or sum the affect tags to arrive at an overall evaluation. Having done this once, of course, the evaluation could be stored and used again later, when the perceiver encounters a similar stimulus configuration, which would subsequently constitute category-based affect. Screening of numerous job or graduate applicants probably operates in this way, as would responding to large numbers of stimulus permutations in an impression formation or attitudes study.

Alternatively, thoughtful processing can occur under conditions of piecemeal processing. For example, subtyping may result from an encounter with inconsistency. The perceiver may try to recall or create a subcategory that fits the particular configuration of inconsistent attributes given (cf. Taylor, 1981; Weber & Crocker, 1983). Such subtypes may be based on exemplars—in effect, one-instance categories—or they may describe an unusual subset of the larger group. In either case, subtyping initially resembles piecemeal processing to the extent that it requires an extended consideration of attribute-level information. Subsequently, subtyping resembles category-based processing in that an affect tag at the subcategory level could be retrieved on the basis of successful subcategorization. Other examples of thoughtful processing might include the generation of an altogether new category or self-reference. Or thoughtful processing could take the form of constructing a causal explanatory system to account for a person's unique combination of attributes. In any case, because of the extended attribute-by-attribute processing time, thoughtful processing resembles piecemeal processing in some crucial respects.

Some evidence for the subtyping form of piecemeal processing comes from consumer research by Sujan (1985). She presented subjects with category labels (35 mm or 110-type cameras) and with attributes that were either consistent or inconsistent with the label. Subjects in the inconsistent conditions often spontaneously thought of a more specific camera that actually possessed the inconsistent attribute configuration, and apparently those subjects used their subtype or one-camera category as a basis for evaluative response. This subtype effect occurred only for subjects who had had sufficient prior experience with cameras.

Hence, there may strictly be two types of piecemeal processing: algebraically combining the attributes' affective tags (as described in the basic model) and resolving the inconsistency of the category and attributes by thoughtful processing (as described here). More important, to the extent that people do examine the inconsistent attributes in an effort to reconcile them with the category, they are engaged in a slower type of processing than category-based processing. Whichever type of piecemeal processing occurs, both are slower than the category-based mode.

A third respect in which the model is oversimplified concerns the dichotomy between piecemeal and category-based processing. The dichotomy is more likely to develop into a continuum as preliminary work tests and elaborates the model. Because inconsistency is a continuous quantity, there may be intermediate levels that cause a mix of the piecemeal and category-based modes. At this stage, however, the dichotomy is a convenient fiction.

Finally, the distinction between the categorization stage and the affect-generation stage is oversimplified. It is possible that the two processes sometimes operate in parallel, with feedback between them. Hence, the two stages may not be as separate and sequential as our preliminary model suggests. Even if the two processes operate in parallel, however, it is still possible that the affect-generation process takes longer when categorization fails and that affect and memory are both attribute-oriented when categorization is relatively unsuccessful.

RELATIONSHIP TO PREVIOUS MODELS

The category-based approach is quite general in its concerns. Thus, it is related to a number of models in social and cognitive psychology. A close examination of those models shows, however, that our approach is distinctive in its concern with affective processes and in other respects.

Our two-stage, two-mode model has several theoretical relatives in research on person perception and social cognition. Notably, a related four-stage (single-mode) model of social judgments (Burnstein & Schul, 1982, 1983) posits initial encoding (of physical features), elaborative encoding (of semantic features), integration (comprehension of features via a common schema), and decision (producing a response). This four-stage model, developed simultaneously and independently with regard to our own, provides a compatible but more complex view of processing stages and a compatible but less complex view of the two modes for generation of an affective response. To compare the Burnstein and Schul (1982, 1983) model and ours, our categorization stage includes both of their kinds of encoding (initial and elaborative), and our affect-generation stage includes both of their later stages (integration and decision). Conversely, their integration and decision stages do not differentiate processing based on category-based versus piecemeal modes.

In another related development, person memory researchers have distinguished between impression judgments based on retrieval of relevant stimulus elements (piecemeal) versus retrieval of a prior abstract judgment (category-based) (Carlston, 1980; Ebbesen & Allen, 1979; Lingle, Geva, Ostrom, Leippe, & Baumgardner, 1979; Lingle & Ostrom, 1979). These models, however, are focused on memory-based judgments, not (as ours is) on stimulus-based affective responses. The distinction is important, for our model hinges on stimulus-based categorization.

One more relevant social memory model attempts to integrate piecemeal and category-based processes in ways that more directly parallel our effort. Wyer and Carlston (1979) proposed that certain circumstances discourage what they call script-based (i.e., category- or schema-based) processing. They suggest that such processing is unlikely, for instance, when there is no meaningful stimulus person— that is, when the person fits no prior conceptions. Such conditions describe our hypothesized piecemeal conditions. We have suggested that categorization fails and piecemeal processing occurs when the person's attributes do not fit the category cued by the provided label or when the attributes alone do not cue any particular category. Wyer and Carlston (1979) suggest that tests of the elemental models of person perception have used precisely such meaningless persons, as well as other techniques that encourage what we call piecemeal processing. They suggest that realistic impression formation and interpersonal attraction are more likely to proceed by processes other than elemental ones.

In cognitive psychology, the piecemeal–configural distinction also has proved interesting. In categorization research, one line of argument holds that configural (holistic) judgments are primary (first and more basic), whereas piecemeal (elemental) judgments are secondary. For example, J. D. Smith and Nelson (1984) proposed that processing on the grounds of overall similarity is rapid, direct, primitive, and basic, whereas processing on the grounds of separable stimulus dimensions is slower, more analytic, and secondary. This parallels the configural versus piecemeal distinction. Configural, category-based processing may be a more primitive mode, suggesting that piecemeal processing occurs primarily when categorization processes are inadequate. Our approach is consistent with this and several other cognitive models, but it is not a decisive test of any of them. Instead, we explicitly address the issue of creating a role for affect in social categorization processes.

In work spanning cognitive and social psychology, other models of affect and cognition are potentially relevant to the current model. For example, Zajonc (1980; Zajonc, Pietromonaco, & Bargh, 1982) proposed that affective reactions can precede cognitive reactions. By this he apparently meant that affect can follow immediately after perception of a stimulus and need not follow from memory for its cognitive content. Besides his own evidence on this point, person perception research corroborates it (Dreben, Fiske, & Hastie, 1979; Riskey, 1979). Our approach indirectly bears on his model, although it is not designed to test it explicitly. As will be seen, we have obtained rapid affective responses along with recall improvement in category-based (versus piecemeal) conditions; this would suggest that we have demonstrated one setting in which affect may depend on cognition. We have also obtained slow affective responses along with poor memory for the attributes on which the affect is based; this would suggest one setting in which affect is relatively independent of memory (but not necessarily independent of all cognition). In any case, our data were not designed to test the Zajonc approach, so they do not allow a definitive statement on this point.

Another relevant theory is G. Mandler's (1982) description of affect as a function of schema fit. This theory differs from ours in two major respects. First,

Mandler's analysis is most relevant to matters of taste and value, not predicated cultural values, of which social categories are a prime example. That is, Mandler was concerned with explaining affective responses to instances of sensory schemata, such as musical melodies. Second, Mandler emphasized affect resulting from variations in degrees of fit to a schema. For example, moderate discrepancies can cause positive affect and severe discrepancies can cause negative affect, depending on how those discrepancies are resolved. His focus thus lay in affective responses based on the ease of categorization, not the result of categorization as linked to affective tags.

Other relevant theories include the work of Bower (1981) and Clark and Isen (1982), who also proposed models of affect and memory. Their models could be fit with ours, but the central concerns differ. Most notably, our model focuses on social knowledge structures, whereas theirs emphasize the connections among structures with similar affective tones. Furthermore, they emphasized the role of affective tone as a cue for memory. It may be that our affective tags are linked to other similarly toned affective tags, so they can, indeed, act as memory cues. Indeed, as suggested earlier, people's current feelings might prime the use of similarly toned categories for stimuli that potentially fit several categories. Nonetheless, our present interest lies not in the role of affect as a memory cue but in different modes of processing affective tags at different levels of a schema.

ALTERNATIVE PREDICTIONS

Before describing the specific hypotheses and some preliminary supporting research, it is important to consider the alternatives to this model. One alternative to our predictions is that people consistently respond in a piecemeal fashion. That is, regardless of the fit of the individual's attributes to an available category, people may generate affective responses on the basis of the affect associated with all the person's attributes. In that case, the processing of affective responses would not differ as a function of category fit. Another alternative to our predictions would be that people consistently respond in a category-based fashion. That is, regardless of category fit, people may generate affective responses on the basis of the affect associated with the most available category. In that case also, processing would not differ as a function of category fit, so long as a category label was available. A third alternative would be that neither the category-based nor the piecemeal modes describe social cognition and social affect. This possibility is testable only to the extent that we can demonstrate that the data are (or are not) consistent with our model. Moreover, most other theories do not address this fine-grained level of analysis. Few of them make predictions about the speed of affective response or about the relationship of affective structure and processing to cognitive structure and processing.

HYPOTHESES AND PRELIMINARY RESEARCH

Hypothesis 1 (Category-based Affect):   *Successful categorization provides a basis for affective response.*

This hypothesis, the central aspect of the model, has been preliminarily tested in a series of studies (Fiske, 1982). One study manipulated categorization to be either successful or unsuccessful according to the consistency or inconsistency of a target's category label and accompanying attributes. In one condition, the attributes as a group were *descriptively inconsistent* with the label; that is, they were inconsistent in meaning with regard to the label. For example, subjects saw photographs of an engineer who wore a T-shirt that read "Civil engineers give a dam" (label) and who played the flute and smoked marijuana (behavioral attributes). In the other condition, the attributes as a group were consistent in meaning with regard to the label. For example, other subjects saw the same engineer working on a computer terminal and sprawling about in relatively unfashionable clothing. *Evaluative inconsistency* was held constant by selecting a group of attributes that all had a slightly more positive evaluative value than the negative category. All categories (i.e., the labels) had been pretested in isolation as moderately negative, whereas all the attributes were pretested in isolation as neutral to positive.

It was predicted that in the consistent combinations, the negative label would trigger a negative evaluation, despite the neutral-to-positive attributes accompanying it. In the inconsistent combinations, however, the negative label and the neutral-to-positive attributes would be combined piecemeal, and the resulting evaluation would be only moderately negative. Note that the isolated evaluations of the information received in each condition were constant; only the consistency of the combinations differed. As predicted, the overall evaluation was more negative in the consistent case than in the inconsistent case. For example, an engineer (negative label) who played the flute (neutral inconsistent attribute) was liked better than an engineer who worked on a computer terminal (neutral consistent attribute). In the inconsistent case, likability was apparently based on label and attributes, whereas in the consistent case, likability was apparently based on the label only.

These results provide partial support for the first hypothesis of category-based or schema-triggered affect. This and other relevant studies are summarized elsewhere (Fiske, 1982).[3] Given the promising results of our early work, we were encouraged to continue testing the model. The next step was to rule out an alternative explanation due to consistency being an imperfect manipulation of category-based affect. Too much else potentially covaries with consistency to make piecemeal versus category-based processing the sole explanation for the results. For example, in the research just described, it is possible that the preference for inconsistent stimulus people is based not on piecemeal processing but instead on a preference for interesting or well-rounded people.

To address this problem, the subsequent research has manipulated the conditions for category-based and piecemeal processing in two separate ways. The manipulations follow from the logic of Hypothesis 1. If successful categorization provides a basis for affective response, category-based affective processing should occur whenever categorization occurs, regardless of the conditions that elicited category-based responses. This has two critical implications. First, category-based affect should result whether elicited by (1) a category label and no additional relevant information or (2) a category label and additional information that fits the category. Second, piecemeal-based affect should result whether elicited by (1) a category label plus attributes that do not fit or (2) attributes received alone that do not suggest any particular category. This allows us to design research in which the piecemeal and category-based processing modes are each elicited in two distinct ways. The weaknesses of any one manipulation of each mode are offset by the presumably nonoverlapping weaknesses of the alternative manipulation of that mode. Thus, the research described next has two separate operationalizations of piecemeal processing and two separate operationalizations of categorical processing.

> *Hypothesis 2 (Efficiency):* Category-based affective responses are faster than piecemeal-based affective responses.

This hypothesis should be true because category-based affect accesses only the category's overall evaluation, rather than the evaluations of each of the individual's attributes. If affect is indeed available immediately after the initial act of categorization, then category-based affect should be relatively fast. Alternatively, if affective responses are based, instead, on a review of the affective tags for the attributes associated with the category, then affective responses should be slower. This follows directly from the theoretical model outlined earlier. The initial step of categorization precedes the evaluative response, which is based either on that categorization (category-based affect) or on the lengthier step of accessing the affective tags of the attributes associated with the category and combining them (piecemeal-based affect). An initial pair of studies tested this reasoning (Fiske & Beattie, 1982; Fiske, Beattie, & Milberg, 1983); one of them (Fiske, Beattie, & Milberg, 1983) will be described here in some detail.

Subjects viewed stimulus people composed of job-category labels and trait attributes. Four conditions were designed—two to elicit category-based processing and two to elicit piecemeal processing. The two category-based conditions were (1) label plus consistent attributes ("consistent" condition) and (2) label plus uninformative attributes ("label-focus" condition). The two piecemeal conditions were (1) label plus inconsistent attributes ("inconsistent" condition) and (2) uninformative label plus attributes ("attribute-focus" condition). The latency of subjects' likability judgments was the primary dependent measure; it was predicted to be faster in the two category-based conditions. To demonstrate more standard schematic information-processing effects on memory, we also measured subjects' recall accuracy and latency, but these were of secondary interest.

The four within-subject conditions were hypothesized to elicit the category-based mode (consistent and label-focus) or the piecemeal mode (inconsistent and

TABLE 7.1 Stimulus Materials and Predictions for Fiske, Beattie, and Milberg (1983) Study: Category Labels and Attributes

Example Stimulus Set[a]

Salesclerk	Construction Worker	Clothing Designer	Person X
Pushy	Ordinary	Curious	Creative
Insensitive	Normal	Energetic	Sophisticated
Pleasant	Nice	Perceptive	Fashionable
Insincere	Typical	Aggressive	Artistic
Fawning	Unremarkable	Liberal	Exacting
(Consistent condition)	(Label-focus condition)	(Inconsistent condition)	(Attribute-focus condition)

Predicted Mode and Rationale

Category-Based Mode	Category-Based Mode	Piecemeal Mode	Piecemeal Mode
Attributes fit undergraduate's salesclerk category	Attributes are essentially uninformative about fit to category	Attributes do not fit category, so attempt to use category will fail because of inconsistency[b]	No label given, and attributes pretested so as not to generate category instantly[c]

[a]There were eight label–attribute sets in all, appropriately counterbalanced and rotated through the four within-subject conditions.

[b]Strictly speaking, not all "inconsistent" combinations were inconsistent in the sense of being opposite to the expected traits, but they all were distinctly not consistent with the expected traits, and some were directly contradictory. Rather than inventing a new term, such as "nonconsistent" or "aconsistent," we will use "inconsistent" here in the sense described—that is, that the attributes were relevant but not consistent.

[c]This is an important point. Clearly, a set of category-relevant attributes can cue category-based processing without benefit of a label. Just such processes are described here as a common basis for categorization. In this study and our other research, the attribute-focus condition was pretested to discourage spontaneous categorization.

attribute-focus). Table 7.1 displays sample stimulus materials and the specific rationale by condition. After reading about each stimulus person, subjects provided a likability response. In this study, unlike the previous study summarized briefly earlier, we were explicitly testing the efficiency of category-based affect. Accordingly, the timing of the likability response was of main interest here. It was thus important to keep the actual likability ratings constant across conditions so as not to confound the likability and processing mode effects on rating time. Because we selected both category labels and attribute sets that averaged neutral to negative, we predicted no difference on likability. The main prediction was that people reacting in a category mode ought to respond faster than people reacting in a piecemeal mode.

The results significantly confirmed our predictions. As predicted, when people were given a category label and consistent attributes, or simply the label and uninformative attributes, they were able to provide a likability response quickly. When they were given a label that did not fit, or no label, they responded more slowly. Planned contrasts supported this specific pattern of results. Thus, the main hypothesis was supported for the difference between category-based and piecemeal modes.

The recall results also supported standard category-based models of person memory (see Fiske & Taylor, 1984, for examples), which suggest that recall will be more efficient (rapid and accurate) when an organizing schema or category is available. Note that for the purposes of memory organization, the consistent condition theoretically was the only one for which memory could be facilitated by drawing directly on the link between the category label and the schema's lower-level attributes. Hence, only the consistent condition was hypothesized to show the efficiency effect, since the other category-based condition (label-focus) involved the uninformative attributes "ordinary, normal, nice, typical, unremarkable." Consequently, the consistent condition was predicted to be faster and more accurate than the two piecemeal conditions and the label-focus category-based condition. The predicted results were obtained.

In sum, the affect results, supplemented by the memory results, supported the hypothesis that both ways of invoking piecemeal processing result in less efficient affective and cognitive responses than does category-based processing. However, it is theoretically possible that the affect results are due not to slower responses at the affect-generation stage, as hypothesized, but instead to slower categorization processes at the initial stage. That is, the first stage (outlined earlier in the basic model) involved judging the fit of the target instance to a category. If that initial step took longer in the two piecemeal conditions (inconsistent and attribute-focus), then the initial categorization stage, not the later affect-generation stage, would account for the affect latency results.

Test of an Alternative Explanation

The alternative explanation was tested in two studies. First, a second set of stimulus materials and a separate judgment task were included in the study just described. (The order of the two tasks was counterbalanced.) In addition to the likability judgments made on the original four stimuli, subjects were asked to judge the consistency of job label and trait attributes for four other stimuli. This operationalized the categorization stage. If the latency of the initial categorization judgment showed the same pattern as the latency for the affect responses, then the alternative explanation would be supported.

The categorization latencies did differ significantly from each other. However, contrast analyses showed that the pattern of means was not at all the same as the pattern for the likability latencies. Because the pattern of categorization latencies differed from the pattern of affect latencies, the alternative explanation is less likely (see Fiske, Beattie, & Milberg, 1983, for details).

In a second and separate study testing this alternative interpretation (Fiske & Neuberg, 1984), subjects made both categorization and affect judgments about the same stimulus person; the sequence of judgments was varied between subjects. This design provided two tests of the alternative hypothesis. First, as before, categorization latencies should not show the same pattern as affect latencies. Under these task conditions, the only significant contrast was orthogonal to the category/piecemeal split; thus, the categorization latencies certainly failed to mimic the affect latencies. Second, the affect latencies should replicate the earlier pattern, regardless of the time taken for the initial categorization judgment. That is, the results should replicate regardless of whether affect latencies were timed as subjects' first judgment or were timed separately after subjects had completed a categorization rating. As before, the essential split between the category and piecemeal modes occurred again, regardless of the time taken for initial categorization ratings.

In addition to these data, two other factors undermine the alternative explanation. First, in testing a related model, Burnstein and Schul (1982) have shown that the latency effects of inconsistency occur primarily at later stages (e.g., affect generation) rather than earlier stages (e.g., categorization) of impression formation. Second, in our tests, the categorization judgments took equally as long or longer than the likability judgments, so it seems less likely that they are the exact component process that accounts for the likability results. Overall, although categorization and affect-generation processes are difficult to disentangle, the alternative explanation is undermined as the primary account for our results.

Summary

The model's overall premise is that social categories enable an affective response based on mere categorization, and its first two hypotheses are (1) category-based affect (successful categorization provides a basis for affective response) and (2) category-based efficiency (category-based affective responses are faster than piecemeal-based affective responses). Both hypotheses were supported by likability latencies that were rapid given either of two category-based conditions—a category label with uninformative traits or a label with consistent traits. In contrast, both piecemeal conditions—an unlabeled list of attributes or a category label with inconsistent traits—elicited longer likability latencies. Recall latencies and accuracy also supported the efficiency hypothesis by showing the schematic memory effects that are now standard in social cognition research.

FUTURE DIRECTIONS: REPRESENTATION AND PROCESSING OF CATEGORY-BASED AFFECT

Thus far, preliminary work has supported the model, but the category-based approach is far from established. Various hypotheses require further investigation to support their plausibility, to extend the theory, and to determine whether the theory is correct and worthy of application.

> *Hypothesis 3 (Set Size):*   *The amount of information that supports successful categorization has no impact on category-based affect.*

If affect is based on the top level of the category, rather than on the lower-level attributes, then the number of associated consistent attributes should not affect category-based processing time. That is, evaluation latencies should show no set-size effect under category-based processing, but they should under piecemeal processing. This hypothesis is critical for both theoretical and practical reasons. Graduated set size would allow a more precise test of inconsistency *per se* than did the preliminary study's comparison of inconsistent information with consistent information. It may be that the chances of a perceiver's changing from category-based to piecemeal mode may increase with the amount of inconsistent information. Alternatively, any amount of inconsistency (beyond a certain minimum) might be sufficient to elicit piecemeal processing. Future research will answer this question.[4]

> ***Hypothesis 4 (Descriptive Versus Evaluative Consistency):*** *Successful categorization depends only on the descriptive consistency of the individual's attributes with the category, not on their evaluative consistency.*

Descriptive consistency refers to compatability of meaning, whereas evaluative consistency refers to compatibility of valence. According to a strong version of our model, category-based efficiency depends only on the descriptive consistency of the attributes with the label. Consequently, in Fiske, Beattie, and Milberg (1983) and in Fiske and Neuberg (1984), the evaluative consistency of label and attributes was held constant but descriptive consistency was varied. However, the preliminary work did not establish Hypothesis 4 because it did not vary both descriptive and evaluative consistency in combination with each other.

Theoretically, descriptive consistency affects the initial categorization stage, whereas evaluative consistency affects the later affect-generation stage. A target person can have evaluatively inconsistent but descriptively consistent attributes and still be categorized as fitting the stereotype. For example, a schizophrenic (negative category label) who is described as "imaginative" (positive attribute) is just as much a schizophrenic as one who is described as "unrealistic" (negative attribute). Evaluative inconsistency does not invalidate the category. Descriptive inconsistency, however, would invalidate the category. For example, a schizophrenic (negative category) who is described as "ploddingly realist" (evaluatively but not descriptively consistent) is not a good example of the category, so categorization should be invalidated. Thus, descriptive, not evaluative, consistency influences the initial categorization stage.

Although evaluative consistency should not affect the categorization stage, it should influence the affect-generation stage. Specifically, evaluative inconsistency can have an impact on evaluation only under piecemeal processing. That is, evaluative consistency should not affect category-based processing of affect, because the attributes themselves are not involved in category-based affect. Given piecemeal processing, however, evaluative consistency can affect the overall evaluation, because each attribute's evaluation contributes to the affective response. Thus, evaluative consistency can affect outcomes at the evaluation stage, but only under piecemeal processing. (Note that this last prediction concerns evaluative outcomes, not processing time.)

Evaluative and descriptive consistency are difficult to disentangle, but previous researchers have had some success (Felipe, 1970; Hartwick, 1979; Higgins & Rholes, 1976; Rosenberg & Olshan, 1970; Wyer & Gordon, 1982). In general, they have found that both kinds of inconsistency matter to such tasks as trait inference, trait evaluation, and trait memory. However, the model helps to specify particular affective processing modes for which each kind of inconsistency matters.

Hypothesis 4 is critical in several respects. First, it potentially will limit the meaning of consistency for our purposes to descriptive consistency. Second, it can more precisely locate the effects of descriptive consistency at the categorization stage and the effects of evaluative consistency at the affect-generation stage. Thus, it can also provide more support for a strong version of the two-stage, two-process model. Finally, it tests the premise that perceivers' access to attributes can be limited to the initial categorization stage and can be absent in the affect-generation stage. In this respect, it is a fine-grained test of Hypotheses 1 and 3—that is, that affective responses are based on the category's overall evaluation and that affective responses based on successful categorization do not depend on the amount of descriptively consistent information supporting the categorization.

Hypothesis 5 (Category Centrality): *Affective responses often focus on the person's social category, rather than on the person's other characteristics.*

The theoretical model gives a special status to the target person's social category. That is, affective reactions are based on social categories, such as age, race, sex, occupation, role, or combinations thereof (e.g., female lawyer), rather than on traits and behaviors. The model is hierarchical, with the social category information organizing the attributes. Thus, if a person is described as a "schizophrenic," that attribute is hypothesized to have stronger links to "bizarre," "obsessive," and the like, than they do to each other. In that sense, "schizo-phrenic" organizes the attributes in memory and provides the summary affective response.

This is not to say that only social categories organize social information and that traits never do. A person described as "sensitive, expressive, perceptive, thoughtful, and female" might elicit reactions primarily as "a sensitive type" (trait) or primarily as "a typical female" (social category). The critical factor is which characteristic is central. A central characteristic may be defined as having many and strong links to other characteristics. In Asch's (1946) research, for example, "warm" and "cold" were central attributes, but "polite" and "blunt" were not. We suspect that social categories often have more links to other characteristics than any of them do to each other—hence their privileged status in the model. In this respect, we draw on an analogy to object perception. The category of "bird," for example, is presumed to have more and stronger links to its attributes "feathered" and "singing" than the attributes do to each other (cf. E. E. Smith & Medin, 1981). Similarly, social categories are presumed typically to organize other information, such as traits. For example, the label "schizophrenic" should have more impact than any single trait, such as "bizarre," assuming that the former has more and stronger links to the other information—that is, if it is central.

Just as social categories are hypothesized to be typically more central than traits, and just as some traits are more central than others, so some social categories will be more central than other social categories. This is a problem that has plagued researchers for some time. Of the several social categories available for labeling someone, which will be dominant? As noted in the basic model, categories that the perceiver learns early in an information set (primacy effects), categories that differentiate the person from others in context (salience effects), categories that the perceiver has used recently or frequently in other contexts (priming effects), and categories that fit the perceiver's current feelings (mood effects) are most likely to be central.

> *Hypothesis 6 (Category Cuing):* *Affect can be cued by a social category label or by attributes strongly associated with the category.*

In the psychology laboratory, categories often are cued by labels; in the real world, however, social categories often are inferred, not given directly. Categorization can occur by direct labeling or by a cluster of attributes strongly associated with the category. The strength of association between a cluster of attributes and a category label should determine whether or not the attributes cue the category when no direct label is present.

FUTURE DIRECTIONS: GENERALIZABILITY AND BOUNDARY CONDITIONS

Thus far, we have focused on the rather fine-grained analysis necessary to describe and test the proposed model of affective–cognitive processing. Fine-grained methods and theories imported from cognitive psychology with few adjustments are appropriate for testing social information-processing models (Taylor & Fiske, 1981), but they sometimes offer limited generalizability to more ecologically valid social settings. It is a major leap from word lists as stimuli to actual people as stimuli, and the differences between the two may be critical in testing the model.

Word lists differ from actual people as targets of perception in several respects. The differences are theoretically important in social cognition research generally (Fiske & Taylor, 1984), and they may create specific problems for this model. The differences include, at a minimum, modality, reciprocity, complexity, time pressure, knowledge, and significance.

As soon as the target becomes a real person instead of a word list, modality and potential for reciprocity are altered. *Modality* differs because word lists bypass the stage of transforming concrete behaviors, appearance, and settings into abstract trait adjectives of the sort used here. One could argue that the proposed model will not hold as well, or at all, when perceivers are not provided with

TABLE 7.2   Design of Neuberg and Fiske (1983) Study

	Conditions			
	Consistent	*Label-Focus*	*Inconsistent*	*Attribute-Focus*
Stimuli	Label plus consistent attributes	Label plus neutral attributes	Label plus inconsistent attributes	Neutral label plus attributes
Replication				
Schizophrenic	"Schizophrenic" label plus "schizophrenic" tape	"Schizophrenic" label plus "neutral" tape	"Schizophrenic" label plus "paraplegic" tape	"Patient" label plus "schizophrenic" tape
Paraplegic	"Paraplegic" label plus "paraplegic" tape	"Paraplegic" label plus "neutral" tape	"Paraplegic" label plus "schizophrenic" tape	"Patient label plus "paraplegic" tape

abstract, ready-made traits and category labels. *Reciprocity* differs because a word list is not a human being who is believed to perceive in return. One could argue that a real target person who is thought to be simultaneously forming impressions of the perceiver would dampen the perceiver's use of rapid, category-based judgments. Given that the target person can also form rapid, category-based judgments of the perceiver (e.g., that the perceiver is an easily prejudiced person), the perceiver could be somewhat more reluctant to reach hasty categorizations about a real target, because the perceiver's presentation of self becomes an issue.

The overall generalizability factors of modality and reciprocity have been tested in some preliminary research. Neuberg and Fiske's (1983) conceptual replication of the Fiske, Beattie, and Milberg (1983) study contained four conditions: consistent, label-focus, inconsistent, and attribute-focus. Subjects were recruited to help with a fictitious local hospital's Patient Reintegration Program. When they arrived, they were told they would be having a 20-minute conversation with a former long-term patient, to help the person get used to everyday encounters and ultimately to ease upcoming job or college admissions interviews. The experimenter provided the category label manipulation by stating that the former patient had been admitted to the hospital a year ago as a schizophrenic or as a paraplegic. Subjects were told that the program had recently found that the conversations went better if the patients made brief introductory videotapes about themselves, which the subjects could view before meeting the patients.

The videotape provided the attribute information about the patient. Although the verbal content of the videotape was held constant (focusing on hobbies, summer jobs, background, plans), its nonverbal manner differed by condition (see Table 7.2). For example, there were four schizophrenic conditions:

1. In the *consistent* condition, subjects expected to meet a person labeled "schizophrenic," and they saw a videotape that depicted the person as having "schizophrenic" traits. (Based on pretesting, these traits were "nervous," "inconsistent," "suspicious.")
2. In the *label-focus* condition, subjects expected to meet a schizophrenic, and they saw a videotape that depicted the person in a neutral, rather deadpan manner.
3. In the *inconsistent* condition, subjects expected to meet a schizophrenic, but they saw a videotape that depicted the person as having "paraplegic" traits ("friendly," "outgoing," "confident," "determined"). These "paraplegic" traits had been pretested as consistent with a paraplegic and inconsistent with a schizophrenic, thus allowing the two stereotypes to be used in a counterbalanced design.
4. In the *attribute-focus* condition, subjects expected to meet an ex-patient of unspecified type, but they saw the "schizophrenic" videotape.

Hence, the first two conditions were expected to produce category-based processing and the last two were expected to produce piecemeal processing. These conditions were replicated for the "paraplegic" stereotype.

After seeing the appropriate videotape, subjects were asked to give their reactions to using videotapes in the program, as it was a recent innovation. The first question assessed the ex-patient's likability, enabling a measure of subjects' affective response latency. Thus, this experiment provided a conservative test of the model: response latencies were measured after a 3-minute videotape, subjects were rating an apparently real person whom they expected to meet, and the setting was highly involving.

Nevertheless, the results replicated our earlier findings from the trait-list studies. In the two category-based conditions, subjects responded significantly faster than in the two piecemeal conditions. The results thus suggest that the model is quite generalizable; affective responses to a videotaped but real person, whom subjects expect to meet, show the same pattern of response latencies as affective responses to a stimulus person depicted by a label and a list of traits. Given this level of generalizability, other hypotheses center on specific aspects of more ecologically valid settings.

Hypothesis 7 (Complexity): Affective responses are more likely to be category-based as stimulus complexity increases.

As previously stated, social categorization occurs in part because it allows perceivers to make sense of complex stimuli. This tendency should increase as social stimuli become more complex. In several respects, real people are more complex than word lists. People adjust upon being perceived; word lists do not. People change over time; word lists are static. People's stable traits must be inferred (as noted earlier); word lists require less inference. Accuracy of inferences cannot be checked as easily for people as for word lists, where it can be assumed. Therefore, because of these complexities, categorization should be more common when the stimulus is a person rather than a word list.

Alternatively, it is possible that complexity might undercut categorization. If a stimulus is sufficiently complex, it is more likely to include attributes that are inconsistent with any given categorization. Thus, category-based processing might be *less* likely when complex information is available. This suggests that sufficient complexity would interfere with category-based processing because of the increased probability of encountering and fully processing inconsistencies. Complexity is less at issue in perceiving word lists than people, and future research must resolve these competing predictions.

> **Hypothesis 8 (Time Pressure):** *Affective responses are more likely to be category-based as time pressure increases.*

Given that social perceivers are notoriously limited in their on-line information-processing capabilities and that categorization simplifies processing, placing time restrictions on social evaluation tasks should increase the use of category-based processing, even in cases of attribute inconsistency. Conversely, increasing available time should discourage perceivers from categorizing. That is, an antidote to increases in real-world stimulus complexity is to increase available time. However, the real world often demands split-second reactions to others. To generalize the model to externally valid settings, one must consider variability in available time.

> **Hypothesis 9 (Knowledge):** *Affective responses are less likely to be category-based if the perceiver is knowledgeable about the social category.*

Another antidote to increasing task complexity is to increase the perceiver's capacity. Knowledgeable people apparently store category-consistent information in a more compact and organized fashion than do those who are less knowledgeable (J. R. Anderson, 1981; Chase & Simon, 1973; Chi & Koeske, 1983). The consistent information is stored in larger chunks, with more interconnections among its components (Hayes-Roth, 1977; Fiske & Dyer, 1985). Because the category-consistent information is more compact, it effectively leaves more on-line capacity available. Hence, those who are knowledgeable not only can process consistent information, as others can, but they also have the added capacity to process inconsistent information when both kinds of information are present. Previous research suggests that knowledge enhances the perceiver's capacity for handling category-discrepant information, under certain very specific conditions: (1) when consistent and inconsistent information are available simultaneously and (2) when the consistent information is known by both more knowledgeable and less knowledgeable people (Fiske, Kinder, & Larter, 1983).

Thus, knowledgeable people have the capacity to be relatively more sensitive to the ways in which others fail to fit stereotypical categories. When the content of those categories is knowledge shared by both more and less knowledgeable people, knowledgeable people may process inconsistent information more fully than less knowledgeable people and thus may rely on social categories to a lesser extent. (Note two caveats to this hypothesis. First, more and less knowledgeable people usually differ in ways other than sheer domain-specific capacity. Second, the predictions specifically address *on-line* capacity differences in *common* knowledge, as noted under the first two conditions earlier. Hence, this hypothesis is relevant to the carefully delimited conditions described.)

> *Hypothesis 10 (Outcome Dependency):* *Affective responses are less likely to be category-based if the perceiver's outcomes depend on the target person.*

In addition to differences based on modality, reciprocity, complexity, time pressure, and knowledge, people are of far greater significance to the perceiver than a word list is. For example, a real person is a causal agent in one's environment; word lists are not. Real people implicate the self because they are more similar to the perceiver than a word list is. Also, real people judge in return, as noted earlier. For all these reasons and more, the perceiver's social outcomes often depend on other people.

Outcome dependency increases attention to inconsistent information (Erber & Fiske, 1984); the outcome-dependent perceiver is more likely to be motivated to think hard than the perceiver who is not outcome-dependent. This does not mean that the outcome-dependent perceiver will necessarily be accurate, only that such a person is more motivated to have a sense of accuracy and hence to pay attention to inconsistency. This, in turn, should encourage piecemeal processing, as noted, so outcome dependency should undercut categorization.

IMPLICATIONS OF THE CATEGORY-BASED APPROACH

Integrating existing ideas about social affect and social cognition is important both theoretically and practically. From a theoretical perspective, an integration of the recent work on social cognition and the classic models of interpersonal evaluation potentially benefits both approaches. In particular, recent insights about cognitive efficiencies can make earlier ideas about constructing evaluations more precise. Similarly, classic insights about evaluative impressions can extend recent social cognition models to the critical problem of interpersonal affect. The proposed approach is primarily directed to such basic theoretical issues.

Nonetheless, this approach has some potential for application. First, it bears repeating that the model supplements traditional insights about stereotyping. The approach also has potential implications for understanding consumer attitudes, for understanding political behavior, and for understanding group decision making. We will briefly illustrate each of these areas to suggest the wider implications of the approach.

The Study of Stereotyping in Social Psychology

Stereotypes have been defined variously by social psychologists (Ashmore & Del Boca, 1981; Brigham, 1971; Brown, 1965; Katz & Braly, 1933; Schneider *et al.*, 1979). For present purposes, stereotypes can be considered to be schemata containing the perceiver's beliefs about a target person's attributes, which are assumed to be true on the basis of classifying the target, and which are assumed without direct evidence that the individual target in fact possesses those attributes. Stereotyping is a process that takes place within the individual observer, but there is often consensus across observers on the content of stereotypes and that content often implies inferiority (Miller, 1982).

Many definitions make the distinction between stereotypes as cognitions or beliefs about a social group and prejudice as a negative affective response to the group. Prejudice, as an affective reaction, often is operationalized as an evaluative judgment on a positive–negative continuum. In practice, prejudice frequently involves intense and complex affective responses (e.g., hate, anger, disgust, fear); however, evaluation is the central dimension in most discussions of affect (Fiske, 1981), and it is the critical feature of prejudice (Allport, 1954). Consequently, as a starting point, we suggest that the foregoing approach to category-based affect bears on prejudice but discusses it in the simplest possible way, as an evaluative judgment on a positive–negative continuum. Precedent for calling such reactions affective comes, for example, from the attitude literature that operationalizes the affective component of attitudes as a simple positive–negative judgment (e.g., Fishbein & Ajzen, 1975).

Historically, research on stereotyping has followed three general approaches: sociological, psychodynamic, and cognitive (Ashmore & Del Boca, 1981). Studied from a sociological viewpoint, stereotypes serve social structural functions in intergroup settings. Studied from a psychoanalytic viewpoint, stereotypes serve motivational functions within the individual's emotional system. Studied from a social cognition viewpoint, stereotypes serve economic functions within the individual's information-processing system. The model described in this chapter focuses on this third set of functions; as such, it makes predictions about affective–cognitive structures and processes, issues about which the more traditional approaches are silent, especially at the fine-grained level now possible. The research described throughout the chapter is evidence for the relevance of social categories to stereotype-based affective responses. However, the content of the specific stereotype should be less important than the general affective–cognitive processes that are presumed to hold regardless of the specific stereotype content.

The Study of Consumer Preferences

Multiattribute models of evaluation have been studied extensively within the field of consumer psychology (Green & Wind, 1973; Shocker & Srinivasan, 1979). Many marketing researchers assume that product evaluations are processed attribute by attribute in what we would call a piecemeal mode; thus, theorists following the piecemeal approach focus on identifying the attributes that consumers use to make their evaluations (Ajzen & Fishbein, 1980).

We would argue, however, that product evaluations are processed piecemeal only in certain instances. Products are members of categories, just as people are (e.g., a Corvette is a member of the American sports car category). Hence, product evaluations may sometimes proceed in a category-based fashion. This is most likely to occur when the salient attributes of the individual brand are consistent with the product category as a whole, which is true for many product categories (e.g., light beer, over-the-counter medicines). Yet, at other times, product evaluations may proceed in a piecemeal fashion. For instance, some individual brands may not fit the larger product category; the attributes of a brand may be clearly inconsistent with the product category as a whole (e.g., a new three-wheeled car), or the brand may simply have one or more features that are unique (e.g., sound-activated lamps). In such inconsistent instances, consumers may well evaluate the product attribute by attribute. Piecemeal processing would also occur when a product as a whole cues no previously existing category (e.g., products with a novel use or purpose, such as "Fuzzbusters").

In a study cited earlier, Sujan (1985) provided data that support this line of reasoning but also point to the importance of expertise or product familiarity. Her data primarily support our model for self-reported experts in a particular product domain (in this case, cameras). Her subjects used category-based processing when attributes were consistent with the product categories (e.g., a standard 35 mm SLR camera versus an Instamatic-type 110 camera); they used piecemeal processing when products were inconsistent. Category-based (versus piecemeal) processing was indicated for all subjects by faster times to impression formation, more verbalizations related to the product category, fewer verbalizations related to the product's attributes, and fewer references to subtypes. Expertise exaggerated these effects.

This study also supports the idea that piecemeal processing can take forms other than attribute-by-attribute averaging, which is consistent with some suggestions made earlier in this chapter. Specifically, Sujan's (1985) data suggest that piecemeal processing can be based on subtypes or one-instance categories. Expert subjects were frequently able to generate a particular type of camera (subtype) that *did* have the apparently inconsistent set of attributes. Novices, on the other hand, processed stimuli categorically, regardless of attribute consistency or inconsistency (cf. Fiske, Kinder, & Larter, 1983). Apparently, novices knew how they felt about cameras in general, but they were not sufficiently familiar with product attributes (e.g., the number of F-stops) to use them as a basis for evaluation.

In sum, Sujan's (1985) data suggest that category-based evaluative responses supplement the piecemeal-based evaluative processing that is more often studied by marketing researchers. More generally, her data extend the category-based model in several respects. First, the data extend the model from the perception of human stimulus objects to nonhuman stimuli. In so doing, the data also emphasize the importance of expertise. Most people are relatively expert (or at least practiced) at social categorizations; in contrast, when the domain is nonsocial categorization, expertise may vary more widely. Finally, the data suggest that piecemeal processing may draw on subtypes as well as on the averaging of attributes.

Other marketing applications are quite plausible. The category-based approach in general separates situations in which people respond to new information in piecemeal fashion from those in which people respond on the basis of prior categories. For example, consider attitudinal responses to product safety information. One question might concern when people respond to a product on the basis of old (safe) categories and when they respond to new discoveries about a product's liabilities, either simply combining all the old and new information or thoughtfully analyzing the relationships among the various product features. Category-based versus piecemeal responding thus captures some potentially helpful distinctions within consumer psychology.

The Study of Political Cognition

On a somewhat speculative note, the category-based approach suggests that political issues can elicit different kinds of processing in different settings. The approach may prove useful here to separate situations that encourage people to respond to new information by considering its implications piecemeal from those that encourage responding on the basis of prior affect-laden representations. When political communicators successfully frame an issue in terms of certain affect-laden categories rather than others, the issue may elicit category-based affect rather than affect based on a piecemeal consideration of the issue's associated attributes.

The importance of framing political issues in terms of particular affect-laden representations is clear across a variety of topics. For example, research on "symbolic politics" addresses, among other issues, people's self-reported political ideology (i.e., the extent to which they assign themselves to the liberal or conservative category). Such self-reports are not strongly based on the component issues that might be expected to make up the attributes of the ideology categories (Kinder & Sears, 1965). Instead, symbolic politics theorists assume, according to Kinder and Sears (1985, p. 668):

> People have strong evaluative commitments to symbols associated with ideological labels and . . . these shape political thinking. The content of these self-identifications may not be rich in policy preferences. . . . Nevertheless, ideological labels are widely recognized and can trigger strong evaluative reactions.

The symbolic politics analysis has been applied to citizen reactions in a range of specific issues: the economy (Kinder & Kiewiet, 1979), Vietnam (Lau, Brown, & Sears, 1978), busing (Sears, Hensler, & Speer, 1979), and the energy crisis (Sears, Tyler, Citrin, & Kinder, 1978). In each case, citizens' policy preferences apparently were not determined by calculating the pros and cons related to their self-interest, a process that may resemble piecemeal processing of the relevant information. Rather, many such political attitudes seem to be determined by affect-laden political labels that shape how the issue is framed. This latter process may possibly reflect category-based affective responding. Recently, Sears, Huddy, and Schaffer (in press) reported survey data largely consistent with citizens' use of an affect-laden equality schema that is not merely equivalent to the simple combination of its component parts. Such political symbols can be usefully conceived as affect-laden schemata that are cued by categorizing a particular issue (e.g., the ERA) with one set of terms (e.g., equality) rather than another (e.g., maintaining traditional family values).

On an even more speculative note, people's perceptions of nuclear disarmament issues especially may lend themselves to analysis in terms of category-based versus piecemeal processing. That is, nuclear issues are dramatically hypothetical compared to other political issues. Hence, they are especially prone to framing in terms of one affect-laden category versus another. For example, antinuclear activists possess particularly concrete images of the devastation of a nuclear war (Fiske, Pratto, & Pavelchak, 1983), and they do not believe it is survivable (Tyler & McGraw, 1983). They may respond to nuclear threat in terms of a nuclear war schema, categorizing related issues as relevant to the extinction of the human race and thus eliciting the attendant affect. In contrast, prodefense activists may possess particularly concrete images of the inexorable and inhuman effects of communist domination. They may respond to nuclear issues in terms of a Russian threat schema, categorizing related issues as relevant to the annihilation of freedom and justice and thus eliciting the attendant affect (see Fischhoff, Pidgeon, & Fiske, 1983, for related points). Although this is all speculative, the importance of framing political issues in terms of affect-laden categories is not. Emotional appeals have a long history in political persuasion (Janis, 1967), and the current approach suggests how affect-laden responses might be structured and processed in the political thinking of ordinary citizens.

The Study of Group Decision Making

Groups make many types of evaluative decisions: about persons (e.g., parole boards or hiring committees), about products (e.g., marketing departments or consumer safety councils), and about issues (e.g., congressional committees or policy boards). Such evaluative decisions may fit the two-stage model outlined here. Consider, first, the categorization stage. When certain decisions are made regularly, groups may develop consensual ways to categorize the entity. Consider, for example, a corporate board of directors and suppose that a competing corporation buys a large portion of their stock. How this purchase is interpreted by the board of directors would probably depend on how they categorized similar events in the past and on the similarity of the present purchase to those events. Some such events may have been labeled as blatant takeovers and others merely as in the greater interest of both companies. Still others might have been categorized as the folly of an eccentric corporate head. Each categorization presumably has an associated evaluative tag, which would be triggered at the evaluation stage if categorization fits successfully. If categorization is not successful, the second stage of evaluation might be based on the details of the particular instance. Thus, evaluations by groups, like those of individuals, may involve two stages: categorization and affect generation. This would parallel N. H. Anderson and

Graesser's (1976) distinction between the attitude-formation and the consensus-formation stages of group decision making (see also Hogarth, 1981; McGrath, 1984).

However, the generation of evaluation by groups probably differs from that by individuals in both the categorization and the affect-generation stages. Categorization requires knowledge, and in groups, knowledge is generally distributed among group members. The sharing of this knowledge facilitates the categorization stage in several ways. Most important, members present arguments that sometimes contain ideas that might not occur to isolated individuals (Burnstein & Sentis, 1981). Sometimes, the ideas are specifically inspired by the group context. For example, ideas that are in a particular group member's memory might be recalled only when other group members provide the proper cues (Wegner, Giuliano, & Hertel, 1983). At other times, group-inspired ideas are insightful, innovative perspectives that emerge only as a function of the group interaction. Group interaction thus increases the number of potential ways in which an entity can be categorized. If preexisting consensual categories do not exist or are not appropriate, the group can create new ways to categorize the entity, ways that draw on the shared knowledge of all group members.

Consensus on categorization may or may not emerge as a result of group interaction, but lack of consensus would be most problematic if alternative views were evaluatively (rather than descriptively) inconsistent. For example, if all group members' categorizations are positive in nature, the entity is "good" for numerous reasons, and a positive decision is reached. On the other hand, if alternative categorizations have polar-opposite evaluative implications (such as guilty/not guilty in jury trials), lack of consensus on categorization necessitates negotiation.

Sometimes, such negotiation will center on finding a consensual category: in other cases, negotiation may simply center on combining the evaluations of individual group members. Much of the existing research on group decision making focuses on such combinatorial processes, and many models have been proposed (e.g., Kerr, 1981; Latané, 1981; Penrod & Hastie, 1979; Stasser & Davis, 1981; Tanford & Penrod, 1983). These models seek to predict a group decision as a function either of the original distribution of preferences or of the state-to-state changes in individual preferences and/or certainty that occur on the "road to consensus." In general, these models do an excellent job of predicting group evaluations in their intended context (jury trials), but their applicability to most other group evaluation tasks is not yet clear. This is because in jury trials, there are only two ways to categorize the "stimulus": guilty or not guilty. Perhaps categorization and evaluation are not distinguished in these models because they are redundant in such settings (i.e., guilty = good, not guilty = bad). The distinction becomes more useful in relatively open groups, where there are fewer limits to categorization and multiple levels of evaluation. Thus, it is possible that a category-based approach to group decision making would prove useful in the study of more complex decision-making situations.

Group evaluations are obviously much more complicated than is implied in this brief section. For example, several aspects of the individual–group relationship (i.e., status differences, mutual levels of attraction and/or commitment, and degree of interdependence) have strong effects on group decisions (Levine & Pavelchak, 1984). In addition, coalitions tend to form within a group, which could reduce the number of alternative categorizations that need be considered (see Murnighan, 1978). Finally, a comprehensive view of group evaluation processes should recognize the power of minorities as well as majorities in the shaping of group decisions (Levine, 1980; Moscovici, 1980; Tanford & Penrod, 1983). Given these caveats, however, there is reason to believe that the model could be extended to groups.

SUMMARY

As suggested by its potential applications to stereotyping, consumer attitudes, political cognition, and group decision-making, the approach described here has potentially broad implications. Such breadth is an advantage as well as a disadvantage. The potential gain is an integrated theory of social information processing that includes a specific role for affect. The potential risk is in prematurely overextending the approach before its terms, hypotheses, and conditions are well defined.

Consequently, our current efforts are focused on category-based versus piecemeal processing of interpersonal impressions. Thus far, our data show (1) that successful categorization provides a basis for affective response and (2) that category-based affective responses are faster than piecemeal-based affective responses. Current research focuses on two further sets of issues. To summarize the first set, representation and processing of category-based affect suggest the following hypotheses: the amount of information that supports successful categorization has no impact on category-based affect; successful categorization depends only on the descriptive consistency of the individual's attributes with the category, not on their evaluative consistency; affective responses often focus on the person's social category, rather than on the person's other characteristics; and affect can be cued by a social category label or by attributes strongly associated with the category. The second major set of issues discussed were limits to the generalizability of the category-based model, as suggested by the following: affective responses are more likely to be category-based if the sitmulus is complex, if the perceiver is under time pressure, if the perceiver is not knowledgeable about the social category, or if the perceiver's outcomes do not depend on the target person.

Overall, the category-based versus piecemeal approach captures a critical distinction in social cognition and social affect: on the one hand, when people respond quickly because something or someone fits a familiar pattern and, on the other hand, when people respond more slowly to the individual merits and demerits of the stimulus.

Acknowledgments

We would like to thank the following people who have commented on earlier versions of this chapter: Sheldon Cohen, Tory Higgins, Sara Kiesler, David Klahr, Brian MacWhinney, David Schneider, Steven Sherman, Herbert Simon, Richard Sorrentino, and Shelley Taylor.

Notes

1. An exception to the recent neglect of the evaluative implications of social categorization is ingroup–outgroup research (e.g., Brewer, 1979; Wilder & Cooper, 1981). However, ingroup–outgroup research does not focus in detail on the mental representation and processing of category-based knowledge and affect. Brewer does elsewhere address the representation and processing of social knowledge (Brewer, Dull, & Lui, 1981; Lui & Brewer, 1983), and indeed, Brewer's approach to knowledge representation is quite close to ours, minus the affect. Other ingroup–outgroup work by Linville (1982a, 1982b; Linville & Jones, 1980) specifically addresses the effects of perceived category complexity on evaluative impressions; it is compatible with our approach but addresses an orthogonal set of issues.

2. In the strictest sense, links can also be either excitatory or inhibitory. That is, an active node may increase *or* decrease activation at its neighbors, depending on the nature of the link. This is consistent with research on implicit personality theories (Rosenberg & Sedlak, 1972; Schneider, 1973), which has shown that certain traits naturally go together and certain other traits naturally contradict each other. One expects a warm person also to be cheerful, but not to be sad. Similarly, a given category label will activate certain constellations of traits but deactivate others. Deactivated traits would be those that are directly inconsistent with the category label. Thus, people's naive theories about other people and the world provide the "glue" that gives person schemata their coherence (Murphy & Medin, 1983). For the purposes of this chapter, however, person schemata will refer to category labels and associated trait constellations that have exclusively excitatory links.

3. A comparison to the earlier, less-developed versions of our approach may be helpful for those who have read it. There were three main points in that work. First, in the initial work on schema-triggered affect, people were represented as instances of categories. This point still holds here, but in much more detailed form. Second, affect was described as linked to categorization in two ways. When an instance fits a category, the instance elicits the affect linked to the category. This point also still holds, although its processes have been much more developed. When an instance does not fit the category, the earlier version proposed that affect typically is moderated. We now believe that piecemeal affect will be more moderate than category-based affect only when the category (in isolation) elicits more extreme affect than do the individual's category-discrepant attributes (in isolation). In all three studies reported in Fiske (1982), the piecemeal moderation effect was obtained because that specific stimulus configuration was designed to produce it, but it need not be true generally. The current model describes several alternative piecemeal processes that can occur when categorization fails, but only some lead to moderation of affect. A related major change is that one of the processes now posited to occur when categorization fails is the piecemeal process of averaging (or summing). Previously, we had claimed that it was cognitively unreasonable. Now we suggest that it is not the preferred mode but that it can occur, given enough time and effort. Third and finally, the earlier approach hypothesized that behavior is linked to categorization. Although this may well prove true, we have no new data or thoughts on this point.

4. We are indebted to Yaacov Trope for suggesting this possibility.

References

Ajzen, I., & Fishbein, M. (1980). *Understanding attitudes and predicting social behavior*. Englewood Cliffs, NJ: Prentice-Hall.

Allport, G. W. (1954). *The nature of prejudice*. Reading, MA: Addison-Wesley.

Anderson, J. R. (Ed.). (1981). *Cognitive skills and their acquisition.* Hillsdale, NJ: Erlbaum.

Anderson, J. R. (1983). A spreading activation theory of memory. *Journal of Verbal Learning and Verbal Behavior, 22,* 261–295.

Anderson, N. H. (1974). Information integration: A brief survey. In D. H. Krantz, R. C. Atkinson, R. D. Luce, & P. Suppes (Eds.), *Contemporary developments in mathematical psychology* (Vol. 2, pp. 236–305). San Francisco: Freeman.

Anderson, N. H. (1983). *Schemas in person cognition* (Center for Human Information Processing Rep. 118). La Jolla: University of California.

Anderson, N. H., & Graesser, C. C. (1976). An information integration analysis of attitude change in group discussion. *Journal of Personality and Social Psychology, 34,* 210–222.

Anderson, N. H., & Lampel, A. K. (1965). Effect of context on ratings of personality traits. *Psychonomic Science, 3,* 433–434.

Asch, S. E. (1946). Forming impressions of personality. *Journal of Abnormal and Social Psychology, 41,* 258–290.

Ashmore, R. D., & Del Boca, F. K. (1981). Conceptual approaches to sterotypes and sterotyping. In D. L. Hamilton (Ed.), *Cognitive processes in stereotyping and intergroup behavior* (pp. 1–35). Hillsdale, NJ: Erlbaum.

Bartlett, F. (1932). *Remembering: A study in experimental and social psychology.* New York: Cambridge University Press.

Bower, G. H. (1981). Mood and memory. *American Psychologist, 36,* 129–148.

Brewer, M. B. (1979). In-group bias in the minimal intergroup situation: A cognitive-motivational analysis. *Psychological Bulletin, 86,* 307–324.

Brewer, M. B., Dull, V., & Lui, L. (1981). Perceptions of the elderly: Stereotypes as prototypes. *Journal of Personality and Social Psychology, 41,* 656–670.

Brigham, J. C. (1971). Ethnic stereotypes. *Psychological Bulletin, 76,* 15–38.

Brooks, L. (1978). Nonanalytic concept formation and memory for instances. In E. Rosch & B. B. Lloyd (Eds.), *Cognition and categorization* (pp. 169–211). Hillsdale, NJ: Erlbaum.

Brown, R. (1965). *Social psychology.* New York: Free Press.

Bruner, J. S. (1957). Going beyond the information given. In J. S. Bruner, H. Gruber, G. Terrell, & M. Wertheimer (Eds.), *Contemporary approaches to cognition* (pp. 151–156). Cambridge, MA: Harvard University Press.

Burnstein, E., & Schul, Y. (1982). The informational basis of social judgments: Operations in forming an impression of another person. *Journal of Experimental Social Psychology, 18,* 217–234.

Burnstein, E., & Schul, Y. (1983). The informational basis of social judgments: Memory for integrated and nonintegrated trait descriptions. *Journal of Experimental Social Psychology, 19,* 49–57.

Burnstein, E., & Sentis, K. (1981). Attitude polarization in groups. In R. E. Petty, T. M. Ostrom, & T. C. Brock (Eds.), *Cognitive responses in persuasion* (pp. 197–216). Hillsdale, NJ: Erlbaum.

Cantor, N., & Mischel, W. (1979). Prototypes in person perception. In L. Berkowitz (Ed.), *Advances in experimental social psychology* (Vol. 12, pp. 3–51). New York: Academic Press.

Carlston, D. E. (1980). The recall and use of traits and events in social inference processes. *Journal of Experimental Social Psychology, 16,* 303–328.

Chase, W. G., & Simon, H. A. (1973). The mind's eye in chess. In W. G. Chase (Ed.), *Visual information processing* (pp. 215–281). New York: Academic Press.

Chi, M. T. H., & Koeske, R. (1983). Network representation of a child's dinosaur knowledge. *Developmental Psychology, 19,* 29–39.

Clark, M. S., & Fiske, S. T. (Eds.). (1982). *Affect and cognition: The 17th Annual Carnegie Symposium on Cognition.* Hillsdale, NJ: Erlbaum.

Clark, M. S., & Isen, A. M. (1982). Toward understanding the relationship between feeling states and social behavior. In A. Hastorf & A. Isen (Eds.), *Cognitive social psychology* (pp. 73–108). Amsterdam: Elsevier North-Holland.

Dreben, E. K., Fiske, S. T., & Hastie, R. (1979). The independence of evaluative and item information: Impression and recall order effects in behavior-based impression formation. *Journal of Personality and Social Psychology, 37,* 1758–1768.

Ebbesen, E. B., & Allen, R. B. (1979). Cognitive processes in implicit personality trait inferences. *Journal of Personality and Social Psychology, 37,* 471–488.

Erber, R., & Fiske, S. T. (1984). Outcome dependence and attention to inconsistent information about others. *Journal of Personality and Social Psychology, 47*, 709–726.

Felipe, A. I. (1970). Evaluative versus descriptive consistency in trait inferences. *Journal of Personality and Social Psychology, 16*, 627–638.

Fischhoff, B., Pidgeon, N., & Fiske, S. T. (1983). Social science and the politics of the arms race. *Journal of Social Issues, 39*, 161–180.

Fishbein, M., & Ajzen, I. (1975). *Belief, attitude, intention, and behavior: An introduction to theory and research.* Reading, MA: Addison-Wesley.

Fiske, S. T. (1981). Social cognition and affect. In J. Harvey (Ed.), *Cognition, social behavior, and the environment* (pp. 227–264). Hillsdale, NJ: Erlbaum.

Fiske, S. T. (1982). Schema-triggered affect: Applications to social perception. In M. S. Clark & S. T. Fiske (Eds.), *Affect and cognition: The 17th Annual Carnegie Symposium on Cognition* (pp. 55–78). Hillsdale, NJ: Erlbaum.

Fiske, S. T., & Beattie, A. (1982, August). *Two modes of processing affect in social cognition.* Paper presented at the meeting of the American Psychological Association, Washington, DC.

Fiske, S. T., Beattie, A. E., & Milberg, S. J. (1983). *Category-based affect: Stereotypic and piecemeal processes in impression formation.* Unpublished manuscript, Carnegie-Mellon University.

Fiske, S. T., & Dyer, L. (1985). The development of social knowledge structures: Evidence from positive and negative transfer effects. *Journal of Personality and Social Psychology, 48*, 839–852.

Fiske, S. T., Kinder, D. R., & Larter, W. M. (1983). The novice and the expert: Knowledge-based strategies in political cognition. *Journal of Experimental Social Psychology, 19*, 381–400.

Fiske, S. T., & Linville, P. W. (1980). What does the schema concept buy us? *Personality and Social Psychology Bulletin, 6*, 543–557.

Fiske, S. T., & Neuberg, S. L. (1984). *Testing an alternative explanation for category-based affect.* Unpublished manuscript, Carnegie-Mellon University.

Fiske, S. T., Pratto, F., & Pavelchak, M. A. (1983). Citizens' images of nuclear war: Content and consequences. *Journal of Social Issues, 39*, 41–65.

Fiske, S. T., & Taylor, S. E. (1984). *Social cognition.* Reading, MA: Addison-Wesley.

Green, P., & Wind, Y. (1973). *Multiattribute decisions in marketing: A measurement approach.* Hinsdale, IL: Dryden Press.

Hamilton, D. L., & Katz, L. B. (1975, August). *A process-oriented approach to the study of impressions.* Paper presented at the meeting of the American Psychological Association, Chicago.

Hamilton, D. L., & Zanna, M. P. (1974). Context effects in impression formation: Changes in connotative meaning. *Journal of Personality and Social Psychology, 29*, 649–654.

Hartwick, J. (1979). Memory for trait information: A signal detection analysis. *Journal of Experimental Social Psychology, 15*, 533–552.

Hastie, R. (1980). Memory for behavioral information that confirms or contradicts a personality impression. In R. Hastie, T. M. Ostrom, E. B. Ebbesen, R. S. Whyer, D. L. Hamilton, & D. E. Carlston (Eds.), *Person memory: The cognitive basis of social perception* (pp. 155–177). Hillsdale, NJ: Erlbaum.

Hastie, R. (1981). Schematic principles in human memory. In E. T. Higgins, C. P. Herman, & M. P. Zanna (Eds.), *Social cognition: The Ontario Symposium* (Vol. 1, pp. 39–88). Hillsdale, NJ: Erlbaum.

Hastie, R., Ostrom, T. M., Ebbesen, E. B., Wyer, R. S., Hamilton, D. L., & Carlston, D. E. (Eds.) (1980). *Person memory: The cognitive basis of social perception.* Hillsdale, NJ: Erlbaum.

Hayes-Roth, B. (1977). Evolution of cognitive structure and processes. *Psychological Review, 84*, 260–278.

Higgins, E. T., Kuiper, N. A., & Olson, J. M. (1981). Social cognition: A need to get personal. In E. T. Higgins, C. P. Herman, & M. P. Zanna (Eds.), *Social cognition: The Ontario Symposium* (Vol. 1, pp. 395–420). Hillsdale, NJ: Erlbaum.

Higgins, E. T., & Lurie, L. (1983). Context, categorization, and recall: The "change-of-standard" effect. *Cognitive Psychology, 15*, 525–547.

Higgins, E. T., & Rholes, W. S. (1976). Impression formation and role fulfillment: A "holistic reference" approach. *Journal of Experimental Social Psychology, 12*, 422–435.

Higgins, E. T., Rholes, W. S., & Jones, C. R. (1977). Category accessibility and impression formation. *Journal of Experimental Social Psychology, 13*, 141–154.

Hogarth, R. M. (1981). *Decision making in organizations and the organization of decision making.* Unpublished manuscript, University of Chicago, Graduate School of Business, Center for Decision Research.

Janis, J. L. (1967). Effects of fear arousal on attitude change: Recent developments in theory and experimental research. In L. Berkowitz (Ed.), *Advances in experimental social psychology* (Vol. 3, pp. 166–224). New York: Academic Press.

Katz, D., & Braly, K. W. (1933). Racial stereotypes in one hundred college students. *Journal of Abnormal and Social Psychology, 28,* 280–290.

Kerr, N. L. (1981). Social transition schemes: Charting the group's road to agreement. *Journal of Personality and Social Psychology, 41,* 684–702.

Kinder, D. R., & Kiewiet, D. R. (1979). Economic grievances and political behavior: the role of collective discontents and symbolic judgments in congressional voting. *American Journal of Political Science, 23,* 495–527.

Kinder, D. R., & Sears, D. O. (1985). Public opinion and political action. In G. Lindzey & E. Aronson (Eds.), *Handbook of social psychology* (3d ed.), pp. 659–741. Reading, MA: Addison-Wesley.

Latané, B. (1981). The psychology of social impact. *American Psychologist, 36,* 343–356.

Lau, R. R., Brown, T., & Sears, D. O. (1978). Self-interest and civilians' attitudes toward the Vietnam War. *Public Opinion Quarterly, 42,* 464–483.

Levine, J. M. (1980). Reaction to opinion deviance in small groups. In P. Paulus (Ed.) *Psychology of group influence* (pp. 375–429). Hillsdale, NJ: Erlbaum.

Levine, J. M., & Pavelchak, M. A. (1984). Conformity and obedience. In S. Moscovici (Ed.), *Social psychology* (pp. 25–50). Paris: Presses Universitaires de France.

Lingle, J. H., Geva, N., & Ostrom, T. M. (1975, August). *Cognitive processes in person perception.* Paper presented at the meeting of the American Psychological Association, Chicago.

Lingle, J. H., Geva, N., Ostrom, T. M. Leippe, M. R., & Baumgardner, M. H. (1979). Thematic effects of person judgments on impression organization. *Journal of Personality and Social Psychology, 37,* 674–687.

Lingle, J. H., & Ostrom, T. M. (1979). Retrieval selectivity in memory-based impression judgments. *Journal of Personality and Social Psychology, 37,* 180–194.

Linville, P. W. (1982a). Affective consequences of complexity regarding the self and others. In M. S. Clark & S. T. Fiske (Eds.), *Affect and cognition: The 17th Annual Carnegie Symposium on Cognition* (pp. 79–109). Hillsdale, NJ: Erlbaum.

Linville, P. W. (1982b). The complexity-extremity effect and age-based stereotyping. *Journal of Personality and Social Psychology, 42,* 193–211.

Linville, P. W., & Jones, E. E. (1980). Polarized appraisals of outgroup members. *Journal of Personality and Social Psychology, 38,* 689–703.

Lippmann, W. (1922). *Public opinion.* New York: Macmillan.

Lopes, L. L. (1982). Toward a procedural theory of judgment (WHIPP 17). Madison, WI: University of Wisconsin, Wisconsin Human Information Processing Program.

Lui, L., & Brewer, M. R. (1983). Recognition accuracy as evidence of category-consistency effects in person memory. *Social Cognition, 2,* 89–107.

Mandler, G. (1982). The structure of value: Accounting for taste. In M. S. Clark & S. T. Fiske (Eds.), *Affect and cognition: The 17th Annual Carnegie Symposium on Cognition* (pp. 3–36). Hillsdale, NJ: Erlbaum.

Mandler, J. (1979). Categorical and schematic organization in memory. In C. R. Puff (Ed.), *Memory organization and structure* (pp. 259–299). New York: Academic Press.

Markus, H. (1977). Self-schemata and processing information about self. *Journal of Personality and Social Psychology, 35,* 63–78.

McClelland, J. L., & Rumelhart, D. E. (1981). An interactive activation model of context effects in letter perception: Part 1. An account of basic findings. *Psychological Review, 88,* 375–407.

McCloskey, M., & Glucksberg, S. (1979). Decision processes in verifying category membership statements: Implications for models of semantic memory. *Cognitive Psychology, 11,* 1–37.

McGrath, J. E. (1984). *Groups: Interaction and performance.* Englewood Cliffs, NJ: Prentice-Hall.

McGuire, W. J., McGuire, C. V., Child, P., & Fujioka, T. (1978). Salience of ethnicity in the spontaneous self-concept as a function of one's ethnic distinctiveness in the social environment. *Journal of Personality and Social Psychology, 36,* 511–520.

Medin, D. L., & Schaffer, M. M. (1978). Context theory of classification learning. *Psychological Review, 85,* 207–238.

Miller, A. G. (1982). Historical and contemporary perspectives on stereotyping. In A. G. Miller (Ed.), *In the eye of the beholder: Contemporary issues in stereotyping* (pp. 1–40). New York: Praeger.

Moscovici, S. (1980). Toward a theory of conversion behavior. In L. Berkowitz (Ed.), *Advances in experimental social psychology* (Vol. 13, pp. 209–239). New York: Academic Press.

Murnighan, J. K. (1978). Models of coalition behavior: Game theoretic, social psychological, and political perspectives. *Psychological Bulletin, 85,* 1130–1153.

Murphy, G. L., & Medin, D. L. (1983). *Determinants of conceptual coherence: Mental glue.* Unpublished manuscript, Brown University.

Neuberg, S. L., & Fiske, S. T. (1983). *The generalizability of category-based affect.* Unpublished manuscript, Carnegie-Mellon University.

Ostrom, T. M. (1977). Between-theory and within-theory conflict in explaining context effects in impression formation. *Journal of Experimental Social Psychology, 13,* 492–503.

Penrod, S., & Hastie, R. (1979). Models of jury decision-making: A critical review. Psychological Bulletin, 86, 462–492.

Riskey, D. R. (1979). Verbal memory processes in impression formation. *Journal of Experimental Psychology: Human Learning and Memory, 5,* 271–281.

Rosch, E. (1978). Principles of categorization. In E. Rosch & B. B. Lloyd (Eds.), *Cognition and categorization* (pp. 27–48). Hillsdale, NJ: Erlbaum.

Rosenberg, S., & Olshan, K. (1970). Evaluative and descriptive aspects in personality perception. *Journal of Personality and Social Psychology, 16,* 619–626.

Rosenberg, S., & Sedlak, A. (1972). Structural representations of implicit personality theory. In L. Berkowitz (Ed.), *Advances in experimental social psychology* (Vol. 6, pp. 235–297). New York: Academic Press.

Rumelhart, D. E., & McClelland, J. L. (1982). An interactive activation model of context effects in letter perception: Part 2. The contextual enhancement effect and some tests and extensions of the model. *Psychological Review, 89,* 60–94.

Rumelhart, D. E., & Ortony, A. (1977). The representation of knowledge in memory. In R. C. Anderson, R. J. Spiro, & W. E. Montague (Eds.), *Schooling and the acquisition of knowledge* (pp. 99–135). Hillsdale, NJ: Erlbaum.

Schneider, D. J. (1973). Implicit personality theory: A review. *Psychological Review, 79,* 294–309.

Schneider, D. J., Hastorf, A. H., & Ellsworth, P. C. (1979). *Person perception.* Reading, MA: Addison-Wesley.

Sears, D. O., Hensler, C. P., & Speer, L. K. (1979). Whites' opposition to "busing": Self-interest or symbolic racism? *American Political Science Review, 73,* 369–384.

Sears, D. O., Huddy, L., & Schaffer, L. G. (in press). Schemas and symbolic politics: The cases of racial and gender equality. In R. R. Lau & D. O. Sears (Eds.), *Political cognition: The 19th Annual Carnegie Symposium on Cognition.* Hillsdale, NJ: Erlbaum.

Sears, D. O., Tyler, T. R., Citrin, J. C., & Kinder, D. R. (1978). Political system support and public response to the energy crisis. *American Journal of Political Science, 22,* 56–82.

Shocker, A. D., & Srinivasan, V. (1979). Multiattribute approaches for product concept evaluation and generation: A critical review. *Journal of Marketing Research, 16,* 159–180.

Smith, E. E., & Medin, D. L. (1981). *Categories and concepts.* Cambridge, MA: Harvard University Press.

Smith, E. E., Shoben, E. J., & Rips, L. J. (1974). Structure and process in semantic memory: A featural model for semantic decisions. *Psychological Review, 81,* 214–241.

Smith, J. D., & Nelson, D. G. K. (1984). Overall similarity in adults' classification: The child in all of us. *Journal of Experimental Psychology: General, 113,* 137–159.

Srull, T. K. (1981). Person memory: Some tests of associative storage and retrieval models. *Journal of Experimental Psychology: Human Learning and Memory, 7,* 440–462.

Srull, T. K., & Wyer, R. S., Jr. (1980). Category accessibility and social perception: Some implications for the study of person memory and interpersonal judgments. *Journal of Personality and Social Psychology, 38,* 841–856.

Stasser, G., & Davis, J. H. (1981). Group decision-making and social influence: A social interaction sequence model. *Psychological Review, 88*, 523–551.

Sujan, M. (1985). Consumer knowledge: Effects on evaluation strategies mediating consumer judgments. *Journal of Consumer Research, 12*, 1–16.

Tanford, S., & Penrod, S. (1983). *Social influence model: A formal integration of research on majority and minority influence processes.* Unpublished manuscript, University of Wisconsin.

Taylor, S. E. (1981). A categorization approach to stereotyping. In D. L. Hamilton (Ed.), *Cognitive processes in stereotyping and intergroup behavior* (pp. 83–114). Hillsdale, NJ: Erlbaum.

Taylor, S. E. & Crocker, J. (1981). Schematic bases of social information processing. In E. T. Higgins, C. P. Herman, & M. P. Zanna (Eds.), *Social cognition: The Ontario Symposium* (Vol. 1, pp. 89–134). Hillsdale, NJ: Erlbaum.

Taylor, S. E., & Fiske, S. T. (1978). Salience, attention, and attribution: Top of the head phenomena. In L. Berkowitz (Ed.), *Advances in experimental social psychology* (Vol. 11, pp. 249–288). New York: Academic Press.

Taylor, S. E., & Fiske, S. T. (1981). Getting inside the head: Methodologies for process analysis. In J. Harvey, W. Ickes, & R. Kidd (Eds.), *New directions in attribution research* (Vol. 3, pp. 459–524). Hillsdale, NJ: Erlbaum.

Tyler, T. R., & McGraw, K. M. (1983). The threat of nuclear war: Risk interpretation and behavioral response. *Journal of Social Issues, 39*, 25–40.

Weber, R., & Crocker, J. (1983). Cognitive processes in the revision of stereotypic beliefs. *Journal of Personality and Social Psychology, 45*, 961–977.

Wegner, D. M., Giuliano, T., & Hertel, P. T. (1983). *Cognitive interdependence in close relationships.* Unpublished manuscript, Trinity University.

Wickelgren, W. A. (1981). Human learning and memory. *Annual Review of Psychology, 32*, 21–52.

Wilder, D. A., & Cooper, W. E. (1981). Categorization into groups: Consequences for social perception and attribution. In J. Harvey, W. Ickes, & R. Kidd (Eds.), *New directions in attribution research* (Vol. 3, pp. 248–277). Hillsdale, NJ: Erlbaum.

Wyer, R. S., Jr., & Carlston, D. E. (1979). *Social cognition, inference, and attribution.* Hillsdale, NJ: Erlbaum.

Wyer, R. S., Jr., & Gordon, S. E. (1982). The recall of information about persons and groups. *Journal of Experimental Social Psychology, 18*, 128–164.

Zajonc, R. B. (1980). Feeling and thinking: Preferences need no inferences. *American Psychologist, 35*, 151–175.

Zajonc, R. B., Pietromonaco, P., & Bargh, J. (1982). Independence and interaction of affect and cognition. In M. S. Clark & S. T. Fiske (Eds.), *Affect and cognition: The 17th Annual Carnegie Symposium on Cognition* (pp. 211–227). Hillsdale, NJ: Erlbaum.

Zanna, M. P., & Hamilton, D. L. (1977). Further evidence for meaning change in impression formation. *Journal of Experimental Social Psychology, 13*, 224–238.

CHAPTER 8

How Do Attitudes Guide Behavior?

RUSSELL H. FAZIO
Indiana University

INTRODUCTION

The theme of this volume is the interfaces among affect, cognition, and behavior. What is the nature of the bidirectional relations among these variables? How does affect influence cognition, and vice versa? To what degree does each of these follow from prior behavior and influence subsequent behavior?

Questions of this sort have long been a crucial concern within the attitude literature. Attitude theorists and researchers probably have devoted a greater degree of their efforts to such issues than any other group of social psychologists. To note just a few examples, Rosenberg (1960) examined the effect of hypnotically induced affect on beliefs toward the attitudinal issue in question. Much of the research on persuasion (for a review, see Eagly & Chaiken, 1984) involves the impact of new information and arguments (cognitions) on favorability (affect) toward the attitude object. Both cognitive dissonance (Festinger, 1957) and self-perception (Bem, 1972) theories have spawned an amazing amount of research concerned with the effects of behavior on subsequent attitudes. Similarly, there has been considerable discussion and research concerning the impact that attitudes may or may not have on subsequent behavior (e.g., Schuman & Johnson, 1976; Wicker, 1969; Zanna, Higgins, & Herman, 1982).

The concern of attitude theorists with the interfaces among affect, cognition, and behavior may be best exemplified by the tricomponent view of attitudes. This perspective essentially defines an attitude as consisting of three interrelated components: an affective component involving feelings about and evaluation of the attitude object, a cognitive component involving beliefs about the object, and a behavioral intentions component (Kothandapani, 1971; Ostrom, 1969).

Although I shall adopt a far simpler definition of attitude—one that views an attitude as essentially affect—I will be concerned with the relations between affect, cognition, and behavior. The focus of this chapter is on the process by which attitudes guide behavior. A model characterizing the attitude-to-behavior process shall be presented, and the results of a program of research testing the process model will be summarized. In so doing, I will be considering the influence of attitude (affect) on subsequent behavior through mediating cognitive processes involving the individual's perceptions of and cognitions about the attitude object in the immediate situation in which the attitude object is encountered. Before detailing the proposed model, a brief historical overview of the literature on attitude–behavior consistency may be useful.

A Brief Historical Overview of the Attitude–Behavior Consistency Issue

Zanna and Fazio (1982) have characterized approaches to the study of attitude–behavior consistency as having progressed through some clear generations of thought and research. Until the mid-1960s, there appears to have been a predominant assumption in the field of a one-to-one correspondence between attitudes and behavior. Early definitions of the attitude concept (e.g., Allport, 1935; Doob, 1947) went so far as to postulate an attitude–behavior link as an explicit part of the definition, ironically implying that if correspondence with behavior was lacking, then there was no attitude. Aside from a few early skeptics (e.g., Corey, 1937; LaPiere, 1934) this assumption remained largely unchallenged until the 1960s, when a number of researchers began to scrutinize the available literature and conduct further investigations of the attitude–behavior relation. These researchers were essentially asking what Zanna and Fazio (1982) have referred to as the "Is" question: "Is there a relation between attitudes and subsequent behavior?" Of these researchers, Allan Wicker (1969) wrote what was undoubtedly the most radical (and impactful) review. He concluded that attitudes typically do not relate to subsequent behavior and, in a later paper (Wicker, 1971), even went so far as to suggest that it may be desirable to abandon the attitude concept.

What Wicker's review did was to spark interest and research. However, later developments have made it clear that Wicker's position was greatly overstated. As a result, recent reviews have portrayed the attitude–behavior relation in a far more optimistic light (Fazio & Zanna, 1981; Schuman & Johnson, 1976). There can be no doubt that, as Wicker indicated, there are a number of reports of minimal or zero attitude–behavior correlations. Nor can there be any doubt that the careful conceptual and empirical scrutiny of the late 1960s and early 1970s has led to a refutation of the notion that a general one-to-one correspondence exists between attitudes and behavior. Yet what has become clear is that fairly impressive attitude–behavior correlations are sometimes observed. Indeed, observed relations have ranged from zero (e.g., Corey's [1937] study of cheating) to the very strong (e.g., Kelly & Mirer's [1974] analysis of voting behavior).

Given the range of observed outcomes, the question of attitude–behavior consistency began to be approached with a new perspective—what Zanna and Fazio (1982) referred to as the "When" approach. Rather than asking whether attitudes relate to behavior, researchers began to search for variables that moderate the extent of the attitude–behavior relation. In its most general form, the crucial question became: "Under what conditions do what kinds of attitudes held by what kinds of individuals predict what kinds of behavior?" (Fazio & Zanna, 1981, p. 165).

Over the past decade, considerable progress has been made in this regard. Many situational and personality variables and many attitudinal qualities have been identified as moderators of the attitude–behavior relation. Normative constraints or inducements have been shown to affect the relation (Ajzen & Fishbein, 1973; Schofield, 1974; Warner & DeFleur, 1969), as have such situational variables as the individual's holding a vested interest in the behavioral issue (Sivacek & Crano, 1982). Various personality factors—such as self-image as a "doer" (McArthur, Kiesler, & Cook, 1969), level of moral reasoning (Rholes & Bailey, 1983), and self-monitoring (Snyder & Swann, 1976; Zanna, Olson, & Fazio, 1980)—have also been found to relate to attitude–behavior consistency. Observed attitude–behavior relations have been found to be enhanced by the employment of attitude and behavior measures of equivalent levels of specificity (Ajzen & Fishbein, 1977). Various attitudinal qualities—including the consistency between affective and cognitive components of attitudes (Norman, 1975), the temporal stability of attitudes (Schwartz, 1978), the confidence with which the attitude is held (Fazio & Zanna, 1978a, 1978b; Sample & Warland, 1973), and how clearly defined the attitude is, as measured by the width of the latitude of rejection (Fazio & Zanna, 1978b; Sherif, Kelly, Rodgers, Sarup, & Tittler, 1973)—have each been shown to relate to attitude–behavior consistency. Also included in the latter class of variables is the manner of attitude formation. Much evidence now exists to suggest that attitudes formed on the basis of direct, behavioral experience with an attitude object are more predictive of later behavior than are attitudes formed via more indirect, nonbehavioral experience (for a review, see Fazio & Zanna, 1981).

There can be no doubt that attitudes do sometimes relate to subsequent behavior and that the field has achieved some understanding of just when that "sometimes" is. As the foregoing listing implies, a number of important moderator variables have been identified successfully. As a result of the many empirical efforts, the field now has a fairly lengthy "catalog" of variables known to moderate the attitude–behavior relation.

The Need for a Process Approach

Despite the resurgence of research on the attitude–behavior relation and despite the now-voluminous literature, little attention has been paid to one very fundamental issue regarding that relation—what Zanna and Fazio (1982) referred to as the "How" question and forecasted as being the central issue of a new third generation of research on attitude–behavior consistency. How do attitudes guide behavior? Throughout the literature (the present author's work being no exception), mention is made of attitudes "guiding" or "influencing" behavior, with little or no accompanying explanation as to how this might occur. What lies behind attitude–behavior consistency? What processes link an attitude to overt behavior and lead it to influence an individual's behavior?

In addition to addressing a very fundamental, yet neglected, question regarding the "translation" of attitudes into behavior, a process approach may have implications for the previous research that has identified moderators of the attitude–behavior relation. As indicated earlier, the product of research stemming from the "When" question has been the identification of a host of seemingly unrelated variables that act as determinants of attitude–behavior consistency. The efforts that have produced this extensive catalog have been primarily empirical in nature, and as commentators on this literature have noted, there has been a marked lack of substantive theory (Cooper & Croyle, 1984).

A model of the process by which attitudes guide behavior can provide the needed theoretical perspective and has the potential of integrating conceptually what is now a mere catalog of moderating variables. Furthermore, such a model may suggest how and why these various factors moderate the attitude–behavior relation. I shall propose such a process model and illustrate how previously identified determinants of attitude–behavior consistency might be linked to the model by focusing on one such moderating variable—the manner of attitude formation.

A MODEL OF THE ATTITUDE-TO-BEHAVIOR PROCESS

The present model is intended to elucidate a step-by-step process by which attitudes guide behavior. The proposed model has been characterized briefly by Fazio, Powell, and Herr (1983), and it will be explicated in more detail here. Then a series of experiments testing various aspects of the process model will be summarized.

Definition of the Situation and the Event

The model begins by assuming that an individual's social behavior is largely a function of his or her perceptions in the immediate situation in which the attitude object is encountered. There is nothing startling or novel about the assumption that behavior is primarily determined by the individual's perceptions in the immediate situation. Indeed, the model simply posits that behavior is largely a function of the individual's definition of the situation. The social world is such that, typically, situations are at least somewhat ambiguous. Social stimuli frequently have multiple meanings. Hence, some degree of interpretation on the part of the individual is required. Such definition of the situation determines the direction and nature of the individual's behavior. This is, of course, a core principle of symbolic interactionism (see Manis & Meltzer, 1972; Rose, 1962). Thomas (1931) argued: "Preliminary to any self-determined act of behavior there is always a stage of examination and determination which we may call the definition of the situation" (p. 41). Similarly,

Stebbins (1972) referred to the term definition of the situation as "a synthesis, interpretation, and interrelation of predispositions, intentions, and elements of the setting" (p. 343) and asserted that "it is the ongoing definition of the situation . . . that guides behavior in the immediate setting" (p. 351).

The concept of definition of the situation has proved useful in experimental social psychology. As a specific example, consider Latané and Darley's (1970) decision-tree analysis of bystander intervention in emergencies. Definition of the event as an emergency is viewed as a critical step if an individual is to intervene. In the classic "smoke-filled room" experiment (Latané & Darley, 1968), subjects who failed to define the smokelike vapors as a potential indicant of a fire were unlikely to report the event to the experimenter. It is in this manner that interpretations of social stimuli and the situations in which they are encountered determine an individual's behavior.

This step of interpretation or definition takes on crucial importance in the context of the attitude-to-behavior process, for, as we shall see, the extent to which the attitude influences such perceptions determines the degree to which the attitude guides behavior. The relevant perceptions when an attitude object is encountered can be considered to involve two components that the discussion up to this point has not attempted to distinguish clearly. One component concerns the individual's perceptions of the attitude object in the immediate situation. Consider, for example, a situation in which the attitude object of interest is some target person. A considerable amount of evidence suggests that a perceiver's behavior toward a target person is influenced by his or her immediate perceptions of that target person (see Snyder & Swann, 1978; Snyder, Tanke, & Berscheid, 1977; Word, Zanna, & Cooper, 1974). As a specific example, consider Kelley's (1950) classic experiment in which students were led to believe that a guest instructor was either a "warm" or "cold" person. Those students with the "warm" expectation tended to participate in the class discussion led by the guest instructor to a greater extent than did those with the "cold" expectation. Thus, perceptions of the target person— that is, the attitude object—influenced behavior.

The second class of relevant perceptions are perceptions of the setting or context in which the attitude object is encountered—that is, the definition of the situation itself. Together, perceptions of the attitude object in the immediate situation and definition of the situation comprise what shall be referred to as the individual's definition of the event. When an individual encounters a target person toward whom he or she has an attitude, the encounter is apt to produce very different definitions of the event if the setting is a funeral parlor, a tennis court, or the individual's home. It is this definition of the event—perceptions that involve both the attitude object and the situation in which the object is encountered—that the model postulates to act as the primary determinant of an individual's behavior.

Attitudes Guide Perceptions

Given the assumption concerning the importance of the individual's definition of the event, the question, in terms of attitudes guiding behavior, centers on the degree to which the individual's attitude will influence the definition of the event. As indicated by the earlier quotation from Stebbins regarding definition of the situation, such definitions have been presumed to be, in part, a function of what the individual brings into the situation. This notion stems from the "New Look" movement (e.g., Bruner, 1957), which so heavily emphasized the constructive nature of perception. Interpretations of objects and situations depend to a large extent on the knowledge structures, affect, values, and expectations that the individual holds.

An individual's attitude thus may influence the individual's perceptions of the attitude object in the immediate situation and, hence, his or her definition of the event. Allport (1935) made this same argument in his highly influential paper on attitudes:

> Without guiding attitudes the individual is confused and baffled. Some kind of preparation is essential before he can make a satisfactory observation, pass suitable judgment, or make any but the most primitive reflex type of response. Attitudes determine for each individual what he will see and hear, what he will think and what he will do. To borrow a phrase from William James, they "engender meaning upon the world"; they draw lines about and segregate an otherwise chaotic environment; they are our methods for finding our way about in an ambiguous universe. (p. 806)

Allport's statements describe what later theorists came to refer to as the object appraisal or knowledge function that attitudes serve. Attitude theorists considered one of the major functions served by attitudes to be that of organizing and structuring a rather chaotic universe of objects (Katz, 1960; Smith, Bruner, & White, 1956). An attitude is thought to provide "a ready aid in 'sizing up' objects and events in the environment" (Smith *et al.*, 1956, p. 41).

As this object appraisal function of attitudes implies, attitudes have been shown empirically to guide information processing. Emphasizing the constructive nature of perception, researchers involved in the "New Look" movement (e.g., Bruner, 1957) demonstrated an association between the value of an object to a given individual and the perception of the object's physical attributes (Bruner & Goodman, 1947; Lambert, Solomon, & Watson, 1949). Similarly, attitudes have been found to relate to what is perceived in an attitudinally relevant pictorial presentation (Proshansky, 1943; Seeleman, 1940). Proshansky, for example, found that an individual's attitude toward organized labor related to the person's description of what he or she "saw" in an ambiguous but labor-relevant picture. Hastorf and Cantril (1954) observed a similar phenomenon with regard to the perception of infractions during a football game.

A corresponding impact of attitude has been observed in more recent research. Lord, Ross, and Lepper (1979) have demonstrated that people's attitudes toward a social policy issue strongly affect their evaluations of relevant empirical evidence. Lingle and Ostrom (1980) have also presented evidence that attitudes provide a framework in terms of which subsequent judgmental decisions are made. In the social perception domain, it is apparent that attitudes toward a target person influence the manner in which ambiguous behavior on the part of the target is interpreted and the causal attributions that are made for nonambiguous behaviors (for a review, see Darley & Fazio, 1980). For example, skilled performers or positive behaviors on the part of a liked other are attributed to the dispositional characteristics of that other, whereas the same behaviors by a disliked other are attributed to situational forces (Regan, Straus, & Fazio, 1974).

In summary, a rich and varied literature exists to document the assumption attitudes influence perceptions relevant to the object. Just as Smith *et al.* (1956) proposed, attitudes appear to serve as convenient and useful summaries by which people "size up" objects in the environment.

Thus, it appears that when an individual encounters an attitude object, his or her attitude will guide perceptions of the object in the immediate situation. These immediate perceptions, congruent as they are with the individual's attitudes, may then prompt attitudinally consistent behavior. For example, if an individual holds a negative attitude toward a target person, that attitude will affect how the perceiver views the target person when they encounter one another. Given the negative attitude, the individual is likely to attend closely to any unpleasant mannerisms exhibited by that target person and to interpret ambiguous comments or behaviors in a negative manner—as signs, perhaps, of aloofness or hostility. In other words, through a process of selective perception, the attitude "colors" the individual's current perceptions of the target person. These immediate perceptions, filtered as they are through the attitude, then influence the individual's behavior response. Having "perceived" aloofness and hostility on the part of the target person, the individual responds in a hostile manner. The end result is behavior consistent with the attitude that initiated and "guided" the entire process.

The Effect of Norms

According to the present model of the attitude-to-behavior process, then, attitudes guide behavior through their mediating impact on perceptions. However, if we assume that the model as described thus far is valid, a crucial issue arises: Why is the answer to the question "Is there an attitude–behavior relation?" a resounding "sometimes"? It is precisely the sort of theorizing that we have engaged in thus far that led to the original presumption of a one-to-one correspondence between attitudes and behavior. Yet empirical findings clearly indicate that attitude–behavior consistency is not at all constant. Hence, there must be more to the process by which attitudes guide behavior. Some factors must prevent the process from reaching its culmination or even prevent it from occurring.

One such factor may be the role of subjective norms. I have argued that behavior is a function of the individual's definition of the event. However, as indicated earlier, the attitude object itself is only one element within the situation, and perceptions of the object in the immediate situation are only one component of the definition of the event at which the individual arrives. The definition of the situation itself is also important. The individual brings into the situation many potentially relevant knowledge structures, only one of which is his or her attitude toward the object. One particularly important set of information that may affect the individual's definition of the event is his or her knowledge of what behaviors are or are not normatively appropriate. Normative guidelines can exert a tremendous impact on the individual's definition of the situation and subsequent behavior. The setting in Milgram's (1963) obedience experiment is a dramatic example of how norms regarding authority figures influence people's definitions of the situation as one in which they have contracted to act as the agent of the experimenter.

Given that perceptions of the attitude object may be only one component of the individual's definition of the event, it is possible for the individual's definition of the situation to override the immediate perceptions of the object. Let us reconsider the target person toward whom an individual holds a negative attitude. The attitude may bias the individual's perception of the behavior of the target person such that the person is perceived as exhibiting hostile, aloof behaviors in the present situation. Thus, immediate perceptions are congruent with the attitude, and this may typically prompt a hostile response. Yet even if the current perceptions of the target are negative, an individual's definition of the event will be far different if the target person is an authority figure who holds some power over the perceiver. Norms may lead the individual to define the situation as one in which remaining calm and overtly friendly is necessary and in which it is important to monitor carefully how he or she responds. As a result, the individual is unlikely to reciprocate the hostility that he or she perceives the target person displaying.

As another example, consider the sort of situation examined in Warner and DeFleur's (1969) study of the impact of norms on attitude–behavior consistency. Imagine a liberal in the segregationist Old South being asked to sign a pro-integration petition. The individual's liberal attitudes are apt to lead him or her to view the petition favorably and to endorse it. Yet the individual's definition of the event is likely to change markedly if he or she is informed that the names of the petition endorsers will be published in the local paper. Knowledge about current normative prescriptions, along with attitudes, can influence the individual's definitions of the situation and the event. Although the individual may continue to perceive the petition itself favorably, his or her definition of the event would include the possibility that he or she might be subjected to negative social sanctions for violating the community's sense of normatively appropriate interracial behavior. As a result, the individual is less likely to sign the petition in a situation involving public rather than private disclosure.

Thus, it appears evident that norms, in addition to attitudinally congruent perceptions of the attitude object in the immediate situation, may affect the individual's definition of the event. To the extent that the normative guidelines are counter to the individual's attitude, the definition of the event will not be attitudinally congruent; nor will it prompt attitudinally congruent behavior. This may be one reason why attitude–behavior consistency does not always occur.

The Role of Attitude Accessibility

Not all situations are normatively prescribed. Even in normatively free situations, considerable variability in attitude–behavior consistency has been observed. The fact that many variables other than normative constraints have been found to moderate the attitude–behavior relation points this out clearly. I suspect that, in many instances, the attitude–behavior process that I have described may not be initiated. The attitude is simply not activated from memory when the individual encounters the attitude object. Unless the attitude is accessed from memory, it cannot produce selective perception of the object in the immediate situation. The individual may never consider the attitude object in evaluative terms.

The crucial importance of attitude activation has been demonstrated in an interesting experiment by Snyder and Swann (1976). This experiment involved judgments of liability in a simulated sex discrimination court case and the relation between attituds toward affirmative action and these liability verdicts. In the conditions relevant to the present concerns, Snyder and Swann found that attitude–behavior correlations were significantly higher in an attitude-salient condition in which subjects were instructed to take some time to consider their views toward affirmative action before reading the court case than in a condition in which subjects were not given such an opportunity. From the perspective of the process model, the experimental instruction amounts to a situational inducement to access the individual's attitude. Once activated, the attitude then guided the processing and interpretation of the case history information and hence influenced the eventual decision. Although more shall be said about this experiment at a later point, it does indicate how crucial it is that an attitude be activated from memory if the attitude is to influence later behavior. Attitude accessibility appears to be an important and central factor in the attitude-to-behavior process.

Figure 8.1 presents a schematic summary of the proposed process model. In essence, the model proposes that a number of steps must occur for behavior toward an object to be influenced by the individual's attitude. First and foremost, the attitude must be accessed from memory upon observation of the attitude object. Unless this step occurs, the attitude will not "guide" the behavior. If the attitude is accessed, then the attitude will serve as a "filter" through which the attitude object will be perceived. This process of selective perception consequently biases the individual's immediate perceptions of the attitude object. If I hold a positive attitude toward a given object and if my attitude has been activated, then I am likely to notice, attend to, and process primarily the positive qualities of the object.

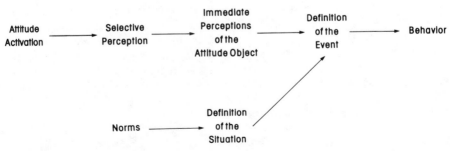

FIGURE 8.1 A diagram of the proposed model of the attitude-to-behavior process.

Similarly, a negative attitude would prompt a perceptual emphasis on the negative qualities of the object. Thus, selective perception, the second step in the model, produces perceptions of the object in the immediate situation that are consistent with the attitude. These immediate perceptions comprise at least a part of the individual's definition of the event. Normative guidelines may affect the individual's definition of the situation and, if counter to the individual's attitude, may result in a definition of the event that does not permit the attitude to be expressed behaviorally. In situations where norms do not dictate the definition of the event, however, the definition will be attitudinally congruent if attitude activation and selective perception have occurred. It is this definition of the event that then determines the direction and nature of the behavior. Approach behaviors are prompted by a definition of the event that consists primarily of positive perceptions of the attitude object in the immediate situation. Likewise, avoidance behaviors are prompted by a negative definition of the event.

Given the crucial role that attitude accessibility occupies in the proposed process model, it becomes important to consider what might determine attitude accessibility. What variables determine whether individuals will access their attitudes upon encountering or observing the attitude object? Attitude activation may occur as a result of some situational cue that defines attitudes as relevant to the immediate situation. In other words, the attitude activation is acute in nature, stemming from some contextual cue. For example, in a recent experiment, Snyder and Kendzierski (1982) exposed subjects with favorable attitudes toward psychological research to a sign posted on the wall of a waiting room. The notice was a request for volunteers to participate in a psychological experiment. Each subject overheard two confederates conversing about the request. When one indicated that he didn't know whether to volunteer or not, the other replied in such a way as to prompt attitude activation or not. In the experimental condition, the reply defined the situation as attitudinally relevant: "[It's] really a question of how worthwhile you think experiments are." In the control condition, no such prompt was delivered, the reply being, simply, "Beats me—it's up to you." Although all the subjects who heard one of these two exchanges had positive attitudes toward psychological research, significantly more of those in the experimental condition acted in accordance with their attitudes and volunteered than those in the control condition. Thus, situations themselves may sometimes provide cues that prompt attitude activation (see also Borgida & Campbell, 1982).

Obviously, not all situations provide such attitude-relevance cues. In cue-free situations, attitudes may still exert an impact on behavior for some individuals. Indeed, 25% of the subjects in the control condition of the Snyder and Kendzierski (1982) experiment did volunteer to participate. Such situations have been my primary interest. My approach has been concerned with the activation of attitudes upon observation of the attitude object without the benefit of prompting from situational cues—in other words, the chronic accessibility of attitudes. What determines whether attitudes are activated in such cue-free settings? To continue with the example, what may distinguish the 25% in the control condition who volunteered, despite having received no attitudinal cue, from those who did not volunteer?

One possible determinant of chronic attitude accessibility, which was noted by Fazio, Chen, McDonel and Sherman (1982), follows from our definition of attitude. Hence, it becomes necessary to digress briefly to offer our working definition. Numerous definitions have appeared in the literature (see Greenwald, 1968; McGuire, 1969), but they all possess one common feature. An attitude is typically considered to involve categorization of an object along an evaluative dimension (e.g., Fishbein, 1963, 1966; Jones & Gerard, 1967; Thurstone, 1946). It is this single feature that has been adopted as a working definition. An attitude is essentially an association between a given object and a given evaluation. This evaluation may range in nature from a very "hot" affect (the attitude object being associated with a strong emotional response) to a "cold," cognitively based judgment of the favorability of the attitude object (see Abelson, Kinder, Peters, & Fiske, 1982; Zanna & Rempel, 1984).

This simple, straightforward definition possesses at least two assets. The first stems from its very simplicity. Unlike some early definitions of attitude (e.g., Allport, 1935; Doob, 1947), it does not postulate the existence of a relation between attitude and subsequent behavior as a part of the definition. Thus, the extent to which the attitude relates to behavior is left as an empirical, not a definitional, issue. Similarly, our simple definition makes no claim about necessary relations among affect, cognition, and behavioral intentions, as does the tricomponent view of attitude. Once again, our definition (which is equivalent to the single affective dimension of the tricomponent view) views such relations as issues to be addressed empirically.

More important, and more relevant to the present concerns, the definition endorsed here implies something interesting about chronic attitude accessibility. An attitude is viewed as an association, and like any construct based on associative learning, the strength of the attitude can vary; that is, the strength of the association between an object and the evaluation can vary. This associative strength may determine the accessibility of the attitude from memory. If it is strongly associated with the object, the evaluation may be accessed easily and quickly upon observation of, or inquiry about, the object. If it is only weakly associated, the evaluation may be much less likely to be accessed and more difficult to access. Even without prompting from situational cues, then, the attitudes of people for whom the object-evaluation association is strong may be activated when they encounter the attitude object and may affect their perceptions of and behavior toward the object. A relatively weak association, on the other hand, may mean that the attitude is never activated in the encounter with the object; hence, behavior occurs without any guidance from the attitude.

In the remaining sections of this chapter, the findings from a series of experiments testing the process model will be presented. We will consider (1) whether attitude accessibility and attitude–behavior consistency do vary, as suggested by the model, as a function of the strength of the object-evaluation association; (2) whether a previously identified moderator of the attitude–

behavior relation—the manner of attitude formation—affects the accessibility of the resulting attitude; (3) whether at least some sorts of attitudes can be activated spontaneously from memory upon mere observation of the attitude object; and finally, (4) the role of selective perception in promoting attitude–behavior consistency.

ATTITUDE ACCESSIBILITY AND THE STRENGTH OF THE OBJECT-EVALUATION ASSOCIATION

The first issue that arises in attempting to test the predictions of the model concerning attitude accessibility is one of operationalization. How can attitude accessibility be measured? We have done so via response time (see Markus, 1977). The latency with which people can respond to an inquiry about their attitudes is considered to be a reflection of the accessibility of the attitude. Typically, our subjects were presented with a series of slides, each of which listed the name of an attitude object followed by an evaluative adjective (e.g., Legalization of Marijuana: Desirable?). The subject's task was to press a "Yes" or a "No" control button as quickly as possible to indicate whether the adjective was or was not descriptive of his or her attitude toward the specified object. The subject was instructed to respond as quickly and accurately as possible. Latency of response, from slide onset to response, was automatically recorded by a microprocessor and served as the datum of interest.

The response time measure is presumed to approximate the likelihood that the attitude is activated spontaneously upon the individual's exposure to the attitude object. That is, we assume that the speed with which people can respond to a direct inquiry about their attitudes covaries with the likelihood of spontaneous attitudinal activation upon mere observation of the attitude object. In the case of a direct attitudinal inquiry, the stronger the object-evaluation association, the faster people can respond. Similarly, in the case of mere observation of the attitude object, the stronger the association, the greater the probability that the attitude spontaneously "comes to mind." Evidence in support of this assumption regarding response latency as an approximation of the likelihood of automatic attitudinal activation will be presented at a later point in the chapter.

Initial work was aimed at testing the hypothesis that the strength of the object-evaluation association determines the accessibility of the attitude from memory. It was reasoned that, like any other concept based on associative learning, the object-evaluation association should be strengthened by inducing people to express their attitudes repeatedly. Each time an attitude is expressed verbally, an instance of noting the association has occurred, thus enhancing associative strength. Fazio *et al.* (1982, Exp. 3) employed this reasoning in attempting to manipulate directly the strength of the object-evaluation association. Subjects were introduced to a set of intellectual puzzles by observing a videotape of an individual working with each type of puzzle. All subjects then evaluated the interest value of each puzzle type. To strengthen the object-evaluation association, the experimenter, using an appropriate ruse, asked half of the subjects to copy their ratings onto two additional forms. The experimenter remarked that the additional forms were for her professor and the computer keypuncher and asked the subjects to help her out by copying their original ratings onto the forms. Since each form was distinct from the original and also involved a different ordering of the five puzzle types, the subjects were forced to find a given puzzle type and its associated rating on the original and then indicate that rating in the appropriate place on each of the other two forms. Essentially, then, these subjects were induced to repeatedly note and express their evaluations of each puzzle type.

This simple manipulation was found to have a profound effect on attitude accessibility, as operationalized by our response-latency measure. Subjects responded to a series of slides, each of which listed the name of a puzzle type followed by an evaluative adjective. Average response latency to the attitudinal inquiries was significantly faster in the repeated-expression condition ($M = 5.94$ s) than in the single-expression condition ($M = 6.77$ s), suggesting that the strength of the object-evaluation association is indeed a critical determinant of attitude accessibility.

Furthermore, a second experiment employing the repeated-expression manipulation revealed that the strength of the object-evaluation association exerts an impact on attitude–behavior consistency (Fazio et al., 1982; Exp. 4). When provided with a "free-play" opportunity during which they could work on any of the puzzle types they had evaluated earlier, subjects in the repeated-expression condition were observed to behave more consistently with their attitudes than subjects in the single-expression condition. For example, the average within-subject rank-order correlation between expressed interest in each puzzle type and the proportion of available problems attempted was .47 in the repeated-expression condition. The average correlation in the single-expression condition was significantly lower (.22). This finding is exactly what would be predicted from the notion that attitude accessibility is a central factor in the attitude-to-behavior process. Any variable that enhances attitude accessibility, as does repeated attitudinal expression, will promote attitude–behavior consistency.

The effect of repeated attitudinal expression on attitude accessibility is by no means limited to attitude objects as trivial as intellectual puzzles. A recent experiment by Powell and Fazio (1984) established the generalizability of the finding across 12 contemporary and socially important attitude issues (e.g., the Equal Rights Amendment, the insanity defense, gun control, nuclear power plants). The experiment involved varying the number of times an attitude was expressed toward each of a subset of the issues in a within-subjects design. Furthermore, unlike the copying procedure used in the previous work, each additional attitudinal expression was made with respect to a different semantic differential scale item. For example, subjects might have evaluated gun control on an approve/disapprove scale, then on a desirable/undesirable scale, and so forth. By varying the number of times a given issue appeared on the questionnaire, the experimenters created a situation in which subjects expressed their attitudes zero, one, three, or six times toward a given issue.

This manipulation produced no effect on attitude extremity. An analysis of

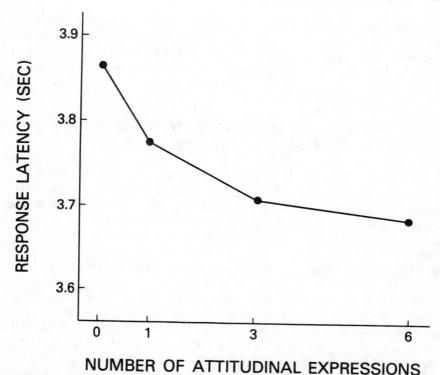

NUMBER OF ATTITUDINAL EXPRESSIONS

FIGURE 8.2 The relation between the number of attitudinal expressions and the latency of response to attitudinal inquiries. (From M. C. Powell and R. H. Fazio, "Attitude Accessibility as a Function of Repeated Attitudinal Expression," *Personality and Social Psychology Bulletin*, Vol. 10, No. 1 (March 1984), pp. 139–148. Copyright © 1984 by Sage Publications, Inc. Adapted by permission of Sage Publications, Inc.)

the final scalar rating revealed that repeated expression did not affect extremity. Nevertheless, the manipulation did produce differences in attitude accessibility, as measured by our standard response time procedure. The greater the number of expressions, the faster the latency of response to an attitudinal inquiry. (The relationship is depicted in Figure 8.2.) Repeated expressions enhanced response latency, with early additional expressions having a greater impact than later ones.

This finding has an important methodological implication. Specifically, it suggests that commonly used attitudinal measurement instruments may actually affect the very attitude they seek to assess. Responding to a measure involves another instance of associating the attitude object with a given evaluation, thus enhancing the strength of the object-evaluation association and, hence, the accessibility of the attitude.

More relevant to the present concerns, the finding attests to the generalizability of the effect of repeated attitudinal expression on attitude accessibility across a variety of important attitude issues. Together with the findings from the "puzzle experiments", the results as a whole provide us with some confidence in the utility of a conceptual framework that views attitudes as object-evaluation associations. The strength of this association appears to be a key determinant of attitude accessibility and of the degree to which the attitude affects later behavior.

RELEVANCE TO MODERATORS OF THE ATTITUDE–BEHAVIOR RELATION

As mentioned earlier, one of the assets of addressing the process, or "How," question is that it may serve to explain how and why variables that have been identified on the basis of "When" research exert their impact. In the present context, consideration of the issue of attitude accessibility may aid our understanding of why some variables determine attitude–behavior consistency.

The Manner of Attitude Formation as a Moderating Variable

As indicated earlier, one such determinant is the manner of attitude formation. Attitudes formed through direct, behavioral experience with the attitude object have been found to be more predictive of later behavior than attitudes based on indirect, nonbehavioral experience (for a review, see Fazio & Zanna, 1981). Support for this hypothesis has now been found in a number of studies. The first investigation (Regan & Fazio, 1977, Exp. 1) was a field study that took advantage of a naturally occurring event. Because of a campus housing shortage, many freshmen had spent the first few weeks of the academic year in temporary housing. Typically, these accommodations consisted of a cot in the lounge of a dormitory. Relative to freshmen who had been immediately assigned to permanent housing, those in temporary quarters had much more direct experience with the housing crisis. Those assigned permanent quarters, on the other hand, had learned about and formed their attitudes toward the housing shortage only through discussions with others and through reading the frequent articles in the campus paper. Thus, a naturally occurring event had created two groups that differed in their manner of attitude formation, the variable of interest. Basically, the two groups were compared for the extent to which they displayed behavior (e.g., agreeing to sign a petition calling upon the university administration to take steps to alleviate the shortage or writing a letter to the university housing office) that was consistent with their attitudes toward the housing crisis, as assessed by questionnaire responses. Despite the fact that the distributions of attitude scores in the two groups were nearly identical, attitude–behavior consistency was much greater among those students who had been assigned to temporary housing (the direct-experience group) than among those assigned to permanent quarters (the indirect-experience group).

    The next step in the research program involved an experimental manipulation of the manner of attitude formation in the laboratory (Regan & Fazio, 1977, Exp.

2). Subjects were introduced to a set of five intellectual puzzles in one of two ways. Half of the subjects were presented previously solved examples of each puzzle and listened to the experimenter describing the type of puzzle and the solution (indirect-experience condition). The remaining subjects were given an opportunity to work the same example puzzles, thus forming their attitudes through direct behavioral experience. After attitudes toward each of the five types of puzzles were assessed, all subjects participated in a "free-play" situation. They were given numerous examples of each puzzle type and were instructed to play with any that they wished. The relation between a given subject's attitudes and his or her "free-play" behavior was examined. On the average, attitude–behavior consistency was much greater in the direct-experience condition than in the indirect-experience condition.

In yet another examination of the hypothesis, college students' attitudes toward participation in psychological research and their willingness to volunteer for participation in future studies were assessed (Fazio & Zanna, 1978a). It was found that the relation between attitudes and volunteering behavior depended on the number of psychological experiments in which the individual had participated in the past. Thus, the greater the amount of direct experience an individual had with participation, the more likely it was that the individual's volunteering behavior corresponded with his or her attitude.

In summary, support was found for the hypothesis that the manner of attitude formation affects attitude–behavior consistency in studies where direct experience was assessed in two naturally occurring groups, manipulated experimentally, and measured as a continuous variable. Furthermore, these investigations involved different attitude objects and different behaviors, thus attesting to the generalizability of the effect. This research illustrates the value of viewing attitudes in the context of behavior. In effect, the distinction between direct and indirect experience involves a comparison of an atttiude inferred from prior behavior toward the attitude object with an attitude developed without the benefit of prior behavioral experience. That is, a prior-behavior-to-attitude-to-later-behavior sequence is compared to an attitude-to-behavior sequence. When the attitude is grounded in and based on prior behavior, the attitude-to-later-behavior relation is stronger than when the attitude is based on indirect experience (sees Zanna, Olson, & Fazio, 1981).

The findings from this program of research on attitude–behavior consistency lead to an important and general conclusion about attitudes. In each of the experiments, differences were found between direct and indirect experience attitudes with regard to attitude–behavior consistency, despite the fact that attitude scores in the two conditions were virtually equivalent. Identical attitude scores cannot be considered to reflect equivalent underlying attitudes. A basic message communicated by the research is that the attitudes of two individuals with identical attitude measurement scores may still differ in important ways. This notion is, of course, at the core of the research mentioned earlier on attitudinal qualities that moderate the strength of the attitude–behavior relation. It also coincides with our definition of attitude as an object-evaluation association.

Although two individuals may hold the same evaluation of an object and thus, when asked, may provide identical attitude ratings, the strength of the association may differ for the two individuals.

Attitude Accessibility and the Manner of Attitude Formation

Research on the manner of attitude formation can serve as an illustration of how the process approach can enhance our understanding of previously identified determinants of the attitude–behavior relation. In considering the question of why attitudes based on direct experience better predict later behavior than attitudes based on indirect experience, it becomes crucial to know how attitudes guide behavior. If we understood how attitudes guide behavior, it would be much easier to discern why certain attitudes do so more than other kinds of attitudes.

In the context of the proposed process model, a hypothesis concerning the manner of attitude formation is generated easily. Conceivably, direct, behavioral experience leads to the formation of an attitude involving a stronger object-evaluation association and, hence, a more accessible attitude than does indirect, nonbehavioral experience. This hypothesis of differential accessibility was tested in an experiment involving the puzzle paradigm and our standard response time measure (Fazio *et al.*, 1982, Exp. 2). Half of the subjects formed their attitudes toward a set of intellectual puzzles after being provided with an opportunity to work examples of each puzzle type (direct experience). The other subjects formed their attitudes after hearing a description and seeing examples of each puzzle type (indirect experience). This manipulation was crossed by an additional factor. To be sure that at least some of the subjects had consolidated their thoughts about and formed their attitudes toward each type of puzzle before the response-time task began, half of the subjects completed a measure of their interest in each type of puzzle immediately after the direct or indirect experience and prior to the response-time task (consolidation condition). The remaining subjects did not complete this measure until after the response-time task (no consolidation).

An analysis of variance on average response time revealed a main effect of consolidation such that subjects in the consolidation condition responded significantly faster than subjects in the no-consolidation condition. This effect suggests that subjects in the no-consolidation condition had not spontaneously formed attitudes toward the objects or, at minimum, had not yet completed the attitude formation process. As in the research by Powell and Fazio (1984), described earlier, this finding has a methodological implication. Commonly employed attitude measures may serve to create attitudes in cases where none initially existed. That is, instead of assessing a preexisting evaluation, an attitude scale can prompt individuals to form attitudes. Fazio, Lenn, and Effrein (1984) have presented a further discussion of this issue and an empirical illustration of how the present response-time procedure can be used to investigate the situational cues that prompt individuals to form attitudes spontaneously.

More relevant to the present concerns, the experimental results also revealed a main effect of the manner of attitude formation, such that subjects in the direct-experience condition were quicker than subjects in the indirect-experience condition. Thus, it appears that direct experience enhances the ease of attitude formation if attitudes have not yet been completely formed, as in the no-consolidation conditions. More important, however, direct experience also appears to enhance attitude accessibility once attitudes have been formed, as in the consolidation conditions.

Fazio *et al.* (1982) discussed this finding of differential accessibility as a function of the manner of attitude formation in relation to the strength of the object-evaluation association. An attitude object may not become as strongly associated with an evaluative category following an indirect experience as compared with a direct experience. Although an individual can and will express an attitude following indirect experience, the association between the object and the evaluation may not be well formed. Hence, when the individual encounters the object, he or she may be relatively unlikely to access the attitude from memory.

Attitudes based on behavior, on the other hand, may involve a stronger object-evaluation bond and consequently may be more readily accessed from memory. Why might behavioral experience lead to such a strong association? A reason is suggested by Bem's (1972) self-perception theory. Central to the theory is the notion that people have difficulty assessing their attitudes (drawing associations between the object and evaluative categories) unless they have engaged in some behavior toward the attitude object. Behavioral information may be considered a more reliable guide to an individual's evaluation of an object than his or her reaction to a medium's description of the object. That is, just as an observer considers knowledge of another's behavior to be the most indicative information concerning the individual's internal disposition, so, too, may a person perceive his or her own behavior as most reflective of his or her evaluation of the object. Hence, following behavioral experience, the individual may strongly associate the evaluation inferred from that behavior with the attitude object.

Support for this argument is provided by some recent research by Fazio, Herr, and Olney (1984). As Bem's (1972) self-perception theory makes clear, not all behavior is such that it can serve as input to an attitude-inference process. Only freely chosen, unmanded behavior can serve this purpose. Behavior that is manded (i.e., obviously attributable to a situational cause) is not considered to reflect internal dispositions. This reasoning leads to the prediction that enhanced accessibility following behavioral preformance will occur if the behavior is unmanded but will not occur if the behavior is manded. In two experiments, Fazio *et al.* (1984) manipulated this variable. The first experiment involved religious behaviors. Subjects completed a lengthy inventory that listed behaviors relevant to religion (e.g., attending services, praying before meals) by checking the behavioral items they had performed. Some subjects completed this inventory with reference to a time frame of the past year. Since the subjects were college students, it was assumed that the behaviors would have been freely chosen. Other subjects completed the inventory with reference to their childhood, on the assumption that the behaviors would have been required by parents and family. The recent and unmanded nature of the behaviors reviewed in the former condition (adult review) make them a more appropriate basis for attitudinal self-inference than the behaviors reviewed in the latter condition (childhood review), which are both more distant in time and manded. (A group of no-review control subjects did not complete the behavioral inventory.) In the conditions that are of relevance here, subjects were then induced to consolidate their attitudes by being forced to complete a measure of their attitude toward religion. The distributions of attitude scores in the three conditions were equivalent.

All subjects then participated in a response-time task involving a number of trials inquiring about attitudes toward a variety of issues. Included among these were two trials regarding religion. As predicted, response latencies were significantly faster for subjects in the adult-review condition than for subjects in each of the other two conditions, who displayed equivalent latencies. Thus, there was indeed something particularly informative and diagnostic about reviewing recent, unmanded behaviors that apparently led to a strengthening of the object-evaluation association.

In a second experiment testing this hypothesis, Fazio *et al.* (1984) employed an induced-compliance procedure. Subjects were induced to perform a new behavior under manded or unmanded conditions. The actual behavior that subjects were committed to perform was held constant, but the conditions under which it was performed served to make it more or less appropriate as a basis for attitudinal inference.

Attitudes toward tuition increases served as the target issue. Subjects first participated in a response time task involving both target and filler trials, which provided preexperimental latency data. The subjects completed a relevant latitudes scale (Halverson & Pallak, 1978) so that we could identify which of nine statements, varying in their support of tuition increases, each subject found most acceptable. In an ostensibly separate experiment, some subjects were then committed to writing an essay regarding tuition increases. In this phase of the experiment, subjects were randomly assigned to one of three conditions: (1) a high-choice condition, in which the subject was asked and committed to writing an essay arguing in support of a specified position regarding tuition increases; (2) a low-choice condition, in which the subject was told that "for experimental control reasons," we could not allow him or her to select a position but instead would assign him or her a specified position to support in writing; or (3) a control condition, in which no mention of an essay was made. To ensure that actual change in attitude extremity would not occur, the specified position for the two essay groups was always the position that the subject had deemed most acceptable on the latitudes scale (cf. Fazio, Zanna, & Cooper, 1977). This procedure did, in fact, prevent the occurrence of attitude change in the high-choice condition.

Following the manipulation, all subjects completed a scale measuring attitudes toward tuition increases to ensure that the high-choice subjects engaged in the necessary self-perception process and consolidated their attitudes. All subjects then participated in the response-time task a second time. For each subject, mean latencies were calculated for the preexperimental filler and tuition items and for the postexperimental filler and tuition items, and then improvement scores (pre—post) for filler and tuition items were calculated. Improvement scores for the filler items, which were equivalent across conditions, provided a control for simply responding to an attitudinal inquiry a second time. Hence, the difference between filler and tuition improvement scores was calculated as the index of interest. The more positive the index score, the greater the improvement was from pre- to postassessment in latency of response for target items than for filler items.

The data pattern was just as predicted, with high-choice subjects displaying more positive scores ($M = 0.25$) than either the low-choice ($M = -0.21$) or control subjects ($M = -0.27$). As in the earlier experiment, this effect was observed despite equivalence in terms of the extremity of attitude scores across the conditions. Thus, there was evidence that the accessibility of attitudes toward tuition increases was enhanced as a function of freely performed behavior.

What emerges from the research summarized here is a view of attitudes based on behavior as being relatively stronger than attitudes based on indirect experience. We have argued that this effect occurs because, as Bem (1972) suggested, people consider freely performed behavior to be such a reliable guide to their attitudes that they form strong associations between the evaluation implied by their behavior and the attitude object. Consequently, the attitude is relatively accessible and likely to be activated when the individual encounters the attitude object. Once activated, it can influence his or her definition of the situation and subsequent behavior. This entire process is less likely to occur for attitudes based on nonbehavioral information, which involve relatively weaker object-evaluation associations.

Thus, the proposed process model has enhanced our understanding of why the manner of attitude formation affects attitude–behavior consistency. Given its value in this regard, the model may suggest how and why various other moderators of the attitude–behavior relation exert their impact. As indicated earlier, the catalog of moderators includes such attitudinal qualities as the degree of correspondence between affective and cognitive measures of the attitude, the confidence with which the attitude is held, its clarity (as measured by the width of the latitude of rejection), and the temporal stability of the attitude. These variables may be reflected in the strength of the object-evaluation association and consequent accessibility of the attitude. The more correspondent the individual's feelings and thoughts about an attitude object, the more accessible the attitude may be. Confidence and clarity may be both causes and consequences of attitude accessibility, as may temporal stability. In a similar manner, the frequently observed moderating impact of the individual-difference measure, self-monitoring, may relate to accessibility. Given the greater functional value of attitudes for low self-monitors, such people may form attitudes that involve greater associative strength and, hence, are more easily and quickly activated than is typical for high self-monitors.

These are clearly speculations that need to be examined empirically. Two findings are at least consistent with these thoughts and suggest that accessibility may relate to two of the aforementioned moderator variables. With respect to clarity of the attitude and width of the latitude of rejection, Fazio *et al.* (1984) did observe a significant correlation between the width of the latitude of rejection concerning tuition increases and preexperimental latency of response to tuition items. The wider the latitude of rejection, the faster the response time. Although the evidence is less direct, there is reason to believe that temporal stability, too, is related to accessibility. Attitudes inferred from behavior have been found to be more stable over time than attitudes formed through nonbehavioral means (Watts, 1967), and as we have seen, attitudes inferred from behavior are also more accessible.

Obviously, more systematic research is needed on the relations between each of the moderators and attitude accessibility. Nevertheless, the present conceptual framework has the potential to integrate the catalog of variables known to affect attitude–behavior consistency.

AUTOMATIC ACTIVATION OF THE ATTITUDE

On the basis of the research described thus far, it appears that a process approach can be quite fruitful. Attitude accessibility appears to play a key role in the process by which attitudes guide behavior. Furthermore, the research suggests that any variable that strengthens the object-evaluation association, such as repeated attitudinal expression, has a corresponding impact on attitude accessibility and attitude–behavior consistency. Finally, the approach has suggested how one particular variable (the manner of attitude formation) moderates the attitude-behavior relation.

Nevertheless, it must be kept in mind that all the research on attitude accessibility has employed the same response-time methodology. Latency of response has served as our operationalization of attitude accessibility. Thus, to assess accessibility, it has been necessary to have the subjects respond to inquiries about their attitudes. In effect, subjects have been asked what their attitudes were. Yet in terms of the process linking attitudes and behavior, the crucial issue is whether individuals access their attitudes upon mere observation of the attitude object, not upon direct inquiry about the object. As argued earlier, it appears plausible to assume that latency of response to an attitudinal inquiry would covary with the likelihood that the attitude will be activated when the individual encounters the attitude object. Yet this assumption remains to be tested. Two approaches have now been used to address this issue. The first examined whether direct experience and repeated attitudinal expression each enhance the likelihood of spontaneous activation of the attitude upon mere observation of the attitude object. In other words, are results parallel to those found with response latency observed when the dependent measure concerns spontaneous activation? The second experiment directly examined the parallel between latency of response to an attitudinal inquiry and automatic attitude activation.

Attitude Activation upon Mere Observation of the Attitude Object

Fazio et al. (1983) examined the spontaneous activation of attitudes via the use of a "priming" paradigm. It has been demonstrated that once a category has been activated, the accessibility of that category is temporarily increased, enhancing the likelihood that the category will be applied to the interpretation of new information (see Higgins, Rholes, & Jones, 1977; Srull & Wyer, 1979, 1980). For example, Higgins *et al.* (1977) exposed subjects to various trait terms and examined whether this priming affected subsequent judgments of a target person in an ostensibly separate experiment. Given that the primed traits were applicable to the provided description of the target person's behavior, they exerted an impact on judgments of the person. Those subjects who had been primed with positive traits perceived the stimulus person as more desirable than those who had been primed with negative traits. Apparently, once the category had been primed via exposure to the specific trait terms, the category was highly accessible and was likely to be applied to the interpretation of the target's ambiguous behavior.

In an initial experiment, Fazio *et al.* (1983) demonstrated that the priming effects that have been observed in the domain of personality traits could be extended to a more attitudinal context and that the specific procedures they employed were capable of revealing the influence of having activated a given category earlier. Priming subjects with positive or negative evaluative adjectives affected their interpretation of ambiguous information presented in a second, ostensibly unrelated study.

In the crucial experiment, subjects were primed with either a positively or a negatively valued attitude object—an intellectual puzzle. Subjects had been introduced to a set of five such puzzles, through either direct or indirect experience, and then had indicated their interest in each puzzle type on an attitude scale. All of the direct-experience subjects and half of the indirect-experience subjects had completed this scale only once. The other half of the subjects in the indirect-experience condition had been induced to express their attitudes repeatedly, via the same ruse employed in the earlier research by Fazio *et al.* (1982). Thus, three conditions had been created in this initial phase of the experiment: (1) direct experience followed by a single attitudinal expression, (2) indirect experience followed by a single attitudinal expression, and (3) indirect experience followed by repeated attitudinal expression. Comparison of the first two conditions permits an examination of the effects of the manner of attitude formation. Comparison of the second and third conditions examines the effect of repeated attitudinal expression.

In the priming phase of the experiment, which presumably was testing color perception, subjects were exposed to either their most or least favorite puzzle type. The procedure involved the presentation of pairs of slides. The first member of each pair was referred to as the "memory word"; it always presented a picture along with the name of the object depicted in the picture. The memory objects employed were neutral fillers, such as umbrella or phone, with the exception of one trial in which the most positively or most negatively valued puzzle served as the memory object. The second member of the slide pair consisted of a colored background and a color name. The subject's task was to identify the background color aloud as quickly as possible and then to recite the memory word that had appeared on the first slide of the pair.

TABLE 8.1   Mean Attribution Scores

	Valence of Attitude Object	
Condition	Positive	Negative
Direct experience	−.309	.285
Indirect experience	.063	−.234
Repeated expression	−.170	.366

Note. More positive scores indicate a stronger attribution to the target's participation because of the money or the wait. More negative scores reflect a stronger attribution to the target's interest in the task. (From "Toward a Process Model of the Attitude–Behavior Relation: Accessing One's Attitude upon Mere Observation of the Attitude Object" by R. H. Fazio, M. C. Powell, and P. M. Herr, 1983, *Journal of Personality and Social Psychology, 44*, p. 731. Copyright 1983 by the American Psychological Association. Reprinted by permission.)

After completing the trials twice and undergoing a bogus debriefing concerning color perception, each subject was asked to participate in a short person perception task. The subject read a brief description concerning the actions of a previous subject who had devoted 10 extra minutes of his time to working at an experimental task. What was deliberately left ambiguous was why this person had done so. Subjects were asked to interpret the reason, first in an open-ended essay and then in response to three scalar items listing three plausible explanations: Did the person agree to participate because he was interested in the task, because he had nothing to do while waiting for his ride to arrive, or because he had been promised a monetary payment?

The data were analyzed according to an index combining judges' ratings of the subjects' essays and the subjects' scalar responses to the questionnaire items. The index was such that the more negative the score, the greater the attribution to the target person's interest in the task. (The means are presented in Table 8.1.) An interactive contrast of valence condition by direct versus indirect experience revealed a statistically significant effect. A contrast involving repeated expression versus indirect experience was also significant. Within both the direct-experience and the repeated-expression conditions, subjects primed with a positively valued object made a significantly stronger attribution to the target's interest in the task than did subjects primed with a negatively valued object.

Thus, the presentation of attitude objects during the color perception phase of the experiment affected subsequent interpretations of the ambiguous information, implying that subjects had accessed their evaluations upon observation of the attitude object. However, such effects were observed only when the subjects' attitudes could be said to involve a relatively strong object-evaluation association. Attitude formation through direct, behavioral experience with the attitude objects resulted in the subjects' accessing the attitude upon mere observation of the object. Attitude formation through indirect, nonbehavioral experience did not, unless the object-evaluation association was strengthened by having the subjects repeatedly express their attitudes. Apparently, given the existence of a strong object-evaluation association, the subjects' attitudes were activated upon presentation of the attitude object during the priming phase. Thus, either positive or negative evaluations had been activated indirectly. Having been activated recently, these evaluations were highly accessible when subjects were interpreting the ambiguous stimulus information. As a result, those for whom a positive evaluation had been activated were relatively likely to view the target's interest in the task as responsible for his or her participation, whereas those for whom a negative evaluation had been activated tended to view the money or the wait as relatively more responsible for the target's action.

It is important to note that this evidence regarding spontaneous activation of attitudes was found in a situation in which the subject was merely exposed to the attitude object. The priming occurred in the context of what was ostensibly a color perception experiment, and the subject was never asked to consider his or her attitude during this phase of the experiment. Nor was it to the subject's advantage to do so, for the subject's task was simply to identify the background color of a slide and to recite the so-called memory word that had been presented on the preceding slide. Despite the irrelevance of an individual's attitude to the immediate concerns, subjects who presumably possessed a strong object-evaluation association apparently accessed their evaluation of the attitude object upon exposure to the object during the color perception task.

Furthermore, these results parallel the findings from the response time research. Apparently, attitude formation through direct experience and repeated attitudinal expression each enhance both the latency with which an individual can respond to an attitudinal inquiry and the likelihood of spontaneous activation of the attitude when the attitude object is encountered.

Response Latency and Automatic Activation

In a second approach to the issue of automatic activation of attitudes, Fazio and Powell (1984) sought to establish directly the parallel between latency of response to an attitudinal inquiry and the likelihood of spontaneous activation. That is, we sought to demonstrate empirically that response latency can serve as an approximation of the likelihood of automatic activation of the attitude upon presentation of the attitude.

The experiment involved a priming procedure modeled after some work done by a number of cognitive psychologists, including Neely (1976, 1977). The chief experimental task involved trials on which a prime word and then a target word were presented on a computer screen. The prime word was an attitude object. It appeared on the screen for 200 ms, then disappeared. After a 100-ms interval, the target word, which was an adjective, appeared. For example, "vodka" might be presented as the prime, followed by the target word "pleasant." The subject's task was to press a key to indicate, as quickly as possible, whether the target adjective had a positive or negative connotation and then to recite the prime word. In this example, the subject would respond as quickly as possible by pressing a key to indicate that "pleasant" had a positive connotation and then would say "vodka" aloud. We asked the subject to pronounce the prime at the end of each trial, simply to ensure that he or she attended to the primes.

The crucial measure was the latency of response regarding the connotation of the target adjective. We reasoned that if the evaluation of the object presented as the prime was automatically activated upon its mere presentation and if the subsequent target word was congruent in valence with that activated evaluation, then the subject's response time should be facilitated. That is, the subject should respond relatively quickly.

Let's assume that vodka is evaluated positively by an individual. Then, presentation of "vodka" as the prime may automatically activate a positive evaluation. If the target adjective that is presented is also positive, the individual may be able to respond relatively quickly, since a positive evaluation has been activated by the prime. That is, facilitation should occur. In a similar manner, facilitation is to be expected if a negatively valued object serves as the prime when it is followed by a negative target adjective, as in "cockroach" followed by "disgusting." What is meant by "facilitation" is simply that the latency is faster in this case than in a trial involving the same target word preceded by a letter string (e.g., "BBB"). Such trials provide a no-prime baseline.

Thus, the presence of facilitation allows us to infer that the evaluation associated with the primed object had been automatically activated upon its mere observation. It is important to remember that the subject is not under any instructions to consider his or her evaluation of the prime word. From the subject's point of view, the prime is simply a word that he or she has to attend to, remember, and recite at the end of the trial.

Of course, we would not expect such facilitation to occur for all attitude objects. It should occur only if the object-evaluation association is quite strong. In this experiment, strong versus weak was operationalized via our old standard response time task, in which the subject was directly asked to indicate his or her attitude toward the object as quickly as possible. If the latency was fast, we considered the object-evaluation association strong and, hence, facilitation should occur in the procedure just described. If the latency was slow, the object-evaluation association was weak and hence no facilitation should occur because the likelihood of automatic activation is low. In this way, the experiment examined directly the relation between our response-latency measure and automatic activation.

The actual experiment was divided into two phases, the first being devoted to prime selection. The subjects were exposed to some 70 objects, for each of which they had to press either a good or a bad key as quickly as possible to indicate their evaluation of the object. These data were then employed to select those objects that would serve as the primes for a given subject in the actual experiment. Four objects were selected in each of four categories: (1) strong good primes and (2) strong bad primes (i.e., objects to which the subject responded "good" or "bad," respectively, most quickly) and (3) weak good primes and (4) weak bad primes (i.e., objects to which the subject responded "good" or "bad" most slowly).

Thus, using our standard response time procedure, we selected primes for each subject. Then, in Phase II, the procedure described earlier occurred. Four different

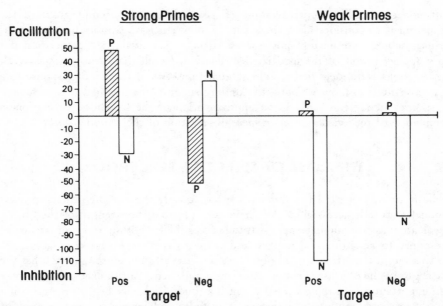

FIGURE 8.3 Mean facilitation scores as a function of the strength of the object-evaluation association for the primed object, the valence of the prime (P = positive; N = negative), and the valence of the target adjective (Pos = positive; Neg = negative). (From Fazio & Powell, 1984.)

classes of objects were presented as primes, along with letter strings to provide a no-prime baseline, and each prime was followed by a positive or negative target adjective toward which the subject had to give a response.

The data, which were analyzed in terms of facilitation scores (differences from the no-prime baseline provided by the letter-string trials), are presented in Figure 8.3. Looking first at the left side, which displays objects involving a strong association, we see that facilitation did occur in the case of congruency between the valence of primed object and the valence of the target adjective. That is, facilitation is found for a positive object when followed by a positive target and for a negative object when followed by a negative adjective. In the cases of incongruency, some inhibition occurs. Most important, a reliable interaction between the valence of the prime and the valence of the target is apparent.

The data pattern is quite different for objects involving a weak association. Most important, there is no interaction and no evidence of facilitation in any case. The only effect here is a main effect of the valence of primed object. Negative objects produced inhibition regardless of the valence of the target adjective. Apparently, negative objects involving a weak association somehow distracted subjects from the central task.

What is crucial is that the evidence for subjects' attitudes having been activated was found in a situation in which the subject was merely exposed to the attitude object. The subject was never asked during the second phase of the experiment to consider his or her attitude. Nevertheless, exposure to objects for which subjects presumably possessed a strong object-evaluation association did prompt activation of the associated evaluation. Recall that strong versus weak associations were identified via our standard measure of latency of response to a direct attitudinal inquiry. Thus, the finding suggests that, as had been assumed, response latency is a fairly good approximation of the likelihood of automatic activation of the evaluation upon mere observation of the attitude object.

THE ROLE OF SELECTIVE PERCEPTION

The research presented thus far has concerned only the first step of the process model—attitude accessibility. We have seen (1) that the strength of the object-evaluation association determines attitude accessibility, both in terms of latency of response to an attitudinal inquiry and in terms of the likelihood of automatic activation of the attitude upon observation of the attitude object and (2) that the strength of the object-evaluation association and, hence, attitude accessibility play an important role in the process by which attitudes influence behavior. According to the proposed model, this influence of attitudes on behavior occurs as a result of the impact that attitudes have on perceptions of the attitude object in the immediate situation and on definitions of the event. The model implies that without such selective perception, attitudes would not affect behavior.

A recent experiment by Fazio and Herr (1984) examined the role of selective perception in the attitude-to-behavior process. The experimental design and procedure were, in part, a replication of the Snyder and Swann (1976) experiment described earlier. Those investigators presented subjects with a legal case history having to do with an affirmative action suit. They found that the degree to which subjects' verdicts in the case were consistent with their attitudes toward affirmative action was enhanced by providing subjects with an instruction to consider their feelings toward affirmative action before reading the case history. As mentioned earlier, in our terms, the instruction amounts to a strong situational cue for the subjects to access their attitudes. When attitudes were made salient in this way, greater consistency was observed than when attitudes were not made salient.

Half of the Fazio and Herr (1984) experimental design simply replicated this experiment. The subjects, who will be referred to as decision-set subjects, were informed that they would read a legal case history concerning affirmative action and then be asked to reach a verdict. Half of these subjects—those in the attitude-salient condition—were also told that they might find it helpful to organize and consider their views regarding the affirmative action issue before reading the case history, just as in Snyder and Swann's (1976) experiment.

The process model would suggest that Snyder and Swann's findings occurred through a process of selective perception. That is, given that attitudes were salient, they affected the subjects' interpretations of the credentials of the two candidates and of the university's actions. For the other half of the subjects in the experiment, we attempted to block selective perception by placing them in what we called a memory set. These subjects were told that the experiment concerned reading comprehension and the recall of detailed information about an actual legal case. They were further instructed: "Try to memorize all the factual details in the information. Attend carefully to each and every detail. You will be asked to repeat as much of the case history as you can in a memory test later in the experiment, so it is important that you remember as much detail as possible." Half of these memory-set subjects were given the attitude-salience instruction, and half were not. Thus, the experiment involved a 2 × 2 design. Subjects' attitudes either had or had not been made salient, and they were in a decision set, as in Snyder and Swann's experiment, or a memory set.

After the manipulations were performed, subjects read the case history, which presented the vitae of both the female plaintiff and the male candidate who was awarded the job. The two were displayed as having very similar qualifications and records. The case history also presented a summary of the case for the female plaintiff and a summary of the case for the defense—the university that was being sued. After the case history had been read by the subjects, they were asked to express a verdict in three different manners: (1) they were presented with a range of possible verdicts and asked to select one, (2) they were asked whether the university's initial decision to hire the male candidate was justified, and (3) they were also asked to write an essay expressing and justifying the verdict that they would deliver. The essays were rated by two judges who were blind to condition for the degree to which they favored the female plaintiff. After the data were standardized, the three verdict measures were summed to form an overall verdict measure. About a week earlier, the subjects had indicated their attitudes toward affirmative action while participating in an ostensibly separate study that had to do with students' attitudes toward a wide variety of issues. This survey had been administered by an experimenter other than the one involved in the affirmative action legal case.

The correlation between attitudes and verdicts within each condition is presented in Table 8.2. Snyder and Swann's results were clearly replicated within the decision-set condition. Subjects for whom attitudes had been made salient displayed greater attitude–behavior consistency than those for whom attitudes

TABLE 8.2 Within-Cell Correlations Between Attitude and Verdict Measures

Attitude Salience	Set	
	Decision	Memory
High	.64	.23
Low	.16	.37

Note. From Fazio and Herr (1984).

TABLE 8.3 Within-Cell Correlations Between Attitude and Perception Measures

Attitude Salience	Set	
	Decision	Memory
High	.71	.12
Low	−.07	.20

Note. From Fazio and Herr (1984).

had not been made salient. Within the memory-set condition, however, no difference was observed as a function of attitude salience. Thus, when subjects were operating under instructions to memorize details of the case, attitude–behavior consistency was relatively low, regardless of whether attitudes had or had not been made salient.

Presumably, this lack of attitude–behavior correspondence within the memory-set/attitude-salient condition occurred because the memory set prevented selective perception from occurring. Some additional evidence supports this view. Subjects were also asked a series of questions concerning their perceptions of the two candidates. For example, they were asked to compare the overall qualifications of the two candidates. An interesting pattern was observed concerning the correlation between attitudes and this item regarding the qualifications of the candidates (Table 8.3). Only in the decision-set/attitude-salient condition was there any evidence that selective perception had occurred. Apparently, the memory-set instructions had succeeded in blocking selective perception.

The findings from the experiment provide further support for the proposed model. In particular, the results indicate that attitudes affect behavior by influencing the individual's perceptions in the immediate situation. To the extent that such selective perception is inhibited, attitudes exert no influence on behavior.

SUMMARY AND IMPLICATIONS

Clearly, more research needs to be conducted to test the present model more extensively. Nevertheless, in light of the research conducted thus far, the model appears to provide a viable explanation of a process by which attitudes guide behavior. As indicated earlier, simply *asking* this process question constitutes a shift in the approach to the study of the attitude–behavior relation. Whereas early investigations and discussion sought to determine *whether* an attitude-to-behavior relation existed (e.g., Corey, 1937; LaPiere, 1934; Wicker, 1969), the more recent goal—apparent in much of the research cited earlier—has been to understand *when* attitudes might predict behavior. Many variables have been identified as moderators of the attitude–behavior relation. In contrast, the present approach is to investigate *how* attitudes guide behavior. Addressing this process question, as we have seen, has a number of benefits.

First and foremost, a much neglected question regarding the attitude–behavior relation has finally begun to be addressed empirically. Despite the centrality and importance of the attitude concept, little consideration has been given to the process question. The proposed model indicates clearly how the "translation" of attitudes into overt behavior can fail to occur. Each step in the process is critical for attitude–behavior consistency to be observed, yet each step provides an opportunity for the system to break down. The attitude may not be activated upon observation of the object, or even if it is accessed, the object may be so clearly and unambiguously positive or negative in the given situation as not to allow any selective perception. Finally, even if immediate perceptions of the object have been influenced by the attitude, some other factors, such as normative constraints, may intervene, affecting the individual's definition of the event and preventing the individual from behaving in accordance with the immediate perceptions.

Second, the proposed model and the research described suggest how and why various factors moderate the attitude–behavior relation. In doing so, the model provides a framework that can be employed to integrate conceptually the catalog of moderators. The research has illustrated this linkage between the process model and previously identified determinants of attitude–behavior consistency with respect to the manner of attitude formation. Attitudes based on direct, behavioral experience with the attitude object have been shown to predict later behavior to a greater extent than attitudes based on indirect, nonbehavioral experience. The research reviewed suggests that, relative to indirect experience attitudes, attitudes based on prior behavior are more likely to be accessed upon mere observation of the object and are more likely to influence perceptions of the object in the immediate situation.

Third, the present conceptualization has the potential for helping to identify further variables that might determine the strength of the attitude–behavior relation. The framework suggests the general principle that any variable that affects the strength of the object-evaluation association will also act as a determinant of attitude–behavior consistency. This suggestion was illustrated by the research on the effects of repeated attitudinal expression.

Finally, because it so heavily emphasizes attitude accessibility and the constructive nature of perception, the model is congruent with the recent orientation in social psychology toward considering the role of cognitive processes. Furthermore, the process view explicitly ties these cognitive features to future behavior, the relative neglect of which has been noted as a shortcoming of social cognition research (Higgins, Kuiper, & Olson, 1981; Snyder, 1980). Thus, the research serves to overcome what many have viewed as a deficiency of research on social cognition.

Generality of the Model

It should be kept in mind that the present definition of attitude equates it with affect. Thus, the model and research essentially describe how affect influences behavior through various mediating mechanisms. Individuals may have affect toward a wide variety of potential attitude objects, including social issues and other people as well as physical objects. The present model can apply to any broadly defined "object" toward which an individual possesses some affective linkage. When an affective association exists toward the specific object that the individual encounters, then the crucial question is whether that association is sufficiently strong that the affect will be activated automatically.

However, in cases where there is no affective linkage to the specific object that is encountered, activation of some relevant affect may occur *following* some preliminary cognitive work. The necessary cognitive work would consist of identifying the object as a member of some category for which an affective linkage does exist. The process of categorization has received considerable empirical and theoretical attention within both social and cognitive psychology (e.g., Cantor & Mischel, 1979; Herr, Sherman, & Fazio, 1983; Smith & Medin, 1981). The degree to which the features of the specific object match the features of the category seems to determine whether the object will be categorized as an instance of the category. Such categorization of the object precedes the various steps involved in the present attitude-to-behavior process model. In effect, then, the present model would represent the second major stage of a two-stage process.

This two-stage process is most applicable to cases in which the individual holds a general attitude that is relevant to a given object but holds no attitude toward the specific object, possibly because it is novel. For example, the person might not have any affective association to *sha char* chicken specifically, but upon categorizing it as a Hunanese dish—a general category toward which the individual does hold an evaluative association—relevant affect may be activated automatically.

Such two-stage processing is particularly relevant to the use of stereotypes regarding categories of people. Upon encountering a stranger, people may attempt to identify the stranger as a member of some social category. Given that they do stereotype the target person, whatever affect is associated with the stereotype may initiate the attitude–behavior process that has been our focus. Fiske (1982; also see Chapter 7 of this volume) has proposed precisely such a two-stage model in a provocative and insightful discussion of stereotypes and schema-triggered affect. She has argued that stereotypes can be viewed as schemata, containing not only the prototypical features of a category member but also an affective or evaluative association. Evaluation of a stranger involves an initial categorization stage. If the stranger's features do not sufficiently match any schema that is retrieved from memory, then categorization has been unsuccessful. In such cases, perceivers consider the target person's characteristics in a relatively slow, time-consuming, piecemeal fashion (i.e., one by one) to arrive at an evaluation of the target. Given successful categorization, on the other hand, perceivers apply the affect associated with the category to the target very rapidly. In other words, categorization as a member of a schema is thought to trigger relevant affect.

The model and research presented in this chapter indicate how schema-triggered affect following successful stereotyping might affect a perceiver's behavior toward the stereotyped target person. The ultimate consequence of such attitudinally consistent action on the part of the perceiver may be a self-fulfilling prophecy. That is, the perceiver's behavior may induce the target person to respond in precisely the manner expected by the perceiver (see Darley & Fazio, 1980, for a review of such social interaction consequences). A second implication of the present work for stereotyping concerns the likelihood that affect will be activated following successful categorization. Just as is the case for attitudes, not all stereotypes are equal in the extent to which they are associated with an affective or evaluative judgment. Whether application of a stereotype to a particular individual will automatically activate any associated affect should depend on the strength of the association between the affect and the category. Weak associations are unlikely to produce schema-triggered affect unless the perceiver is induced by specific instruction or some situational cue to evaluate the target person. Relatively strong affective associations, on the other hand, should be activated quickly and spontaneously by successful categorization. For example, a perceiver may have stereotypes of both "people who wear eyeglasses" and "political conservatives." Categorization of a target into the latter stereotype appears far more likely to trigger affect automatically than does categorization into the former stereotype.

Also relevant to the present discussion of a two-stage process is the recent research of Lord, Lepper, and Mackie (1984). In considering the role of general, as opposed to specific, attitudes, these researchers suggested that general attitudes will promote consistent behavior only to the extent that the specific instance in question matches the prototype of the general attitude object. These researchers examined the consistency between subject's attitudes toward a typical member of a Princeton University eating club and the extent to which the subjects would like to work with a specific member of the eating club on a joint task. Greater consistency was observed when this ostensible club member was described in such a way as to embody subjects' prototyped characteristics of members of the eating club than when the target was described as an atypical member. This finding again illustrates the importance of an initial categorization stage when we are concerned with general attitudes or stereotypes. Once again, however, the model and research presented in this chapter suggest that such attitude–behavior consistency following successful categorization can be expected only to the extent that the association between the general object category and an individual's evaluation of that category is sufficiently strong to prompt automatic activation of the attitude. Otherwise, successful categorization will not activate any affective reaction and will not initiate the attitude-to-behavior process that has been discussed.

Automatic Versus Controlled Processing Models of the Attitude–Behavior Relation

Before concluding, it may be useful to consider the relation between the present model and other potential models of the attitude-behavior process. As Fazio *et al.* (1983) themselves note, the proposed model is by no means the only conceivable process by which attitudes might guide behavior. Although no existing model has addressed the process concern directly, suggestions regarding other conceivable processes can be gleaned from past work on the attitude–behavior relation. A predominant approach to the study of attitude–behavior consistency has been that taken by Azjen and Fishbein (1980). This approach centers on a multiple regression equation involving the prediction of intentions to perform (or not to perform) a given act from individuals' attitudes toward the specific act and their normative beliefs about the behavior in question (i.e., perceptions regarding how significant others perceive the act). This behavioral intention is presumed to serve as the immediate determinant of the behavior. Ajzen and Fishbein's model has successfully predicted both behavioral intentions and behavior in a considerable number of domains, including voting behavior, career intentions, and family planning (for a review, see Ajzen & Fishbein, 1980).

Although the regression model of Ajzen and Fishbein has been subject to some serious criticisms at both the conceptual and methodological levels (e.g., Abelson, 1982; Bentler & Speckart, 1979; Sherman, 1980; Sherman, Presson, Chassin, Bensenberg, Corty, & Olshavsky, 1982), it raises an interesting point about the attitude-to-behavior process. To the extent that the regression equation can be considered to capture the phenomenology of the individual, rather than serving as a simple predictive device, it suggests a very different process from that proposed by the present model. As implied by its name—the "theory of reasoned action"—and by the central role occupied by intentions, the Ajzen and Fishbein approach focuses on a very deliberate decision process. When faced with a decision, people consider closely their beliefs toward the act in question and then summate those beliefs to arrive at a specific attitude toward the act. This attitude and normative beliefs are each weighted appropriately before the people decide to intend to perform (or not to perform) the given action.

Yet another suggestion regarding the attitude-to-behavior process is provided by self-awareness theory (Wicklund, 1975). This theory is motivational in nature. Under conditions of heightened self-awareness, individuals *strive* to behave consistently with their internal attitudes. Indeed, a wide variety of investigations have found enhanced attitude–behavior consistency when either the attitude measure or the behavior occurred in a situation that served to heighten self-focused attention (for a review, see Wicklund, 1982).

What distinguishes the latter two approaches from the present model is their rather deliberate and conscious nature. These models imply an activation of attitudes as a consequence of some situational cue that prompts people to view their attitudes as relevant (Borgida & Campbell, 1982; Snyder, 1982; Snyder & Kendzierski, 1982; see Salancik, 1982, for a broad discussion of attitude relevance as a function of contextual cues) or, more generally, as a consequence of heightened self-awareness. (Abelson [1982] refers to such attitude-eliciting conditions as individuating.) Once the attitude is activated, the individual carefully considers the attitude in a deliberate reasoning process to arrive at a behavioral decision, possibly, as suggested by Ajzen and Fishbein (1980), by first deciding upon a behavioral intention. On the other hand, the process explicated by the present model is far less deliberate and far more spontaneous. The model and the research conducted to test it center on spontaneous activation of the attitude upon mere observation of the attitude object. As indicated by the research findings, such spontaneous activation can be expected only in the case of attitudes involving strong object-evaluation associations. If the association is only weakly established, the attitudinal evaluation is unlikely to be activated unless the individual is prompted to do so. Once activated, the attitude biases perceptions of the object in the immediate situation, and behavior simply follows from these perceptions without any necessary conscious reasoning process. That is, the individual's construction or definition of the event directs his or her behavior.

The distinction drawn here corresponds at least roughly to the distinction offered by cognitive psychologists between automatic versus controlled attention and memory processes (e.g., Schneider & Shiffrin, 1977; Shiffrin & Schneider, 1977). Shiffrin and Dumais (1981) characterize as automatic any process that leads to the activation of some concept or response "whenever a given set of external initiating stimuli are presented, regardless of a subject's attempt to ignore or bypass the distraction" (p. 117). Controlled processes, in contrast, require the active control or attention of the individual. The present model essentially centers on automatism. Neither the activation of the attitude nor the selective perception component requires conscious effort, intent, or control on the part of the individual. Indeed, it is within an entirely automatic sequence that the components take on a necessary role if attitude is to guide behavior. On the other hand, the process implicit in the Ajzen and Fishbein (1980) theory of reasoned action and in objective self-awareness theory involve more controlled processes. Some cue directs the individual's attention to his or her attitude and induces him or her to access the attitude and to consider it in arriving at a behavioral decision.

It appears that both automatic and controlled processes can be involved in the manner by which attitudes guide behavior. The crucial question that arises concerns the conditions under which an automatic attitude–behavior process versus a controlled one might operate. (See Sherman & Fazio, 1983, for a more detailed discussion of this issue.) The controlled process appears to require some motivational or inducing force. People do not, at every moment in their daily lives, engage in deliberate reasoning processes by which they decide how they intend to behave. Nor are people continuously in a state of self-awareness. Constant reliance on such effortful, controlled processes would be enormously dysfunctional for daily living. Instead, some situational cue must induce heightened self-awareness; some situational factor must motivate the individual to engage in the effortful, controlled process. What such factors might be is not entirely evident from past research. However, one likely candidate is simply the importance of the behavioral decision. Highly consequential behaviors may prompt a careful analysis. When deciding what college to attend, what job to pursue, and the like, people clearly focus attention on the self. They may assume the approach of rational decision makers who carefully consider their attitudes and relevant normative beliefs to arrive at a behavioral intention.

It appears that most daily behaviors are not sufficiently consequential to induce people to undertake a controlled analysis. Instead, most daily behaviors are probably fairly spontaneous and nondeliberative. Such behaviors flow from people's definitions of the events they experience. In such cases, the crucial question is whether the individual's attitude has influenced his or her definition of the event. It is for this reason that the present model focuses on the functionality of attitudes. Attitudes that adequately serve the object appraisal function guide behavior in a fairly automatic manner and free the individual from having to engage in deliberate, reasoned, controlled processes. However, such an automatic process will only operate to the extent that a strong association has been established toward the object. Only then will encountering the attitude object spontaneously activate the associated evaluation. If the relevant association is too weak to be activated, then behavior will follow from a definition of the event that is not attitudinally based. Instead, the behavior may be determined by whatever features of the situation and the attitude object are sufficiently salient to influence the individual's immediate perceptions.

Obviously, a more comprehensive model that conceptually integrates the present approach and more controlled processes, such as that implicit in the Ajzen and Fishbein (1980) theory of reasoned action, would be desirable. An integrative model might involve the possibility of the present automatic process if the attitude is activated from memory upon mere observation of the attitude object. If the attitude is not activated automatically, then a more controlled process (possibly along the lines suggested by Ajzen & Fishbein) may still produce attitude–behavior consistency, provided that some situational variable (such as highly consequential decision settings) motivates the individual to retrieve from memory and carefully consider his or her attitudes. If the object-evaluation association is too weak for automatic activation to occur, and if the situation does not motivate a controlled analysis, then attitudes cannot be expected to influence the behavior. More research on both the automatic and the controlled processes is needed before any formal, detailed attempt to integrate the two into a comprehensive model can be pursued realistically. Nevertheless, the development of such a comprehensive model is necessary if social psychology is to arrive at an understanding of what may be the multiple processes by which attitudes, and affect in general, influence behavior.

Acknowledgments

Preparation of this chapter and some of the reported research was supported by Grant MH 38832 from the National Institute of Mental Health. Other research was supported by Grant BNS 80-23301 from the National Science Foundation and Grant MH 34227 from the National Institute of Mental Health. The author thanks Paget Gross, Edward Jones, Steven Sherman, and Mark Zanna, along with the editors, for their helpful comments on an earlier draft.

References

Abelson, R. P. (1982). Three modes of attitude-behavior consistency. In M. P. Zanna, E. T. Higgins, & C. P. Herman (Eds.), *Consistency in social behavior: The Ontario Symposium* (Vol. 2, pp. 131–146). Hillsdale, NJ: Erlbaum.

Abelson, R. P., Kinder, D. R., Peters, M. D., & Fiske, S. T. (1982). Affective and semantic components in political person perception. *Journal of Personality and Social Psychology, 42,* 619–630.

Ajzen, I., & Fishbein, M. (1973). Attitudinal and normative variables as predictors of specific behaviors. *Journal of Personality and Social Psychology, 27,* 41–57.

Ajzen, I., & Fishbein, M. (1977). Attitude–behavior relations: A theoretical analysis and review of empirical research. *Psychological Bulletin, 84,* 888–918.

Ajzen, I., & Fishbein, M. (1980). *Understanding attitudes and predicting social behavior.* Englewood Cliffs, NJ: Prentice-Hall.

Allport, G. W. (1935). Attitudes. In C. Murchison (Ed.), *Handbook of social psychology* (pp. 798–844). Worcester, MA: Clark University Press.

Bem, D. J. (1972). Self-perception theory. In L. Berkowitz (Ed.), *Advances in experimental social psychology* (Vol. 6, pp. 1–62). New York: Academic Press.

Bentler, P. M., & Speckart, G. (1979). Models of attitude–behavior relations. *Psychological Review, 86,* 452–464.

Borgida, E., & Campbell, B. (1982). Belief relevance and attitude–behavior consistency: The mediating role of personal experience. *Journal of Personality and Social Psychology, 42,* 239–247.

Bruner, J. S. (1957). On perceptual readiness. *Psychological Review, 64,* 123–152.

Bruner, J. S., & Goodman, C. C. (1947). Value and need as organizing factors in perception. *Journal of Abnormal and Social Psychology, 42,* 33–44.

Cantor, N., & Mischel, W. (1979). Prototypes in person perception. In L. Berkowitz (Ed.), *Advances in experimental social psychology* (Vol. 12, pp. 3–52). New York: Academic Press.

Cooper, J., & Croyle, R. T. (1984). Attitudes and attitude change. *Annual Review of Psychology, 35,* 395–426.

Corey, S. M. (1937). Professed attitudes and actual behavior. *Journal of Educational Psychology, 28,* 271–280.

Darley, J. M., & Fazio, R. H. (1980). Expectancy confirmation processes arising in the social interaction sequence. *American Psychologist, 35,* 867–881.

Doob, L. W. (1947). The behavior of attitudes. *Psychological Review, 54,* 135–156.

Eagly, A. H., & Chaiken, S. (1984). Cognitive theories of persuasion. In L. Berkowitz (Ed.), *Advances in experimental social psychology* (Vol. 17, pp. 268–359). New York: Academic Press.

Fazio, R. H., Chen, J., McDonel, E. C., & Sherman, S. J. (1982). Attitude accessibility, attitude–behavior consistency, and the strength of the object-evaluation association. *Journal of Experimental Social Psychology, 18,* 339–357.

Fazio, R. H., & Herr, P. M. (1984). [On the role of selective perception in the attitude–behavior rocess]. Unpublished data, Indiana University.

Fazio, R. H., Herr, P. M., & Olney, T. (1984). Atttiude accessibility following a self-perception process. *Journal of Personality and Social Psychology, 47,* 277–286.

Fazio, R. H., Lenn, T. M., & Effrein, E. A. (1984). Spontaneous attitude formation. *Social Cognition, 2,* 217–234.

Fazio, R. H., & Powell, M. C. (1984). [Automatic activation of attitudes]. Unpublished data, Indiana University.

Fazio, R. H., Powell, M. C., & Herr, P. M. (1983). Toward a process model of the attitude–behavior relation: Accessing one's attitude upon mere observation of the attitude object. *Journal of Personality and Social Psychology, 44,* 723–735.

Fazio, R. H., & Zanna, M. P. (1978a). Attitudinal qualities relating to the strength of the attitude–behavior relationship. *Journal of Experimental Social Psychology, 14,* 398–408.

Fazio, R. H., & Zanna, M. P. (1978b). On the predictive validity of attitudes: The roles of direct experience and confidence. *Journal of Personality, 46,* 228–243.

Fazio, R. H., & Zanna, M. P. (1981). Direct experience and attitude–behavior consistency. In L. Berkowitz (Ed.), *Advances in experimental social psychology* (Vol. 14, pp. 161–202). New York: Academic Press.

Fazio, R. H., & Zanna, M. P., & Cooper, J. (1977). Dissonnace and self-perception: An integrative view of each theory's proper domain of application. *Journal of Experimental Social Psychology, 13,* 464–479.

Festinger, L. (1957). *A theory of cognitive dissonnace.* Stanford, CA: Stanford University Press.

Fishbein, M. (1963). An investigation of the relationships between beliefs about an object and attitude toward that object. *Human Relations, 16,* 233–240.

Fishbein, M. (1966). The relationship between beliefs, attitudes, and behavior. In S. Feldman (Ed.), *Cognitive consistency* (pp. 199–223). New York: Academic Press.

Fiske, S. T. (1982). Schema-triggered affect: Applications to social perception. In M. S. Clark & S. T. Fiske (Eds.), *Affect and cognition: The Seventeenth Annual Carnegie Symposium on Cognition* (pp. 55–78). Hillsdale, NJ: Erlbaum.

Greenwald, A. G. (1968). On defining attitude and attitude theory. In A. G. Greenwald, T. C. Brock, & T. M. Ostrom (Eds.), *Psychological foundations of attitudes* (pp. 361–388). New York: Academic Press.

Halverson, R. R., & Pallak, M. S. (1978). Commitment, ego-involvement, and resistance to attack. *Journal of Experimental Social Psychology, 14,* 1–12.

Hastorf, A. H., & Cantril, H. (1954). They saw a game: A case study. *Journal of Abnormal and Social Psychology, 49,* 129–134.

Herr, P. M., Sherman, S. J., & Fazio, R. H. (1983). On the consequences of priming: Assimilation and contrast effects. *Journal of Experimental Social Psychology, 19,* 323–340.

Higgins, E. T., Kuiper, N. A., & Olson, J. M. (1981). Social cognition: A need to get personal. In E. T. Higgins, C. P. Herman, & M. P. Zanna (Eds.), *Social cognition: The Ontario Symposium* (Vol. 1, pp. 395–420). Hillsdale, NJ: Erlbaum.

Higgins, E. T., Rholes, W. S., & Jones, C. R. (1977). Category accessibility and impression formation. *Journal of Experimental Social Psychology, 13,* 141–154.

Jones, E. E., & Gerard, H. B. (1967). *Foundations of social psychology.* New York: Wiley.

Katz, D. (1960). The functional approach to the study of attitudes. *Public Opinion Quarterly, 24,* 163–204.

Kelley, H. H. (1950). The warm-cold variable in first impressions of persons. *Journal of Personality, 18,* 431–439.

Kelley, S., & Mirer, T. W. (1974). The simple act of voting. *American Political Science Review, 68,* 572–591.

Kothandapani, V. (1971). Validation of feeling, belief, and intention to act as three components of attitude and their contribution to the prediction of contraceptive behavior. *Journal of Personality and Social Psychology, 19,* 321–333.

Lambert, W. W., Solomon, R. L., & Watson, P. D. (1949). Reinforcement and extinction as factors in size estimation. *Journal of Experimental Psychology, 39,* 637–641.

LaPiere, R. T. (1934). Attitudes vs. actions. *Social Forces, 13,* 230–237.

Latané, B., & Darley, J. M. (1968). Group inhibition of bystander intervention in emergencies. *Journal of Personality and Social Psychology, 10,* 215–221.

Latané, B., & Darley, J. M. (1970). *The unresponsive bystander: Why doesn't he help?* New York: Appleton-Century-Crofts.

Lingle, J. H., & Ostrom, T. M. (1981). Principles of memory and cognition in attitude formation. In R. E. Petty, T. M. Ostrom, & T. C. Brook (Eds.), *Cognitive responses in persuasion* (pp. 399–420). Hillsdale, NJ: Erlbaum.

Lord, C. G., Lepper, M. R., & Mackie, D. (1984). Attitude prototypes as determinants of attitude-behavior consistency. *Journal of Personality and Social Psychology, 46*, 1254–1266.

Lord, C. G., Ross, L., & Lepper, M. R. (1979). Biased assimilation and attitude polarization: The effects of prior theories on subsequently considered evidence. *Journal of Personality and Social Psychology, 37*, 2098–2109.

Manis, J. G., & Meltzer, B. N. (Eds.). (1972). *Symbolic interaction.* Boston: Allyn & Bacon.

Markus, H. (1977). Self-schemata and processing information about the self. *Journal of Personality and Social Psychology, 35*, 63–78.

McArthur, L. A., Kiesler, C. A., & Cook, B. P. (1969). Acting on an attitude as a function of self-percept and inequity. *Journal of Personality and Social Psychology, 12*, 295–302.

McGuire, W. J. (1969). The nature of attitudes and attitude change. In G. Lindzey & E. Aronson (Eds.), *Handbook of social psychology* (2d ed., Vol. 3, pp. 136–314). Reading, MA: Addison-Wesley.

Milgram, S. (1963). Behavioral study of obedience. *Journal of Abnormal and Social Psychology, 67*, 371–378.

Neely, J. H. (1976). Semantic priming and retrieval from lexical memory: Evidence for facilitatory and inhibitory processes. *Memory and Cognition, 4f*, 648–654.

Neely, J. H. (1977). Semantic priming and retrieval from lexical memory: Roles of inhibitionless spreading activation and limited-capacity attention. *Journal of Experimental Psychology: General, 106*, 226–254.

Norman, R. (1975). Affective-cognitive consistency, attitudes, conformity, and behavior. *Journal of Personality and Social Psychology, 32*, 83–91.

Ostrom, T. M. (1969). The relationship between the affective, behavioral, and cognitive components of attitude. *Journal of Experimental Social Psychology, 5*, 12–30.

Powell, M. C., & Fazio, R. H. (1984). Attitude accessibility as a function of repeated attitudinal expression. *Personality and Social Psychology Bulletin, 10*, 139–148.

Proshansky, H. M. (1943). A projective method for the study of attitudes. *Journal of Abnormal and Social Psychology, 38*, 393–395.

Regan, D. T., & Fazio, R. H. (1977). On the consistency between attitudes and behavior: Look to the method of attitude formation. *Journal of Experimental Social Psychology, 13*, 38–45.

Regan, D. T., Straus, E., & Fazio, R. H. (1974). Liking and the attribution process. *Journal of Experimental Social Psychology, 10*, 385–397.

Rholes, W. S., & Bailey, S. (1983). The effects of level of moral reasoning on consistency between moral attitudes and related behaviors. *Social Cognition, 2*, 32–48.

Rose, A. M. (1962). A systematic summary of symbolic interaction theory. In A. M. Rose (Ed.), *Human behavior and social processes* (pp. 3–19). Boston: Houghton Mifflin.

Rosenberg, M. J. (1960). Cognitive reorganization in response to the hypnotic reversal of attitudinal affect. *Journal of Personality, 28*, 39–63.

Salancik, G. R. (1982). Attitude–behavior consistencies as social logics. In M. P. Zanna, E. T. Higgins, & C. P. Herman (Eds.), *Consistency in social behavior: The Ontario Symposium* (Vol. 2, pp. 51–74). Hillsdale, NJ: Erlbaum.

Sample, J., & Warland, R. (1973). Attitude and prediction of behavior. *Social Forces, 51*, 292–304.

Schneider, W., & Shiffrin, R. M. (1977). Controlled and automatic human information processing: I. Detection, search, and attention. *Psychological Review, 84*, 1–66.

Schofield, J. W. (1974). Effect of norms, public disclosure, and need for approval on volunteering behavior consistent with attitudes. *Journal of Personality and Social Psychology, 31*, 1126–1133.

Schuman, H., & Johnson, M. P. (1976). Attitudes and behavior. *Annual Review of Sociology, 2*, 161–207.

Schwartz, S. H. (1978). Temporal instability as a moderator of the attitude–behavior relationship. *Journal of Personality and Social Psychology, 36*, 715–724.

Seeleman, V. (1940). The influence of attitudes upon the remembering of pictorial material. *Archives of Psychology*, No. 258.

Sherif, C. W., Kelly, M., Rodgers, H. L., Sarup, G., & Tittler, B. I. (1973). Personal involvement, social judgment, and action. *Journal of Personality and Social Psychology, 27*, 311–328.

Sherman, S. J. (1980). On the self-erasing nature of errors of prediction. *Journal of Personality and Social Psychology, 39*, 211–221.

Sherman, S. J., & Fazio, R. H. (1983). Parallels between attitudes and traits as predictors of behavior. *Journal of Personality, 51*, 308–345.

Sherman, S. J., Presson, C. C., Chassin, L., Bensenberg, M., Corty, E., & Olshavsky, R. W. (1982). Smoking intentions in adolescents: Direct experience and predictability. *Personality and Social Psychology Bulletin, 8*, 376–383.

Shiffrin, R. M., & Dumais, S. T. (1981). The development of automatism. In J. R. Anderson (Ed.), *Cognitive skills and their acquisition* (pp. 111–140). Hillsdale, NJ: Erlbaum.

Shiffrin, R. M., & Schneider, W. (1977). Controlled and automatic human information processing: II. Perceptual learning, automatic attending, and a general theory. *Psychological Review, 84*, 127–190.

Sivacek, J., & Crano, W. D. (1982). Vested interest as a moderator of attitude–behavior consistency. *Journal of Personality and Social Psychology, 43*, 210–221.

Smith, E. E., & Medin, D. L. (1981). *Categories and concepts.* Cambridge, MA: Harvard University Press.

Smith, M. B., Bruner, J. S., & White, R. W. (1956). *Opinions and Personality.* New York: Wiley.

Snyder, M. (1980). Seek, and ye shall find: Testing hypotheses about other people. In E. T. Higgins, C. P. Herman, & M. P. Zanna (Eds.), *Social cognition: The Ontario Symposium* (Vol. 1, pp. 277–303). Hillsdale, NJ: Erlbaum.

Snyder, M. (1982). When believing means doing: Creating links between attitudes and behavior. In M. P. Zanna, E. T. Higgins, & C. P. Herman (Eds.), *Consistency in social behavior: The Ontario Symposium* (Vol. 2, pp. 105–130). Hillsdale, NJ: Erlbaum.

Snyder, M., & Kendzierski, D. (1982). Acting on one's attitude: Procedures for linking attitude and behavior. *Journal of Experimental Social Psychology, 18*, 165–183.

Snyder, M., & Swann, W. B. (1976). When actions reflect attitudes: The politics of impression management. *Journal of Personality and Social Psychology, 34*, 1034–1042.

Snyder, M., & Swann, W. B. (1978). Behavioral confirmation in social interaction: From social perception to social reality. *Journal of Experimental Social Psychology, 14*, 148–162.

Snyder, M., Tanke, E. D., & Berscheid, E. (1977). Social perception and interpersonal behavior: On the self-fulfilling nature of social stereotypes. *Journal of Personality and Social Psychology, 35*, 656–666.

Srull, T. K., & Wyer, R. S. (1979). The role of category accessibility in the interpretation of information about persons: Some determinants and implications. *Journal of Personality and Social Psychology, 37*, 1660–1672.

Srull, T. K., & Wyer, R. S. (1980). Category accessibility and social perception: Some implications for the study of person memory and interpersonal judgments. *Journal of Personality and Social Psychology, 38*, 841–856.

Stebbins, R. A. (1972). Studying the definition of the situation: Theory and field research strategies. In J. G. Manis & B. N. Meltzer (Eds.), *Symbolic interaction* (pp. 339–355). Boston: Allyn & Bacon.

Thomas, W. I. (1931). *The unadjusted girl.* Boston: Little, Brown.

Thurstone, L. L. (1946). Comment. *American Journal of Sociology, 52*, 39–40.

Warner, L. G., & DeFleur, M. L. (1969). Attitude as an interaction concept: Social constraint and social distance as intervening variables between attitudes and action. *American Sociological Review, 34*, 153–169.

Watts, W. A. (1967). Relative persistence of opinion change induced by active compared to passive participation. *Journal of Personality and Social Psychology, 5*, 4–15.

Wicker, A. W. (1969). Attitudes versus actions: The relationship of verbal and overt behavioral responses to attitude objects. *Journal of Social Issues, 25*, 41–78.

Wicker, A. W. (1971). An examination of the "other variable" explanation of attitude–behavior inconsistency. *Journal of Personality and Social Psychology, 19*, 18–30.

Wicklund, R. A. (1975). Objective self-awareness. In L. Berkowitz (Ed.), *Advances in experimental social psychology* (Vol. 8, pp. 233–275). New York: Academic Press.

Wicklund, R. A. (1982). Self-focused attention and the validity of self-reports. In M. P. Zanna, E. T. Higgins, & C. P. Herman (Eds.), *Consistency in social behavior: The Ontario Symposium* (Vol. 2, pp. 149–172). Hillsdale, NJ: Erlbaum.

Word, C. O., Zanna, M. P., & Cooper, J. (1974). The nonverbal mediation of self-fulfilling prophecies in interracial interaction. *Journal of Experimental Social Psychology, 10,* 109–120.

Zanna, M. P., & Fazio, R. H. (1982). The attitude–behavior relation: Moving toward a third generation of research. In M. P. Zanna, E. T. Higgins, & C. P. Herman (Eds.), *Consistency in social behavior: The Ontario Symposium* (Vol. 2, pp. 283–301). Hillsdale, NJ: Erlbaum.

Zanna, M. P., Higgins, E. T., & Herman, C. P. (Eds.). (1982). *Consistency in social behavior: The Ontario Symposium* (Vol. 2). Hillsdale, NJ: Erlbaum.

Zanna, M. P., Olson, J. M., & Fazio, R. H. (1980). Attitude–behavior consistency: An individual difference perspective. *Journal of Personality and Social Psychology, 38,* 432–440.

Zanna, M. P., Olson, J. M., & Fazio, R. H. (1981). Self-perception and attitude–behavior consistency. *Personality and Social Psychology Bulletin, 7,* 252–256.

Zanna, M. P., & Rempel, J. K. (1984, June) *Attitudes: A new look at an old concept.* Paper presented at the Conference on Social Psychology of Knowledge, Tel Aviv.

CHAPTER 9

Affect, Cognition, and Motivation

MARTIN L. HOFFMAN
New York University

Research on affect and motivation was all but done in during the 1960s and 1970s by the cognitive revolution in psychology. Except for Tomkins and a few others, along with the psychoanalysts who were largely divorced from mainstream psychology, affect and motivation were virtually ignored. When they were considered, they were usually viewed as the products of cognition.[1] The dominant approach to affect was, and indeed may still be, that of Schachter and Singer (1962), Mandler (1975), and Lazarus (1982, 1984), in which feelings are the consequences of cognitive appraisal. Motivational concepts, too, were rarely in evidence in psychological journals, except for the motivation to reduce cognitive dissonance or disequilibrium.

Things appear to be changing now, even (perhaps especially) among cognitive psychologists. Leaders in cognition, such as Bower (1981), Norman (1980), and Simon (1982), have discussed the limitations of studying thought as though it were free of emotional influence and are trying to incorporate affect into their models. Zajonc (1980) has argued for the proposition that affective systems operate independently of cognition. Even Piaget (1981) has viewed affect as important in determining the tendency to approach or avoid situations, and thus in determining the amount of intellectual effort expended and the rate of acquisition of knowledge obtained in different domains. Moreover, Carnegie-Mellon University, a bastion of cognitive science, devoted its entire 1982 symposium to the interaction of affect and cognition (Clark & Fiske, 1982). Although some participants in the symposium (e.g., Mandler, 1982) reiterated the traditional view that appraisal is necessary for affect to be experienced, others viewed the interaction of affect and cognition as more complex. Fiske (1982), for example, suggested that some of the categories stored in memory may be charged with affect, and the affect may be conferred on stimulus events that activate such a category. It may not be an exaggeration to suggest that psychology is in the early stages of a paradigm shift in which affect no longer takes a back seat.

As for the connection between affect and motivation, psychology has always assumed that such a connection existed. If one is angry at someone, one wants to strike that person. If one loves someone, one wants to embrace him or her. If one grieves at the loss of someone, one wishes for his or her return. For the learning theorists of the 1940s and 1950s, affect was often thought to be an essential part of reinforcement, which underlay motivation. For psychoanalysis, objects invested with affect are objects that one is motivated to possess. Some of these objects are also forbidden, and the availability of forbidden objects, though eliciting desire, also evokes anxiety, which provides the motivational basis for activating a variety of cognitive defenses. It thus seems clear that anything we learn about affect may tell us something important about motivation.

This chapter is written with the view that whether affect is or is not merely the product of cognition, it is most profitable to consider affect as it relates to cognition. I find it helpful to view the relationship between affect and cognition in terms of several broad questions: What are the modes of information processing that mediate between a stimulus event and an affective response? How does an affective response influence subsequent information processing? What is the impact of language development and socialization on affective expression and control? To deal with these questions, I reviewed the literature and constructed a scheme for how affect and cognition interact. The scheme seems capable of organizing most of the findings and concepts in the literature, and it also helps identify problems for further research. It may also provide a perspective on the issue of whether appraisal is necessary for affective experience—an issue that continues to generate heat in the literature (Lazarus, 1982, 1984; Zajonc, 1984). Furthermore, with the addition of certain assumptions, the scheme can generate hypotheses about the interplay of cognitive and affective processes and how they influence each other in complex life situations. The scheme may thus represent a step toward a comprehensive theory.

The scheme encompasses three broad, increasingly complex modes of information processing that generate affective responses to a stimulus event: (1) direct affective response to the physical or sensory aspects of a stimulus (sight, sound, smell, feel); (2) affective responses to the match between the physical or sensory aspects of a stimulus and an internal representation or schema; and (3) affective responses to the meaning of a stimulus beyond its physical and sensory aspects (its causes, consequences, implications for the self). Three other processes—mental juxtaposition of a stimulus, construction of a stimulus, and semantic interpretation—also involve transformation of the stimulus, but they do not generate affect on their own. What they do is put the stimulus into a form that allows the three affect-generating modes to operate. I therefore call them "preparatory transformations." As an example, young children may know the semantic meaning of a parent's losing his job, yet not generate the appropriate affect unless they understand the implications. Finally, the scheme includes the ways in which the affect elicited through any of the modes may influence subsequent information processing: Affect may initiate, terminate, accelerate, or disrupt information processing; it may determine which sector of the environment is processed and which processing modes operate; it may organize recall and influence category accessibility; it may contribute to the formation of emotionally charged schemata and categories; it may provide input for social cognition; and it may influence decision making.

In all that follows, the stimulus in question may be a thing, a person, one's self, an event, an idea, an internal state, an action by oneself or another, or a verbal message. As will be evident, some of these types of stimuli are more likely to be associated with certain processes, other types of stimuli with other processes.

BASIC MODES OF AFFECT AROUSAL

The information-processing modes that mediate affect arousal are presented here in rough developmental order.

Direct Affective Response to Physical Features of a Stimulus

This mode, an essentially physical-sensory one, is cognitively "shallow." All that is needed to elicit affect is registration of the stimulus event and a minimum of perceptual organization.

Unconditioned Response

Included here are unconditioned affective responses to stimuli that appear to be involuntary (and perhaps sometimes unconscious). Since learning is not necessary, the stimuli involved may be thought of as "autochthonous" generators of affect. The stimulus–affect connections may be biologically based, in keeping with Gibson's (1979) notion that the organism's perceptual system has evolved to be "attuned" to information pertinent to survival. Also, these connections may operate for the first time and in purest form in early infancy, before complex cognitive appraisal processes are possible. Examples are the infant's show of fear in response to an apparently looming object, distress in response to the sound of another infant's cry (G. B. Martin & Clark, 1982; Sagi & Hoffman, 1976; Simner, 1971), and anger in response to physical constraint or interruption of an ongoing activity (Stenberg, Campos, & Emde, 1983). Research on this topic, which bears on the fundamental issue of the early ontogeny of emotion, has only recently begun. Stenberg et al. (1983) found that when a 1-month-old infant's forearm is held firmly though not painfully against his side, his face shows signs of anger but also signs of other affects; at 4 months and at 7 months, the infant shows only anger, which suggests that by 4 months, anger has become the primary response to physical constraint. Stenberg et al. have also shown that 4-month-old infants respond with anger when a biscuit they are eating is taken away. Izard, Hembree, and Spizzirri (1983) reported that fear emerges as a response to acute pain (during inoculation) by about 7 or 8 months, which is approximately the same time fear of heights is manifested (Campos, Hiatt, Ramsay, Henderson & Svejda, 1978). Watson and Ramey (1972) found evidence that exerting control over one's environment may be a joy-eliciting stimulus in 10-month-olds: The infants coo and smile when given the opportunity to control the rotation of a mobile; they show far less joy if someone else rotates the mobile.

Conditioned Response

It seems likely that almost any stimulus can be conditioned to produce an affective response. For example, infants can be conditioned to grimace at the sound of a tone that is otherwise ignored (Papousek, 1967). In nature, however, certain stimuli are more likely than others to be paired with a stimulus or an event that is an autochthonous generator of affect.

Among the important stimuli that often become conditioned elicitors of affect are the sounds of words. There is evidence that words (and nonsense syllables) can become conditioned stimuli for eliciting an affect by being paired with an unconditioned stimulus for that affect, such as an electric shock. Words can also become conditioned elicitors of affect by being paired with other words that were previously conditioned to elicit the affect (Staats & Staats, 1957; Zanna, Kiesler, & Pilkonis, 1970). Examples from life are fear in response to the sound of the word "cancer" and anger or fear in response to the sound of the word "hate," when these affects result not from the semantic meaning of the words but from their previous association with affectively charged events. J. J. Campos (personal communication, May 1983) reported that when mothers vocalize sadness using a nonsense word, their 12-month-old children *look* sad. What may have happened is that the mother's sad tone of voice has become a conditioned stimulus for eliciting a sad feeling in the child, and the feeling is expressed in the child's face. Besides word sounds, verbal messages have other "paralinguistic" features, including shifts in inflection and intonation, stress, and temporal markers such as pauses and hesitations, which may become conditioned stimuli that elicit affective responses.

Mimicry

An affect-eliciting mode that is peculiar to social stimuli—that is, to facial expressions and postural movements that reflect another person's affective state—is mimicry. As defined by Lipps (1906), mimicry is an automatic two-step process in which one first imitates the changes in another person's facial expression, voice, or posture that reflect that person's feeling. This creates internal kinesthetic cues that contribute through afferent feedback to one's experiencing the other's feeling. This mechanism has been neglected in the literature, and it has not yet been demonstrated empirically, but there is recent supportive evidence (reviewed by Hoffman, 1978) for each of the two steps. Thus, people are found to blink and make mouth movements when someone blinks or stutters. And when their facial muscles are artificially set in the patterns corresponding to a particular emotion, they may experience that emotion (Laird, 1984). Campos *et al.*'s (1978) work on the visual cliff may be relevant. Ten-month-old infants typically start crossing the cliff to get to the mother on the other side. Part of the way over, they look down and appreciate the depth and then look up at the mother. They are more likely to continue to cross the cliff if the mother displays a joy face (75% cross) than if she displays a sad face (30% cross), an angry face (10% cross), or a fear face (none cross). In some cases, the infant's facial expression approximates the mother's, which may indicate the occurrence of mimicry. (It is also possible that the infant's crossing behavior and facial response are both direct responses to the emotional message from the mother.) A possible early precursor of mimicry was reported by Meltzoff and Moore (1983) who found that an hour after birth, infants imitate certain facial gestures (mouth opening and tongue protrusion), although no evidence was presented for a connection between mimicry and affect.

Affective Response to the Match Between Stimulus and Representation

When the child is capable of object permanence—representing an object that is not in one's immediate perceptual field—he or she can then compare the physical features of a stimulus to the representation of an object (pattern matching, recognition). From that point on, the child is open to a new class of affect-eliciting stimuli. If an object is an unconditioned elicitor of affect, or if it has become a conditioned elicitor, the child's representation of that object—its schema—may be affectively charged, or "hot." Later, when a stimulus is encountered that resembles this schema, it may activate the schema and evoke the same affect. If, on closer inspection, the resemblance breaks down and there is no match (the stimulus is not the object), the affective response may change dramatically. In short, the affect elicited may depend on (1) the match between the stimulus and the schema and (2) the affective charge of the schema. A fourfold classification results (see Table 9.1): The stimulus may match (1) or not match (2) an emotionally charged schema; it may match (3) or not match (4) a neutral schema. This classification is useful, because it organizes some diverse findings in the literature.

Cells 1 and 2 in Table 9.1 are illustrated by stranger anxiety in 8–12-month-old infants (Bronson, 1972; Campos, Emde, Gaensbauer, & Henderson, 1975). An approaching woman who, from a distance, appears to fit the infant's mother-schema may evoke a joyful smile (cell 1), but when the woman gets closer, the mismatch is evident; the smile then disappears and the infant's expression may turn to fear, sadness, or anger (cell 2). There are several theories of stranger anxiety, in some of which the affective charge of the mother-schema is central. Spitz (1957) attributed stranger anxiety to a sense of disappointment or loss. The approaching

TABLE 9.1   Fourfold Classification Based on Stimulus Match or Mismatch with an Emotionally Charged or Neutral Schema

	Match	Mismatch
Charged schema	1	2
Neutral schema	3	4

stranger creates an expectancy for the mother, hence anticipatory joy, which disappears when the mother does not show up. As Spitz (1957) put it:

> The stranger's face is compared to the memory traces of the mother's face and found wanting. This is not mother, she is still lost. Unpleasure is experienced and manifested. (p. 54)

Spitz's theory fits the experimental research findings on the process of attaining a percept, in which the sequence appears to be from a global structuring of a visual scene to an analysis of its local features (Navon, 1977). Also fitting this experimental research are the cognitive primacy theories that attribute stranger anxiety entirely to the cognitive discrepancy between stimulus and schema; that is, the inability to assimilate a stimulus is viewed as inherently upsetting (e.g., Kagan, 1974). (The cognitive primacy theories may have difficulty explaining the finding, discussed later, that when it comes to inanimate objects, infants often prefer the novel to the familiar.)

The preference for novelty, often found in subjects of all ages, presumably includes positive feelings toward novel objects and is thus illustrative of cell 4 in Table 9.1. The preference for novelty suggests that the degree of match between stimuli and schemata may be relevant to affect arousal even when the stimuli and schemata are emotionally neutral, or "cold." Piaget and other cognitive psychologists believe that moderate discrepancies between stimulus events and schemata may be a prerequisite for cognitive processing and growth. According to these writers, such discrepancies may arouse an affect—a mild "perturbation" or a more pronounced feeling of "surprise" (Charlesworth, 1969)—that provides the motivation for trying to make sense out of the discrepancy.

When a stimulus matches an affectively neutral or "cold" schema (cell 3 in Table 9.1) we might expect that there will be little or no affective response. The literature generally supports this expectation. The one big exception is Zajonc's (1968) finding that when adults are repeatedly exposed to a stimulus, they develop a positive feeling toward it. This phenomenon, known as the "mere exposure" effect, has been found for a wide variety of stimuli and is quite robust in adults (Harrison, 1977). Infants also show a preference for the familiar, but not for long. For example, 3–6-month-olds preferred a familiar stimulus when they were first exposed to it, but after 15–30 seconds, they shifted to a preference for a novel stimulus (Rose, Gottfried, Melloy-Carminar, & Bridger, 1982). In another study, 8- and 12-month-olds showed a similar progression from familiarity preference to novelty preference, and the process occurred repeatedly as new stimuli were encountered (Hunter, Ames, & Koopman, 1983). The difference between the adult and infant findings is probably not due to the subjects' age, since adults also get bored. It may be due to important differences in the procedure, however. In the adult studies, subjects observed a set of stimuli that were interspersed and presented at varying frequencies and then rated how much they liked each one. They preferred the most frequently presented stimuli. The subjects were thus *repeatedly* exposed to both familiar and nonfamiliar objects. They may thus be assumed to have repeatedly engaged in the process of pattern matching and recognition. Thus, "mere exposure" is not an altogether appropriate description. If they had, indeed, been merely exposed to the stimulus, as in the infancy studies, they might well have preferred something new. If so, this would suggest that preference for the familiar may be a transitory phenomenon. More specifically, infants and adults alike may find that the process of matching or assimilating a stimulus is inherently pleasurable, as suggested by cognitive psychologists (e.g., McCall, 1972), but once a stimulus is assimilated or comprehended as matching a schema, it may lose its interest (unless the schema is emotionally charged).

To summarize, when a stimulus appears to match a schema charged with a particular affect, it may be expected to elicit that affect; if there turns out to be no match, the anticipatory affect may disappear and be replaced by a differently valenced affect. When a stimulus matches an affectively neutral schema, positive affect may be aroused, though only momentarily. A mismatch between a stimulus and an affectively neutral schema may produce a feeling of perturbation, surprise, or relief from boredom.

Affective Response to the Meaning of a Stimulus

Thus far, whether the stimulus is an unconditioned or conditioned affect elicitor or whether it elicits affect because it matches an affectively charged schema, the person is responding to the physical features of the stimulus. We now turn to higher order cognitive processing, in which the affective response is based on the meaning of a stimulus beyond its physical features. The processes involved, often interrelated and overlapping, are categorization and appraisal of the stimulus.

Categorization

A category may be acquired by abstracting the properties shared by a number of items (objects, events, actions) or by forming a prototype representing the central tendency of any one of the items. In the simplest type of category, items are grouped because they are similar in physical appearance. Items may also be grouped according to their function—what they can do or what can be done with them. One type of function neglected in the categorization literature is the function that items may have for oneself—a function that may be assumed to be associated with affect. Items that differ in physical appearance may nevertheless satisfy a need or interfere with its satisfaction; consequently, these items may evoke the same affect despite their physical differences. Thus, over time, one may form categories consisting of joy-producing items, anger-producing items, fear-producing items, and the like. These categories may be formed on the basis of having direct experience with desired or dreaded events (getting good grades, receiving an award, being mugged, or being punished by authority) or of imagining that they have happened.

One's repertoire of categories may thus include categories charged with different affects in varying levels of intensity. This is important because if one identifies a stimulus as an instance of a category charged with a particular affect (assimilates the stimulus to the category), the stimulus should evoke the same affect.

In Fiske's (1982) terms: "Affect may generalize from experiences with prior instances to the category as a whole and hence back to new instances" (p. 61). Fiske found, in keeping with this conception, that when a stimulus person was a good match to the subject's positively charged, idiosyncratic schema of "old flame," the stimulus person elicited positive affect; when the stimulus person matched a negatively charged, culturally stereotyped schema ("politician"), negative affect was elicited.

The same stimulus can be categorized in different ways. If a book is categorized with school failure experiences, it should evoke rather unpleasant, perhaps shameful feelings; but if it is categorized with objects one used as a child to stand on to get things out of reach, it might evoke pleasant feelings associated with mastery and nostalgia. We may also assume that categories are often charged with more than one affect. In Freud's (1936) anxiety theory, for example, an action schema may be charged with positive and negative affect (anxiety) because of past experiences (perhaps in socialization) in which the action was associated with pleasure followed by punishment.

Because people may have many categories—emotionally charged and neutral—stored in memory, and a stimulus may potentially be associated with any category, we might ask what makes a person identify a stimulus as fitting a particular emotionally charged category. This is part of the larger question of what conditions lead to activation of a category and enable it to "capture" the sensory input. The usual answers found in the cognition literature (e.g., Bargh & Pietromonaco, 1982; Higgins & King, 1981) may also apply here. First, it seems obvious that the most natural reason for a category to be activated is that it has many features in common with the stimulus. "Material for wrapping packages" may be among the highly accessible categories when the stimulus is a ball of string. Second, a category may be activated because of the context. Given the appropriate mood music and suggestive camera work, movie audiences might categorize the string as a weapon for strangulation. Contextual cues of which one is unaware may also heighten a category's accessibility. Bargh and Pietromonaco (1982) presented hostile cues outside the subjects' awareness, which resulted in a temporary increase in accessibility of categories charged with hostile affect. (The subjects subsequently made negative social judgments.) Third, a category may be activated because of its relevance to another category that has been activated.[2]

When we assimilate a stimulus to a category, we are responding not to the idiosyncratic features of the stimulus but to the characteristics it has in common with other exemplars of the category. Since we do the same with the other exemplars of the category, categorization inevitably must have a "leveling" effect on affective experience; that is, we respond to different stimuli with similar affect (less intensely to some exemplars, more intensely to others). On the other hand, categorization may also have an "enriching" effect, especially when the category is affectively charged and the stimulus activating it is otherwise neutral. If, on approaching one's car, one perceives a piece of paper on the windshield as a parking ticket, this may activate the category "parking tickets," along with certain schemata and scripts about policemen and fines, and the affects associated with them. These schemata, scripts, and affects may in turn, in some individuals, activate the broader, more ancient category of being caught and punished by parental authority, along with its associated affects. This example not only illustrates the potential affect-enriching property of categorization but also indicates that the affect elicited can be powerful: Intense affect can be elicited by an otherwise neutral stimulus.

It may be rare for a stimulus to be totally assimilated to a category. Consequently, one's response may usually be partly to the idiosyncratic, noncategorized properties of the stimulus and partly to the categorized properties of the stimulus. Consider a stimulus that, unlike the piece of paper in the foregoing example, has affect-eliciting properties of its own, that activates an affectively charged category. It may be useful in this case to distinguish between two components of an affective response: the affect elicited by the idiosyncratic stimulus component and the affect elicited by the categorical component. We can then talk about affective responses that are primarily stimulus-driven and those that are primarily category-driven. The categorical component presumably increases with age.

Appraisal

Whether or not one categorizes the stimulus event, one can determine its importance for oneself (or for someone else) and respond affectively as the result of assessing its consequences, inferring its causes, or comparing it with a standard.

ASSESSING CONSEQUENCES   One's affective response to a stimulus, in this case usually an event or an action by someone or by oneself, can be influenced by one's assessment of its consequences—that is, whether the consequences will occur immediately or in the future and whether they will be minor and short-term or will exert a powerful influence over one's life. For example, the government's economic policy, which may ordinarily elicit little or no affect, may elicit a great deal of affect when we become aware of its impact on us, or, if we are empathic, its impact on others. Our own actions may not ordinarily elicit affect in us unless we are aware of their consequences for us or for others. If, after winning a game or a battle, we become aware of the harmful consequences for the loser, this may diminish the joy of winning. There is considerable evidence (Hoffman, 1983a) that the awareness of harming others typically produces guilt feelings in people of all ages.[3]

One's level of cognitive development is obviously important in assessing consequences. Consider an adult who responds with intense anxiety to a barely perceptible body ache because he or she knows that it may be a sign of cancer. The anxiety may become even more intense, and prolonged as well, if the adult engages in a series of assessments that escalate in importance—for example, if he or she ruminates about the many ways in which cancer can change one's life. The same body ache may elicit little or no affect in a young child, whose only concern is the degree of physical discomfort.

Assessing consequences and categorization are not necessarily mutually exclusive. One may assimilate a stimulus to a category (e.g., illegal acts), assess the consequences of the category (punishment), and then experience the appropriate affect. Or one may assimilate a stimulus to a category that is already defined in terms of consequences (acts that are punished). When one does this, one's affective response is not the result of assessing consequences in the present. Rather, one has made assessments of the consequences of similar events in the past, resulting in the construction of a category that includes the stimulus and its consequences. One may now experience the affect as an immediate response to categorizing the act, without going through the process of assessing consequences.

INFERRING CAUSALITY   One's affective response to an action or state can be influenced by one's inference about its cause—that is, whether it was intentional or accidental, whether it was under the person's control, and whether there were mitigating circumstances. One is more likely to respond sympathetically to another's distress, for example, if its cause is perceived as beyond the other person's control (Hoffman, 1982). If it is perceived as within the person's control, one's sympathy may be diminished, and if a third person is perceived as the cause, one may feel angry at that person (Hoffman, 1982). Similar factors have been found to operate in achievement contexts (Weiner, 1982). Teachers tend to sympathize with children who fail because of low ability, and they are more likely to be angry at a child who does not complete assignments if the child is very bright. Here are some other anecdotal examples: A friend misses an appointment, and we feel angry at the oversight. If we attribute his behavior to his attitude toward us, we may feel sad at being rejected; if he then gives a plausible explanation, we may feel better. A bus driver passes us by and we feel angry, but our anger may be tempered if we find out that he supports a family and that his job depends on meeting unrealistic rush-hour schedules, with the result that he often has to pass people up. Perhaps sympathy is aroused in this case, which interferes with the initial anger. Or some of the anger may be redirected toward the bus company. There is experimental evidence that provoked anger may be reduced by mitigating information, especially if such information is presented before the provocation. Kremer and Stephens (1983) suggested that when one assesses cause without having mitigating information, one constructs causal attributions; these causal attributions may then interfere with the processing of mitigating information presented later. I would add that this later processing of mitigating information may also be impaired by the affect associated with the earlier causal attribution.

One's level of cognitive development is obviously important here, too. Infants, for example, often infer causality on the most primitive basis, which, according to Heider (1958), is the simple contiguity of events. An infant falls and expresses anger toward the mother who is present, as if the mother had caused the infant to fall. Zahn-Waxler, Radke-Yarrow, and King's (1979) study of 15–18-month-old infants is also interesting in this connection. A child is playing with her mother, who looks sad, and the child—who has done nothing wrong—says, "I sorry, did I hurt you mommy?" or proceeds to spank herself. Such a response may reflect a rudimentary guilt feeling, although the child may also look upset because of a fear of punishment. In a recent developmental study (Pazer, Slackman, &

Hoffman, 1981), 6-, 8-, and 10-year-old children were asked how "mad" they would feel if someone harmed them in some way (e.g., stole their cat). The 8- and 10-year-olds who were given mitigating background information about the culprit (e.g., he had lost his own cat and his parents wouldn't replace it) said that they would be less mad than the children of the same age who were not given background information. The younger children who were given the background information understood it, but it apparently had no influence on their affective response. This suggests that a certain level of maturity may be necessary before attributions—at least those that pertain to background factors beyond the immediate situation ("distal" attributions)—will be effective in determining one's affective response.

It is clear from the examples cited that inferring the causality of an act and assessing its consequences often occur together and interact. The rejection example indicates that knowing an act's cause may lead to a reassessment of its consequences ("I have [or have not] been rejected"). The bus driver example and the study by Pazer *et al.* (1981) suggest that knowing an act's cause may elicit affect (empathy, sympathy) that conflicts with the initially elicited, consequence-determined affect.

COMPARISON WITH A STANDARD   When one compares an instance of behavior, such as one's own behavior, to a standard of performance or a standard of morality—whether the behavior fits the standard, exceeds it, misses it, or violates it—an affective response may be elicited. The performance standards used to evaluate one's actions may be absolute or relative to the performance of others, and one may or may not have internalized them. The social comparison research suggests that information about the relative performance of self and others may be available at a very early age but that it does not begin to influence self-evaluation, and hence become an important source of feelings, until about 7 or 8 years of age (Ruble, Boggiano, Feldman, & Loebl, 1980).[4]

Research has indicated that experimentally induced success and failure can make one feel happy or sad and, furthermore, that certain causal attributions can lead to more specific feelings, such as pride and shame (Weiner & Graham, 1984). Success, for example, is more likely to generate pride when subjects are induced to attribute it to their ability rather than to characteristics of the task. The reason for this may be that ability attributions help assure a connection between one's performance and one's self-system. It seems reasonable to assume that the self-system is charged with affect, and there is evidence that when one's attention is focused on oneself, affect is evoked (Scheier & Carver, 1977). It thus makes sense that attributing one's success to one's ability should make one think about competence and should evoke a competence-relevant affect, such as pride. It should be noted, however, that the self-system is complex, and there is evidence that affect may or may not be elicited, depending on how complex it is (Linville, 1982). For example, one may supplement the attribution with a kind of balancing out ("I may not do well on this, but I do well on something else").

Regarding moral standards, considerable research has suggested that children as well as adults tend to experience guilt when their actions violate a moral standard (Hoffman, 1983b). Furthermore, if they resist the temptation to act in a way that violates the standard, they often experience a positive feeling of self-approval that resembles past feelings associated with approval from others.

An internalized standard may be viewed as a subcategory of the self-system that is charged with affects relevant to self-evaluation (pride, shame, guilt). The earlier discussion of factors determining accessibility and activation of categories may thus be applicable here. The role of context in activating a moral standard and eliciting its affect is illustrated in story-completion responses that I obtained some time ago (Hoffman, 1970). In one item, a child the same age and sex as the subjects (fifth and seventh graders) cheats in a race without getting caught, wins the prize, and is congratulated by everyone. This story is frequently completed as follows: The story child is initially filled with joy, but later that night, when alone in bed and in the dark, he thinks about what he did, realizes it was wrong, and is consumed with guilt. The role of context is also indicated in a study designed to test "self-focused awareness" theory (Duval & Wicklund, 1972). Trick-or-treating children entering a home were told from another room to take only one candy from a large bowl on a table near the front door. Children were more likely to take only one candy when the bowl was placed in front of a large mirror. Putting this finding together with Scheier and Carver's (1977) report that affect is aroused when attention is focused on oneself, it would appear that seeing their own image may have activated the children's self-related, affectively charged moral standards.

PREPARATORY TRANSFORMATIONS

One can transform a stimulus into another form and then respond with affect to the transformed stimulus. For example, one can imagine that what is happening to someone else is happening to oneself, or one can ignore the immediate situation and imagine a totally different one and respond affectively to the imagined event. Or one can interpret a verbal message and respond to its semantic meaning rather than to its physical characteristics. These transformations may not elicit affect themselves, but they may put the stimulus into a form that makes it possible for the previously discussed affect-eliciting modes to operate.

Juxtaposition of the Stimulus: Role Taking

Taking the role of someone in an affect-eliciting situation may produce an empathic affective response in the observer (Hoffman, 1978). There appear to be two distinct role-taking modes that can have this effect (Hoffman, 1984). In the first, one simply focuses attention on the other's behavior (e.g., facial expression, posture, tone of voice) and/or situation and imagines how the other is feeling. This may be enough to generate empathic feeling. Even if the other is not present, so long as one has the necessary information, one can construct a representation—

imaginal (e.g., visual) or propositional—of the other's behavior and situation and respond affectively to this representation. The underlying process may be a combination of conditioning and mimicry (Hoffman, 1978) or the application of social category knowledge (Higgins, 1981).

In the second role-taking mode, one transforms the stimuli impinging on someone else into stimuli impinging on oneself. One may then respond to those stimuli as if they really were impinging on oneself and thereby experience some of the other's affect. Furthermore, one's affective response may be heightened if one is reminded of similar events in one's own past when one actually experienced the same affect and one may employ imagery to recapture those events. There is suggestive experimental evidence that this mode may generate more intense empathic affect, measured phsyiologically, than the first (Stotland, 1969). The reason may be that it connects more directly to the self-system. There is also evidence, however, that the connection to the self-system may make this a relatively fragile mode for eliciting empathic affect. When one focuses on how it would feel to be in the other's place and recalls one's own relevant past experiences, one may get caught up in egoistic concerns, and the image of the other that started the process may consequently fade away—a phenomenon I call "egoistic drift" (Hoffman, 1984).

Constructing the Stimulus

If one can juxtapose a stimulus event, one can also ignore it altogether and imagine some other affectively charged event. The imagined event may have occurred in the past, it may be anticipated in the future, or it may be made up anew. Many examples can be found in the research literature, including the burgeoning mood-induction experiments showing that almost any affect can be generated by imagining oneself in a relevant situation. The subjects of these experiments have been mostly adults, although Harris and Siebel (1975) found that when third-graders were asked to think happy or sad thoughts, it had an effect on their subsequent altruistic and aggressive behavior. Mischel and Moore (1973) reported that it was more difficult for children to delay gratification when they imagined the desired object in ways that highlighted its consummatory characteristics more than its nonconsummatory characteristics. Also, according to J. Singer (personal communication, May 1985), when subjects are in the process of trying to remember an affect-laden situation, their faces take on an expression that is congruent with the affect. Finally, consider a practical application from an airline flight attendant training session, in which the objective was to teach the control of anger toward certain passengers. The question was, "How do you rid yourself of anger?" The answer was, "Imagine a reason that excuses the other person's behavior" (Sheehy, 1983).

The foregoing examples are simple instances in which one imagines an event and experiences the appropriate affect. More interesting and important are examples in which one repeats this process many times with regard to the same hypothetical or anticipated event and, as a result, builds up an event schema that carries a powerful affective charge. Consider an example. In thinking about a questionable deduction on one's income tax return, one may imagine the possible consequences of being called up by the tax authorities—the unpleasantness of being challenged, compelled to produce documentation, and possibly brought to court. One may also imagine the long-term consequences of a huge fine or a jail term. These ruminations may take place over a period of weeks or months, and each time a certain amount of anticipatory affect may be experienced. As a result, one may build up an affectively charged schema for the event of receiving a letter from the Internal Revenue Service. If one then actually receives such a letter, its very appearance in the mailbox may be enough to trigger an immediate, intense emotional response. Stated more generally, by thinking about certain dreaded or desired events and anticipating their various consequences over a period of time, one may build highly charged anticipatory event schemata. This process, which suggests a schematic model rather than a spreading-activation model, may explain the powerful emotional reactions people sometimes have to an event that they have never before experienced. It may also explain how such a powerful emotional response can be triggered so quickly—too quickly for the kind of appraisal to have been made that would justify its intensity. (The appraisal, of course, was accomplished many times before the event.)

These event schemata are often bipolar. Consider the graduate school applicant who is waiting to hear whether he was accepted or rejected by the school of his choice or to find out whether he did well or poorly on the Graduate Record Exam; the assistant professor waiting to find out whether or not she is to be granted tenure; the trial defendant awaiting the verdict as to his guilt or innocence. In each case, over time, the person may have repeatedly imagined the various ways in which his or her life would be affected by the alternative outcomes and thus may have built up a bipolar, affectively charged schema. Consequently, the person is primed to respond immediately, with intense joy or dejection, to the slightest hint of the outcome.

Semantic Interpretation of a Stimulus

When a stimulus is in verbal form, as increasingly occurs with age, one normally interprets and responds, at least partly, to its semantic meaning. Verbal communications usually also have physical, nonsemantic components, however—word sounds, stress, intonation, inflection, pauses, hesitations—that may have become conditioned elicitors of affect, as discussed earlier. For this reason, it may often be difficult to isolate affective responses resulting from pure semantic interpretation. And when verbal communication occurs in an interpersonal, face-to-face context—probably the prototypical mode in the evolution of human communication—semantic meanings are additionally confounded with changes in the communicator's posture, gaze, and facial expression. I cited evidence earlier that words and nonsense syllables can become conditioned elicitors of affect, and it seems reasonable to expect that the same is true of the other nonsemantic features of verbal communications. But can the purely semantic component of an affectively charged message—together with an assessment of causes or consequences—generate affect? What is the evidence?

Several American and Russian experiments have shown that pure semantic meaning can become a conditioned stimulus for autonomic arousal (Razran, 1971). When older children or adults, for example, are conditioned to salivate, sweat, or constrict their blood vessels in response to a particular word, the conditioning generalizes more readily to semantically related words than to phonetically related words (more from "surf" to "waves" than from "surf" to "serf"; more from "dog" to "terrier" than from "flower" to "glower"). It is also interesting that younger children and adults in states of fatigue and intoxication transfer conditioning more along phonetic than semantic dimensions. These studies suggest that pure semantic meaning can become a conditioned stimulus for eliciting an affective response. An interesting implication of this research is that semantic interpretation may produce affect with a minimum of categorization or appraisal. The research suggests, further, that since meanings are independent of the particular organization of letters and words, different verbal messages that have the same meaning may elicit the same affect.

Although the pure semantic component of a verbal communication may mediate affect through conditioning, the research does not tell us whether a verbal communication that refers to an event not previously associated with affect can produce an affective response—that is, whether semantic meaning can actually *generate* affect. It seems likely that it can. Consider the negative affect-generating potential of the message "The department's decision was to deny [or grant] you tenure," even when it is delivered in a calm or friendly and supportive voice. One's affective response to such a message is presumably not due to conditioning, since one may not previously have had the experience of being up for tenure. The affective response is probably the result of interpreting the message and assessing the consequences of the event, or of assimilating the message content to other affectively charged schemata, such as those revolving around wish fulfillment and denial. It might also be the result of having previously ruminated about the consequences and having built up a highly charged event schema that is activated by the message, in the manner described earlier.

This is conjecture, of course. To demonstrate convincingly that semantic meaning (and appraisal) can generate affect may require controlling the non-semantic, stylistic components. This could be done in several ways. Perhaps the most stringent technique would be to communicate across languages—to present the subject with an affectively charged message that is translated literally into the subject's language from another language that has an entirely different rhythm and style. If subjects who understand the message also have the appropriate affective response, this would constitute strong evidence for affect arousal through semantic interpretation. Another technique would be to see if words that elicit one affect elicit a different affect when put in combinations that have a different meaning. Higgins and Rholes (1976) found that evaluative responses (which presumably have an affective component) depend on the meaning of the combination, rather than the meaning of each word. Although subjects evaluated the words "casual" and "surgeon" positively, they evaluated "casual surgeon" negatively.

Still another technique would be to employ written messages, removing those aspects of style that might evoke affect independently of semantic meaning. I used an approximation of this procedure in my empathy research by asking people to think about a recent time when they read about someone's misfortune in a letter and to try to remember what went through their minds. They described the two role-taking modes that I discussed earlier. Although these are vicarious rather than direct arousal modes, they suggest that one way semantic interpretation may generate affect is through a sequence of transformations: transforming written words into semantic meanings; then transforming the semantic meanings into affectively charged images of stimuli impinging on another person; and finally, transforming these images into images of stimuli impinging on oneself.

The same thing may happen in face-to-face verbal communication, except that the first step involves transformation of spoken rather than written words. The face-to-face condition may also be more complicated because of the presence of nonverbal cues that elicit affect directly through sensory and perceptual processes. These processes may begin generating affect before semantic interpretation is completed, at least in those cases in which the message is long and requires a great deal of semantic interpretation before the affective meaning becomes clear. In any case, the face-to-face condition may best be conceptualized as a network of verbal and nonverbal affect-eliciting processes. These processes are ordinarily congruent, although they may conflict at times, such as when the communicator attempts deception.

A final word should be added about semantic interpretation. Verbal messages vary in degree of clarity and ease of comprehension and hence in the amount of mental effort they require to be understood. To the degree that one's mental effort is directed to the processing of verbal information, one is distracted from the content and therefore is presumably less responsive to the meaning of the message. If two messages have the same affective meaning, the one that requires more processing to abstract the meaning should therefore be the less effective elicitor of affect. In other words, controlling for affective content, the greater the amount of processing required, the less intense (as well as more delayed) the affective response is likely to be. Also, if too much processing is required, this may render an affectively meaningful message incapable of eliciting affect, even though its semantic meaning is eventually comprehended.

To summarize, there appear to be three ways in which semantic interpretation of a stimulus may result in affect: (1) it may yield meanings that produce affect through conditioning, with a minimum of categorization or appraisal; or it may produce meanings that are followed by (2) categorization or (3) appraisal, which in turn generate affect. The effectiveness of these processes, especially 2 and 3, as affect elicitors may depend on the amount of mental effort required to abstract the meaning.

THE INFLUENCE OF AFFECT ON COGNITION

We now turn to ways in which affect, elicited through the various information-processing modes just described, may have an impact on cognition. Intuitively, as noted by Higgins, Herman, and Zanna (1981), affect could have various effects on cognition. One might attend more to affectively important stimuli and events or be more likely to rehearse and ruminate about them, or one might find affectively charged schemata more accessible than neutral ones. The problem is specifying the characteristics of the affective experience (intensity, valence) and the aspect of the cognitive process involved. An interesting question is whether Piaget and other cognitive psychologists are right when they claim that although affect motivates cognition and may determine the situations in which one engages in cognitive processing, affect cannot structure cognition. It probably depends on what is meant by "structure." If affect simply increased or decreased the speed or accuracy of cognitive processing, that would not reflect a change in structure. But it might reflect a change in structure if affect produced a change in the sector of the environment that is the primary target of processing or in the cognitive response hierarchy—that is, in the likelihood of one or another information-processing mode being utilized.

Affect May Initiate, Terminate or Disrupt Information Processing

As already mentioned, cognitive psychologists often view affect as providing the motivating force for initiating cognitive processes. There is considerable experimental evidence that moderate levels of affect intensity can enhance, and high-intensity levels can disrupt or terminate information processing in such complex tasks as deriving meaning from verbal cues (Kahneman, 1973). There is also evidence that positive affect improves performance by adults on such cognitive tasks as digit span and naming multiple uses for common objects, that positive affect results in faster shape discrimination learning in 4-year-old children (Masters, Barden, & Ford, 1979), that the affects associated with depressed states may curtail processing (Teasdale & Fogarty, 1979), and that unconscious affect may influence selective attention (Erdelyi, 1974). In Piaget's (1981) view, affect determines the tendency to approach or avoid situations and thus the amount of intellectual effort one chooses to exert in different domains, which in turn influences the rate of acquisition of knowledge—accelerating it in some domains and slowing it down in others. For Freud (1936), one hypothesized type of affect—anxiety—is responsible for touching off cognitive processes (defense mechanisms) whose function is to keep other affects that are associated with pain from conscious awareness.

Affect May Result in Selective Processing

Some time ago, Easterbrook (1959) summarized research evidence for the proposition that the number of cues utilized in any situation tends to become smaller with an increase in negative emotion. Not all cues are neglected equally; those most likely to be neglected are background contextual cues. This reduction in the range of background cue utilization may harm performance on tasks that require the use of a wide range of cues, and an increase in negative affect may be said to be disorganizing with regard to such tasks. Furthermore, more to the point, if an increase in negative affect intensity makes foreground cues the center of attention, this may mean that the automatic, nonverbal processing modes (sensory, perceptual), which are adaptive in processing background environmental cues, are less likely to be utilized. In those tasks in which proficiency demands concentration on the foreground, irrelevant cues are excluded, and negative affect can be said to be organizing. Thus, there seems to be an optimal range of cue utilization—hence, negative affect intensity—for each task. If negative affect does, indeed, foster processing of foreground cues, it may be appropriate to mention Broadbent's (1971) distinction between reacting to stimuli with immediate associations only and relating stimuli to many background experiences. We might expect that the number of background experiences associated with a stimulus may tend to diminish with increase in negative affect intensity, although immediate associations may be unaffected. An increase in positive affect, on the other hand, appears to result in an increase in unusual (presumably less immediate) word associations (Isen, Johnson, & Robinson, in press). Affect may thus play a role in determining which sector of the environment—foreground or background—becomes the primary target of cognitive processing.

In a review by Mueller (1979), it was found that intense anxiety directs one's attention to physical features of words (acoustic properties, order of presentation, phonetic similarities) and that this occurs to the relative neglect of semantic content. This suggests that affect can determine the extent to which semantic and nonsemantic processing modes are brought into play. In attempting to explain certain repeated findings in the parent discipline literature, I have similarly hypothesized (Hoffman, 1983a) that the anger and fear aroused by power-assertive discipline by parents (force, threats, commands) may direct children's attention to the consequences of their deviant action for themselves (punishment). This interferes with the semantic processing of the information contained in the verbal component of the parent's message that may also be present (reason). To summarize, affect may determine the sector of the environment that is processed and the modes of processing that are brought into play.

Affect May Organize Recall

The influence of affect on recall, which has long interested psychologists (e.g., Bartlett, 1932; Freud, 1914), is so far the most heavily researched topic in the affect–cognition literature (Bartlett, Burleson, & Santrock, 1982; Bower, Monteiro, & Gilligan, 1978; Isen, Shalker, Clark, & Karp, 1978; Laird, Wagener, Halal, & Szegda, 1982; Nasby & Yando, 1982). The best documented finding, obtained at all age levels—5 years, 8 years, 10–12 years, adulthood—is that one's affective state facilitates recall of information congruent with the affect. This is particularly true of positive affect. Several investigators found that positive but not negative affect influences recall (Bartlett *et al.*, 1982; Isen *et al.*, 1978;

Natale & Hantas, 1982; Teasdale & Fogarty, 1979) and several others found that negative affect also influences recall, but to a lesser extent than positive affect (Bower et al., 1978; Nasby & Yando, 1982; Teasdale, Taylor, & Fogarty, 1980). Laird et al. (1982) found no differences between positive and negative affect, but this may have been because task difficulty was not controlled. Subjects recalled passages that had different emotional content, and the positive-affect passages were rated by the subjects as being more difficult. Had the passages been equally difficult, the positive-affect passages might have had a greater effect on recall. Isen et al. (1978) suggested that positive affect contributes to recall of mood-congruent information because of a human tendency to maintain positive and avoid negative internal states. To account for the entire pattern of findings (including those for negative affect), I would add that negative affect also contributes to recall of mood-congruent information but that this effect is neutralized, in part, by the disposition to maintain a positive internal state. As a result, positive and negative affect both contribute to recall of mood-congruent information, but the effect is more pronounced for positive affect. A more cognitive explanation recently suggested by Isen (in press) is that the asymmetry of positive and negative affect on memory may be due to the structure of the cognitive schemata (or networks) of the two affects (e.g., sad material may be less well elaborated and interconnected in the cognitive system than happy material). Though cognitive, this explanation still highlights the importance of mood, since Isen suggests that the sad material may lack structure as a result of "habits of mood-repair."

The influence of affect on encoding processes is less clear-cut. Gilligan and Bower (1984), who did not find evidence for recall of mood-congruent information, did find evidence for encoding of mood-congruent information, and this finding was obtained for both happiness and sadness. Isen et al. (1978) found no such effect; Nasby and Yando (1982) found it for positive affect and anger but not for sadness in children. Gilligan and Bower also obtained better recall when the subjects' affect at the time of recall was the same as their affect at encoding (state-dependent memory)—a finding that other investigators, except Bartlett et al. (1982), have not obtained. Recently, Bower and Mayer (in press) have reported repeated failure to replicate this effect. It is too soon to tell, but the clear-cut symmetrical results for positive and negative affect obtained by Gilligan and Bower may be due to the use of hypnosis, which gave the subjects a more intense and focused affective experience.

The question may be asked whether schemata for life events are organized in memory around certain affects, and thus whether affect may be one of the factors contributing to schema accessibility. Consider Nelson and Gruendel's (1981) observation that young children quickly acquire certain scripts, such as the script for eating at McDonald's. Although Nelson did not study affect, I suggest that the restaurant-eating experience may be a life event that is charged with family-connected, mainly positive affect. This affect may have been the child's major basis for organizing the script. Asking the child "What happens at McDonald's?" may evoke that affect and call up the script. This hypothesis could be tested by seeing how quickly children acquire equally complex scripts that are affectively neutral.

Affect Contributes to Formation of Emotionally Charged Categories and Schemata

I suggested earlier that assimilating a stimulus to an affectively charged category may result in the category's affect being conferred on the stimulus—that one responds to the stimulus with the category's affect. That formulation put the focus on the process of categorization as an elicitor of affect. When we examine affectively charged categories and schemata from the standpoint of how they are formed, however, the focus is put on affect as a contributing factor. That is, it seems reasonable to assume that people have feelings in connection with certain events, real or imagined, before they group the events into a category. Thus, affective experiences contribute to the construction of an affectively charged category. When a new stimulus event is assimilated to the category and acquires its affective charge, the process may be viewed as one in which past affect is transferred to the stimulus event through the mechanism of categorization.

The point can be illustrated with the self-system. We assume that the physical, mental, and dispositional characteristics making up the self are charged with affect because of their past association with affective experiences. Because of this past history, the self-system develops as an affectively charged category. When the self-system is activated, one should therefore experience affect, and the affect may be expected to operate in the ways discussed earlier; for example, it should play a role in organizing memory. There is evidence that it does. Rogers, Kuiper, and Kirker (1977) found that memory for a trait word (e.g., "shy") is enhanced if one thinks about whether the word describes oneself ("Does the word describe you?") and that the effect is greater than the effect of thinking about the word in other ways ("Is the word a synonym of X?"). A possible explanation is that thinking about a word in relation to the self activates the self-system and elicits affect—more often positive than negative affect, owing to the human tendency to protect one's self-image. This affect then becomes attached to the word, resulting in enhanced memory for the word. Such an explanation can focus on the importance of the cognitive contribution (assimilating the word to the self-system) or the importance of the affective contribution (past affective experiences that account for the self-system's affective charge).

Affect May Provide Input for Social Cognition

As I noted earlier, when one mimics the facial and postural movements accompanying another's affective experience, the afferent feedback from the muscular contraction patterns involved in these movements may enable one to experience some of the other's feelings. Awareness of these feelings in oneself may, in turn, inform one that the other is having the same feeling, and this knowledge may alter one's subsequent processing of information about that person. The same kind of information may be obtained without mimicry. One may have conditioned or unconditioned affective responses to the other's facial and postural movements or to the other's situation, and the awareness of these feelings in oneself may suggest that the other is having similar feelings.

By enabling one to be sensitive to nonverbal cues with little cognitive effort, mimicry and conditioning may thus alert one to another's affective response, as well as providing one with initial information about what the specific affect is. When the other tries to deceive verbally, mimicry and conditioning may provide one with clues about what the other's true feelings really are, because people's feelings may be "leaked" through changes in their facial response, posture, or tone of voice. These clues, imprecise though they may be, may alert one and lead one to examine and appraise the other's behavior more closely. Affects generated by mimicry and conditioning may thus contribute to social cognition because they provide important cues about one of the major sources of unpredictability in people—their feelings (Hoffman, 1981).

Affect May Influence Decision Making and Problem Solving

Isen, Means, Patrick, and Nowicki (1982) reported several experimental studies showing that people who are experiencing low to moderate levels of positive affect tend to adopt the simplest strategy and consider fewer alternatives. They also do little or no checking of information. The result is either a faster, more efficient decision or a biased, incomplete, and incorrect one, depending on the nature of the task and the validity of the person's initial hunches. There is evidence that these effects may not be obtained when the person is provided with feedback or when the task is defined as extremely important. Finally, protocol analysis suggests that the strategy used by positive-affect subjects is efficient rather than sloppy (Isen & Means, 1983).

THEORETICAL ASSUMPTIONS

What has been presented so far is a taxonomy of information-processing modes that elicit affect and various ways in which affect influences information processing. This taxonomy encompasses a broad range of facts and theoretical conceptions about affective–cognitive interaction, and it provides a framework for organizing the literature and identifying gaps in research. Furthermore, as I hope to make clear, by adding certain assumptions, the taxonomy becomes a scheme that may help illuminate and generate hypotheses about the interplay among processes and the complex ways in which they influence one another in real life. Before presenting these assumptions, it should be noted that the processes are not mutually exclusive, since they utilize different aspects of a person's sensory, perceptual, and cognitive apparatus and may operate at different levels of consciousness. Although they were presented and discussed one at a time, they may often operate together in various combinations, as in complex interpersonal interactions. This raises the question of how the processes combine and under what conditions they facilitate or interfere with one another. It also raises questions about the differences in latency among them—for example, whether the faster processes generate affect that then influences the slower processes. The assumptions that deal with these matters follow.

All Processing Modes Are Used

The first assumption, shared by traditional information-processing theories, is that it is adaptive to extract as much meaning as possible in most situations. Therefore, when one is exposed to a relevant stimulus, most if not all of the information-processing modes in one's repertoire are utilized. The sensory and perceptual modes are relatively automatic and may operate in virtually all situations. The cognitive modes are more under voluntary control, and people may often stop processing when they have what seems to them to be a reasonable conclusion.

Infants may be limited to the sensory mode, as in the primitive fear and avoidance of a looming object. Older children and adults may respond to a network of sensory, perceptual, and cognitive cues. On seeing a rapidly approaching truck they, like infants, may experience a primitive fear, but there may also be a cognitive overlay—that is, an awareness of potential consequences that may heighten the fear. Although all the cues in a network may contribute to an affective response, one cue may be predominant. Sometimes, the sensory aspect of the stimulus is salient and the affective response is primarily stimulus-driven. At other times, the affective response may be category- or schema-driven or driven by the context. The affect elicited by the different processes may ordinarily be congruent, as in the truck example, but they are sometimes incongruent, as when a person attempts to deceive someone.

Processing Modes Elicit Affect Sequentially

Whether the processes are congruent or not, an important aspect of how they interact is the temporal relationship among them. Do they generate affect simultaneously or sequentially? Our assumption is that they generate affect sequentially. This follows logically from the fact that the simplest mode requires only sensory registration of the stimulus (which takes only about 40 or 50 ms) and perhaps a minimum of perceptual organization, whereas the more complex modes require sensory registration plus additional cognitive processing. We would thus expect that a direct response to a physical stimulus takes the least amount of time. Pattern recognition should take longer because of the additional step of matching the stimulus to a schema. Categorization should take still longer, the exact amount of time depending on the complexity and number of categories available and the extent to which one is primed to use certain categories. The time required to assess the consequences of a stimulus event or relate it to one's self-system may be expected to vary greatly, depending on the number of consequences considered and how explicitly relevant they are to the self-system. Finally, we would expect the time required for categorizing and assessing consequences to be longer when the stimulus is verbal rather than physical because of the additional intervening step of semantic interpretation. This becomes obvious when a verbal message consists of strings of words, perhaps sentences, that must be semantically interpreted before the affect-generating meaning can be apprehended.

There has been no systematic research on processing times for the different modes, but there are scattered findings that may give us some idea of the magnitudes involved. Regarding recognition of the physical features of a stimulus, Potter (1975) found that subjects could recognize an object if a line drawing of it was flashed for as little as 44 ms. Blum (1954) found that only 30 ms were required for subjects with certain personality conflicts to recognize pictorial stimuli ("Blackie" test pictures) symbolizing these conflicts. These figures provide a rough tentative estimate of pattern recognition time, although the actual time required varies with, among other factors, the intensity (e.g., loudness, illumination) of the stimulus.

The time required for responding to the semantic meaning of a stimulus appears to vary, as expected, with the complexity of the task. In studies of unconscious processing, to be discussed later, subjects were able to catch a bit of the meaning of words flashed for as little as 50 ms (Marcel, Katz, & Smith, 1974; Wickens, 1972). Categorizing words takes much longer. Gitomer, Pellegrino, and Bisanz (1983) presented a list of words and asked subjects to identify the one that fit a category (e.g., fruit). This task could be done in about 300–500 ms if the correct word was the first on the list, which suggests that it takes about a third of a second to fit a simple stimulus word to a highly accessible category. If the correct word was not first, thus requiring more scanning time, the task took more than 500 ms. Craik and Tulving (1975) flashed words for 200 ms and asked subjects, before exposing each word, whether it fit a certain category ("Is the word a type of fish?"). The subjects took about 700 ms to respond, and they did not respond at all in a third of the trials. Potter's (1975) subjects also took about 700 ms in a similar task, although when the stimulus was a drawing of an object (hat), instead of a word, it took about 10% less time to determine whether it fit a category (clothing). In the study by Rogers *et al.* (1977), cited earlier, which used more complex trait words and a more demanding task (judging whether the word was a synonym of another word), the task took much longer—about 2.5 s. And when the subjects judged whether the trait word was descriptive of themselves, the task took about 3 s.

These processing times tell us nothing about affect. How long does it take from the time the stimulus is processed, regardless of the processing mode involved, until one experiences the affect? There are no data on this essentially physiological question, but we can get some idea of how long it takes for a processed stimulus to travel through the system and produce an affective response from Landis and Hunt's (1939) classic study of the startle response. The startle response may not be an affect (Ekman, 1984), but it does resemble negative affective responses to physical stimuli in several ways. The subjects' facial expressions "immediately following" the startle response and the words they use to describe the experience resemble fear and anger, and there is the same autonomic nervous system involvement (decrease in galvanic skin response) as in affect arousal (Hunt, 1937). Landis and Hunt (1939) found that the eyeblink, which is the quickest measureable part of the startle pattern, has a latency of about 50 ms. The spreading of the mouth takes about 80 ms. Since mouth movements often accompany affect expressions, it may be that 80 ms, or roughly a tenth of a second, is a reasonable approximation of the time an adult takes from processing a stimulus to having an affective response. The time it takes to experience the feeling is presumably somewhat less than this because of the time it takes to go from feeling to response.

Our speculations about sequential processing and the likelihood that sensory processing precedes cognitive processing thus appear to be borne out empirically. The difference in processing time ranges from virtually zero to very large, depending on whether extensive semantic interpretation is required to apprehend the affective meaning of the stimulus event. In any case, sequential operation of the different processing modes suggests that they influence one another, which leads to the third assumption.

Processing Modes Influence One Another

The affect elicited by early-acting modes may be expected to serve as input to the later modes and thus influence them in the ways described earlier (e.g., it may cause selective processing of information). As a result, the affect elicited by a later mode may have two components—one that is due to earlier modes and another that is independent. The independent component may, in turn, feed back and have an impact on affect elicited earlier. It may simply confirm and perhaps fine-tune the early affect, or it may contradict it. In the case of confirmation, the net resultant affect may simply be a heightened, more elaborated version of the initial affect (e.g., when one assesses the consequences of being hit by a truck after having an immediate fear response to the onrushing stimulus). When the affect produced by a later mode contradicts that produced by an earlier mode, a blend of the conflicting affects may result. A second possibility, which seems likely to occur more often because of its potentially adaptive value, is that one of the contradictory affects ultimately prevails—ordinarily the one having the most compelling implications for the actor's welfare (in the case of empathy, implications for someone else's welfare).

We might expect that there is a temporal limit to the impact that affect elicited by one processing mode can have on a subsequent mode. That is, if the earlier affect were largely dissipated before the subsequent mode began to operate, it would have little or no impact. The autonomic-arousal component of affective responses may be relevant here. It is known by psychophysiologists and medical practitioners who measure blood pressure that although the latency of autonomic arousal from stimulus onset may be several seconds, the arousal duration may range from several seconds to 10 or 15 minutes or longer (traumatic autonomic upheaval may elevate the heart rate for hours or even days).[5] We may conclude, along with Clark (1982), that although the facial component of an affective response might dissipate quickly, the autonomic arousal component may often endure for quite a while afterward. If so, it seems reasonable to expect that the affective state, including its associated feeling tone, may be prolonged (though the feeling component may not persist as long as the physiological), thus extending the period during which it can influence subsequent processing. In other words, the autonomic arousal component may operate like a flywheel that keeps affect elicited early in a sequence "alive" long enough for it to influence subsequent processing. In this way, the arousal component may help maintain the dynamic interplay among processing modes and the affect they generate. This seems more likely to occur in real-life settings; there is evidence that experimentally induced affect is often short-lived.

Processing May Be Unconscious

The question of whether processing can occur outside awareness has long been debated (e.g., Shevrin & Dickman, 1980). Behaviorists ruled it out; and cognitive psychologists tended to assume, until recently (Nisbett & Wilson, 1977), that people are always aware of the content and the underlying processes of their cognitive functioning. One might engage in certain habitual functions without awareness, but certainly not in the kind of mental activity involved in semantic processing. There is now a growing body of evidence that even semantic processing can be unconscious. As mentioned earlier, Bargh and Pietromonaco (1982) found that hostile cues presented outside awareness influenced subjects' social judgments. More direct evidence for unconscious semantic processing was obtained by Marcel *et al.* (1974). They found that although subjects could not correctly identify single words briefly flashed on a screen (followed by a pattern mask), their erroneous responses, though showing little graphic or phonological relationship to the stimulus word, sometimes bore a striking semantic relationship to it.[6] Thus, *green* led to responses such as "blue" and "yellow," *queen* to "king," *apple* to "orange," *light* to "dark," *happy* to "joy," and so forth. The subjects thus showed some knowledge of the semantic meaning of a word without knowing what the word was. In an earlier experiment, Wickens (1972) found that subjects could not identify flashed (and masked) single words but were able to judge whether or not the word was similar in meaning (in terms of semantic differential) to a newly presented word. Marcel (1983a) recently improved Wickens's procedure and obtained the same results. This research suggests that once people learn to read, the meaning of words can register quickly without conscious intention or awareness. Furthermore, the meaning that unconscious processing affords may be an integral part of and make a direct contribution to the analysis and comprehension of a message. Unconscious semantic processing may thus be adaptive because it facilitates quick identification of meanings and, hence, determination of the proper course of action (e.g., fight or flee) in a situation. (See Erdelyi [1974] and Marcel [1983] for theories about the cognitive basis of unconscious processing.)

Can unconscious semantic meaning elicit affect? The fact that semantic meaning can become a conditioned stimulus for eliciting affect, noted earlier, suggests a positive answer to this question. There is also the demonstration by Kunst-Wilson and Zajonc (1980) that people who were shown geometric shapes so fast that they were unaware of having seen them were later found to prefer these shapes to forms they were genuinely seeing for the first time. Although semantic meaning may not have been involved, this finding suggests that unconsciously perceived stimuli can elicit affect.

If unconscious processing is always going on and if it can elicit affect, what happens if the affect is highly aversive? The "perceptual defense" or "subception" research in the 1940s and 1950s found that when an emotionally loaded stimulus (a socially tabooed word or a nonsense syllable previously conditioned to produce affect by associating it with electric shock) was flashed rapidly enough, subjects could not identify it; their galvanic skin responses, however, revealed that they had recognized its meaning and responded affectively (Lazarus & McCleary, 1951; McGinnies, 1949). More recently, H. Shevrin (personal communication, April 1985) reported that patients have stronger evoked potentials to flashed words that are related to their emotional problems than to neutral words, even though they cannot identify the words and often are unaware that any word was flashed. In light of the perceptual defense research, it seems reasonable to infer that the subjects experienced aversive affect, though unaware of the meaning of the verbal stimuli that produced that affect. We may tentatively conclude with the hypothesis that unconscious semantic processing may sometimes be initiated by motivational and emotional states: motivation and emotion may lead to a selective, unconscious sensitivity, a lowered threshold to relevant verbal stimuli.

What happens if the exposure time of a threatening stimulus is gradually increased to the point at which conscious processing becomes possible? Psychoanalytic theory would predict that people with emotional problems would have *higher* thresholds of conscious recognition of words relevant to their problems. Blum's (1954) research speaks to this issue. Blum found that subjects whose aggressive and sexual impulses were experimentally aroused had lower thresholds for recognizing pictorial stimuli symbolizing these impulses when the stimuli were flashed for 30 ms—too fast for conscious recognition. This finding fits those obtained by Shevrin and by the perceptual defense researchers. More interesting, Blum's subjects had higher thresholds when the stimuli were flashed for 200 ms, which was just enough time for minimal conscious recognition. Blum interpreted the findings as supporting two interrelated psychoanalytic hypotheses: (1) the unconscious striving for expression of underlying impulses (vigilance) and (2) the warding off of these threatening impulses as they begin to approach consciousness (defense). Should further research substantiate the existence of such a vigilance-defense process, it would indicate that there may be a conflict-based type of processing in which meaning is rendered unconscious to avoid threat or pain. In contrast to the previously discussed (conflict-free) unconscious processing, which I suggested may be an integral part of the analysis and comprehension of messages, the stimulus meaning in this case is not admitted to consciousness and thus cannot contribute to analysis and comprehension. This conflict-based process may be adaptive because it reduces pain and thus enables the individual to continue what he or she was doing, but the cost may be a diminished ability to comprehend certain messages because of lost access to potentially important information. Such a process, if it exists, must be clearly differentiated from conflict-free unconscious processing.

The notion that pain avoidance may underlie unconscious processing leads to our fifth and last assumption.

Processing Is Biased Positively

The fifth assumption is that there is a motivational bias in information processing; that is, other things being equal, processing is biased to maximize the experience of positive affective states and to minimize the experience of negative affective states.[7] This assumption is shared by traditional psychoanalytic and learning theorists, especially operant learning theorists, as well as by some contemporary social learning theorists. Mischel, Ebbeson, and Zeiss (1976) used it to explain their finding of selective memory about the self; and, as noted earlier, Isen *et al.* (1978) used it to explain their finding that recall of mood-congruent information is stronger for positive than for negative affect. The findings that, in a neutral mood, people tend to remember more pleasant than unpleasant childhood events (Gilligan & Bower, 1984) and more pleasant than unpleasant words in a list (Isen *et al.*, 1978) are also in keeping with this assumption. Finally, the research on perceptual defense and motivated unconscious processing suggests that one may shut off the processing of certain stimuli to avoid a painful emotional experience.[8]

The assumption of motivational bias may have a bearing on accessibility of schemata and categories. It suggests that such representations are more likely to be accessible if they carry a positive affective charge; that is, there may be a tendency to assimilate stimuli to positively charged schemata and categories. What happens with negatively charged representations is less clear. They should certainly be less accessible than positively charged representations, but how do they compare with neutral representations? The memory research, as noted, is inconclusive. The perceptual defense research suggests, on the one hand, that negatively charged schemata may be readily activated and may quickly assimilate relevant stimuli. But the research also suggests that one may be largely unaware of the assimilation process, the resulting affect, and the impact on subsequent processing of the stimulus. In short, the research seems to suggest the tentative hypothesis that negatively charged schemata may be more accessible, but primarily to unconscious processing.

What about bivalent schemata and categories? These appear to be similar to negatively charged representations, but they are also charged with positive affect, presumably because the past experiences of pain or punishment were preceded by pleasure. Such representations may be highly accessible because of their positive affective charge, but they may be accessible primarily to unconscious processing because of their negative charge. The end result, suggested by Blum's previously discussed research, may be that bivalent representations are readily activated by appropriate (tempting) stimuli (vigilance) and that these stimuli are then processed unconsciously (defense).

To summarize, the fifth assumption states that affect-eliciting processes are biased to maximize positive and to minimize negative affect. One important implication of this assumption is that a positive affective charge should add to a schema's or a category's accessibility. We may also speculate, pending necessary research, (1) that a negative charge may also increase accessibility, though to a lesser degree, and (2) that the activation of negatively and bivalently charged schemata or categories and the processing that results may be largely unconscious.

COMPLEX AFFECTIVE–COGNITIVE INTERACTION SEQUENCES

The addition of the five assumptions to our scheme leads to expectations about how the various processes described earlier may flow and interact in complex life situations. As an illustration, we might expect that when a stimulus can be responded to in terms of both its physical features and appraisal, the affect generated by the physical features may be evoked first and may influence the appaisal process. Consider the following incident. A professor thought he saw a bear entering the classroom. He wondered why a student would wear a bear outfit, and his first thought was that the student was emotionally disturbed. The professor then became very frightened, because he remembered that a disturbed student had walked into a professor's office a few weeks earlier and shot him. We may ask why the professor categorized the student as disturbed and a potential murderer, rather than as someone participating in a harmless, frivolous act (e.g., a fraternity initiation rite, which would probably be far closer to the base rate of reasonable explanations for that kind of student behavior). On questioning, it turned out that the professor had an initial fear at seeing a bear, which was quickly dismissed as absurd, before he began wondering about the student. It seems reasonable that the initial, fleeting fear may have served to activate fear-charged categories, such as crazy and potentially dangerous students. If so, what first appeared to be a simple example of categorization leading to affect (crazy and dangerous student, leading to fear) becomes, on closer inspection, an example of a more complex, three-step sequence: (1) the affect aroused by physical features of a stimulus (fear of bear) is quickly dismissed as a result of appraisal (it can't be a bear); (2) the affect nonetheless activates a category charged with the same affect; and (3) activating this category produces the same affect, although it is now in a form that is more acceptable and compelling because it has a far more realistic basis.

Here is another example. A young adult male saw the driver of an expensive sports car being wheeled in a stretcher to an ambulance. He had not seen the accident, having come on the scene just after it happened. He reported:

> I first assumed it was probably a rich, smart-aleck kid driving while drunk or on dope and I did not feel for him. I then thought, this might be unfair, maybe he was rushing because of some emergency, suppose he was taking someone to the hospital, and then I felt for him. But then I thought, that was no excuse, he should have been more careful even if it was an emergency, and my feeling for him decreased. Then I realized the guy might be dying and I really felt bad for him again.

This response nicely illustrates the shifts in causal attribution and the resulting changes in feeling that may occur in ambiguous situations. Here again, however, the actual process may have been more complex. We may ask, first, what made the observer change his attribution in the first place? In an interview, the observer, who is a generally empathic person, remembered that his first response to the physical features of the stimulus event was an intensely aversive empathic distress. This was followed by the derogatory attribution. I suggest, in keeping with the notion of "empathic overarousal" (Hoffman, 1978), that the derogatory attribution was a cognitive operation that served to temporarily reduce the painful empathic feelings. This made the situation more tolerable and gave the observer time to gain control over his emotional response to the event. He was then able to respond to the stark reality of the victim's condition, which remained in view, and again empathize, this time without having to derogate the victim.[9] It is interesting to note that, as in the previous example, the person was more aware of the effect of his cognitive attribution on his feelings than the effect of his feelings on his cognitive attributions. Research is needed to establish whether this is generally true, and whether it reflects this society's value on rationality.

These anecdotes suggest the impact that affect elicited by physical features of stimuli can have on appraisal. It may thus appear that appraisal has a subordinate, secondary role in eliciting affect. This is not always true, of course. When the meaning of a stimulus is clear and compelling (signifying powerful, long-term consequences) appraisal processes may not be readily modifiable by simpler processes, except perhaps temporarily. An example is that cited earlier, in which a dull body ache may make one intensely anxious because of its association with a life-threatening illness. Another example comes from the empathy domain. When a mature observer sees someone, who does not know he is terminally ill, having fun, the observer is less likely to respond with empathic joy than with empathic distress or some combination of joy and distress—because the illness is a far more compelling indicator of the person's condition than the facial and other body cues reflecting his affective state in the immediate situation.

I have not yet discussed interpersonal interactions, but we can only assume that in such interactions, one responds to a network of verbal and nonverbal cues, and the previous discussion of processing sequences presumably applies. Before one can interpret a verbal message, one may have already responded affectively to cues at the nonverbal, physical-feature level, and the resulting affect may influence one's interpretation of the verbal message and the affect that results from that interpretation. If the nonverbal cues and verbal message are discrepant, there is a question of which one will be the major determiner of affect. I suggest that this will depend primarily on which one provides the affectively more compelling information. If neither is compelling (the situation is ambiguous), one should ordinarily tend to favor the source that makes one feel good.

When interacting with someone, one may not only respond to verbal and nonverbal cues, but one may also assimilate the interaction to a representation or schema of past interactions with that person. To the extent that this is done, one is responding not to the immediate stimulus value of the other or of the interaction, but to the accumulated value of past interactions. Thus, assimilating an interaction to one's interaction schema may, in a sense, create a barrier (R. M. Martin, 1968) between oneself and the other person. This may have a "leveling" effect, thus limiting spontaneity. On the other hand, it may also have a social-regulation function. It may, for example, operate as a brake that prevents extreme emotional responses to specific acts of provocation by the other. Consider the following statement by a 12-year-old child who was describing his emotional reactions during a fight with a friend:

> "You have known your friend so long and loved him so much, and then all of a sudden you are so mad at him, you say, I could just kill you and you still like each other, because you have always been friends and you know in your mind you are going to be friends in a few seconds anyway." (Rubin, 1983, p. 254)

We see here a possibly important point of connection between ahistorical information-processing approaches to affect and approaches to the study of affect as a feature of enduring relationships. Person and interaction schemata that are developed in the course of building a relationship with someone may often play a significant role in determining one's affective response to a particular action by that person.

When interacting with someone, one may also respond in terms of emotionally charged representations of past interactions with *someone else*. Consider the psychoanalytic notion of transference, which appears to be a case of assimilating the therapist to one's parent-schema. Why would someone do this? I suggest that one may do it because the feelings engendered when one is in the dependent role of patient—affection, desire for nurturance and approval—may activate long-held schemata of one's interaction with the parent that are charged with these same feelings ("mother-gives-and-I-receive-affection" schema). One may then have these feelings in the therapy session, and they may influence how one categorizes and appraises what the therapist says and does and, in general, how one constructs the therapist–patient relationship. Furthermore, the feelings and resulting cognitive constructions affect one's behavior toward the therapist. It seems reasonable to assume that these transference processes are mostly unconscious. Why else would a rational person persist in acting toward the therapist as though the therapist were the parent? In short, transference may be described in part as a largely unconscious, affect-based assimilation of therapist–patient interactions to schemata of parent–child interactions.[10]

Transference may be an extreme form of what normally occurs in many, if not all, interactions—with one's spouse, one's boss, one's friends. And if we broaden the definition of transference to include schemata of past interactions with other people besides parents, it seems likely that one may always, to some extent, assimilate the individuals with whom one is currently interacting to schemata of past interactions that are activated by currently engendered feelings.

IS COGNITIVE EVALUATION NECESSARY FOR AFFECT?

Our framework may provide a helpful perspective on the continuing debate regarding whether a cognitive evaluation process is necessary for eliciting affect. Those who believe it is necessary have not specified what they mean by "cognitive evaluation." Their illustrations, however, suggest that they mean what I have called "categorization" and "appraisal." Since these are but two of several processes, some of which are minimally cognitive and operate outside awareness, the most reasonable conclusion would seem to be that cognitive evaluation is not necessary for eliciting affect. Those holding the cognitive-evaluation-is-necessary position have responded to this challenge either by excluding the minimally cognitive processes from consideration or by defining cognitive evaluation broadly enough to include these processes. Thus, Mandler (1982) excludes "innate preferences" from his analysis of what accounts for taste. Lazarus (1982), on the other hand, argues that even what I have called "direct affective responses to physical stimuli" may be viewed as instances of cognitive evaluation processes. According to Lazarus, the concept of appraisal includes

> . . . the type of process described by ethologists in which a fairly rigid, built-in response to stimulus arrays differentiates danger from no-danger. An evaluative perception, hence appraisal, can operate at all levels of complexity, from the most primitive and inborn to the most symbolic and experienced-based. If this is reasonable, then it is also possible to say that cognitive appraisal is *always* involved in emotion, even in creatures far more primitive than humans. (Lazarus, 1982, p. 1023)

I suggest that we gain very little by postulating in advance, as Lazarus does, that cognitive evaluation is always necessary and by defining cognitive evaluation so broadly as to include all ways of processing stimuli. We are more likely to enhance our understanding, first, by recognizing that although some kind of information processing is necessary for having an affective experience, the type of processing may vary from the exceedingly simple to the highly complex; and second, by trying to specify the types of processes and their activating conditions, as has been attempted here.

If cognitive evaluation is but one of several affect-eliciting processes, and if it is often influenced by the affect elicited by earlier, more primitive processes, the question may be raised regarding just how important cognitive evaluation is for affect. As noted earlier, categorization and appraisal can be very important, even in situations in which they are not the primary affect-eliciting process. Indeed, even when categorization and appraisal enter the affect-eliciting sequence relatively late and are biased by earlier, more primitive processes, they may still end up being the most powerful and enduring determinant of one's affective response in the situation. Furthermore, this may be true whether the affect elicited by these evaluative processes merely confirms or strongly contradicts the affect elicited earlier (as in the "dull ache" example cited earlier).

It may thus be true that "preferences need no inferences" (Zajonc, 1980) and that preferences may bias inferences, sometimes outside awareness. Inferences once made, however, may often be the more compelling indicator of what is truly important in a situation. When that happens, inferences may undermine preferences.

Notes

1. An exception was the research on affect as a retrieval cue (Isen, Shalker, Clark, & Karp, 1978).

2. The concept of "spreading activation" comes to mind, but the assumption that activation is automatic and hierarchically structured and that it spreads out equally in all directions from a node has been questioned on empirical grounds (Johnson & Tversky, 1983).

3. I have advanced a moral development theory that capitalizes on this fact, focusing on disciplinary practices that point up the consequences of the child's action for others (Hoffman, 1983a).

4. However, such comparison information is used by 4–5-year-olds to evaluate *others* (Ruble, 1983) and therefore could influence their affective response to others.

5. Some components of autonomic arousal (e.g., heart rate) may dissipate more quickly than others.

6. This is not effective processing, however, as it just exceeds chance expectations.

7. The other things that must be equal for this bias to operate are the degree of explicitness of the stimulus and the degree to which the stimulus has compelling implications for the actor's welfare (see the discussion of how processing modes influence one another). A stimulus that is perceptually explicit for negative affect (an onrushing truck, a failing grade on an exam) will not ordinarily elicit positive affect. The positive bias may be expected to operate when there is a lack of explicitness.

8. None of these findings deny the possible influence of enduring negative affect as a personality characteristic. Depressed people, for example, may tend to recall unpleasant information and may process feedback about the outcomes they achieve differently than happy people do.

9. An alternative explanation is that the derogatory attribution reflects a "belief in a just world" (Lerner & Simmons, 1966), which was activated independently of empathy. This explanation cannot explain why the attribution immediately followed an intense empathic distress response, why it negated the empathic distress ("I didn't feel for him"), and why it was in turn negated by a thought ("this might be unfair") that accompanied a less intense empathic distress response. I suggest, in keeping with my "defense" interpretation, that the derogatory attribution may have reflected a belief in a just world, but the belief may have been activated to alleviate the pain associated with the intense empathic distress initially aroused.

10. A major objective of Freudian therapy is to bring the patient to the point at which he or she can experience the inappropriate feelings while knowing that they are inappropriate and that they originated in past interactions with parents. Experiencing the feelings is not enough, and understanding their source is not enough. One must do both—engage in transference and know one is doing so—simultaneously and continue to do so ("working through"). The resulting synthesis of affect and cognition may then undermine the transference.

References

Bargh, J., & Pietromonaco, P. (1982). Automatic information processing and social perception: The influence of trait information presented outside of conscious awareness on impression formation. *Journal of Personality and Social Psychology, 43*, 437–449.

Bartlett, F. C. (1932). *Remembering.* Cambridge: Cambridge University Press.

Bartlett, J., Burleson, G., & Santrock, J. (1982). Mood-congruent memory in children. *Journal of Experimental Child Psychology, 34*, 59–76.

Blum, G. S. (1954). An experimental reunion of psychoanalytic theory with perceptual vigilance and defense. *Journal of Abnormal and Social Psychology, 49*, 94–98.

Bower, G. H. (1981). Mood and memory. *American Psychologist, 36*, 129–148.

Bower, G. H. & Mayer, D. (in press). Failure to replicate mood-dependent retrieval. *Bulletin of the Psychonomic Society*.

Bower, G. H., Monteiro, K. P., & Gilligan, S. G. (1978). Emotional mood as a context for learning and recall. *Journal of Verbal Learning and Verbal Behavior, 17*, 573–587.

Broadbent, D. E. (1971). *Decision and stress*. London: Academic Press.

Bronson, G. (1972). Infants' reactions to unfamiliar persons and novel objects. *Monographs of the Society for Research in Child Development, 32* (4, Serial No. 112).

Campos, J. J., Emde, R. N., Gaensbauer, T. J., & Henderson, C. (1975). Cardiac and behavioral interrelationships in the reactions of infants to strangers. *Developmental Psychology, 11*, 589–601.

Campos, J., Hiatt, S., Ramsay, D., Henderson, C., & Svejda, M. (1978). The emergence of fear on the visual cliff. In M. Lewis & L. Rosenblum (Eds.), *The origins of affect* (pp. 149–182). New York: Plenum.

Charlesworth, W. R. (1969). The role of surprise in cognitive development. In D. Elkind & J. Flavell (Eds.), *Studies in cognitive development*. London: Oxford University Press.

Clark, M. S. (1982). A role for arousal in the link between feeling states, judgments, and behavior. In M. Clark & S. Fiske (Eds.), *Affect and cognition: The 17th Annual Carnegie Symposium on Cognition* (pp. 263–290). Hillsdale, NJ: Erlbaum.

Clark, M. S., & Fiske, S. T. (1982). *Affect and cognition: The 17th Annual Carnegie Symposium on Cognition*. Hillsdale, NJ: Erlbaum.

Craik, F. I. M., & Tulving, E. (1975). Depth of processing and the retention of words in episodic memory. *Journal of Experimental Psychology: General, 104*, 268–294.

Duval, S., & Wicklund, R. A. (1972). *A theory of objective self-awareness*. New York: Academic Press.

Easterbrook, J. A. (1959). The effect of emotion on cue utilization and the organization of behavior. *Psychological Review, 66*, 183–201.

Ekman, P. (1984). Expression and the nature of emotion. In K. R. Scherer & P. Ekman (Eds.), *Approaches to emotion* (pp. 319–344). Hillsdale, NJ: Erlbaum.

Erdelyi, M. H. (1974). A new look at the new look: Perceptual defense and vigilance. *Psychological Review, 81*, 1–25.

Fiske, S. F. (1982). Schema-triggered affect: Applications to social perception. In M. S. Clark & S. T. Fiske (Eds.), *Affect and cognition: The 17th Annual Carnegie Symposium on Cognition* (pp. 55–78). Hillsdale, NJ: Erlbaum.

Freud, S. (1914). *On the psychopathology of everyday life*. New York: Macmillan.

Freud, S. (1936). *The problem of anxiety*. New York: Norton.

Gibson, J. J. (1979). *The ecological approach to visual perception*. Boston: Houghton Mifflin.

Gilligan, S. G., & Bower, G. H. (1984). Cognitive consequences of emotional arousal. In C. Izard, J. Kagan, & R. Zajonc (Eds.), *Emotions, cognition, and behavior* (pp. 547–588). New York: Cambridge University Press.

Gitomer, A., Pellegrino, H., & Bisanz, J. (1983). Developmental changes and invariance in semantic processing. *Journal of Experimental Child Psychology, 35*, 56–80.

Harris, M. B., & Siebel, C. E. (1975). Affect, aggression, and altruism. *Developmental Psychology, 11*, 623–627.

Harrison, A. A. (1977). Mere exposure. In L. Berkowitz (Ed.), *Advances in experimental social psychology* (Vol. 10, pp. 40–83). New York: Academic Press.

Heider, F. (1958). *The psychology of interpersonal relations*. New York: Wiley.

Higgins, E. T. (1981). Role taking and social judgment: Alternative developmental perspectives and processes. In J. H. Flavell & L. Ross (Eds.), *Social cognitive development: Frontiers and possible futures* (pp. 119–153). New York: Cambridge University Press.

Higgins, E. T., Herman, C. P., & Zanna, M. P. (1981). *Social cognition: The Ontario Symposium* (Vol. 1). Hillsdale, NJ: Erlbaum.

Higgins, E. T., & King, G. (1981). Accessibility of social constructs: Information processing consequences of individual and contextual variability. In N. Cantor & J. F. Kihlstrom (Eds.), *Personality, cognition, and social interaction.* Hillsdale, NJ: Erlbaum.

Higgins, E. T., & Rholes, W. S. (1976). Impression formation and role fulfillment: A "holistic reference" approach. *Journal of Experimental Social Psychology, 12,* 422–435.

Hoffman, M. L. (1970). Conscience, personality and socialization techniques. *Human Development, 13,* 90–126.

Hoffman, M. L. (1978). Empathy, its development and prosocial implications. In C. B. Keasey (Ed.), *Nebraska Symposium on Motivation* (Vol. 25, pp. 169–218). Lincoln: University of Nebraska Press.

Hoffman, M. L. (1981). Perspectives on the difference between understanding people and understanding things. In J. Flavell & L. Ross (Eds.), *Advances in social cognitive development* (pp. 67–81). New York: Cambridge University Press.

Hoffman, M. L. (1982). Development of prosocial motivation: Empathy and guilt. In N. Eisenberg-Berg (Ed.), *Development of prosocial behavior* (pp. 281–313). New York: Academic Press.

Hoffman, M. L. (1983a). Affective and cognitive processes in moral internalization: An information processing approach. In E. T. Higgins, D. Ruble, & W. Hartup (Eds.), *Social cognition and social development: A socio-cultural perspective* (pp. 236–274). New York: Cambridge University Press.

Hoffman, M. L. (1983b). Empathy, guilt, and social cognition. In W. F. Overton (Ed.), *The relationship between social and cognitive development* (pp. 1–52). Hillsdale, NJ: Erlbaum.

Hoffman, M. L. (1984). Interaction of affect and cognition in empathy. In C. Izard, J. Kagan, & R. Zajonc (Eds.), *Emotions, cognition, and behavior* (pp. 103–131). New York: Cambridge University Press.

Hunt, W. A. (1937). The reliability of introspection in emotion. *American Journal of Psychology, 49,* 650–653.

Isen, A. M. (1983). Some specific effects of four affect-induction procedures. *Personality and Social Psychology Bulletin, 9,* 136–143.

Isen, A. M., Johnson, M. M. S., & Robinson, G. F. (in press). The influence of positive affect on the unusualness of word associations. *Journal of Personality and Social Psychology.*

Isen, A. M., Means, B., Patrick, R., & Nowicki, G. (1982). Some factors influencing decision-making strategy and risk taking. In M. S. Clark & S. T. Fiske (Eds.), *Affect and cognition: The 17th Annual Carnegie Symposium on Cognition* (pp. 243–262). Hillsdale, NJ: Erlbaum.

Isen, A. M., Shalker, T. E., Clark, M., & Karp, L. (1978). Affect, accessibility of material in memory and behavior: A cognitive loop? *Journal of Personality and Social Psychology, 36,* 1–12.

Izard, C. E., Hembree, L. M., & Spizzirri, C. C. (1983). Changes in facial expressions of 2- to 19-month-old infants following acute pain. *Developmental Psychology, 19,* 418–426.

Johnson, E. J., & Tversky, A. (1983). Affect, generalization, and the perception of risk. *Journal of Personality and Social Psychology, 45,* 20–31.

Kagan, J. (1974). Discrepancy, temperament, and infant distress. In M. Lewis & L. Rosenblum (Eds.), *The origins of fear* (pp. 229–248). New York: Wiley.

Kahneman, D. (1973). *Attention and effort.* Englewood Cliffs, NJ: Prentice-Hall.

Kremer, J. F., & Stephens, L. (1983). Attributions and arousal as mediators of mitigation's effect on retaliation. *Journal of Personality and Social Psychology, 45,* 335–343.

Kunst-Wilson, W. R., & Zajonc, R. B. (1980). Affective discrimination of stimuli that cannot be recognized. *Science, 207,* 557–558.

Laird, J. D. (1984). The real role of facial response in the experience of emotion. *Journal of Personality and Social Psychology, 47,* 909–917.

Laird, J. D., Wagener, J. J., Halal, M., & Szegda, M. (1982). Remembering what you feel: Effects of emotion on memory. *Journal of Personality and Social Psychology, 42,* 646–657.

Landis, C., & Hunt, W. A. (1939). *The startle pattern.* New York: Farrar and Rinehart.

Lazarus, R. S. (1982). Thoughts on the relations between emotion and cognition. *American Psychologist, 37,* 1019–1024.

Lazarus, R. S. (1984). On the primacy of cognition. *American Psychologist, 39,* 124–129.

Lazarus, R. S., & McCleary, R. A. (1958). Autonomic discrimination without awareness: A study of subception. *Psychological Review, 58*, 113–122.

Lerner, M. J., & Simmons, C. (1966). Observer's reaction to the innocent victim: Compassion or rejection? *Journal of Personality and Social Psychology, 4*, 203–210.

Linville, P. W. (1982). Affective consequences of complexity regarding the self and others. In M. S. Clark & S. T. Fiske (Eds.), *Affect and cognition: The 17th Carnegie Symposium on Cognition* (pp. 79–110). Hillsdale, NJ: Erlbaum.

Lipps, T. (1906). Das Wissen von fremden Ichen. *Psychologische Untersuchungen, 1*, 694–722.

Mandler, G. (1975). *Mind and emotion.* New York: Wiley.

Mandler, G. (1982). The structure of value: Accounting for taste. In M. S. Clark & S. T. Fiske (Eds.), *Affect and cognition: The 17th Annual Carnegie Symposium on Cognition.* Hillsdale, NJ: Erlbaum.

Marcel, A. J. (1983a). Conscious and unconscious perception: Experiments on visual masking and word recognition. *Cognitive Psychology, 15*, 197–237.

Marcel, A. J. (1983b). Conscious and unconscious perception: An approach to the relations between phenomenal experience and perceptual processes. *Cognitive Psychology, 15*, 238–300.

Marcel, A. J., Katz, L., & Smith, M. (1974). Laterality and reading proficiency. *Neuropsychologia, 12*, 131–139.

Martin, G. B., & Clark, R. D. (1982). Distress crying in neonates: Species and peer specificity. *Developmental Psychology, 18*, 3–9.

Martin, R. M. (1968). The stimulus barrier and the autonomy of the ego. *Psychological Review, 75*, 478–493.

Masters, J., Barden, R. C., & Ford, M. (1979). Affective states, expressive behavior, and learning in children. *Journal of Personality and Social Psychology, 37*, 380–389.

McCall, R. (1972). Smiling and vocalization in infants as indices of perceptual-cognitive processes. *Merrill-Palmer Quarterly, 18*, 341–347.

McGinnies, E. (1949). Emotionality and perceptual defense. *Psychological Review, 56*, 244–251.

Meltzoff, A. N., & Moore, M. K. (1983). Newborn infants imitate adult facial gestures. *Child Development, 54*, 702–709.

Mischel, W., Ebbesen, E., & Zeiss, A. (1976). Determinants of selective memory about the self. *Journal of Consulting and Clinical Psychology, 44*, 92–103.

Mischel, W., & Moore, B. (1973). Effects of attention to symbolically-presented rewards on self-control. *Journal of Personality and Social Psychology, 28*, 172–179.

Mueller, J. H. (1979). Anxiety and encoding processes in memory. *Personality and Social Psychology Bulletin, 5*, 288–294.

Nasby, W., & Yando, R. (1982). Selective encoding and retrieval of affectively valent informaiton: Two cognitive consequences of children's mood states. *Journal of Personality and Social Psychology, 43*, 1244–1253.

Natale, M., & Hantas, M. (1982). Effects of temporary mood states on memory about the self. *Journal of Personality and Social Psychology, 42*, 927–934.

Navon, D. (1977). Forest before trees: The precedence of global features in visual perception. *Cognitive Psychology, 9*, 353–383.

Nelson, K., & Gruendel, J. M. (1981). Generalized event representations: Basic building blocks of cognitive development. In A. Brown & M. Lamb (Eds.), *Advances in developmental psychology* (Vol. 1). Hillsdale, NJ: Erlbaum.

Nisbett, R. E., & Wilson, T. D. (1977). Telling more than we can know: Verbal reports on mental processes. *Psychological Review, 84*, 231–259.

Norman, D. A. (1980). Twelve issues for cognitive science. In D. A. Norman (Ed.), *Perspectives on cognitive science: Talks from the La Jolla Conference.* Hillsdale, NJ: Erlbaum.

Papousek, H. (1967). Conditioning during early postnatal development. In Y. Brackbill & G. Thompson (Eds.), *Behavior in infancy and early childhood* (pp. 259–274). New York: Free Press.

Pazer, S., Slackman, E., & Hoffman, M. (1981). *Age and sex differences in the effect of information on anger.* Unpublished manuscript, City University of New York.

Piaget, J. (1981). *Intelligence and affectivity: Their relationship during childhood.* Palo Alto, CA: Annual Reviews. (Original work published 1954)

Potter, M. (1975). Time to understand pictures and words. *Science, 253*, 437–438.

Razran, G. (1971). *Mind in evolution.* Boston: Houghton Mifflin.

Rogers, T. B., Kuiper, N. A., & Kirker, W. S. (1977). Self-reference and the encoding of personal information. *Journal of Personality and Social Psychology, 35*, 677–688.

Rose, S. A., Gottfried, A. W., Melloy-Carminar, P., & Bridger, W. H. (1982). Familiarity and novelty preferences in infant recognition memory: Implications for information processing. *Developmental Psychology, 18*, 704–713.

Rubin, Z. (1983). What is a friend? In W. Damon (Ed.), *Social and personality development* (pp. 249–257). New York: Norton.

Ruble, D. N., (1983). The development of social-comparison processes and their role in achievement-related self-socialization. In E. T. Higgins, D. N. Ruble, & W. W. Hartup (Eds.), *Social cognition and social development: A sociocultural perspective* (pp. 134–157). New York: Cambridge University Press.

Ruble, D. N., Boggiano, A. K., Feldman, N. S., & Loebl, J. H. (1980). Developmental analysis of the role of social comparison in self-evaluation. *Developmental Psychology, 16*, 105–115.

Sagi, A., & Hoffman, M. L. (1976). Empathic distress in the newborn. *Developmental Psychology, 12*, 175–176.

Schachter, S., & Singer, J. (1962). Cognitive, social, and physiological determinants of emotional state. *Psychological Review, 69*, 379–399.

Scheier, M. F., & Carver, C. S. (1977). Self-focused attention and the experience of emotion: Attraction, repulsion, elation, and depression. *Journal of Personality and Social Psychology, 35*, 625–636.

Sheehy, G. (1983, October 23). [Review of *Commercialization of human feeling*, by A. R. Hochschild]. *New York Times*, p. 7.

Shevrin, H., & Dickman, S. (1980). The psychological unconscious: A necessary assumption for all psychological theory? *American Psychologist, 35*, 421–434.

Simner, M. L. (1971). Newborn's response to the cry of another infant. *Developmental Psychology, 5*, 136–150.

Simon, H. A. (1982). Comments on affective underpinnings of cognition. In M. S. Clark & S. T. Fiske (Eds.), *Affect and cognition: The 17th Annual Carnegie Symposium on Cognition* (pp. 333–342). Hillsdale, NJ: Erlbaum.

Spitz, R. A. (1957). *No and yes: On the genesis of human communication.* New York: International Universities Press.

Staats, C. K., & Staats, A. W. (1957). Meaning established by classical conditioning. *Journal of Experimental Psychology, 54*, 74–80.

Stenberg, C., Campos, J., & Emde, R. (1983). The facial expression of anger in seven month old infants. *Child Development, 54*, 178–184.

Stotland, E. (1969). Exploratory investigations of empathy. In L. Berkowitz (Ed.), *Advances in experimental social psychology* (Vol. 4). New York: Academic Press.

Teasdale, J. D., & Fogarty, S. J. (1979). Differential effects of induced mood on retrieval of pleasant and unpleasant events from episodic memory. *Journal of Abnormal Psychology, 88*, 248–257.

Teasdale, J. D., Taylor, R., & Fogarty, S. J. (1980). Effects of induced elation-depression on the accessibility of memories of happy and unhappy experiences. *Behavioral Research and Therapy, 18*, 339–346.

Watson, J. S., & Ramey, C. T. (1972). Reactions to response-contingent stimulation in early infancy. *Merrill-Palmer Quarterly, 18*, 219–228.

Weiner, B. (1982). The emotional consequences of causal attribution. In M. S. Clark & S. T. Fiske (Eds.), *Affect and cognition: The 17th Annual Carnegie Symposium on Cognition* (pp. 185–210). Hillsdale, NJ: Erlbaum.

Weiner, B., & Graham, S. (1984). An attributional approach to emotional development. In C. Izard, J. Kagan, & R. Zajonc (Eds.), *Emotions, cognition, and behavior* (pp. 167–191). New York: Cambridge University Press.

Wickens, D. D. (1972). Characteristics of word encoding. In A. W. Melton & E. Martin (Eds.), *Coding processes in human memory* (pp. 191–216). Washington, DC: Winston.

Zahn-Waxler, C., Radke-Yarrow, M., & King, R. A. (1979). Childrearing and children's prosocial initiations towards victims of distress. *Child Development, 50*, 319–330.

Zajonc, R. B. (1968). Attitudinal effects of mere exposure. *Journal of Personality and Social Psychology Monograph Supplement, 9*(2, Pt. 2), 1–27.

Zajonc, R. B. (1980). Feeling and thinking: Preferences need no inferences. *American Psychologist, 35*, 151–175.

Zajonc, R. B. (1984). On the primacy affect. *American Psychologist, 39*, 117–123.

Zanna, M. P., Kiesler, C. A., & Pilkonis, P. A. (1970). Positive and negative affect established by classical conditioning. *Journal of Personality and Social Psychology, 14*, 321–328.

CHAPTER 10

Attribution, Emotion, and Action

BERNARD WEINER
University of California, Los Angeles

PRINCIPLES FOR A THEORY OF MOTIVATION

The history of the study of motivation is now sufficiently rich that we may use our experience with prior culs-de-sac, prior errors of omission and commission, and prior successes to create new and more adequate conceptions. I suggest that these new theories may benefit by adhering to the following principles, although I privately suspect that these rules reflect my personal biases more than an objective analysis of the history of motivation. The precepts to be offered overlap; no attempt has been made to dispense with a rule if it is not independent of other principles.

1. A Theory of Motivation Must Be Based on a Concept Other Than Homeostasis

From the origins of the scientific study of motivation (circa 1920) until perhaps 1955, psychoanalytic (Freudian) and drive (Hullian) theories dominated the field. Both conceptions are based on the notion that people strive to reduce internal tension; their fundamental motivational principle is that any deviation from equilibrium produces a motivational force to return to the prior state of internal balance. The prototypical observation from which this tenet may be derived is exhibited in the behavior of a newborn infant. When all biological needs are satisfied—that is, when internal equilibrium is attained and no tension from biological deficits exists—the infant rests. There is a state of sleep or quiescence. The onset of hunger or thirst, which may cause tissue damage, gives rise to activity

---

This Chapter was written while the author was supported by grant MH38014 from the Public Health Service, National Institute of Mental Health.

281

such as reflexive sucking, which may reduce the need states of hunger and thirst. If the instrumental activity results in goal attainment, then there is an offset of the need and a return to the quiet state. But this tranquility is only temporary; because of the cyclical nature of needs, behavior is reinitiated. Hence, disequilibrium cannot be avoided, and behavior fluctuates from rest to activity and back again to inactivity.

An array of clinical and empirical evidence supports this intuitively appealing homeostatic principle. There can be little doubt that, given a biological deficit, behaviors typically are instigated to reduce that deficit. After all, we generally eat when we are hungry (given the availability of food), drink when we are thirsty, and attempt to flee from pain. Furthermore, some psychogenic (as opposed to viscerogenic) need states also can be conceptualized with homeostatic principles. For example, conflicting cognitions create a state of "mental disequilibrium" (e.g., I smoke, and smoking causes cancer; I like Jane and the president, but Jane dislikes the president). The individual then may bring the system back into balance by, for example, discounting the smoking–cancer evidence or devaluing his or her opinion of Jane.

Given the seeming robustness of the homeostatic principle, why shouldn't it then provide the foundation for a theory of human motivation? The major difficulty with this rule of conduct is that the greater part of human behavior cannot be subsumed within the concept of homeostasis. Humans often strive to induce states of disequilibrium—we ride roller coasters, read scary mystery stories, seek new and exciting forms of entertainment, and quit comfortable jobs and even comfortable marriages for more challenge. Furthermore, the prominent psychogenic motivations—such as the desires to attain success, win friends, gain power, and help others—apparently fall beyond the range of homeostatic explanations. Motivational concerns, including hunger and thirst, may even be overlooked when we are striving for achievement success, affiliative goals, or spiritual growth. As I am writing this, a leader of the Irish Revolutionary Army is dying while on a hunger strike.

In addition—though somewhat less central—not all bodily needs instigate behavior. Theorists who posit automatic connections between internal disequilibrium and behavior have difficulty dealing with this fact. For example, oxygen deprivation may not be motivating unless it is accompanied by an awareness of this need or by an associated panic reaction. This is beautifully illustrated in the following story from Tomkins (1970):

> Consider anoxic deprivation. Almost any interference with normal breathing will immediately arouse the most desperate gasping for breath. Is there any motivational claim more urgent than the demand of one who is drowning or choking to death for want of air? Yet it is not simply the imperious demand for oxygen that we observe under such circumstances. We also are observing the rapidly mounting panic ordinarily recruited whenever the air supply is suddenly jeopardized. . . . We have only to change the rate of anoxic deprivation to change the nature of the recruited affect. . . . Thus, in the Second World War, those pilots who refused to wear their oxygen masks at 30,000 feet suffered a more gradual anoxic deprivation. They did not panic for want of oxygen. They became euphoric. It was the affect of enjoyment which the more slowly developing anoxic

signal recruited. Some of these men, therefore, met their deaths with smiles on their lips. (pp. 101–102)

To summarize, homeostatic mechanisms often govern viscerogenic or bodily needs and goal-oriented instrumental behavior, and some psychogenic needs may be guided by the same principle. Hence, the homeostatic analysis was an important conceptual advance in the history of motivation. But the concept of homeostasis cannot account for the manifold of human actions, and biologically based needs may not instigate action unless they are accompanied by appropriate cognitions or emotional states. Moreover, my personal belief is that the behaviors best explained by homeostatic principles (eating, drinking, and pain avoidance) may be the least interesting aspects of human activity.

2. A Theory of Motivation Must Embrace More Than Hedonism

An axiom of virtually all the earlier and the extant theories of motivation is that organisms strive to increase pleasure and to decrease pain. The unassailable acceptance of hedonism—known as the pleasure–pain principle—characterizes psychoanalytic and drive theories as well as the influential cognitive theories of motivation proposed by Atkinson (achievement theory), Lewin (field theory), and Rotter (social learning theory). Regarding this fundamental law of behavior, Freud (1920/1955) stated: "The impressions that underlie the hypothesis of the pleasure principle are so obvious that they cannot be overlooked" (p. 1). In addition to "impressions," hundreds of experiments have documented that reward (pleasure) increases the probability of repeating a response, whereas punishment (pain) decreases the probability of the response preceding the negative outcome. Homeostatic theories are closely linked with hedonism, for they assume that a return to a state of equilibrium produces pleasure.

There can be no doubt that the pleasure–pain principle guides human (and infrahuman) conduct; prior theories have not been remiss in having this principle as the foundation of their conceptions. But reward (pleasure) does not inevitably increase the likelihood of a response, nor does punishment (pain) assuredly decrease the probability of the reoccurrence of the punished behavior. For example, expected reward for the performance of an intrinsically interesting activity (e.g., telling children they will get candy for playing a game they like) can, under some circumstances, reduce the interest in that game. The children engage in the game less when reward is withdrawn because they come to believe that "playing" was due to the external reward (Deci, 1975; Lepper, Greene, & Nisbett, 1973). In addition, success is considered rewarding, yet if the task is easy, goal attainment reduces motivation and produces boredom (Atkinson, 1964). Finally, the absence of an anticipated reward produces increased motivation to attain the goal (Amsel, 1958) and may stimulate creative vigor.

In addition to behaviors that are decreased by reward and increased by punishment, Freud pointed out that some of life's activities, including traumatic dreams, games of disappearance ("peek-a-boo"), and aspects of transference (reenacting significant conflicts with one's parents through a therapist) apparently do not increase pleasure. The pleasure–pain principle also cannot account for the focus of thoughts on, for example, past or present wrongs that others are perceived as having perpetuated (paranoia), goods that one does not possess but others do (envy), or the success of rivals (jealousy). One might contend that such deployment of attention has instrumental value in that goal attainment is promoted. That is, the unpleasant thoughts or behaviors serve the pleasure principle. Quite often, however, this clearly is not the case. What instrumental value is there in becoming obsessed over neighbors' more beautiful homes or their more considerate children?

If humans do not always act as hedonic maximizers, then other motivational principles are needed. As motivational psychologists progressed from the study of infrahuman actions to the study of human actions, nonhedonic aspects of thinking and acting became increasingly evident. One of the most important of these other "motive forces" is the desire to understand the environment and oneself—what might be called cognitive mastery. Cognitive mastery has been thought to instigate behaviors ranging from the acquisition of language to the selection of actions that can reveal information about one's capacities.

Motivational goals are often interrelated and complexly intertwined. For example, cognitive mastery or knowledge aids in goal attainment, which increases pleasure. Thus, it might be contended that mastery is subsumed under hedonic motivation. However, as already indicated, some knowledge has no apparent value for reaching end states. A different reason to believe that mastery is incorporated within the pleasure principle is that information search is influenced by the hedonic desire to increase self-esteem and to protect oneself from anxiety. For example, cancer patients tend to compare themselves with other, more seriously ill victims. This promotes the conclusion that life could be worse—a reassuring thought for the sick as well as the healthy (Taylor, 1983). Here again, mastery or knowledge seems to be in service of hedonic goals. On the other hand, truth is often sought even though the information might cause great displeasure. We can all remember an occasion when an inquiry was preceded by the phrase, "Now, tell me the truth . . . " although the inquirer knew full well that the answer might "hurt." Hence, cognitive mastery cannot merely be subsumed within the pleasure–pain principle.

3. A Theory of Motivation Must Include the Full Range of Cognitive Processes

Prior to the advent of behaviorism, thoughts and other mental events played a crucial role in theories of human action. Behaviorism buried this belief, conceiving of humans as machines or robots with input–output connections. Behaviorism no longer plays a dominant role in psychology, in part because a mechanistic approach to human motivation is not tenable. After all, we are not robots, machines, or hydraulic pumps! A broad array of mental processes—including information search and retrieval, short- and long-term memory, categorization, judgment, and decision making—play essential roles in determining behavior. Just as behavior often is functional, aiding in goal attainment, cognitions also serve adaptive functions for reaching desired end states. Thus, cognitive functionalism must play as central a role in a theory of motivation as behavioral functionalism.

Earlier cognitive conceptions of motivation—such as those formulated by Atkinson (1964), Lewin (1935), Rotter (1954), and Tolman (1925)—focused on the expectancy of goal attainment as a major determinant of action. They unfortunately neglected a multitude of other mental structures and processes that influence behavior. This restriction greatly limits the capacities of these theories to account for human conduct.

4. A Theory of Motivation Must Be Concerned with Conscious Experience

Motivation has been inseparably linked with the study of overt behavior. Throughout the history of this field, well-known books have had behaviorally oriented titles, such as *Principles of Behavior* (Hull, 1943), *The Motivation of Behavior* (Brown, 1961), and *The Dynamics of Action* (Atkinson & Birch, 1970). However, we experience, feel, and think, as well as act, and all these processes have a place within the study of motivation. A theory of motivation is responsible for examining the experiential state of the organism and the meaning of an action. Hence, the theory must embrace phenomenology and accept the position, so clearly articulated by Lewin (1935), that organisms act on a perceived rather than an objective world.

Associated with this position is my belief that many (but not all) significant thoughts and feelings are conscious and are known by the actor. As Gordon Allport (1960) noted, one should ask an individual directly to gain information about him or her. We may not be aware of psychological processes, or the "how's" of psychology (how we learn, how we perceive, how we remember), but we often are aware of psychological content, or the "what's" of psychology (what we want, what we feel, for what reason we engage in an activity). If one focuses on very conflicting actions of extreme emotional involvement, as Freud did, then repression and other dynamic processes may produce a discrepancy between the conscious and the "true" determinants of action. In addition, if attention is primarily directed to complex judgments, as exemplified in the work of decision theorists, or to inferences in esoteric, multistimuli situations, then the limits of human information processing may give rise to inaccuracies regarding self-observations. However, for the typical and prevalent aspects of being—that is, considering how life is spent and what is reflected upon—direct access to the determinants of motivation and emotion is quite possible. For most of us at most times, a royal road to the unconscious is less valuable to the motivation researcher than the dirt road to consciousness.

5. A Theory of Motivation Must Include the Self

This principle is closely related to the prior contention that a theory must be concerned with consciousness and the subjective world, for the experience of the self is part of phenomenal reality. There are numerous indications that the self plays a fundamental role in human motivation: many actions serve to sustain or enhance self-esteem; an individual's self-concept frequently determines thoughts and behaviors; people tend to maintain self-consistency in their actions; and self-perception provides one thread to the stability of personality and behavior over time. The concept of the self has been relatively neglected in the study of motivation (see the exceptions in this book!). It surely did not fit into behavioristic conceptions, which used lower organisms as the main source of experimental evidence. In addition, the cognitive theories of motivation focused on the more manageable concept of subjective expectancy, perhaps preferring to postpone a consideration of the subtle and vague role played by a concern with the self. However, the self lies at the very core of human experience and must be part of any theoretical formulation in the field of human motivation.

6. A Theory of Motivation Must Include the Full Range of Emotions

One might anticipate that the study of motivation and the study of emotion would be intimately linked. In support of this expectation, there is a psychological journal with the title *Motivation and Emotion*, and many psychology courses carry the same name. It is surprising, however, that theories of motivation have incorporated only the pleasure–pain principle of emotions, even though this crude delineation is manifestly inadequate for describing feelings. Even the pleasures associated with aggression and sexual fulfillment, which formed the basis for the all-embracing notion of pleasure advanced by Freud, are quite likely to be distinct. I doubt that the emotion associated with the killing of father is akin to the pleasure of sleeping with mother! In addition, these feelings certainly are distinguishable from the pleasures derived from occupational attainment or social success, such as pride or feelings of competence. In a similar manner, distinct "pains" surely are linked with unsatisfied hostility and incompleted sexual desires, and these doubtlessly differ from the feelings that accompany failure to achieve or social rejection.

The theory of achievement motivation formulated by Atkinson (1964) does consider emotions characterized by labels other than pleasure–pain. Atkinson suggested that whether one approaches or avoids an achievement-related goal depends on the affective consequences of pride and shame. However, this conception does not acknowledge other emotions that are manifest in achievement contexts, such as happiness and unhappiness, anger and gratitude, and humiliation and pity. Thus, Atkinson's theory also fails to give emotions their rightful place in motivation.

People experience a great diversity of emotions that are intertwined with thoughts and actions. One of the goals of the theory presented in this chapter is to set forth precisely the relationships among the tripartite divisions in psychology of cognition, affect, and behavior. In approaching this goal, I will demonstrate that motivation cannot be understood without a detailed analysis of emotion.

7. A Theory of Motivation Must Be Neither Too General nor Too Precise

Based on the fate of psychoanalytic and drive theory, one could draw the conclusion that a theory must have some optimal level of breadth and precision. Perhaps the greatest virtue of the psychoanalytic conception of motivation was its range of convenience—the capability of addressing phenomena as disparate as war, wit, and neurosis. In psychology, however, the range of a theory correlates inversely with its capability of making exact predictions. Thus, the strength of the psychoanalytic conception also greatly contributed to its declining position in the field of motivation.

In sharp contrast to the psychoanalytic approach, drive theory, as formulated by Clark Hull and Kenneth Spence, has limited breadth but, in certain contexts, great precision. The rather exact theoretical predictions were most often tested with laboratory rats engaged in a simple behavior, such as running down a straight alleyway for food. Unfortunately, these data were not of great value in the attempt to generalize laboratory findings to complex human activities.

In sum, if a theory is too broad (like psychoanalytic theory), then at this point in the history of motivation it will have little exactness; if it is too precise (like drive theory), then at this point it will have little breadth and generality. Hence, a careful path must be taken between the two-headed challenges of predictability (precision) and generalizability.

8. A Theory of Motivation Must Be Built upon Reliable (Replicable) Empirical Relationships

An adequate theory of motivation provides the opportunity for the creation of a laboratory course or some other setting in which a variety of derivations from the theory can be demonstrated *with certainty*. This is true of theories in the natural sciences, and it should apply to psychology as well. One of the reasons for the acceptance and popularity of Skinnerian psychology is its demonstration that the frequency of a response increases when an organism is rewarded for a particular behavior. Watching pigeons play table tennis seems to be a sufficient antecedent for conversion to radical behaviorism!

Motivational theories are deficient in this respect. For example, regarding the unequal recall of completed versus incompleted tasks—what is known as the Zeigarnik effect—Lewin (1935) stated: "All later experimental investigations were built upon this" (p. 240). However, the differential recall observed by Lewin and Zeigarnik is not a reliable finding. In a similar manner, Atkinson (1964) contended that individuals classified as high versus low in achievement needs exhibit opposing risk preferences given tasks that differ in perceived difficulty. This central prediction from Atkinson's conception is not found reliably, which is probably partially responsible for the lessening influence of his conception. Furthermore, differences in expectancy shifts between people labeled internal versus external in perceptions of control cannot be demonstrated reliably, but this is a fundamental prediction of Rotter's (1966) social learning theory.

One cannot build a theory on a weak "reference experiment"—that is, an experiment that provides the standard for evaluating the theory. Motivational theories must have reference experiments with results as certain as the outcome of mixing two parts hydrogen and one part oxygen, or as certain as the consequences of giving a hungry rat food when it engages in a particular behavior.

9. A Theory of Motivation Must Be Based on General Laws Rather Than Individual Differences

Atkinson (1964) has been especially visible and persuasive among the motivational psychologists who argue that individual differences play a central role in the study of motivational processes. As already indicated, in Atkinson's theory of achievement strivings, persons labeled high in achievement needs are predicted to exhibit different risk-taking behavior than persons low in achievement needs. Therefore, disparities between individuals are central to the testing of this conception. Atkinson's theory then falls prey to all of the complex issues and obstacles faced by trait psychologists. For example, people are not equally motivated to achieve in all situations; that is, there is discriminativeness in behavior. People may be highly motivated to achieve in competitive activities, such as tennis, but not in the classroom, or perhaps not even in other sports, such as baseball. Atkinson's theoretical formulation does not recognize this possibility; people are merely classified as high or low in achievement needs. Thus, it is not surprising that tests of this theory, which occur in many disparate situational contexts, often prove unsatisfactory.

In a similar manner, Rotter's (1966) current conception of social learning is linked with an individual difference labeled locus of control. But people are not equally motivated to have or to relinquish control in all settings, and they might perceive control of reinforcement as possible in some situations but not in others. For example, perceptions of success as due to internal (personal) factors is uncorrelated with perceptions of failure as controlled by internal causes (see review in Weiner, 1980b). Specificity is not well integrated into the theory, and hypotheses using perceptions of control as a predictor variable often are disconfirmed. Again, the classroom demonstrator in a laboratory course would be embarrassed.

In sum, given the difficulties of personality measurement and the situational specificity of behavior, it would be more fruitful to search, first, for general laws rather than exploring Person × Situation interactions. This search could then be followed, if necessary, by the inclusion of individual differences to refine the generalizations that have been made or to uncover more complex associations that might have been overlooked.

An identical position was expressed previously by the behaviorists. For example, Berlyne (1968) stated:

It is perfectly obvious that human beings are different from one another in some respects but alike in other respects. The question is whether we should first look for statements that apply to all of them or whether we should first try to describe and explain their differences. The behavior theorist feels that the search for common principles of human and animal behavior must take precedence. This, he would point out, is how scientific inquiry must proceed. . . . Until we can see what individuals of a class or species have in common, we cannot hope to understand how their dissimilarities have come about or even to find the most fruitful way to describe and classify these dissimilarities. (p. 640)

This is perhaps the only instance in this chapter where agreement with a behaviorist is found and/or admitted.

10. A Theory of Motivation Must Include Sequential (Historical) Causal Relationships

The prominent theories of motivation, with the exception of the psychoanalytic approach, are ahistorical. These theories attempt to identify the immediate determinants of action, such as drive and habit or expectancy and value, and specify the manner in which they influence behavior at a given moment in time. The antecedent historical conditions, or why an individual perceives the present situation as he or she does, is not necessary to predict behavior. What is essential is the specification of the present determinants of action.

One of the shortcomings of an ahistorical approach is that the influence of the components of the theory on one another have to be ignored. In expectancy-value theories, for example, if value is biased upward by high expectancy (one likes what one can get), or if high value biases expectancy upward (one expects to get what one likes), then a temporal sequence is implicated. In these instances, the magnitudes of the components in the theory cannot be determined simultaneously; that is, value cannot be ascertained prior to expectancy nor expectancy prior to value. This is illustrated in the following diagram:

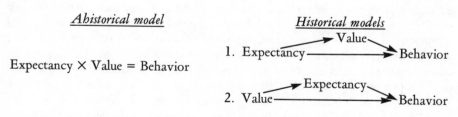

Ahistorical model

Expectancy × Value = Behavior

Historical models

1. Expectancy ⟶ Value ⟶ Behavior

2. Value ⟶ Expectancy ⟶ Behavior

The ahistorical analysis of motivational processes was enhanced by the growth of parametric statistics, particularly the analysis of variance. This technique enables investigators to determine which factors are affecting the dependent variable at a moment in time, and to specify the mathematical relationships between these factors. A newer approach in statistical analysis is causal modeling, including path analysis. This methodology helps in uncovering the causal chain of influencing factors. Acceptance of a historical sequence suggests that one should search for the causal relations between the determinants of action.

One of the essential sequences examined in this chapter concerns the relationships among thinking, feeling, and acting. I have already contended that a theory of motivation should include the full range of both thoughts and feelings. But how do these factors influence behavior? Many possibilities arise. It might be (1) that thoughts produce both feelings and behavior; (2) that thoughts antedate feelings, whereas feelings give rise to action; or (3) that thoughts generate feelings, while thoughts and feelings together produce behavior. These possible permutations are shown in the following diagram:

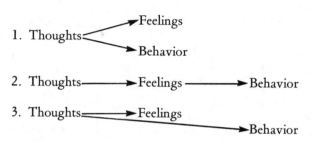

The historical position adopted in this chapter permits exploration of these different possibilities.

11. A Theory of Motivation Must Explain Rational and Irrational Actions, Using the Same Concepts for Both

Human behavior is varied and complex. Many behaviors are quite rational: consciously selected strategies help control stress and anxiety (consider the current jogging craze); goal expectancies are calculated; information is sought and processed; and self-insight is attained. On the other hand, many aspects of our conduct are quite irrational: plans that could control stress, anxiety, smoking, and obesity are abandoned; expectancies are biased; information is improperly utilized; and there is great personal delusion. Psychoanalytic theory has best explained some of the apparent unreasonableness in our lives, while the cognitive conceptions and decision theories are more adept at dealing with the sensibility of action, although these theories are increasingly pointing out the boundaries of rationality.

Kant (1869/1956) contended that reason guides moral behavior, whereas passions determine all other aspects of life. Psychological research, however, has documented that passions such as anger, pity, and sympathy partly direct moral actions, whereas a variety of intelligent judgments influence other motivated behaviors. Therefore, the division suggested by Kant is not justified. Rather, behavior has both ego (thinking) and id (emotional) components. A theory of human behavior must be able to explain the moral and the amoral using the same principles. This belief reaffirms the notion that an adequate theory must include diverse cognitions and emotions and must clarify the relationships among the basic motivational components of reason, passion, and action.

12. A Theory of Motivation Must Be Able to Account for Achievement Strivings and Affiliative Goals

A theory has a focus and a range of convenience—observations that can be best explained and observations to which the theory can be generalized. The focus of convenience of a theory of human motivation should be activities that are most prevalent in everyday life. It would be unwise to base a general theory of human motivation on very uncommon behaviors. Hence, psychoanalytic theory—which is grounded on sexual and aggressive relationships among family members—and Hullian theory—which examined the behavior of hungry and thirsty rats—developed conceptual frameworks that were inadequate to account for the modal activities of humans. Psychological theory and experiments have been overly focused on the esoteric—the behaviors or thoughts that account for little of life's variance.

In our culture, two sources of motivation are most dominant: achievement strivings and social bonding. Freud recognized these with the more general terms of *Arbeit und Liebe* (work and love). Most preadults are either in school, doing schoolwork, engaged in some other achievement-related activity, such as sports or a hobby, or spending their time with their friends of the same or the opposite sex. Adults typically are working in their selected occupations or are engaged in social activities with their friends or family. Of course, there are many other motivational pursuits—aggression, altruism, curiosity, lust, and power, to name just a few. But the most prevalent concerns are achievement success and social acceptance. Self-esteem has been documented to be determined by experiences of competence and incompetence in the achievement domain and acceptance and rejection in the interpersonal arena (see Epstein, 1979). Therefore, these topics should be at the focus of a theory of human motivation.

If the foregoing advice is followed, then the formulated theory undoubtedly would not readily account for the unconscious desires pointed out by psycho-analytic theory or the behavior generated by food and water deprivation. A single conception cannot account for the supposed desire to sleep with mother and kill father, the longing for food when hungry and water when thirsty, and the strivings to accomplish success and enhance social networks. In light of this, a reasonable strategy is to explain those behaviors that are most common, most usual, and most exhibited. I believe that these behaviors are the pursuits of social and emotional bonds and life accomplishments.

Summary

Twelve principles have been outlined that form the foundation for the general theory of motivation and emotion presented in this chapter. A theory of motivation must:

1. Be based on a concept other than homeostasis
2. Embrace more than hedonism
3. Include the full range of cognitive processes
4. Be concerned with conscious experience
5. Include the self
6. Include the full range of emotions
7. Be neither too general nor too precise
8. Be built upon reliable (replicable) empirical relationships
9. Be based on general laws rather than individual differences
10. Include sequential (historical) causal relationships
11. Explain rational and irrational actions, using the same concepts for both
12. Be able to account for achievement strivings and affiliative goals

AN ATTRIBUTIONAL THEORY OF MOTIVATION AND EMOTION

For many years now, I have attempted to create an attributional theory of motivation that could include some of the foregoing principles (see Weiner, 1979, 1980b). More recently, my endeavors have been guided by two distinct subgoals: (1) to delineate the specific linkages between the structure of attributional thinking and qualitatively distinct emotional reactions and (2) to specify the relationships among cognition, emotion, and action. These two issues provide the focus for the remainder of the chapter.

The guiding principle of attribution theory is that people search for understanding, seeking to discover why an event has occurred (Heider, 1958; Kelley, 1967; Weiner, 1980b). This presumption serves the same function for attribution theory that the pleasure–pain principle serves for most other theories of motivation. Both point out the basic "springs of action" and result in a focus on a particular set of phenomena.

The events that people attempt to explain include: "Why doesn't Johnny like me?" "Why did she get a poor mark on the spelling quiz?" "Why did I fail to get a hit in the baseball game?" and "Why did our political party lose the election?" Causal search is not indiscriminately displayed in all situations, for this would place great cognitive strain on the organism. Rather, search is most evident when there has been an unexpected outcome (e.g., failure when success was anticipated), when a desire has not been fulfilled (e.g., there is interpersonal rejection) (see Folkes, 1982; Lau & Russell, 1980; Weiner, 1985; Wong & Weiner, 1981), and/or when the outcome is important. The reader might note that all of the "why" questions listed here involve nonattainment of desired outcomes. People do not usually ask "Why *does* Johnny like me?" unless this is an unexpected or very important occurrence.

There are a number of speculations that account for the instigation of causal search given unexpected, aversive, and/or important outcomes. One function of causal search and explanation is to reduce surprise (Pettit, 1981). For example, a person might be startled if he is rejected for a date by his fianceé. The response to a "why" query—such as "I must meet a friend" or "I have a terrible headache"—produces the explanation needed to account for the rejection, thereby reducing surprise and uncertainty. Another function of causal search is to aid in subsequent goal attainment. Knowing why one has failed might increase later chances for success, inasmuch as pertinent instrumental actions can now be undertaken. Attributional analyses, therefore, are functional, and attribution theory falls within the broader study of cognitive functionalism.

As hinted earlier, causal search is not confined to any single motivational domain. People desire to know, for example, why their team has been defeated—an achievement concern (Lau & Russell, 1980); why they have been refused for a date—an affiliative concern (Folkes, 1982); and why they have lost an election—a power concern (Kingdon, 1967). The number of perceived causes is virtually infinite and depends on the particular activity under consideration. The dominant causes for success and failure at a school exam (e.g., ability, study habits, help from others) differ from the perceived causes of success and failure at sporting events (e.g., the quality of the opposition, weather conditions), from the perceived causes of interpersonal acceptance or rejection (e.g., personality, physical attractiveness), and from the perceived reasons for winning or losing an election (e.g., stance on issues, party identification). Inasmuch as the potential list of causes is considerable within any motivational domain or activity, and because the specific causes differ between domains and activities, it is essential to create a classification scheme or a taxonomy of causes. In so doing, the underlying properties of causes can be ascertained and their similarities and differences can be determined. The discovery of these bases for comparison, which are referred to as causal dimensions, has proved to be the key step in the construction of this attributional theory of motivation and emotion.

There have been two approaches to the study of the underlying properties or structure of perceived causes. The method first employed, which has been labeled dialectic (see Rychlak, 1968), characterizes the work of my colleagues and me (Rosenbaum, 1972; Weiner, 1979; Weiner et al., 1971). The general procedure was to group a set of causes (thesis), to discover an apparent contradiction in reasoning by demonstrating that causes within the same grouping differ in some respect (antithesis), and then to resolve the inconsistency by postulating an additional causal dimension to capture the dissimilarity (synthesis). This approach was guided by the prior causal analyses of Heider (1958). The second method, which emerged from a dissertation by Passer (1977), is best labeled experimental or empirical. The empirical procedure has involved an analysis of responses from subjects, primarily using the quantitative methodologies of factor analysis or multidimensional scaling.

Because of space limitations, I will not examine these procedures and the data in any detail. Rather, I ask the readers to accept that both methods reveal three underlying dimensions of causality, or properties of causes (see Weiner, 1979, 1980b): locus, stability, and controllability. Locus refers to the location of a

TABLE 10.1 Perceived Causes of Achievement Failure and Social Rejection on the Basis of a Locus × Stability × Controllability Classification Scheme

	Motivational Domain	
Dimension Classification	Achievement	Social
Internal-stable-uncontrollable	Low aptitude	Physically unattractive
Internal-stable-controllable	Never studies	Always unkempt
Internal-unstable-uncontrollable	Sick on the day of the exam	Coughing when making the request
Internal-unstable-controllable	Did not study for this particular test	Did not call sufficiently in advance
External-stable-uncontrollable	School has hard requirements	Religious restrictions
External-stable-controllable	Instructor is biased	Rejector always prefers to study at night
External-unstable-uncontrollable	Bad luck	Rejector must stay with sick mother that evening
External-unstable-controllable	Friends failed to help	That night the rejector wants to watch television

cause—internal or external to the actor. Stability relates to the temporal duration of a cause—relatively constant over time or changing from moment to moment or from period to period. Controllability concerns the possible volitional alteration of a cause—relatively controllable or uncontrollable. Each of these properties is conceived as a bipolar continuum. For present purposes, however, we shall assume that causes fall within discrete categories, such as internal or external. Table 10.1 presents eight causes for achievement failure and eight causes for social rejection that intuitively represent the meanings of the dimensions. The dimensions apply equally in the achievement and affiliative contexts, thus permitting direct comparisons between phenotypically distinct causes across disparate motivational domains. Of course, this helps in the construction of a general theory that includes these two dominant motivational themes. Now that the structure of causal thinking has been addressed, I can turn my attention to emotions and causal attribution-emotion linkages. Then I will integrate causal thinking and feeling within a general motivational theory.

AN ATTRIBUTIONAL APPROACH TO EMOTION

The field of emotion is vast and complex, and the formulation of a "compleat" theory of emotion is not my goal. Rather, the aims of this chapter are to document the relationships between causal ascriptions and emotion, to show the significance of these postulates in everyday life, and to propose general laws linking thinking, feeling, and action. To do this, some basic issues in the field of emotion must be addressed, if only briefly.

The most embracing presumption guiding this chapter is that how we think influences how we feel. This clearly is a cognitive approach to emotion. Cognitive emotion theory assumes that emotions are guided by the construal or appraisal of a situation (Arnold, 1970; Ellis, 1974; Lazarus, 1966). Thinking is believed to give rise to qualitative distinctions between feelings and therefore is responsible for the richness and diversity in emotional life. The cognitive perspective, as adopted here, does not deny that some emotions may be elicited without intervening thought processes. For example, conditioned fear and hormonally induced depression may not be preceded by higher level thinking. Neither do I deny that emotional states influence cognitive processes. For example, a person in a depressed mood may be prone to recall unpleasant memories and to perceive the world as a hostile or demanding place. Rather, I merely postulate that cognitions quite typically precede and determine affective reactions. In the present context, this more specifically connotes that perceptions of what caused a positive or a negative outcome determines, in part, the affective reactions to that outcome.

It also is assumed that there is no fixed demarcation point between a "hot" affect and a "cold" cognition. At times, research participants have reported "feeling dumb" or "feeling incompetent" when failure is ascribed to lack of ability. But "feeling dumb" or "feeling incompetent" certainly sound like cognitions as well as affects. On the other hand, it is also evident that the "hot" emotion of anger can be distinguished from a "cold" thought, such as "This is a chair." The differentiation between emotion and cognition is based, in part, on the definition of emotion. Along with many other theorists (e.g., Averill, 1982), I define emotion as a complex syndrome or a composite of many interacting factors. Emotions are presumed to have a positive or a negative quality of a certain intensity; they frequently are preceded by an appraisal of a situation and give rise to a variety of actions. This combination of features (hedonic direction, intensity, antedating cognition, and consequent action) does not characterize "cold" cognitions. In the present discussion, no position is taken regarding other possible correlates or parts of the emotional syndrome, including nonspecific or specific physiological activity and facial or postural involvement. Although these components are central in some approaches to emotion, they are not relevant to the concerns expressed in this chapter.

Finally, within the present attributional approach to motivation, emotions are assumed to be postattributional (after the cause of an event has been decided) and prebehavioral (prior to subsequent action). Affects, therefore, come at a juncture between behavioral events, summarizing the past and instigating the future:

Action 1 ⟶ Outcome 1 ⟶ Attribution 1 ⟶ *Affect* ⟶

Action 2 ⟶ Outcome 2 ⟶ Attribution 2

As such, they play a pivotal role in behavioral sequences (see Kelley, 1984).

The Cognition–Emotion Process

Most emotion theorists with a cognitive bent conceive of emotional experience as a temporal sequence involving cognitions of increasing complexity (e.g., Arnold, 1970; Lazarus, 1966; Schachter & Singer, 1962). The attributional framework advanced here also assumes a sequence in which cognitions of increasing complexity enter into the emotion process to further refine and differentiate experience. I contend that, following the outcome of an event, there is a general positive or negative reaction (a "primitive" emotion) based on the perceived success or failure of that outcome (the "primary" appraisal). For example, after receiving an A in a course, hitting a home run in a baseball game, or being accepted for a date, an individual will feel happy or pleased. In a similar manner, after receiving an F in a course, failing to get a hit in a baseball game, or being rejected for a date, the person will experience frustration or sadness. These emotions are labeled "outcome-dependent/attribution-independent," for they are determined by the attainment or nonattainment of a desired goal, not by the cause of that outcome.

Following the appraisal of a situation as positive or negative, a causal ascription for the outcome may be sought, and a different set of emotions is generated by the chosen attribution. For example, success perceived as due to help from others produces gratitude, whereas success due to long-term effort tends to give rise to relaxation and calmness. On the other hand, failure due to hindrance from others generates anger, whereas failure due to lack of effort often results in guilt. Emotions such as gratitude and anger are labeled "attribution-dependent," inasmuch as they are determined by the perceived cause of the prior outcome. Note that increasing cognitive complexity generates more differentiated emotional experience.

Causal dimensions also play a key role in the emotion process. Each causal dimension is uniquely related to a set of feelings. For example, success and failure perceived as due to internal causes—such as personality and effort, respectively raise or lower self-esteem and self-worth. That is, feelings related to self-esteem are influenced by causal properties (dimensions), rather than by a specific cause.

The temporal sequence assumed for the cognition–emotion process is depicted in the following diagram:

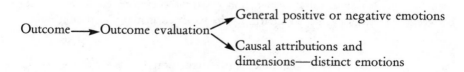

Note that the emotion process is initiated with the interpretation of an outcome (success or failure at an exam, rejection or acceptance for a social engagement), and that general affective reactions and more differentiated emotional experiences are assumed to coexist over time. More specifically, consider the situation in which a student receives feedback regarding an important exam. The grade is low (subjective failure), and the student feels sad. She thinks that the failure was due to a lack of sufficient effort, which produces guilt. In addition, inasmuch as effort expenditure is an internal cause, there is a lowering of self-esteem or self worth. Hence, there is simultaneous experience of outcome- and attributional-mediated emotions (sadness, guilt, and lowered self-esteem).

A number of prevalent human emotions can be incorporated within this approach. In determining the most common emotions, Davitz (1969) identified 400 words in *Roget's Thesaurus* and had subjects indicate which labels they would agree upon as representing emotions. Of the 137 reliably identified emotions, 50 were selected by Davitz for further examination. Of these, 14 were found to have high-frequency usage on the basis of an established word count procedure. In another attempt to ascertain the most predominant emotions, Bottenberg (1975) identified 30 emotions named as most frequently experienced by a large sample of college students. A combination of the research endeavors of Davtiz and Bottenberg reveals that five emotions have been identified as high-frequency by word count and also are reported as frequently experienced: anger, happiness, love, pity, and pride. The present attributional approach addresses four of these—anger, happiness, pity, and pride. Thus, although a full theory of emotions is not being offered, I do think that some of the most prevalent emotional experiences can be accounted for within this attributional approach. I will first turn to the emotion of happiness and then examine pride, anger, and pity.

OUTCOME-DEPENDENT AFFECTS (HAPPINESS)

A few years ago, an enigmatic article appeared in the sports pages. A championship soccer match was being held, and the visiting team spent the night at a local hotel. During the evening, the townspeople walked around the hotel making as much noise as possible, attempting to keep the visiting team from sleeping, which would impede their play the next afternoon. I naively wondered why people would want to win in this manner? Could positive affect be experienced (rather than, say, guilt) given this unseemly behavior as the cause of success?

An answer to this question was provided in studies I subsequently conducted with my associates (Weiner, Russell, & Lerman, 1978, 1979). In an initial investigation (Weiner *et al.*, 1978), we compiled a dictionary list of approximately 250 potential affective reactions to success and failure. The list began with the emotions of amazed, amused, and appreciative and ended with wonderment, worried, and wretched. Then a cause for success or failure was given within a brief story format, and participants reported the intensity of the affective responses they thought would be experienced in this situation. Intensity was indicated by marking rating scales for each of the positive affects, given a success outcome, and each of the negative affects, given a failure. For example, one story read:

> It was extremely important for Pat to receive a high score on an exam about to be taken. Pat has very high ability. Pat received a high score on the test and felt that score was received because of ability. After receiving the score, what do you think the feelings were?

TABLE 10.2   Success: Top Five Affective Intensity Ratings by Attribution for Success

Ability	Unstable Effort	Stable Effort	Task Difficulty	Mood
Pleased	Good	Satisfied	Pleased	Cheerful
Satisfied	Happy	Good	Contented	Good
Confident	Satisfied	Pleased	Happy	Delighted
Competent	Delighted	Secure	Secure	Happy
Happy	Gratified	Comfortable	Satisfied	Pleasant

Personality	Other's Effort	Other's Motivation and Personality	Luck	Intrinsic Motivation
Pleased	Pleased	Good	Happy	Pleased
Happy	Happy	Happy	Thankful	Happy
Contented	Appreciative	Delighted	Delighted	Satisfied
Proud	Satisfied	Satisfied	Pleased	Proud
Satisfied	Proud	Cheerful	Relieved	Confident

Note. Data derived from Weiner, Russell, and Lerman (1978).

Ten attributions were supplied for success and 11 for failure, including ability, stable and unstable effort, task difficulty, luck, mood, and help or hindrance from others. Table 10.2 shows the most intensely rated affects as a function of the causal attribution for success. It is evident that, regardless of the ascription, feelings of good, happy, pleased and satisfied were reported.

TABLE 10.3   Percentage of Emotional Recollections as a Function of the Causal Attribution for Success

Affect	Ability	Unstable Effort	Stable Effort	Personality	Others	Luck
Competence	30	12	20	19	5	2
Confidence	20	19	18	19	14	4
Contentment	4	4	12	0	7	2
Excitement	3	9	8	11	16	6
Gratitude	9	1	4	8	43	14
Guilt	1	3	0	3	2	18
Happiness	44	43	43	38	46	48
Pride	39	28	39	43	21	8
Relief	4	28	16	11	13	26
Satisfaction	19	24	16	14	9	0
Surprise	7	16	4	14	4	52
Thankfulness	0	1	0	0	18	4

Note. From "The Cognition–Emotion Process in Achievement-Related Contexts" by B. Weiner, D. Russell, and D. Lerman, 1979, *Journal of Personality and Social Psychology, 37*, p. 1214. Copyright 1979 by the American Psychological Association. Reprinted by permission.

To overcome some of the weaknesses of this simulational and respondent procedure, participants in a follow-up investigation (Weiner *et al.*, 1979) were asked to report a critical incident in their lives when they actually succeeded or failed in an exam because of a specified cause. Six causes were supplied: ability, stable and unstable effort, personality, others, and luck. The respondents recalled the event and their three most dominant affects at that time. The data from this study for successful outcomes are shown in Table 10.3. The most dominant affect reported was happy; about 45% of the subjects reported experiencing this affect in all the causal conditions.

What, then, would the townspeople have felt if their soccer team had won because the opposition was fatigued. I now suspect that, following a victory, they would have described their feelings as happiness. This reaction would have been experienced whether the team succeeded because of the actions of the townspeople, good team performance, the poor performance of the opposition, good luck, or any other cause. As mentioned earlier, affects such as happy for success (I am not dealing with failure in this chapter) are labeled "outcome-dependent/attribution-independent" because their elicitation depends on attainment or nonattainment of a goal, not on the causes of those outcomes.

The investigations by Weiner *et al.* (1978, 1979) provide the main source of empirical evidence to support the notion of outcome-linked affects. But other theorizing and data also buttress the existence of this affective category (see Bryant & Veroff, 1982; Gollwitzer, Earle, & Stephan, 1982; Smith & Kluegel, 1982). In his analysis of interpersonal relationships, Kelley (1983) also reasoned that there are outcome- as well as attribution-related sources of emotion:

> I am pleased or displeased by the more specific or concrete things I experience. ... So when my wife prepares a picnic lunch for our afternoon's outing, my pleasure–displeasure comes partly from the quality of the lunch itself, but also (as a partly separate matter) from the quality of the love and thoughtfulness I attribute to her for the effort. In general, then, people evaluate interaction on a dual basis, partly in terms of the concrete outcome ... and partly in terms of the interpersonal tendencies ... that they and their partners manage to express. (p. 15)

Although it has been proposed that happiness (and displeasure) derive from concrete outcomes, this does not imply that these affects are free from cognitive determination. As indicated in the diagram of the emotion process, success and failure depend on outcome evaluation. In addition, in Chapter 2 of this book, Higgins, Strauman, and Klein contend that success and failure produce differential outcome-linked affects as a function of standards of comparison. Also, De Rivera (1977) has shown that highly positive affects such as elation versus gladness can be discriminated according to the perceived likelihood of goal attainment. Greater differentiation among the outcome-related affects thus appears to be required and remains a task for the future.

ATTRIBUTION-LINKED AFFECTS

I have contended that the emotion process begins with the interpretation of an event as a success or a failure; that is, the environment is evaluated as "good" or "bad." This results in a generally positive (happy) reaction if the outcome is perceived as a success. Causal attributions and their underlying properties of locus, stability, and controllability in turn generate differentiated affective reactions that are presumed to coexist with the initial broad emotional response. I will now turn to the remaining dominant affects—pride, pity, and anger—and establish their associations with causal perceptions.

Causal Locus and Pride

The hypothesis of a relationship between causal locus and pride has long been entertained and recognized by well-known philosophers. Hume, for example, believed that what a person is proud of must belong to the person; Spinoza reasoned that pride consists of knowing one's merits, or power; and Kant nicely captured the locus–pride union by noting that everyone at a meal might enjoy the food, but only the cook of that meal can experience pride.

The attributional literature most germane to a locus–pride association is included under the general category of attributional biasing, or what is known more specifically as the "hedonic" or "self-serving" bias. Substantial research has revealed that people are more likely to make self-attributions for positive than for negative outcomes. For example, in the achievement domain, there is a tendency to attribute success to ability and effort (internal factors) and to ascribe failure to task difficulty and luck (external factors). Although there has been controversy regarding the interpretation of these data, and alternative nonmotivational explanations have been offered, the operation of ego-enhancing and ego-defensive biases generally has been accepted as explaining the experimental findings. As Harvey and Weary (1981) note: "By taking credit for good acts and denying blame for bad outcomes, the individual presumably may be able to enhance or protect his or her self-esteem" (p. 33). The documentation of self-serving attributional biases can be considered strong evidence supporting the hypothesized locus–esteem relation.

To ascertain more directly the effects of underlying causal properties on affective reactions, the data gathered by Weiner *et al.* (1978, 1979) are again relevant. Recall that in two investigations, causal ascriptions were specified for success and failure, and the participants either indicated on rating scales the intensity of affect they thought would be experienced or recalled the emotions they did experience in these situations. To determine whether locus influences affect, the combined responses for internal causes (e.g., ability, effort, personality) were compared with the combined responses for external causes (e.g., task difficulty, luck, others). The differences for successful outcomes in the two investigations are shown in Table 10.4. The table indicates that in both studies, internal ascriptions for success augmented reports of pride, confidence, competence, and satisfaction.

TABLE 10.4 Dimension-Linked Affects for Success as a Function of Locus of Causality

Affects reported in Weiner et al. (1979)	Affects reported in Weiner et al. (1978)
Pride	
Competence	Pride
Confidence	Competence
Satisfaction	Confidence
	Satisfaction
	Zest

These affects can be subsumed within the rubric of self-esteem or self-worth; the labels connote pride in oneself, belief that one is competent, self-confidence, and self-satisfaction. These data confirm that positive feelings about oneself are augmented when success is self-attributed. Although attributions to the self in situations of failure lower self-esteem, this affective reaction can be further differentiated as a function of the attributional context. Whereas both ability and effort attributions for success augment pride, lack of ability as the perceived cause of failure elicits shame, whereas failure ascribed to insufficient effort produces guilt (Brown & Weiner, 1984). Both of the negative affective reactions lower self-esteem, although they are quite distinct. Unfortunately, space does not permit further pursuit of this issue here.

The bias to ascribe success rather than failure to the self and to ascribe failure rather than success to external factors demonstrates that people may bias attributions and, in so doing, alter or manage feelings toward the self. In addition, the linkage between locus and self-esteem is consciously used to influence the emotional lives of others. That is, the association between internal attributions for outcomes and self-esteem is not only recognized by philosophers and psychologists—it is an integral part of everyday interpersonal interaction.

Perhaps the most evident conscious or calculated use of the locus–esteem association occurs in affiliative contexts. Frequently, people are asked to take part in a social engagement, such as a date or a party. The recipient of this request may prefer to refuse and will communicate a rejection. Inasmuch as a rejection is a negative outcome for the requester—perhaps unexpected—the rejected person is likely to ask "why" to determine the cause of the refusal. The rejecter may then tell the truth or not. One question that arises is under what conditions the rejecter will withhold the truth and communicate a false cause (i.e., tell a lie).

Guided by the prior methodology of Folkes (1982), Weiner and Handel (1985) examined this question and the development of the locus–esteem relation. Children 5–12 years of age were asked to respond to the following:

> Pretend that a boy (girl) from your class asks if you would like to go out and play with him (her). You decide not to go out and play because . . .

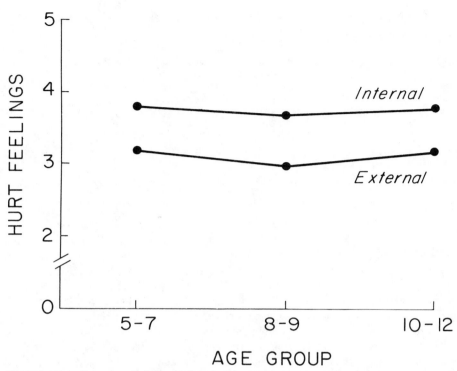

FIGURE 10.1 Reports of "hurt feelings" as a function of the locus of the cause of rejection. (Data from Weiner & Handel, 1985.)

This was followed by eight causes—four internal to the requester (e.g., "Your classmate always cheats at games," "Your classmate is never good at games") and four external to him or her (e.g., "You are sick with a bad cold," "You can't get to his or her house"). Following each cause of rejection, the experimenter asked how much the classmate's feelings would be hurt if that cause was conveyed. It was reasoned that "hurt feelings" captures the emotion of self-esteem.

The data revealed that, among all age groups, "hurt feelings" were anticipated to be greater with communication of internal rather than external causes (see Figure 10.1). This finding was equally evident across the age groups; a developmental trend was not displayed. In addition, children in all age groups indicated that they would be more likely to lie and withhold internal rather than external causes. Thus, the data were entirely consistent with the prior findings reported by Folkes (1982). Young children already are sophisticated (and benevolent) liars, knowing how to manipulate the affective lives of others and how to maintain and enhance the self-worth and self-esteem of others by changing what they think.

Causal Controllability Related to Anger and Pity

I have contended that affects are generated by the subjective outcome of an event as well as by the attributions for (or the perceived causes of) that outcome. One property of causes—their locus—influences self-esteem. I now turn to a second property of phenomenal causality—the perceived control over causes—and document how this influences anger and pity. Recall that four of the most dominant human emotions are happiness, pride, anger and pity.

A large survey study by Averill (1982, 1983) illustrated the attributional antecedents of anger. Averill asked his respondents to describe a situation in which they were made angry; he then examined the characteristics of these situations. He concluded:

> The major issue for the person in the street is not the specific nature of the instigating event; it is the perceived *justification* for the instigator's behavior. Anger, for the person in the street, is an accusation. . . . Over 85% of the episodes described by angry persons involved either an act that they considered voluntary and unjustified (59%) or else a potentially avoidable accident (e.g., due to negligence or lack of foresight, 28%). . . . To summarize, the typical instigation to anger is a value judgment. More than anything else, anger is an attribution of blame. (Averill, 1983, p. 1150)

Averill (1983) also noted that others "have pointed out that anger involves a normative judgment, an attribution of blame" (p. 1150). For example, in one of the first pertinent investigations, Pastore (1952) demonstrated that blame attributions influence the relationship between frustration and aggression. He found that aggression (and, by implication, anger) is not merely the result of nonattainment of a desired goal, but rather follows when a barrier imposed by others is "arbitrary" rather than "nonarbitrary." Among the arbitrary, aggression-instigating conditions identified by Pastore (1952) was "Your date phones at the last minute and breaks an appointment without an adequate explanation." The so-called nonarbitrary equivalent situation was "Your date phones at the last minute and breaks an appointment because he (she) had suddenly become ill."

In contrast to the linkage between controllability and anger, it is hypothesized that uncontrollable causes are associated with pity. (In this context, emotions such as compassion and sympathy are not distinguished from pity, although they might indeed be discriminable). Another's loss of a loved one because of an accident or illness (a cause external to the target of the pity and uncontrollable) or the failure of another because of a physical handicap (internal to the target of pity and uncontrollable) are prevalent situations that elicit pity. Uncontrollability, however, is not likely to be a sufficient condition for the generation of pity. After all, we may not pity a child who is not tall enough to reach a toy on a shelf. It appears that objects of pity must be suffering a severe distress, perhaps central to their lives. In addition, another person might have to be defined as "fundamentally different" to be the recipient of a full-blown pity reaction.

Inasmuch as pity is associated with perceptions of uncontrollability and a fundamental and adverse difference, communicated pity could serve as a cue promoting the self-perception of difference, deficiency, and inadequacy (see Graham, 1984; Weiner, Graham, Stern, & Lawson, 1982). For this reason, when the teacher of Helen Keller began her training, it is reported that she stated to Ms. Keller's family: "We do not want your pity." Similarly, Robertson Davies, a contemporary author, wrote: "I will not expose myself to the pity of my inferiors," thus conveying that a target of pity is associated with some deficiency.

There has been little research examining the emotion of pity, and what research has been done typically has involved comparisons with anger. In one investigation conducted by Weiner, Graham, and Chandler (1982), college students were asked to describe instances in their lives in which the emotions of pity and anger were experienced. After they had recounted two experiences for each emotion, the concept of causal dimensions was introduced and defined. The subjects then rated the cause of the event in question, if applicable, on each of the three dimensions.

Concerning pity, 71% of the causes were rated as stable and uncontrollable, with equal apportionment between the internal and external alternatives. The following two instances were typical:

1. A guy on campus is terribly deformed. I pity him because it would be so hard to look so different and have people stare at you.
2. My great grandmother lives in a rest home, and everytime I go there I see these poor old half-senile men and women wandering aimlessly down the halls. . . . I feel pity every time I go down there.

For the affect of anger, 86% of the situations involved an external and controllable cause, as Averill (1982) and others have also documented. The following two anger-arousing situations were typical:

1. My roommate brought her dog into our no-pets apartment without asking me first. When I got home she wasn't there, but the barking dog was. . . . As well, the dog had relieved itself in the middle of the entry.
2. I felt angry toward my boyfriend for lying to me about something he did. All he had to do was tell me the truth.

The use of excuses in everyday interpersonal interactions demonstrates that the relations between causal controllability–anger and uncontrollability–pity are part of naive psychology (i.e., the average person's understanding of psychological principles). Picture a scenario in which you are waiting for someone to arrive for an appointment, either of a social or business nature. You wait 10, 30, and finally 60 minutes until the person finally appears. During the waiting period, you might have many emotional reactions, ranging from worry (Did something happen?) and self-doubt (Is this the right place?) to frustration and anger (Where the hell is he?). When the person does appear, it is likely that an explanation will be immediately offered or asked for (inasmuch as unexpected negative events elicit attributional search). Imagine that the tardy person states: "It was so nice out that I took my time getting here" or "I decided to first watch this program on television." As you read these responses, you probably intuitively recognized that they are not "good" excuses. A good excuse lessens personal responsibility. By giving such an excuse, one anticipates that anger will be mitigated, that one's positive image will be maintained, and that the interpersonal relationship will not be weakened. Thus, a better strategy would be to state: "My car broke down" or "There was a tie-up on the freeway" or "I temporarily became dizzy" (transportation and medical excuses are among the most common types). These are "good" excuses because the perception of the cause of lateness is changed from uncertain, or controllable, to uncontrollable. Of course, there are other acceptable ways to deal with a broken social contract, including accepting responsibility and retribution, offering an apology, providing a justification, and the like. The functions of these alternative strategies are not examined in this context.

The function of excuse-giving as a moderator of anger was documented by Weiner and Handel (1985). We gave children ranging in age from 5–12 the following scenario: "You promised to play with a friend after school, but then did

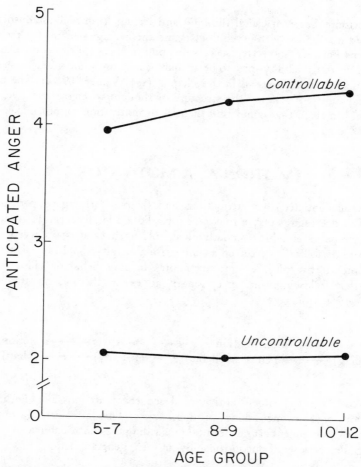

FIGURE 10.2 Reports of anticipated anger as a function of the controllability of the cause of not appearing for an appointment. (Data from Weiner & Handel, 1985.)

not show up. The real reason was . . . " Four controllable causes (e.g., "You decided to watch TV") and four uncontrollable causes (e.g., "Your bike had a flat tire") were then provided. The subjects were asked how angry their friend would be if that reason was communicated. The data, depicted in Figure 10.2, reveal that among all age groupings, controllable causes for nonappearance are believed to elicit more anger than uncontrollable causes. In addition, children of all age groups indicated that they would be more likely to communicate uncontrollable than controllable causes. That is, if they would be perceived as personally responsible, there was an inclination to lie. It is thus evident that 5-year-olds already have learned the art of excuse-making and perceive the relationship between controllable causes for a social "failure" and anger from others.

Summary

The associations between causal thinking and feeling form well-established and robust laws, known by both psychologists and the average person. I perceive the relationships between subjective success–happiness, locus–pride, controllability–anger, and uncontrollability–pity to be unequivocal, as are some other attribution–emotion linkages not discussed in this chapter (see Weiner, 1982). The present theory's capability of relating the structure of thought to emotion as well as to motivation is a claim that competing theories of motivation cannot make.

EMOTION AS A MOTIVATOR

It is well substantiated that attributions and their underlying properties guide feelings. But do feelings play a role in action? To aid in answering this question, assume a scenario in which an individual holding a cane is observed to fall. Inasmuch as disability is perceived as uncontrollable, pity should be elicited. One might contend that pity, in turn, promotes helping behavior. This scenario suggests that following the perception of an event, there is an attribution–emotion–action sequence:

$$\text{Outcome} \longrightarrow \text{Attribution} \longrightarrow \text{Affect} \longrightarrow \text{Action}$$
$$\text{(Falling)} \longrightarrow \text{(Uncontrollable)} \longrightarrow \text{(Pity)} \longrightarrow \text{(Help)}$$

Of course, many other motivational sequences are possible. Perhaps the observation of someone falling produces pity. This affective reaction then influences the subsequent causal ascription regarding the controllability of the cause of falling. Perceptions of uncontrollabiliy, in turn, generate help:

$$\text{Falling} \longrightarrow \text{Pity} \longrightarrow \text{Uncontrollable} \longrightarrow \text{Help}$$

Still another possibility is that the observed outcome simultaneously generates both affect and an attribution. Outcome, attribution, and/or affect then influence action

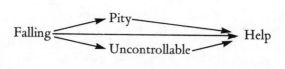

Given this model, the affect and/or attribution may be epiphenomena in that they have no influence on behavior and may or may not precede or accompany help-giving.

Yet another possibility is that the perception of falling elicits (or fails to elicit) helping behavior. Helping partly determines affect and perceptions regarding controllability. This sequence also has many possible variations, with action directly influencing both affect and attribution or directly influencing only one of these two reactions:

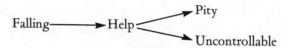

All of the possible permutations and combinations of these four variables have not yet been exhausted, and there is good reason to believe that the models are not mutually exclusive. Rather, there are likely to be direct and indirect bidirectional influences between all of the variables: thought influences affect, and affect influences thought; affect influences action, and action influences affect; and so on. The sequence that I think is dominant, however, is "we feel the way we think and act on the basis of those feelings." That is, the tripartite division of psychology into thinking, feeling, and behaving also represents the predominant temporal order, or the typical motivational episode (also see Tomkins, 1970).

In a series of investigations, evidence has been provided to support this line of reasoning (Meyer & Mulherin, 1980; Weiner, 1980a, 1980c). In one investigation, subjects read the following scenario:

> At about 1:00 in the afternoon you are walking through campus and a student comes up to you. The student says that you do not know him, but that you are both enrolled in the same class. He asks if you would lend him the class notes from the meeting last week, saying that notes are needed because he skipped class to go to the beach. (Alternate form: Notes are needed because of eye problems.) (Weiner, 1980c, p. 676)

Another scenario used was the following:

> At about 1:00 in the afternoon you are riding a subway car. There are a number of other individuals in the car and one person is standing, holding on to the center pole. Suddenly, this person staggers forward and collapses. The person apparently

is drunk. He is carrying a liquor bottle wrapped in a brown paper bag and smells of liquor. (Alternate form: The person is carrying a black cane and apparently is ill.) (Weiner, 1980a, p. 190)

In these investigations, perception of the controllability of the cause of the need (in these instances, "beach," "eye problems," "drunk," or "disabled"), ratings of pity and anger (which are known to be linked to perceived controllability), and the likelihood of helping were assessed. The data revealed positive relationships among perceived controllability, anger, and lack of help, as well as among perceived uncontrollability, pity, and help-giving. Thus, subjects tended to perceive the causes of the "eye problem" student and the "disabled" individual as uncontrollable; they reported feeling pity and indicated that they would help. On the other hand, the causes of the "beach" student and the "drunk" were perceived as controllable; subjects reported feeling anger and indicated that they would not help.

These correlational data also provide evidence concerning the temporal organization of behavior, including the linkage between affect and action. The logic of the analysis is that if affect mediates the relationship between thought and action, then partialling affect from the cause (controllability)–helping correlation will greatly modulate the magnitude of that correlation. On the other hand, partialling thoughts from the affect–helping correlation should not influence the magnitude of that correlation. And that, indeed, has been the pattern of findings. The data from one pertinent study (Weiner, 1980c) reveal that perceived controllability relates negatively with helping ($r = -.37$), whereas helping relates positively with feelings of pity ($r = .46$) and negatively with reports of anger ($r = .71$). The correlations between the two affects and helping were only slightly altered when perceptions of controllability were statistically taken from the relationships, with the pity–helping correlation lowered more than that of anger–helping (from $r = .46$ to $r = .30$). On the other hand, the correlation between controllability and help-giving was reduced to near zero when the reactions of pity or anger were statistically held constant. In sum, the data support the position that emotions, rather than causal perceptions, appear to be the immediate or direct motivators of behavior, whereas causal perceptions are indirectly linked to action. As previously hypothesized, thoughts give rise to feelings, and feelings guide behavior.

This analysis can be applied to any number of situations. For example, assume that a person succeeds and that success is ascribed to volitional help from others. On the basis of the prior discussion, this is expected to give rise to gratitude. One might think that gratitude, in turn, promotes actions instrumental to the mainten- ance of the relationship, such as the purchase of a gift:

Outcome (success)———►Attribution (help from others) ———►
———►Affect (gratitude)———►Action (gift purchase)

Or consider a school setting in which a bright pupil fails because of lack of effort. Being a controllable cause, this should produce teacher anger (see Prawat,

Byers, & Anderson, 1983, for confirmatory data). Anger, in turn, is anticipated to give rise to some form of punishment:

Outcome (failure of a pupil) ⟶ Attribution (lack of effort) ⟶
⟶ Affect (anger) ⟶ Action (punishment)

It has been documented many times that pupil failure because of lack of effort does maximize negative evaluation (e.g., Weiner & Kukla, 1970). What remains to be demonstrated, based on the analysis presented here, is that this punishment is mediated by teacher reactions of anger.

Thus far, the cause–affect–behavior sequence has been discussed in the contexts of help-giving and achievement strivings. It can also be readily applied to affiliative strivings. For example, assume that a person ascribes personal rejection to some internal characteristic such as an unpleasant personality. This should produce "hurt feelings" and feelings of shame and inadequacy. Such experiences are likely to result in subsequent avoidance behavior in interpersonal contexts.

In sum, it is postulated that an attribution–affect–behavior sequence is the form of a typical motivational episode. Of course, not all sequences of motivated behavior need follow this ordering, but I suggest that many do.

NONATTRIBUTION THOUGHTS, AFFECT, AND ACTION

One question that emerges from the foregoing analysis is whether any thoughts are directly, as opposed to indirectly, linked to motivated behavior. The cognition that motivational theorists stress as directly related to action is the expectancy of goal attainment. This concept has been perceived by many so-called expectancy-value theorists (e.g., Lewin, Rotter, Atkinson) as a key determinant of behavior. Social learning proponents have been especially lucid in pointing out that regardless of level of need, behavior is not undertaken unless there is some likelihood that the action will result in goal attainment. Considering the foregoing discussion, it might be contended that even if great pity is experienced, helping behavior is not extended unless the action has some reasonable, subjective likelihood of resulting in a positive outcome. Thus, although pity might be experienced at the sight of a drowning person, observers will not jump into the water if they cannot swim. On the other hand, they might run for help or engage in other actions that are instrumental to their altruistic goals.

Even in these cases, however, one can take the position that expectancy is not directly linked to action, but rather is associated with mediating affects. High or low expectancy of goal attainment may be related to anticipatory excitement (hope) or anticipatory fear. These affects, in turn, are suggested to be directly linked to approach or withdrawal:

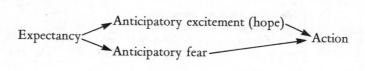

Expectancy ⟨ Anticipatory excitement (hope) ⟶ Action
Anticipatory fear ⟶

Perhaps surprisingly, neobehaviorists such as Spence (1956, p. 135) advanced a similar proposal regarding the mechanisms that might mediate what cognitivists label as expectancy or anticipation of a reward.

A FINAL NOTE

A number of assumptions about the construction of a viable theory of motivation were outlined at the beginning of this chapter. To reiterate, a theory of motivation must include the full range of emotions—emotions that are qualitatively distinct and not merely subsummed within the broad heading of pleasure–pain. Furthermore, a theory of motivation must specify sequential (temporal) relationships among the determinants of behavior. It thus should be based more on linear models and path analysis than upon the analysis of variance techniques used so well in the testing, for example, of Hullian theory. These two principles guided the theoretical construction and empirical data presented in this chapter.

To end on a speculative note, I would like to suggest that the immediate determinants of motivation are not so complex as others might have us believe. Cognitive psychologists have become more and more aware of the bounded rationality that describes human beings and the necessity of people's attempts to reduce cognitive strain. In a similar manner, humans cannot possibly be immediately guided by all of the variables that have been suggested as determinants of action. If they were, they surely would become buried in process. For example, expectancy-value theorists postulate that behavior is determined by expectancy of goal attainment multiplied by (or added to) the value of the anticipated goal. Expectancy, in turn, is suggested to be determined by factors such as the primacy, recency, and frequency of the attainment of the goal, as well as by such factors as the recency and frequency of attainment of similar goals and generalized beliefs about perceived control. Values also are determined by an array of factors, such as the quality and the quantity of the goal. It is likely that an individual calculates all these variables and finally adds or multiplies expectancy and value before acting? I think that asks too much of humans. Rather, I propose that at any particular moment in time, one or two emotions known by the actor will be the prime movers of most actions.

References

Allport, G. (1960). *Personality and social encounter: Selected essays*. Boston: Beacon Press.
Amsel, A. (1958). The role of frustrative nonreward in noncontinuous reward situations. *Psychological Bulletin, 55*, 102–119.
Arnold, M. B. (1970). Perennial problems in the field of emotion. In M. B. Arnold (Ed.) *Feelings and emotions* (pp. 169–186). New York: Academic Press.
Atkinson, J. W. (1964). *An introduction to motivation*. Princeton, NJ: Van Nostrand.
Atkinson, J. W., & Birch, D. (1970). *The dynamics of action*. New York: Wiley.
Averill, J. R. (1982). *Anger and aggression: An essay on emotion*. New York: Springer-Verlag.
Averill, J. R. (1983). Studies on anger and aggression. *American Psychologist, 38*, 1145–1160.

Berlyne, D. (1968). Behavior theory as personality theory. In E. F. Borgatta & W. W. Lambert (Eds.), *Handbook of personality theory and research* (pp. 629–690). Chicago: Rand McNally.

Bottenberg, E. H. (1975). Phenomenological and operational characterization of factor-analytically derived dimensions of emotion. *Psychological Reports, 37*, 1253–1254.

Brown, J., & Weiner, B. (1984). Affective consequences of ability versus effort ascriptions: Controversies, resolution, and quandaries. *Journal of Educational Psychology, 76*, 146–158.

Brown, J. S. (1961). *The motivation of behavior*. New York: McGraw-Hill.

Bryant, F. B., & Veroff, J. (1982). The structure of psychological well-being: A sociohistorical analysis. *Journal of Personality and Social Psychology, 43*, 653–673.

Davitz, J. R. (1969). *The language and emotion*. New York: Academic Press.

Deci, E. L. (1975). *Intrinsic motivation*. New York: Plenum.

De Rivera, J. (1977). *A structural theory of emotions*. New York: International Universities Press.

Ellis, A. (1974). Rational-emotive therapy. In A. Burton (Ed.), *Operational theories of personality*. New York: Brunner/Mazel.

Epstein, S. (1979). The ecological study of emotions in humans. In P. Pliner, K. R. Blankstein, & I. M. Spigel (Eds.), *Perception of emotion in self and other* (pp. 47–84). New York: Plenum.

Folkes, V. S. (1982). Communicating the reasons for social rejection. *Journal of Experimental Social Psychology, 18*, 235–252.

Freud, S. (1955). Beyond the pleasure principle. In J. Strachey (Ed.), *The standard edition of the complete psychological works of Sigmund Freud* (Vol. 18). London: Hogarth Press. (Original work published 1920)

Gollwitzer, P. M., Earle, W. B., & Stephan, W. G. (1982). Affect as a determinant of egotism: Residual excitation and performance attributions. *Journal of Personality and Social Psychology, 43*, 702–709.

Graham, S. (1984). Communicating sympathy and anger to black and white children: The cognitive (attributional) consequences of affective cues. *Journal of Personality and Social Psychology, 47*, 40–54.

Harvey, J. H., & Weary, C. (1981). *Perspectives on attribution processes*. Dubuque, IA: Brown.

Heider, F. (1958). *The psychology of interpersonal relations*. New York: Wiley.

Hull, C. L. (1943). *Principles of behavior*. New York: Appleton-Century-Crofts.

Kant, I. (1956). *The critique of practical reason*. New York: Bobbs-Merrill. (Original work published 1869)

Kelley, H. H. (1967). Attribution theory in social psychology. In D. Levine (Ed.), *Nebraska Symposium on Motivation* (Vol. 15, pp. 192–238). Lincoln: University of Nebraska Press.

Kelley, H. H. (1983). The situational origins of human tendencies: A further reason for the formal analysis of structures. *Personality and Social Psychology Bulletin, 9*, 8–30.

Kelley, H. H. (1984). Affect in interpersonal relations. *Review of Personality and Social Psychology, 5*, 89–115.

Kingdon, J. W. (1967). Politicians' beliefs about voters. *American Political Science Review, 61*, 137–145.

Lau, R. R., & Russell, D. (1980). Attributions in the sports pages: A field test of some current hypotheses in attribution research. *Journal of Personality and Social Psychology, 39*, 29–38.

Lazarus, R. S. (1966). *Psychological stress and the coping process*. New York: McGraw-Hill.

Lepper, M. R., Greene, D., & Nisbett, R. E. (1973). Undermining children's intrinsic interest with extrinsic reward: A test of the overjustification hypothesis. *Journal of Personality and Social Psychology, 28*, 129–137.

Lewin, K. (1935). *A dynamic theory of personality*. New York: McGraw-Hill.

Meyer, J. P., & Mulherin, A. (1980). From attribution to helping: An analysis of the mediating effects of affect on expectancy. *Journal of Personality and Social Psychology, 39*, 201–210.

Passer, M. W. (1977). *Perceiving the causes of success and failure revisited: A multidimensional scaling approach*. Unpublished doctoral dissertation, University of California, Los Angeles.

Pastore, N. (1952). The role of arbitrariness in the frustration–aggression hypothesis. *Journal of Abnormal and Social Psychology, 47*, 728–732.

Pettit, P. (1981). On actions and explanations. In C. Antaki (Ed.), *The psychology of ordinary explanations* (pp. 1–26). London: Academic Press.

Prawat, R. S., Byers, J. L., & Anderson, A. H. (1983). An attributional analysis of teachers' affective reactions to student success and failure. *American Educational Research Journal, 20*, 137–152.

Rosenbaum, R. M. (1972). *A dimensional analysis of the perceived causes of success and failure.* Unpublished doctoral dissertation, University of California, Los Angeles.

Rotter, J. B. (1954). *Social learning and clinical psychology.* Englewood Cliffs, NJ: Prentice-Hall.

Rotter, J. B. (1966). Generalized expectancies for internal versus external control of reinforcement. *Psychological Monographs, 80* (Whole No. 609).

Rychlak, J. F. (1968). *A philosophy of science for personality theory.* New York: Houghton Mifflin.

Schachter, S., & Singer, J. E. (1962). Cognitive, social and physiological determinants of emotional state. *Psychological Review, 69*, 379–399.

Smith, E. R., & Kluegel, J. R. (1982). Cognitive and social bases of emotional experience: Outcome, attribution, and affect. *Journal of Personality and Social Psychology, 43*, 1129–1141.

Spence, K. W. (1956). *Behavior theory and conditioning.* New Haven: Yale University Press.

Taylor, S. E. (1983). Adjustment to threatening events: A theory of cognitive adaptation. *American Psychologist, 38*, 1161–1173.

Tolman, E. C. (1925). Purpose and cognition: The determinants of animal learning. *Psychological Review, 32*, 285–297.

Tomkins, S. S. (1970). Affect as the primary motivational system. In M. B. Arnold (Ed.), *Feelings and emotion* (pp. 101–110). New York: Academic Press.

Weiner, B. (1979). A theory of motivation for some classroom experiences. *Journal of Educational Psychology, 71*, 3–25.

Weiner, B. (1980a). A cognitive (attribution)–emotion–action model of motivated behavior: An analysis of judgments of help-giving. *Journal of Personality and Social Psychology, 39*, 186–200.

Weiner, B. (1980b). *Human motivation.* New York: Holt, Rinehart & Winston.

Weiner, B. (1980c). May I borrow your class notes? An attributional analysis of judgments of help giving in an achievement-related context. *Journal of Educational Psychology, 72*, 676–681.

Weiner, B. (1982). The emotional consequences of causal attributions. In M. Clark & S. T. Fiske (Eds.), *Affect and cognition: 17th Annual Carnegie Symposium on Cognition* (pp. 185–209). Hillsdale, NJ: Erlbaum.

Weiner, B. (1985). "Spontaneous" causal thinking. *Psychological Bulletin, 97*, 74–84.

Weiner, B., Frieze, I., Kukla, A., Reed, L., Rest, S., & Rosenbaum, R. M. (1971). *Perceiving the causes of success and failure.* Morristown, NJ: General Learning Press.

Weiner, B., Graham, S., & Chandler, C. (1982). Causal antecedents of pity, anger, and guilt. *Personality and Social Psychology Bulletin, 8*, 226–232.

Weiner, B., Graham, S., Stern, P., & Lawson, M. E. (1982). Using affective cues to infer causal thoughts. *Developmental Psychology, 18*, 278–286.

Weiner, B., & Handel, S. (1985). Anticipated emotional consequences of causal communications and reported communication strategy. *Developmental Psychology, 21*, 102–107.

Weiner, B., & Kukla, A. (1970). An attributional analysis of achievement motivation. *Journal of Personality and Social Psychology, 15*, 1–20.

Weiner, B., Russell, D., & Lerman, D. (1978). Affective consequences of causal ascriptions. In J. H. Harvey, W. J. Ickes, & R. F. Kidd (Eds.), *New directions in attribution research* (Vol. 2). Hillsdale, NJ: Erlbaum.

Weiner, B., Russell, D., & Lerman, D. (1979). The cognition–emotion process in achievement-related contexts. *Journal of Personality and Social Psychology, 37*, 1211–1220.

Wong, P. T. P., & Weiner, B. (1981). When people ask "why" questions and the heuristics of attributional search. *Journal of Personality and Social Psychology, 40*, 650–663.

PART III

Goals and Orientations

CHAPTER 11

Motivation and the Self-System

JOEL O. RAYNOR
DEAN B. McFARLIN
State University of New York at Buffalo

INTRODUCTION AND OVERVIEW

Theoretical Background

The self is a topic that currently demands a great deal of attention in the field of psychology. Thousands of studies examining self issues have been conducted over the past two decades (Wylie, 1979), and numerous theoretical perspectives have attempted to account for self-system development and functioning (see reviews by Greenwald & Pratkanis, 1984; Tesser & Campbell, 1983). In spite of this large research literature and variety of theories, understanding of the self and its motivational implications for behavior is far from complete. On the other hand, many theories of motivation have failed to systematically consider the role of self-system functioning as a determinant of action (Raynor, 1982b).

A necessary first step toward greater understanding of the self-system and its link to behavior is the development of more unified, systematic theory. The theoretical approach taken here represents such a step. The framework presented here integrates the study of the self and behavioral systems. It is intended to provide the basis for an emerging conception of personality that deals with the bidirectional relationship between the self and behavior.

This theory of self-system development and functioning represents the application of principles of motivation derived from a conceptual analysis of the determinants of overt action—particularly achievement-oriented action (cf. Atkinson & Birch, 1978; Atkinson & Feather, 1966; Atkinson & Raynor, 1974; Raynor & Entin, 1982a). It is embedded in a theory of personality functioning (Raynor, 1982b) and a step-path theoretic approach to the study of overt action (Raynor & Entin, 1982a, 1983). The goal is to provide a systematic account of motivation in *both* the behavioral and self-systems, using the same principles and assumptions. A virtue of this theory is its ability to derive phenomena heretofore treated with different (often antagonistic) theoretical perspectives from the same conceptual framework. For example, behaviors usually associated with either a self-consistency or a self-enhancement perspective can be derived from principles dealing with the maximizing of positive value and the minimizing of negative value.

Focus and Plan

The present chapter provides a brief but current statement of our theoretical position. New to this presentation is the functional distinction between motivation concerning sources of value at *some* psychological distance from the individual and motivation concerning sources of value at *zero* psychological distance (i.e., those being experienced by the individual).

The plan of the chapter is (1) to outline our theoretical integration of self and behavioral system functioning; (2) to reinterpret major theory and research from the self literature using this approach; and (3) to summarize the implications suggested by the theory and discuss directions for future research.

This chapter is not intended to discredit or disprove existing conceptual schemes. Rather, we hope to illustrate that current theory and research can be conceptualized in a more systematic fashion using our approach. Just as previous affective theories largely ignored the role of cognition in human functioning, many current cognitive and information-processing theories are conceptually imbalanced in that they tend to ignore the role of affect. We believe a conceptual integration of affective and cognitive processes is an essential first step toward a more complete understanding of motivation, action, and self-system functioning. Our approach represents just such an integration.

A THEORY OF MOTIVATION IN THE SELF AND BEHAVIORAL SYSTEMS

Assumptions

Basic Functions of Personality

Our primary assumption is that there are two basic functions of personality: to maximize positive value and to minimize negative value. These basic functions result in adaptive behavior that is more or less successful in achieving these goals. Thus, all behavior is adaptive in that the individual is constantly striving to maximize positive value and minimize negative value.

In this theory the concept of value is defined in terms of (1) its functional impact on motivation, (2) distinctions between different *sources* of value, and (3) distinctions between different *types* of value.

The Functional Role of Value

The functional role of value depends on three factors: (1) the psychological distance of the individual from a source of value (i.e., psychological distance is zero

TABLE 11.1   Motivation as a Function of Psychological Distance to and Direction of Sources of Value

Psychological Distance	Direction of Value	
	Positive	Negative
Zero (experiencing outcomes)	*Maintenance*: Motivation to think/act in ways expected to maintain or retain positive value	*Removal*: Motivation to think/act in ways expected to minimize or remove negative value
Greater than zero (anticipating or recalling outcomes)	*Production*: Motivation to think/act in ways expected to produce positive value	*Resistance*: Motivation to resist thoughts/acts expected to produce negative value

when a person *experiences* value and greater than zero when a person *recalls* or *anticipates* value), (2) the direction of value (positive or negative), and (3) the magnitude of value. When people experience positive value, they are motivated to maintain that source of value.[1] Similarly, when an individual recalls or anticipates positive value, a tendency to think or act is aroused. Attaining that positive value becomes a goal. When an individual recalls or anticipates negative value, however, a tendency to resist engaging in thought or action that would produce that value is aroused. On the other hand, when people experience negative value, they are motivated to minimize or remove that source of value. To summarize, although both positive and negative value function regardless of psychological distance, they function *differently*. Action is initiated (1) to recall or attain anticipated positive value, (2) to retain positive value that is experienced, or (3) to remove negative value that is experienced. Action is inhibited, on the other hand, by the anticipation of attaining or recalling negative value.[2] Table 11.1 summarizes the four basic functional roles of value identified here.

Sources of Value

Value can also be defined in terms of its source. We have identified five possible sources of both positive and negative value: (1) outcomes of action (e.g., success or failure at a task); (2) self-images (e.g., "tennis player," "psychology professor"); (3) abilities (e.g., mathematical, artistic); (4) attributes (e.g., kind, selfish); and (5) psychological careers (see later discussion). These sources of value are not necessarily grounded in the present. For instance, a person who was an "Olympic athlete" in 1960 may derive a great deal of positive value from that past self-image. Similarly, an athlete who is on the current U.S. Olympic Team may derive positive value from that present self-image. Finally, a person may view "becoming an Olympian" as a source of positive value. In short, we argue that the five sources of value are time-linked in that they are determined by the anticipated future, the evaluated present, or the retrospected past.

General Types of Value

We distinguish between different types of value that people must deal with in trying to maximize positive and minimize negative value. There are two general types of value: affective value and information value.

Affective value refers to the emotional functioning of personality. The concept of affective value specifies how emotional states (feeling good or bad) influence adaptive behavior. When positive affective value is recalled or anticipated (e.g., feeling good about having received tenure last year or the possibility of receiving it next year), the individual is motivated to initiate action to produce that source of good feelings (e.g., reminiscing about key publications that led to tenure in the past, redoubling efforts to publish to attain tenure in the future). Similarly, when positive affective value is experienced (e.g., feeling good about having just graduated from college), the individual is motivated to initiate action to maintain or retain the source of good feelings (e.g., telling friends, buying a college ring). However, when negative affective value is experienced (e.g., feeling bad about being in a traffic accident), the individual is motivated to engage in activity to remove the source of bad feelings (e.g., blaming the other driver). On the other hand, when negative affective value is recalled or anticipated (e.g., recalling a bad drinking binge, anticipating feeling bad if one gets drunk), the individual is motivated to resist engaging in activity that might produce the source of bad feelings (e.g., resisting remembering the amount of liquor consumed on a drinking binge, avoiding drinking excessively).

Information value refers to the cognitive functioning of personality. The concept of information value specifies how cognitive states (clarity or confusion) influence adaptive behavior. When positive information value is recalled or anticipated (e.g., having known or coming to know one's ability to play golf), the individual is motivated to initiate action to produce that recalled or anticipated source of knowing (e.g., reminiscing about past golf matches, playing a great deal of golf). Similarly, when positive information value is experienced (e.g., knowing one is high [or low] in mathematical ability) the individual is motivated to continue action to maintain that source of clarity (e.g., continuing to see oneself as high [or low] in mathematical ability). However, when negative information value (confusion or ambiguity) is recalled or anticipated (e.g., recalling the outcome of a previous match or thinking about an upcoming match with a tennis pro, which may confuse an amateur about his or her own level of tennis ability), the individual is motivated to resist engaging in activity that might obtain that source of confusion (e.g., resisting remembering details of the previous match, avoiding playing the tennis pro). On the other hand, when negative informtion value is experienced (e.g., being given information casting doubt on one's level of mathematical ability), the individual is motivated to engage in activity to minimize or remove the source of confusion (e.g., ignoring confusing information, taking a highly diagnostic math test).

Substantive Types of Value

Finally, five different substantive types of value may operate in the behavioral or self systems. We assume that these substantive types of value can arouse both

TABLE 11.2 Value in the Self and Behavioral systems: Dimensions and Distinctions

Dimensions	*Distinctions*
Direction of value	Positive, negative
Possible sources of value	Outcomes of action, self-images, abilities, attributes, psychological careers
Time linkages associated with value	Retrospected past, evaluated present, anticipated future
General types of value	Affective, information
Substantive types of value	Intrinsic, difficulty, instrumental, extrinsic, cultural

Note. Adapted from Raynor (1982b).

information and affective value. *Intrinsic value* refers to the amount of information or affective value aroused by the inherent properties of (1) an activity that an individual engages in or (2) an attribute or self-image. *Difficulty value* is determined by (1) an individual's perceived chances of attaining, maintaining, or evaluating a given outcome or (2) an individual's perceived degree of possession of attributes, competencies, or skills. *Instrumental value* refers to the number of opportunities for obtaining value that are believed to be ensured by (1) the attainment, maintenance, or evaluation of an outcome or (2) possession of some attribute or self-image. *Extrinsic value* refers to value that is immediately dependent on (1) attainment of other outcomes of action or (2) possession of some attribute or self-image. *Cultural value* refers to a moral-evaluative source of value—the extent to which a person (1) sees an outcome as good or bad, right or wrong, proper or improper in the person's culture or (2) believes that possession of an attribute or self-image makes him or her a good or bad, right or wrong, proper or improper person in his or her culture. Table 11.2 summarizes the dimensions we have identified and the distinctions we have made regarding the concept of value.

Motivation as a Multiplicative Function

At this point, we need to clarify the concept of motivation. In this theory, motivation to think (covert activity) or behave (overt activity) is actually a multiplicative function of the amount of positive value that is anticipated, recalled, or experienced and the subjective probability of attaining or retaining it. Motivation to resist or remove is a multiplicative function of the amount of negative value that is anticipated, recalled, or experienced and the subjective probability of experiencing or removing it. Resultant tendency to think or act is a function of the difference between motivation to think or act and resistance to thought or action. Thus, the theory builds on the basic logic of expectancy-value theory (Atkinson, 1964; Atkinson & Feather, 1966; Atkinson & Raynor, 1974; Feather, 1982; Lewin, Dembo, Festinger, & Sears, 1944; Raynor & Entin, 1982a; Tolman, 1955).

Resultant value determines motivation for thinking about and doing (holding expectancy constant). Resultant value can involve the difference between (1) positive and negative affective value, (2) positive and negative information value, (3) positive affective value and negative information value, or (4) positive information value and negative affective value. The experiencing of negative information or affective value produces motivation to reduce or eliminate negative value. An infinite variety of thoughts or actions may be equally functional in terms of minimizing or eliminating experienced negative value. Specification of the particular means of minimizing value depends on the ability to indicate the sources of positive value for an individual in a given situation. Similarly, the function of recalled or anticipated negative value *per se* does not allow for specific predictions. The theory specifies the *amount* of resistance to be overcome for a particular thought or action to emerge. Determination of thought or action also requires the specification of the resultant value of options available to a person in a particular situation and the probability of experiencing those sources of value.

Thus, our position is essentially a two-factor theory in which positive and negative value are independent. Removal of experienced negative value is not synonymous with maximization of positive value. For example, if a college student feels bad about getting a low grade on a test (experiences negative value), he or she may be motivated to get relief from the shame of failure by getting drunk. In this case, the student is attempting to remove experienced negative value rather than to produce positive value. Furthermore, if the student anticipates that the low test grade will lead to a bad grade for the entire course, he or she may drop the course as a way of resisting activity expected to produce such negative value. On the other hand, the student may decide that by studying harder for subsequent tests, he or she could get a good grade in the course. In this case, the student is studying hard to *produce* anticipated positive value (i.e., feeling good about getting a high grade in the course) rather than to resist anticipated negative value.

Defining the Self-System

The self-system constitutes an individual's phenomenological or experienced sense of self. This position is consistent with the views of many theorists (e.g., Allport, 1955; Epstein, 1973; James, 1890; Kelly, 1955; Lecky, 1945; Maslow, 1954; Mead, 1934; Rogers, 1951; Snygg & Combs, 1949). We do not, however, share the assumption made (at least implicitly) by these theorists—namely, that all people need a "theory" (i.e., the self-system) that organizes experience in a way that gives predictability and meaning to life (Epstein, 1981, 1983).

Our theory's basic assumption regarding positive and negative value makes no reference to "self." People do not *require* or *need* to have a self-system to function in society. Rather, the self-system is something that may or may not emerge as a phenomenal means of self-identity. Once people have developed the capacity for self-consciousness, various sources and amounts of information and affective value will dictate whether or not a self-system emerges. If substantial sources of positive information and affective value exist that are associated with potential self-images, than a self-system will emerge. An area of activity (e.g., academic performance) will serve as the basis for phenomenal self-identity when the outcomes associated with that area of activity have strong positive value for the individual. For example, people with strong cultural value for a particular self-image (e.g., becoming a physician) will come to see themselves in terms of that self-image. People with an emergent self-system possess a source of motivational impetus in addition to that provided by the behavioral system (see Raynor & Entin, 1982a, for research dealing with the functional role of importance for positive self-evaluation). The structure of the self-system results from the functional property of personality to maximize positive value—in short, to find out and feel good about onself.

Value in the Behavioral and Self-Systems

Value in the Behavioral System

Value in the behavioral system refers to the attractiveness or repulsiveness of the informational and affective consequences of *outcomes of action*. Motivation for action is seen as a multiplicative function of the value of an outcome and the expectancy of attaining, maintaining, or evaluating that outcome (Raynor & Entin, 1982b). When an outcome is psychologically distant in the behavioral system, action results spontaneously from the interaction between value (i.e., retrospected or anticipated consequences of action) and characteristics of the individual. Both information and affective value in the behavioral system result spontaneously from experiencing the outcomes of action. For example, placing one's hand on a hot stove has both informational (e.g., "I burned my hand by placing it on the stove") and affective consequences (e.g., "My burned hand hurts"). Actions and cognitions are consequences of arousal in the behavioral system without phenomenal self-awareness. Neither thought nor action in the behavioral system is mediated by, or requires, conscious self-awareness. Obviously, people attend to and may be aware of different sources of value in the behavioral system. But phenomenal self-awareness is not necessary for personality functioning in the behavioral system.

Value in the Self-System

Motivation in the self-system, however, does require phenomenal awareness of a source of value associated with an ability, attribute, or self-image. Affective value in the self-system refers to positive and negative esteem income (i.e., answering the question "How good or bad do I feel about myself?"). Information value in the self-system refers to phenomenal clarity or confusion derived from perceived abilities, attributes, and self-images (i.e., answering the question "Who am I?"). In other words, people's phenomenal, time-linked abilities, attributes, and self-images provide value in the self-system.

People with phenomenal self-systems are motivated to maximize positive value and minimize negative value regarding their past ("who I have been") and future self-images ("who I am becoming") as well as their currently possessed abilities and attributes. Motivation for self-evaluation is a multiplicative function of the expectancy of attaining, maintaining, or evaluating a particular ability, attribute, or self-image and the amount of value associated with it. In the self-system, outcome expectancies refer to the probabilities of recalling, attaining, maintaining, or evaluating a particular attribute or self-image that serves as a source of value.

Information Versus Affective Value in the Self-System

We distinguish between time-linked self-images and the amount of positive or negative value associated with them. Time-linked abilities, attributes, or self-images define the substance of the self as a phenomenological construct. Value, however, is defined in quantitative terms. More specifically, positive information value in the self-system refers to the extent to which an individual feels he or she knows or is clear about a particular time-linked ability, attribute, or self-image. Negative information value refers to the extent to which an individual is ambiguous or confused about a particular ability, attribute, or self-image. Positive affective value in the self-system refers to the extent to which an individual feels good about a particular time-linked ability, attribute, or self-image. Negative affective value refers to the extent to which an individual feels bad about a particular ability, attribute, or self-image. Although information value and affective value are conceptualized in parallel fashion, they may operate orthogonally. In other words, being clear about one's self-image does not necessarily imply feeling good about it, and being confused about one's self-image does not necessarily imply feeling bad about it.

In addition, a particular self-image may have both informational and affective value to an individual. For example, a student who anticipates that he or she will become competent in math can both clarify his or her future self-image as a math student and make himself or herself feel good. All combinations of affective and information value are possible in a given situation.

The primary goal or threat in an individual's self-system depends on the amount and direction of both affective and information value for that individual. When information value is relatively strong and affective value is relatively weak, finding out and remaining clear about the self will be the primary goal in the self-system, whereas the primary threat will be confusion and ambiguity about the self (e.g., clarity versus confusion about one's competence or incompetence in math). Conversely, when affective value is strong and information value weak, feeling good about the self will be the primary goal in the self-system, whereas feeling bad about the self will be the primary threat (e.g., feeling good versus feeling bad about one's competence or incompetence in math).

When both affective and information value are weak, however, motivation in the self-system will be negligible. In this case, the self-system will have little impact on behavior, and self-consciousness will be minimal. Action can then be accounted for primarily via behavioral system functioning.

Stability Versus Change in the Self-System

An important implication of this theory is that there are no necessarily stable structural elements in the phenomenal self-system. The relative stability of the self-system depends on the relative stability of sources and amounts of value. If the source and amount of value remains constant, then the self-system will be "stable." If value changes, old self-images will disappear and new ones will emerge if they are associated with substantial positive value. This idea is congruent with the notion of "dynamic self-concept" elaborated by Cantor, Markus, Niedenthal, and Nurius in Chapter 4 of this volume. In our terminology, Cantor *et al.* suggest that an individual may have a number of self-images in his or her self-system. The influence of a particular self-image on behavior will depend, however, on how much positive or negative value that self-image holds for the individual at a given point in time.

In our view, the stable functions of personality are to maximize positive and minimize negative value. We distinguish, however, between personality and the self-system. The self-system refers to phenomenological concepts (self-images) that have clear implications regarding the perceived importance of activities for positive or negative self-evaluation.

Negative Affective Value and the Self-System

An obvious question arises concerning "negative" self-images. How does this position account for people with clear, negative self-images (e.g., "I am stupid")? We predict that a negative self-image will not emerge if affective value is the only determinant of self-system functioning. Negative self-images can provide people with a large amount of positive information value, and this positive information value may override the negative affective value associated with a "negative" self-image. For example, an individual may have a clear, well-maintained self-image as someone who is "unintelligent," because it is the only way that individual can have a clear self-identity (i.e., answering the question, "Who am I?"). The positive information value obtained by having such clarity about the self may overwhelm the negative affective cultural value associated with the self-image of "unintelligent." In other words, resultant positive information value can motivate the emergence of a clear but affectively negative self-image. Any behavior directed toward finding out about, clarifying, and knowing oneself may ultimately lead to a self-attribution that produces a relatively stable *negative* self-image if negative affective value is associated with that self-image.

Negative Affective Value and Psychological Defensiveness

We argue that the strong negative value associated with self-images eventually leads either to self-destructive behavior or to the mobilization of the kind of psychological defenses characterized in psychodynamic approaches to personality functioning (cf. Janis, 1969). Automatic (i.e., unconscious) psychological defenses are triggered when the negative affective value associated with self-images becomes so intense that self-destructive thoughts and actions may result. Psychological defenses, once implemented, change the motivational dynamics in the self-system. The individual who is "protected" by these defenses is now primarily motivated to minimize negative value rather than to maximize positive value (informational and affective). The individual's phenomenal self-system is no longer functional, because psychological defenses now preclude phenomenal self-awareness. The mobilization of such defenses to minimize negative value is a function of *personality* rather than of the self-system.

This position can account for the "abnormal" motivation of certain people and can integrate the functioning of normal and abnormal motivation. There are two kinds of "abnormal" functioning without a phenomenal self-system: (1) when positive information and affective value are minimal and (2) when negative affective value predominates. The former case is exemplified by the "apathetic" individual, who is indifferent to self-relevant information because it does not result in feeling either good or bad. The latter case is exemplified by the alcoholic, who has psychological defenses mobilized that preclude phenomenal self-awareness (Johnson, 1973).

The Psychological Career: An Integrative Concept

Up to this point, we have discussed value separately in terms of the behavioral and self-systems. We have linked value to outcomes in the behavioral system and to phenomenal abilities, attributes, and self-images in the self-system. We use the integrative concept of *psychological career* to deal with those people for whom value is available in *both* the behavioral and self-systems. People with an emergent self-system possess a source of motivational impetus in addition to that provided by the behavioral system when the outcomes of action in the behavioral system define the emergent self-system. We refer to this dual functioning as a psychological career— that is, a behavioral opportunity for phenomenal self-identity.

More specifically, when an individual's phenomenal self is seen in terms of the outcomes of action, arousal occurs simultaneously in both behavioral and self-systems. When large amounts of value are involved, the outcomes of action are perceived to be important for positive or negative self-evaluation. As a behavioral opportunity for phenomenal self-identity, the psychological career is the concept that integrates the study of the determinants of thought and action (motivation) with the development and functioning of the self-system.

In a psychological career, people are motivated both to find out who they are and to feel good about themselves when information *and* affective value are positive and come from the same source. When value is positive, the behavioral opportunity is represented as (1) an opportunity for positive self-evaluation and (2) the immediate next step in a path toward attaining some future goal, evaluating some present outcome, or maintaining some past accomplishment. In this context, change in the phenomenal self-system results from (1) the emergence of particular substantive psychological careers, (2) the disappearance of a psychological career when the self is no longer defined in terms of the outcomes of action associated with that career path, and (3) alterations in psychological careers determined by changes in time-linked sources of value (from the anticipated future, the evaluated present, and the retrospected past).

A psychological career emerges when an individual perceives that substantial amounts of positive value may be obtained from the outcomes of activities associated with a particular life path. "Knowing who I am" and "feeling good about myself" become tied to the outcomes of action along this path. Younger people tend to emphasize the future to find out who they will become and to feel good about themselves. Older people tend to emphasize the past to be certain of who they have become and to feel good about their past accomplishments. In other words, the study of stages of striving in a psychological career (cf. Brown, 1982; Raynor, 1982b; Raynor & Brown, in press) has important implications for the study of motivation and the self-system.

Changes in phenomenal self-identity result when new psychological careers replace old ones as predominant sources of positive value. This occurs when major patterns of life activity change. Such changes have a major impact on the content and structure of the self-system—for example, when new competencies are required as prerequisites for success along a new career path. An "identity crisis" results when people no longer know and feel good about who they are becoming, who they have been, or what attributes currently define them. People who pursue the same substantive life path will have much greater stability in the structure of their self-systems than people who make major changes in life activities. The particular structure and ordering of life paths interacts with people's personal sources of value to determine the various psychological careers that are pursued in life activity.

At this juncture, we would like to point out that our conceptualization of psychological career bears striking similarity to Cantor *et al.*'s notion of "predominant life tasks" (see Chapter 4 of this volume). On the other hand, Cantor *et al.*'s interpretation of the functional consequences of psychological careers is more cognitively orientated than ours.

REINTERPRETING THEORY AND RESEARCH FROM THE SELF LITERATURE

The basic elements of our theory have now been presented. We have argued elsewhere (Raynor, 1982b) that different theories in psychology have dealt with different aspects of time-linked sources of value. Traditional expectancy-value theory has dealt primarily with the anticipated future (cf. Atkinson & Raynor, 1974). Cognitive consistency theory has dealt primarily with the retrospected past (cf. Festinger, 1957). Theories concerned with information seeking and processing have dealt primarily with the evaluated present (cf. Trope, 1975). Finally, theories concerned with psychological defenses have dealt primarily with circumstances in which the predominance of negative value leads to unconscious motivation concerned with its removal (cf. Janis, 1969).

We now turn to a reinterpretation and reanalysis of theory and research from the self literature. We use our theoretical framework (1) to redefine conceptual variables used in the self literature, (2) to reassess current methodological issues relevant to self-esteem, and (3) to reinterpret research concerned with self-enhancement, self-evaluation maintenance, self-consistency, self-confirmation, and self-assessment.

Reevaluating Conceptual Variables in the Self-System

The "self" in our framework refers to phenomenal time-linked abilities, attributes, and self-images. In other words, we define what many theorists call the "self-concept" in terms of a person's phenomenal self-descriptions (abilities, attributes, and self-images) of who he or she has been, is now, and is becoming. As pointed out earlier, the view of self as a phenomenal entity is one shared by many theorists (Combs, 1981). We disagree with those theorists (e.g., Allport, 1955; Lecky, 1945) who also assume (1) that a person's sense of self always consists of an organized set of perceptions and (2) that people *need* a "self-theory" (i.e., a self-concept) to organize their life experiences. In our framework, there is no principle that *necessitates* viewing the self as a set of organized perceptions. Furthermore, we argue that there is no need for a self-system *per se*; people can function without a phenomenal self-system. Our basic motivational principles—that people are motivated to maximize positive and to minimize negative value—are functions of *personality*. But these principles are *not* linked to phenomenal self-awareness. We can specify the actions of people who lack a phenomenal sense of self for a particular path in society, substantive ability, attribute, or self-image by applying these principles within either (1) the behavioral system or (2) a system characterized by unconscious psychological defenses.

The Self as Process

Although it is not a new issue (cf. James, 1890), a number of theorists within the self literature have recently argued that the self-concept can be viewed as a *process* as well as a cognitive structure (cf. Markus, 1980). The self can be thought of as a continuing process of information search, interpretation, and assimilation that also contributes to the structure of the self-concept. The distinction between self as structure and self as process has been made quite eloquently by Markus (1977, 1980; Markus, Smith, & Moreland, 1982). Markus defines the self-concept as a set of self-schemata that both structure the individual's experience and aid in the processing of self-relevant information. A self-schema is conceived as a "cognitive generalization about the self, derived from past experience, that organizes and guides the processing of self-relevant information contained in the individual's social experiences" (Markus, 1977, p. 64).

In our framework, the self-system involves a self-evaluative process in which the individual is motivated to find out (information value) and feel good (affective value) about particular time-linked self-images. Thus, process goes beyond merely organizing information. It determines the direction, vigor, and persistence of action, particularly along life paths that are important for positive self-evaluation—that is, in a psychological career (cf. Brown, 1982; Raynor, 1982a, 1982b; Raynor & Brown, in press).

However, both traditional "structured content" and newer "process-oriented" approaches to the self-system tend to be too limited in scope. For example, Markus's self-schemata are defined only in terms of *past* experience. Similarly, Wylie (1979) argues that the "structured content" of the self-concept (i.e., organized perceptions regarding one's abilities and attributes) is derived from *past* experience. Wylie also contends that people possess an "ideal self" that is based on some anticipated *future* self-image. Our approach, in contrast, considers past, present, and anticipated future experiences that may have an impact on self-relevant cognitions. We argue, for instance, that the "ideal self" may encompass past self-images that the individual would like to maintain (particularly older individuals) and that self-schemata may be defined in terms of future abilities, attributes, and self-images that the individual anticipates (particularly younger individuals).

Level of Possession, Expectancy, and Value

In our view, researchers need to draw clear distinctions between conceptual variables that are often confounded in both structure- and process-oriented approaches to the self-system. We make explicit conceptual distinctions among (1) the degree of possession of some attribute, competence, and so forth, as representing the substantive focus of the individual's present self-image; (2) the degree of confidence (expectancy) in attaining or maintaining some outcome for which a given substantive attribute is believed to be a necessary prerequisite; and (3) affective evaluations (positive and negative) associated with both the perceived level of possession of specific attributes and more global perceptions of competence or incompetence. Although degree of possession of certain attributes, level of self-confidence, and affective reactions may be positively correlated, they are conceptually distinct variables that should be examined systematically but given separate conceptual status in a theory integrating self- and behavioral system functioning. This is particularly necessary when considering degree of possession of attributes or self-images that have negative affective value.

Some Methodological Issues

Assessing Self-Esteem

The "evaluative aspect" of the self-system, self-esteem, is perhaps the most widely assessed concept relevant to the self in the literature. This is partly because of the ease of operationalizing self-esteem (as opposed to tapping into specific content areas or structural components within the self-system). In addition, the fact that researchers have been able to derive ostensibly clear-cut predictions regarding the effects of individual differences in self-esteem on behavior from "competing" theoretical perspectives (see later discussion) has undoubtedly contributed to the ever-growing self-esteem literature.

The concept of self-esteem has been assessed using scales originally designed to tap global self-worth (e.g., the Rosenberg, 1965, scale), social competencies (e.g., the Janis & Field, 1959, scale), and self-esteem in children (e.g., the Coopersmith, 1967, self-esteem inventory). Hundreds of paper-and-pencil "self-esteem" scales are currently available (Wylie, 1979). As Robinson and Shaver (1978) have pointed out, however, there is a general lack of good evidence concerning the reliability and validity (construct, discriminant, and convergent) of these instruments. Unfortunately, researchers tend to assume that these instruments have generic properties—that is, that all scales are equally good at assessing something called self-esteem.

Wylie (1979) noted that self-esteem research continues to suffer from a variety of unresolved measurement and methodological problems. These problems are traceable to what we argue has been the tendency of researchers to confound three conceptually distinct variables in their assessment of self-esteem: (1) level of possession of some more or less positively or negatively valued attributes, (2) cognitive expectations regarding the attainment, maintenance, or removal of a particular source of value (e.g., expectations concerning the attainment of a successful career or failure on a task), and (3) affective value associated with the possession of some level of positively or negatively valued attributes.

In our theory, self-esteem refers to positive and negative affective value in the self-system (i.e., esteem income); level of possession of attributes refers to the structural components of the self-system; and motivation in the self-system is a multiplicative function of value and the expectancy of experiencing it. From our perspective, using instruments that combine these three distinct variables invites conceptual ambiguity (see Janis & Field, 1959, and Helmreich & Stapp, 1974, for examples of scales assessing at least two of these types of variables).

Self-Esteem as an Independent and Dependent Variable

An important issue concerns how self-esteem should best be operationalized as an independent or dependent variable. As an independent variable, self-esteem tends to be conceptualized as a reflection of level of competency, specific or general (positive information value). Nicholls, Licht, and Pearl (1982) made the point that high self-esteem most often means high perceived competence, whereas low self-esteem means low perceived competence. High self-esteem people are often thought of as being highly self-confident people who expect success, whereas low self-esteem people lack confidence and expect failure (cf. Ellis & Taylor, 1983; McFarlin & Blascovich, 1981). But it is the difference in *perceived competence* that provides the basis for hypothesized differences in self-confidence and subsequent behavior (e.g., persistence, performance).

Researchers who use self-esteem as an independent measure often use categories created by median splits on the distribution of available self-esteem scores. Swann (1983) pointed out that this technique may be problematic when distributions of scores are skewed. He argued that since self-esteem tends to be fairly high in college populations (the source of subjects for most laboratory research), what has been called "low" self-esteem is probably low *positive* self-esteem. He concluded that the current empirical ambiguity in the self literature may result partly from the methodology used to create self-esteem categories. With skewed distributions of scores, this methodology may prevent researchers from making clear tests of theoretically derived predictions relevant to high and low self-esteem people. From our perspective, it also prevents a distinction between positive and negative affective value associated with a level of possession of some attribute or competence.

As a dependent variable, self-esteem tends to be conceptualized in *affective* terms (Jones, 1973). Typically, some manipulation is introduced to effect change in subjects' self-esteem, with change being described in terms of increases or decreases in good or bad feeling about the self (either in general or with regard to specific competencies). But many measures of self-esteem contain items that reflect both level of possession of an attribute (e.g., "I see myself as socially skilled") and affective reactions (e.g., "I feel good about myself").

From our perspective, resolving the foregoing measurement and methodological issues requires restricting the concept of positive and negative self-esteem to affective evaluations (i.e., distinct from the concept of the degree of possession of an attribute, set of attributes, or overall competence). Operationally, we would assess self-esteem in terms of "feeling good or bad about yourself." For example, such questions as "How necessary is seeing yourself as a hard worker for feeling good about yourself?" or "How necessary is getting a good grade in this course for feeling good about yourself?" are consistent with our conceptual definition of self-esteem. On the other hand, such questions as "To what extent do you see yourself as being a hard worker?" or "How competent do you now believe yourself to be as a parent?" are consistent with our conceptual definition of degree of possession of an attribute (cf. Raynor, 1982a; Raynor, Atkinson, & Brown, 1974; Raynor & English, 1982). This operational distinction allows for empirical investigation of the relationship between ratings of degree of possession of some attribute and (1) the subjective probability of success (confidence) when utilizing that attribute and (2) the amount of self-esteem or esteem income associated with possessing a given level of that attribute. Our definition of self-esteem allows us to be very specific in terms of the important sources of affective value for people's self-systems.

Our restricted definition of self-esteem as esteem income (affective value in the self-system) suggests that researchers should not use traditional measurement instruments when self-esteem is to be treated as an independent variable. To treat self-esteem as an independent variable requires that researchers place people into categories based on their endorsement of items assessing the level of *positive and negative* affective value (esteem income) and on separate items assessing levels of possession of self-relevant attributes. This would result, for example, in people being described as having either high-positive, low-positive, neutral, low-negative, or high-negative esteem income and being high, moderate, or low on degree of possession of self-relevant attributes. The result of using scales that often confound level of possession of an attribute, confidence, and esteem income is conceptual ambiguity. This is particularly the case when (1) positive versus negative affectively valued attributes are compared and (2) correlations are obtained between "self-esteem" and degree of possession of a negatively valued attribute. In fact, previous theories have tended not to distinguish between level of possession and value *associated with* level of possession.

What is often seen in the literature are such statements as "high self-esteem subjects are predicted to expect success" and "high self-esteem subjects should feel better after success than low self-esteem subjects." As descriptions of empirical findings, these statements reflect two ways of measuring the same construct when items assessing level of possession, self-confidence, and good or bad feelings are included in a measure of self-esteem. Rather than providing implications for construct validity of a theory of self-system functioning, these statements refer more to measurement issues. They reflect different methods of measuring the same thing, or convergent validity (Campbell & Fiske, 1959). Since the various measures of self-esteem often measure more than one construct (i.e., level of possession, confidence, and affective value), the discovery of positive associations between these measures and perceived ability, confidence, and affective self-evaluations adds little to the construct validity of a theory in which the meaning of self-esteem is embedded. Positive correlations between degree of possession, confidence, and positive affect do, however, provide a set of empirical relationships to be explained by a theory of self-system functioning (Raynor, 1982a, 1982b). This is particularly the case when degree of possession of certain attributes is *not* found to correlate positively with confidence or positive affect. We would predict just such a lack of positive association for an attribute that has little positive or negative affective value associated with it. For example, most middle-aged adults probably have very little affective value associated with their driving skills. For most of these people, driving is taken for granted and is simply not very important in terms of their self-systems. Thus, for these people, we would expect a weak relationship between driving ability and positive affect (esteem income). A stronger relationship, however, might be expected for 16-year-olds. For many adolescents, being able to drive represents a significant "rite of passage" into adulthood.

Value in the Self-System and Laboratory Research

This brings us to a major methodological issue heretofore not addressed. The widespread use of research paradigms in which input involving the self is provided in a laboratory context has the disadvantage of often dealing with aspects of the self-system of little value to the individual. Exceptions to this include the presentation of attributes (e.g., intelligence) that are widely recognized by subjects both as having large positive affective value and as being prerequisites for important life activity. We acknowledge that laboratory research is valuable and essential because of the degree of control it provides, but we must not lose sight of the ultimate goal—to understand and predict life activity. An exclusive emphasis on laboratory research paradigms may preclude investigation of important (value-laden) self-relevant information. On the other hand, successful induction of large negative value in laboratory settings carries with it an ethical responsibility not to produce permanent psychological harm to the subject. What often happens is that an implicit or explicit "contract" is entered into between the researcher and subjects to the effect that there is no link between what occurs in the laboratory and important life behavior. In effect, such an understanding prevents the functioning of large negative affective value and precludes the study of motivation to minimize large negative affective value.

PERSPECTIVES FROM THE SELF LITERATURE

In this section, we consider theory and related research from five theoretical perspectives: (1) self-enhancement, (2) self-evaluation maintenance, (3) self-consistency, (4) self-confirmation, and (5) self-assessment. Since much of the research cited in this section employed traditional measures of self-esteem, it is difficult, in terms of our theory, to know whether affective value (esteem income), confidence, or level of perceived possession of an attribute was being addressed. For the sake of clarity, however, our use of the terms "high self-esteem" and "low self-esteem" in this section should be interpreted as assuming high-positive affective value in the self-system and high-negative affective value in the self-system, respectively.

Reinterpreting Self-Enhancement Theory and Research

Several theorists have endorsed the idea that individuals are self-enhancing. For example, self-enhancement is an important part of Thibaut and Kelley's (1959) social exchange theory and the self theories of Epstein (1973), Snygg and Combs (1949), and Rogers (1951).

According to the self-enhancement position, people have a need to maximize self-esteem or, to use our terminology, to maximize positive affective value in the self-system. If this need is not satisfied, it becomes stronger (in a drive sense). The self-enhancement view predicts that all people should react more favorably to positive evaluations (even if unexpected) and less favorably to negative evaluations (even if expected). In addition, those with the greatest need for favorable self-perceptions (i.e., low self-esteem people) should react most favorably to positive evaluations and least favorably to negative evaluations.

More recently, some researchers have conceptualized self-enhancement and self-consistency as competing motives (cf. Dipboye, 1977; Jones, 1973). Although evidence from the self literature suggests that "competing" may not be the right word (McFarlin & Blascovich, 1981), this position has led researchers interested in the self to test the sometimes contrasting predictions made by the self-enhancement and self-consistency theorists. Unfortunately, however, most efforts in this regard have tended to focus on either cognitive (informational) or affective reactions to evaluation—rarely both.

As Shrauger (1975) has noted, the strongest evidence supporting the self-enhancement perspective comes from studies assessing *affective reactions* to evaluation—for example, task enjoyment, satisfaction with evaluation, attraction for the evaluator. Some research also suggests that certain *behavioral reactions* to evaluation may plausibly be interpreted in terms of self-enhancement (McFarlin, 1984). In terms of affective reactions to evaluation, however, the general finding is that people, regardless of their level of self-esteem, react more favorably to positive feedback than to negative feedback.

We interpret this general self-enhancement finding as meaning that people feel good (positive affective value) following success and feel bad (negative affective value) following failure. We believe that the concept of self-enhancement as used by researchers in the self literature usually refers to motivation to maximize positive affective value in the self-system (with information value being held constant). In our terms, when the goal of maximizing positive affective value is attained (e.g., via success) the individual feels good, whereas when he or she fails to minimize negative affective value (e.g., after failure) he or she feels bad.

This set of predictions is congruent with empirical findings in the self-enhancement literature. For example, subjects receiving positive feedback regarding task performance have been found to enjoy the task more (e.g., Leonard & Weitz, 1971), to be more satisfied with the feedback received (e.g., Feather, 1969; Shavit & Shouval, 1980), and to like the evaluator more (e.g., Dittes, 1959; Ilgen, 1971; Jacobs, Berscheid, & Walster, 1971; Krauss & Critchfield, 1975, Walster, 1965; Weaver & Brickman, 1974) than subjects receiving negative feedback, regardless of their level of self-esteem. In addition, McFarlin and Blascovich (1981) showed that subjects preferred success to failure on a future task, regardless of their level of self-esteem.

In terms of *behavioral reactions* to evaluation, some studies have been interpreted as showing support for the self-enhancement position. For instance, if people are self-enhancing and they believe success is possible, they should try to maximize their chances for success. This should especially be true for low self-esteem people. Relative to high self-esteem people, low self-esteem people have been shown to be especially likely to pursue positive outcomes if they believe the probability of success is high (cf. Sigall & Gould, 1977; Weiner, 1970, 1973).

Rather than interpreting these findings in terms of a need for self-enhancement, however, we argue that since they tend to feel worse about themselves than high self-esteem people do, low self-esteem people may be motivated to minimize negative affective value in most performance situations (information value being held constant). We interpret the fact that low self-esteem subjects tend to pursue positive outcomes if success appears likely in "one-shot" situations as behavior designed to minimize negative affective value. By succeeding in these "easy" performance situations, low self-esteem subjects anticipate reducing negative affective value associated with their bad feelings about themselves.

Although there has been a general finding that high self-esteem people tend to outperform low self-esteem people especially after failure (McFarlin, 1984; Shrauger, 1975, 1982), this does not necessarily imply that low self-esteem people lack a self-enhancement motive. When faced with failure, low self-esteem people may employ a self-enhancing strategy in which they "give up" to minimize the impact of future failure and preserve what little self-regard they have (Archibald, 1974). If failure occurs with such a self-handicapping strategy, the low self-esteem individual has a ready excuse—lack of effort (Jones & Berglas, 1978).

Several recent studies have suggested that it is high rather than low self-esteem people who employ a *compensatory* strategy following negative evaluations (Baumeister, 1982; McFarlin, Baumeister, & Blascovich, 1984; McFarlin & Blascovich, 1981). Baumeister (1982), for instance, confronted high and low self-esteem subjects with "negative" evaluations (in the form of bogus personality traits). Subjects were then asked to describe themselves to partners with whom they were to interact later. When high self-esteem subjects were under the impression that their partners were aware of their "negative" personality traits, their self-descriptions did not directly contradict these "bad" aspects but stressed unrelated positive traits. In their interactions with their partners, however, high self-esteem subjects did behave in ways that directly disconfirmed the negative trait information. This phenomenon has been labeled "compensatory self-enhancement" (Baumeister & Jones, 1978). Low self-esteem subjects, on the other hand, appeared to conform to negative evaluations presented to their partners, in terms of both their self-descriptions and their subsequent behavior. We reinterpret the tendency of low self-esteem people to engage in "self-handicapping" and high self-esteem people to engage in "compensatory self-enhancement" in terms of positive and negative affective value.

Rather than seeing self-handicapping as a self-protective strategy (motivated by a need for self-enhancement), we argue that the anticipation of future failure (i.e., psychological distance greater than zero) will be a source of great negative affective value (holding information value constant) for low self-esteem people. These people should be motivated to resist thoughts or actions expected to produce negative affective value. One way to accomplish this would be to avoid any behaviors that might lead to failure that could be attributed to the self. Thus, "giving up" or not exerting much effort would be one method of ensuring that subsequent failure will be attributed to lack of effort, not lack of ability.

On the other hand, a failure experience simply increases motivation to do well for high self-esteem people. Anticipated future success takes on greater positive affective (difficulty) value. This can account for the tendency of high self-esteem people to predict higher levels of future success for themselves (McFarlin & Blascovich, 1981) and exert more effort to succeed (McFarlin *et al.*, 1984) following failure, rather than success.

The Baumeister (1982) study, however, requires more explanation. For high self-esteem subjects, the negative personality profiles probably were a source of negative information value (i.e., potentially confusing) *and* negative affective value. By stressing unrelated positive traits (i.e., minimizing feeling bad) and rejecting the negative profile directly via interaction with a partner (i.e., minimizing confusion), high self-esteem subjects may have been able to remove experienced negative value. On the other hand, low self-esteem subjects' acceptance of the negative profiles suggests that the resultant motivation was due to positive information value (i.e., negative personality profiles were seen as *valid*, providing clarity).

Reinterpreting Self-Evaluation Maintenance Theory and Research

The term "self-evaluation maintenance" (formerly "self-esteem maintenance") continues to be associated with the work of Tesser and his colleagues (Tesser, 1980; Tesser & Campbell, 1980, 1982, 1983; Tesser & Paulhus, 1983; Tesser & Smith, 1980). Basically, they have proposed a model to account for the effects that social relationships have on self-evaluation.

The self-evaluation maintenance (SEM) model has two basic assumptions: (1)

individuals are motivated to maintain positive self-evaluations, and (2) social relationships have important effects on self-evaluation. The impact of social relationships on self-evaluation is described in terms of two processes: (1) reflection—the extent to which people try to enhance their own self-evaluation by "magnifying" the achievement of others—that is, "basking in reflected glory" (Cialdini et al., 1976); and (2) comparison—the extent to which people's self-evaluation suffers when they compare their achievements in an area to others' achievements. Both processes depend on an "interactive combination" of two variables—closeness and performance. People who are "close" (e.g., relatives) and perform well will have a greater impact on an individual's self-evaluation than people who are "distant" (e.g., strangers) and perform poorly. "Relevance" determines which process will dominate in a given situation. Essentially, others' performances are relevant if they have implications for attributes considered important to the individual's self-definition. Tesser argued that when others' performances are relevant, the comparison process dominates, whereas reflection dominates when relevance is low (see Tesser and Campbell, 1983, for a detailed treatment of the SEM model).

The SEM assumption that people are motivated to maintain positive self-evaluations is congruent with a self-enhancement position. Although the model represents a more unified and more systematic theoretical position than traditional self-enhancement approaches, it is limited to the extent that it does not (1) distinguish between positive and negative value (information and affective) and (2) allow for time-linked sources of value (past, present, future). The closest the model comes to our conception of value is the contention that, depending on the situation, people will attempt either to maximize positive self-evaluations or to minimize loss to self-evaluation (Tesser & Campbell, 1983). Similarly, "closeness" is not synonymous with our conception of psychological distance, because it is based on proximity or similarity rather than on time (i.e., experiencing versus recalling or anticipating). The SEM model basically attempts to predict how situational variables associated with social relationships shape self-definition. It is not, as Tesser and Campbell (1983) admit, a model that can account for individual differences. We can plausibly reinterpret the SEM research in terms of our framework.

The SEM research typically involves a paradigm in which subjects are given the opportunity to maximize gain or minimize loss in self-evaluation by changing the interpretation of others' performance, closeness, or relevance in a given situation (Tesser & Campbell, 1983). By manipulating two of these three variables, specific predictions regarding the remaining variable can be made using the model. Usually, pairs of subjects are asked to perform some task that has vague or nonobvious implications for possession of particular skills or attributes. This ostensibly allows for facile manipulations or performance feedback or relevance of the task.

For example, Tesser and Smith (1980) asked two pairs of male friends to work together on a word identification task. Subjects were told either that the task assessed important verbal skills (i.e., high relevance) or that it was unrelated to important skills (i.e., low relevance). Each person took turns trying to identify words on the basis of clues provided by other members of the work group. The results showed that when task relevance was high, those subjects who were given negative feedback regarding their ability to identify words subsequently were more likely to try to hinder the performance of others in their group (by providing difficult clues) than when task relevance was low. This was especially true for friends. Subjects gave easier clues to friends than to strangers, however, when task relevance was low. Congruent with the SEM model, these findings suggested that relevance has an important impact on whether the reflection or comparison process will dominate in a given situation.

Other tests of the SEM model have controlled performance and closeness and have treated relevance as the major dependent variable. For example, Tesser and Campbell (1982) had subjects perform two separate tasks (one assessing "social sensitivity," the other assessing "esthetic judgment") with a confederate. Subjects were told that the confederate was either a "close" or a "distant" other. Subjects were asked to rate the relevance of the tasks to their own self-definition both before and after they completed the experiment. Congruent with the SEM model, subjects who were outperformed by the confederate on one of the two tasks reduced the perceived self-relevance of that task, especially when the confederate was seen as a "close" other.

We reinterpret the SEM research as supporting our basic contention that people are motivated to maximize positive value and to minimize negative value. As was the case with the self-enhancement literature, "value" within the context of SEM research seems to mean *affective value* (information value being held constant). Without refering to a need for self-evaluation maintenance *per se*, we predict that in situations in which the reflection process operates (i.e., irrelevant task dimension, close other), people are trying to maximize positive affective value in the *behavioral system* by "basking in reflected glory." We assume that if a particular attribute is really irrelevant to the phenomenal self-system, then the motivating source of value must lie within the behavioral system. In short, people who exemplify the "reflective process" are trying to "feel good," not "feel good about themselves." Conversely, people who attempt to hinder the performance of close others on self-relevant attributes (i.e., exemplifying the comparison process) are trying to minimize experienced negative affective value in the self-system.

To be sure, the methodology used in many SEM laboratory studies may make our reinterpretation problematic. Typically, ambiguous tasks are used to manipulate performance or induce self-relevance on fictitious traits. It is unclear, therefore, how "relevant" such tasks are to subjects in any absolute sense (e.g., in terms of esteem income or level of competence). The positive information and affective value provided by these tasks may be minimal. The use of this methodology may partially explain the failure of SEM research to find any strong links between such individual-difference variables as self-esteem and so-called SEM strategies (see Tesser & Campbell, 1983). If these tasks and the attributes they ostensibly reflect are irrelevant to the self-system, predictions relevant to self-esteem cannot be made.

On the other hand, Tesser has also conducted several nonlaboratory tests of the SEM model with generally supportive results (see Chapter 12 of this volume), and he argues that these studies did tap self-relevant traits that were "important" to people (A. Tesser, personal communication, May 15, 1984). Assuming that Tesser's contention is correct, we must nevertheless point out that from our perspective, the SEM model fails to distinguish among (1) affective and information value (positive and negative), (2) behavioral and self-systems, and (3) different time-linked sources of value. Reconceptualizing the SEM model to account for these distinctions would transform it into a model that could make predictions regarding individual differences in perceptions of social relationships.

Reinterpreting Self-Consistency Theory and Research

The basic idea behind consistency theory is quite simple: Individuals are motivated to maintain consistency in the attitudes and beliefs they hold. This notion is a key element in several theories, such as the balance theories of Heider (1958) and Newcomb (1959, 1961), Festinger's (1957) cognitive dissonance theory, Korman's (1970) theory of work motivation and occupational choice, and Osgood and Tannenbaum's (1955) congruity theory.

Self-concept theorists have also emphasized the importance of self-consistency. Lecky (1945), for example, concluded that people have only one basic self need—to maintain self-consistency. Other self theorists have suggested that although individuals have a number of basic needs, self-consistency is of critical importance (e.g., Epstein, 1973; Rogers, 1951; Snygg & Combs, 1949).

Many theorists contend that maintaining self-consistency is necessary for psychological survival. To maintain consistency with respect to the attitudes one holds toward oneself is to preserve the integrity and unity of the self-concept system one has developed. As Lecky (1969) has argued, it is the individual's unified conceptual system (i.e., the structured, organized way people view themselves and the world around them) that allows him or her to bring predictability and order to an otherwise incoherent world of experience. Failure to uphold what Lecky calls the "principle of unity" (self-consistency) invites disorganization of the conceptual system. The result of this would be the "death" of one's personality. In effect, many self-consistency theorists seem to have a *reactive* view of the self-concept. An implicit underlying assumption for these theorists is that the adult person *has* an organized, unified self that he or she is motivated to defend (i.e., the conceptual starting point is a unified, organized sense of self).

In our framework, however, we view the concept of self-consistency as defined by self theorists as an *outcome* rather than a goal in the self-system. We do not posit a need for self-consistency, just as we do not posit the need for a self-system. We cannot agree with the assumption that all adults have an organized, unified sense of self that they are motivated to defend. In our view, self-consistency is merely a descriptive term, and we take it upon ourselves to specify the conditions under which this term will apply to the outcomes of thought or action. Thus, we reinterpret research findings said to support the existence of a "need" for self-consistency in terms of the outcomes of people's motivation to maximize positive and minimize negative value.

To test the extent to which a need for self-consistency exists, psychologists have typically employed a paradigm in which subjects who differ in their level of self-esteem (as assessed by traditional instruments) are given either positive or negative evaluations (about their performance on a task, personality traits, etc.). Subjects' affective, cognitive, and behavioral reactions to such feedback are then assessed. The rationale behind this paradigm is as follows. As the evaluative component of the self-concept, self-esteem involves expectancies for success and failure based on past experience (Cohen, 1959). Thus, one would assume that high self-esteem people tend to deal with life confidently; they expect success and are accustomed to it; and they prefer to receive favorable feedback about themselves. On the other hand, one would assume that low self-esteem people tend to deal with life less confidently; they expect failure and are accustomed to it; and they are more willing to accept negative feedback (McFarlin & Blascovich, 1981; Schlenker, Soraci, & McCarthy, 1976).

Given these assumptions, the self-consistency position predicts that high self-esteem people will respond more favorably to positive evaluations (i.e., evaluations consistent with a high level of self-esteem) and less favorably to negative evaluations (i.e., evaluations inconsistent with a high level of self-esteem) than will low self-esteem people. This prediction has been labeled the "moderate consistency effect" (Shrauger, 1975). More controversial is the counterintuitive prediction that low self-esteem individuals should respond more favorably to negative (i.e., consistent) evaluations than positive (i.e., inconsistent) evaluations. In effect, low self-esteem individuals should embrace failure and avoid success to be consistent with their own negative expectancies. This prediction is known as the "strong consistency effect" (Shrauger, 1975).

The research evidence regarding these two basic self-consistency predictions is mixed. Very few studies support the "strong consistency effect" (see reviews by Dipboye, 1977; Shrauger, 1975). The "moderate" prediction enjoys considerable support, but as Shrauger (1975) has pointed out, it appears limited to cognitive (informational) responses to evaluation.

Our reinterpretation of the basic self-consistency paradigm is as follows. This paradigm involves assessing *reactions* to evaluative information. In our terms, this means that individuals are reacting to the experience of certain outcomes (i.e., psychological distance is zero). Thus, we can predict the conditions under which the strongest "self-consistency" patterns should be manifested. If evaluative information produces confusion in a particular self-image (i.e., is "inconsistent") and the resultant motivation is to reduce the confusion (i.e., to reduce negative information value), then we should see some kind of "rejection" of that "inconsistent" information as a way of reducing confusion. If, on the other hand, evaluative information produces clarity (i.e., is "consistent" with a particular self-image) and resultant motivation is to maintain that clarity (i.e., to maximize positive information value), then we should see some kind of "acceptance" of the "consistent" evaluative information as a way of maintaining clarity. Notice that the key notion here is *resultant motivation*. The so-called consistency effect, in its purest form, depends on the dominance of information value over affective value. When affective value in the self-system is weak, the primary goal is to find out, know, or remain clear about a self-image, and the primary threat is to face confusion, ambiguity, or uncertainty about a self-image. It is not surprising that the evidence supporting self-consistency theory tends to come primarily from studies with cognitive (i.e., informational) rather than affective assessments of reactions to evaluative information.

More specifically, we reinterpret self-consistency research assessing the reception or retention of evaluative information in terms of information value. To reduce confusion about a particular self-image, evaluative information "inconsistent" with that self-image may be distorted or inaccurately recalled. Conversely, information "consistent" with a particular self-image may be accurately recalled to maintain clarity (cf. Crary, 1966; Mischel, Ebbesen, & Zeiss, 1973; Shrauger, 1972; Shrauger & Terbovic, 1976; Silverman, 1964; Stotland, Thorley, Thomas, Cohen, & Zander, 1957; Suinn, Osborne, & Page, 1962). Similarly, people also tend to rate evaluations and evaluators that deliver self-consistent information as more credible (i.e., maximizing positive information value) than those that deliver self-inconsistent information (i.e., minimizing negative information value) (e.g., Crary, 1966; Shrauger & Kelly, 1984; Shrauger & Lund, 1975).

Reinterpreting Self-Confirmation Theory and Research

The term "self-confirmation," or "self-verification" has recently gained attention in the self literature as an important link between the self and behavior in evaluative settings. In reviewing the relevant literature, one cannot avoid noting the apparent similarity between this term and the concept of self-consistency.

The term "self-confirmation" was coined by Swann and his colleagues (Swann, 1982, 1983; Swann & Hill, 1982; Swann & Read, 1981a, 1981b; Swann, Read, & Hill, 1981). Their basic contention is that people are motivated to *actively* seek out information that confirms or verifies their own self-conceptions.

Swann *et al.* argue that people should be highly motivated to ensure their self-concept's reliability and predictive power. This entails more than simply reacting favorably to feedback that confirms self-perceptions; people should be motivated to seek out and elicit self-confirmatory information from others. This information-seeking propensity serves to "bring [people's] social environment into harmony with their self-conceptions" (Swann & Read, 1981b, p. 353).

Research conducted by Swann and his colleagues seems to support these ideas. For example, Swann and Read (1981b) found that subjects were more likely to seek (Exp. 1), elicit (Exp. 2), and accurately recall (Exp. 3) self-confirming information than self-disconfirming information. In Experiment 1, subjects who were "self-likable" (i.e., high in self-esteem) spent more time studying bogus statements from their "future conversation partners" when they suspected that the statements might indicate they were rated as likable than if they suspected that they might be rated not likable. The opposite pattern was found for "self-dislikables" (i.e., low in self-esteem). Thus, subjects appeared to be more interested in self-confirmatory information than in self-disconfirmatory information. In Experiment 2, prior to a "getting acquainted" conversation with "social interaction" partners, subjects were led to believe that their partners had already formed either a favorable or unfavorable impression of them. The results indicated that high self-esteem subjects succeeded in eliciting more favorable evaluations from their partners than did low self-esteem subjects. The tendency to elicit self-confirming evaluations was especially pronounced when subjects believed that their partners' initial impression might disconfirm their self-conceptions. It was also revealed that high self-esteem subjects tended to resort more to self-presentational tactics (e.g., praise, compliments) than low self-esteem subjects to elicit favorable evaluations. Finally, Experiment 3 demonstrated that both high and low self-esteem subjects tended to recall self-confirmatory appraisal information more than disconfirmatory information.

Swann contended that, taken together, his line of research indicates that people are both active information *seekers* and information *shapers*. People even appear willing to manipulate the environment to ensure that they will receive self-confirmatory feedback (Swann, 1982; Swann & Read, 1981b). What is unique about Swann's research is that it goes beyond existing self-consistency notions, with its emphasis on individuals as *proactive* rather than merely *reactive* in the quest for self-consistency.

In terms of our framework, Swann's research is similar to much of the work in the self-consistency area in that it tends to focus on cognition (i.e., information value). On the other hand, some of Swann's studies dealt with *anticipated* information value (i.e., where outcomes are psychologically distant), whereas most of the self-consistency literature tends to deal only with *experienced* information value. We reinterpret Swann's findings in terms of maximizing positive information value. We would argue, for example, that Swann and Read's (1981b, Exp. 1) subjects expected to clarify who they were; when they subsequently did so, they were maximizing positive information value. On the other hand, when people fail to minimize negative information value, they experience confusion about who they are. This motivates them to remove the confusion (but not necessarily strive for clarity) in a manner that depends on the resultant positive value of possible alternative actions. We would contend, for instance, that subjects in Swann and Read's (1981b, Exp. 3) study who were given self-disconfirming information were, in effect, confused by the experimental manipulation. Inaccurate recall of this information would be a way of minimizing negative information value (i.e., not thinking about the confusion).

We believe that Swann's evidence that people are active information seekers and information shapers is really a reflection of an experimentally induced opportunity to maximize positive information value—that is, to strive for clarity about oneself. If they were given such an opportunity, we would expect people to seek out self-confirming rather than self-disconfirming information if the resultant motivational impetus was to maximize positive information value. The fact that subjects in Swann *et al.*'s studies sought self-confirmatory information even when it had negative affective value (e.g., for the "self-dislikables") lends further credence to the suggestion that information value was dominant (i.e., stronger than affective value) in these investigations. We would not expect such an effect, however, when affective value is dominant.

Reinterpreting Self-Assessment Theory and Research

Possession of Attributes and Positive Value

A derivation of our position has to do with the implied positive association between level of possession of an attribute and positive value. For certain attributes (e.g., intelligence), increasing levels of possession are associated with increasing levels of positive affective value (difficulty value in the self-system). Knowing that one has a certain level of intelligence (high, moderate, low), however, yields an equivalent amount of positive information value. Research by Trope (1975; Trope & Brickman, 1975) disassociated an attribute from strong positive affective value and made people uncertain about how much of the attribute they possessed. Under these circumstances, they were motivated to find out more about their particular level of possession of that attribute, rather than to feel good about their level of possession.

In many cases, however, there is substantial affective value associated with a given attribute, particularly attributes that are important prerequisites for life success in various substantive areas (i.e., those with instrumental value in the self-system). When positive affective value is large, motivation to feel good about possession of an attribute increases as level of possession increases. We contend that when this occurs, motivation to find out about degree of possession should increase as anticipated level of possession increases because of positive affective value rather than positive information value.

Consistent with these ideas, work by Nochajski and Raynor (1984) found a substantial positive correlation for both male and female college students between degree of possession of a perceived attribute (athletic competence) and motivation to find out and demonstrate competence by engaging in sports competition. Similarly, when high possession of Trope's "integrative orientation" attribute was experimentally induced to have positive value (i.e., was desirable), subjects high in this attribute constructed a test of integrative orientation in a way that maximized their chances of scoring "high" relative to "low." Similarly, when low integrative orientation was seen as desirable, subjects low on this attribute constructed tests in a way that maximized their chance of scoring "low" relative to "high." When both high and low levels of integrative orientation were induced to have negative affective value (i.e., were undesirable), subjects high and low on this attribute constructed tests with greater zero diagnosticity; that is, they constructed tests so that they could not find out their respective levels of ability (Raynor & Nochajski, 1984).

In terms of our theory, demonstrating a high level of competence is not a goal of action *per se*. Rather, motivation to feel good (i.e., to maximize positive affective value) by demonstrating a high level of competence that has positive affective value is the goal of action. On the other hand, we predict resistance to finding out or demonstrating a highly negative attribute (e.g., selfishness). Raynor and Nochajski (1984) found just such an effect when "integrative orientation" was induced as an undesirable attribute. Although finding out one is smart provides both positive information and affective value, finding out one is selfish provides negative affective value and positive information value. Nicholls's (1984) contention that the goal of achievement-oriented activity is to demonstrate high ability may hold only because competence in such activity yields a large amount of positive affective value. People can feel good about demonstrating competence at achievement tasks. If certain achievement activities were seen primarily as diagnostic of negatively valued attributes such as incompetence, we predict that people would resist demonstrating their incompetence at these activities to minimize negative affective value (Raynor & Nochajski, 1984).

Individual Differences in Possession of Attributes and Positive Value

An important expansion of the present formulation into the realm of individual differences comes from research by Sorrentino and his colleagues (Sorrentino & Hewitt, 1984; Sorrentino, Short, & Raynor, 1984). These authors challenged Trope's (1975, 1979) arguments (1) that *all* people will make use of an opportunity to discover information about their own ability and (2) that differences in behavior often linked to achievement-related motives are actually due to relative differences in such cognitive information seeking (i.e., success-oriented persons being more interested than failure-threatened persons).

In an attempt to replicate Trope (1979), Sorrentino and Hewitt (1984) found (1) that uncertainty-oriented people appear to be interested in reducing uncertainty with regard to their ability, whereas certainty-oriented people actually avoid an opportunity to reduce such uncertainty; and (2) that success-oriented people approach and failure-threatened people avoid this opportunity *only* where the attribute could be one of high ability.

Sorrentino and Hewitt's explanation of these differences is similar to our approach in that they argue that uncertainty orientation is primarily concerned with cognitive information seeking, whereas achievement-related motives are primarily concerned with the affective consequences of success and failure. Put in our terms, the uncertainty-oriented person is high in the desire to attain clarity and low in the desire to avoid confusion. The certainty-oriented person, however, is more concerned with avoiding confusion than in attaining clarity. This individual does not, therefore, engage in situations that are initially confusing, even though such activity could ultimately reduce confusion. Congruent with these notions, uncertainty-oriented subjects in the Sorrentino and Hewitt (1984) study chose to be tested on items that would reduce uncertainty about their own ability, whereas certainty-oriented subjects avoided such items.

Differences in achievement-related motives are synonymous with our distinction between positive and negative affective value. Consistent with Raynor and Nochajski (1984), Sorrentino and Hewitt (1984) found that success-oriented subjects chose items that would tell them if they had high ability (because they anticipated feeling good about demonstrating high competence), whereas failure-threatened subjects avoided these items (because they anticipated feeling bad about failing to demonstrate high competence).

SUMMARY AND CONCLUSIONS

Implications for Theory and Research

Implications for Self-System Concepts

We have already noted that current definitions of self-concept and self-esteem confound several conceptual variables that researchers should assess orthogonally: level of possession of an attribute, cognitive expectations, and affective value. Traditional measures of self-esteem often provide a confounded index of motivational impetus. To the extent that such measures tap a positively correlated syndrome of high ability, confidence, and positive esteem income, affective value should dominate.

To use self-esteem as an independent variable requires greater precision than has been evidenced heretofore. There are many situations in which a positive correlation between high scores on traditional self-esteem measures and resultant positive affect may exist. On the other hand, low scores may be associated with resultant negative value. Thus, "high self-esteem" people may be motivated primarily to maximize affective positive value, whereas "low self-esteem" people may be motivated primarily to minimize negative affective value. In other situations, however, low self-esteem may be associated with weak affective value, and information value may dominate. In short, researchers should try to determine the level of positive and negative value (both informational and affective) before they attempt to predict actions and reactions to evaluative situations.

Implications for Self Theory and Research

Our *post hoc* reinterpretation of theory and research from the self literature presents a plausible alternative explanation for these findings. We recognize that this chapter is but a starting point for the development of research that will determine the utility and validity of our position. In general, we feel that the best way to test our theory is to design research that makes orthogonal assessments of affective and informational value (positive and negative) in a given situation. This would avoid some of the conceptual, measurement, and methodological problems already discussed.

We have reinterpreted positions referred to as self-enhancement, self-evaluation maintenance, self-consistency, self-confirmation, and self-assessment as different manifestations of the basic motivation to maximize positive value and minimize negative value. Research supporting self-enhancement and self-evaluation maintenance positions comes mainly from studies in which affective value appears to dominate, whereas support for self-consistency and self-confirmation comes mainly from studies in which information value appears to dominate. Support for the self-assessment position comes mainly from studies in which affective value is positive and subjects are unclear about their level of possession of an attribute. Interpretation of the motivation to demonstrate competence cannot ignore the role of affective value associated with level of possession of a competence. We interpret what researchers have called the "affective–cognitive dichotomy" in the self literature (cf. McFarlin, 1984; Shrauger, 1975) in a fairly simple fashion. Studies assessing affective reactions ignore or hold constant information value. Studies assessing cognitive reactions have done the same with affective value. Studies on self-assessment emphasize information value rather than affective value. Thus, the affective–cognitive distinction is an issue that is produced by the paradigms employed and neglect of the "other" determinant.

To verify our contentions, researchers need to create conditions under which we would predict that patterns analogous to those found in self-enhancement, self-evaluation maintenance, self-consistency, self-confirmation, and self-assessment studies should and should not hold. For example, the so-called "strong" consistency position predicts that people should continue to view themselves as "stupid" on subsequent occasions to the extent that they have a clearly defined image of a stupid person. We would predict, however, that the motivation to maintain this self-image will occur only when the positive information value in maintaining that clear self-image outweighs the negative affective value of seeing themselves as stupid. If little affective value is associated with the self-image of stupidity, a pattern of results analogous to a "need for self-consistency" should emerge. In this case, motivation to maintain a clear self-image will predominate. As noted earlier, however, this "strong" consistency effect has had only modest support (although Swann's work can be viewed as a major new source of support for this position). We suspect that researchers have had difficulty demonstrating strong consistency effects because of the large amounts of negative affective value associated with failure or "bad" attributes (e.g., stupidity). Similarly, research on self-assessment should take into account the amount and direction of affective value associated with a particular level of possession of some attribute or competence.

Toward a Theory of Personality, Motivation, and Self

In this chapter, we have attempted to present a unified theoretical approach that integrates the study of self- and behavioral systems with both affective and cognitive perspectives. We have tried to do more than merely redefine terms. It is our hope that this integration will provide the basis for an emerging theory of personality, motivation, and self that focuses on psychological careers and the self–behavior interface.

In our integrative approach, it is assumed that the direction of value (positive or negative) is determined by the interaction between (1) a particular source of value in the situation or life circumstance of an individual and (2) those personal characteristics that an individual brings into a situation that color his or her interpretation of a particular source of value. Thus, the notion of value as a motivational variable assumes that individual differences interact with the different life circumstances faced by people to determine the value that influences thoughts and actions.

For example, individual differences in achievement-related motives are now conceived of as relatively stable factors that determine whether resultant affective value in the achievement domain is negative, zero, or positive (cf. Atkinson & Feather, 1966; Atkinson & Raynor, 1974; Raynor & Entin, 1982b). In addition, individual differences in uncertainty-related motives are now conceived of as relatively stable factors that determine whether resultant information value is negative, zero, or positive (cf. Sorrentino & Hewitt, 1984; Sorrentino, Short, & Raynor, 1984).

An important new area for research suggested by this approach concerns the interaction between individual differences in resultant value and the emergence, content, and functioning of associated self-systems. For example, what are the joint effects of (1) individual differences in resultant value in the achievement domain (e.g., success-oriented versus failure-threatened people) and (2) sources of positive or negative self-esteem derived from achievement-related attributes (i.e., skill-demanding competencies) or self-images (e.g., occupational roles)? What specific effects result when an individual's self-image has positive affective value but negative information value (or vice versa)?

We suggest that researchers take seriously both affective and cognitive determinants of action. In addition, researchers should examine both personal and situational determinants of value in trying to understand functioning in the behavioral system, the self-system, and psychological careers. Dichotomies between affect and cognition and between personal and situational determinants are common in the current literature. Many psychologists have negative evaluations of motivational psychology as involving affective value exclusively and of personality psychology as involving stable personal sources of value exclusively. Such evaluations stand in the way of building an integrative theory of personality, motivation, and self-system functioning that is empirically based and subject to continuing refinement in light of subsequent research.

Notes

1. We agree with Atkinson and Birch's (1978) contention that attainment of a positive outcome reduces motivation to strive for that outcome. It is unclear, however, whether the resultant *value* of that outcome declines over time. In our view, maintaining or retaining value is part of the process of instigation to action and is independent of any consummatory force. For example, attaining food may reduce motivation to strive for food, and once the individual begins to get filled up, there will be some consummatory force that will lower motivation to eat. Independent of this, however, is motivation to *maintain* the positive experience of eating (e.g., the good taste of food).

2. In this theory, action is associated only with the maintenance or production of positive value and the removal of *experienced* negative value. Individuals do not act to avoid anticipated or recalled negative value *per se*. Rather, they resist activity expected to produce negative value. The only aim of this resistance is to prevent anticipated or recalled negative value; it does not involve feeling good.

References

Allport, G. H. (1955). *Becoming: Basic considerations for a psychology of personality.* New Haven: Yale University Press.

Archibald, W. P. (1974). Alternative explanations for self-fulfilling prophecy. *Psychological Bulletin, 81,* 74–84.

Atkinson, J. W. (1964). *An introduction to motivation.* Princeton, NJ: Van Nostrand.

Atkinson, J. W., & Birch, D. (1978). The dynamics of achievement-oriented activity. In J. W. Atkinson & J. O. Raynor (Eds.), *Personality, motivation, and achievement* (pp. 143–197). Washington, DC: Hemisphere.

Atkinson, J. W., & Feather, N. T. (Eds.). (1966). *A theory of achievement motivation.* New York: Wiley.

Atkinson, J. W., & Raynor, J. O. (Eds.). (1974). *Motivation and achievement.* Washington, DC: Hemisphere.

Baumeister, R. F. (1982). Self-esteem, self-presentation, and future interaction: A dilemma of reputation. *Journal of Personality, 50,* 29–45.

Baumeister, R. F., & Jones, E. E. (1978). When self-presentation is constrained by the target's prior knowledge: Consistency and compensation. *Journal of Personality and Social Psychology, 36,* 608–618.

Brown, E. T. (1982). *Parenting as a psychological career path for women.* Unpublished doctoral dissertation, State University of New York at Buffalo.

Campbell, D. T., & Fiske, D. W. (1959). Convergent and discriminant validation by the multitrait multimethod matrix. *Psychological Bulletin, 56,* 81–105.

Cialdini, R. B., Borden, R. J., Thorne, A., Walker, M. R., Freeman, S., & Sloan, L. R. (1976). Basking in reflected glory: Three football field studies. *Journal of Personality and Social Psychology, 34,* 366–375.

Cohen, A. R. (1959). Some implications of self-esteem for social influence. In C. Hovland & I. Janis (Eds.), *Personality and Persuasibility* (pp. 102–120). New Haven: Yale University Press.

Combs, A. W. (1981). Some observations on self-concept research and theory. In M. D. Lynch, A. A. Norem-Hebeisen, & K. Gergen (Eds.), *Self-concept: Advances in theory and research* (pp. 5–17). Cambridge, MA: Ballinger.

Coopersmith, S. (1967). *The antecedents of self-esteem.* San Francisco: Freeman.

Crary, W. G. (1966). Reactions to incongruent self-expectancies. *Journal of Consulting Psychology, 30,* 246–252.

Dipboye, R. L. (1977). A critical review of Korman's self-consistency theory of work motivation and occupational choice. *Organizational Behavior and Human Performance, 18,* 108–126.

Dittes, J. E. (1959). Attractiveness of group as a function of self-esteem and acceptance by the group. *Journal of Abnormal Social Psychology, 59,* 77–82.

Ellis, R. A., & Taylor, M. S. (1983). Role of self-esteem within the job search process. *Journal of Applied Psychology, 68,* 632–640.

Epstein, S. (1973). The self-concept revisited, or a theory of a theory. *American Psychologist, 28,* 404–416.

Epstein, S. (1981). The unity principle versus the reality and pleasure principles, or the tale of the scorpion and the frog. In M. D. Lynch, A. A. Norem-Hebeisen, & K. Hergen (Eds.), *Self-concept advances in theory and research* (pp. 27–37). Cambridge, MA: Ballinger.

Epstein, S. (1983). The unconscious, the preconscious, and the self-concept. In J. Suls & A. G. Greenwald (Eds.), *Psychological perspectives on the self* (Vol. 2, pp. 219–247). Hillsdale, NJ: Erlbaum.

Feather, N. T. (1969). Attribution of responsibility and valence of success and failure in relation to initial confidence and task performance. *Journal of Personality and Social Psychology, 13,* 129–144.

Feather, N. T. (Ed.). (1982). *Expectations and actions: Expectancy-value models in psychology.* Hillsdale, NJ: Erlbaum.

Festinger, L. (1957). *A theory of cognitive dissonance.* Evanston, IL: Row, Peterson.

Greenwald, A. G., & Pratkanis, A. R. (1984). The self. In R. S. Wyer & T. K. Srull (Eds.), *Handbook of social cognition* (pp. 111–150). Hillsdale, NJ: Erlbaum.

Heider, F. (1958). *The psychology of interpersonal relations*. New York: Wiley.

Helmreich, R., & Stapp, J. (1974). Short forms of the Texas Social Behavior Inventory (TSBI), an objective measure of self-esteem. *Bulletin of the Psychonomic Society, 4*, 473–475.

Ilgen, D. (1971). Satisfaction with performance as a function of the initial level of expected performance and the deviation from expectations. *Organizational Behavior and Human Performance, 6*, 345–361.

Jacobs, L., Berscheid, E., & Walster, E. (1971). Self-esteem and attraction. *Journal of Personality and Social Psychology, 17*, 84–91.

James, W. (1890). *The principles of psychology* (Vols. 1 & 2). New York: Holt.

Janis, I. L. (Ed.). (1969). *Personality: Dynamics, development and assessment.* New York: Harcourt, Brace & World.

Janis, I., & Field, P. (1959). Sex differences and personality factors related to persuasibility. In C. Hovland & I. Janis (Eds.), *Personality and persuasibility*. New Haven: Yale University Press.

Johnson, V. E. (1973). *I'll quit tomorrow*. New York: Harper & Row.

Jones, E. E., & Berglas, S. (1978). Control of attributions about the self through self-handicapping strategies: The appeal of alcohol and the role of underachievement. *Personality and Social Psychology Bulletin, 4*, 200–206.

Jones, S. C. (1973). Self- and interpersonal evaluations: Esteem theories versus consistency theories. *Psychological Bulletin, 79*, 185–199.

Kelly, G. A. (1955). *The psychology of personal constructs* (Vols. 1 & 2). New York: Norton.

Korman, A. (1970). Toward a hypothesis of work behavior. *Journal of Applied Psychology, 54*, 31–41.

Krauss, H. H., & Critchfield, L. L. (1975). Contrasting self-esteem theory and consistency theory in predicting interpersonal attraction. *Sociometry, 38*, 247–260.

Lecky, P. (1945). *Self-consistency: A theory of personality*. New York: Island Press.

Lecky, P. (1969). *Self-consistency*. Garden City: Doubleday.

Lewin, K., Dembo, T., Festinger, L., & Sears, P. S. (1944). Level of aspiration. In J. McV. Hunt (Ed.), *Personality and the behavior disorders* (Vol. 1, pp. 333–378). New York: Ronald Press.

Leonard, S., & Weitz, J. (1971). Task enjoyment and task perseverance in relation to task success and self-esteem. *Journal of Applied Psychology, 55*, 414–421.

Markus, H. (1977). Self-schemata and processing information about the self. *Journal of Personality and Social Psychology, 35*, 63–78.

Markus, H. (1980). The self in thought and memory. In D. M. Wegner & R. R. Vallacher (Eds.), *The self in social psychology* (pp. 102–130). New York: Oxford University Press.

Markus, H., Smith, J., & Moreland, R. L. (1982, October). *The role of the self in social perception: A cognitive analysis*. Paper presented at the meeting of the Society for Experimental Social Psychology, Nashville, IN.

Maslow, A. H. (1954). *Motivation and personality*. New York: Harper & Row.

McFarlin, D. B. (1984). *Motivational links between the self-concept and behavior in evaluative settings*. Unpublished manuscript, State University of New York at Buffalo.

McFarlin, D. B., Baumeister, R. F., & Blascovich, J. (1984). On knowing when to quit: Task failure, self-esteem, advice, and nonproductive persistence. *Journal of Personality, 54*, 138–155.

McFarlin, D. B., & Blascovich, J. (1981). Effects of self-esteem and performance feedback on future affective preferences and cognitive expectations. *Journal of Personality and Social Psychology, 40*, 521–531.

Mead, G. H. (1934). *Mind, self, & society*. Chicago: University of Chicago Press.

Mischel, W., Ebbessen, E. B., & Zeiss, A. R. (1973). Selective attention to the self: Situational and dispositional determinants. *Journal of Personality and Social Psychology, 27*, 129–142.

Newcomb, T. M. (1959). Individual systems of orientation. In S. Koch (Ed.), *Psychology: A study of a science* (Vol. 3, pp. 384–422). New York: McGraw-Hill.

Newcomb, T. M. (1961). *The acquaintance process*. New York: Holt, Rinehart and Winston.

Nicholls, J. G. (1984). Achievement motivation: Concepts of ability, subjective experience, task choice, and performance. *Psychological Review, 91*, 328–346.

Nicholls, J. G., Licht, B., & Pearl, R. (1982). Some dangers of using personality questionnaires to study personality. *Psychological Bulletin, 92*, 572–580.

Nochajski, T., & Raynor, J. O. (1984, August). *Motivation to evaluate competence vs. do well in individual sports competition.* Paper presented at the American Psychological Association Convention, Toronto.

Osgood, C. E., & Tannenbaum, P. H. (1955). The principle of congruity in the prediction of attitude change. *Psychological Review, 62*, 42–55.

Raynor, J. O. (1982a). Self-possession of attributes, self-evaluation, and future orientation: A theory of adult competence motivation. In J. O. Raynor & E. E. Entin (Eds.), *Motivation, career striving, and aging* (pp. 207–226). Washington, DC: Hemisphere.

Raynor, J. O. (1982b). A theory of personality functioning and change. In J. O. Raynor & E. E. Entin (Eds.), *Motivation, career striving, and aging* (pp. 249–302). Washington, DC: Hemisphere.

Raynor, J. O., Atkinson, J. W., & Brown, M. (1974). Subjective aspects of achievement motivation immediately before an examination. In J. W. Atkinson & J. O. Raynor (Eds.), *Motivation and achievement* (pp. 155–171). Washington, DC: Hemisphere.

Raynor, J. O., & Brown, E. T. (in press). Motivation at different stages of striving in a psychological career. In D. A. Klieber (Ed.), *Advances in motivation and achievement: Vol. 4. Motivation and adulthood.* Greenwich, CT: JAI Press.

Raynor, J. O., & English, L. D. (1982). Relationships among self-importance, future importance, and self-possession. In J. O. Raynor & E. E. Entin (Eds.), *Motivation, career striving, and aging* (pp. 197–205). Washington, DC: Hemisphere.

Raynor, J. O., & Entin, E. E. (1982a). *Motivation, career striving, and aging.* Washington, DC: Hemisphere.

Raynor, J. O., & Entin, E. E. (1982b). Theory and research on future orientation and achievement motivation. In J. O. Raynor & E. E. Entin (Eds.), *Motivation, career striving, and aging* (pp. 13–82). Washington, DC: Hemisphere.

Raynor, J. O., & Entin, E. E. (1983). The function of future orientation as a determinant of human behavior in a step-path theory of action. *International Journal of Psychology, 18*, 25–49.

Raynor, J. O., & Nochajski, T. (1984). *Affective and information value as determinants of motivation for self-assessment.* Unpublished manuscript, State University of New York at Buffalo.

Robinson, J. P., & Shaver, P. R. (1978). *Measures of social psychological attitudes.* Ann Arbor: University of Michigan, Institute for Social Research.

Rogers, C. (1951). *Client-centered therapy.* Boston: Houghton Mifflin.

Rosenberg, M. (1965). *Society and the adolescent self-image.* Princeton, NJ: Princeton University Press.

Schlenker, B. R., Soraci, S., & McCarthy, B. (1976). Self-esteem and group performance as determinants of egocentric perceptions in cooperative groups. *Human Relations, 29*, 1163–1176.

Shavit, H., & Shouval, R. (1980). Self-esteem and cognitive consistency effects on self–other evaluation. *Journal of Experimental Social Psychology, 16*, 417–425.

Shrauger, J. S. (1972). Self-esteem and reactions to being observed by others. *Journal of Personality and Social Psychology, 23*, 192–200.

Shrauger, J. S. (1975). Responses to evaluation as a function of initial self-perceptions. *Psychological Bulletin, 82*, 581–596.

Shrauger, J. S. (1982). Selection and processing of self-evaluative information: Experimental evidence and clinical implications. In G. Weary & H. L. Mirels (Eds.), *Integrations of clinical and social psychology* (pp. 128–153). New York: Oxford University Press.

Shrauger, J. S., & Kelly, R. (1984). *Self-confidence and endorsement of external evaluations.* Unpublished manuscript, State University of New York at Buffalo.

Shrauger, J. S., & Lund, A. (1975). Self-evaluations and reactions to evaluations from others. *Journal of Personality, 43*, 94–108.

Shrauger, J. S., & Terbovic, M. L. (1976). Self-evaluation and assessments of performance by self and others. *Journal of Clinical and Consulting Psychology, 44*, 564–572.

Sigall, H., & Gould, R. (1977). The effects of self-esteem and evaluator demandingness on effort expenditure. *Journal of Personality and Social Psychology, 35*, 12–20.

Silverman, I. (1964). Self-esteem and differential responsiveness to success and failure. *Journal of Abnormal and Social Psychology, 69*, 115–119.

Snygg, D., & Combs, A. W. (1949). *Individual behavior: A new frame of reference for psychology.* New York: Harper & Row.

Sorrentino, R. M., & Hewitt, E. C. (1984). Uncertainty-reducing properties of achievement tasks revisited. *Journal of Personality and Social Psychology, 47*, 884–899.

Sorrentino, R. E., Short, J. C., & Raynor, J. O. (1984). Uncertainty orientation: Implications for affective and cognitive views of achievement behavior. *Journal of Personality and Social Psychology, 46*, 189–206.

Stotland, E., Thorley, S., Thomas, E., Cohen, A. R., & Zander, A. (1957). The effects of group expectations and self-esteem upon self-evaluation. *Journal of Abnormal and Social Psychology, 54*, 55–63.

Suinn, R. M., Osborne, D., & Page, W. (1962). The self-concept and accuracy of recall of inconsistent self-related information. *Journal of Clinical Psychology, 18*, 473–474.

Swann, W. B. (1982, August). *Reaffirming self-conceptions through social interaction.* Paper presented at the American Psychological Association Convention, Washington, DC.

Swann, W. B. (1983). Self-verification: Bringing social reality into harmony with the self. In J. Suls and A. G. Greenwald (Eds.), *Social psychological perspectives on the self* (Vol. 2, pp. 33–66). Hillsdale, NJ: Erlbaum.

Swann, W. B., & Hill, C. A. (1982). When our identities are mistaken: Reaffirming self-conceptions through social interaction. *Journal of Personality and Social Psychology, 43*, 59–66.

Swann, W. B., & Read, S. J. (1981a). Acquiring self-knowledge: The search for feedback that fits. *Journal of Personality and Social Psychology, 41*, 1119–1128.

Swann, W. B., & Read, S. J. (1981b). Self-verification processes: How we sustain our self-conceptions. *Journal of Experimental Social Psychology, 17*, 351–372.

Swann, W. B., Read, S. J., & Hill, C. A. (1981, August). *Bringing others to see us as we see ourselves.* Paper presented at the American Psychological Association Convention, Los Angeles.

Thibaut, J. W., & Kelley, H. H. (1959). *The social psychology of groups.* New York: Wiley.

Tesser, A. (1980). Self-esteem maintenance in family dynamics. *Journal of Personality and Social Psychology, 39*, 77–91.

Tesser, A., & Campbell, J. (1980). Self-definition: The impact of the relative performance and similarity of others. *Social Psychology Quarterly, 43*, 341–347.

Tesser, A., & Campbell, J. (1982). Self-evaluation maintenance and the perception of friends and strangers. *Journal of Personality, 50*, 261–279.

Tesser, A., & Campbell, J. (1983). Self-definition and self-evaluation maintenance. In J. Suls and A. G. Greenwald (Eds.), *Social psychological perspectives on the self* (Vol. 2, pp. 1–31). Hillsdale, NJ: Erlbaum.

Tesser, A., & Paulhus, D. (1983). The definition of self: Private and public self-evaluation management strategies. *Journal of Personality and Social Psychology, 44*, 672–682.

Tesser, A., & Smith, J. (1980). Some effects of friendship and task relevance on helping: You don't always help the one you like. *Journal of Experimental Social Psychology, 16*, 582–590.

Tolman, E. C. (1955). Principles of performance. *Psychological Review, 62*, 315–326.

Trope, Y. (1975). Seeking information about one's own ability as a determinant of choice among tasks. *Journal of Personality and Social Psychology, 32*, 1004–1013.

Trope, Y. (1979). Uncertainty-reducing properties of achievement tasks. *Journal of Personality and Social Psychology, 37*, 1505–1518.

Trope, Y., & Brickman, P. (1975). Difficulty and diagnosticity as determinants of choice among tasks. *Journal of Personality and Social Psychology, 31*, 918–925.

Walster, E. (1965). The effect of self-esteem on romantic liking. *Journal of Experimental Social Psychology, 1*, 184–197.

Weaver, D., & Brickman, P. (1974). Expectancy, feedback, and disconfirmation as independent factors in outcome satisfaction. *Journal of Personality and Social Psychology, 30*, 420–428.

Weiner, Y. (1970). The effects of "task" and "ego-oriented" performance on two kinds of over-compensation inequity. *Organizational Behavior and Human Performance, 5*, 191–208.

Weiner, Y. (1973). Task, ego-involvement, and chronic self-esteem as moderators of situationally devalued self-esteem. *Journal of Applied Psychology, 58*, 225–232.

Wylie, R. C. (1979). *The self-concept* (Vol. 2). Lincoln: University of Nebraska Press.

CHAPTER 12

Self-Enhancement and Self-Assessment in Achievement Behavior

YAACOV TROPE

Hebrew University

INTRODUCTION

A recurrent theme in a great deal of psychological research is the influence of needs, motives, and wishes on judgmental processes. Social psychologists have been particularly interested in the biasing effects of people's need to enhance or protect their self-esteem. In the last decade, most of the work on self-serving biases has been conducted by students of attribution processes and social cognition (e.g., Bradley, 1978; Greenwald, 1980; Kruglanski & Ajzen, 1983; Snyder, Stephen, & Rosenfield, 1978; Tetlock & Levi, 1982; Zuckerman, 1979). The general question these psychologists addressed was whether people take credit for their successes by attributing them to internal causes, such as ability and effort, and deny responsibility for their failures by attributing them to external causes, such as task difficulty and bad luck.

From its start, the attribution literature contrasted the notion of self-serving biases with the alternative view that people strive to attain a veridical assessment of themselves (Darley & Goethals, 1980; Jones & Davis, 1965; Kelley, 1967, 1972). In this alternative view, people may be imperfect information processors, frequently handicapped by insufficient and unrepresentative information and by normatively inappropriate inferential rules. However, this view claims that self-serving attributions can be accounted for by informational variables rather than by motivated distortions (Ajzen & Fishbein, 1975; Miller & Ross, 1975; Nisbett & Ross, 1980). Many studies have attempted to pit the notion of self-serving biases against the informational interpretation (for reviews, see Tetlock & Levi, 1982; Zuckerman, 1979). However, inspection of this literature reveals that it has been almost exclusively concerned with inferences, attributions, and other cognitive

350

processes. The vast amount of work on cognitive processes has not been matched by theorizing and research on behavior and decision making. There is very little research to tell us whether people *act* on their environment in a manner that will assure enhancement of their self-esteem or, alternatively, in a manner that will enable them to assess their competencies.

In the typical research paradigm, the experimenter predetermines the kind of task subjects perform and the kind and amount of feedback they receive. Subjects are constrained to interpreting this fixed-outcome information. In real life, however, people are frequently free to select and even construct their own tasks and then to decide how much effort to expend and how long to persist. People can choose, for example, among a variety of academic courses that differ in the kinds of abilities they require (e.g., mathematical, verbal, or artistic). Within each ability domain, people are frequently free to determine the difficulty of the tasks they undertake. Furthermore, on any given task, people can actively regulate their effort expenditure and decide how much time to devote to the task before shifting to alternative tasks. It is apparent, then, that the kinds of outcomes available for self-inference depend on the logically preceding behavioral stage—that is, the kinds of situations people actively construct for themselves and the manner in which they perform in these situations. Even if people were perfectly impartial attributors, biased strategies of choice, effort expenditure, and persistence could still trap them in perpetual confirmation of their unrealistically high self-regard. It is theoretically important, therefore, to study the operation of self-serving biases in the behavioral domain independent of their operation in the inferential domain.

Task choice, effort expenditure, and persistence may appear to be fertile testing grounds for self-serving biases because of the wealth of data available on these achievement-related decisions, data that have accumulated in three decades of extensive research on achievement motivation (see Atkinson, 1957; Atkinson & Raynor, 1974; Kukla, 1978; McClelland, Atkinson, Clark, & Lowell, 1953; Ruble, 1980; Weiner, 1980). Despite their theoretical diversity, most contributors to this area implicitly share a self-enhancement viewpoint. People presumably select tasks, expend effort, and persist at tasks to attain outcomes that enhance their self-esteem. However, this achievement motivation research was not specifically designed to contrast self-enhancement and self-assessment. It tested various self-enhancement formulations, but it did not contrast them with the motivation to attain veridical self-assessment.

This chapter first explicates the self-enhancement assumptions of the major achievement behavior theories and then integrates these assumptions in a formal self-enhancement model of achievement behavior. This model is subsequently contrasted with a self-assessment model wherein choice, effort expenditure, and persistence are construed as means for people to attain veridical information about their capabilities. The final section examines self-assessment as a means for future maximization of self-esteem. Self-assessment is assumed to require immediate but short-term achievement costs for the sake of remote but long-term achievement gains.

SELF-ENHANCING ACHIEVEMENT BEHAVIOR

The major achievement theories share two fundamental assumptions. One assumption is that people seek to maximize the subjective expected utility of performance outcomes. The other assumption identifies this utility with esteem-related affect; that is, success produces *positive* esteem-related affect (e.g., pride, satisfaction) and failure produces *negative* esteem-related affect (e.g., shame, dissatisfaction). Achievement behavior is self-enhancing in that it strives to maximize positive esteem-related affect and to minimize negative esteem-related affect. The differences among the various theories are in the postulated antecedents of these affective reactions to success and failure. This section first examines the antecedents postulated by the major achievement theories and then develops a new self-enhancement model. Finally, it discusses relevant research and explores some extensions of the new self-enhancement model.

Probability of Success and Esteem-Related Affect

Atkinson's (1957, 1964) achievement theory and its subsequent revisions (Atkinson & Birch, 1970; Atkinson & Raynor, 1974) are the most explicit in adopting the subjective expected utility (SEU) principle and in equating the utility of performance outcomes with esteem-related affect. Specifically, the amount of positive affect experienced after success (U_s) and the amount of negative affect experienced after failure (U_f), weighted by the subjective probabilities of the outcomes (P_s and $1 - P_s$), combine according to the SEU principle into the tendency to achieve success (T_a), as follows:

$$T_a = P_s U_s + (1 - P_s) U_f. \tag{12.1}$$

The theory postulates personality and situational determinants of experienced pride (U_s). The personality determinant is the motive to achieve success (M_s), conceived as a disposition to derive pride from success. The situational contribution—the incentive value of success (I_s)—is inversely related to the probability of success; that is, $I_s = 1 - P_s$. The lower the probability of success, the greater the pride derived from success. These two factors combine multiplicatively to determine the amount of pride experienced given success; that is, $U_s = M_s(1 - P_s)$. The amount of shame experienced after failure (U_f) is analogously defined as a multiplicative function of the motive to avoid failure (M_f), which is conceived as a personality disposition to experience shame given failure, and the incentive value of failure (I_f). The latter is assumed to be directly related to the probability of success—that is, $I_f = -P_s$—and $U_f = M_f(-P_s)$. Substituting these assumptions into Equation 12.1 and simplifying, we obtain

$$T_a = (M_s - M_f)P_s(1 - P_s). \tag{12.2}$$

This equation specifies the expected utility of performing a given task—that is, the expected amount of pride when $M_s > M_f$ and the expected amount of shame when $M_s < M_f$. Equation 12.2 suggests that a person with $M_s > M_f$ can maximize pride by working on intermediate P_s tasks and a person with $M_s < M_f$ can minimize shame by working on low P_s or high P_s tasks.

In subsequent revisions of the theory, Atkinson and his colleagues suggested additional assumptions to take into account changes in achievement tendencies over time (Atkinson & Birch, 1970). The expected esteem-related affect, as defined in Equation 12.2, is assumed to determine the rate of increase in the tendencies to approach or avoid achievement tasks. Furthermore, consummatory and resistance forces accumulating over time are postulated to reduce the rates of increase in the approach and avoidance tendencies, respectively. From the present perspective, the important point is that in Atkinson's original and revised models, the amount of esteem-related affect associated with past and present activities—as determined by achievement motives and success probability in these activities—predicts choice, performance, and persistence.

Internal Attribution and Esteem-Related Affect

Like Atkinson's theory, Weiner's attribution theory (Weiner, 1979; Weiner, Frieze, Kukla, Reed, Rest, Rosenbaum, 1971) assumes that the utilities of outcomes reflect their esteem-related affective consequences and that these utilities are weighted by the outcome probabilities, as specified by the SEU principle, to determine the attractiveness of achievement tasks. Unlike Atkinson, however, Weiner proposed a cognitive theory to account for affective reactions to outcomes and for assessment of their probabilities. This theory is based on people's intuitive beliefs regarding the causes of performance outcomes. Briefly, attribution of outcomes to stable factors of ability and task difficulty is presumably the prime determinant of probabilities of success and failure. Thus, attribution of success or failure to ability or task difficulty results in pronounced changes in subjective success probabilities, whereas attribution to unstable factors, effort and luck, results in small changes in these probabilities. According to Weiner, affective reactions are largely determined by attribution to effort and ability, which are seen as internal causes. Presumably, attribution of success to ability or effort produces intense pride and attribution of failure to lack of effort or lack of ability produces intense shame, whereas attribution of these outcomes to external causes, such as difficulty and luck, produces less intense emotional reactions. Weiner accepts Atkinson's assumption that the intensity of the affective reaction to an outcome is inversely related to its probability. In Weiner's theory, however, this relationship is mediated by the inverse relationship between internal attribution of an outcome and its probability; for example, the higher the probability of success (or the easier the task), the less success is attributed to ability and effort.

In light of recent evidence, Weiner extended the set of achievement causes and elaborated on the links between causal attribution, on the one hand, and probability assessments and affective reactions, on the other (Weiner, 1979). However, the extended framework retains the basic assumption that in their task choice, effort expenditure, and persistence, people strive to attribute success to internal causes and failure to external causes. Such self-enhancing achievement behavior is designed to maximize the amount of positive esteem-related affect and to minimize the amount of negative esteem-related affect.

A Self-Enhancement Model

In Weiner's attribution model, effort attribution is the prime determinant of affective reactions to outcomes. Attributions to ability are assumed to have little affective consequences. In contrast, the present model starts from the assumption that the affective value of outcomes derives from their inferential relationship to distinct ability categories (see Berglas & Jones, 1978; Darley & Goethals, 1980; Kukla, 1978; Nicholls, 1979; Trope & Brickman, 1975). This approach recognizes ability not only as *internally caused* but also as more *general* than other achievement causes; that is, its effects may extend over a greater time span and across a greater range of tasks and circumstances than the effects of other achievement causes (see Abramson, Seligman, & Teasdale, 1978). Outcomes serve as pieces of information on the basis of which inferences are made about ability. Success produces positive esteem-related affect to the extent that it demonstrates high ability, and failure produces negative esteem-related affect to the extent that it discloses lack of ability.

This line of reasoning seems to be at variance with Weiner and his colleagues' earlier findings of the centrality of effort attribution and the inverse relationship between affect and attributed ability (see Weiner, 1974). It should be noted, however, that in these studies, outcomes were devoid of informational value regarding ability; that is, subjects were typically asked to *assume* a given ability level and to consider success and failure in hypothetical achievement situations. If ability levels were inferred from outcomes, instead of being assumed, the results might have been different. Indeed, several studies found that inference of high ability in light of success and inference of lack of ability in light of failure intensified affective reactions to these outcomes (Trope, 1975, 1980; Trope & Brickman, 1975). Furthermore, several authors have argued that the dependent measures in the studies by Weiner and his colleagues tapped moral evaluations or reinforcement strategies designed to influence the person's own performance or that of another person (Kukla, 1978; Nicholls, 1976). Such evaluations and reinforcements are responsive to effort expenditure but insensitive and perhaps inversely related to stipulated ability. Indeed, recent work by Weiner and his colleagues, tapping a wide range of affective reactions, showed that pride, happiness, and feelings of competence were directly related to attributed level of ability (Weiner, Russell, & Lerman, 1978).

In sum, like Atkinson's and Weiner's theories, the present self-enhancement model assumes that achievement behavior is predictable from the amount of esteem-related affect one expects to derive. Unlike previous theories, however, this model explicitly defines this affect in terms of (1) the diagnostic value of outcomes regarding possession or lack of ability and (2) the esteem-related affect associated with possessing or lacking the ability.

The Diagnostic Value of Performance Outcomes

It is suggested that the amount of esteem-related affect a person expects to derive from performance outcomes is a function of the extent to which outcomes are expected to produce a change in the person's initial beliefs about his or her ability level. The person's initial beliefs or knowledge about his or her ability, prior to receiving performance outcomes, can be represented by the subjective probability distribution over the ability dimension under consideration. In Light of performance outcomes, the person expects to revise this prior probability distribution into a posterior probability distribution. Success should result in an upward revision, whereas failure should lead to a downward revision of the probability distribution. The amount of revision depends on the informational value of the outcome with regard to the person's ability level, which, in turn, is defined in terms of outcome diagnosticity—that is, the extent to which the probability of the outcome is believed to vary as a function of the person's ability level. When the outcome is thought to be equally probable under the alternative ability levels, its occurrence will not produce any revision in the person's prior beliefs about the ability. The greater the perceived variability in the outcome probability given the alternative ability levels, the greater is the expected impact of the occurrence of the outcome on the person's prior beliefs.

Diagnosticity is viewed here as a subjective judgment based on the perceived validity of task performance with regard to underlying ability. This judgment is assumed to depend on two sources of information: *task outcomes* and *task features* (for a detailed discussion, see Trope, 1983). The judgment of diagnosticity from task outcomes is guided by the person's assumptions about ability. A task is judged diagnostic to the extent that its outcomes match the expectations derived from these assumptions. One such assumption is that ability varies across people (Kelley, 1967). The resulting expectation is that the outcome of a diagnostic task should vary across people—the greater the performance differences among people, the greater the inferred diagnosticity. Another assumption is that abilities are stable and general properties of people. The corresponding expectation is that on a diagnostic task, a given person's performance should exhibit minimal fluctuation over time and circumstances. To the extent that fluctuations occur, they should not mask individual differences; that is, repeated performances should be correlated across persons (Kelley, 1967).

Like judgment of diagnosticity from outcomes, judgment of diagnosticity from features of the task itself are based on people's intuitive theories of ability. A task will be judged diagnostic of an ability if it incorporates the features that are assumed to define the ability. If social sensitivity is defined as the ability to identify another's psychological characteristics, a task will be judged diagnostic of that ability to the extent that success in the task requires correct identification of these characteristics. At a more abstract level, the assumption that ability is a stable property implies that a task is diagnostic to the extent that it requires repeated performances—that it includes multiple items rather than a single item. The assumption that ability is general leads to the expectation that a diagnostic task should include heterogenous items. Judged diagnosticity also depends on the exclusion of nonability factors. To the extent that the task is composed of multiple and heterogenous items, it will be seen as minimizing the influence of extraneous, momentary, and specific factors. Similarly, a task that compares simultaneous performances by different people is also expected to eliminate some nonability factors, such as facilitating or interfering circumstances, and will therefore be judged as more diagnostic than a task that does not allow such comparison between performers.

The Esteem Associated with Abilities

Affective reactions to outcomes depend not only on the certainty with which they diagnose possession or lack of an ability but also on how enhancing or damaging to self-esteem possession or lack of the ability is. It is surprising that previous achievement theories have ignored differences among abilities in their self-enhancement implications. In these theories, the kind of ability diagnosed by an outcome does not influence the affective reaction to that outcome.

A number of factors may determine the amount of esteem attendant upon possession or lack of an ability. One such factor is the perceived *generality* of the ability (Darley & Goethals, 1980). Abilities differ in the range of achievement performances they are believed to affect. A specific ability is believed to manifest itself in a narrow range of performances, whereas a general ability is believed to manifest itself in a broad range of performances. The distinction may be an intuitive version of the parallel distinction between general and specific abilities in the theory of intelligence. It is also similar to Abramson *et al.*'s (1978) distinction between global and specific causal attributions. Related to generality is the *temporal stability* of abilities. Some abilities are seen as relatively stable and as having a long-term influence on performance, whereas other abilities are seen as more likely to change over time and thus as having only a short-term influence on performance. Another relevant factor is the importance of the activities that the ability is believed to affect. Activities are important to the extent that their outcomes are either highly desirable or undesirable. For example, spatial ability probably affects more important activities in the life of a pilot than in the life of a clinical psychologist, and social sensitivity probably affects more important activities in the life of the clinical psychologist than in the life of the pilot. The greater the importance of the activities affected by an ability, the more positive the affect attendant upon possession of that ability and the more negative the affect attendant upon lack of it. Thus, an esteemed ability is one that is believed to have prolonged influence on a broad range of activities that are important to the individual. Individual differences in achievement motive may also affect ability-related esteem. Possession of high ability may produce more positive esteem and possession of low ability may produce less negative esteem among people who are high in achievement motive, as compared to people who are low in achievement motive.

The Esteem-Related Utility of Achievement Tasks

It is assumed that the diagnostic value of success regarding possession of an ability (D_s) and the positive esteem attendant upon actual possession of the ability (E_a) combine multiplicatively to determine the positive esteem-related utility of success (E_s). Thus, $E_s = D_s E_a$. The negative esteem-related utility of failure (E_f) is similarly defined as $D_f(-E_a^-)$, where D_f denotes the diagnostic value of failure regarding lack of an ability and $-E_a^-$ denotes the amount of negative esteem attendant upon lack of the ability.

The esteem-related utility of a task (E_t) is defined as the subjective expected utility of the outcomes at the task—that is, the sum of the utilities of success and failure, each weighted by its subjective probability, as follows:

$$E_t = P_s D_s E_a - (1 - P_s)D_f E_a^-. \tag{12.3}$$

Note that P_s is not the same as difficulty; it refers to a given person's probability of success, which can be determined by various factors other than difficulty (e.g., effort, ability).

If achievement behavior is oriented toward self-enhancement, it should maximize E_t, the expectancy that the outcome will diagnose an ability level that enhances rather than lowers the person's self-esteem. According to Equation 12.3, an achievement task should be attractive when success is expected to demonstrate unequivocally the possession of an esteemed ability, and it should be repulsive to the extent that failure is expected to uncover incompetence. Each of these factors is necessary for the task to be attractive or repulsive. For example, a task would not be attractive when (1) the probability of success is low, (2) success is undiagnostic of ability, or (3) possession of the ability does not enhance the person's self-esteem.

Equation 12.3 can be simplified (1) when success is as diagnostic of the possession of ability as failure is diagnostic of lack of ability (i.e., $D_s = D_f = D$) and (2) when the positive esteem attendant upon possession of the ability is as extreme as the negative esteem attendant upon lack of the ability (i.e., $E_a = -E_a^- = E$). Substituting these values into Equation 12.3 and rearranging, we obtain

$$E_t = DE(2P_s - 1). \tag{12.4}$$

This equation highlights an important implication of the ability enhancement model—that the effects of diagnosticity (D) and extremity of the esteem associated with possessing or lacking an ability (E) depend on the subjective probability of success. When $P_s > .5$, achievement tasks will be approached, because performance is more likely to enhance than to lower the person's self-esteem. Under these circumstances, achievement motivation should increase with the diagnosticity of performance and with extremity of esteem. In contrast, when $P_s < .5$, achievement tasks should be avoided, because they are more likely to lower than to enhance the person's self-esteem. Furthermore, under these circumstances, achievement motivation should decrease as diagnosticity and extremity of esteem increase.

Relevant Research

There has been very little research bearing directly on the predictions that are unique to the present self-enhancement model. However, the extensive research on the effect of task difficulty on achievement behavior is indirectly relevant. This research, conducted mainly in the framework of Atkinson's theory of achievement motivation, has demonstrated that people prefer and work harder at intermediate-difficulty tasks than at easy or hard ones (Heckhausen, 1977; Ruble, 1980). Theoretical considerations and a large amount of past research suggest that intermediate-difficulty tasks are ordinarily judged as more diagnostic than easy or hard ones (Trope, 1983). From the present perspective, it might be argued, then, that the documented superiority of intermediate tasks is mediated by their greater diagnostic value. Furthermore, past research has found that the preference for intermediate tasks is stronger among subjects with high achievement motive than among subjects with low achievement motive. This effect of achievement motive can be interpreted in several ways. First, as suggested by a number of investigators (e.g., Buckert, Meyer, & Schmalt, 1979; Kukla, 1978; Nicholls, 1979), the higher the achievement motive, the higher the perceived ability level and, therefore, the higher the probability of success. If so, the dependence of the intermediate-difficulty preference on achievement motive is consistent with our model's assumption that the diagnostic value of a task and the probability of success interact to determine the motivation to perform a task. Second, it was suggested earlier that achievement motive may determine the amount of esteem-related affect attendant upon possession of high ability. Again, the dependence of task difficulty preference on achievement motive is consistent with the model's prediction of an interactive effect of diagnosticity and the amount of esteem-related affect on task attractiveness. Finally, Trope (1975) found that individuals with high achievement motive are more sensitive to task diagnosticity than individuals with low achievement motive. Hence, it is possible that the former individuals are more attracted to intermediate-difficulty tasks because they perceive a greater difference in diagnosticity between intermediate and easy or hard tasks.

Although diagnosticity and difficulty are ordinarily correlated, the two can, in principle, vary independently of each other. Indeed, a study that actually unconfounded diagnosticity from difficulty found that the inference of ability depends on diagnosticity independent of difficulty (Trope & Brickman, 1975). The same study also investigated the effects of diagnosticity and difficulty on task preference, thus providing evidence that is directly pertinent to the present model's postulated effects of diagnosticity (see also Buckert *et al.*, 1979; Forsterling & Weiner, 1981; Trope, 1975; Zuckerman, Brown, Fischler, Fox, Lathin, & Minesian, 1979). Consistent with the model, it was found that subjects preferred high-diagnosticity tasks to low-diagnositicty tasks, independent of intermediate task difficulty. Furthermore, Trope (1975) found that subjects with high achievement motive displayed a stronger preference for high-diagnosticity tasks than did subjects with low achievement motive. Since subjective probability of success (P_s) is positively related to achievement motive (Kukla, 1978), this result is consistent with the prediction that high P_s increases the interest in diagnostic tasks. More recently, Zuckerman *et al.* (1979) directly manipulated probability of success by providing prior success or failure feedback. As the present model would predict, subjects who experienced success were more inclined to attempt highly diagnostic tasks than subjects who experienced prior failure. Similar results were obtained by Trope (1979). These studies bear out the interactive effect of probability of success and task diagnosticity on task preference, as postulated by the present self-enhancement model. Clearly, more research is needed to test the joint effect of these and other variables of the model. Such research should also be extended from task preference to other aspects of achievement behavior, such as quantity and quality of performance and persistence.

Elaborations and Extensions of the Model

Prior Probabilities of Abilities and Esteem

Theoretical considerations and empirical observations suggest that the amount of esteem associated with an ability is negatively related to its prevalence or base-rate probability (P_a). Specifically, the possession of scarce, low-probability abilities is associated with high *positive* esteem, and the lack of common, high-probability abilities is associated with high *negative* esteem. These hypotheses are consistent with Helson's (1964) adaptation level theory (see also Brickman and Campbell, 1971) and Merton and Kitt's (1950) relative deprivation theory in assuming that satisfaction or dissatisfaction with positive or negative events is high when the events deviate from expectancies or are rare among relevant comparisons others. The present hypotheses are also consistent with a wealth of data relating satisfaction to expectancies (see Janoff-Bulman & Brickman, 1981). Thus, as the base-rate probability of the ability (P_a) increases, the *positive* esteem associated with possessing the ability decreases (i.e., $E_a = 1 - P_a$) and the *negative* esteem associated with lacking it increases (i.e., $E_a = -P_a$). Substituting in Equation 12.3, we obtain

$$E_t = P_s D_s (1 - P_a) - (1 - P_s) D_f P_a. \qquad (12.5)$$

In this equation, an achievement task would be attractive to the extent that success is expected to diagnose the possession of an ability that many people lack, and the task would be repulsive to the extent that failure is expected to diagnose the lack of an ability that many people possess.

Assuming that success and failure are equally diagnostic (i.e., $D_s = D_f = D$) and substituting into Equation 12.5, we can write

$$E_t = D(P_s - P_a). \tag{12.6}$$

In this version of the model, achievement motivation should be a positive function of the subjective probability of success at the task and a negative function of the base rate of the inferred ability. These effects are more pronounced when diagnosticity is high than when it is low. Furthermore, the relative magnitudes of P_s and P_a determine the effect of diagnosticity. When probability of success is greater than the base rate of ability, the attractiveness of the task increases with its diagnosticity; conversely, when the probability of success is smaller than the prior probability of the ability, attractiveness decreases as diagnosticity increases.

A Self-Presentation Version of the Self-Enhancement Model

Like the self-enhancement formulations just cited, recent self-presentation approaches to social interaction have been almost exclusively concerned with attributions, inferences, and self-descriptions (Arkin, Appelman, & Burger, 1980; Bradley, 1978; Jones & Pittman, 1982; Schlenker, 1981; Tedeschi, 1981; Ungar, 1980). Application of these approaches to achievement behavior would suggest that task choice, persistence, and performance can be viewed as self-presentations aiming at public demonstration of high ability. These approaches can be reformulated in terms of my self-enhancement model. Specifically, self-presentation concerns should be manifested in public definitions of the diagnostic values of success and failure (D_s and D_f) and the amounts of esteem attendant upon possession or lack of an ability (E_a and E_a^-). Thus, D_s and D_f would reflect the person's assessments of the diagnostic values the audience imputes to success and failure, respectively. In public situations, E_a and E_a^- would represent assessments of how esteemed possession or lack of an ability is in the eyes of the audience. Like their private counterparts, the public esteems may be related to the prevalence of the ability (P_a). In this case, however, P_a may reflect the prevalence of the ability in the audience or the audience's prior probability (as assessed by the actor) that the actor possesses the ability. Note that P_s remains a private, rather than public, assessment of the probability of success.

Expressed in terms of these socially defined variables, Equations 12.3–12.6 specify a self-presentation model in which task choice, performance, and persistence are designed to maximize the expectancy of publicly demonstrating a socially esteemed ability. A task would be attractive to the extent that the person expects to succeed and the audience believes success is diagnostic of an esteemed competency; a task would be repulsive to the extent that the person expects to fail and failure is seen by the audience as diagnostic of a negative incompetency. In terms of Equation 12.4, tasks that are publicly recognized as diagnostic of esteemed abilities will be sought after to the extent that the person expects to succeed, but they will be avoided to the extent that the person expects to fail.

An important implication of the self-presentation version of the model is that the aforementioned preferences would be displayed even when they conflict with private assessments of the diagnosticity of the task and the value of possessing the ability. For example, the self-presentation version of the model suggests that the individual would welcome extrinsic facilitating factors to the extent that the audience is unaware of their operation. Such illicit extrinsic facilitators may raise the person's probability of success without lowering the public diagnosticity of the task; a lowering of the privately assessed diagnosticity should not affect motivation. From a self-presentation point of view, the person would be tempted to use any illicit facilitating means in performing tasks whose successful completion is publicly defined as requiring an esteemed ability.

Individual Differences in the Self-Enhancement Model

Past research has related achievement behavior to various personality variables such as anxiety, self-esteem, and internal versus external locus of control (Weiner, 1980), but the personality variable that has been most extensively studied is the achievement motive. In fact, all of the major achievement theories have postulated that perceived environmental characteristics interact with achievement motive to determine achievement behavior. Thus, in Atkinson's mode, achievement motive is conceptualized as an affective disposition to experience pride following success or shame following failure. According to Weiner (1979), the relationship between achievement motive and affect is mediated by disparate attributions of people with low achievement motive and people with high achievement motive. Presumably, the latter attribute success to ability and effort and failure to lack of effort, whereas the former attribute success to luck and task facility and failure to lack of ability. Kukla (1978) conceptualized achievement motive as individual differences in perceived ability—the higher the achievement motive, the higher the perceived ability.

Individual differences in achievement motive can be manifested in each of the components of the ability-enhancement model. First, achievement motive may directly influence E_a and E_a^- so that the higher the achievement motive, the more intense the positive esteem derived from possession of an ability and the less intense the negative esteem associated with lack of ability. This possibility is analogous to Atkinson's conception of the achievement motive as an affective disposition. A more cognitive interpretation of achievement motive would suggest that it affects the perceived diagnostic value of success and failure, so that as achievement motive increases, the perceived diagnostic value of success increases and that of failure decreases. This interpretation would parallel Weiner's attribution model, in which achievement motive is postulated to affect attributions of outcomes. Finally, achievement motive could affect the probability of success—the higher the motive, the higher the person's probability of success. This possibility is congruent with Kukla's (1978) analysis, in which achievement motive is related to perceived ability, which should, in turn, be related to probability of success. Although previous theorizing has argued for one possibility, all three are plausible, and they need not be treated as if they were mutually inconsistent.

SELF-ASSESSMENT OF ABILITIES

The theories reviewed in the preceding section trace the motivational properties of performance outcomes to one general factor—the extent to which they enhance the person's self-esteem. People are presumably biased in favor of tasks that can reveal their competence and against tasks that can reveal their incompetence. Fundamentally different factors are suggested by the view that people strive to attain a realistic assessment of their strengths and weaknesses. In the last three decades, this view has been proposed by students of social comparison processes (Festinger, 1964; Ruble & Boggiano, 1981; Suls & Miller, 1977), attribution processes (Kelley, 1972; Meyer, Folkes, & Weiner, 1976), and the self (Janoff-Bulman & Brickman, 1981). Based on these past contributors, this section presents a formal model of self-assessment of abilities. The model treats achievement tasks as means for self-assessment and assumes that the value of performance outcomes derives from their informativeness regarding the person's abilities.

A Self-Assessment Model

Both person and task factors are postulated to determine how much information the person can gain about his or her ability. The person factors are represented by the person's *prior* uncertainty regarding his or her ability and the task factors by the amount of information that can be extracted from task outcomes. Prior uncertainty regarding the person's ability level, denoted by U_a, reflects the person's prior beliefs about his or her ability. These beliefs are represented by subjective prior probabilities of the various ability levels. In the proposed model, prior uncertainty is derived from the prior probability distribution according to the information theory index of entropy (see Shannon & Weaver, 1949), as follows: $U_a = -\Sigma P_a \log_2 P_a$, where P_a denotes the prior probability of a given ability level. Prior uncertainty is at a maximum when all ability levels are equally probable; it is at a minimum when the prior probability of one ability is unity and the prior probability of all other ability levels is zero.

The achievement of a performance outcome revises the prior uncertainty into a new *posterior* level of uncertainty, denoted by $U_{a/o}$, which specifies the amount of uncertainty conditional upon the achievement of a particular outcome o. The definition of posterior uncertainty is analogous to that of prior uncertainty. Specifically, posterior uncertainty is obtained from the posterior probabilities of the ability levels, given that a particular outcome was achieved ($P_{a/o}$). According to information theory, $U_{a/o} = -\Sigma P_{a/o}\log_2 P_{a/o}$. Again, posterior uncertainty increases with the dispersion of the posterior probability distribution over the ability dimension.

The amount of uncertainty reduced by success can be defined, then, as the difference between prior uncertainty (U_a), or the amount of uncertainty before knowing which outcome was attained, and the amount of posterior uncertainty given success ($U_{a/s}$). The difference between prior and posterior uncertainty is similarly defined for failure. Accordingly, the amount of ability uncertainty a task is expected to reduce (U) can be expressed as the expected value of uncertainty reduction—that is, the sum of the amounts of uncertainty reduced by success and failure, weighted by the probability of success (P_s) and failure ($1 - P_s$), as follows:

$$U = P_s(U_a - U_{a/s}) + (1 - P_s)(U_{a - U_{a/f}})$$

or, more simply:

$$U = U_a - [P_s U_{a/s} + (1 - P_s)U_{a/f}]. \tag{12.7}$$

Note that the second term on the right-hand side of the equation specifies the expected amount of uncertainty remaining after learning which outcome was in fact achieved. Thus, the amount of uncertainty task performance is expected to reduce is defined as the difference between the amount of uncertainty in the absence of outcome information and the amount of uncertainty expected after knowing what outcome was achieved.

Posterior probabilities can be viewed as revisions of the corresponding prior probabilities in light of a particular outcome. The amount of revision is, in turn, a function of the diagnostic value of the outcome—that is, the extent to which its conditional probability varies with ability level. When the outcome is equally probable under the various ability levels, the outcome has no diagnostic value and the posterior probability distribution should remain the same as the prior probability distribution. The greater the variation in the outcome probability under the various ability levels, the greater the diagnostic value of the outcome (i.e., its accuracy in discriminating between the ability levels) and the greater the amount of revision from prior to posterior probabilities.

It should be pointed out that outcome diagnosticity is similarly defined in the self-assessment model and in the self-enhancement model. In both models, it represents a subjective judgment of the relationship between task performance and ability levels. As noted earlier, this judgment can be based on task features (i.e., the extent to which they are representative of the ability schema) and properties of the outcome distribution (e.g., the relative stability of outcomes within persons and variability across persons). Both models allow for inaccuracies and biases in the judgment of diagnosticity. The difference between the models is in the postulated influence of judged diagnosticity on choice, performance, and persistence.

To reiterate, before undertaking a task, the person presumably assesses the prior probabilities of the ability levels under consideration, using the available prior information. The dispersion of the prior probability distribution reflects the person's prior uncertainty. The person's knowledge about the task is represented in the model by the diagnostic values of the different outcomes, which, in turn, determine posterior probabilities. The difference between prior and posterior uncertainty yields the amount of uncertainty a particular outcome could reduce if it were actually achieved. Before performing the task, the person cannot be sure which outcome will be attained. Hence, he or she can only estimate the expected amount of uncertainty task performance will reduce by combining the amounts of uncertainty reduction conditional upon the various outcomes, each weighted by the probability of the outcome.

Forms of Ability Assessment

Five forms of ability assessment through task performance can be distinguished. First, the person can construct tasks designed to diagnose particular abilities. Second, he or she may select from among the available tasks the one that is most diagnostic of the abilities under consideration. Third, the person may transform various aspects of the task to maximize its diagnosticity; for example, by working independently, a person can attain more ability information than by using others' direct help. Fourth, diagnosticity can be controlled by varying effort expenditure; for example, if diagnosticity is believed to be positively related to effort, people can work hard if they wish to maximize diagnosticity. It is reasonable to suppose that for a broad range of tasks and kinds of abilities, diagnosticity indeed increases with effort. However, effort may reach a point at which the rate of improvement in the performance associated with low ability equals or even exceeds the rate of improvement in performance associated with high ability. From this point, diagnosticity may decrease as effort increases. Thus, both very little effort and extreme effort may mask performance differences between ability levels. Effort may function, then, like task difficulty with respect to diagnosticity; that is, diagnosticity may be related in a curvilinear fashion to both difficulty and effort expenditure. The relationship between diagnosticity and effort may depend on task difficulty. For easy tasks, performance may reach its maximal diagnostic value when a small amount of effort is exerted. Further increments in effort may act to diminish performance differences between ability levels, as even incapable persons start performing well. The more difficult the task, the greater the amount of effort that extracts maximal diagnosticity from the task. Finally, for any given level of effort at a self-constructed or self-selected task, the person can control ability information by the number of items attempted. Given that the items are not redundant, the person can compensate for the low diagnostic value of a task by working on a relatively large number of items.

CONTRASTING SELF-ENHANCEMENT AND SELF-ASSESSMENT

As noted earlier, self-enhancement achievement theories have generated a large amount of supporting empirical research (see, e.g., Atkinson & Raynor, 1974; Weiner, 1980). However, although this research has frequently contrasted alternative self-enhancement formulations, it has not been designed to contrast self-enhancement and self-assessment. In fact research traditionally cited as supporting self-enhancement is interpretable in self-assessment terms. This section first illustrates these self-assessment reinterpretations and then discusses research paradigms that can pit self-enhancement against self-assessment in achievement behavior.

The Effects of Diagnosticity and Difficulty on Task Choice

An important prediction made by all major theories of achievement motivation is that people will prefer and work harder on intermediate-difficulty tasks than on easy or hard tasks. In an earlier section, these predictions were related to task diagnositicty, and it was argued that intermediate-difficulty tasks are ordinarily seen as more diagnostic than easy or hard tasks. The superiority of intermediate-difficulty tasks was therefore interpreted as consistent with the present self-enhancement model, wherein task attractiveness depends on the expectancy that performance will demonstrate a high level of ability. In support of this model, it was shown that when diagnosticity is varied independently of difficulty, subjects prefer highly diagnostic tasks irrespective of their difficulty.

These results are also interpretable in self-assessment terms. In this view, diagnostic tasks are attractive because they can reduce a greater amount of uncertainty regarding the person's ability level than undiagnostic tasks can. The problem is that the manipulation of diagnosticity and task difficulty in past research (e.g., Trope, 1975) confounded the amount of uncertainty that can be reduced and the level of ability that can be demonstrated. Hence, that research could not discriminate between self-enhancement and self-assessment.

Shifts in Level of Aspiration

Another research paradigm that has been used extensively by achievement theorists provides subjects with performance feedback on an initial task and then allows them to shift to either easier or harder tasks. Many studies, from early work on level of aspiration (Lewin, Dembo, Festinger, & Sears, 1944) to current research on Atkinson's dynamics-of-action theory (Kuhl & Blankenship, 1979), have demonstrated that people shift to increasingly harder tasks after repeated success and to increasingly easier tasks after repeated failure. These patterns of task choice, called "typically shifts in level of aspiration," are viewed in the various self-enhancement formulations as attempts to maximize pride.

The self-assessment interpretation of this phenomenon is based on two observations. First, a large amount of research has shown that the diagnosticity of success increases and the diagnosticity of failure decreases as difficulty increases Trope (1983). Thus, in relatively easy tasks, failure is more diagnostic than success, whereas in relatively hard tasks, success is more diagnostic than failure. Second, previous outcomes affect the probability of success, so that prior success increases the probability of success and prior failure decreases this probability. Hence, with repeated success, harder tasks become increasingly more informative, because the person is more likely to attain success—the highly diagnostic outcome of the tasks—rather than failure—the nondiagnostic outcome of the tasks. Analogously, repeated failure increases the informativeness of easy tasks because the person is more likely to fail—the diagnostic outcome of the tasks—rather than succeed—the nondiagnostic outcome of the tasks. Thus, typical shifts in level of aspiration, previously viewed as self-enhancing attempts to obtain pride, are readily interpretable as attempts to keep the amount of new ability-relevant information at a maximum.

Perceived Ability and Task Choice

Related to the effect of previous outcomes is the effect of preexisting differences in perceived ability on task choice. According to several self-enhancement formulations, the higher the perceived ability, the harder the tasks people are willing to undertake (Kukla, 1978). The self-assessment interpretation of this finding is similar to the interpretation of typical shifts in level of aspiration. For individuals with high perceived ability, hard tasks are more informative because success, which is highly diagnostic in hard tasks, is more probable. Similarly, easy tasks are more informative for people with low perceived ability because failure, which is highly diagnostic in easy tasks, is more probable.

Self-Handicapping Research

One interesting self-enhancement formulation is Berglas and Jones's (1978) notion of self-handicapping achievement behavior. These authors proposed that individuals "select the available environment best designed to protect their image of self-competence" (p. 410). According to Berglas and Jones, individuals who initially receive incontingent success suspect deterioration in their future performance. To avoid diagnostic ability information, these individuals subsequently handicap themselves by working on hard tasks. These findings are also open to a self-assessment interpretation. First, compared to Berglas and Jones's contingent-success subjects, their incontingent-success subjects initially worked on harder tasks and, in one experiment, were actually told that they performed better. As argued earlier, the harder the task on which the person initially succeeds, the harder the task that person should subsequently attempt if he or she wishes to maximize the diagnostic value of subsequent task performance. The greater task difficulty preferred by Berglas and Jones's incontingent-success subjects is therefore consistent with the self-assessment model.

Second, the task selected by incontingent-success subjects was closer to the *intermediate difficulty* point than the task selected by contingent-success subjects. In fact, the former group expressed a stronger preference for the "no drug" task, the one that neither artificially facilitated nor inhibited performance. Thus, the incontingent-success subjects actually displayed a stronger preference for performing a task under relatively diagnostic circumstances. The self-assessment model would suggest that such an enhanced interest in ability information is likely to occur when the person is uncertain about his or her ability. Indeed, Berglas and Jones's procedures were designed to induce greater uncertainty in incontingent-success subjects than in contingent-success subjects.

Previous Outcomes, Performance, and Persistence

Several self-enhancement formulations predict that the effect of previous outcomes on subsequent performance and persistence depends on the individual's achievement motive (Atkinson & Raynor, 1974; Kukla, 1972). Indeed, people with low achievement motive have been found to persist more and perform better after success than after failure, whereas people with high achievement motive have been found to persist more and perform better after failure than after success (Weiner, 1965, 1966). Similar results have been reported in the literature on task anxiety. People with a low level of anxiety profit most from failure, whereas people with a high level of anxiety profit most from success (see Sarason, 1959).

In the self-assessment model, each attempt at the task is viewed as an informational query regarding the person's ability level, and whether these attempts will persist depends on the amount of uncertainty remaining after previous outcomes. The effects of previous outcomes on high-achievement and low-achievement individuals are interpretable in self-assessment terms if it is assumed that the former individuals have a higher level of perceived ability than the latter. Specifically, when perceived ability is high (individuals with high achievement motive), the prior probability distribution is peaked at the high ability levels. Failures may raise the probabilities of the lower ability levels and thereby increase the dispersion of the probability distribution. In contrast, successes are likely to further decrease the probabilities of the lower ability levels and thereby decrease the dispersion. Thus, failure may increase ability-related uncertainty, whereas success may decrease it. Given these assumptions, the self-assessment model predicts that failure will enhance persistence and success will diminish it, as past research has found. When perceived ability is low (individuals with low achievement motive), the probability distribution is peaked at low levels of ability. Under these circumstances, success and failure are predicted, and were found, to have the opposite effects: success should increase uncertainty and thereby enhance subsequent persistence, whereas failure should decrease uncertainty and thereby dampen persistence.

Beyond individual differences, it is reasonable to assume that, on the average, college students believe they are more likely to have high ability than low ability. If so, failure should have an overall enhancing effect. However, although failure may initially increase uncertainty about the person's ability, continued failure may reduce it, as low ability levels become subjectively more probable than high ability levels. The corresponding curvilinear effect of amount of failure on persistence has actually been obtained in learned helplessness studies (see Wortman & Brehm, 1975).

Finally, research conducted in the framework of attributional achievement theories has found that subjects exhibit pronounced decrements in performance following repeated failure to the extent that they attribute their failures to lack of ability (see Dweck & Reppucci, 1973; Weiner, Heckhausen, Meyer, & Cook, 1972). In the self-assessment model, outcomes that are attributed to ability have a higher diagnostic value and should therefore reduce uncertainty at a faster rate than outcomes that are not attributed to ability. Hence, as past research has shown, the effect of previous outcomes on subsequent performance should increase with the diagnosticity of outcomes.

The foregoing discussion by no means exhausts self-enhancement achievement studies. Nevertheless, it amply demonstrates the ability of the self-assessment model to account for a broad range of self-enhancement achievement research. This is not to say that the two motivations are indistinguishable; rather, it illustrates that past self-enhancement research was not specifically designed to rule out self-assessment interpretations. The remainder of this section describes two research paradigms that do pit self-enhancement against self-assessment.

The Joint Effects of the Diagnosticity and Probability of Success and Failure

In both the self-assessment and the self-enhancement models, outcome diagnosticity determines task attractiveness. However, a fundamental difference between these models concerns the contributions of the diagnostic values of success and failure (D_s and D_f, respectively) to task attractiveness. In all self-enhancement formulations, including my own (see Equation 12.3), the diagnostic values of success and failure have opposite effects on task attractiveness: D_s increases task attractiveness, whereas D_f decreases it. In contrast, the self-assessment model treats success and failure as potentially equivalent pieces of information regarding the individual's ability. Both outcomes can increase task attractiveness as long as they can reduce some uncertainty regarding the person's ability. Success can reduce uncertainty by diagnosing high ability in the same way that failure can reduce uncertainty by diagnosing low ability.

As noted earlier, the finding that people prefer diagnostic tasks or intermediate-difficulty tasks (Buckert *et al.*, 1979; Trope, 1975; Trope & Brickman, 1975; Zuckerman *et al.*, 1979) may reflect the person's interest in demonstrating high ability as well as a wish to reduce uncertainty regarding his or her ability. Evidently, to determine unequivocally whether the diagnostic value of failure is substracted from the diagnostic value of success, as the self-enhancement formulations assume, or added to the diagnostic value of success, as the self-enhancement model assumes, it is necessary to manipulate the two kinds of diagnosticity independently. This can be achieved by presenting to subjects the performance distributions associated with high and low ability. The greater the overlap between the two distributions, the lower the diagnosticity of the task. However, the degree of overlap does not have to be uniform over the range of performance scores that can be attained at the task. The overlap over high scores can be equal to, greater than, or smaller than the overlap over low scores, thus rendering the diagnosticity of high scores (success) equal to, greater than, or smaller than the diagnosticity of low scores (failure). By independent variation of the overlap between the ability level distributions over high and low performance scores, it is thus possible to vary independently the diagnosticity of success and failure. If people seek self-enhancement, their preference for a task should increase with the diagnosticity of high scores but decrease with the diagnosticity of low scores. They should be maximally attracted to a task for which high scores are diagnostic and low scores are undiagnostic. On such a task, the range of performance scores that is unique to high ability is relatively large, whereas the range of scores that is unique to low ability is relatively small. In other words, the performances associated with low ability are a *subset* of the performances associated with high ability. Such a task is ideal for self-enhancement purposes, because it can unequivocally demonstrate high ability but cannot disclose low ability. In contrast, on a task for which failure is diagnostic and success undiagnostic, the performances associated with high ability are a subset of the performances associated with low ability. Such a task poses the greatest threat for self-enhancement, because poor performance can uncover low ability, but good performance cannot demonstrate high ability.

A different pattern of preferences is dictated by self-assessment. Specifically, both success and failure should contribute to task attractiveness in direct proportion to their diagnostic value. Thus, a task for which neither success nor failure is diagnostic should be the least attractive, a task for which both success and failure are diagnostic should be the most attractive, and both a task for which only success is diagnostic and a task for which only failure is diagnostic should be intermediate in attractiveness.

By introducing the variable of probability of success into this paradigm, we can derive additional contrasting predictions from the self-enhancement and self-assessment models. In the self-enhancement model (see Equation 12.3), the higher the probability of success, the greater the weight of D_s, which adds to task attractiveness, and the smaller the weight of D_f, which detracts from task attractiveness. Hence, task attractiveness is always positively related to P_s. The diagnostic values D_s and D_f can affect only the strength of this relationship—the higher the D_s and D_f, the stronger the relationship between task attractiveness and P_s; they cannot affect the sign of the relationship. In contrast, in the self-assessment model, the sign of the relationship between task attractiveness and P_s depends on D_s and D_f. In this model (see Equation 12.7), P_s and $(1 - P_s)$ serve as weights for D_s and D_f, respectively, both of which add to task attractiveness. Hence, when $D_s > D_f$, task attractiveness is positively related to P_s, when $D_s < D_f$ task attractiveness is negatively related to P_s, and when $D_s = D_f$ task attractiveness is unrelated to P_s. Furthermore, for any given difference between D_s and D_f, the self-assessment model predicts that task attractiveness will always be positively related to diagnosticity. In contrast, the self-enhancement model predicts that the sign of the relationship depends on P_s. For example, given that $D_s = D_f = D$, task attractiveness will be positively related to D when $P_s > .5$, negatively related to D when $P_s < .5$, and unrelated to D when $P_s = .5$.

This set of contrasting predictions has not yet been subjected to empirical test. One study on task choice (Trope, 1980) varied orthogonally D_s and D_f, but not P_s. The results of that study were consistent with the self-assessment model but not with the self-enhancement model. Specifically, task preference was found to be a positive function of both D_s and D_f. Further research is needed on various forms of achievement behavior other than task choice, such as task performance and persistence. This research should also vary P_s independently of D_s and D_f.

Prior Uncertainty Regarding Abilities

Another fundamental difference between self-enhancement and self-assessment formulations concerns the role of prior uncertainty regarding abilities. Prior information may leave different amounts of uncertainty about different abilities. According to the self-assessment model (see Equation 12.7), as prior uncertainty increases, outcomes of given diagnosticity can reduce more uncertainty regarding the person's ability. Hence, this model predicts that the individual will undertake tasks, expend effort, and persist in ability domains in which prior information left the greatest amount of uncertainty. In contrast, self-enhancement formulations predict that people will be motivated to perform tasks in ability domains in which they expect to demonstrate high ability—that is, domains in which perceived ability is high. Furthermore, according to the self-assessment model, prior uncertainty and task diagnosticity should have an interactive effect on task motivation. As uncertainty increases, the difference between the amounts of uncertainty that can be reduced by high-diagnosticity and low-diagnosticity tasks increases. The corresponding effect on task motivation should be expressed in a more pronounced effect of diagnosticity when uncertainty is high than when it is low. In contrast, self-enhancement formulations predict that the effect of task diagnosticity should depend on perceived ability. People with high perceived ability should be attracted to diagnostic tasks, whereas people with low perceived ability should be attracted to undiagnostic tasks.

One study tested these predictions with respect to task performance (Trope, 1982). Subjects performed an initial task and then received predetermined results. To induce high uncertainty, subjects received conflicting results—some indicating high ability, some low ability, and some intermediate ability. Low uncertainty was induced by reporting unequivocal results, all showing that the subject's ability was either high, intermediate, or low. Later, subjects performed a new task whose diagnosticity was either high or low. The results confirmed the self-assessment predictions. Specifically, subjects who were uncertain of their ability level expended more effort than subjects who were certain about their ability level, whether low, intermediate, or high. Also, subjects worked harder on the diagnostic task than on the undiagnostic task. More important, the effect of task diagnosticity was more pronounced when prior uncertainty was high than when it was low. Contrary to the self-enhancement prediction, subjects performed better at the highly diagnostic task regardless of whether they were certain of possessing high, intermediate, or low ability.

Again, further research is needed on other kinds of achievement behavior before firm conclusions can be drawn. The paradigm developed by Trope (1982) can be used in research on task choice and persistence. At the very least, this study illustrates the feasibility of contrasting self-enhancement and self-assessment.

Individual Differences in Self-Assessment

As noted earlier there has been a large amount of theoretical and empirical work on personality factors in self-enhancing achievement behavior. There has been very little work, however, on personality determinants of self-assessment in achievement behavior. An important exception is the work by Sorrentino and his colleagues on uncertainty orientation (Sorrentino & Hewitt, 1984; Sorrentino, Short, & Raynor, 1984). These authors conceptualized uncertainty orientation as a general disposition to seek or avoid reduction of uncertainty regarding future self-relevant events. Given that ability assessment can reduce such uncertainty, it should depend on the individual's uncertainty orientation. Indeed, in a recent study, Sorrentino and Hewitt (1984) found that uncertainty-oriented subjects preferred tasks that diagnosed ability levels about which they were uncertain, whereas certainty-oriented subjects preferred tasks that diagnosed ability levels of which they were certain.

The effect of achievement motive on self-assessment is less clear. The finding that individuals with high achievement motive are more interested in diagnostic tasks, cited earlier as supporting a self-enhancement interpretation of achievement motive, is also interpretable in self-assessment terms. That is, individuals with high achievement motive may be more interested in diagnosing their ability. Indeed, Trope (1980) found that compared to subjects with low achievement motive, subjects with high achievement motive were more interested in diagnosing *both* low and high ability levels. However, Sorrentino and Hewitt (1984) found that the difference between the motive groups is in their interest in diagnosing high rather than low ability—a finding that tends to support the self-enhancement interpretation of achievement motive. Unfortunately, the different experimental designs and achievement motive measures employed by Sorrentino *et al.* (1984) and Trope (1980) do not permit direct comparisons.

Subjective Asymmetries Between Success and Failure

A valid test of self-enhancement and self-assessment requires accurate estimates of the *subjective* diagnostic values of outcomes and their probabilities. These subjective values and their objective counterparts are not necessarily the same. As noted earlier, various motivational and informational factors produce overestimation of the diagnostic value of past successes and underestimation of the diagnostic value of past failures (Miller & Ross, 1976; Zuckerman, 1979). These factors may also influence prior judgments—those that are made before the task is actually undertaken. As a result, the same objective information may produce different subjective judgments for success and failure. Therefore, I will discuss several biasing factors that have received little attention in past work on self-enhancing biases.

First, success often refers to a set of performance features or events that are better defined than those represented by failure. In fact, failure is frequently represented merely by the absence of the features or events that define success. As a result, the relationship between success and high ability may be more readily perceived than the relationship between failure and low ability. Second, when people are planning to perform a task, they may give more attention to the way in which success can be achieved than to the way in which failure can be avoided. Consequently, success is likely to be perceptually more salient and to receive greater weight in determining task attractiveness than failure.

A third factor that may create an asymmetry between success and failure concerns the person's knowledge about the ability scale under consideration. People may have more distinct, better differentiated schemata for high ability levels than for low ability levels; they may perceive a greater difference between mediocrity and competence than between mediocrity and incompetence. Given that success discriminates better at the upper part of the ability scale and failure discriminates better at the lower part of the ability scale, it follows that success will be more diagnostic than failure. The upper part of the ability scale may also be better differentiated than the lower part in terms of the desirability of possessing the various ability levels. All levels below mediocrity may be equally undesirable, but each level above mediocrity may be distinctively more desirable. Consequently, the importance of discriminating at the upper part of the ability scale (i.e., the importance of the diagnosticity of success) may be greater than the importance of discriminating at the lower part of the ability scale (i.e., the importance of the diagnosticity of failure).

There are undoubtedly situations that favor the informational value of failure over that of success. In some situations, failure may be better defined and more salient than success, and the lower part of the ability scale may be better differentiated than the upper part. Further, theoretical and empirical work is needed to identify the circumstances that favor success and those that favor failure. For the present discussion, the important point is that without an accurate assessment of subjects' own beliefs about success and failure, various factors may act to give an artificial advantage to success, and thus to self-enhancement predictions, or to failure, and thus to self-assessment predictions.

CONCLUSION: THE INSTRUMENTAL VALUE, COSTS, AND REGULATION OF SELF-ASSESSMENT

The preceding section demonstrated the feasibility of pitting self-enhancement against self-assessment and thus gauging their relative importance in achievement behavior. Whereas that discussion was confined to the level of the immediate behavior, this section examines the relationship between the two motivations from a broader behavioral perspective. From this perspective, self-assessment may be instrumental for the long-term satisfaction of self-enhancement needs. It is therefore argued that an immediate activity will be used for self-assessment only to the extent that the long-term benefits of self-assessment are more influential than its immediate costs.

The Instrumental Value and Cost of Self-Assessment

According to the self-enhancement model presented earlier in this chapter, the esteem an individual derives from performance outcomes depends on the level of ability those outcomes demonstrate. Frequently, however, people are uncertain about the level of ability they can demonstrate in future achievement-related activities. Acquisition of information regarding their abilities may reduce this uncertainty, thus improving the perceived chances of selecting the activities that will demonstrate their highest abilities. In the absence of prior ability information, people may commit themselves to activities that will demonstrate only mediocrity or even incompetence. For such long-term activities as fields of study and careers, making decisions without sufficient prior ability information may result in chronic frustration of self-enhancement needs. With prior ability information, people can avoid such activities and can concentrate their endeavors in domains in which they can demonstrate their best abilities. In short, the value of using an immediate task for self-assessment may derive from its instrumental value for the attainment of long-term self-enhancement benefits. Self-assessment may also be instrumental for the attainment of other long-term achievement utilities. Prior ability information can help identify domains in which people can publicly present their highest abilities, derive intrinsic satisfaction from the performance itself (Nicholls, 1979; Trope, 1978; Trope & Burnstein, 1977), or attain various social and material gains.

The costs of self-assessment result from the kind of ability information it yields and from the self-assessment process itself. Regarding the first factor, it was noted earlier that self-assessment may require undertaking tasks that diagnose uncertain abilities and tasks for which failure is more diagnostic than success. Although they maximize informational input, the outcomes of such tasks may disclose the person's incompetencies and, consequently, lower his or her immediate self-esteem. Thus, the cost of using an immediate task for self-assessment may involve the same kind of esteem-related utilities the individual eventually wishes to maximize.

In addition, the process of self-assessment itself may have negative affective and behavioral consequences. Self-assessment induces a focus on the self as an object of evaluation, which is likely to be experienced as aversive (Wicklund, 1975). Obviously, self-enhancement may also entail self-focus. However, the two orientations direct the person's attention to different aspects of the self. In self-enhancement, the person concentrates on his or her best abilities to identify the one in which he or she can demonstrate the highest level. This biased attention may nullify and even reverse the negative affective consequences of self-focus. In contrast, in self-assessment, the person searches for abilities in which his or her standing is uncertain. The resulting awareness of relatively undesirable aspects of the self is likely to exacerbate negative affect. Moreover, self-assessment entails a prolonged appraisal of future achievement-related options. Instead of the person fully commiting himself or herself to some job, field of study, or hobby, self-assessment requires continued appraisal of various options in light of incoming ability information. The prolonged lack of an *unequivocal behavioral orientation* (Jones & Gerard, 1967) may result in a loss of emotional gratification and efficient performance.

It is conceivable that some negative consequences of self-assessment have future, long-term effects. For example, a diagnostic failure may result in enduring damage to the person's self-esteem. It is also possible that self-assessment has immediate short-term value in the form of gratification that is intrinsic to the mere reduction of ability uncertainty (Berlyne, 1960). However, the foregoing discussion suggests that, on the whole, the negative consequences of self-assessment operate earlier and for a shorter duration than its positive consequences. It is reasonable, therefore, to characterize the decision to assess oneself as depending on the individual's willingness to endure immediate but short-term achievement costs for the sake of remote but long-term achievement benefits. In assessing his or her abilities, the individual incurs, for example, a short-term loss of self-esteem for the sake of its ultimate enhancement.

The Regulation of Self-Assessment

The temporal arrangement of self-assessment contingencies relates the decision to assess oneself to the general category of delay-of-gratification decisions, such as the decision to invest in education or in long-term saving programs. As past research in this area has demonstrated (Karniol & Miller, 1983; Mischel, 1974, 1979), the individual does not react passively to the situational contingencies. Given an initial decision to assess his or her abilities, the individual may employ a variety of self-regulatory strategies to maintain self-assessment. Some of these strategies may involve manipulation of the motivational structure of the situation. Thus, to minimize the cost of unflattering ability information, the individual may, for example, perform the task privately rather than publicly or at least may prevent public knowledge of the outcomes. Even more interesting, the individual may precommit himself or herself to self-assessment by irreversible elimination of alternatives or, in the less extreme case, may impose on herself or himself high costs for failure to complete a self-assessing task. When situational contingencies are beyond the individual's control, she or he may control the impact of self-assessment outcomes by self-regulation of the mediating emotional and cognitive processes. If the immediate aversiveness of self-assessment is believed to be ameliorated by a good mood, the individual may time his or her self-assessment to coincide with a good mood. Prior to self-assessment, she or he may engage in activities that induce a positive mood. Even in the most restrictive environments, the individual may still retain the freedom to direct his or her attention to the positive aspects of self-assessment (i.e., the optimization of future achievement-related decisions) and away from the negative aspects (i.e., the immediate costs). Mischel's (1974) work suggests that self-regulation may involve even more subtle aspects of information processing, such as the encoding of the immediate costs of self-assessment in nonemotional terms.

Although these self-regulatory strategies may sometimes be employed automatically, they all seem to derive from the person's intuitive theories about his or her cognitive and emotional processes (see Flavell, 1977; Mischel, 1984). These knowledge structures may be highly complex and may give rise to a large variety of self-regulatory strategies that go well beyond those mentioned here. It may be useful to document and classify the various strategies. However, a more important challenge for future work is to develop a general theory of the antecedents and consequences of people's use of the various types of self-regulatory strategies in decisions to assess or enhance themselves.

References

Abramson, L. Y., Seligman, M. E. P., & Teasdale, J. D. (1978). Learned helplessness in humans: Critique and reformulation. *Journal of Abnormal Psychology, 87*, 49–74.

Ajzen, I., & Fishbein, M. (1975). A Bayesian analysis of attribution processes. *Psychological Bulletin, 82*, 261–272.

Arkin, R. M., Appelman, R. J., & Burger, J. M. (1980). Social anxiety, self-presentation, and self-serving bias in causal attribution. *Journal of Personality and Social Psychology, 38*, 23–35.

Atkinson, J. W. (1957). Motivational determinants of risk-taking behavior. *Psychological Review, 64*, 359–372.

Atkinson, J. W. (1964). *An introduction to motivation.* Princeton, NJ: Van Nostrand.

Atkinson, J. W., & Birch, D. (1970). *The dynamics of action.* New York: Wiley.

Atkinson, J. W., & Raynor, J. O. (Eds.). (1974). *Motivation and achievement.* Washington, DC: Winston.

Berglas, S., & Jones, E. E. (1978). Drug choice as a self-handicapping strategy in response to noncontingent success. *Journal of Personality and Social Psychology, 36*, 405–417.

Berlyne, D. (1960). *Conflict, arousal, and curiosity.* New York: McGraw-Hill.

Bradley, G. W. (1978). Self-serving biases in the attribution process: A reexamination of the fact or fiction question. *Journal of Personality and Social Psychology, 36*, 56–71.

Brickman, P., & Campbell, D. T. (1971). Hedonic relativism and planning the good society. In M. H. Appley (Ed.), *Adaptation-level theory* (pp. 287–302). New York: Academic Press.

Buckert, U., Meyer, W. U., & Schmalt, H. D. (1979). Effects of difficulty and diagnosticity on choice among tasks in relation to achievement motivation and perceived ability. *Journal of Personality and Social Psychology, 37,* 1172–1178.

Darley, J. M., & Goethals, G. R. (1980). People's analyses of the causes of ability-linked performances. In L. Berkowitz (Ed.), *Advances in experimental social psychology* (Vol. 13, pp. 2–39). New York: Academic Press.

Dweck, C. S., & Reppucci, N. D. (1973). Learned helplessness and reinforcement responsibility in children. *Journal of Personality and Social Psychology, 25,* 109–116.

Festinger, L. (1954). A theory of social comparison processes. *Human Relations, 7,* 117–140.

Flavell, H. H. (1977). *Cognitive development.* Englewood Cliffs, NJ: Prentice-Hall.

Forsterling, F., & Weiner, B. (1981). Some determinants of task preference and the desire for information about the self. *European Journal of Social Psychology, 11,* 399–408.

Greenwald, A. G. (1980). The totalitarian ego. *American Psychologist, 35,* 603–618.

Heckhausen, H. (1977). Achievement motivation and its constructs: A cognitive model. *Motivation and Emotion, 1,* 283–329.

Helson, H. (1964). *Adaptation-level theory: An experimental and systematic approach to behavior.* New York: Harper.

Janoff-Bulman, R., & Brickman, P. (1981). Expectations and learning from failure. In N. T. Feather (Ed.), *Expectancy, incentive and action* (pp. 207–240). Hillsdale, NJ: Erlbaum.

Jones, E. E., & Davis, K. E. (1965). From acts to dispositions: The attribution process in person perception. In L. Berkowitz (Ed.), *Advances in experimental social psychology* (Vol. 2). New York: Academic Press.

Jones, E. E., & Gerard, H. B. (1967). *Foundations of social psychology.* New York: Wiley.

Jones, E. E., & Pittman, T. (1982). Toward a general theory of strategic self-presentation. In J. Suls (Ed.), *Psychological perspectives on the self* (pp. 231–262). Hillsdale, NJ: Erlbaum.

Karniol, R., & Miller, D. T. (1983). The development of self-control in children. In S. Brehm, S. Kassin, & F. Gibbons (Eds.), *Developmental social psychology* (pp. 141–170). New York: Oxford University Press.

Kelley, H. H. (1967). Attribution theory in social psychology. In D. Levine (Ed.), *Nebraska Symposium on Motivation* (Vol. 15, pp. 192–238). Lincoln: University of Nebraska Press.

Kelley, H. H. (1972). Attribution in social interaction. In E. E. Jones, D. E. Kanouse, H. H. Kelley, R. E. Nisbett, S. Valius, & B. Weiner (Eds.), *Attribution: Perceiving the courses of behavior* (pp. 1–26). Morristown, NJ: General Learning Press.

Kruglanski, A. W., & Ajzen, I. (1983). Bias and error in human judgment. *European Journal of Social Psychology, 13,* 1–44.

Kuhl, J., & Blankenship, V. (1979). Behavioral change in a constant environment: Moving to more difficult tasks in spite of constant expectations of success. *Journal of Personality and Social Psychology, 37,* 551–563.

Kukla, A. (1972). Foundations of an attributional theory of performance. *Psychological Review, 79,* 454–470.

Kukla, A. (1978). An attributional theory of choice. In L. Berkowitz (Ed.), *Advances in experimental social psychology* (Vol. 11, pp. 113–144). New York: Academic Press.

Lewin, K., Dembo, T., Festinger, L., & Sears, P. S. (1944). Level of aspiration. In J. McV. Hunt (Ed.), *Personality and the behavior disorders* (Vol. 1, pp. 333–378). New York: Ronald Press.

McClelland, D. C., Atkinson, J. W., Clark, R. W., & Lowell, E. L. (1953). *The achievement motive.* New York: Appleton-Century-Crofts.

Merton, R. K., & Kitt, A. S. (1950). Contributions to the theory of reference group behavior. In R. K. Merton & P. F. Lazarsfeld (Eds.), *Continuities in social research: Studies in the scope and method of "The American soldier"* (pp. 40–105). Glencoe, IL: Free Press.

Meyer, W. U., Folkes, V. S., & Weiner, B. (1976). The perceived informational value and affective consequences of choice behavior and intermediate difficulty task selection. *Journal of Research in Personality, 10,* 410–423.

Miller, D. T., & Ross, M. (1975). Self-serving biases in the attribution of causality: Fact or fiction. *Psychological Bulletin, 82*, 213–225.

Mischel, W. (1974). Processes in delay of gratification. In L. Berkowitz (Ed.), *Advances in experimental social psychology* (Vol. 7, pp. 249–293). New York: Academic Press.

Mischel, W. (1979). On the interface of cognition and personality: Beyond the personality-situation debate. *American Psychologist, 34*, 740–754.

Mischel, W. (1984). Counergences and challenges in the search for consistency. *American Psychologist, 39*, 351–364.

Nicholls, J. G. (1976). Effort is virtuous, but it's better to have ability. *Journal of Research in Personality, 10*, 306–315.

Nicholls, J. G. (1979). Quality and equality in intellectual development: The role of motivation in education. *American Psychologist, 34*, 1071–1084.

Nisbett, R. E., & Ross, L. (1980). *Human inferences: Strategies and shortcomings of social judgment.* Englewood Cliffs, NJ: Prentice-Hall.

Ruble, D. N. (1980). A developmental perspective on theories of achievement motivation. In L. J. Fyans (Ed.), *Achievement motivation: Recent trends in theory and research* (pp. 225–245). New York: Plenum.

Ruble, D. N., & Boggiano, A. K. (1981). Optimizing motivation in an achievement context. In B. Keogh (Ed.), *Advances in special education* (pp. 183–238). Greenwich, CT: JAI Press.

Sarason, S. B. (1959). *Psychological problems in mental deficiency.* New York: Harper.

Schlenker, B. R. (1981). *Impression management: The self-concept, social identity, and interpersonal relations.* Monterey, CA: Brooks/Cole.

Shannon, C. E., & Weavor, W. (1949). *The mathematical theory of communication.* Urbana: University of Illinois Press.

Snyder, M. J., Stephen, W. G., & Rosenfield, D. A. (1978). Atributional egotism. In J. H. Harvey, W. Ickes, & R. F. Kidd (Eds.), *New directions in attributional research* (Vol. 2, pp. 91–120). Hillsdale, NJ: Erlbaum.

Sorrentino, R. M., & Hewitt, E. C. (1984). The uncertainty-reducing properties of revisited. *Journal of Personality and Social Psychology, 46*, 884–903.

Sorrentino, R. M., Short, J. C., & Raynor, J. D. (1984). Uncertainty orientation: Implications for affective and cognitive views of achievement behavior. *Journal of Personality and Social Psychology, 46*, 189–206.

Suls, J. M., & Miller, R. L. (1977). *Social comparison processes: Theoretical and empirical prospectives.* New York: Hemisphere.

Tedeschi, J. T. (Ed.). (1981). *Impression management theory and social psychological research.* New York: Academic Press.

Tetlock, P. E. & Levi, A. (1982). Attribution bias: On the inconclusiveness of the cognitive-motiation debate. *Journal of Experimental Social Psychology, 18*, 68–88.

Trope, Y. (1975). Seeking information about one's own ability as a determinant of choice among tasks. *Journal of Personality and Social Psychology, 32*, 1004–1013.

Trope, Y. (1978). Extrinsic rewards, congruence between dispositions and behavior, and perceived freedom. *Journal of personality and social psychology, 36*, 93–106.

Trope, Y. (1979). Uncertainty reducing properties of achievement tasks. *Journal of Personality and Social Psychology, 37*, 1505–1518.

Trope, Y. (1980). Self-assessment, self-enhancement and task preference. *Journal of Experimental Social Psychology, 16*, 116–129.

Trope, Y. (1982). Self-assessment and task performance. *Journal of Experimental Social Psychology, 18*, 201–215.

Trope, Y. (1983). Self-assessment in achievement behavior. In J. M. Suls & A. G. Greenwald (Eds.), *Psychological perspectives on the self* (Vol. 2, pp. 93–121). Hillsdale, NJ: Erlbaum.

Trope, Y., & Brickman, P. (1975). Difficulty and diagnosticity as determinants of choice among tasks. *Journal of Personality and Social Psychology, 31*, 918–925.

Trope, Y., & Burnstein, E. (1977). A disposition-behavior congruity model of perceived freedom. *Journal of Experimental Social Psychology, 13*, 357–368.

Ungar, S. (1980). The effects of the certainty of self-perceptions on self-presentational behaviors: A test of the strength of self-enhancement motives. *Social Psychological Quarterly, 43*, 165–172.

Weiner, B. (1965). The effects of unsatisfied achievement motivation on persistence and subsequent performance. *Journal of Personality, 38*, 428–442.

Weiner, B. (1966). The role of success and failure in the learning of easy and complex tasks. *Journal of Personality and Social Psychology, 3*, 339–344.

Weiner, B. (Ed.). (1974). *Achievement motivation and attribution theory.* Morristown, NJ: General Learning Press.

Weiner, B. (1979). A theory of motivation for some classroom experiences. *Journal of Educational Psychology, 71*, 3–25.

Weiner, B. (1980). *Human motivation.* New York: Holt, Rinehart and Winston.

Weiner, B., Frieze, T. H., Kukla, A., Reed, L., Rest, S., & Rosenbaum, R. M. (1971). *Perceiving the causes of success and failure.* Morristown, NJ: General Learning Press.

Weiner, B., Heckhausen, H., Meyer, W. U., & Cook, R. E. (1972). Causal ascriptions and achievement behavior: A conceptual analysis of effort and reanalysis of locus of control. *Journal of Personality and Social Psychology, 21*, 239–248.

Weiner, B., & Kukla, A. (1970). An attributional analysis of achievement motivation. *Journal of Personality and Social Psychology, 15*, 1–20.

Weiner, B., Russell, D., & Lerman, D. (1978). Affective consequences of causal ascriptions. In J. H. Harvey, W. J. Ickes, & R. F. Kidd (Eds.), *New directions in attribution research* (Vol. 2, pp. 59–90). Hillsdale, NJ: Erlbaum Press.

Wicklund, R. A. (1975). Objective self-awareness. In L. Berkowitz (Ed.), *Advances in experimental social psychology* (Vol. 8, pp. 233–277). New York: Academic Press.

Wortman, C. B., & Brehm, J. W. (1975). Responses to uncontrollable outcomes. An integration of reactance theory and the learned helplessness model. In L. Berkowitz (Ed.), *Advances in experimental social psychology* (Vol. 8, 278–336). New York: Academic Press.

Zuckerman, M. (1979). Attribution of success and failure revisited, or: The motivational bias in alive and well in attribution theory. *Journal of Personality, 47*, 245–287.

Zuckerman, M., Brown, R. H., Fischler, G. L., Fox, G. A., Lathin, D. R., & Minesian, A. J. (1979). Determinants of information seeking behavior. *Journal of Research in Personality, 13*, 161–174.

CHAPTER 13

Uncertainty Orientation, Motivation, and Cognition

RICHARD M. SORRENTINO
JUDITH-ANN C. SHORT
University of Western Ontario and St. Thomas Psychiatric Hospital

The theme of this Handbook is the "Warm Look"—the synergistic inter-dependence of motivation and cognition in predicting behavior (see Chapter 1). In the present chapter, we shall stress this interdependence from an informational and affective perspective. We believe we have discovered an important informational individual-difference variable that is critical to furthering the understanding of the Warm Look. In addition, we may have clearly delineated an important affective variable—the achievement motive. As shall be seen, other chapters in this volume not only have furthered our understanding of what we are about but also have provided what may be important implications for other contributions to the Handbook.

The informational variable we have discovered is what we call uncertainty orientation (see Sorrentino & Hewitt, 1984; Sorrentino, Short, & Raynor, 1984). This involves the degree of uncertainty surrounding the outcome of one's activity. It is cognitive in nature and has much to do with what many have called cognitive information seeking. Its two strongest implications for the other contributions to this Handbook are (1) that this variable not only has a great deal to do with cognitive information seeking but also has a great deal to do with maintenance and preservation of current knowledge; and (2) that uncertainty orientation has often been and continues to be confused with achievement motivation. In terms of the first implication, we wish to draw the attention of many cognitive theorists, as well as proponents of the Warm Look, to the fact that there are many people who simply are not interested in finding out information about themselves or the world, who do not conduct causal searches, who could not care less about socially comparing themselves with others, and who "don't give a hoot" for resolving discrepancies or inconsistencies about the self. Indeed, such people (we call them certainty oriented) will go out of their way not to perform activities such as these (we call people who *do* go out of their way to do such things uncertainty oriented).

The second factor bears on the fact that, in contrast to cognitive alternatives (cf. Trope, 1975; Weiner, 1972), we believe that achievement motivation is primarily an affective variable, as was originally theorized (cf. Atkinson, 1964; McClelland, Atkinson, Clark, & Lowell, 1953). Success-oriented people are not any more interested in finding out information about their own ability than failure-threatened people are; they simply have greater pride in accomplishment and less shame over failure. On the other hand, in contrast to affective approaches (cf. Atkinson & Raynor, 1974), the degree of perceived difficulty or subjective probability of success—which in effect is the degree of certainty about success or failure—does not fit nicely into a neat package of interaction with achievement-related motives. Rather, it is in the service of uncertainty orientation. In this chapter, we shall present a brief history of theory and research into the realm of uncertainty orientation. We shall then discuss its relevance to the Warm Look both by itself and in combination with achievement-related motives.

A THEORY OF UNCERTAINTY ORIENTATION

The prototype for uncertainty orientation comes straight from Rokeach's *The Open and Closed Mind* (1960). For Rokeach's approach, one must distinguish among types of people on a continuum ranging from "gestalt types" on one end to "psychoanalytic types" on the other. The former were characterized by the "need for a cognitive framework to know and understand," whereas the latter were characterized by the "need to ward off threatening aspects of reality" (Rokeach, 1960, p. 67). Although this harks back to Freudian notions regarding basic trust and mistrust of the world (with the open-minded person passing successfully through the oral stage and seeking out the new world and the closed-minded person still fixated, hanging onto Mommy's skirts and Daddy's coat tails—or vice versa), it is also not unlike current notions of category accessibility or cognitive schemata (Higgins & King, 1981; Markus, 1977). Rokeach (1960) argued that the open-minded person possesses a cognitive belief system oriented toward new beliefs and/or information, whereas the closed-minded person possesses a belief system oriented toward familiar and/or predictable events. In his book, he presented an impressive series of studies to show that these differences in belief systems (or schemata) account for differences in general authoritarianism, prejudice, cognitive problem solving (e.g., the classic case of Joe Doodlebug), music appreciation, perceptions, political and religious opinionation, and religious dogma.

An important point we will make throughout this chapter and elsewhere is that cognitive theories in general and cognitive information-seeking interpretations of achievement behavior in particular stress Rokeach's "gestalt type," to the relative (or absolute) neglect of the "psychoanalytic type." This is most unfortunate, given (1) that the majority of the adult population is probably more the latter—that is, closed-minded and authoritarian (cf. Kirscht & Dillehay, 1967; Kohlberg, 1976) and (2) that many cognitive theorists are misled into thinking that all persons are gestalt types and shape their theories accordingly.

A second major influence in our development of uncertainty orientation was Kagan's (1972) article on motives and development. According to Kagan, uncertainty resolution is a primary determinant of behavior. People will sometimes approach and sometimes avoid uncertain situations, depending on the availability of coping mechanisms and the voluntary or involuntary nature of the involvement. Their primary motive will always be to resolve the uncertainty, however; other motives are considered to be secondary and idiosyncratic. For example, in some people, the dependency motive will be aroused in response to uncertainty, whereas other people may have affiliation, achievement, or dominance motives aroused. In each case, though, these motives and their associated behaviors are designed to resolve the individual's uncertainty. Although Kagan (1972) does not discuss individual differences in the need to resolve uncertainty, it seems possible that, as a function of developmental history, some people will evolve an orientation toward uncertain situations and others toward certain situations. Finally, similar to our position, Kagan (1972) views other sources of motivation, such as achievement, as being in the service of uncertainty resolution.

We stumbled on uncertainty orientation quite by accident. Soon after our discovery of the "mysterious moderates"—that is, the finding that people who score as moderate on motive measures tend to behave in a most peculiar fashion (Sorrentino & Short, 1977)—we searched for some factor present in every situation that might account for this phenomenon. Perhaps moderates were higher on some personality factor relevant to this dimension, causing the moderates phenomenon. To our delight, we realized that every situation varies with the amount of uncertainty regarding the outcome of that situation. Some outcomes are very certain, some very uncertain, and some in between. Hence, perhaps in addition to some source of motivation specific to a given situation (e.g., achievement, affiliation, power), people also vary with respect to how they handle the uncertainty regarding the outcome of a situation.

It turns out that we were right about the importance of uncertainty orientation (although it does not account for the moderates phenomenon). In a series of studies, some of them to be reported here, things worked out fairly well. Unfortunately, it took years to figure out why they were working well; that is, we could successfully predict three factor interactions, but we could not understand precisely why they worked. After consulting with dozens of people, banging our heads against the wall many times, and—not least—reading first drafts of chapters in this Handbook, we think we also have the "why."

UNCERTAINTY ORIENTATION AS INFORMATION VALUE

In their chapter of the Handbook (Chapter 11), Raynor and McFarlin make an important distinction between two types of value: information value and affective value. Basically, it is the distinction between finding out versus feeling good (see also Chapter 14, by Trope, which presents two separate theories of achievement behavior, one affective and one informational). To the extent that one or both of these opportunities exist in a given situation, the person will be motivated to undertake that activity. We believe now that uncertainty orientation is primarily concerned with information value. The uncertainty-oriented person seeks to attain clarity about his or her self or environment (Raynor and McFarlin's self versus behavioral systems). Certainty orientation is also concerned with information value, but in terms of maintaining present clarity about the self or the environment. People who score high in n-uncertainty and low in authoritarianism are considered uncertainty oriented; people who score low in n-uncertainty and high in authoritarianism are considered certainty oriented (see Sorrentino & Hewitt, 1984).

Although we think of uncertainty orientation as a cognitive rather than a motivational variable, we claim that it is the uncertainty-oriented person who is similar to Rokeach's "gestalt type." It is he or she who will search for meaning, attempting to make sense out of his or her environment, and will seek out new or novel situations. The certainty-oriented person is similar to the "psychoanalytic type," maintaining information value by adhering to situations that do not entail uncertainty about the self or environment. This person was an enigma to us at first, until we realized that we, too, thought of everyone as more or less a "gestalt type." But such a person will not seek to find out anything about his or her self or environment if it requires changing what is already known and clear to the person.

A case in point is our replication of one of two studies done by Trope (1979). Trope set out to demonstrate that people will prefer to find out about their ability regardless of whether the outcome is positive or negative. In his study, people in one group (ascending condition) were made to believe that they did not have low ability on a test of a new ability, but it was uncertain whether they had intermediate or high ability. In another group (descending condition), people were made to believe that they did not have high ability, but it was uncertain whether they had low or intermediate ability. When they were given the opportunity to construct a further test made up of items of their choice, subjects in both conditions were more likely to choose test items that would resolve this uncertainty. Hence, Trope (1979) found, as predicted, that subjects were more likely to choose uncertainty-reducing items than other items, regardless of whether the chosen items would indicate high or low ability.

Although this was an ingenious experiment, from our perspective it relates only to the uncertainty-oriented person. The certainty-oriented person would probably not choose such items, as he or she is not interested in finding out new information about the self. Figure 13.1 shows the results of our replication of

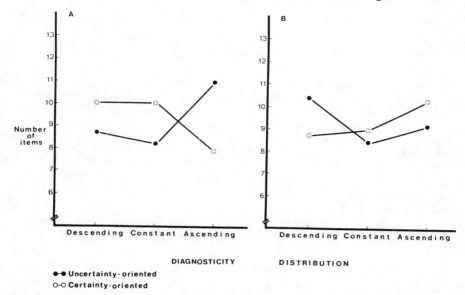

FIGURE 13.1 Mean number of items chosen from each subtest as a function of uncertainty orientation (uncertainty-oriented versus certainty-oriented) and experimental conditions (A = ascending, B = descending). (From "Uncertainty-Related Properties of Achievement Tasks as a Function of Uncertainty-Orientation and Achievement-Related Motives" by R. M. Sorrentino and E. Hewitt, 1984, *Journal of Personality and Social Psychology, 47,* pp. 892. Copyright 1984 by the American Psychological Association. Reprinted by permission.)

Trope's (1979) study. Based on subjects' estimates of their own ability (i.e., they knew that they did not have low ability but did not know whether they were of intermediate or high ability—ascending condition; or they knew they did not have high ability but were uncertain whether they had intermediate or low ability—descending condition), they were given the opportunity to take a further test of that ability. The test was divided into three subtests, and subjects could choose as many items as they wished from the three subtests, up to a total of 28 items. Subjects were then shown charts in which it was evident that one of the subtests would reduce uncertainty about their ability (ascending portion of diagnositicty distribution for Ascending condition, descending portion for descending condition in Figure 13.1). Note that, as we expected, the tendency to choose items most diagnostic of their ability (i.e., ascending subtest items in the ascending condition, descending subtest items in the descending condition) was shown only by the uncertainty-oriented subjects. Indeed, the certainty-oriented subjects appeared to prefer items in both conditions that either would reaffirm what they already know about their new ability (descending or ascending items in opposing conditions) or would tell them nothing new at all (constant items in both conditions). Thus, these people chose items that would preserve the status quo over items that would provide potentially important information about the self. Certainty-oriented people simply were not interested in being placed in a situation that we uncertainty-oriented types (i.e., most of us in academia) would prefer. The certainty-oriented person simply does not act like a "normal" person. We will discuss this further later in the chapter.

ACHIEVEMENT MOTIVATION AND AFFECTIVE VALUE

Whereas we have been examining the uncertainty aspects of achievement situations in terms of a personality variable directly related to the uncertainty of the situation, others have attributed these differences to achievement-related motives. Like us, Schneider and Posse (1982) pointed out that the uncertainty of the outcome in achievement-oriented situations may be the important situational determinant. They believed, however, that the uncertainty may directly affect differences resulting from achievement-related motives. Heckhausen (1968) believed that curiosity may be an important factor, but he also treated it as inherent to achievement motivation. It is interesting that Kuhl and Geiger (1984; see also Kuhl, Chapter 14 of this volume) provided evidence that the curiosity motive *per se* does not show properties similar to the achievement motive; they concluded that either their dependent measure, speed of drawing, is a valid index only for the achievement motive, or "cumulative effects (in strength of motivation over time) are especially strong in the achievement domain whereas, in other domains, behavior may be more context specific or episodic" (Kuhl & Geiger, 1984, p. 28). These conclusions are consistent with our argument that curiosity or cognitive information seeking is neither related to nor has the affective arousal properties of the achievement motive.

The biggest challenge to the theory of achievement motivation, however, has come from Weiner (e.g., Weiner, 1972) and Trope (e.g., Trope, 1975, 1979; Trope & Brickman, 1975). These investigators argued that the major difference between success-oriented and failure-threatened people is not affective (feeling good about success, feeling bad about failure), as Atkinson and Raynor (1974) would argue, but is primarily a difference in cognitive information seeking. That is, the success-oriented person is more interested than the failure-threatened person in finding out about his or her ability. Hence, the success-oriented person is most interested in highly diagnostic tasks.

Some support for this notion comes from a study by Trope (1975), in which he demonstrated that success-oriented people choose to take a test most diagnostic of their ability; this difference was greater than a similar preference by failure-threatened people. We argue, however, that this experiment was not a true test of the cognitive information-seeking alternative, as diagnosticity was confounded with affective value. That is, the highly diagnostic condition was the only condition in which the success-oriented person would know that success meant he or she had high ability. Since high ability is something most people are proud of,

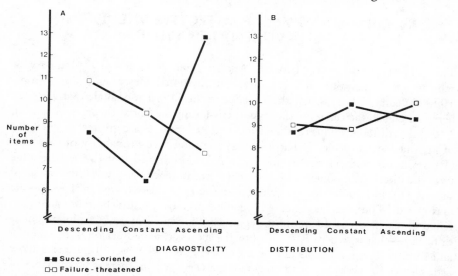

FIGURE 13.2 Mean number of items chosen from each subtest as a function of achievement-related motives (success-oriented versus failure-threatened) and experimental conditions (A = ascending, B = descending). (From "Uncertainty-Related Properties of Achievement Tasks as a Function of Uncertainty-Orientation and Achievement-Related Motives" by R. M. Sorrentino and E. Hewitt, 1984, *Journal of Personality and Social Psychology, 47,* pp. 893. Copyright 1984 by the American Psychological Association. Reprinted by permission.)

the greatest pride in accomplishment should occur here. If this experiment had controlled for level of ability (e.g., if it had been highly diagnostic of low ability) and still had found predicted differences for achievement-related motives, then a cognitive information seeking explanation would have received support. Actually, the previous study cited (Trope, 1979) did control for level of ability, but it did not examine differences resulting from achievement-related motives. When we replicated that study (Sorrentino & Hewitt, 1984), we did examine such differences. Our findings are shown in Figure 13.2. Note that where subjects could find out whether they did or did not have high ability (ascending condition), success-oriented people most preferred and failure-threatened people least preferred the most diagnostic task (ascending diagnosticity subtest). However, where subjects already knew they did not have high ability but could not find out whether it was low or intermediate (descending condition), differences due to achievement-related motives were extinguished. Apparently, there is little affective value to a task in which the person already knows that he or she is mediocre at best (see Raynor and McFarlin, Chapter 11, for similar arguments). Thus, affective value, not cognitive information seeking, appears to be the primary goal of achievement motivation. This is not to say that information seeking is unimportant to achievement *behavior*; indeed, in the next section we argue that it is crucial.

INFORMATION VALUE, AFFECTIVE VALUE, AND ACHIEVEMENT BEHAVIOR

The crux of the difference between Atkinson and Raynor's (1974) theory of achievement motivation and cognitive informational viewpoints (e.g., Trope, 1975; Weiner, 1972) is that the affective versus informational alternatives cited here can equally account for the hypothesis (from the initial theory—Atkinson, 1964) that differences due to achievement-related motives are greatest in situations of intermediate difficulty—that is, where the subjective probability of success is .50. From his mathematical formulation, Atkinson argued that this is where the two situational components of the achievement tendency—incentive value of success (I_s) and subjective probability of success (P_s), where $I_s = 1 - P_s$—are maximized. Thus, success-oriented people are most positively motivated and failure-threatened people are most negatively motivated by tasks of intermediate difficulty—that is, where $P_s = .50$. For the success-oriented person, succeeding at an easy task does not enable him or her to feel good, whereas difficult tasks allow little chance to succeed. For the failure-threatened person, there is little chance of failing at an easy task and little shame at failing at a difficult task. Hence, affective arousal for both types of motivation is greatest where $P_s = .50$.

Cognitive information theorists argue, however, that a P_s of .50 is where persons can find out most about their ability. A task for which P_s is too low (i.e., a difficult task) or too high (i.e., an easy task) gives less information about ability, as success or failure may be attributed to chance or task factors. Hence, the true goal of the achievement motive is to determine the person's ability—to find out rather than to feel good.

We argue that both approaches are only partially correct. Although differences due to achievement-related motives are affective and the important situational determinant is informational, the two do not go together. What really happens is that they interact with a third variable—uncertainty orientation. In addition to task difficulty, situations of intermediate difficulty entail two separate but related cognitive components: (1) they provide the most information about the person's ability, as the cognitive theorists state; and (2) the outcome of the activity is at its highest uncertainty, as we (Sorrentino *et al.*, 1984) and others (e.g., Schneider & Posse, 1982) point out. Thus, situations of intermediate difficulty should be of relevance to uncertainty-oriented persons, as they offer the opportunity to attain new information about the self ("How good am I?") and the environment ("What will happen?"). On the other hand, situations of low or high difficulty are of relevance to the certainty-oriented person, as they maintain clarity about the self ("I know I'm bad/good at this") and the environment ("I know what should happen").

In terms of affective arousal due to achievement-related motives, the important point is that this arousal will be greatest in situations relevant to the person's uncertainty orientation. Situations that *attain* clarity about the self lead to the greatest arousal of achievement-related motives for uncertainty-oriented people; situations that *maintain* clarity about the self lead to the greatest arousal of achievement-related motives for certainty-oriented people.

This general hypothesis can be translated here to the prediction that although levels of intermediate difficulty will lead to the greatest arousal of achievement-related motives for uncertainty-oriented people, easy and difficult levels will lead to the greatest arousal of achievement-related motives for certainty-oriented people.

In the first of three studies by Sorrentino, Short, and Raynor (1984), we demonstrated that this was, indeed, the case. For the uncertainty-oriented group, the greatest differences on a test of complex arithmetic ability, in which success-oriented people outperformed failure-threatened people, was at $P_s = .50$. For the certainty-oriented group, however, the reverse occurred. That is, the greatest differences due to achievement-related motives occurred at $P_s = .20$ and $P_s = .80$ (highest certainty of failure and success in the study). The results of this study were especially pleasing, as they were with female subjects and they actually showed avoidance behavior on the part of failure-threatened subjects where $P_s = .50$ (but *only* for the uncertainty-oriented group, as we had predicted). The theory of achievement motivation has been severely criticized because of the paucity of results on both counts: predicting the behavior of females (see Horner, 1974), and predicting that avoidance behavior of failure-threatened people will occur where $P_s = .50$ (Trope, 1975; Weiner, 1972).

Two other experiments were reported in the Sorrentino *et al.* (1984) article. Both argued that Raynor's (1969, 1974) elaborated theory of achievement motivation, now called the general theory of achievement motivation (Atkinson & Raynor, 1974), held only for uncertainty-oriented people. Raynor's elaboration expanded the initial theory (Atkinson, 1964; Atkinson & Feather, 1966) to include the effect of future goals on performance at the immediate activity. Where it is necessary to succeed at the immediate activity to move on to the next step toward some future goal, success-oriented people will be more positively motivated and failure-threatened people will be more negatively motivated than where performance at the immediate activity has no direct future consequences. In support of his theory, Raynor demonstrated that performance differences due to achievement-related motives were greater on a test of complex arithmetic ability in a contingent than in a noncontingent condition (Entin & Raynor, 1973; Raynor & Rubin, 1971)—that is, where it was or was not necessary to succeed at each step of a path to move on to the next step—and in a field study, where subjects perceived their performance in an introductory psychology course as instrumental or noninstrumental to future goals. Differences on final grade point averages for the course as a function of achievement-related motives was greater for the high-perceived-instrumentality subjects than for the low-perceived-instrumentality subjects (Raynor, 1969).

We argued that a critical factor in Raynor's elaboration is the uncertainty of the outcome. That is, the ultimate outcome of any activity that is one step in a series of obstacles the individual must overcome before reaching the final goal must be more uncertain than the outcome of a similar activity that is not connected to future goals. In addition, future goal-oriented situations offer still further information about the self ("How far can I go?" "What will I become?"), whereas situations about present goals deal with the here and now ("This is what it is," "This is what I am").

Given that future goal orientation leads to further attainment of clarity about the self and the environment, whereas situations without future goals are more likely to maintain clarity about the self or environment, we argued that Raynor's predictions would hold only for people who are uncertainty-oriented. For certainty-oriented people, we predicted precisely the opposite outcome. Differences in arousal of achievement-related motives should be greater where the final outcome of the immediate activity and information about the self is less uncertain—that is, in the noncontingent condition of the Raynor and Rubin (1971) study—and where students actually perceived their course as unrelated to future goals—the low-perceived-instrumentality subjects in the Raynor (1969) study. In Studies 2 and 3 reported by Sorrentino *et al.* (1984), we replicated the two Raynor studies, but we also examined individual differences in uncertainty orientation. Our predictions were confirmed.

Taken together, these three studies supported our general theory of the interaction between information value and affective value. Differences in arousal of achievement-related motives are greatest in situations relevant to the person's uncertainty orientation. Hence, although the general theory of achievement motivation predicts (and much of the lay community accepts) that success-oriented people perform best and failure-threatened people perform worst at tasks of intermediate difficulty, on contingent paths, and where the course is perceived as instrumental to future goals, this occurs *only* if the people are also uncertainty-oriented. Indeed, if they are also certainty oriented, success-oriented people perform best and failure-threatened people worst at easy and difficult tasks, on noncontingent paths, and where the course has little perceived relevance to future goals (low perceived instrumentality).

Even though we predicted all of this, the results for the certainty-oriented group were mind-boggling when we looked at their behavior as a function of achievement-related motives. It is difficult to think of a success-oriented person as really "turned on" by simple or impossible tasks, or by trivial ones, and the failure-threatened person as extremely inhibited by these very tasks, as opposed to more challenging ones. Table 13.1 shows the results of the grade study (Sorrentino *et al.*, 1984, Study 3). The table indicates the actual performance of students in an introductory psychology course as a function of their perceived instrumentality of the course to future goals. Bear in mind that these actual grades were obtained from 3 months (for midterm exams) to 7 months (for final exams and grades) after students were assessed for achievement-related motives, uncertainty orientation, and perceived instrumentality of the course. For the uncertainty-oriented group, we not only have perfect data in support of the general theory of achievement motivation, but we can understand it. Success-oriented people *should* perform better where they perceive the course as instrumental to future goals than where they do not. Failure-threatened people, of course, should be more anxious and

TABLE 13.1 Mean Percentage Scores on Three Measures of Classroom Performance as a Function of Resultant Uncertainty Orientation × Achievement-Related Motives × Perceived Instrumentality (Study 3)

Subjects' Orientation	Midterm Examinations		Final Examinations		Final Course Grade	
	Noninstrumental	Instrumental	Noninstrumental	Instrumental	Noninstrumental	Instrumental
Uncertainty oriented						
Success oriented	64.27	72.06	62.33	71.75	67.33	74.94
	($n = 15$)	($n = 15$)	($n = 15$)	($n = 16$)	($n = 15$)	($n = 16$)
Failure threatened	69.12	59.62	61.50	53.92	68.88	59.46
	($n = 8$)	($n = 13$)	($n = 8$)	($n = 13$)	($n = 8$)	($n = 8$)
Certainty oriented						
Success oriented	63.71	53.17	64.71	58.00	67.71	62.67
	($n = 7$)	($n = 12$)	($n = 7$)	($n = 12$)	($n = 7$)	($n = 12$)
Failure threatened	56.93	60.43	52.93	56.43	59.33	60.43
	($n = 15$)	($n = 21$)	($n = 15$)	($n = 21$)	($n = 15$)	($n = 21$)

Note: From "Uncertainty Orientation: Implications for Affective and Cognitive Views of Achievement Behavior" by R. M. Sorrentino, J. C. Short, and J. O. Raynor, 1984, *Journal of Personality and Social Psychology, 46,* p. 201. Copyright 1984 by the American Psychological Association. Reprinted by permission.

inhibited where they also perceive the course as relevant to future goals. These are "normal" people—males and females alike (no sex differences were found across the three factors). Now look at the certainty-oriented group. Here we had success-oriented people performing better and failure-threatened people performing worse where the course was irrelevant to future goals.

At about the same time these results were coming in, comedian Steve Martin included in his act a skit in which he did nothing but state repeatedly, "What the hell is that?" Although the object of his perplexity was never revealed, we are certain it was our data concerning the certainty-oriented person. At this point, we turn to cognitive theorists to help us answer Mr. Martin's question.

THE COGNITIVE DYNAMICS OF UNCERTAINTY ORIENTATION

Our original foray into the realm of uncertainty orientation was with the belief that we were dealing with a "hot," or motivational, variable. Indeed, we thought we were dealing, basically, with an approach–avoidance source of motivation (e.g., motive for uncertainty versus motive to avoid uncertainty). This, does not appear to be the case, however. If, for example, certainty-oriented people were motivated to avoid uncertainty, then such anxiety should have added to fear of failure in uncertain situations. This did not occur, however. Rather, in our research, fear of failure appeared to be neutralized for certainty-oriented people in uncertain situations.

Table 13.1 illustrates this point. Note that where perceived instrumentality (PI) is high, the certainty-oriented, failure-threatened people do better in their courses than where PI is low. If the certainty-oriented people were anxious about uncertainty (i.e., high PI), then the opposite effect should have occurred. This absence of an additive effect for certainty orientation and fear of failure in uncertain situations occurred in the other two studies reported by Sorrentino *et al.* (1984) and in subsequent research (e.g., Sorrentino & Roney, in preparation). The astute observer may note that similar reasoning applies to the failure-threatened, uncertainty-oriented person, who should show less rather than greater inhibition in uncertain situations if uncertainty orientation were a source of positive motivation. This also did not occur in our research. Hence, there does not appear to be any clear evidence that uncertainty orientation is a "hot" motivational variable.

As previously stated, however, we did show that differences in performance due to achievement-related motives are greatest in situations relevant to the person's uncertainty orientation. Hence, we do have apparent affective differences due to achievement-related motives where the situation is relevant to uncertainty orientation, and little or no difference in the expected direction (i.e., success-oriented people outperforming failure-threatened people) where the situation is not relevant.

Given that we appear to have affective differences as a function of achievement-related motives but not as a function of uncertainty orientation, we turned to other avenues of explanation for the underlying dynamics of uncertainty orientation. Thanks to Tory Higgins, we were directed to a literature that helps explain this phenomenon. This literature is in the area of individual differences in either self-schemata (e.g., Markus, 1977; Rogers, Kuiper, & Kirker, 1977) or accessible constructs (Higgins & King, 1981). These authors have suggested that individual differences in the relevance or accessibility of schemata can influence the processing of information. For Markus (1977), self-schemata are "cognitive generalizations about the self, derived from past experience, that organize and guide the processing of self-related information" (p. 64). Whereas Markus discussed the role of self-schemata in the processing of relevant information within specific content areas (e.g., dependence–independence), our conceptualization refers to a more general class of self-schemata—namely, the cognitive domain of certain versus uncertain outcomes.

Higgins and King (1981) postulated that constructs that are related to a person's goals, expectations, or previous social experience become more accessible, thereby increasing the likelihood that they will be utilized in processing subsequent information. These authors also suggested that various personality differences may be mediated by individual differences in construct accessibility.

From these notions, we took the position that certainty is a readily accessible construct within the cognitive domain of certainty-oriented people, whereas uncertainty is a readily accessible construct for uncertainty-oriented people. When these constructs are tapped by situational cues, relevant sources of motivation (such as achievement-related motives) are aroused. These sources of motivation are unlikely to be aroused when the construct is inaccessible.

This position fits the data nicely. Uncertainty orientation is a cognitive component, and achievement-related motives are affective components. Hence, motivational arousal occurs when the relevant construct is accessed. Uncertainty orientation can also continue to be considered as an individual difference in information value (see Raynor and McFarlin, Chapter 11 of this volume). That is, uncertainty-oriented people attend to situations that attain clarity, whereas certainty-oriented people attend to situations that maintain clarity.

Our position is also very close to the general model of social cognition and affect put forward by Fiske and Pavelchak (Chapter 7 of this volume), who state that "social categories enable a rapid affective response to an instance of the category—a response that does not require an attribute-by-attribute evaluation of the instance" and that "the outcome of the initial categorization stage determines the mode of the second major stage—affective responses." As can be seen, the core of their cognition and affect model is strikingly similar to our cognition and motivation model. Here, uncertainty orientation would be viewed as a general construct (rather than only social), and the affect would be directly linked to specific sources of motivation.

What is particularly exciting about this similarity is that the model offers a basis for a number of testable hypotheses. For example, the first two hypotheses put forward by Fiske and Pavelchak (Chapter 7) can be easily transformed to test our model:

Hypothesis 1 (Category-Based Affect): Successful categorization provides a basis for affective response.

Hypothesis 2 (Efficiency): Category-based affective responses are faster than piecemeal-based affective responses.

These can be transformed to read as follows:

1. Successful categorization of relevant uncertainty-oriented information leads to a more intense motivational response than unsuccessful categorization.
2. Affective responses due to motivational arousal are faster when they are category-based (with appropriate uncertainty categories) than when they are piecemeal-based.

Hypothesis 1 is straightforward and is consistent with our position. In Chapter 7, Fiske and Pavelchak argue that Hypothesis 2 is correct "because category-based affect accesses only the category's overall evaluation, rather than the evaluations of each of the individual's attributes. . . . The initial step of categorization precedes the evaluative response, which is either based on that categorization (category-based affect) or based on the lengthier step of accessing the affective tags of the attributes associated with the category and combining them (piecemeal-based affect)." This may be what uncertainty orientation is all about. That is, it is an efficient filtering device for directing affective arousal from appropriate sources of motivation. Hence, the situation is screened for new information (for uncertainty-oriented people) or for maintaining clarity (for certainty-oriented people), and if accessed, appropriate motive arousal is immediately engaged. If this notion is correct, then affect due to motivational arousal derived from uncertainty categories is relatively fast.

Finally, three recent studies in support of our position have been completed. The first, by Sorrentino and Hewitt (in preparation), was an attempt to demonstrate that uncertainty orientation is a general class variable (i.e., it applies to all domains). We argued that if this were the case, even in a game of chance, uncertainty-oriented people should select intermediate risks, whereas certainty-oriented people should be more likely to select less or more extreme risks (again, intermediate risks are those where the outcome is of the highest uncertainty). The results supported our predictions. This study is important in that it shows that uncertainty is not limited to information about the person's ability but also includes the uncertainty of a given outcome. An interesting additional finding in this study was that sex differences did occur, but only for the certainty-oriented group. The differences were as one might expect according to traditional sex role stereotypes. That is, certainty-oriented males took greater risks and certainty-oriented females exhibited greater caution than both uncertainty-oriented males and females. Hence, certainty-oriented males and females both chose more certain outcomes (i.e., certain success, certain failure) but differed according to sex-typed characteristics.

Put in Raynor and McFarlin's (Chapter 11) terms, then, uncertainty orientation incorporates both the self (self-assessment) and the behavioral (uncertain outcomes) system. Thus, in Study 1 of Sorrentino *et al.* (1984), a P_s of .50 was the most uncertain outcome and provided the greatest information that would reduce uncertainty about the person's ability. Both are relevant to uncertainty orientation. It remains to be seen what happens when one empirically varies the two sources of uncertainty.

In the second study, King (1980) sought to determine whether individual differences in uncertainty orientation could be conceived as individual differences in construct accessibility. In her experiment, King (1980) had subjects read an essay containing behavioral descriptions of a person that contained both certainty- and uncertainty-related interpersonal constructs. One week after this task, subjects were asked to reproduce the descriptions. Consistent with an accessibility effect for uncertainty orientation, subjects over time revealed the expected patterns of distortion and recall of certainty- and uncertainty-related information. That is, both uncertainty-oriented and certainty-oriented subjects recalled and showed memory distortion in the direction relevant to their cognitive domain.

The third study, Sorrentino and Roney (in preparation), returns to the cognitive information-seeking domain to test yet another of Trope's (1981) hypotheses in light of our findings (Sorrentino & Hewitt, 1984). In his study, Trope (1982) found, as he had predicted, that people would perform better on a test of complex arithmetic ability if they felt that the test was diagnostic of their ability than if they did not. In other words, people work harder if they can find out about their ability than if they cannot. Consistent with our arguments, we predicted that performance differences due to diagnosticity conditions would interact with uncertainty orientation and achievement-related motives. Our hypothesis was supported by the results. In the uncertainty-oriented group, success-oriented people performed better and failure-threatened people performed worse in diagnostic than in nondiagnostic conditions. In the certainty-oriented group, success-oriented people performed better and failure-threatened people worse in nondiagnostic than in diagnostic conditions.

In essence, uncertainty orientation may be viewed as a cognitive individual-difference variable related to information value. It serves as a situational screening device that, when identifying a relevant situation, arouses appropriate sources of motivation. Further understanding of uncertainty orientation alone or in interaction with affective variables can contribute to numerous areas of motivation and cognition.

IMPLICATIONS FOR MOTIVATION AND COGNITION

There are several obvious implications of uncertainty orientation for the Warm Look (many related to other contributions to this Handbook), including implications for self-assessment, social comparison, self-inconsistencies, self-concept discrepancies, and risk taking in achievement-oriented situations. Other general assumptions also come into question.

Self-Assessment

As we believe we demonstrated in the Sorrentino and Hewitt (1984) study, certainty-oriented people do not take the opportunity when it is provided, to find out what they are like. Only uncertainty-oriented people do so. Trope's discussion of the cost of self-assessment (Chapter 12) provides a very good explanation of how this lack of interest in self-assessment may have come about. Citing Wicklund (1975), Trope points out that self-assessment induces a focus on the self as an object of evaluation, which is likely to be experienced as aversive. Also, he notes that "in self-assessment, one searches for abilities on which one's standing is uncertain. The resulting awareness of relatively undesirable aspects of the self is likely to exacerbate negative affect." Furthermore, Trope considers the fact that self-asessment often entails a prolonged appraisal of future achievement-related options, which could come at the expense of emotional gratification and efficient performance. He goes on to point out that there may be negative consequences of self-assessment that have future long-term affects. As an example, he cites the possibility that a diagnostic failure "may result in an enduring loss of self-esteem."

These costs tie in nicely with the heretofore apparently bizarre behavior of the certainty-oriented group in Studies 2 and 3 of Sorrentino et al. (1984). Recall that in both these studies, differences in performance (complex arithmetic ability, introductory psychology course grades) due to achievement-related motives were greatest where performance had no future relevance—in the noncontingent condition of Study 2 and the low-perceived-instrumentality condition in Study 3. One might characterize these situations as relevant for the certainty-oriented group, as they do not require prolonged appraisal, which would hamper emotional gratification and efficient performance, and they are less likely than future goal-oriented situations to lead to diagnostic failures, which might result in an enduring loss of self-esteem.

Trope continues his discussion with the statement: "It therefore seems reasonable to characterize the decision to assess oneself as depending on the individual's willingness to endure immediate but short-term achievement costs for the sake of remote but long-term achievement benefits." Given the aforementioned results, it seems reasonable to conjecture that the certainty-oriented group is not so willing. Self-assessment, then, may be a goal only of the uncertainty-oriented person. The certainty-oriented person simply does not wish to be bothered with such prolonged appraisal or with the confusion such tasks entail—a perfectly "normal" reaction.

Social Comparison

Elsewhere (Sorrentino & Hewitt, 1984) we pointed out that both the theory of achievement motivation (Atkinson & Raynor, 1974) and social comparison theory (Festinger, 1954) have their historical roots in early work on level of aspiration (e.g., Lewin, Dembo, Festinger, & Sears, 1944). The former theory dealt with the affective component (feeling good or bad about success or failure); the latter dealt with the cognitive component (i.e., self-assessment and cognitive information seeking). Why neither theory saw the merits of combining the two approaches is still a mystery. Just as we we have shown that the theory of achievement motivation (Atkinson & Raynor, 1974) must be modified to incorporate information value, it is also reasonable to argue that social comparison theory must account for affective value (as well as individual differences in information value). First, the principal hypothesis that the individual has a need to know and evaluate his or her abilities, opinions, and attitudes (Hypothesis 1 of Festinger's [1954] theory) may be appropriate only for uncertainty-oriented people. Certainty-oriented people may find such situations irrelevant. Similar to our findings in Sorrentino and Hewitt (1984), when given the opportunity to compare their ability with others, they probably won't take it. Second, to the extent that a certainty-oriented person has to choose a person with whom to compete, it will not necessarily be a similar other. The choice will be made *in combination* with relevant sources of motivation. For example, research plans are underway to conduct a study in which subjects are to choose their competitors in a game of Master Mind. They will see a rank ordering of competitors in terms of their closeness to the subjects' ability. We predict that in the uncertainty-oriented group, success-oriented people will be most likely and failure-threatened people least likely to choose a similarly skilled other. However, in the certainty-oriented group, success-oriented people will be most likely and failure-threatened people least likely to choose a dissimilar other (better *or* worse).

Theoretically, this prediction is not very different from Study 1 of Sorrentino *et al.* (1984), in that people are most uncertain of how they will perform against a similar as opposed to a dissimilar other, and such a choice would provide the most information about their ability. Hence, the greatest difference is due to achievement-related motives for the uncertainty-oriented group. On the other hand, uncertainty about success, failure, and one's actual ability is less with a dissimilar other; hence, differences due to achievement-related motives are greatest here for the certainty-oriented group. We would go too far beyond the bounds of this chapter if we were to incorporate other hypotheses from social comparison theory. It seems, however, that individual differences in information value and/or affective value are important to its predictions. By taking account of these differences, social comparison theory may finally accrue the support it so richly deserves (see Goethals, 1984).

Self-Inconsistencies and Self-Concept Discrepancies

Upon reading the other chapters in this Handbook, it has become apparent that in addition to self-assessment, notions regarding the self-concept play a central role in developing the Warm Look. Ideas regarding self-enhancement, self-systems, facets of the self, self-consistency, self-standards, self-esteem maintenance, self-concept discrepancies, possible selves, and so forth, abound (see Breckler and Greenwald, Chapter 6; Cantor, Markus, Niedenthal, and Nurius, Chapter 4; Tesser, Chapter

15; Ross and Conway, Chapter 5; Higgins, Strauman, and Klein, Chapter 2; Raynor and McFarlin, Chapter 11; Trope, Chapter 12). As we pointed out earlier, however, many of these authors either assume that all people are interested in these "hyphenated selfs" or assume that they are relevant to individual differences in achievement-related motives. As a case in point, the chapter by my coeditor (Higgins *et al.*, Chapter 2), in relating self-concept discrepancies to achievement-related motives, states: "Moreover, in our model, the amount of pleasure produced by success or the amount of displeasure produced by failure would depend on the extent to which the performance decreased or increased, respectively, a person's self-concept discrepancies." These authors view reduction in self-concept discrepancies as an accentuator of motivational arousal due to achievement-related motives. (Their argument is similar to Trope's [1975] argument for cognitive information seeking.) We argue that such is not the case. According to our theory, self-concept discrepancies clearly fall within the domain of uncertainty orientation, not achievement motivation. Indeed, we argue that for certainty-oriented people, differences in performance due to achievement-related motives would simply not occur (or at least would be relatively small) in situations where self-concept discrepancies exist. Having to attend to the discrepancy would detract from rather than engage achievement-related motives. In this group, success-oriented people may derive a great deal of pleasure from a task in which there is no self-concept discrepancy, and failure-threatened people may derive a great deal of fear or shame. Similar arguments could be made, of course, for the other "self-" concepts listed. To the extent that there is some confusion, inconsistency, or discrepancy about the self, uncertainty-oriented people will seek clarity; however, certainty-oriented people will not. This effect will interact with any source of affective value (e.g., achievement, affiliation) that is also present in the situation.

Achievement-Related Motives, Positive Information Value, and Risk Taking

One of the major phenomena investigated by researchers of achievement motivation has been risk taking. The theory of achievement motivation (Atkinson & Raynor, 1974) specifies that in a one-step contingent path, success-oriented people should prefer intermediate risk, where the probability of success or failure is .50 (this prediction does change for a contingent path with more than one step; see Raynor, 1974). Failure-threatened people will avoid this type of risk. Research testing these predictions has indicated that success-oriented people do indeed prefer intermediate risk (see Atkinson & Litwin, 1960); however, the findings for failure-threatened people are much less consistent with the theory. These people do not seem to display a strong avoidance response and often show none beyond chance level. Because of this problem, the theory has been strongly criticized (e.g., Weinstein, 1969). We note, however, that inherent in any risk situation is the element of uncertainty, and the stable individual-difference variable—uncertainty orientation—should be influential in risk-taking situations. We have already demonstrated in Study 1 of Sorrentino *et al.* (1984) that performance differences due to achievement-related motives are greatest where $P_s = .50$, but only for the uncertainty-oriented group; for the certainty-oriented group, performance differences due to achievement-related motives were least where $P_s = .50$. The study also showed avoidance of a P_s of .50 for failure-threatened people, but only if they were also uncertainty oriented. We would expect similar differences in a risk-taking study that involves skill and a clear standard of excellence (i.e., an achievement-oriented situation). The failure of the theory to receive support, then, may be because it did not consider information value when predicting risk-taking behavior. Both social comparison theory and theory of achievement motivation could thus benefit from considering implications from one another.

Other General Assumptions

In addition to the foregoing implications, we take the opportunity here to make note of several statements by contributors to this Handbook in light of our discovery of individual differences in uncertainty orientation. We take issue with Weiner's (Chapter 10) ninth principle: "A theory of motivation must be based on general laws rather than individual differences." We believe we have demonstrated by research presented in this chapter that failure to account for individual differences could lead to erroneous assumptions and conclusions. For example, self-assessment and cognitive information-seeking theories of achievement behavior (e.g., Trope, 1975, 1979; Weiner, 1972) apply only to uncertainty-oriented people. Certainty-oriented people behave in a manner opposite to what these theories predict.

Our hunch is that the certainty-oriented person's refusal to engage in opportunities to assess his or her ability (Sorrentino & Hewitt, 1984) pervades many other areas of cognitive information seeking. We wonder, for example, whether Hoffman's (Chapter 9) first assumption—that everyone tries to get as much meaning as possible out of a situation—really does apply to everyone. We don't think certainty-oriented people can be so described. Similarly, Weiner's (Chapter 10) statement that "the guiding principle of attribution theory is that people search for understanding, seeking to discover why an event has occurred" is also "up for grabs." His arguments supporting this principle are basically those of seeking new information about the self or environment; yet certainty-oriented people may not care about new information. Thus, theories that attempt to relate affect to cognition must be careful to note that their underlying assumptions may be questionable for some people.

Another area that comes to mind is the degree to which people in general actually engage in rational or cognitive strategies as outlined by some contributors. Consider, for example, the arguments put forth by Cantor, Markus, Niedenthal, and Nurius (Chapter 4). They state: "In general it seems that most people are naturally inclined to work through cognitive simulations or play through a series of scenarios in which they imagine themselves in different plausible outcomes for the situation in question." We have serious doubts at this time that certainty-oriented people behave in such a manner. Raynor and McFarlin (Chapter 11), for example, point out that a self-system is not necessary for human functioning. They state: "We do not, however, share the assumption . . . that all people need a 'theory' (i.e., the self-system) that organizes experience in a way that gives predictability and meaning to life." Thus, it may be that certainty-oriented people do not use the self to direct motivational functioning, as Cantor *et al.* theorize.

A second cognitive issue may be found within the theory of action emergence (Wegner and Vallacher, Chapter 18). These authors argue that simple lateral movement in an identity structure is not allowed. That is, although people can go from high to low levels and from low to high levels of action identification, they cannot go from one high level to another: "This, then, is what keeps people from accepting, willy-nilly, any high-level identification that is offered for an act they already know at a high level." It is our contention that certainty-oriented people *will* go "willy-nilly." One of the predominant features of closed-minded people, for example, is that they do not go through a process of evaluating new information on its merits (see Rokeach, 1960). Thus, if a person is told by an appropriate source of authority that "lobbying for a larger national defense budget" is actually "promoting nuclear war," this new action identification would be accepted, possibly, without going through lower levels. Thus, the certainty-oriented person, who is similar, conceptually, to the closed-minded person, may not need to go from higher to lower levels before a new high-level action identification takes place.

Finally, we have discussed elsewhere (Sorrentino & Hancock, in press) the relevance of uncertainty orientation to the social influence literature. There, too, we have pointed out that various theories may be restricted to an uncertainty-oriented view of behavior. For example, one of the contributors to this volume, Fazio (Chapter 8), applies the distinction offered by cognitive psychologists between automatic and controlled processes (Schneider & Shiffrin, 1977; Shiffrin & Schneider, 1977) to the area of attitude change and persuasion. He states that automatic processing requires "no conscious effort, intent, or control on the part of the individual." Controlled processing, in contrast, requires engaging in "deliberate reasoning," whereby people "assume the role of rational decision makers who carefully consider their attitudes and relevant normative beliefs to arrive at a behavioral intention." Fazio argues that the more important the decision (e.g., deciding on going to college), the more we would rely on controlled than on automatic processing. We argue (Sorrentino & Hancock, in press), first, that uncertainty-oriented people are more likely to rely on controlled processing, whereas certainty-oriented people are more likely to rely on automatic processing. Second, although we agree that uncertainty-oriented people are more likely to increase their reliance on controlled processing as the importance of the decision increases, it is likely that certainty-oriented people are still more likely to rely on automatic processing. In other words, when the final decision to go to college must be made, the uncertainty-oriented person will seek further clarity by rationally weighing all the pros and cons to see if there is any reason to change or alter his or her inclination. The certainty-oriented person will seek to maintain the clarity he or she already has (i.e., the inclination). If he or she has been told by parents and society that college is good, and if that attitude has been internalized, the attitude will automatically be activated, without any further rational or conscious deliberate planning. The certainty-oriented person, then, may think in terms of black or white, good or bad. Indeed, we make the case elsewhere (Raynor, McFarlin, Zubek, & Sorrentino, in preparation; Sorrentino & Hancock, in press) that certainty-oriented people are at, or below, Kohlberg's (1976) level of moral authority (Level 4), as most adults probably are. Such people may, indeed, rely on what they already know or have been told, especially for important decisions.

In sum, a theory of motivation and cognition must be based on general laws that can account for individual differences.

CONCLUSIONS

Although much of what we have to say is mere conjecture at this point, in this final section we would like to present our idea of what uncertainty-oriented and certainty-oriented people are like. It is important to note that, for both types, motivational variables can systematically alter the actual affective state and the subsequent behavior exhibited.

The Uncertainty-Oriented Person

This person is similar to Rokeach's (1960) "gestalt type." He or she attempts to integrate new events or beliefs into already existing belief systems, changing the new or old belief accordingly. Thus, a thought, an idea, a person, is evaluated on its own merits. This person probably made it through the oral and anal stage of development fairly successfully, developing a basic trust in the world and a sense of autonomy. What is important for this person is that he or she attain clarity about the self and the environment. Thus, situations that offer information are accessed by this person. Hence, we have our "need to know" type so readily advocated by rational and/or gestalt psychologists. Self-assessment, social (and physical) comparison, dissonance reduction, causal searches and attributions, possible selves, self-concept discrepancy reduction, self-confrontation, balance, cognitive dissonance, social justice, and equity are all characteristics that this person has or is susceptible to.

This person is unlikely to be prejudiced, bigoted, opinionated, or sexist. (Clayton [1981] found that uncertainty orientation correlates positively with adrogyny, using Bem's [1974] sex role inventory; and Sorrentino & Hewitt [in preparation] found that uncertainty-oriented people do not take risks in accordance with traditional sex role stereotypes, whereas certainty-oriented people do.) This does not mean that such a person will necessarily exhibit positive behavior in all situations, however. A case in point is a study by Sorrentino, Hancock, and Fong (1979), in which low authoritarians (who tend to be uncertainty oriented, on the average) were found to be more likely than high authoritarians to derogate an innocently suffering victim in the classic teacher–learner paradigm of Lerner and Simmons (1966). We predicted that this would be the case, given that uncertainty-oriented people would attempt to make sense out of the fact that the person was suffering innocently. Since this suffering contradicted their belief in a just world (see Lerner, Miller, & Holmes, 1976), they derogated the victim to preserve that belief. Authoritarians (who tend to be certainty oriented, on the average) did not derogate, as they do not attempt to resolve, nor are they threatened by, inconsistencies in their environment.

In addition to the possibility that uncertainty-oriented people can exhibit negative as well as positive behaviors to attain clarity about themselves or their environment, it is important to note that when relevant sources of motivation are engaged, positive or negative behaviors toward the self or others can occur. Thus, although an achievement-oriented situation with an uncertain outcome engages achievement-related motives for the uncertainty-oriented person, the failure-threatened person will feel anxious in that situation. In other words, because the uncertain outcome engages the motive to avoid failure, the person's performance will be more inhibited than if he or she were in an achievement-oriented situation where there was a certain outcome (see Table 13.1). Similarly, for the certainty-oriented person, we would expect that where a social situation with a relatively clear outcome (e.g., where it does not involve a self-concept discrepancy or an inconsistent attitude) may be positively motivating for an approval-oriented, certainty-oriented person, it will be more inhibiting than an uncertain situation for a rejection-threatened, certainty-oriented person. In other words, when situations relevant to a person's uncertainty orientation are accessed, they engage appropriate sources of motivation. These can be positive (e.g., approval-oriented) or negative (e.g., rejection-threatened) sources of motivation.

The Certainty-Oriented Person

This person is the "cold" version of Rokeach's (1960) "psychoanalytic type." He or she likes to stick to familiar events and traditional beliefs. Thus, a thought, an idea, a person, is rejected if it is unfamiliar or different (unless an authority figure endorses it). This person probably did not make it through the oral and anal stage of development successfully, thus developing a basic mistrust in the world, a dependence on authority, and a low sense of autonomy in an unfamiliar environment. What is important for this person is that he or she maintain clarity about the self and the environment. This person, however, is no longer an affective or "hot" psychoanalytic type but has developed a "cold" cognitive style that adheres to what is already known or familiar. Self-assessment, social (and physical) comparison, dissonance reduction, causal searches and attributions, possible selves, self-concept discrepancy reduction, self-confrontation, social justice, and equity are all characteristics that this person does not have or is not susceptible to.

This person is likely to be prejudiced, bigoted, opinionated, and a sexist. This does not mean that such a person will necessarily exhibit negative behavior in all situations, however. Witness, for example, the fact that the authoritarian (who tends to be certainty oriented, on the average) is less likely to derogate an innocently suffering victim, as described earlier. On the other hand, Sorrentino *et al.* (1979) did show that authoritarians would derogate a victim if they themselves were held responsible for the victim's suffering. Whereas low authoritarians derogate to resolve a logical inconsistency, high authoritarians derogate to avoid blame.

Many years ago, when I (RMS) was first starting out in graduate school, I read an article in which the author pointed out that consistency theories of attitude change might be merely the Zeitgeist and that in the future inconsistency theories might prevail in social psychology. To date, such theories have not emerged. I believe now, however, as I wondered then, that resolving inconsistencies about the self or the environment may be a primary concern to people like ourselves (i.e., people in academia). However, perhaps *most* people aren't like that at all. Maybe they just go about their ordinary, everyday life without future goals, in noncontingent paths, and without trying to resolve a single inconsistency. Hence, we present to you, who are not convinced, the certainty-oriented personality.

Acknowledgments

Our thanks to Michael Atkinson, Ramona Bobcocel, Erin Hewitt, E. Tory Higgins, Todd Hogue, Gillian King, Joel Raynor, and Chris Roney for their helpful comments on earlier drafts.

References

Atkinson, J. W. (1964). *An introduction to motivation.* Princeton, NJ: Van Nostrand.

Atkinson, J. W., & Feather, N. T. (1966). *A theory of achievement motivation.* New York: Wiley.

Atkinson, J. W., & Litwin, G. H. (1960). Achievement motivation and test anxiety conceived as motive to approach success and motive to avoid failure. *Journal of Abnormal and Social Psychology, 60,* 52–63.

Atkinson, J. W., & Raynor, J. O. (1974). *Motivation and achievement.* Washington, DC: Winston.

Bem, S. L. (1974). The measurement of psychological androgyny. *Journal of Consulting and Clinical Psychology, 42,* 155–162.

Clayton, J. P. (1981). *Uncertainty orientation, sex role identity and performance in achievement situations.* Unpublished master's thesis, University of Western Ontario.

Entin, E. C., & Raynor, J. O. (1973). Effects of contingent future orientation and achievement motivation on performance in two kinds of task. *Journal of Experimental Research in Personality, 6,* 314–320.

Festinger, L. (1954). A theory of social comparison processes. *Human Relations, 2,* 117–140.

Goethals, G. R. (1984, August). *Social comparison theory: Psychology from the lost and found.* Paper presented at the 92nd Annual Convention of the American Psychological Association, Toronto.

Heckhausen, H. (1968). Achievement motive research: Current problems and some contributions toward a general theory of motivation. In S. P. Grossman, G. E. McClearn, S. Levine, H. Heckhausen, R. S. Lazarus, & J. Aronfreed (Eds.), *Nebraska Symposium on Motivation* (Vol. 16, pp. 103–174). Lincoln: University of Nebraska Press.

Higgins, E. T., & King, G. (1981). Accessibility of social constructs: Information processing consequences of individual and contextual variability. In N. Cantor & J. F. Kihlstrom (Eds.), *Personality, cognition, and social interaction* (pp. 69–121). Hillsdale, NJ: Erlbaum.

Horner, M. S. (1974). The measurement and behavioral implications of fear of success. In J. W. Atkinson & J. O. Raynor (Eds.), *Motivation and achievement* (pp. 91–117). Washington, DC: Winston.

Kagan, J. (1972). Motives and development. *Journal of Personality and Social Psychology, 22*, 51–66.

King, G. (1980). *Individual differences in construct accessibility: A cognitive structural approach to uncertainty orientation.* Unpublished doctoral dissertation, University of Western Ontario.

Kirscht, J., & Dillehay, R. (1967). *Dimensions of authoritarianism.* Lexington: University of Kentucky Press.

Kohlberg, L. (1976). Moral state and moralization. In T. Lickman (Ed.), *Moral development and behavior* (pp. 31–53). New York: Holt, Rinehart and Winston.

Kuhl, J. & Geiger, E. (1984). The dynamic theory of the anxiety–behavior relationship: The champagne-cork effect. In J. Kuhl & J. W. Atkinson (Eds.), *Motivation, thought, and action* (pp. 242–276). New York: Praeger.

Lerner, M. J., Miller, D. T., & Holmes, J. G. (1976). Deserving and the emergence of forms of justice. In L. Berkowitz & E. Walster (Eds.), *Advances in experimental social psychology* (Vol. 9, pp. 133–162). New York: Academic Press.

Lerner, M. J., & Simmons, C. H. (1966). Observer's reaction to the innocent victim: Compassion or rejection? *Journal of Personality and Social Psychology, 4*, 203–210.

Lewin, K., Dembo, T., Festinger, L., & Sears, P. S. (1944). Level of aspiration. In J. McV. Hunt (Ed.), *Personality and the behavior disorders* (pp. 333–378). New York: Ronald Press.

Markus, H. (1977). Self-schemata and processing information about the self. *Journal of Personality and Social Psychology, 35*, 63–78.

McClelland, D. C., Atkinson, J. W., Clark, R. A., & Lowell, E. (1953). *The achievement motive.* New York: Appleton-Century-Crofts.

Raynor, J. O. (1969). Future orientation and motivation of immediate activity: An elaboration of the theory of achievement motivation. *Psychological Review, 76*, 606–610.

Raynor, J. O. (1974). Future orientation in the study of achievement motivation. In J. W. Atkinson & J. O. Raynor (Eds.), *Motivation and achievement* (pp. 121–154). Washington, DC: Winston.

Raynor, J. O., McFarlin, R., Zubek, J. M., & Sorrentino, R. M. (in preparation). *Information value and cognitive functioning: Reinterpretation of cognitive-developmental and ego-identity theory in terms of uncertainty and certainty orientation.* Manuscript in preparation.

Raynor, J. O., & Rubin, I. S. (1971). Effects of achievement motivation and future orientation on level of performance. *Journal of Personality and Social Psychology, 17*, 36–41.

Roger, T. B., Kuiper, N. A., & Kirker, W. S. (1977). Self reference and the encoding of personal information. *Journal of Personality and Social Psychology, 35*, 677–688.

Rokeach, M. (1960). *The open and closed mind: Investigations into the nature of belief systems and personality systems.* New York: Basic Books.

Schneider, K., & Posse, N. (1982). Risk-taking in achievement oriented situations: Do people really maximize affect or competence information? *Motivation and Emotion, 6*, 259–271.

Schneider, W., & Shiffrin, R. M. (1977). Controlled and automatic human information processing: I. Detection, search, and attention. *Psychological Review, 84*, 1–66.

Shiffrin, R. M., & Schneider, W. (1977). Controlled and automatic human information processing: II. Perceptual learning, automatic attending, and a general theory. *Psychologial Review, 84*, 127–190.

Sorrentino, R. M. (1984). [Life styles of uncertainty oriented persons: A field study]. Unpublished raw data.

Sorrentino, R. M., & Hancock, R. D. (in press). Implications of affective and information value for the study of social influence. In M. P. Zanna, J. Olson, & P. Herman (Eds.), *Social influence: The Ontario Symposium* (Vol. 4).

Sorrentino, R. M., Hancock, R. D., Fong, K. K. (1979). Derogation of an innocent victim as a function of authoritarianism and involvement. *Journal of Research in Personality, 13*, 39–48.

Sorrentino, R. M., & Hewitt, E. (1984). Uncertainty-related properties of achievement tasks as a function of uncertainty-orientation and achievement-related motives. *Journal of Personality and Social Psychology, 47*, 884–899.

Sorrentino, R. M., & Hewitt, E. (in preparation). *Uncertainty orientation: Another look at the Atkinson & Birch bead jar study.* Manuscript in preparation.

Sorrentino, R. M., & Roney, C. (in preparation). *Task diagnosticity as a determinant of action.* Manuscript in preparation.

Sorrentino, R. M., & Short, J. C. (1977). The case of the mysterious moderates: Why motives sometimes fail to predict behavior. *Journal of Personality and Social Psychology, 35,* 478–484.

Sorrentino, R. M., Short, J. C., & Raynor, J. O. (1984). Uncertainty orientation: Implications for affective and cognitive views of achievement behavior. *Journal of Personality and Social Psychology, 46,* 189–206.

Trope, Y. (1975). Seeking information about one's own ability as a determinant of choice among tasks. *Journal of Personality and Social Psychology, 32,* 1004–1013.

Trope, Y. (1979). Uncertainty-reducing properties of achievement tasks. *Journal of Personality and Social Psychology, 37,* 1505–1518.

Trope, Y. (1982). Self-assessment and task performance. *Journal of Experimental Social Psychology, 18,* 201–215.

Trope, Y., & Brickman, P. (1975). Difficulty and diagnosticity as determinants of choice among tasks. *Journal of Personality and Social Psychology, 31,* 918–925.

Weiner, B. (1972). *Theories of motivation: From mechanism to cognition.* Chicago: Markham.

Weinstein, M. S. (1969). Achievement motivation and risk preference. *Journal of Personality and Social Psychology, 13,* 153–172.

Wicklund, R. A. (1975). Objective self-awareness. In L. Berkowitz & E. Walster (Eds.), *Advances in experimental social psychology* (Vol. 8, pp. 233–275). New York: Academic Press.

CHAPTER 14

Motivation and Information Processing
A New Look at Decision Making, Dynamic Change, and Action Control

JULIUS KUHL
Max Planck Institute for Psychological Research, Munich

Since technological innovations are the most explicit expressions of advances in our knowledge, it comes as no surprise that models of the human mind frequently emulate the architecture of new technical systems. After Freud's and Lewin's steam engine models of the human mind and the behavioristic switchboard model, today's technological metaphor is the information-processing computer. One might be tempted to belittle the latter paradigm by arguing that it will be outmoded as soon as another technical innovation takes place. I believe, however, that there is no alternative for an experimental science but to take advantage of the best currently available paradigm that has the potential for generating new insights. Paradigms are not chosen at random. Not every technical innovation has the potential of being heuristically useful for generating new psychological research, but information-processing models undoubtedly have been very fruitful in generating new insights about human cognitive functioning. Information-processing models of human cognition provide a finer grained analysis of the mechanisms that mediate the acquisition and representation of knowledge than earlier models of human cognition. In this chapter, I will discuss some advantages and some limitations of an information-processing perspective for the study of human motivation.

Since most theories of human motivation assume a close interaction between cognitive and motivational processes, a more detailed account of cognitive processes should facilitate the elaboration of models of the interaction between cognition and motivation. Current models of motivation take account of *outcomes* of cognitive processes rather than the functional characteristics of the processes themselves. However, developing an information-processing perspective for the study of motivation is not confined to an analysis of cognitive determinants of motivation. The information-processing approach is defined by a certain level of analysis rather than by one specific mental function. I will discuss some evidence suggesting that information-processing mechanisms operating on motivational states differ in some respects from cognitive information processing. Similarly, the information processing underlying emotional phenomena seems to differ in many ways from cognitive information processing (Kuhl, 1983a; Leventhal, 1980; Zajonc, 1984). Although the focus of this chapter is on exploring the usefulness of an information-processing perspective for the study of human motivation, the chapter also addresses the neglect of motivation in current cognitive models. Even those few cognitive models that do not leave people "buried in thought" (Guthrie, 1935, p. 172) provide a simplistic shortcut from cognition to action that ignores most questions about the functional relationship between cognitive processes and motivational states and the functional characteristics of motivational processes.

In this chapter, I will relate motivational phenomena (e.g., choice, persistence, effort) and motivational constructs (e.g., value, expectancy, wish, intention) to several cognitive structures and mechanisms. Specifically, I will discuss the interaction between three motivational processes and several cognitive processes. The motivational processes relate to (1) deliberate choice among goals and action alternatives (*decision making*), (2) simultaneous changes in several competing motivational tendencies that are not necessarily mediated by conscious thought (*dynamic change*), and (3) the maintenance and enactment of intentions—that is, action tendencies the organism has committed itself to execute despite the press resulting from many alternative action tendencies (*action control*). I will try to show how a comprehensive motivational theory of human action can help integrate research findings regarding various cognitive functions that are usually studied separately (e.g., semantic memory, passive and active attention, consciousness, subconscious processing). Finally, I will discuss reasons for maintaining the distinction between motivational and cognitive processes despite the close interaction between these two types of processes.

COGNITIVE, EMOTIONAL, AND MOTIVATIONAL PROCESSES

At the outset, it may be useful to discuss several terminological problems. I will argue, in a nutshell, that cognitive psychologists use the term "cognitive" in an overinclusive way and the term "information processing" in an underinclusive way. A negative side effect of the remarkable progress achieved in cognitive psychology over the past two decades has been an inflationary use of the term "cognitive." It seems as though any process that is going on in the human mind is called a cognitive process. Even the distinction between emotional processes and cognitive processes has now become blurred. Although cognitive psychologists have widely ignored emotions until very recently, some of them now tend to subsume emotions under the broad conceptual hood that describes their field. Emotions are considered "nodes" in a propositional network of associations between semantic concepts (Bower, 1981), one of the "twelve issues" for a cognitive science (Norman, 1980), or simply indistinguishable from cognitive processes (Mandler, 1983). There is a vast amount of phylogenetic (Plutchik, 1980), neurophysiological (Dawson & Schell, 1982; Izard, 1984; Routtenberg, 1978; Sperry, 1964; Tucker, 1981) and psychological (Izard, 1977; Lazarus, 1982, 1984; Zajonc, 1980, 1984) evidence suggesting structural and functional differences between the mechanisms underlying emotional and cognitive processes. The temporal characteristics (latency, decay, and so forth) of cognitive processes differ both from motivational (goal-related) processes (Anderson, 1983; Ovsiankina, 1928; Zeigarnik, 1927) and from emotional processes (Zajonc, 1980, 1984). In light of these findings, the evidence suggesting close interactions between cognitive and emotional processes should not entice us to give up the distinction altogether.

The concept of "motivation" does not fare better in the cognitive literature. Even an author who believed that "motivation is indeed important, worthy of serious study, and a major determiner of our behavior" was reluctant to grant it a separate status because "the phenomena of motivation come from various aspects of several [presumably "cognitive"] issues: Belief Systems, Emotion, Consciousness" (Norman, 1980, p. 27). If one accepted the dependence of one mental process on other processes as a justification for denying the former a separate psychological status, one could, of course, apply a similar argument and describe cognitive processes as "derived phenomena" by pointing to experimental findings demonstrating the dependence of cognitive processes on emotional and motivational processes (e.g., Blum & Barbour, 1979; Bower, 1981; Bruner & Goodman, 1947; Erdelyi, 1974; McClelland & Atkinson, 1948).

I believe that the difficulties some cognitive psychologists have in understanding motivation derive in part from the fact that they use the term "cognitive" in an overinclusive way. The term "cognitive" derives from the Latin word for "knowing" (*cognoscere*). Although it originally referred to *conscious* knowledge about some aspect of the world, it now seems feasible to apply it to some subconscious representations as well, because experimental psychologists have learned that many knowledge structures available to their subjects can be inferred from indirect signs of behavior without being accessible to conscious introspections. A perhaps less useful broadening of the term "cognitive," however, is one that identifies it with *any mental representation*. Although emotional and motivational states probably never occur in the absence of any reference to a ("cognitive") knowledge structure, the first two differ from the last in so many ways that it is useful to maintain the traditional terminological distinctions among the concepts. Since this chapter addresses the question of how cognitive and motivational processes interact, I will focus on cognitive mechanisms that may affect motivational processes. Despite this emphasis, however, I will also discuss several functional differences among cognitive and motivational processes that suggest that they be conceived of as interacting but separate "modules" (Fodor, 1983), rather than as three aspects of one *unified* "cognitive" architecture (Anderson, 1983; Hamilton, 1983) or three "intentional" states (Searle, 1983, p. 3), none of which has a special status of its own. (See Kuhl & Atkinson, in press, for a detailed discussion of the distinctive features of motivational processes.)

Fodor (1983) discussed several reasons for distinguishing separate "modules" (or "vertical faculties") even *within* the cognitive subsystem. He acknowledged, however, that there may be several subsystems that are common to all mental functions—for example, short-term memory and other "horizontal faculties." However, the fact that such horizontal faculties may be common to emotional, motivational, and cognitive processes should not obscure the functional differences among those processes. The degree of similarity between any two processes cannot be determined in an absolute sense; it depends on the level of analysis one adopts and the specific purpose on which one focuses.

If one focuses on the commonalities rather than the differences between various mental processes, the acknowledgment of fundamental differences between any pair of mental processes need not keep one from maintaining a "unitary" conception of the mind. In his unitary theory of cognition, Anderson (1983) discussed a fundamental difference between motivational and cognitive mechanisms: Whereas ordinary memory structures are subject to rapid decay after being activated, aroused goal states persist over extended periods of time without decreasing in strength. Since Freud (1915/1949) and Lewin (1935), motivational psychologists have claimed that this property of persistence is the basis for several functional differences between motivational and cognitive processes. Recently, several implications of the property of persistence have been demonstrated in a series of computer simulations of a dynamic model of motivation based on this property (Atkinson & Birch, 1970). The simulations revealed many nonobvious distinctive features of motivational processes, but none of these features applies to cognitive processes, which do not have the property of persistence. (See Kuhl & Atkinson, in press, for a detailed report of this work.) In light of these findings, I base my preference for a modular approach on a pragmatic purpose: A theoretical approach (i.e., the modular approach) that focuses on potential differences among the phenomena investigated is more likely to help discover existing differences than one that emphasizes the similarities among those phenomena (i.e., the unitary approach).

A rough taxonomy of the three subsystems addressed in this chapter is given in Figure 14.1. It is assumed that cognitive, emotional, and motivational subsystems relate to the world in three different ways. The term "cognition" is reserved for those processes that mediate the acquisition and representation of knowledge about the world—that is, processes that have a *representative* relation to the world of objects and facts. "Emotional" processes evaluate the personal significance of those objects and facts. "Motivational" processes relate to the world in an actional way; that is, they relate to goal states of the organism in its attempt to produce desired changes in its environment. Within each of these subsystems, various mental states can be distinguished on the basis of an intensity-

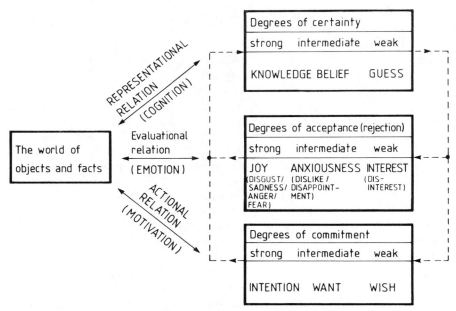

FIGURE 14.1 A taxonomy of cognitive, emotional, and motivational states.

related aspect—that is, degrees of certainty associated with cognitive representations, degrees of acceptance or rejection associated with emotional states, and degrees of commitment associated with various motivational states.

Despite the functional differences among the three subsystems, the model assumes close interactions among them at a later stage of processing. First, emotional and motivational processes operate on the representation of the world as provided by the cognitive system. Second, cognitive processes are affected by the emotional and motivational states of the organism. Third, the cognitive system operates on the output of the emotional and motivational systems in the sense that emotional and motivational states of the organism may be represented on various levels of the cognitive system. This third aspect of the interdependence of cognitive processes on the one hand and emotional and motivational processes on the other may have contributed to the confounding of the three types of processes by some authors. The distinction between cognitive representations of emotions and emotional processes themselves is important (Mandler, 1975), as is the distinction between motivational states and their cognitive representations. Children seem to develop "declarative" knowledge about their own motivational states rather late, considerably later than they develop knowledge about the external world (Olson & Astington, 1983; Piaget, 1952). Thus, the functional effects of emotional and motivational states have to be carefully distinguished from the effects of the cognitive representations of these states.

Since the focus of this chapter is on motivational processes, I will confine the discussion to those cognitive processes that have a direct functional significance for the three aspects of motivation mentioned earlier. The first of these aspects, which is related to deliberate decision making, presumably draws upon the (cognitive) representation of action-related knowledge. Therefore, after briefly discussing the limitations of traditional expectancy-value approaches to decision making, I will discuss a model that stresses the functional significance of the way action-related knowledge is represented in memory. The second aspect of motivation is related to "dynamic" factors that control temporal changes in motivational states. These dynamic processes seem to be more closely related to emotional processes, and they seem to be less easily accessible to conscious awareness. I will discuss them in light of several recent findings regarding functional differences between conscious and subconscious modes of information processing. Finally, I will briefly discuss theory and evidence regarding a third aspect of motivation that presumably supports the maintenance of the currently activated intentional state of an organism.

DECISION MAKING

Most motivational psychologists consider that the problem of *choice* is the most fundamental question to be answered. Once we can predict which goal people deliberately select in a given situation and which action alternative they choose to attain that goal, we should be able to predict their behavior. Although I will discuss two additional questions that need to be studied to explain goal-directed behavior, the problem of choice remains an important one. Most models of motivation assume a deliberate decision-making process to explain choice among goals and action alternatives. During the past three decades, *expectancy-value models* have dominated the scene (Feather, 1982). According to these models, an individual's motivation to perform a certain activity is a function of the algebraic product of two parameters: the expectancy that she or he will be able to perform the activity and obtain the desired outcomes and the personal value of all outcomes associated with that activity. Rather than testing the universal validity claim of this theory, research has focused on elaborating or reformulating expectancy and value parameters (Kuhl, 1982b). Elaborated models have been developed to account for many additional variables, such as perceived responsibility for outcomes (Feather, 1967), the instrumentality of immediate action for the attainment of future goals (Raynor, 1969), perceived goal distance (Gjesme, 1981), personal standards for self-evaluation (Kuhl, 1978), causal attribution of success and failure (Weiner, 1972, 1980), self-concepts of own ability (Kukla, 1972; Meyer, 1973), the need for optimal self-stimulation (Nygard, 1977; Schneider, 1973), and dynamic processes affecting temporal changes of motivational tendencies (Atkinson & Birch, 1970). In this research, the expectancy-value paradigm was the theoretical basis rather than the target of empirical investigation.

Limitations of Expectancy-Value Models

Attempts have been made to test the validity of the basic assumptions of expectancy-value models (Graen, 1969; Hackman & Porter, 1968; Lawler &

Porter, 1967; Lynch & Cohen, 1978; Pritchard & Sanders, 1973). However, these studies do not permit any firm conclusions because of several unresolved methodological problems (Kuhl, 1982b; Schmidt, 1973). One of these problems arises from the fact that one cannot test the assumption regarding a multiplicative relationship between expectancy and value parameters unless one has developed a method that guarantees at least interval-scale measurement of these parameters. Although many models of psychological testing have claimed to provide interval measurement, there is no consensus about any method that would actually justify that claim. (See Kuhl, 1982b, for a fuller discussion of this issue.) I have proposed a method of *logical statement analysis* to circumvent some of the problems that render the test of expectancy-value models so difficult. This method is based on a count of the number of individuals for whom a logical statement describing the basic assumptions of the model to be tested is true. In several applications of this method, we found that subjects' behavior does not always seem to be a function of the *conjunction* of expectancy and value (as the logical analogue of a multiplicative relationship). Some subjects seem to base their decisions entirely on value-related information, ignoring the subjective chances of success, at least in some situations. Others focus on expectancy-related information and ignore value-related information. Similar individual differences regarding the type of information affecting motivation have been found in achievement-related contexts (see Chapter 11, by Raynor and McFarlin, and Chapter 13, by Sorrentino and Short, in this book). Some subjects even combine expectancy- and value-related information *disjunctively* (Kuhl, 1977, 1982b). These results are inconsistent with the basic postulate underlying all expectancy-value models—namely, that all people base all their decisions on one particular rule for combining expectancy- and value-related information. People seem to have idiosyncratic and highly context-specific rules that specify the type of information to be considered and the way that information is to be combined to arrive at a decision (Kruglanski & Klar, 1985; Kuhl, 1982b). This conclusion suggests that we should pay more attention to the specific ways in which individuals represent decision-related knowledge (Kuhl, 1983b, pp. 104–118).

A Propositional Network Model of Action-Related Knowledge

Most of the recent research into semantic memory has been based on the assumption that knowledge structures are encoded in the format of a *propositional network*. According to this assumption, semantic memory can be described in terms of a complex network of interconnected propositional structures, each of which consists of an organized set of conceptual *nodes* (Anderson & Bower, 1973; Kintsch, 1974; Norman & Rumelhart, 1975). Thus, concepts are described as intersections (nodes) in a network of semantic relations. Although some authors have assumed that any knowledge (including spatial imagery) is represented in a propositional format (Anderson & Bower, 1973; Olson & Bialystok, 1983; Pylyshyn, 1973), many recent findings suggest that we can distinguish several codes: a propositional code, a quasi-pictorial code for images (Anderson, 1983; Kosslyn, 1980; Shepard & Cooper, 1983), a string code for temporally

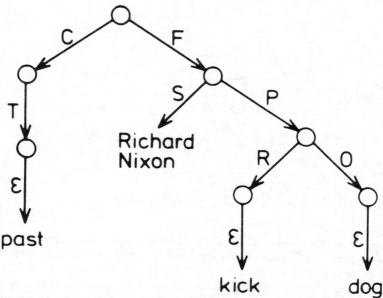

FIGURE 14.2 Propositional representation of the sentence "Richard Nixon kicked a dog" in semantic memory (after Anderson & Bower, 1973).

structured information (Anderson, 1983; Ornstein, 1969), and a kinesthetic and/ or motor code (Posner, 1973). Since propositionally coded information seems to be especially important for decision making, I will focus on this format.

Anderson and Bower (1973) describe propositional memory structures in terms of a network of binary relations between conceptual nodes. These propositional structures encode information about facts (F) and about the context (C) to which these facts are related. As illustrated in Figure 14.2, the fact component is subdivided into a subject node (S) and a predicate node (P). The predicate is further subdivided into a relational node (R) and an object node (O). The context component may be subdivided into a temporal node (T) and a locational node (L).

Since we are interested in propositional representations of action-related knowledge, a question arises regarding the particular characteristics of this type of knowledge. I have proposed (Kuhl, 1983b, p. 107) that structures encoding motivationally significant knowledge differ from other knowledge structures in four ways. First, in action-related propositions, the subject node refers to some aspect of the *self* as the agent of an action. Second, the context node describes the temporal and spatial *conditions* under which the intended action is to be performed. Third, the object node refers to an action plan or *production system* (Anderson, 1983). Finally, the relational component of action-related knowledge structures specifies the *type* of the motivational state it encodes. In accordance with earlier cognitive models of motivation (e.g., Ajzen & Fishbein, 1973), four types of motivational states are of particular interest: expectations, wishes (or "attitudes"

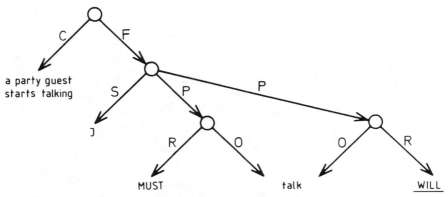

FIGURE 14.3 Propositional representation of an intentional state.

toward an act), obligations, and intentions. Whereas traditional expectancy-value models do not make any assumptions regarding how these motivational states are encoded in memory, I have assumed that the type of state to which an action-related structure relates is encoded by the relational component. Specifically, the verbs *can, wish, must,* and *will* presumably encode expectations, wishes, social norms, and intentions, respectively.

The intentional state is of particular interest because in many expectancy-value models, intentions do not have a status separate from other motivational states. As a result, the functional significance of the personal *commitment* to an action that presumably distinguishes an intention from other motivational states has been neglected in theories of motivation since Kurt Lewin's (1926) seminal paper in which he denied intentional states any special status. (See Kuhl, 1984, for a fuller discussion of Lewin's paper.) In a later section of this chapter, I will discuss the assumption that the intentional format is particularly important because it controls access to an individual's repertoire of self-regulatory strategies.

How can one conceive of the memory processes involved in decision making? Two cases can be distinguished. In the first case, illustrated in Figure 14.3, the individual encounters a situation for which she or he has already stored an intentional proposition. As soon as the context component of such a proposition is matched to the encoded situation, the action specified in the proposition can be retrieved. It should be noted, however, that the "object node" encoding the action intended in that situation ought not be confounded with the *procedural* knowledge structure containing the action programs that must be activated to execute the actions. During the decision-making process, these procedural knowledge structures need not be activated. It is important to note the difference between the declarative structure illustrated in Figure 14.3 and the procedural structure to which it refers. Since declarative structures encode knowledge *about* one's intentions, a declarative representation of an intention can be activated without executing the (procedural) action program to which it refers. Although the

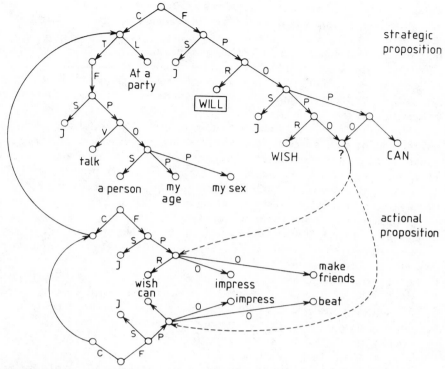

strategic
proposition

actional
proposition

FIGURE 14.4 Semantic network representation of strategic and actional propositions.

declarative structures encoding this knowledge may have associative links to the corresponding *production systems* (Anderson, 1983), the activation of the former need not activate the latter.

It should be noted that according to the present model, humans can function perfectly well *without* a declarative representation of their intentions. In fact, during the early years of life, infants are not even capable of forming such a declarative representation. In their interactions with the environment, young children progressively differentiate *enactive* knowledge structures (Piaget, 1952). Nevertheless, the development of declarative representations seems to be an important requirement for many self-regulatory abilities that develop later in childhood (Olson & Astington, 1983; Piaget, 1952).

Let us turn to the second case of how memory processes can mediate decision making. Besides *actional* propositions (Figure 14.3), individuals seem to store many *strategic* propositions, which specify the strategy for searching an action alternative rather than specifying the action itself (see Figure 14.4). The actional proposition illustrated in Figure 14.3 specifies an individual's intentional commitment to start a conversation when approached by another guest at a party, whereas

Figure 14.4 illustrates the case, perhaps, of a less experienced party guest, who has not yet developed an actional proposition. However, this person may retrieve a decision rule, such as "When a woman starts talking to me and she is my age, I *will* do what I *wish* to do and *can* do." As soon as this rule is activated, several action alternatives may be activated that are specified in expectational (i.e., *can*) structures or wish-related structures. If one action alternative is found in both an expectational and a wish-related structure, that action may be selected for further processing (Figure 14.4).

The finding mentioned earlier—that, in a given situation, different subjects seem to employ quite different decision rules—suggests that there are substantial individual differences in strategic propositions. In the example illustrated in Figure 14.4, some individuals may focus on wish-related action propositions only, disregarding their personal abilities (i.e., *can* propositions), others may focus on socially desired actions (i.e., *must* propositions) rather than on personal preferences, and so on. One implication of this aspect of the model is that we do not see any simple way to predict all people's behavior at all times unless we seriously attempt to assess exhaustively all people's action-related memory structures. The futility of a similar task became very obvious when investigators started to implement tiny portions of one individual's associative memory on a computer (Anderson & Bower, 1973). An attempt to predict "all people's behavior all the time" (Bem, 1983) would be unrealistic. It would require not only an exhaustive description of all people's action-related memory structures but also a prediction of all future conditions with which all people will be confronted. Even though physicists know the law predicting the speed of falling objects, nobody would expect them to predict when each of the apples hanging on a tree will actually fall down.

Empirical Evidence

What would be a more realistic task for motivational psychology? I believe that the level of analysis assumed in information-processing models has great heuristic value for generating many answerable questions to be investigated in the future. For example, what is the functional significance of the *type* of action-related structure as encoded in the relational component (i.e., *can, wish, must*, and *will* propositions)? In a recent study, we found one interesting hint that deserves to be followed up in future experiments (Heckhausen & Kuhl, 1985). When our subjects reported many wishes and behavioral intentions they had during the day, it was interesting that wishes seemed to be activated in memory especially at times when no intentional state claimed memory capacity.

Another question suggested by the propositional model relates to the subject node of a motivational proposition. What happens if it does *not* specify the self as the agent of an intended action? I have proposed the assumption that the self-referential component is necessary in an intentional structure for obtaining access to the individual's repertoire of self-regulatory strategies (Kuhl, 1984). This assumption provides an interesting explanation of experimental results demonstrating the facilitative effects of self-awareness (Carver & Scheier, 1981; Wicklund, 1975). By the present account, enhanced self-awareness facilitates the enactment of action-related structures because it provides access to self-regulatory mechanisms mediating the transition from cognition to action. Also, the motivational enhancement associated with increased self-confidence (Bandura, 1977; de Charms, 1968; Kukla, 1972; Rotter, 1954) can be explained more parsimoniously by the self-regulation hypothesis than by traditional models. These models assume a separate judgmental process for assessing the actor's ability to reach a desired goal. If perceived ability is low, motivation is reduced. The self-regulation hypothesis assumes that the motivation-reducing effects of decreased confidence are not always mediated by an explicit judgmental process. In many cases, decreased confidence may simply weaken the self-referential component of an intentional structure (Figure 14.3), thereby impeding access to self-regulatory functions. This assumption is consistent with the early findings of Ach (1910) and the many findings showing facilitation of performance as a result of experimentally induced ego-involvement (Atkinson, 1958; Greenwald, 1982).

Another interesting question suggested by the propositional model refers to the degeneration of the object node, which specifies action alternatives. The action component of an intention seems to degenerate when subjects are exposed to a series of uncontrollable failures and all available action alternatives have been unsuccessful. Elsewhere, I have summarized experimental findings supporting the hypothesis that a degeneration of the action-related component results in a reduction of working memory capacity due to the intrusion of degenerated intensions that cannot be carried out (Kuhl, 1984). This hypothesis provides an alternative explanation for generalized performance deficits observed after an experimental treatment that exposes subjects to uncontrollable failure (Brunstein & Olbrich, in press; Kuhl, 1981; Kuhl & Weiss, 1984). According to our data, *generalized* performance deficits following exposure to uncontrollable failure are not attributable to a reduced expectation of control and the motivational deficit resulting from it. When subjects were given a new task after failure pretreatment, expectancy and motivation ratings were not reduced. Nonetheless, we found several indications for a memory overload due to subjects' preoccupation with their (degenerated) intention to solve the pretreatment task even while trying hard to solve the new problem.

A currently controversial issue relates to the mechanisms involved in the activation of propositional structures. Does activation spread from node to node (Anderson & Bower, 1973), or are propositional structures activated as a whole— for example, by some resonance mechanism (Carr & Bacharach, 1976; Gibson, 1966)? In the latter case—which seems to be more compatible with recent findings (Ratcliff & McKoon, 1981)—the complexity of a decision rule should not affect the speed of processing, at least so long as an *automatic* mode of processing is involved. In an active, "consciously" controlled mode in which activation may proceed from node to node, complex rules should take more processing time than simple rules. As a result, an overly deliberate decision maker may find himself or herself performing a rather unattractive routine activity rather than one that reflects her or his latent preference if the preferred activity happens to be encoded in a more complex propositional structure. We found support for this hypothesis in a study in which subjects were given an opportunity to switch to an interesting activity while working at a rather boring routine task (Kuhl & Eisenbeiser, in press). A personal disposition toward deliberate and lengthy decision making was assessed by a questionnaire administered prior to the experiment. Deliberate decision makers ("state-oriented" subjects) significantly more often failed to switch to the more attractive activity than "impulsive" ("action-oriented") decision makers, whereas a significantly *greater* proportion of action-oriented subjects switched to the more attractive activity.

Another question suggested by the propositional model refers to the effects of a degenerated, ill-defined, or lacking context component. The context component presumably encodes the conditions under which an intended action is to be performed (Figure 14.3). What happens, for instance, when a *will* proposition (i.e., an intention) specifies a goal and an action but does not contain sufficient information about the context in which the action is to be performed? If our assumption is correct that *will* propositions are assigned a rather high priority for access to working memory, an intentional structure that has a degenerated context component should intrude into working memory at inappropriate times—that is, when the current situation does not permit it to be executed. This intrusi᠎ n is less likely to occur when an intention has a fully developed context componer ᠎; in this case, any mismatch between the encoding of the current situation and the context component of an intentional memory structure would prevent the intentional structure from being admitted to working memory. Hence, whenever the context component of an intention degenerates (e.g., when a person intends to perform an action but does not specify when and where), available memory capacity should be reduced, and the individual's ability to perform appropriate actions may deteriorate.

In a recent study (Kuhl & Helle, 1984), we tested whether the problems depressives have initiating even simple activities might result from their encoding motivational propositions in an intentional format even if the context of execution is not specified. A group of hospitalized depressive patients and three control groups (hospitalized schizophrenics, hospitalized alcoholics, and a group of university students) participated in the experiment. Within each group, half of the subjects were exposed to a manipulation that was designed to induce a degenerated intention. These subjects were asked to tidy up the papers, computer cards, and pens that were scattered on a desk. Subsequently, the experimenter told each subject that she or he was not allowed to start at that task because "we have to do several other things first. It is actually up to you to decide when there will be an opportunity to tidy up the desk." This instruction was meant to render unspecified the conditions under which the subject should clear up the table. We assumed that, because of the ill-defined context component, nondepressive subjects would encode this instruction in a format that was less self-committing than an intention (e.g., a wish), because people do not commit themselves to execute an instruction when they do not even know *when* they are supposed to execute it. If our assumption was correct that depressives would tend to adhere rigidly to the intentional format despite the ill-defined context, they should have had a reduced working memory capacity in the experimental condition, compared to the memory capacity in the control group of subjects who were not asked to clear up the desk. Our findings were consistent with this prediction. The short-term memory capacity assessed subsequent to the experimental manipulation was significantly reduced in the depressive subjects compared to the control subjects. Subjects with low depressive symptoms did not show any impairment of short-term memory capacity in either the experimental or the control condition.

Although the studies summarized here illustrate the heuristic value of the propositional model, much additional work needs to be done to test the various assumptions of the model. Specifically, more direct methods need to be developed to induce and assess structural aspects of action-related memory representations. Nevertheless, I hope that the studies summarized in this section have shown that it is worthwhile to replace the goal of predicting "all people's behavior all the time" with the less ambitious but more realistic goal of investigating some of the basic mechanisms affecting human motivation.

DYNAMIC CHANGE

Although decision making and choice have been the major topics in motivational psychology, *persistence* is also an important aspect of motivation. To account for it, one has to explain the temporal changes of motivational tendencies. Within the framework of expectancy-value theory, these changes are attributed to changes in expectancy and value aspects (Atkinson & Feather, 1966; Nygard, 1977). However, the waxing and waning of motivational tendencies over time does not depend only on changes in those cognitive structures. A motivational tendency also increases as a result of the *cumulation* of past arousal of the same or similar tendencies (Atkinson & Cartwright, 1964). For example, the repeated ringing of a telephone may cause a cumulative increase in the tendency to pick it up, even if there is no change in the cognitive evaluation of expectancy- and value-related information (Kuhl & Atkinson, 1984). Persevering motivational tendencies may be *displaced* to situations that are semantically unrelated to the context in which they were aroused. For example, a clerk who has been humiliated by his boss may act out his aggressive tendencies at home against his wife. Expression of a motivational tendency in action seems to result in a *reduction* of that tendency, even if there are no changes in expectancy- or value-related cognitions. These dynamic principles of cumulative instigation and behavioral consummation have been inferred from the well-known results of Lewin's students, Zeigarnik (1927) and Ovsiankina (1928). Atkinson and Birch (1970) developed a formal theory that spells out the implications of these dynamic principles for the *stream of behavior*. Atkinson, Bongort, and Price (1977) summarized the basic assumptions as follows:

> If a certain kind of activity has been intrinsically satisfying or previously rewarded in a particular situation, there will be an *instigating force* (F) for that activity, attributable in part to strength of motive in the person and in part to the magnitude of incentive for that activity in that situation. This will cause a more or less rapid arousal and increase in the strength of an inclination to engage in that activity, an *action tendency* (T), depending on the magnitude of the force. If a

certain kind of activity has been frustrated or punished in the past, there will be an *inhibitory force* (*I*) and a more or less rapid growth in the strength of a disinclination to act. This is what we now call a *negation tendency* (*N*) and conceive as a tendency *not* to do it. The duration of these forces will determine how strong the action tendency or negation tendency becomes. The latter, the tendency not to do something, will produce *resistance* to the activity. It opposes, blocks, dampens; that is, it subtracts from the action tendency to determine the *resultant action tendency* ($\bar{T} = T - N$). The resultant action tendency competes with other resultant action tendencies for other incompatible activities. The strongest of them is expressed in behavior. The expression of an action tendency in behavior is what reduces it. Engaging in activity produces a *consummatory force* (*C*), which depends in part on the consummatory value (*c*) of the particular activity and in part on the strength of tendency being expressed in behavior (i.e., $C = c\bar{T}$). Similarly, the resistance to an action tendency, produced by the opposition of a negation tendency, constitutes an analogous *force of resistance* (*R*), which reduces, in a comparable way, the strength of the negation tendency. (p. 5)

Since a more detailed discussion of this theory is beyond the scope of this chapter, I will confine myself to a brief summary of several experimental findings illustrating perseverance, cumulative instigation, and behavioral consummation of action tendencies. (See Kuhl & Atkinson, in press, for a fuller account of the experimental research into the dynamic principles of motivation).

Evidence for Perseverance and Cumulation Effects

Weiner (1965) showed that subjects with a strong motive to succeed and a weak fear of failure became increasingly motivated to work on several achievement tasks when they were made to fail on successive trials. He attributed this result to a cumulative increase of motivation over the failure trials.

Perseverance of unconsummated action tendencies was demonstrated in several recent studies on *symbolic self-completion*. According to Wicklund and Gollwitzer (1982), humans have a need to establish their identity in their social environment by acquiring symbols that are indicative of their desired self-definition. In their experiments, they aroused this need in their subjects and subsequently gave them an opportunity to express the need in various situations unrelated to the situation in which it was aroused. The results confirmed the hypothesis that aroused action tendencies persevere and affect behavior in a variety of situations (Wicklund & Gollwitzer, 1981). In one experiment, for example, the subjects' self-definition associated with personal hobbies (e.g., "I like hang-gliding") was aroused by having them write essays about their hobbies that allegedly were to be published. One group of subjects was interrupted before completing their essays, whereas a control group was not interrupted. In a subsequent experiment, which was allegedly unrelated to the first one, the interrupted group showed an increased willingness to help improve a text that was meant to encourage adolescents from underprivileged environments to participate in certain leisure activities. Unknown to the subjects, the activity chosen corresponded to the hobbies they had written about in the first experiment (Wicklund & Gollwitzer, 1981, Exp. 3).

A similar motivational carry-over effect was found in an achievement-related context (Kuhl & Koch, 1984). Subjects participated in two allegedly unrelated experiments that were conducted in different rooms by different experimenters. In the first experiment, the subjects were asked to work on an achievement task. Half of the subjects were interrupted before finishing the task by the second experimenter, who entered the room and asked the subjects to come with him because he "was running out of time." Subjects with a high motive to achieve success—as assessed by a projective test administered prior to the experiment— showed facilitated performance in a target-shooting game when they had been exposed to the interruption treatment, compared to the performance of the no-interruption control group. The performance of failure-oriented subjects, whether or not they had been interrupted in the first experiment, was as high as the performance of success-oriented subjects exposed to the interruption treatment.

That perseverance of a motivational tendency across different situations can in fact produce a cumulative effect was confirmed in another achievement-related context (Kuhl & Blankenship, 1979a). In a free-choice situation, the tendency of subjects to choose very difficult tasks gradually increased during the course of the experiment, even though they had been given so many practice trials that actual and perceived performance (i.e., expectancy of success) did not show any increment over trials. These results were interpreted as an indication that dynamic factors affected motivation even when cognitive variables were held constant. The dynamic theory predicts a gradual increase even under these conditions, because the continuous exposure of subjects to the various tasks should result in successive and cumulative instigations of their tendencies to work on the tasks (Kuhl & Blankenship, 1979b).

A cumulative increase in strength of motivation over time was demonstrated in another experiment in which children were given an opportunity to engage in three different activities (Kuhl & Geiger, in press). For one of these activities—an attractive "fun-pad" drawing game—an inhibitory tendency was aroused by inducing a mild degree of anxiety. The children were told that the pen they were given to play the game was a very expensive one and that it could break easily. This manipulation effectively increased the average latency of initiating the drawing activity, as compared to a no-anxiety control group. Within the anxiety group, subjects had been randomly assigned to one of three subgroups. In two of these subgroups, an attempt was made to reduce the anxiety 1 min and 5 min after anxiety induction, respectively, by telling the subjects a "trick" to avoid breaking the pen. In the third group, anxiety was not reduced. According to the dynamic principle of motivational cumulation (Atkinson & Birch, 1970), the tendency to initiate the drawing activity should have increased over time and should have been suddenly set free when the inhibitory tendency was reduced. Evidence for such a cumulation effect was found in one group of subjects with a strong motive to achieve success, as assessed by a multimotive projective test (see Figure 14.5). In this group, speed of drawing as an index of motivational strength was highest in the group in which anxiety was reduced after 5 min, lower in the 1-min anxiety group, and lowest in the no-reduction anxiety group. The question of why this cumulative "bottling-up" effect did not occur in two other groups (i.e., in subjects

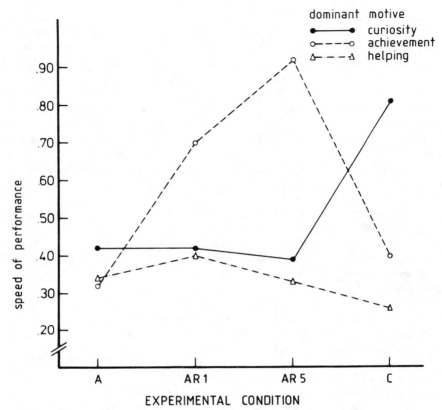

FIGURE 14.5 Speed of performance as a function of dominant motive and experimental condition. (A = anxiety/no removal, AR1 = anxiety/removal after 1 min, AR5 = anxiety/ removal after 5 min, C = no-anxiety control group.)

with a strong curiosity motive or a strong helping motive) remains open. One simple explanation that can be tested in future research is that the speed-of-drawing measure was a valid index of strength of motivation only in subjects with a strong achievement motive. Another interpretation is that cumulative effects are especially strong in the achievement domain whereas, in other domains, behavior may be more context specific or "episodic" (Kuhl, 1983b, p. 174).

Although the assumption regarding the consummatory effect of expressing an action tendency in behavior is intuitively very plausible, consummation has not been studied in great detail experimentally. In the Kuhl and Geiger (in press) study, we did find significant negative correlations between times spent in an activity during the first and second halves of the experiment. Blankenship (1982) developed a sophisticated experimental technique to assess the *consummatory value* expressing an action tendency in behavior. The most extensive research regarding consummatory mechanisms dates back to Karsten's (1928) early work on *mental satiation*.

Dynamic Principles and Information Processing: The Moderating Role of Consciousness

Although the research summarized in the preceding section supports the assumption that dynamic processes such as perseverance, cumulation, and consummation affect behavior, it obviously does not show that these processes are effective all the time. Is it plausible to assume that human decisions are *always* affected by the relative strengths of motivational tendencies that are aroused before processing of decision-related information begins? The theory of the *dynamics of action* (Atkinson & Birch, 1970) criticizes rationalistic approaches that maintain that decisions are *never* affected by those dynamic factors. A "rational" decision is conceived of as *episodic*—that is, as entirely based on information processed during the decision-making episode. A rational decision should not depend on the decision maker's "prejudice" toward one of the outcomes, as would be the case if his or her decision were affected by persevering motivational tendencies aroused on prior occasions. Similarly, a rational decision should not be affected by any consummatory effects resulting from the fact that the decision maker has taken certain actions in the past. Are decisions rational and context specific, or are they affected by cross-situational carry-over effects that are not reflected in the cognitions processed to arrive at a decision? Rather than putting the question in this all-or-nothing form, it may be heuristically more useful to question the *degree* to which dynamic or cognitive-episodic processes affect behavior in various situations. Even though some clerks may act out the aggression aroused at work against their spouses, not all clerks do so, and even those who do may not always do so. If the relative impact of dynamic and cognitive-episodic factors varies across situations and across individuals, as was suggested by some of the findings summarized earlier, it seems necessary to look for processes that affect the relative weight of dynamic and cognitive-episodic factors.

Recent findings regarding functional differences between conscious and subconscious information processing suggest that the *phenomenal status* of the knowledge structures affecting motivation might determine the relative weight of dynamic and cognitive-episodic processes. Specifically, conscious representation of action-related knowledge and of emotional and motivational states may mediate context-specific, episodic decision making, whereas subconscious processing may be associated with such dynamic processes as cross-situational cumulation, displacement, and substitution. Evidence supporting this assumption derives from Marcel's (1983a) work on functional differences between subconscious and conscious processing. Marcel (1983b) rejected the widely accepted *identity assumption*, according to which conscious processing is basically identical with subconscious processing, except that the former is characterized by a stronger intensity of the processes involved.

One finding contradicting the identity assumption (Marcel, 1983a, Exp. 5) showed that conscious identification of a subliminally projected (pattern-masked) stimulus word was *not* facilitated when that word had been shown up to 20 times in rapid succession. That the memory structure representing that word had been intensified on a subconscious level as a function of the number of stimulus repetitions could be demonstrated by the fact that response times at a *lexical* decision task—requiring subjects to decide whether or not *any* word had been shown—decreased when the number of stimulus repetitions increased. If conscious awareness depended only on the intensity of a stimulus representation exceeding a critical threshold, the number of stimulus repetitions should have affected the probability of conscious identification as well.

Marcel (1983b) assumed that consciousness is based on a constructive process that may alter the information represented on subconscious levels according to the current intentions and expectations of the individual. Conscious processing seems to differ from subconscious processing in several ways. First, conscious processing seems to be much less affected by cumulative processes than subconscious processing is. A similar conclusion was derived from a recent series of studies comparing children's and adults' mechanisms for representing spatial knowledge (Olson & Bialystok, 1983). The results were inconsistent with the traditional belief that children's spatial representations are affected by only one of the various frames of reference (i.e., the egocentric one). Olson & Bialystok (1983) were able to demonstrate that children's perceptions were affected by the same referential information as adults' perceptions, except that children processed the information in a summative and holistic way. Adults seemed to break up the holistically encoded pattern of information and combine the pieces of information extracted from several frames of reference according to an explicit and sequential binary logic. This step-by-step processing seems to be typical of conscious processing (Kuhl, 1983a).

The latter conclusion relates to the second distinctive feature of consciousness, which is closely related to the noncumulative aspect of conscious processing. Consciousness seems to be related to the ability to exert active control over the type of information extracted from the complex informational structures represented on subconscious levels. Consciousness seems to break up complex structures and isolate specific pieces of information in accordance with the current context and the current goals of the organism. Marcel (1980) presented words with multiple meanings to his subjects—for example, "palm" (a tree or a body part). If such a word is shown without providing any context information, both meanings of the word are activated. This can be inferred from the fact that, at a lexical decision task, words related to either meaning of the stimulus word (e.g., "wrist" or "coconut") are identified more quickly than words unrelated to the stimulus word. When the word "palm" was placed in a context favoring one of the two meanings, by showing the sequence "hand-palm" or the sequence "tree-palm" before showing the word to be identified ("wrist"), only the meaning suggested by the context word ("hand" or "tree") was activated. This reduction of complex information seems to be confined to conscious processing. In an experimental condition in which the word "palm" was deprived conscious representation by showing a pattern mask a few milliseconds after its appearance, *both* meanings of the stimulus word were activated, irrespective of which meaning was suggested by the context word.

The third functional difference between conscious and subconscious processing relates to the direction of processing. The traditional view (Craik & Lockhart, 1972) that information processing proceeds from the most simple levels (e.g., extracting the physical features of objects) to the most complex levels (e.g., extracting semantic information) does not seem to be valid for conscious processing. Marcel's results suggest that conscious recovery of information proceeds from the most complex to the most primitive levels of processing. In one experiment (Marcel, 1983a, Exp. 1), subjects were able to consciously retrieve the meaning of subliminally presented words, although they were not able to recognize beyond chance whether they had seen a word or a blank field. A similar finding was reported by Kunst-Wilson and Zajonc (1980) and by Seamon, Brody and Kauff (1983). Under tachistoscopic viewing conditions, subjects were able to extract the (emotional) meaning of the stimulus words, although they were not able to discriminate them graphically from unfamiliar words.

Although the applicability of these findings to complex motivational phenomena remains to be investigated in the future, Marcel's results are suggestive enough to encourage future research regarding the hypothesis that the phenomenal status of action-related knowledge determines the relative weight of dynamic and cognitive-episodic processes. The episodic and context-specific type of decision making that is not affected by motivational tendencies aroused prior to the decision-making episode may very well be mediated by the reductionistic aspect of consciousness. If consciousness breaks up complex informational structures represented on a subconscious level and isolates those pieces of information that are related to the current context, motivational carry-over effects from past situations should be minimized.

Many questions need to be answered, however, to develop a fuller understanding of the motivational significance of consciousness. First, there is still no evidence that consciousness is a unitary mechanism, as is assumed by many authors (Mandler, 1983; Marcel, 1983b; Norman, 1980). Although it seems plausible to conceive of consciousness as a horizontal faculty (Fodor, 1983)—that is, a unitary mechanism across all mental processes—it appears equally conceivable that consciousness is defined by quite different sets of characteristics in different domains. Conscious representation of motivational states may involve mechanisms different from those involved in conscious representation of emotional or cognitive information. However, to the extent that cognitive processes affect motivational states, findings regarding conscious processing of cognitive information would still be relevant for a motivational analysis even if conscious processing within the motivational system were different from conscious processing in the cognitive system.

Recent research suggests that conscious processing of cognitive information affects goal-directed behavior in a different way than subconscious processing affects it. Silverman (1976) reported a series of studies suggesting that motivational carry-over effects occur even across semantically unrelated situations, provided that the relevant information is processed in the subconscious mode. In one experiment (Silverman, Ross, Adler, & Lustig, 1978), the dart-throwing performance of male college students was impaired when a sentence presumably activating an unconscious father–son conflict ("Beating daddy is wrong") was presented subliminally. No impairment was observed in a condition in which the likelihood that this sentence could reach awareness was increased (by increasing the luminance of the stimulus). Although it would be premature to draw any firm conclusions from these results, they encourage us to pursue our hypothesis concerning the motivational significance of consciousness in future research.

ACTION CONTROL

We know from everyday experience that we do not always carry out our intentions. Choice of a goal and persistence in striving for it do not guarantee that goal-related intentions will be actually performed. In many cases, a certain amount of effort is needed to enact an intention. It takes effort to maintain an intention, to shield it from the press resulting from competing action tendencies, and to strengthen it if necessary until it has been carried into effect. I assume that this type of self-regulatory effort is required not only for enacting "difficult" intentions (e.g., to quit smoking) but also for enacting seemingly easy intentions (e.g., to make a phone call). Since "effort" is a phenomenal summary term that probably refers to a variety of mechanisms, our task is to investigate the specific mechanisms that mediate the enactment of intentions. I have proposed the term "action control" to refer to these self-regulatory mechanisms. The neglect of action-control processes in motivational psychology, which resulted from Lewin's (1926) seminal paper on motivation and volition, has impeded research into the functional differences among motivational states (e.g., wishes, action tendencies, intentions). Since the study of action control reveals many functional differences among motivational states (e.g., intentions versus wishes) and between motivational processes and other mental processes (i.e., cognitive and emotional processes), it supports the modularity hypothesis proposed earlier, rather than a unitary conception of motivational states (Searle, 1983) or even of all mental processes (Anderson, 1983).

In what ways are intentional states functionally different from other mental states? First, the memory mechanisms underlying the retention of intentional states seem to differ in several respects from those underlying other mental states. This difference, which was demonstrated in a series of studies by Birenbaum (1930), has been neglected in the information-processing literature until very recently. Anderson (1983) recognized the fact that activation of an intentional state—or, in his terms, the "goal element"—does not decay as rapidly as activation of other "cognitive" elements. To account for this fact, he defined the memory structure encoding the actor's current goal as a "source node" that maintains its level of activation until the goal is actually attained. Assuming a permanent source of activation does not provide much explanatory depth regarding the mechanisms underlying the maintenance of intentional states, although this level of explanation may suffice within a theory of cognition.

A comprehensive theory of motivation requires a detailed analysis of the specific mechanisms mediating the maintenance of intentional states. Experimental research into this problem suggests that this maintenance function is supported by several systems, ranging from certain subcortical neurophysiological mechanisms to complex cognitive strategies. In one experiment, mother rats seemed to have lost their ability to maintain their "intention" to pick up their offspring and take them to the nest after certain parts were removed from the limbic brain (Stamm, 1955). After a lesion of the hippocampus, they became distracted by all sorts of environmental stimuli that had not interrupted a similar behavior before the surgery. Pribram (1971) reported similar observations of humans with lesions in the limbic system. These patients showed a specific inability to recall intentions, especially when they were trying to perform complex actions, whereas retention of nonintentional information seemed to be undisturbed.

Our own research has focused on information-processing mechanisms supporting the maintenance and enactment of intentions. Since this research has been described elsewhere (Kuhl, 1983b, 1984, 1985), a brief summary of some of the findings will suffice here. Self-regulatory efficiency may be considered a function of two factors: the *self-regulatory abilities* of the individual and the *difficulty of enactment*—that is, the amount of self-regulatory ability needed to enact the current intention.

Difficulty of Enactment: Action and State Orientations

Most models of self-regulation do not specify the determinants of the demands placed on the self-regulatory system in various situations. According to my present model (Kuhl, 1984), the difficulty of enactment is a function of three factors: (1) the number and strengths of self-generated action tendencies competing with the current intention, (2) the compatibility of socially demanded actions with the current intention, and (3) the mode of control that is currently activated.

Individuals do not always perform actions that they wish or intend to perform. Recently, I proposed a distinction between a *metastatic* and a *catastatic* mode of control (Kuhl, 1984). The catastic mode is characterized by a high difficulty of enactment, whereas the metastatic mode is characterized by facilitated enactment of intention. When a computer is operating in an editing mode, instructions are not executed even if they are activated. Similarly, action-related memory structures can be activated in an individual on a fantasy-related level without being executed.

In our research, we have focused on another determinant of metastatic and catastatic modes of control—action and state orientation, respectively. An organism is said to be *action-oriented* if attention is focused on a fully developed action structure. If attention is focused on some internal or external state, the organism is said to be *state-oriented*. This state may be characterized by perseverating cognitions related to some present, past, or future state or even by the absence of any coherent conscious thought. I have developed a questionnaire to assess individual differences in state versus action orientation (Kuhl, 1985). In

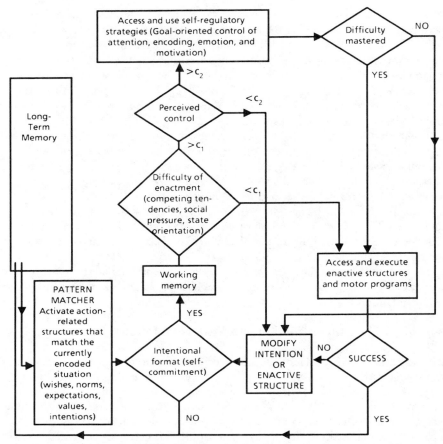

FIGURE 14.6   Outline of a model of action control. (*Note*: c_1 and c_2 are numerical constants that serve as threshold values in the model: c_1 = amount of difficulty of enactment necessary to activate self-regulatory processes; c_2 = amount of perceived control necessary to activate self-regulatory processes.)

several studies, we found that state-oriented subjects show weak relationships between projective measures of their motives and motive-related behavior (Kuhl & Geiger, in press) and between their intentions and their actual behavior (Kuhl, 1982a). These relationships were significantly stronger in action-oriented subjects. Also, after state-oriented subjects have been exposed to a series of uncontrollable failures, they seem to have considerably more problems than action-oriented subjects in fully concentrating on an intention to perform well at a new (solvable) task (Brunstein & Olbrich, in press; Kuhl, 1981; Kuhl & Weiss, 1984).

Self-Regulatory Abilities

According to the model of action control (Figure 14.6), an action-related (declarative) memory structure stored in long-term memory is activated when a match is found between the encoding of the current situation and the context component (see Figure 14.6) of that structure. If this action-related structure is an intentional structure (as defined by the *will* relation), it is "admitted" to working memory. Nonintentional structures (i.e., wishes, values, norms, and expectations) are transformed into an intentional structure and admitted to working memory if they conform to certain "admission rules" (Kuhl, 1984, p. 121). Self-regulatory strategies are activated if two requirements are met. First, the difficulty of enactment—as defined by the strengths of competing tendencies, the amount of social pressure to engage in alternative activities, and the current degree of state orientation—has to exceed a critical value (c_1). Second, the actor's perceived ability to control successfully the implementation of the intended action has to exceed a critical value (c_2). If these conditions are met, the six self-regulatory strategies to be discussed here may be invoked to facilitate the enactment of the current intention. These six closely related processes presumably mediate action control; they facilitate the protection and maintenance of a current intention against the pressure exerted by the competing action tendencies.

1. Active attentional selectivity facilitates the processing of information supporting the current intention and inhibits the processing of information supporting competing tendencies. Mischel and Mischel (1983) reported a series of experimental findings that children learn to maintain an experimentally induced intention against a seducing action alternative by avoiding visual contact with the source of distraction. Our experimental data suggest that, compared to action-oriented subjects, state-oriented subjects are less effective in actively attending to information that supports the current intention (Kuhl, 1984, p. 269).

2. Encoding control presumably facilitates the protective function of volition by selectively encoding those features of a stimulus that are related to the current intention. This assumption is in line with recent experimental evidence of a biasing of pattern-matching resources in favor of memory structures involving the current goal (Anderson, 1983; La Berge, 1973; Posner & Snyder, 1975) and with the notion of goal-directed encoding and representation (Hamilton, 1981; Higgins, 1981). Several studies have demonstrated that *perceptual tuning*—that is, the preconscious selection of perceptual input on the basis of higher order conceptual structures—occurs at very early stages of perceptual processing (Carr & Bacharach, 1976).

3. Emotion control presumably facilitates the protective function of volition by inhibiting emotional states that might undermine the efficiency of the protective function of volition. It has been suggested and found that certain emotional states (e.g., sadness) render it difficult to protect and maintain an intention to avoid a tempting action alternative (Izard, 1977; Mischel, Ebbesen, & Zeiss, 1972). We are currently investigating in our laboratory when—and depending on what developmental precursors—children learn to control their emotions to facilitate the enactment of current intentions against powerful alternative tendencies.

4. Motivation control refers to a feedback relation from self-regulatory processes to their own motivational basis (Kuhl, 1984). This process is especially important when the current intention is supported by a nondominant action tendency. When a mismatch is detected—indicating that the current intention is insufficiently strong—a self-regulatory process is activated that increases the strength of the current intention by selectively processing information that supports it. This function of motivation control may or may not involve the selective attentional process. The central characteristic of motivation control is that it explicitly aims at the strengthening of the current intention by enhancing its motivational basis. For example, if I form the intention of mowing my lawn while feeling afraid that I will not be able to pull myself together and actually do it, a very useful strategy would be to think about what would happen if I should fail to perform the intended action—that is, my neighbors would be irritated, the grass would rapidly grow to a height that would make it much more difficult to cut later, and so forth. In a recent study (Beckmann & Kuhl, 1984), action-oriented subjects seemed to use a motivation-control strategy. Whereas state-oriented subjects did not increase the subjective attractiveness of tentatively chosen alternatives during the course of the decision-making process, action-oriented subjects facilitated the final choice by increasing the attractiveness of tentatively chosen alternatives compared to rejected alternatives.

5. Environment control describes a strategy that may develop from the more basic strategies for dealing with emotion control and motivation control. Emotional and motivational states may be controlled by manipulation of the environment. Making a social commitment is such a manipulation. People who intend to stop smoking may inform a relevant other person about their intention because they know having informed another person will create some social pressure that might help maintain the intention. Clinically oriented theories of self-control (e.g., Thoresen & Mahoney, 1974) place particular emphasis on the process of environment control, probably because deficits in this process are more easily removed than deficits in the other, less easily observable processes.

6. Parsimony of information processing is an aspect of volitional control that relates to the definition of stop rules for information processing. Theoretically, an actor could forever go on processing new information about various consequences of potential action alternatives without ever performing any of them. Efficient action control requires optimalizing the length of the decision-making process. Whenever the actor believes that further processing of information bearing on potential action alternatives may jeopardize the execution of the current intention, the process of appraising action alternatives should be brought to a halt, especially if further processing may reveal information that undermines the motivational power of the current intention. In one study (Kuhl & Beckmann, 1983), action-oriented subjects used a simple decision rule when making their choices among various games of dice. In contrast, state-oriented subjects continued to use a more complex rule that made it necessary to process information that did not increase expected utility substantially.

CONCLUSION

In this chapter, I have discussed three motivational phenomena—choice, persistence, and effort—and I have suggested three information-processing mechanisms that presumably affect these phenomena. First, to understand choice among goals and action alternatives, we need to investigate the structural aspects of the representations of action-related knowledge in human memory. Second, the study of persistence requires an analysis of the dynamic processes affecting temporal changes in action tendencies that cannot be fully attributed to changes in action-related knowledge. The extent to which dynamic principles—such as perseverance and cross-situational cumulation of action tendencies—affect behavior may increase with an increasing amount of subconscious processing. Conscious processing of action-related information seems to support context-specific (episodic) decision making that is relatively free from motivational carryover effects from the individual's past. Finally, the maintenance and enactment of intentional states seems to be mediated by attentional mechanisms and strategies that individuals use to shield their current intentions against competing action tendencies.

Although I have discussed several cognitive mechanisms affecting motivation, one should not overlook the functional differences between motivational and cognitive processes. Dynamic processes may affect motivational states independent of any cognitive mediation. Action control functions, which are even supported by subcortical mechanisms, do not affect cognitive or emotional processes and not even all motivational processes. They seem to be confined to one category of motivational states—intentional states.

Finally, it should be noted that an information-processing approach to the study of motivation is defined by a certain level of analysis, rather than by a reduction of all mental events to cognitive processes. The fact that research into human information processing has almost exclusively focused on cognitive processes is a historical coincidence, rather than a logical or psychological necessity. Mental mechanisms such as memory, attention, and consciousness are not necessarily unitary phenomena. I have cited some evidence suggesting that these mechanisms differ in some respects across psychological systems. Information-processing principles may also be different across cognitive, emotional, and motivational systems. In the absence of conclusive data, it is a more useful research strategy to look for potential differences among these systems than to deny functional differences and confine our research into memory, attention, and consciousness to one of these systems.

Acknowledgments

This chapter was written during my term as a Fellow at the Center for Advanced Study in the Behavioral Sciences, Stanford, California. I am grateful for the support received from the center's staff and for helpful suggestions from Torgrim Gjesme.

References

Ach, N. (1910). *Über den Willensakt und das Temperament* [On the act of will and the temperament]. Leipzig: Quelle und Meyer.

Ajzen, I., & Fishbein, M. (1973). Attitudinal and normative variables as predictors of specific behaviors. *Journal of Personality and Social Psychology, 27,* 41–57.

Anderson, J. R. (1983). *The architecture of cognition.* Cambridge, MA: Harvard University Press.

Anderson, J. R., & Bower, G. H. (1973). *Human associative memory.* Washington, DC: Hemisphere.

Atkinson, J. W. (1958). *Motives in fantasy, action, and society.* Princeton, NJ: Van Nostrand.

Atkinson, J. W., & Birch, D. (1970). *The dynamics of action.* New York: Wiley.

Atkinson, J. W., Bongort, K., & Price, L. H. (1977). Explorations using computer simulation to comprehend thematic apperceptive measurement of motivation. *Motivation and Emotion, 1,* 1–27.

Atkinson, J. W., & Cartwright, D. (1964). Some neglected variables in contemporary conceptions of decision and performance. *Psychological Reports, 14,* 575–590.

Atkinson, J. W., & Feather, N. T. (1966). *A theory of achievement motivation.* New York: Wiley.

Bandura, A. (1977). Self-efficacy: Toward a unifying theory of behavioral change. *Psychological Review, 84,* 191–215.

Beckmann, J., & Kuhl, J. (1984). Deforming information to gain action control: Functional aspects of the veridicality of human information processing. *Journal of Research in Personality, 18,* 223–237.

Bem, D. J. (1983). Toward a response style theory of persons in situations. In R. A. Dienstbier (Ed.), *Nebraska Symposium on Motivation 1982. Personality: Current theory and research* (pp. 201–231). Lincoln: University of Nebraska Press.

Birenbaum, G. (1930). Untersuchungen zur Handlungs- und Affektpsychologie [Studies on the psychology of action and affect]. *Psychologische Forschung, 13,* 218–284.

Blankenship, V. (1982). The relationship between consummatory value of success and achievement-task difficulty. *Journal of Personality and Social Psychology, 42,* 901–914.

Blum, G. S., & Barbour, J. S. (1979). Selective inattention to anxiety-linked stimuli. *Journal of Experimental Psychology: General, 108,* 182–224.

Bower, G. H. (1981). Mood and memory. *American Psychologist, 36,* 129–148.

Bruner, J. S., & Goodman, C. C. (1947). Value and need as organizing factors in perception. *Journal of Abnormal and Social Psychology, 42,* 33–44.

Brunstein, J. C., & Olbrich, E. (in press). Personal helplessness and action-control: An analysis of achievement-related cognitions, self-assessments, and performance. *Journal of Personality and Social Psychology.*

Carr, T. H., & Bacharach, V. R. (1976). Perceptual tuning and conscious attention: Systems of input regulation in visual information processing. *Cognition, 4,* 281–302.

Carver, C. S., & Scheier, M. F. (1981). *Attention and self-regulation: A control-theory approach to human behavior.* New York: Springer.

Craik, F. I. M., & Lockhart, R. S. (1972). Levels of processing: A framework for memory research. *Journal of Verbal Learning and Verbal Behavior, 11,* 671–684.

Dawson, M. E., & Schell, A. M. (1982). Electrothermal responses to attended and nonattended significant stimuli during dichotic listening. *Journal of Experimental Psychology: Human Perception and Performance, 8,* 315–324.

de Charms, R. (1968). *Personal causation.* New York: Plenum.

Erdelyi, M. H. (1974). A new look at the New Look: Perceptual defense and vigilance. *Psychological Review, 81,* 1–25.

Feather, N. T. (1967). Valence of outcome and expectation of success in relation to task difficulty and perceived locus of control. *Journal of Personality and Social Psychology, 7,* 372–386.

Feather, N. T. (Ed.). (1982). *Expectations and actions: Expectancy-value models in psychology.* Hillsdale, NJ: Erlbaum.

Fodor, J. A. (1983). *Modularity of mind.* Cambridge, MA: MIT Press.

Freud, S. (1949). *Collected papers* (Vol. 4). New York: Basic Books. (Original work published 1915)

Gibson, J. J. (1966). *The senses considered as perceptual systems.* Boston: Houghton Mifflin.

Gjesme, T. (1981). Is there any future in achievement motivation? *Motivation and Emotion, 5,* 115–138.

Graen, G. (1969). Instrumentality theory of work motivation. Some experimental results and suggested modifications. *Journal of Applied Psychology, 53* (Whole No. 2, Pt. 2).

Greenwald, A. G. (1982). Ego task analysis: An integration of research on ego-involvement and self awareness. In A. H. Hastorf, & A. M. Isen (Eds.), *Cognitive social psychology* (pp. 105–147). New York: Elsevier North-Holland.

Guthrie, E. R. (1935). *The psychology of learning.* New York: Harper.

Hackman, J. R., & Porter, L. W. (1968). Expectancy-theory predictions of work effectiveness. *Organizational Behavior and Human Performance, 3,* 417–426.

Hamilton, D. L. (1981). Cognitive representations of persons. In E. T. Higgins, C. P. Herman, & M. P. Zanna (Eds.), *Social cognition: The Ontario Symposium* (Vol. 1, pp. 135–159). Hillsdale, NJ: Erlbaum.

Hamilton, V. (1983). *The cognitive structures and processes of human motivation and personality.* New York: Wiley.

Heckhausen, H., & Kuhl, J. (1985). From wishes to action: The dead ends and short-cuts on the long way to action. In M. Frese & J. Sabini (Eds.), *Goal-directed behavior: Psychological theory and research on action.* Hillsdale, NJ: Erlbaum.

Higgins, E. T. (1981). The "communication game": Implications for social cognition and persuasion. In E. T. Higgins, C. P. Herman, & M. P. Zanna (Eds.), *Social cognition: The Ontario Symposium* (Vol. 1, pp. 343–392). Hillsdale, NJ: Erlbaum.

Izard, C. E. (1977). *Human emotions.* New York: Plenum.

Izard, C. E. (1984). Emotion-cognition relationships and human development. In C. E. Izard, J. Kagan, & R. B. Zajonc (Eds.), *Emotions, cognition, and behavior* (pp. 17–37). New York: Cambridge University Press.

Karsten, A. (1928). Psychische Sättigung [Psychic satiation]. *Psychologische Forschung, 10,* 142–254.

Kintsch, W. (1974). *The representation of meaning in memory.* Hillsdale, NJ: Erlbaum.

Kosslyn, S. M. (1980). *Image and mind.* Cambridge, MA: Harvard University Press.

Kruglanski, A. W., & Klar, Y. (1985). Knowing what to do: On the epistemology of actions. In J. Kuhl & J. Beckmann (Eds.), *Action control: From cognition to behavior.* New York: Springer-Verlag.

Kuhl, J. (1977). *Mess-und prozesstheoretische Analysen einiger Person- und Situationsparameter der Leistungmotivation* [Personal and situational determinants of achievement motivation: Computer simulation and experimental analysis]. Bonn: Bouvier.

Kuhl, J. (1978). Standard setting and risk preference: An elaboration of the theory of achievement motivation and an empirical test. *Psychological Review, 85,* 239–248.

Kuhl, J. (1981). Motivational and functional helplessness: The moderating effect of state versus action orientation. *Journal of Personality and Social Psychology, 40,* 155–170.

Kuhl, J. (1982a). Action vs. state-orientation as a mediator between motivation and action. In W. Hacker, W. Volpert, & M. von Cranach (Eds.), *Cognitive and motivational aspects of action.* Amsterdam: North-Holland.

Kuhl, J. (1982b). The expectancy-value approach in the theory of social motivation: Elaborations, extensions, critique. In N. T. Feather (Ed.), *Expectations and actions: Expectancy-value models in psychology.* Hillsdale, NJ: Erlbaum.

Kuhl, J. (1983a). Emotion, Kognition und Motivation: II. Die funktionale Bedeutung der Emotionen für das problemlösende Denken und für das konkrete Handeln [Emotion, cognition, and motivation: II. The functional significance of emotions for problem-solving and action]. *Sprache und Kognition, 4,* 228–253.

Kuhl, J. (1983b). *Motivation, Konflikt und Handlungskontrolle* [Motivation, conflict, and action control]. Heidelberg: Springer.

Kuhl, J. (1984). Volitional aspects of achievement motivation and learned helplessness: Toward a comprehensive theory of action control. In B. A. Maher (Ed.), *Progress in experimental personality research* (Vol. 12, pp. 99–170). New York: Academic Press.

Kuhl, J. (1985). Volitional mediators of cognition-behavior consistency: Self-regulatory processes and action versus state orientation. In J. Kuhl & J. Beckmann (Eds.), *Action control: From cognition to behavior.* New York: Springer-Verlag.

Kuhl, J., & Atkinson, J. W. (1984). Perspectives in human motivational psychology: A new experimental paradigm. In V. Sarris & A. Parducci (Eds.), *Perspectives in psychological experimentation: Toward the year 2000.* Hillsdale, NJ: Erlbaum.

Kuhl, J., & Atkinson, J. W. (Eds.). (in press). *Motivation, thought, and action.* New York: Praeger.

Kuhl, J., & Beckmann, J. (1983). Handlungskontrolle und Umfang der Informationsverarbeitung: Wahl einer vereinfachten (nicht optimalen) Entscheidungsregel zugunsten rascher Handlungsbereitschaft. [Action control and parsimony of information processing in decision making]. *Zeitschrift für Sozialpsychologie, 14,* 241–250.

Kuhl, J., & Blankenship, V. (1979a). Behavioral change in a constant environment: Moving to more difficult tasks in spite of constant expectations of success. *Journal of Personality and Social Psychology, 37,* 551–563.

Kuhl, J., & Blankenship, V. (1979b). The dynamic theory of achievement motivation: From episodic to dynamic thinking: *Psychological Review, 86,* 141–151.

Kuhl, J., & Eisenbeiser, T. (in press). Mediating vs. meditating cognitions in human motivation: Action control, inertial motivation, and the alienation effect. In J. Kuhl & J. W. Atkinson (Eds.), *Motivation, thought, and action.* New York: Praeger.

Kuhl, J., & Geiger, E. (in press). The dynamic theory of the anxiety-behavior relationship: The champagne-cork effect. In J. Kuhl & J. W. Atkinson (Eds.), *Motivation, thought, and action.* New York: Praeger.

Kuhl, J., & Helle, P. (1984). *Motivational and volitional determinants of depression: The degenerated-intention hypothesis.* Manuscript submitted for publication.

Kuhl, J., & Koch, B. (1984). Motivational determinants of motor performance: The hidden second task. *Psychological Research, 46,* 143–153.

Kuhl, J., & Weiss, M. (1984). *Performance deficits following uncontrollable failure: Impaired action control or global attributions and generalized expectancy deficits?* Manuscript submitted for publication.

Kukla, A. (1972). Foundations of an attributional theory of performance. *Psychological Review, 79,* 454–470.

Kunst-Wilson, W. R., & Zajonc, R. B. (1980). Affective discrimination of stimuli that cannot be recognized. *Science, 207,* 557–558.

La Berge, D. (1973). Attention and the measurement of perceptual learning. *Memory and Cognition, 1,* 268–276.

Lawler, E. E., & Porter, L. W. (1967). Antecedent attitudes of effective managerial job performance. *Organizational Behavior and Human Performance, 2,* 122–142.

Lazarus, R. S. (1982). Thoughts on the relation between emotion and cognition. *American Psychologist, 37,* 1019–1024.

Lazarus, R. S. (1984). On the primacy of cognition. *American Psychologist, 39,* 124–129.

Leventhal, H. (1980). Toward a comprehensive theory of emotions. In L. Berkowitz (Ed.), *Advances in experimental social psychology* (Vol. 13, pp. 139–207). New York: Academic Press.

Lewin, K. (1926). Untersuchungen zur Handlungs- und Affekt-Psychologie: II. Vorsatz, Wille und Bedürfnis [Studies on action and affect psychology: Intention, will, and need]. *Psychologische Forschung, 7,* 330–385.

Lewin, K. (1935). *A dynamic theory of personality: Selected papers.* New York: McGraw-Hill.

Lynch, J. G., & Cohen, J. L. (1978). The use of subjective expected utility theory as an aid to understand variables that influence helping behavior. *Journal of Personality and Social Psychology, 36,* 1138–1151.

Mandler, G. (1975). *Mind and emotion.* New York: Wiley.

Mandler, G. (1983). *Consciousness: Its function and construction* (Report No. 117). La Jolla, CA: Center for Human Information Processing.

Marcel, A. J. (1980). Explaining selective effects of prior context on perception: The need to distinguish conscious and pre-conscious processes. In J. Requin (Ed.), *Anticipation and behavior.* Paris: Centre National de la Recherche Scientifique.

Marcel, A. J. (1983a). Conscious and unconscious perception: Experiments on visual masking and word recognition. *Cognitive Psychology, 15,* 197–237.

Marcel, A. J. (1983b). Conscious and unconscious perception: An approach to the relations between phenomenal experience and perceptual processes. *Cognitive Psychology, 15*, 238–300.

McClelland, D. C., & Atkinson, J. W. (1948). The projective expression of needs: I. The effect of different intensities of the hunger drive on perception. *Journal of Psychology, 25*, 205–232.

Meyer, W. U. (1973). *Leistungsmotiv und Ursachenerklärung von Erfolg und Misserfolg* [Need achievement and causal attribution of success and failure]. Stuttgart: Klett.

Mischel, W., Ebbesen, E., & Zeiss, A. R. (1972). Cognitive and attentional mechanisms in delay of gratification. *Journal of Personality and Social Psychology, 21*, 204–218.

Mischel, H. N., & Mischel, W. (1983). The development of children's knowledge of self-control strategies. *Child Development, 54*, 226–254.

Norman, D. A. (1980). Twelve issues for cognitive science. *Cognitive Science, 4*, 1–32.

Norman, D. A., & Rumelhart, D. (1975). *Explorations in cognition.* San Francisco: Freeman.

Nygard, R. (1977). *Personality, situation, and persistence.* Oslo: Universitetsforlaget.

Olson, D. R., & Astington, J. W. (1983). *Children's acquisition of metalinguistic and metacognitive verbs.* Manuscript submitted for publication.

Olson, D. R., & Bialystok, E. (1983). *Spatial cognition.* Hillsdale, NJ: Erlbaum.

Ornstein, R. E. (1969). *On the experience of time.* Baltimore: Penguin.

Ovsiankina, M. (1928). Die Wiederaufnahme unterbrochener Handlungen [The resumption of interrupted tasks]. *Psychologische Forschung, 11*, 302–379.

Piaget, J. (1952). *The origins of intelligence in the child.* New York: International Universities Press.

Plutchik, R. (1980). *Emotion: A psychoevolutionary synthesis.* New York: Harper & Row.

Posner, M. I. (1973). *Cognition: An introduction.* Glenview, IL: Scott, Foresman.

Posner, M. I., & Snyder, C. R. R. (1975). Attention and cognitive control. In R. L. Solso (Ed.), *Information processing and cognition.* Hillsdale, NJ: Erlbaum.

Pribram, K. H. (1971). *Languages of the brain.* Englewood Cliffs, NJ: Prentice-Hall.

Pritchard, R. D., & Sanders, M. S. (1973). The influence of valence, instrumentality, and expectancy on effort and performance. *Journal of Applied Psychology, 57*, 55–60.

Pylyshyn, Z. W. (1973). What the mind's eye tells the mind's brain: A critique of mental imagery. *Psychological Bulletin, 80*, 1–24.

Ratcliff, R., & McKoon, G. (1981). Does activation really spread? *Psychological Review, 88*, 454–462.

Raynor, J. O. (1969). Future orientation and motivation of immediate activity: An elaboration of the theory of achievement motivation. *Psychological Review, 76*, 606–610.

Rotter, J. B. (1954). *Social learning and clinical psychology.* Englewood Cliffs, NJ: Prentice-Hall.

Routtenberg, A. (1978, November). The reward system of the brain. *Scientific American*, pp. 154–164.

Schmidt, F. L. (1973). Implications of a measurement problem for expectancy theory research. *Organizational Behavior and Human Performance, 10*, 243–251.

Schneider, K. (1973). *Motivation unter Erfolgsrisiko* [Motivation under uncertainty of success]. Göttingen: Hogrefe.

Seamon, J. J., Brody, N., & Kauff, D. M. (1983). Affective discrimination of stimuli that are not recognized: Effects of shadowing, masking, and cerebral laterality. *Journal of Experimental Psychology: Learning, Memory, and Cognition, 9*, 544–555.

Searle, J. (1983). *Intentionality: An essay in the philosophy of mind.* New York: Cambridge University Press.

Shepard, R. N., & Cooper, L. A. (Eds.). (1983). *Mental images and their transformations.* Cambridge, MA: MIT Press.

Silverman, L. H. (1976). Psychoanalytic theory. The reports of my death are greatly exaggerated. *American Psychologist, 31*, 621–637.

Silverman, L. H., Ross, D. L., Adler, J. M., & Lustig, D. A. (1978). Simple research paradigm for demonstrating subliminal psychodynamic activation: Effects of oedipal stimuli on dart-throwing accuracy in college males. *Journal of Abnormal Psychology, 87*, 341–357.

Sperry, R. W. (1964, January). The great cerebral commissure. *Scientific American*, pp. 42–52.

Stamm, J. S. (1955). The function of the median cerebral cortex in maternal behavior of rats. *Journal of Comparative and Physiological Psychology, 48*, 77–88.

Thoresen, C. E., & Mahoney, H. J. (1974). *Behavioral self-control.* New York: Holt, Rinehart and Winston.

Tucker, D. M. (1981). Lateral brain function, emotion, and conceptualization. *Psychological Bulletin, 89,* 19–46.

Weiner, B. (1965). The effects of unsatisfied achievement motivation on persistence and subsequent performance. *Journal of Personality, 33,* 428–442.

Weiner, B. (1972). *Theories of motivation: From mechanism to cognition.* Chicago: Markham.

Weiner, B. (1980). *Human motivation.* New York: Holt, Rinehart and Winston.

Wicklund, R. A. (1975). Objective self-awareness. In L. Berkowitz (Ed.), *Advances in experimental social psychology* (Vol. 8, pp. 233–275). New York: Academic Press.

Wicklund, R. A., & Gollwitzer, P. M. (1981). Symbolic self-completion, attempted influence, and self-deprecation. *Basic and Applied Social Psychology, 2,* 89–114.

Wicklund, R. A., & Gollwitzer, P. M. (1982). *Symbolic self-completion.* Hillsdale, NJ: Erlbaum.

Zajonc, R. B. (1980). Feeling and thinking: Preferences need no inferences. *American Psychologist, 35,* 151–175.

Zajonc, R. B. (1984). On the primacy of affect. *American Psychologist, 39,* 117–123.

Zeigarnik, B. (1927). Über das Behalten von erledigten und unerledigten Handlungen [On the recall of completed and uncompleted tasks]. *Psychologische Forschung, 9,* 1–85.

CHAPTER 15

Some Effects of Self-Evaluation Maintenance on Cognition and Action

ABRAHAM TESSER

University of Georgia, Institute for Behavioral Research

This chapter describes a research program that has been ongoing for the past few years. The research started with the assumption that people are motivated to maintain a positive self-evaluation. It further assumed that there are two antagonistic social-psychological processes through which one's self-evaluation is maintained. Outcroppings of the maintenance process can be seen in an individual's actions and in his or her beliefs. In the sections that follow, the self-evaluation maintenance (SEM) model is described in some detail, the dynamics of the model are elaborated, and evidence concerning the effects of the hypothesized process on cognition and action is reviewed. The chapter also addresses a variety of issues, including the systemic nature of the SEM processes, distortion, awareness, self-presentation, and affect.

THE SELF-EVALUATION MAINTENANCE PROCESSES

The Core Assumption

The SEM model has at its heart the assumption that people are motivated to evaluate themselves positively. That is, they will change their behavior and/or their beliefs so as to see themselves in a positive light. This assumption does not imply that people do not have other motives—such as to see themselves accurately or consistently (see Raynor and McFarlin, Chapter 11 of this volume). It does imply, however, that all things being equal, the individual prefers to feel positive rather than negative about himself or herself.

Although such an assumption seems reasonable (after all, who would want to see himself in a negative light?), it has not gone unchallenged in the psychological literature. The locus of the challenge centers on people who habitually tend to evaluate themselves negatively—people who are depressed and/or of relatively low self-esteem. The theoretical impetus for the assumption that people who have a negative view of themselves may actually seek out negative information about themselves comes from balance theory (Heider, 1958). This theory suggests that people have a preference for balanced cognitive structures—that is, structures in which "good" things go with "good" things, "bad" things go with "bad" things, and good and bad are separate. Thus, if an individual views himself or herself in negative terms, negative information about the self is balanced and positive information is not.

Shrauger (1975) has done an extensive review of the literature on reactions to information about the self as a function of initial self-evaluation. On the basis of that review, he has concluded that there is evidence for both the consistency view and the evaluation maintenance view. On the one hand, feedback is better retained and is seen as more accurate and as caused by one's own abilities if that feedback is consistent with one's prior evaluation of the self than if it is inconsistent with one's prior evaluation. Score one for balance theory. On the other hand, one's *affective* response to feedback tends to be self-enhancing. The affective response is generally positive to favorable feedback and negative to unfavorable feedback. Moreover, Shrauger (1975) noted that "this was as much, if not more, the case for people with negative expectancies as for those with positive expectancies" (p. 581). These affective responses to feedback argue for the tenability of the assumption that people are motivated to maintain a positive self-evaluation.

The conclusion from Shrauger's review has been explicitly tested by McFarlin and Blascovich (1981). These investigators had women whose self-esteem had been previously measured work on an analogies test. Feedback about their performance was randomly determined: One-third were told they had done well, one-third were told they had done poorly, and one-third were given no feedback. Subjects were then asked about their performance on an upcoming task. The questions concerned preference for successful performance (an affective measure) and their expectations for performance. Self-esteem affected expectations for future performance, whereas feedback did not, and those who were high in self-esteem expected to do better than those who were low in self-esteem. However, consistent with the self-evaluation maintenance assumption, all subjects, regardless of their self-esteem and regardless of the previous feedback, *wanted* to do well on the subsequent task.

Are depressed individuals not motivated to maintain a positive evaluation of the self? According to psychoanalytic theory (e.g. Freud, 1917/1953), the answer to this question is no. Mechanisms of self-deception and distortion help us maintain a positive view of ourselves. When these mechanisms break down, the result is depression. It is not that depressives don't wnat to feel positively about themselves, they simply don't have appropriate defenses.

Some exciting recent work on the cognitive functioning of depressives and nondepressives is relevant to this issue. In a variety of studies, Alloy and Abramson (1979) have found that it is normals who tend to show distortion in their perception of control. They overestimate their control for positive outcomes and underestimate their control for negative outcomes, whereas depressed individuals are relatively accurate about their control. Most recently, Alloy (1982) has studied the accuracy of depressives and nondepressives in their perception of other persons. The findings were the mirror image of those for self-perception.

Alloy (1982) tied these latter data to the psychoanalytic hypothesis as follows: If the biases observed in the nondepressives' view of themselves are the result of defenses associated with self-esteem maintenance, then there is little reason to expect much bias in their view of others. Similarly, if depressives are accurate about themselves because of a breakdown in their defenses, there is no reason to expect that dysfunction to play itself out in their perception of other persons. "Thus, the reversal of depressive realism and nondepressive distortion observed in judgments about others is consistent with the self-esteem maintenance hypothesis, although it is not specifically predicted by this hypothesis" (Alloy, 1982, p. 12).

The SEM model assumes that people are motivated to maintain a positive self-evaluation. It also spells out two social-psychological processes through which this motive operates: a reflection process and a comparison process. The important parameters for each process are the same, but their impacts on self-evaluation are opposite. I will describe each of these antagonistic processes and then describe how they operate in concert.

Increasing Self-Evaluation: The Reflection Process

All of us have encountered people who tell us about their next-door neighbor who was in the Olympics, or about their cousin who plays first violin in the Houston Symphony, or about having gone to the same high school as Woody Allen. The stories are usually told with great animation and apparent pride on the part of the storytellers. Why? They are not talking about their own accomplishments, and they have played no instrumental role in the accomplishments of these outstanding others. Cialdini and his colleagues (Cialdini *et al.*, 1976; Cialdini & Richardson, 1981) have argued that "BIRGing" (basking in the reflected glory of another) raises self-evaluation. Indeed, their data indicate that threats to self-evaluation increase the use of this strategy.

The reflection process has two components: the degree of association between an actor and another—the *closeness* parameter—and the quality of the other's *performance*. These combine "multiplicatively" to affect self-evaluation. That is, if there is no association between an actor and another, then regardless of how outstanding that other's performance is, there is little to be gained by reflection. Similarly, if the other's performance is mediocre, there is little to be gained by reflection, regardless of how close the association is between the actor and the other. To the extent that one is in a close association with an outstanding other, the reflection process results in raised self-evaluation.

The closeness parameter associated with the reflection process is a cognitive-perceptual variable. Although the term "closeness" often connotes a positive affective bond, my own experience with the model (e.g., Pleban & Tesser, 1981) suggests that it is best to exclude the affective component from the definition. (Attraction researchers, such as Berscheid [1982], seem to be coming to a similar conclusion; that is, we often have intense negative affective responses to those to whom we are closest in other ways.) From the current perspective, closeness is a quantitative variable similar to Heider's (1958) notion of a unit relation or Osgood, Suci, and Tannenbaum's (1958) notion of an associative bond. Closeness increases with similarity, physical proximity, family ties, similarity in place of origin, and the like. In sum, anything that tends to put two persons into a unit relationship increases closeness. (See Campbell & Tesser, 1985, for a more complete discussion of the closeness variable.)

The performance parameter is concerned with the quality of the other person's performance. However, the quality of another's performance often is made meaningful through comparison to one's own performance. Therefore, the other's performance is generally defined in terms relative to the actor's performance.

Decreasing Self-Evaluation: The Comparison Process

The logic of the reflection process suggests that if one wants to raise self-evaluation, one ought to put oneself into a close association with an outstanding other. But being in close association with an outstanding other can easily have the opposite effect; it could make one look bad by comparison. Furthermore, the same combination of variables that maximizes increases in self-evaluation by reflection also maximizes decreases in self-evaluation by comparison.

Again, if the other's performance is mediocre, one will not suffer by comparison regardless of how close the association is. And if there is no association between self and other, comparisons are unlikely, regardless of how good the other's performance is. It follows, then, that the comparison process will cause one's self-evaluation to suffer most given a close association with an outstanding other.

The Relative Importance of the Reflection and Comparison Processes

The reflection process and the comparison process are mirror images of one another. Being in a close association with another can raise self-evaluation by reflection or lower self-evaluation by comparison. If the two processes were equally important, their effects would cancel one another out and lead to the conclusion that the closeness and performance of others have little to do with self-evaluation. The SEM model suggests that the two processes are generally not equally important. Sometimes the reflection process will predominate and sometimes the comparison process will predominate, depending on the *relevance* of the performance dimension to one's self-definition.

A performance dimension is any dimension that has a consensually agreed-upon "good" pole and "bad" pole and on which it is possible to rank-order people in terms of their "goodness." Tennis playing, tightrope walking, and physical beauty are examples of performance dimensions. Obviously, there are a huge number of such dimensions. For any particular individual, however, it will be important to do well on only a small subset of these dimensions. An individual may acknowledge good tightrope walking, for example, but not particularly want to be a good tightrope walker. That same individual, however, might very well want to be a good tennis player. Another's performance is *potentially* relevant to an individual's self-definition to the extent that the performance dimension is one on which the individual wishes to do well.

There is a second necessary condition that must be met if another's performance is to be relevant to one's self-definition. Following Festinger's (1954) theory of social comparison processes, the other's performance cannot be too discrepant from one's own. If another's performance is so much better than one's own that it puts him or her into a qualitatively different class, then that person's performance will not be relevant. Thus, the pitching performance of a major league baseball player will not be relevant to the self-definition of a sandlot ball player, even if it is very important for the sandlot player to be good at baseball. In sum, another's performance is relevant to one's self-definition to the extent that it is on a dimension that is important to the self and to the extent that the other's performance is not too discrepant from one's own.

Relevance is crucial because it determines the relative importance of the comparison process and the reflection process. To the extent that another's performance is relevant to one's self-definition, the comparison process will be relatively more important than the reflection process: A good performance by a close other will result in a loss in self-evaluation by comparison. To the extent that another's performance is not relevant to one's self-definition, the reflection process will be relatively more important than the comparison process: A good performance by a close other will result in a gain in self-evaluation by reflection. Thus, for example, if John's sister Mary has just given a triumphal piano concert, John will suffer by comparison if he also aspires to being a concert pianist, but he will glow in the reflection of her accomplishment if he has no such personal aspiration.

SELF-EVALUATION MAINTENANCE DYNAMICS

Thus far, I have argued that people are motivated to protect their self-evaluation. I have described two processes that can affect their self-evaluation, and I have introduced the notion of relevance—the variable that determines the importance of each process in any particular situation. The description, however, has been one of static pieces. This section attempts to put the pieces together and show how they form a dynamic system—a system that is useful for understanding a variety of social behaviors.

Perhaps the best way to illustrate the dynamics of the model is through example. Suppose that Albert's good friend Bob makes a 90 on a biology test on which Albert made an 80. Suppose, further, that it is important to Albert's self-definition to do well in biology. Relevance is high, so the comparison process should be more important than the reflection process. Also, since Bob is close and performs better than Albert, there is a potential loss in self-evaluation for Albert. To prevent this loss, Albert can do a variety of things: He can alter the closeness of his relationship with Bob, for example, by spending less time with him or focusing on ways in which the two of them are different. By reducing closeness, the impact of Bob's better performance is reduced. Albert can also attempt to affect Bob's performance. For example, he can mislabel or hide Bob's slides for the next test, or he can can come to believe that Bob's good performance was based on luck. By reducing Bob's performance, he also reduces the threat of comparison. Finally, Albert can change his self-definition. For example, he can spend less time studying biology, or he can decide that art is much more interesting. By reducing the importance of biology to his self-definition, the relevance of Bob's performance is reduced. The reflection process thus becomes relatively more important, with the consequence that Albert may actually gain in self-evaluation through his close friend Bob's good performance.[1]

There are several things to notice in the example. First, attempts to maintain self-evaluation take place on three variables: closeness, performance, and relevance. In all of the research to be described in this chapter, it is these three variables that are either manipulated or measured. There is no attempt to measure self-evaluation. Indeed, from the current perspective, self-evaluation is simply a hypothetical entity that has no empirical indicants. Its primary function is to help make understandable the relationships among closeness, performance, and relevance. (See Tesser & Campbell, 1983, for a more extended discussion of this point.)

Second, the model is systemic; that is, the variables operate like a system. There are no independent and dependent variables in the usual sense. A change in closeness, for example, can produce a change in relevance or a change in performance, and a change in performance or relevance can produce a change in closeness. It is possible to manipulate and fix any two of these variables and observe the impact of those manipulations on the third variable. (This has been done in some laboratory studies to be described later.) However, it is important to keep in mind that such manipulations are simply research strategies intended to illuminate aspects of the model; they do not reflect the overall systemic nature of the model.

The third thing to notice in the example is that attempts to maintain self-evaluation show themselves both in action and in cognition. For example, one can change closeness by changing one's beliefs about the relationship to another or by actually changing the relationship. The following discussion of the research is organized to point up this duality. Each of the empirical variables—performance, closeness, and relevance—is taken in turn, and I indicate how that variable should be affected by the remaining two variables and review evidence from the laboratory and the field showing how relevant cognitions and actions are actually affected.

THE IMPACT OF CLOSENESS AND RELEVANCE ON AFFECTING ANOTHER'S PERFORMANCE

The SEM system suggests that the relevance of another's performance and the closeness of that other should interact in affecting how an individual deals with the other's performance. If the other's performance is low in relevance to one's self-definition, the reflection process will be relatively more important than the comparison process: The better the other's performance, the greater the boost to self-evaluation, particularly if the other is close. Therefore, given low relevance, the closer the association between the self and the other, the more the self should be motivated to facilitate the other's performance (either cognitively or behaviorally). On the other hand, if the other's performance is high in relevance to one's self-definition, the comparison process will be more important than the reflection process: The better the other's performance, the greater the threat to self-evaluation, particularly if the other is close. Under these circumstances, the model makes a prediction that clashes with conventional wisdom. The model suggests, given high relevance, that the closer the association between the self and the other, the more the self should be motivated to interfere with the other's performance (either cognitively or behaviorally).

Cognitions About Another's Performance

Tesser and Campbell (1982) recently completed a laboratory study designed to examine the effects of relevance and closeness on one's beliefs about another's performance. Two pairs of female friends participated in each session. When they arrived, each participant was given a few minutes to describe herself to the others so that they might form an impression of her. Then each participant was privately seated before a microcomputer, which administered a series of questions dealing with social sensitivity and esthetic judgment. Most of the social sensitivity items described a human relations predicament and gave two potential responses to the predicament. The participant was to choose the response that was "the best thing to do in the situation." The esthetic judgment items consisted of pairs of pictures from the Meier Art Judgment Test (Meier, 1940), and the participant was to pick the "better" picture. After the subjects responded to each item, the computer indicated whether their answer was correct or incorrect. (This was done randomly, and each participant recieved 50% correct feedback.) Following this, on half of the items, the computer prompted the participant to indicate how she thought her friend (a close other) responded to the item; on the remaining items, the computer prompted the participant to indicate how she thought one of the women she had met for the first time earlier in the session (a distant other) responded to the item.

After completing the computer phase of the study, each participant filled out a questionnaire concerning the relevance of social sensitivity and esthetic judgment to their self-definition.

The SEM model predicts that closeness of other and relevance of task should interact in determining the guesses participants make about the correctness of the other's response to each item posed by the computer. Participants should be relatively more generous to a friend than to a stranger when the items are low in relevance (and the reflection process is important); they should be relatively less generous to a friend than to a stranger when the items are high in relevance (and the comparison process is important). Competing predictions concerning these data can be generated from some other perspectives. Balance theory (Heider, 1958) might predict that since friends are generally better liked than strangers, a participant should be more generous to a friend than to a stranger, regardless of task relevance. Also, since friends are generally more similar to one another than to strangers, an information-processing perspective might predict that a participants would guess that the friend responded like she did more than the stranger, regardless of correctness of response or relevance of task.

The balance theory hypothesis was not supported: Overall, participants were no more generous in the guesses they made about their friends' performance than they were in the guesses they made about the strangers' performance. Nor was the information-processing hypothesis supported: Participants did not guess that the responses made by their friends were more similar to their own responses than were the responses made by the strangers. On the other hand, the SEM predictions were well supported: Relevance of task and closeness of target interacted in determining the participants' guesses about the others' performance. If social sensitivity was more relevant to the participant than esthetic judgment, she was more charitable in her guesses about her friend's performance than in those about the stranger's performance on the esthetic judgment task but more charitable toward the stranger than toward her friend on the social sensitivity task. If esthetic judgment was more relevant to the participant than social sensitivity, she was more charitable in her guesses about her friend's performance than in those about the stranger's performance on the social sensitivity task but more charitable toward the stranger than toward her friend on the esthetic judgment task. In sum, one's cognitions about the performance of others seem to conform to the expectations generated by the SEM model.

Some nonlaboratory evidence concerning the impact of closeness and relevance on the cognitions concerning another's performance comes from a study carried out on fifth- and sixth-graders in the Nashville, Tennessee, school system (Tesser, Campbell, & Smith, 1984). At an initial session, students were given a list of school-related activities, such as football, arithmetic, and playing a musical instrument. They were asked to indicate the activity on which it was most important for them to do well (high relevance) and the activity on which it was least important for them to do well (low relevance). They were also given the names of the other children in their class. On this list, they indicated the child with whom they most liked to spend their time (close other) and the child with whom they least liked to spend their time (distant other). A week later, the students made performance ratings on the activity they indicated was relevant and on the activity they indicated was irrelevant to their self-definition. They rated their own performance and the performance of the the child they selected as close and the child they selected as distant.

Let us first focus on a comparison of the self-ratings with the ratings of the close other. When the performance ratings were averaged over the relevant and the irrelevant activities, the ratings of self and the ratings of the close other were virtually identical. Furthermore, the pattern of ratings was the same: Both the self and the close other were rated as performing better on the activity designated as relevant than on the activity designated as irrelevant. These results are certainly no surprise to those who have even a passing acquaintance with the interpersonal attraction literature. One doesn't need the SEM model to understand a similarity effect.

The unique prediction from the SEM model is an interaction: The self should be seen as performing better on the relevant activity and more poorly on the irrelevant activity. (Such a configuration would minimize the threat associated with comparison and would maximize the gain associated with reflection.) The expected interaction did emerge and was highly significant ($p < .001$). Furthermore, both aspects of the hypothesis were significant. Participants rated themselves as significantly better on the relevant activity ($p < .001$) and the close other as significantly better on the irrelevant activity ($p < .001$). The results for the distant other can be summarized quickly. They were derogated across the board and were seen as performing significantly more poorly than the self or close other on both the relevant and the irrelevant activity.

Again, the SEM model seems to do a reasonable job of ordering data in connection with the cognitions associated with another's performance. These particular data also help refine the model. A strong interpretation of the model is that people want to be around others who do poorly at those activities that are important to the self. Obviously, such an expectation is too strong, and these data illustrate that. The respondents did not rated close others as doing poorly on the activity that was most relevant; the close other was rated as doing well on that activity but simply not as well as the respondent himself or herself. This suggests that we want to be around others who are highly competent, so long as their competence doesn't exceed our own on those dimensions that are important to our self-defintion.

Actions to Affect Another's Performance

The preceding section reviewed some evidence showing that one's beliefs concerning another's performance are affected by the interaction of closeness and relevance. It is also true that these variables will affect one's *actions*? Will people act out behaviors that will facilitate or interfere with the performance of others? One of the first studies in this research program addressed that question.

Tesser and Smith (1980) had two male subjects who were unacquainted with one another (distant other) report to the laboratory, each with a friend (close other). The four subjects present at each session were told that they were to participate in a word identification task. Each participant would be given the opportunity to identify target words from clues provided by the other participants. Half of the subjects were led to believe that performance on this task was related to important verbal skills (high relevance), and the remaining subjects were led to believe that performance in the "game" was uncorrelated with important skills (low relevance). The experimenter arranged for the first two participants, one from each friendship pair, to do poorly. These participants then had an opportunity to provide clues for for their friends and for the strangers who had not yet "played." All the potential clues were graded for difficulty. If the subject wanted to facilitate the other's performance, he could provide easy clues; if he wanted to hinder the other's performance, he could provide difficult clues. Thus, the behavior of interest was the difficulty of the clue chosen for the other.

Recall the SEM prediction. When the task is low in relevance, the reflection process is important; the closer the other, the more there is to be gained from the other's good performance. Therefore, given low relevance, the closer the other, the more one should try to facilitate that other's performance—that is, one should give less difficult clues. When the task is high in relevance, the comparison process is important; the closer the other, the greater the threat from the other's good performance. Therefore, given high relevance, the closer the other, the *less* one should try to facilitate that other's performance; that is, one should give more difficult clues.

The results were consistent with the expectations. First, overall, participants gave more difficult clues when the task was high in relevance than when it was low in relevance. More interesting was the interaction between relevance and target. When the task was low in relevance, the subjects behaved the way common sense might suggest they would behave—they gave their friends easier clues than the strangers. However, when the task was high in relevance, not only did this effect attenuate, it reversed itself. Participants actually gave the strangers easier clues than they gave their friends.

These data provide some support for the idea that closeness and relevance interact to affect the actions we take to affect another's performance. Furthermore, the data suggest that a friend may not always have an advantage over a stranger. When the task is relevant and another's performance threatens to surpass our own, we may take action to prevent that from happening, particularly when the other is close. In short, the song is wrong: You don't *always* hurt the one you love-only sometimes.

THE IMPACT OF QUALITY AND RELEVANCE OF PERFORMANCE ON INTERPERSONAL CLOSENESS

This section deals with changes in closeness as a self-evaluation maintenance strategy. The focus is on changes in cognitions and changes in action concerning interpersonal closeness as a result of changes in the quality and relevance of another's performance. Recall the implications of the model. If another performs on a task that is relevant to one's self-definition, the comparison process is more important than the reflection process: The better the other performs, the greater the potential threat, particularly if the other is close. Therefore, when the task is relevant, the better the other performs, the more distance the individual should put between self and other. If the task is not relevant, the reflection process will be more important than the comparison process: The better the other performs, the greater the potential gain in self-evaluation, particularly if the other is close. Therefore, when the task is low in relevance, the better the other performs, the closer the individual should put the self to the other. We will examine data relevant to these predictions using indices of closeness that are either cognitive or behavioral.

Cognitions About the Closeness of Another

A laboratory study (Pleban & Tesser, 1981) was conducted in which participants were randomly assigned to work on a task that was either high or low in relevance and on which another performed more poorly, at about the same level, or better than the participant. The experiment was framed in terms of a "College Bowl" kind of question-answering competition. When a male participant arrived at the laboratory, he and another "participant" were given a questionnaire asking them to indicate the personal importance of a number of subject areas, such as football and rock music. The other "participant" was actually a confederate of the experimenter who had memorized the answers in each of the topic areas so that he could vary his performance at will. Half of the participants answered questions about a topic they rated as important (high relevance), and half answered questions about a topic they rated as low in importance (low relevance). Since one's score was supposed to be determined by a complex formula that took into account speed of answering, difficulty of question, and number of correct answers, and since the confederate's performance was preprogrammed, it was possible to give the participants false feedback about relative performance. All participants learned that they had scored at about the 50th percentile. The other's performance scores varied; participants were told that the other performed at the 20th, or the 40th, or the 60th, or the 80th percentile. Following this feedback, participants went into another room to fill out a questionnaire that included some measures of closeness. This section will discuss only the cognitive measure (how much you and the other have in common) and affective measures (how much you like the other).

Recall the SEM prediction. When the task is high in relevance, the better the other does (relative to the self), the less the resulting closeness; when the task is low in relevance, the better the other does (relative to the self), the greater the resulting closeness. Preliminary analyses that included relevance and all four levels of relative performance yielded no significant effects. However, an analysis of the cognitive measure that included only levels of performance superior to that of the participant—that is, 60th and 80th percentiles—revealed a significant interaction in the appropriate direction. That is, the more decisively the confederate outperformed the participant, the less similar the confederate was seen to be when the task was high in relevance. More surprisingly, when the task was low in relevance, the more decisively the confederate outperformed the participant, the more similar he was seen to be. The affective measure of closeness revealed no significant effects.

There are two points worth making about the results of this study. First, the model did not seem to work when the other performed worse than the self. This seems to echo the implications of the Nashville School Study discussed earlier. It does not appear that people want to be close to others who perform poorly on tasks that are relevant to their self-definition (or that they necessarily distance themselves from others who perform poorly on low-relevance tasks). Second, although the cognitive measure of closeness worked as predicted, the affective measure did not. It could simply be that participants were unwilling to say that they did not like someone they had just met; that is, the measure may have been insensitive. Or it could be something more fundamental—namely, that the closeness construct simply should not include affective responses. (I am inclined to believe the latter.)

The Pleban and Tesser (1981) study indicated that it is possible to affect cognitions about closeness in the laboratory. Can one also find evidence that cognitions about closeness are affected by another's relative performance in "real-world" settings, such as the family? To answer this question I (Tesser, 1980) undertook a secondary analysis of some biographical data collected by William Owens on college students (Owens & Schoenfeldt, 1979).

One of the questions Owens asked concerned the relevant performance of siblings: "During the time you spent at home, how successful was your brother or sister in such things as popularity, skills, possessions and appearance?" (Since there were many cases, it was possible to focus on respondents who had only one sibling.) The response categories indexed relative performance: the sibling was less successful, equally successful, or more successful than the self. Although siblings are from the same family, closeness can vary depending on how far apart they are in age. For purposes of this analysis, siblings were classified as close if they were less than 3 years apart and distant if they were more than 3 years apart. The present study is concerned with cognitions concerning closeness. It is difficult to imagine anyone changing their belief about differences in age. However, Owens asked a series of seven questions concerning the relationship between the respondent and the sibling. For example, one item dealt with amount of friction/fighting as a measure of closeness of relationship. Such items, which are more amenable to interpretation by the respondent, were summed to yield a cognitive index of closeness.

Since Owens's question appears to measure performance high in relevance, the comparison process should be important: The better a sibling's performance, the less close the respondent should believe he or she is to the sibling. However, some siblings are already distant—that is, more than 3 years apart—so there would be less need for such respondents to *cognitively* distance themselves than there would be for respondents with siblings who are less than 3 years apart. Therefore, the specific prediction was in terms of a closeness-in-age effect: When a sibling's performance is better than the respondent's performance, respondents who are close in age should report more distance than respondents who are distant in age. When a sibling's performance is not better than the respondent's performance, then the difference in reported distance between respondents who are close and distant in age should be attenuated or reversed. Although this hypothesis is rather complex, the data were consistent with it. The appropriate pattern clearly emerged for first- and second-born males and for first-born females. It was there but less clear among second-born females.

In sum, the evidence seems to be consistent with the idea that the relevance and quality of another's performance affects our beliefs about our association with the other. We tend to see ourselves as distant from others who outperform us on relevant dimensions, and the laboratory data suggest that we tend to see ourselves as close to others who outperform us on less relevant dimensions.

Actions Affecting the Closeness of Others

We have seen that beliefs about closeness are affected in ways suggested by the SEM model. Here we review evidence bearing on the question of whether actions taken to affect closeness are similarly affected by the relevance and quality of another's performance.

The Pleban and Tesser (1980) study described in the peceding section included two action measures of closeness. When the participant completed the "College Bowl" competition, he went into an adjoining room to fill out a questionnaire. The other "participant" was already seated. Literally, the distance at which the actual participant sat from the confederate served as a behavioral measure of closeness. A "behavioroid" measure (Aronson & Carlsmith, 1968) of closeness was constructed from responses to questions concerning each participant's desire and willingness to work with the other "participant" again.

The results on these action-related measures of closeness were quite consistent with the results of the cognitive measure. When the other's performance was lower than that of the participant, closeness was unaffected. However, when the other's performance was better than that of the participant, the SEM predictions were confirmed: Quality and relevance of performance interacted to affect closeness. When the task was relevant, the better the other's performance (relative to the participant's performance), the farther the participant sat from the other and the less willing he was to work with the other; when the task was low in relevance, the better the other's performance, the closer the participant sat to the other and the more willing he was to work with the other.

To see whether this set of relationships obtains in action taken in the "real world," we took another look at within-family dynamics. This time we used an archival methodology to interrogate the relationship between fathers and sons (Tesser, 1980, Study 3). We consulted standard biographies of outstanding scientists and noted three pieces of information for each scientist: the scientist's field, the occupation of the scientist's father, and any comments pertaining to the relationship between the scientist and his father (e.g., his father did not provide financial support). A group of judges independently rated the similarity between the occupations of father and son and the closeness of their relationship.

What kind of relationship between similarity of occupation and closeness should we expect? The performance of the scientist was generally better than that of the father; after all, it was the son's achievements that earned entry into the standard biographies. Since the son's achievement was outstanding, there was the potential for gain by reflection or pain by comparison. If the son's performance was not relevant, the closer they were, the more the father might gain by reflection; if the son's performance was relevant, the closer they were, the more the father might be threatened by comparison. Therefore, the more similar—that is, relevant—the son's field was to that of the father, the less close should be the relationship of father to son. The relationship between rated similarity of occupation and rated closeness of relationship was, as expected, negative and significant.

Taken together, the data suggest that the quality and relevance of another's performance interact to affect beliefs and actions concerning the closeness of association with that other. From the laboratory, the Pleban and Tesser (1981) study provided experimental evidence that both beliefs and actions are affected as expected. Outside the laboratory, the sibling study held relevance constant at a high level and showed that beliefs about closeness were affected by the performance of one's sibling (and the closeness in age of that sibling). To the extent that the sibling performed better than the self, the closer that sibling was in age, the greater the perceived distance was on a cognitive measure. In the scientist study, the son's performance was held constant at a high level and the distance between father and son was seen to be negatively associated with the relevance of the son's performance to the father's self-definition. The data from the Pleban and Tesser study also suggest that closeness in terms of the SEM model may not manifest itself in affect and that people may be relatively insensitive to the performance of another that is poorer than their own performance.

SELF-DEFINITION: THE IMPACT OF PERFORMANCE AND CLOSENESS ON RELEVANCE

In this section, the concern is with the circumstances under which people change their *self-definition* as a SEM strategy. Self-definition is tied to the relevance parameter of the model, the parameter that determines the relative importance of the reflection and comparison processes. The system for making predictions should be quite clear by now: If the self is outperformed by another, particularly a close other, the self will suffer by comparison if relevance is high or will gain by reflection if relevance is low. Therefore, the better another's performance, the more likely one is to change one's self-definition so as to make that performance low in relevance, particularly if the self and the other have a close association. This section examines data relevant to this prediction, focusing first on cognitive and then on action measures of self-definition. (A more complete discussion of the implications of the SEM model for self-definition can be found in Tesser & Campbell, 1983.)

Cognitive Changes in Self-Definition

In one of our early studies, Jennifer Campbell and I (Tesser & Campbell, 1980) manipulated closeness and other's performance to examine their effects on several measures of self-definition. During a first, large-group session, females participating in a "Personality Validity Study" filled out a variety of questionnaires in which were imbedded a few items designed to measure the importance of esthetic judgment and social sensitivity to their self-definition. The purported purpose of a second session was to get performance measures on tasks related to esthetic judgment and social sensitivity. When participants arrived for the second session, they found another "participant" (an experimental accomplice) present. Closeness was manipulated by telling each participant that according to the tests she had taken previously, she and the other "participant" were similar in a number of ways (close other) or dissimilar in a number of ways (distant other).

Participants were told that they could work on only one performance test but that they would be given a sample of each test before they indicated their preference. Participants then worked on several tasks presumed to reflect social sensitivity and several presumed to reflect esthetic judgment. To manipulate performance, each participant was told that both she and the other "participant" had performed equally but poorly on one dimension and that although they both had performed better on the second dimension, the confederate had outperformed the naive participant on that dimension. (Social sensitivity and esthetic judgment were counterbalanced as the equal and unequal performance dimensions.)

This kind of feedback allows for a stronger test of the SEM prediction. That is, one might argue that one's self-definition simply reflects the things one does best, regardless of the performance of others. The SEM model, on the other hand, suggests that the performance of others, particularly close others, is crucial. Since the dimension on which the other does better than the subject—that is, the unequal dimension—is also the dimension on which the subject herself does best, the two hypotheses make competing predictions regarding the change in the importance of the dimension to self-definition. The former hypothesis predicts that the unequal dimension should become more important than the equal performance dimension, since this is the dimension on which the participant does best. The SEM model predicts that the unequal dimension should become *less* important than the equal performance dimension, since this is the dimension on which the participant can suffer by comparison to the other. Furthermore, this difference should be more pronounced in the close-other condition than in the distant-other condition. Participants were given an opportunity to rate the importance of social sensitivity and esthetic judgment to their self-definition after receiving the feedback. An analysis of change in importance (from the first session) yielded results perfectly consistent with the expectations of the SEM model.

More recently, Tesser and Paulhus (1983) completed a conceptual replication of this study. The experiment was complex and will be discussed more later. For present purposes, it is enough to say that male participants learned that they either outperformed or were outperformed by another participant on a dimension called "cognitive-perceptual integration." The other was described as either similar or dissimilar to the participant. The rated importance of cognitive-perceptual integration to the participant's self-definition was affected by the interaction of performance feedback and closeness of association: The better the participant's performance relative to the other, the more important cognitive-perceptual integration was to the participant's self-definition; this was particularly true when the other was described as similar.

The laboratory evidence seems clear enough. Cognitions about one's self change as a result of the relative performance of others in combination with the closeness of association with those others. We seem to reduce the relevance of a close other's outstanding performance so that we may bask in their reflected glory (or reduce the threat of comparison). The Owens sibling data (Owens & Schoenfeldt, 1979) provide an opportunity to see whether such cognitive changes in self-definition can also be found in a nonlaboratory context.

Recall that respondents in the Owens study who had one sibling were classified in terms of relative performance. They were further cross-classified in terms of closeness in age. The hypothesis with which we are currently working suggests that one sibling should make the other's performance irrelevant to the extent that the other performs better, particularly if the other is close. Although Owens did not directly ask respondents how important the particular performance classification dimensions were to their self-definition, he did provide an indirect means to this end. If one wants to make another's activities irrelevant to one's self-definition, one can simply "deidentify" with the other (Schacter, Shore, Feldman-Rotman, Marquis, & Campbell, 1976)—that is, one can simply say that he or she is very different from oneself. Owens asked "How much were you like your brother or sister in skills and abilities? . . . ways of acting in social situations?" Responses to these items were summed to yield an identification index (Tesser, 1980, Study 1), which served as the dependent variable for the present analysis.

Again, the hypothesis predicts that the better the sibling's relative performance, the more closeness in age will result in deidentification. Separate analyses were conducted for male and female respondents. The predicted effects were not found for females. However, the males did respond as predicted by the SEM model. When their sibling outperformed them, the closer they were in age, the less they identified with the sibling; when they outperformed their sibling, the closer they were in age, the more they identified with the sibling.

This nonlaboratory study supplements the laboratory studies. Although the evidence is indirect, the sibling data suggest that cognitions about self are affected by the closeness and performance of others, even in family settings. This was true, however, only for male respondents. Perhaps there is a fundamental sex difference in the extent to which SEM processes are important. Although I do not have a compelling alternative explanation for these data, I tend to reject that possibility becuase several other studies have worked quite well with women participants—for example, the study by Tesser and Campbell (1980) described earlier in this section.

Changes in Self-Definition: Some Action Indicators

We have reviewed some evidence that the closeness of another and the quality of that other's performance interact to affect cognitions about the importance of the performance dimension to the self—that is, in SEM terms, the relevance of the other's performance. This section attempts a similar review looking for changes in self-definition that manifest themselves in action.

Both the Tesser and Campbell (1980) study and the Tesser and Paulhus (1983) study included action-related measures of self-definition. Recall that Tesser and Campbell gave female participants feedback concerning their relative performance on some sample items measuring social sensitiivty and esthetic judgment. We assumed that people's self-definition often plays itself out in the choices they make about what they want to do. Therefore, participants were asked to choose which task they wanted to work on and to scale how strongly they felt about the choice. Although they did not actually work on the task, we classify this choice as an action measure because participants believed that it would result in actually working on the task (cf. Aronson and Carlsmith, 1968). This choice measure worked just like the cognitive measure described earlier: Participants tended to avoid choosing to work on the dimension on which they were outperformed, particularly when the other was described as similar (close).

Tesser and Paulhus (1983) gave their male participants feedback concerning their performance on cognitive-perceptual integration. Following this, participants were left alone in a room containing two loose-leaf notebooks. One of the books contained biographies of people high on cognitive-perceptual integration; the other contained biographies of people low on cognitive-perceptual integration. We assumed that the amount of time an individual spent looking at the biographies of people high on cognitive-perceptual integration would reflect the importance of cognitive-perceptual integration to his own self-definition. Therefore, the amount of time spent looking at each of these books was surreptitiously recorded. Again, the results on this action measure of self-definition echoed the results on the cognitive measure: Participants who were outperformed on cognitive-perceptual integration spent less time with the high cognitive-perceptual integration biographies than subjects who outperformed the other participant; this relationship was more pronounced when the other participant was described as similar.

A high school setting provided a nonlaboratory site for collecting action-related data on self-definition. (This unpublished study is described in more detail in Tesser & Campbell, in press.) Students were asked how much more education they would like to have. We assumed that the answers to this question would reflect the importance of school to the respondent's self-definition and a commitment to action—that is, continuing in school, if conditions permit. In this study, closeness was defined in terms of the similarity of race and sex of the respondents' classmates. We used five pieces of information simultaneously to predict how much more school the respondent wanted: the student's grade point average and her or his performance relative to (1) same race, same sex classmates, (2) same race, different sex classmates, (3) different race, same sex classmates, and (4) different race, different sex classmates. Only one of these variables was a significant predictor of this action index of self definition—the respondent's performance relative to close classmates (same race, same sex).

Taken as a whole, the data seem to support the SEM model predictions concerning self-definition. To the extent that another, particularly a close other, performs well, it is to the individual's advantage to lower the relevance of the other's performance to his or her own self-definition. In this way, the threat from comparison is reduced and the potential gain through reflection is increased. We have reviewed evidence that people's beliefs about themselves and their actions that can be construed as indexing their self-definition are affected by the performance of close others. In particular, the Tesser and Campbell (1980) study has shown that it is performance *relative to similar others* that is important in this process, rather than one's absolute performance.

SOME ADDITIONAL ISSUES

The Systematic Nature of SEM Processes

Earlier, I indicated that the SEM model is really a system of variables; there are no causes or effects as such. Each of the operational variables—performance, closeness, and relevance—can be thought of as an effect or, in combination with one of the other variables, as an interactive cause of the third. Indeed, that is the way the preceding review of the evidence proceeded. (A summary of that review is presented in Tables 15.1–15.3.)

In the laboratory studies, it was possible to fix two of the variables and observe their impact on the third. This is not the case in the nonlaboratory studies. Since none of the variables are manipulated, we are simply observing a set of relationships among the three variables, with none having a logical causal priority over the others. The classification of one of the variables as "the dependent variable" is arbitrary and simply reflects the way of thinking about the data that is easiest for me.

Saying that the model is systemic implies that a change in any one variable can result in a change in either or both of the other variables. This is disquieting in that there is no well-developed component of the model that can be used to specify the circumstances under which any of these options will occur. There are several tacks that might be taken to address this problem.

TABLE 15.1 The Impact of Closeness and Relevance on Affecting Another's Performance

Study/Setting	Independent Variables: Closeness/Relevance	Dependent Variable: Other's Performance	Outcome
Tesser & Campbell (1982)/laboratory	*Closeness:* Friends versus strangers *Relevance:* Rated importance of social sensitivity versus esthetic judgement	*Cognition:* Guesses about correctness of others' responses to social sensitivity and esthetic judgment items	More positivity in guesses about friend compared to stranger on low-relevance dimension; reversed on high-relevance dimension
Tesser, Campbell, & Smith (1984)/nonlaboratory	*Closeness:* Classmate most like to spend time with versus classmate least like to spend time with *Relevance:* Activity rated most versus least relevant from among a set of school-related activities	*Cognition:* Rating of own and others' performance	Self and close other rated as similar in overall performance; both rated as better on self's relevant activity; self rated higher than other on relevant activity, lower than other on irrelevant activity; distant other derogated on both activities
Tesser & Smith (1980)/laboratory	*Closeness:* Friends versus strangers *Relevance:* Told task measures important characteristics (e.g., verbal intelligence) versus task unrelated to important characteristics	*Action:* Difficulty of clues given to others to guess "password"	Friend given easier clues than stranger when task relevant, reversed when task not relevant

TABLE 15.2   The Impact of Quality and Relevance of Performance on Interpersonal Closeness

Study/Setting	Independent Variables: Other's Performance/Relevance	Dependent Variable: Closeness	Outcome
Pleban & Tesser (1981)/ laboratory	*Performance*: Feedback on college bowl competition *Relevance*: Topic rated most relevant versus least relevant.	*Cognition*: Ratings of general similarity of other	The more decisively one is outperformed on a high-relevance dimension, the less the general similarity; reversed when dimension is of low relevance; performance poorer than own had no impact on closeness
Tesser (1980, Study 2)/ nonlaboratory	*Performance*: Sibling rated as performing poorer versus equal versus better *Relevance*: Presumed to be high; performance on popularity, skills, possession, and appearance	*Cognition*: Sum of items dealing with sibling friction	When respondent was outperformed by sibling, the closer they were in age, the greater the friction (i.e., beliefs about distance); relationship attenuated when respondent was not outperformed by sibling
Pleban & Tesser (1981)/ laboratory	See above	*Action*: (1) Distance participant sits from other (2) Willingness to work with other again	The more decisively one is outperformed by another on a high-relevance dimension, the farther away one sits and the less willing one is to work with the other; relationship reversed on low-relevance dimension; performance poorer than own had no impact on closeness
Tesser (1980, Study 3)/ nonlaboratory	*Performance*: Presumed to be high, since found in standard biography *Relevance*: Ratings of similarity of occupation	*Action*: Ratings of closeness from biographical information given about a scientist and his father.	The more similar the son's accomplishment to the father's profession, the more distant the relationship

Cognitive consistency theories faced a similar dilemma in trying to specify how inconsistencies would be resolved. A number of creative and potentially useful answers emerged. Rosenberg and Abelson (1960) suggested a least-effort principle. That is, all things being equal, the individual will be more likely to operate on one dimension than on two or on all three. They also allude to a utility principle: The individual is more likely to operate on a dimension that will minimize his or her losses and maximize his or her gains in other ways. For example, people with a high need for affiliation should be less likely to decrease closeness and more likely to increase closeness to affect self-evaluation than people with a low need for affiliation. It has also been suggested that an individual is less likely to distort—that is, cognitively change—a dimension if such beliefs are subject to "reality constraints" (Tesser, 1976; Walster, Berscheid, & Barclay, 1967). Since relevance (one's self-definition) is often less subject to external reality constraints than another's performance or closeness, this notion implies that one's self-definition is more likely to be changed than the quality of another's performance or closeness.

There are other individual difference variables that suggest themselves as determinants of SEM strategies. For example, people who find it easy to change their behavior to fit the situation (see Snyder, 1979) might find it easier to change their self-definition than people whose behavior is less situationally variable. There are also other situational variables that could produce preferences for particular maintenance strategies. For example, if people expect others to reciprocate in kind (Foa & Foa, 1974), they might consider it more costly to interfere with the others' performance than to reduce closeness or change their own self-definition. Obviously, any number of principles can be brought to bear in trying to predict the differential use of SEM strategies. Although such principles serve a valuable heuristic function, they are, at this stage, *ad hoc*.

A question related to the choice of SEM strategy concerns the relationships among the uses of different strategies. There may be a hydraulic relationship such that the use of one strategy reduces the level of use of another. Or the use of one strategy may be independent of the use of another; for example, an individual who changes closeness is no more nor less likely to change relevance than an individual who does not change closeness. Finally, there may be a positive association among strategies; for example, an individual who operates on another's performance is more likely to operate also on relevance than an individual who does not operate on performance.

Few data address this question, but there are some. Across the studies dealing with siblings (Tesser, 1980, Studies 1 & 2), two SEM strategies were measured: changes in relevance (identification) and changes in closeness (friction). Those cells of the design that produce the most threat to self-evaluation should produce the most pronounced attempts to maintain self-evaluation. Since changing relevance and changing closeness are both ways of maintaining self-evaluation, they should, *on the average*, covary across the cells of the design. However, if an *individual* seeks to maintain self-evaluation by reducing relevance, he or she may or may not also choose to decrease closeness. Indeed, if he or she decreases relevance, there may be

TABLE 15.3   Self-Definition: The Impact of Closeness and Performance on Relevance

Study/Setting	Independent Variables: Closeness/Performance	Dependent Variable: Self-Definition (Relevance)	Outcome
Tesser & Campbell (1980)/laboratory	*Closeness*: Manipulated personality similarity *Performance*: Feedback of relative performance on social sensitivity and esthetic judgment	*Cognition*: Change in rated importance of social sensitivity and esthetic judgment to self	The poorer one's performance relative to the other, the less important the performance dimension to self-definition; this relationship was stronger for similar than for dissimilar others
Tesser & Paulhus (1983)/laboratory	*Closeness*: Manipulated similarity of age, major, personality *Performance*: Feedback of relative performance on "cognitive-perceptual integration"	*Cognition*: Rated importance of cognitive-perceptual integration	The poorer one's performance relative to the other, the less important cognitive-perceptual integration to self-definition
Tesser (1980, Study 1)/nonlaboratory	*Closeness*: Siblings less than 3 years apart versus more than 3 years apart *Performance*: Sibling rated as performing poorer, equal, or better on popularity skills, possessions, and appearance	*Cognition*: Identification/deidentification with sibling on performance dimensions	No effects for females; for males, when the sibling outperformed the respondent, the closer the sibling, the less the identification; this relationship was reversed when the respondent was outperformed by the sibling

Tesser & Campbell (1980)/laboratory	*Closeness*: Manipulated personality similarity *Performance*: Feedback of relative performance on social sensitivity and esthetic judgment	*Action*: Choice of task on which to work	The poorer one's performance relative to another's performance, the more that performance dimension is avoided; this relationship was stronger for similar than for dissimilar others
Tesser & Paulhus (1983)/laboratory	*Closeness*: Manipulated similarity of age, major, personality *Performance*: Feedback of relative performance on "cognitive-perceptual integration"	*Action*: Amount of time spent looking at biographies of person high on cognitive-perceptual integration	The poorer one's performance on cognitive-perceptual integration relative to another, the less time spent looking at the biographies of people high in cognitive-perceptual integration; this relationship was stronger for similar than for dissimilar others
Described in Tesser & Campbell (in press)/nonlaboratory	*Closeness*: Similar sex/similar race versus dissimilar sex/race *Performance*: Relative grade point average in school	*Action*: How much additional school desired	The only significant predictor of additional school desired was grade point average relative to similar sex/race classmates

less of a need to decrease closeness (and vice versa). If this line of reasoning is correct, then the average *within-cell* correlation between relevance and closeness should be lower than the correlation of the average level of relevance and closeness *across cells*.

This turned out to be the case. Both correlations were positive and significantly different from zero, but the correlation across cell means ($r = .58$) was significantly larger than the mean within-cell correlation ($r = .26$). This analysis suggests that the uses of strategies such as operating on relevance or operating on closeness are relatively independent. Furthermore there is no sign of a hydraulic relationship; the use of one strategy did not reduce the propensity to use the other. (Indeed, there is a slight tendency for people who use one strategy also to use the other.) What is even clearer, however, is the need for more data and theoretical development to guide the collection of such data.

The Distortion Issue

In reviewing the evidence for the SEM model we examined changes in cognition regarding other's performance, closeness, and self-definition. When someone reports what he or she *believes* about something, one question that comes to mind is whether that belief is accurate or inaccurate. That is, are people distorting the world to maintain their self-evaluation? In general, this is a difficult question with which to deal (cf. Nisbett & Ross, 1980), because it is often difficult to know the "truth." Furthermore, in this particular case, we have not set out to address the accuracy question. However, there are some data that can be coaxed to address this issue.

Recall the study (Tesser, Campbell, & Smith, 1985) in which student respondents rated performance: They rated the self higher than the close classmate on a relevant activity and lower than the close classmate on an irrelevant activity. One way to determine whether these ratings are a distortion is to compare them with ratings of an "unbiased" source. In this case, the students' ratings were compared to those of the teacher. On the whole, there was no more distortion of own ratings than ratings of close other; and there was no more distortion on relevant activities than on irrelevant activities. However, there was a pattern of distortion: The student's own performance was distorted upward on the relevant activity and downward on the irrelevant activity; and the close other's performance was distorted downward on the relevant activity and upward on the irrelevant activity. These data suggest that there is distortion and that the distortion is in a direction anticipated by the SEM model.

The sibling study (Tesser, 1980, Study 2) concerning closeness (friction) also argues for some distortion. What the respondents reported about closeness differed depending on whether they reported themselves as being outperformed by their sibling or outperforming their sibling. However, both the better performing and poorer performing sibling are in the same relationship. Therefore, if respondents were reporting accurately about the relationship, they should be giving identical reports of degree of closeness, and there should be no difference as a function of relative performance. That there is such a difference argues for at least some distortion of one's views in the service of self-evaluation maintenance.

The data don't even begin to address the question of the pervasiveness of distortion. Also, although we have touched on the distortion of performance and of closeness, we have not touched on the distortion of self-definition. Indeed, questions of accuracy of self-definition raise a variety of thorny issues (e.g., is there a "true" self), which probably would best be dealt with in another place. It is sufficient at this point simply to say that there is evidence of distortion of the world in the service of self-evaluation maintenance.

The Awareness Issue

I have reviewed evidence that some changes in cognitions and actions in social life can be understood using the SEM model. I have also suggested that some of the cognitive changes are distortions. Given the recent interest in cognitive psychology, another question that often emerges about cognitive and behavioral changes is whether or not people are aware of making them. This question has not been systematically pursued in this research program, but some data from a couple of studies do address the issue.

Recall the study (Tesser & Campbell, 1982) in which participants made guesses about the performance of a friend and a stranger on a variety of computer-generated items dealing with high- and low-relevance dimensions. Following their interaction with the computer, the participants were asked a variety of questions about the guesses they had made. Participants *said* that they guessed that their friend was correct more often than they guessed the stranger was correct. However, there was no difference between how often they *actually* guessed their friend and the stranger were correct.

Subjects were also asked to indicate the importance of each of the following strategies in determining their guesses: random (guessed at random), projection (guessed same as own answer), and thoughtful (tried to figure out how other would respond). Participants said that the random strategy was more important for the stranger and that the projection and thoughtful strategies were more important for the friend. Again, this self-report was inconsistent with what was actually observed: There was no difference between friend and stranger in the number of times the participant projected her own answer. Furthermore, the computer kept track of response latencies. One would think that a thoughtful strategy would require more time than the other strategies. However, participants' guesses were actually made slightly more quickly for their friends than for the strangers.

Tesser and Smith (1980) had participants provide a friend and a stranger clues for a password task that was described as more or less relevant to their self-definition. On a postexperimental questionnaire, *regardless of the relevance condition*, participants indicated that they gave friends and strangers equally difficult clues. In fact, they gave friends easier clues when the task was low in relevance and gave strangers easier clues when the task was high in relevance.

In each case, there is an inconsistency between what a participant reports and what he or she actually does. Perhaps the participant is quite aware of his or her behavior but simply provides a self-report intended to make him or her look good to the experimenter. This seems unlikely, however, in that the experimenter is also aware of the previous behavior. If anything, a "lie" about earlier behavior might make the participant look worse. Therefore, although there aren't many data on the question, it appears that at least some of the changes associated with the model are made without awareness.

Private Self-Evaluation Maintenance or Public Image Management?

Recently, there has been an upsurge of interest among social psychologists in self-presentation (Baumeister, 1982) and impression management (Schlenker, 1980). To this point, changes in performance, closeness, and relevance have been discussed as though they exclusively serve "private" needs for a positive self-evaluation. This section is concerned with the question of whether these changes can also be interpreted as strategies intended to convey a particular public impression.

Suppose that an individual performs poorly relative to a close other on a particular task and that an audience asks that individual how important the task is to his or her self-definition. Suppose, as the SEM model predicts, that the individual tells the audience that the task is unimportant. Such a statement could be intended to affect the audience's belief about the self, it could reflect an attempt to maintain private self-evaluation, or both. One way to disentangle these motives (in this context) is to vary *independently* what the individual believes about his or her relative performance and what he or she thinks the audience believes about his or her relative performance. If the individual's self-description is affected by what he or she believes about his or her relative performance, then private motives are important; if the self-description is affected by what he or she thinks the audience believes about his or her relative performance, then impression management is important; if the self-description is affected by both what he or she thinks and what he or she believes the audience thinks, then both motives are important.

The necessary conditions were set up by Tesser and Paulhus (1983). Recall that the participants were given feedback that they had done better or worse than either a similar or dissimilar participant on cognitive-perceptual integration. The participants were also told that they would be interviewed by the experimenter's supervisor but that when the experimenter entered the participants' scores in the computer for the supervisor, he became confused about the order in which to enter them. The participants were told that the information the supervisor would read about their performance might be confused, but they were asked not to reveal the mistake. In this way, it was possible to vary independently what the participants believed about their performance and what the supervisor (audience) believed about their performance. What the participant told the supervisor about his performance was affected by both what the participant believed about his performance and what he thought the supervisor believed about his performance. Thus, it appears that the kinds of changes in behavior documented in this chapter can serve both public and private motives.

It is not too surprising that public and private self-images tend to be similar— that is, that the images one creates for an audience are similar to those one holds privately. Holding different public and private self-images can create cognitive overloads in social interaction, can produce the undesirable view of self as "liar," and can create an uncomfortable state of dissonance. Furthermore, there is evidence that one's public image tends to have an impact on one's private view. There are reality and social structural constraints on what one can believe about one's self as well as the operation of consistency and self-perception mechanisms. There is also evidence that one's private view of self tends to have an impact on the kinds of public images one tries to create. The recent work on symbolic self-completion theory (Wicklund & Gollwitzer, 1982) has put together an impressive array of data to suggest that one's private view of self is manifested and maintained through the manipulation of public symbols.

Threats to Self-Evaluation and the Intrusion of Negative Affect

In describing the SEM model and reviewing the evidence collected to test the model, we focused only on cognitive and action-oriented changes in other's performance, other's closeness, and one's self-definition. We did not consider the affective consequences of being confronted by a set of circumstances that threaten self-evaluation. Such circumstances should produce negative affect—anxiety, depression, and the like. We have not collected data relevant to this hypothesis in any of our studies, but a recently completed study by Salovey and Rodin (1984) and one by Nadler, Fisher, and Ben-Itzhak (1983) do provide some pertinent data.

In the course of studying what Salovey and Rodin (1984) call "social-comparison jealousy," they completed an experiment in which they gave participants feedback that they did well or poorly on a dimension that was relevant or irrelevant to their self-definition. They also provided information that another participant had done well on either the relevant or the irrelevant dimension. From the perspective of the SEM model, the condition that poses the greatest threat to self-evaluation is the one in which the participant does poorly on a relevant dimension and the other does well on this dimension. Salovey and Rodin compared this condition to the remaining seven conditions in the experiment and found that participants in this condition reported more anxiety, more depression, and less positivity of mood than participants in the other conditions.

When one person helps another, the person who is receiving help is implicitly demonstrating inferior performance. Therefore, if the help is on a dimension that is relevant to the recipient's self-definition, comparison processes should come into play, and the closer the relationship of the helper, the greater the threat to self-evaluation. In a recently completed study, Nadler *et al.* (1983) had participants try to solve a mystery. The task was described as tapping important skills (high relevance) or luck (low relevance). The participant's solution was wrong and he was given a clue from either a friend (close other) or a stranger (distant other). Some participants went through this experience once, and some went through it twice. Participants then rated their affect on a series of scales. From the perspective of the SEM model, the most threatening condition was the one in which help was received twice from a friend on the task that was described as relevant. Indeed, this turned out to be the condition associated with the most negative affect; none of the other conditions appeared to differ from one another.

The two studies described here suggest that conditions presumed to result in a threat to self-evaluation are also associated with negative affect. Obviously, more research is needed. For example, do conditions presumed to maximize self-evaluation—that is, the outstanding performance of a close other on a low-relevance dimension—produce positive affect? Does the negative affect associated with threatening conditions play a causal role in some of the changes in closeness, relevance, and performance that have been observed? Do appropriate changes in relevance, closeness, and performance produce positive affect? It is hoped that the answers to these questions will be forthcoming soon.

Acknowledgment

Much of the research discussed in this chapter was completed with the support of National Science Foundation grant number BNS-8003711.

Notes

1. A couple of additional possibilities are open to Albert. He could claim that Bob is a genius and view Bob's performance as so discrepant from his own performance that it is low in relevance. With low relevance, Albert could bask in the reflected glory of Bob's performance. Another possibility is that Albert could work harder for the next exam and thereby attempt to outperform Bob. Although each of these possibilities is derivable from the model, they have not been given as much attention in our research as the other possibilities. Therefore, I will have little more to say about them in this chapter.

References

Alloy, L. B. (1982, October). *Depression and social comparison: Illusory self or other perceptions?* Paper presented at the meeting of the Society for Experimental Social Psychology, Nashville, IN.

Alloy, L. B., & Abramson, L. Y. (1979). Judgment of contingency in depressed and nondepressed students: Sadder but wiser? *Journal of Experimental Psychology: General, 108*, 441–485.

Aronson, E., & Carlsmith, J. M. (1968). Experimentation in social psychology. In G. Lindzey & E. Aronson (Eds.), *The handbook of social psychology* (2d ed., pp. 1–79). Reading, MA: Addison-Wesley.

Baumeister, R. F. (1982). A self-presentational view of social phenomena. *Psychological Bulletin, 91*, 3–26.

Berscheid, E. (1982). Attraction and emotion in interpersonal relationships. In M. S. Clark & S. T. Fiske (Eds.), *Affect and cognition: The 17th Annual Carnegie Symposium on Cognition* (pp. 37–54). Hillsdale, NJ: Erlbaum.

Campbell, J. D., & Tesser, A. (1985). Self-evaluation maintenance processes in relationships. In S. Duck & D. Perlman (Eds.), *Personal relationships* (Vol. 1). London: Sage.

Cialdini, R. B., Borden, R. J., Thorne, A., Walker, M. R., Freeman, S., & Sloan, L. R. (1976). Basking in reflected glory: Three (football) field studies. *Journal of Personality and Social Psychology, 34,* 366–375.

Cialdini, R. B., & Richardson, K. D. (1980). Two indirect tactics of image management: Basking and blasting. *Journal of Personality and Social Psychology, 39,* 406–415.

Festinger, L. (1954). A theory of social comparison processes. *Human Relations, 7,* 117–140.

Foa, U. G., & Foa, E. (1974). *Societal structures of the mind.* Springfield, IL: Thomas.

Freud, S. (1953). Mourning and melancholia. In J. Strachey (Ed. and Trans.), *The standard edition of the complete psychological works of Sigmund Freud* (Vol. 14, pp. 237–260). London: Hogarth Press. (Original work published 1917)

Heider, F. (1958). *The psychology of interpersonal relations.* New York: Wiley.

McFarlin, D. B., & Blascovich, J. (1981). Effects of self esteem and performance feedback on future affective preference and cognitive expectations. *Journal of Personality and Social Psychology, 40,* 521–531.

Meier, N. C. (1940). *The Meier art tests: 1. Art judgment.* Iowa City: University of Iowa, Bureau of Educational Research and Service.

Nadler, A., Fisher, J., & Ben-Itzhak, S. (1983). With a little help from my friend: Effect of single or multiple act aid as a function of donor and task characteristics. *Journal of Personality and Social Psychology, 44,* 310–321.

Nisbett, R., & Ross, L. (1980). *Human inference: Strategies and shortcomings of social judgment.* Englewood Cliffs, NJ: Prentice-Hall.

Osgood, C. E., Suci, G. J., & Tannenbaum, P. H. (1958). *The measurement of meaning.* Urbana: University of Illinois Press.

Owens, W. A., & Schoenfeldt, L. F. (1979). Toward a classification of persons [Monograph]. *Journal of Applied Psychology, 64,* 569–607.

Pleban, R., & Tesser, A. (1981). The effects of relevance and quality of another's performance on interpersonal closeness. *Social Psychology Quarterly, 44,* 278–285.

Rosenberg, M. J., & Abelson, R. P. (1960). An analysis of cognitive balancing. In C. I. Hovland & I. L. Janis (Eds.), *Attitude organization and change* (pp. 112–163). New Haven: Yale University Press.

Salovey, P., & Rodin, J. (1984). Some antecedents and consequences of social comparison jealousy. *Journal of Personality and Social Psychology, 47,* 780–792.

Schachter, F. F., Shore, E., Feldman-Rotman, S., Marquis, R. E., & Campbell, S. (1976). Sibling deidentification. *Developmental Psychology, 12,* 418–427.

Schlenker, B. R. (1980). *Impression management.* Monterey, CA: Brooks/Cole.

Shrauger, J. S. (1975). Responses to evaluation as a function of initial self-perceptions. *Psychological Bulletin, 82,* 581–596.

Snyder, M. (1979). Self-monitoring processes. In L. Berkowitz (Ed.) *Advances in experimental social psychology* (Vol. 12, pp. 86–126). New York: Academic Press.

Tesser, A. (1976). Thought and reality constraints as determinants of attitude polarization. *Journal of Research in Personality, 10,* 183–194.

Tesser, A. (1980). Self-esteem maintenance in family dynamics. *Journal of Personality and Social Psychology, 39,* 77–91.

Tesser, A., & Campbell, J. (1980). Self-definition: The impact of the relative performance and similarity of others. *Social Psychology Quarterly, 43,* 341–347.

Tesser, A., & Campbell, J. (1982). Self-evaluation maintenance and the perception of friends and strangers. *Journal of Personality, 50,* 261–279.

Tesser, A., & Campbell, J. (1983). Self-definition and self-evaluation maintenance. In J. Suls & A. G. Greenwald (Eds.) *Psychological perspectives on the self* (Vol. 2, pp. 1–31). Hillsdale, NJ: Erlbaum.

Tesser, A., & Campbell, J. (in press). A self-evaluation maintenance model of student motivation. In C. Ames & R. Ames (Eds.), *Research on motivation in education: The classroom milieu.* New York: Academic Press.

Tesser, A., Campbell, J., & Smith, M. (1984). Friendship choice and performance: Self-evaluation maintenance in children. *Journal of Personality and Social Psychology, 46*, 561–574.

Tesser, A., & Paulhus, D. (1983). The definition of self: Private and public self-evaluation management strategies. *Journal of Personality and Social Psychology, 44*, 672–682.

Tesser, A., & Smith, J. (1980). Some effects of task relevance and friendship on helping: You don't always help the one you like. *Journal of Experimental Social Psychology, 16*, 582–590.

Walster, E., Berscheid, E., & Barclay, A. M. (1967). A determinant of preference among modes of dissonance reduction. *Journal of Personality and Social Psychology, 7*, 211–215.

Wicklund, R. A., & Gollwitzer, P. M. (1982). *Symbolic self-completion*. Hillsdale, NJ: Erlbaum.

CHAPTER 16

The Paradigmatic and Narrative Modes in Goal-Guided Inference

HENRI ZUKIER
New School for Social Research

THE SOCIAL DIMENSIONS OF COGNITION

Current research in social cognition often is founded on a set of characteristic assumptions and guided by an image (though not a formal model) of cognitive processes that emphasizes their social dimensions. This distinctive social cognitive perspective is said to entail new levels of analysis and new conceptual approaches that take account of the motivational components of inference and memory and consider information processing within the full context of interpersonal interaction (e.g., Fiske & Taylor, 1984; Ostrom, 1984; Zajonc, 1980). Yet the theory and research that have evolved from this perspective have largely eschewed any far-reaching reconceptualizations. Despite some important exceptions, many social-psychological models of cognition are decidedly informed by cognitive psychology and tend to relegate the specifically social dimensions of cognition to the background. The typical study often extends traditional non-social cognitive models and measures to studies about people—the quintessential social stimuli (usually, though, considered outside their social setting).

The cognitive studies of social stimuli have proved so remarkably fruitful that they have often come to define the field. Hence, the distinctiveness of social-cognitive research frequently is articulated in terms of the phenomena and the content areas to which it applies ("people thinking about people") rather than in terms of the explanatory principles or processes involved. However, it again has become evident from these studies that non-cognitive personal and motivational factors, such as goals and values or attitudes and needs, are not merely adjuncts to cognition that color judgments and either interfere with or impel cognitive

465

activity. Rather, these factors emerge as a constitutive part of cognition, and their neglect often results in very partial descriptions of the cognitive processes themselves.

The social dimensions of cognition are reflected in at least three features of everyday judgments. These features are characteristic of the cognitive processes, quite independently of the properties of the social, or nonsocial, objects of judgment.

The Purposive and Deliberative Nature of Inference

First, judgments typically have a deliberative, purposive aspect. Information is neither given nor processed in a neutral way. The input attracts varying amounts of attention and processing as it is sieved through and often blended with a person's interests and needs, preferences, and purposes and as the input is coordinated with the individual's motivational and intentional inclinations. Indeed, motivation itself typically is taken to involve some form of preference, implying both intentionality and choice. The intentionality may be deliberate, as it often is in achievement motivation or attribution theories; or the intentionality may be less articulated and conscious, as it is in Freudian and other psychodynamic frameworks. Cognitive processing is equally, though not as self-evidently, coordinated with the individual's goals and intentions. The purposefulness engenders a selective mindfulness and cognitive attunement to particular kinds of information and alternatives.

For example, in impression formation and in communication, information is structured and processed differently, depending on the purposes and the uses the observer has in mind. Thus, it appears that people may be particularly inclined to interpret an individual's behavior in terms of global personality traits and to commit the "fundamental attribution error" (Nisbett & Ross, 1980) if they expect to communicate verbally to someone else their impression of that individual. By contrast, when people do not envisage conveying their impression, they structure the descriptions in a more differentiated way (Hoffman, Mischel, & Baer, 1984). People also pay more attention to inconsistent information about another individual and primarily consider the individual's stable characteristics if they expect to interact with the person subsequently (Erber & Fiske, 1984).

Three broad classes of goals can be identified that underlie people's behavior and affect information processing: cognitive goals, expressive goals, and pragmatic goals. Cognitive purposiveness seeks to bring the universe within the grasp of intelligence. The cognitive grasp primarily affords a pragmatic grip on the environment and makes it more readily manageable. At the general level, the cognitive purposefulness yields sweeping theories and constructs, laws of physics or of psychology, or schemes of history. At the specific information-processing level, a person's goals for a given problem modulate the very definition and understanding of the task and the type of solution that will seem appropriate.

The goal specification does not merely serve to describe the task; it often evokes an overall representation of the problem and of the kinds of alternatives and resolutions that the individual should be alert to and strive for. The perceived goal or purpose imposes a directionality, at times a program, for the solution (see Newell & Simon, 1972). Thus, slight differences in the framing of choices may reverse people's preferences for a particular course of action, presumably because the alternatives are evaluated in terms of different points of reference.

Although cognitive goals are pursued mostly for their promise of pragmatic control, intellectual activity for its own sake may also hold considerable appeal. Imaginative activity or intellectual playfulness (and their products) can yield remarkable pleasures through the attainment of expressive goals. The expressive purposiveness that animates a great deal of human activity entails a wide range of motives: aesthetic goals in perception and understanding, emotional life, the pursuit of affective interests, and the regulation of the affective quality of interpersonal relationships. Expressive goals also influence the judgment process. On some psychodynamic accounts, such ill-articulated goals indeed are determining; at least, they provide a set of decision contingencies. For instance, many decisions in ordinary life involve considerations of "self-presentation" (e.g., Goffman, 1959) and of the likely impact of a behavior on the maintenance or modification of social relationships.

The cognitive and expressive goals are coordinated to with the pursuit of pragmatic goals, which reflect people's concrete concerns and represent the constant endeavor to translate mental grasp into empirical grip, understanding into control and prediction of the environment.

The Context-Embeddedness of Inference

One aspect of the purposiveness of inference is its responsiveness to the immediate context and the larger cultural environment. As has been noted about language comprehension: "There is no such thing as the zero or null context for the interpretation [of many sentences] . . . we understand the meaning only against a set of background assumptions" (Searle, 1979, p. 117). The context endows behavior and inference with a personal viewpoint, with relevance, and with passion. In part, this keen awareness of how large the context often looms led experimental psychology to "evacuate" the context from the laboratory. The reality of the laboratory typically has been designed to be austere, "culture-free," and devoid of the extrinsic cues and "noise" that might provide programs or procedures for solution of the problem. A "veil of ignorance" (Rawls, 1971) is thrust upon subjects in the laboratory, and "cultural deprivation" is assumed to be their desirable, if not natural, state (Zukier, 1983). Similarly, the multiplicity of goals and the conflicts engendered by their incompatibility are also excluded from the typical study of inference. In the laboratory, the experimenter carefully spells out the objective of the task (e.g., recall, impression formation) and only after a shared understanding has been attained does the experiment proceed.

The austerity of the laboratory often leads, however, to a poverty of behavior and of the theorizing about it. Indeed, even early classic studies of animal learning and human problem solving vividly demonstrated that the structure of the physical environment (or the lack thereof) could produce either seemingly "stupid," blind trial-and-error behavior (e.g., Thorndike, 1911) or intelligent and insightful behavior (e.g., Köhler, 1925; Maier, 1931). The context may thus provide cues for the solution by structuring the problem or by defining the appropriate patterns and conditions for the deployment of particular strategies. Thus, studies of cross-cultural cognition have concluded that cultural differences are unlikely to occur in basic component cognitive processes but occur only in functional cognitive systems and in their deployment, as a function of different cultural contexts (Cole & Scribner, 1974, pp. 193–194).

The context sensitivity of judgments has been underrepresented in social cognition studies—and not only through the austerity of the laboratory. Typically, the studies have examined the final stages of processing, when the problem already is understood and an appropriate strategy is applied. Research has only rarely considered the prior stage of processing, at which people select the strategies to be deployed from the available options. The context probably is particularly crucial at the early stages of processing, when the problem is first reconstructed and its points of reference are articulated.

Action-Linked Inference

The purposiveness and context sensitivity of inference reflect, in some way, designs of future action on the basis of the judgment or uses of the information. The centrality of action has been a long-standing theme in numerous works, though not in recent social-cognitive research. Aristotle (1973) already underscored the primacy of action concepts as the organizing elements for many forms of understanding and explanation and the connection between action and purposiveness. The second chapter of *Poetics* emphatically begins with the argument that "Artists imitate men involved in action". Indeed

> Tragedy is essentially an imitation not of persons but of action and life. . . . All human happiness or misery takes the form of action; the end for which we live is a certain kind of activity, not a quality. . . . In a play accordingly they do not act in order to portray the characters; they include the characters for the sake of the action. So that it is the action in it, i.e., its Fable or Plot, that is the end and purpose of the tragedy; and the end is everywhere the chief thing. (p. 678)

This Aristotelian emphasis also underlies, for example, a great deal of contemporary literary theory. Thus both formalists and many structuralists (e.g. Barthes, 1975; Greimas, 1966; Todorov, 1977) consider the characters of a story as secondary byproducts subordinated to the action or plot. In a different way, Piaget also postulated a close connection between action and the emergence of intelligence. Cognition is rooted in action, both at the earliest levels of sensorimotor adaptation and at the highest levels of formal operational and scientific thought: "From the most elementary sensorimotor actions (such as pulling and pushing) to the most sophisticated intellectual operations, which are interiorized actions, carried out mentally, . . . knowledge is constantly linked with actions or operations" (Piaget, 1970, p. 704).

There are several links between social cognition and action. First, information is processed differently, depending on how it will be utilized. For instance, people tend to structure information quite differently, depending on what they intend to communicate, to whom, and in what context (Higgins, McCann, & Fondacaro, 1982; Zajonc, 1960). Also, action-linked processing provides a distinctive mode of understanding, a characteristic logic and language for structuring information that are closely coordinated with behavior and everyday interaction, with the intentionality and context-embeddedness of ordinary inference. Action-linked knowledge, in its elementary forms, appears very early in development and may, in fact, provide the early building blocks of cognitive development. For instance, it has been suggested that young children first organize knowledge around events in episodic systems and only later shift to a decontextualized, categorically organized knowledge system (Brown, 1977; Mandler, 1979, 1983; Nelson, 1977; Nelson & Gruendel, 1981).

These social dimensions of cognition—its purposive, context-sensitive, and action-linked components—are articulated in the concept of personal and sociocultural goals (see Burke, 1969; Garfinkel, 1967; Goffman, 1959; Mead, 1934; Wittgenstein, 1958). In the study of cognition, these notions have had a checkered history.

GOAL-GUIDED INFERENCE

Reactive Selectivity

Early studies of thinking were guided by a behaviorist framework, in which the individual was a passive organism responding to reinforcement contingencies in the environment. In this conception, thinking was but another instance of the learning process, like rote memory or mnemonic reproduction. In the 1960s, the focus shifted to a "cognitive" perspective, which emphasized the active learning of the individual and the constructive, organizational nature of the inference process. Experience was not simply "given" to the individual. Thinking, or cognition, involved transformation of the environmental input through a set of operations and integration of it into a broader system of knowledge. That is, chunks of experience were assigned meaning and identity and regrouped on that basis into equivalence classes or categories. Henceforth, thinking was treated as an active, anticipatory activity, not as a mimetic one. Research examined the strategies deployed by the individual to reorganize and integrate the information in inference and also in memory and recall (see Hastie *et al.*, 1980; Wyer & Srull, 1984; Zukier & Hagen, 1978).

The constructive and organizing nature of inference involves, at the strategy execution stage, a range of unifying processes that integrate disparate facts. The execution stage is preceded by a stipulative stage, involving selective processes that determine the appropriate strategies to be deployed, the relative relevance of various facts for the judgment, and the weight they are to be accorded. By necessity, inference entails such extensive selectivity in attentional, encoding, and retrieval processes. Inference thus also entails standards or criteria of reference, in terms of which the selectivity occurs. For example, in judgments of category membership, the features of the prototypical category representative may serve as criteria for determining whether a given individual is or is not likely to belong to that category—say, whether this person behaves like the prototypical introvert (Cantor & Mischel, 1979). In decisions under uncertainty, people will prefer a risk-aversive or risk-seeking behavior, involving, for example, possible monetary gains or losses, as a function of the reference points used in their judgments (Kahneman & Tversky, 1984).

The importance of such processes of selectivity in judgment has led a number of researchers to examine the determinants of the criterion selection that guides judgment. Criterion selection may occur deliberately, guided by the goals and objectives of the inference process and by the functional importance of the information attended to. Alternatively, criterion selection may occur rather inadvertently from the subject's point of view, in unintentional reaction to stimulus features or contexts that may be entirely irrelevant to the judgment. It is primarily the passive, reactive kind of selectivity that has been examined in most current research. The determinants of reactive selectivity either are contemporaneous (but often nonfunctional) features of the information—such as its vividness, salience, distinctiveness, or ease of retrieval—or they involve past experiences, stored in schemata. The schematized experiences may serve as reference points, or they may activate certain categories and thereby render them more accessible.

For instance, research on judgmental heuristics has identified several cognitive strategies that underlie everyday decision making (Kahneman, Slovic, & Tversky, 1982; Kahneman & Tversky, 1973). The heuristics reduce the complexity of the judgmental task by selectively considering some features of the available information at the expense of other features that are equally or more relevant. Although they often serve as efficient shortcuts for decision making, the heuristics also lead to systematic errors, through the inappropriate selectivity they introduce. The availability heuristic, for example, is used to estimate the likelihood of an event or the size of a class, such as the relative frequency of various natural hazards (Slovic, Fischhoff, & Lichtenstein, 1976) or the risk of heart attack among middle-aged people. The availability heuristic leads people to assess these probabilities by the ease with which particular instances can be recalled or imagined. Ease of retrieval, however, is at least partly a function of factors largely unrelated to the probability of the event. Vividness of direct experience with a similar event, recency of occurrence, and extremity or distinctiveness of the event all render the event more available in memory and therefore will (erroneously) increase its perceived likelihood.

The representativeness heuristic is involved in judgments of category assignment, in determining whether a particular person or object belongs to a given class (for example, whether an individual is likely to be a lawyer or an engineer). Judgments of representativeness are based primarily on the similarity between the individual and the possible groups under consideration. As a consequence, probability judgments based on representativeness tend to neglect the prior probability of outcomes, the degree of predictability, and other relevant factors. Thus, in judgments of both availability and representativeness, people are attuned to various, sometimes irrelevant, stimulus features (vividness, similarity) and neglect more important formal properties of the information.

Another line of research on priming and category activation has shown how irrelevant experiences bias subsequent judgments in different contexts (Higgins, King, & Mavin, 1982; Higgins, Rholes, & Jones, 1977; see also Srull & Wyer, 1979, 1980; Wyer & Srull, 1981). The research examined the effects of differential construct accessibility on impression formation and recall. Specifically, the focus was on several nonfunctional factors that affect the readiness with which a stored construct is utilized in social inference and on the extent to which it will influence the organization and interpretation of the information. For example, in one study (Higgins *et al.*, 1977), subjects were primed for either positive or negative traits and then read several ambiguous descriptions of a person (e.g., "adventurous" or "reckless"). Subjects' impressions and evaluations of the person were consistently biased by the unrelated trait categories that had been previously activated.

Salience effects constitute a form of reactive selectivity that is linked not to previously stored information or past experiences but to contemporaneous features of the information. Salience influences perceptual processes (McArthur, 1981) and memory retrieval processes (Fiske, Kenny, & Taylor, 1982; Taylor & Fiske, 1978). Research on salience has also focused on the stimulus features that may draw the observer's attention, independently of any processing goals. For example, an individual who is brightly lit, moving, or novel will draw a disproportionate amount of attention. Similarly, solo status or distinctiveness (e.g., a black or a woman in an otherwise all-white, male group, or a handicapped person) is very salient, and will be given disproportionate weight in impression formation or retrieval (see Taylor, 1982).

In all these studies, the information that receives special attention rarely does so because it is called for by the individual's judgmental objectives or by the use to which he or she intends to put the information. The salient information is not actively selected, but imposes itself and "engulfs" the observer. Thus, an inappropriate criterion or point of reference may often be activated, guide further processing and recall, and produce systematic distortions.

The judgmental reference points may be provided by schemata (Bartlett, 1932; Markus, 1977; Rumelhart, 1984) or by similar generic categories that articulate a set of general conceptions and expectations about people or events (cf. Cantor & Mischel, 1979; Minsky, 1975; Ostrom, Lingle, Pryor, & Geva, 1980; Schank & Abelson, 1977). In the schema-processing view, the inference process essentially consists of an examination of the fit between the new information and the internally stored expectations called up by the activation of preestablished schemata formed through prior experience. When inappropriate or conflicting schemata become accessible (naturally or experimentally), reactive selectivity again occurs. For example, Langer (1975) has documented an "illusion of control." She altered people's behavior in a chance situation, in which the participants in effect had no control over the outcome, by introducing into the situation some irrelevant factors typically associated with the exercise of skill and control (e.g., choice, or competition between the participants). The irrelevant skill elements presumably evoked a schema of controllable situations; as a consequence, participants behaved as if they indeed had control over the situation. Conversely, Seligman and his associates (e.g., Abramson, Seligman, & Teasdale, 1978) demonstrated how the activation of a "no control" schema may induce "learned helplessness" in people and lead them to relinquish effective control in situations where such control is, in fact, easily available and discernible.

Goal-Guided Selectivity

In contrast to the emphasis on reactive selectivity, the more deliberative, goal-oriented selectivity in inference has received significantly less attention. The goal-guided approach examines planned forms of inferential selectivity, where selectivity is not affected by the irrelevant or haphazard availability of concepts at the time of judgment, but is determined by the judgmental objectives to which the particular concepts are distinctively relevant. In the category-based views of processing, and in the studies of reactive selectivity, inference essentially is linked to the individual's *past experiences*, organized in schema-like structures (or prototypes, scripts, etc.). The generic categories serve as criteria for recognition and for assessing the goodness of fit between current experience and past, normative experience. By constrast, in the goal-guided framework, inference is linked to the individual's *future behavior*, to normative expectations associated with social roles and with the construction of meaning in the context of social interaction (e.g., Burke, 1969; Garfinkel, 1967; Goffman, 1959). Specifically, the structuring of information depends on its intended use. An individual's goals influence which information receives particular attention, how it is encoded and organized, and how it is given meaning or interpreted. Goals represent the individual's personal point of view and intentions in the situation and the coordination of the judgmental process with anticipated interaction and with the present context and environment.

A future-oriented, contextual goal emphasis reflects not so much the active as the interactive nature of inference. The "New Look" in cognitive psychology demonstrated compellingly that the characteristics of the individual problem solver, rather than the objective features of the stimulus-task, are primary determinants of judgment. Hence, subsequent research has examined people's internal knowledge structures and mental models to process information (e.g., schemata, prototypes, etc.) and the cognitive strategies that peope use to handle complex information despite limited processing capacity (e.g., research on judgmental heuristics). In all these studies, the individual made judgments in the splendid isolation of the laboratory.

This individualistic approach proved illuminating, but it took insufficient account of the task environment. For example, a classic phenomenon in problem solving involves the elicitation of dramatic changes and reversals in people's answers to alternative but formally equivalent formulations of problems, and even to identical problem formulations in different domains (see Duncker, 1945; Johnson-Laird & Wason, 1977; Kahneman & Tversky, 1984). The effects are obtained even with slight changes in the formulation of the problem isomorphs, which are formally devoid of significance; the same steps are required to achieve the appropriate solution. These reversals have been taken, at times, as an indication of inconsistency and irrationality, produced by the great context susceptibility (that is, reactive selectivity) of individuals. It is also possible, however, that people's response changes to problem isomorphs reflect considerable *context sensitivity* rather than *susceptibility*. To the extent that the individual's internal representations of the problem are constructed partly in response to the task environment, even minor variations in that environment may lead to a restructuring of the problem and of the kinds of solutions it calls for. The considerable differences in processing times that alternative problem isomorphs require also indicate that the different formulations indeed produce different internal representations of the problem (Hayes & Simon, 1977; Simon & Hayes, 1976). In effect, then, the patterns of results for response changes to alternative problem isomorphs are consistent with the view that inference is essentially an interactive process, highly flexible and adaptive to the perceived demands and cues of the task-environment—and the social context. Inference involves a negotiation of meanings (for example, the meaning of a task negotiated between the subject and the experimenter) and a coordination of various information-processing and interpersonal objectives. An adequate model of cognition must therefore redress both the stimulus and the individualistic overemphases and consider the interaction between people and context.

The following sections explore some dimensions of interactional processing and its purposive, context-sensitive, and action-linked components. The interactional dimensions are articulated in the concept of goal orientation. In particular, two contrasting fundamental orientations are examined—the paradigmatic and the narrative orientations, which constitute very general modes of structuring and processing information. The two orientations are related to the more pointed processing and interpersonal objectives described in current social-cognitive research and to broader sociocultural orientations. Together, the orientations constitute an important aspect of the social context factors that affect cognition. Each will be examined in turn.

NARRATIVE AND PARADIGMATIC ORIENTATIONS

At the most fundamental level, the goal orientation framework identifies two basic orientations that generally characterize inference in varying degrees and combinations: the paradigmatic mode and the narrative mode. The two modes constitute distinctive and irreducible cognitive competences, and each is characterized by a particular logic for organizing representation, understanding, and explanation. The two modes involve different cognitive operations and strategies, and they result in different products. They represent two forms of knowing that are available to people, which are deployed, alone or together, deliberately or not, as a function of individual objectives and task representation.

The paradigmatic mode of thinking is constituted by the traditional scientific logic for description and explanation. The paradigmatic mode involves the construction and coordination of equivalence classes (e.g., categories, schemata, prototypes). The categories are organized in a hierarchical system, and they stand in inclusional relationship to one another, however fuzzy their boundaries may be (see Rosch, 1978). The construction of and assignment to categories involve the logic of classes and principles of logical induction. The paradigmatic mode tends toward context-free propositions and formal, timeless abstractions. It is typical of the scientific-normative model, and it has been the near-exclusive focus of current inference research. Indeed, studies of thinking have been concerned primarily with forms of categorization, from early investigations of concept attainment and problem solving, which examined people's strategies for identifying category assignment rules and criterial categorical attributes, to current models of schema-based and heuristic processing, in which the informational input is matched to prototypical mental models.

The second basic orientation, the narrative mode, has been left out of many current accounts of inference. It is best represented in outcomes such as discourse, story, and historical accounts, and it also is characteristic of many everyday judgments. The narrative mode of thinking involves combinatorial rules of connectedness and relations of concatenation. Narrative arguments are articulated in temporal sequences, around intentionality and action. The narrative mode is highly context-sensitive; its output is thematic, situated in time and place; and its formal expression is through the topic-comment structure, rather than the paradigmatic category.

One can readily identify some elements of narrative structure and constraints and some of the formal conditions under which narrative structuring emerges and operates. However, the full logic of the narrative mode cannot be articulated yet. It should be clear, nevertheless, that the two modes are not antithetical and that the narrative mode is no less rigorous than the paradigmatic mode. Just as the poet selects words very carefully from the available equivalence class (i.e., a para-digmatic operation) but articulates those selections differently than the scientist, so people use different modes of articulation and strategies to construe events or information in various ways. Thus, although all thinking and inference are founded on classification and categories, the articulation between the categories need not be structured like the propositional model. In fact, many everyday judgments and beliefs cannot be justified in formal deductive–inductive terms, nor do they fit the systematic structure of scientific theory. The narrative explanation incorporates elements of the paradigmatic explanation but also goes beyond it and is bound by a different set of constraints. The two orientations are not equally prevalent in everyday judgments; in some combination, however, they are always present.

The proposed framework for the description of the two modes is still largely programmatic. Although a preliminary formulation and some experimental evidence are already available (Zukier & Pepitone, 1984), this formulation can serve only to highlight important issues and to delineate the directions in which the framework must be elaborated.

In the paradigmatic orientation, the individual is concerned with the relationship between the individual case and population referents or general conceptual categories. The paradigmatic mode emphasizes "vertical" relationships of subordination and superordination, member-to-category relationships, and the subsumption of different instances under generic categories. Information is articulated along dimensions of likeness, equivalence, prototypicality, and contrast.

The narrative orientation is a "horizontal" orientation, concerned with developing or uncovering sequential relationships of concatenation, conjunction, or combination. The narrative mode emphasizes "action-related" structuring and the "pulling together" of the available information into a connected narrative and pattern or network; this pattern reveals the common thread and internal coherence of the story—its plot rather than its paradigmatic theme.

The distinction between the paradigmatic and the narrative modes makes contact with related dichotomies in the literature. For example, it is related to the distinction between nomothetic and idiographic approaches to the study of social behavior; the nomothetic approach attempts to describe behavior in terms of broad and general laws or dimensions, whereas the idiographic approach seeks to capture the unique specificity of the individual case (Allport, 1961). The distinction also makes contact with the double articulation of language in terms of the paradigmatic and syntagmatic relations between linguistic units (e.g., Lyons, 1969).

The two orientations represent fundamental modes of thinking and structuring processes and generate distinctive forms and products. Thus, the narrative mode, in particular, must be distinguished from paradigmatic categories that spell out a temporal sequence of actions, such as "scripts" and "scenarios" (Abelson, 1981; Schank & Abelson, 1977). Scripts are paradigmatic products—categories about social situations (e.g., the "restaurant" script); they are preestablished constructs stored in memory, which, like all categories, serve to identify new members of the class ("This is a restaurant?!"). The script categories are temporally organized around actions and plans simply because they map schematically social episodes.

The paradigmatic and narrative modes are best characterized in terms of some "loose" contrasting properties (see Zukier & Pepitone, 1984). The paradigmatic mode is concerned with general laws about causal relationships and with general, context-free propositions, on the model of the language of natural science (e.g., the laws of gravity, the dynamics of the authoritarian personality). By contrast, the narrative mode is concerned with the logic of human action and intentionality: reasons rather than causes; intentions, beliefs, and goals; the motivational underpinnings of behavior. Narrative structuring draws on the arguments of action: the agent, the action itself, the situation, the intention or goal, and the instruments of action (Burke, 1969). The narrative mode also emphasizes the relationship of the part to the whole, rather than the relationship of the instance to the general class of such events. In the narrative mode, the observer attempts to capture the "full picture"—the unique pattern and distinctive personality of the individual.

The paradigmatic mode emphasizes a small set of similarities and commonalities between various phenomena, in order to classify and construct types that subsume the particular instances. The paradigmatic mode is extensive; it sacrifices specificity and comprehensiveness of description for wide applicability of its propositions and trades richness for rigor. By contrast, the narrative mode is intensive; it focuses as much on differences as on similarities and trades generality for singular comprehensiveness, rigor for richness. It seeks to consider more aspects of a phenomenon, even though it thereby reduces the phenomenon's prototypicality and the explanation's (predictive) power.

The paradigmatic and narrative modes also involve different "truth" criteria. Paradigmatic accounts must be verifiable, or "falsifiable" (Popper, 1968), by *external* validation—that is, by a demonstration of the facts they invoke. Narrative accounts primarily call for an *internal* validation and are justified not in terms of their veridicality but in terms of their verisimilitude, plausibility, internal coherence, and persuasiveness. Thus, narrative structuring is more flexible and can more readily accommodate discontinuities, contradictions, and exceptions in its accounts.

Few studies have directly examined the narrative mode. References to narrative thought are mostly included in studies of paradigmatic thinking, when the investigators note in passing the indications emerging from the data that point to the existence of another mode of understanding. For instance, in a recent study of paradigmatic probability judgments, Tversky and Kahneman (1983) concluded that their data illustrate "people's affinity for nonextensional reasoning" and "demonstrate with exceptional clarity the contrast between the extensional logic that underlies most formal conceptions of probability and the natural assessments that govern many judgments and beliefs." Indeed, "the representativeness heuristic generally favors outcomes that make *good stories*" (emphasis added); hence, "a comprehensive account of human judgment must reflect the tension between compelling logical rules and seductive nonextensional intuitions" (p. 311, 314). Tversky and Kahneman's project was not concerned with this nonextensional reasoning and thus treated its manifestations primarily as failures or absences of paradigmatic thinking. The narrative mode embodies the very structure and logic their data evoke.

The paradigmatic and the narrative mode are both commonly available to individuals, and either one may dominate in a particular context. Internal or external factors may lead to the deployment, deliberate or not, of a given mode and of the strategies associated with it. These factors may involve contingent judgmental objectives, contextual determinants, or more enduring individual differences in preferences or in inclination to adopt one or the other mode. Each of these factors will be examined as they are manifested in a series of experimental investigations.

CONTINGENT SITUATIONAL DETERMINANTS OF JUDGMENTAL MODE

Role Assignment: Judgmental Mode and the Use of Base Rate Information

The operation of the paradigmatic and narrative modes was explored in a series of studies by Zukier and Pepitone (1984) on the limiting conditions of the base rate fallacy in prediction. The base rate fallacy, a very robust and well-documented phenomenon in social inference, involves the relative underutilization of prior probabilities, or base rate information, in probabilistic judgments. In the classic experiment (Kahneman & Tversky, 1973), subjects read several brief sketches of individuals, supposedly sampled at random from a group of 100 engineers and lawyers. After reading each description, subjects were asked to indicate the probability that the sketch was of one of the engineers or one of the lawyers in the sample. In some conditions, the sample was said to be composed of 70% lawyers and 30% engineers; in the other conditions, this proportion was reversed. Despite the different base rate information, subjects in both conditions made very similar probability judgments for each description. Moreover, when the sketch contained only information that was useless for the determination of the individual's group membership, subjects still neglected the prior probabilities and judged both outcomes equiprobable. The results have been replicated numerous times, and various explanations have been offered for this apparent insensitivity to base rate information (for a review, see Borgida & Brekke, 1981). Most explanations suggest that the base rate fallacy results from some particular feature of the information: its abstractness (e.g., Nisbett & Borgida, 1975), its noncausal format (e.g., Ajzen, 1977; Tversky & Kahneman, 1980), or its generality (Bar-Hillel, 1980).

In terms of the orientation framework, base rate information clearly is paradigmatic information: it summarizes a general proposition about a particular feature (e.g., profession) of a class of people or events. Base rate information carries no direct information about any individual case; it only has implications that can be deductively derived for a particular instance. The implications specify one aspect of the relationship between the individual case and the general category—the prior probability that the case indeed belongs to the general category. This led Zukier and Pepitone (1984) to examine the possibility that the base rate fallacy may not reflect a general insensitivity to this type of "statistical" information. Instead, it could result from a mismatch in the task representation of the experimenter and subjects. Indeed, although base rate information is highly relevant in a paradigmatic mode, it is only of secondary importance in a narrative mode. The solution of the problem requires a paradigmatic operation; thus, if subjects should construe or interpret the task in a narrative mode (inadvertently, from the experimenter's viewpoint), the neglect of base rate information would signify not simply the failure of paradigmatic thinking but the operation of narrative thinking. This argument suggests that subjects would appropriately consider base rate information in a paradigmatic judgmental mode, but not in a narrative mode, and that controlling for mode of judgment may attenuate the base rate fallacy.

In a first experiment (Zukier & Pepitone, 1984), this possibility was examined by manipulating the roles to which subjects were assigned, which were presumably associated with a paradigmatic or narrative mode. Subjects received the base rate problems from the original Kahneman and Tversky (1973) study and were asked to adopt the role of a scientist or a clinical counselor. They then assessed the category membership of two individuals about whom they read brief descriptions. The roles of scientist and clinical counselor were outlined so as to evoke a paradigmatic and a narrative orientation, respectively. The descriptions and other instructions were adapted from Kahneman and Tversky (1973).

Thus, subjects in both conditions were told that the personality descriptions were sampled at random from a group of 30 engineers and 70 lawyers, and they were asked to indicate for each description the probability that it belonged to an engineer. One vignette described the individual—"Jack"—in terms of the popular stereotype of an engineer (e.g., "shows no interest in political and social issues; spends most of his free time on his many hobbies which include home carpentry . . . and mathematical puzzles"). The other "neutral" vignette of "Dick" was designed to be completely uninformative about the individual's profession (e.g., "He is married with no children . . . he promises to be quite successful in his field . . . he is well respected by his colleagues").

In addition, subjects in the paradigmatic condition were told that the study was conducted by the "Center for Research in Scientific Thinking" at the Graduate School of Management. The study, it was explained, "examines how much people will use scientific thinking when making decisions." Subjects were told; "Make your judgments as if you were a scientist analyzing data."

In the narrative condition, the experiment was presented as a study by the "Center for Job Counselor Training," which examined "an individual's general sensitivity and intuitive understanding of another person and in particular of professional interests." Subjects were urged to "try to understand the individual's personality, professional inclinations and interests as best you can. Call on your general knowledge, sensitivity and empathy."

Thus, in this study, the base rate information indicated a low *a priori* probability that any of the descriptions sampled at random would belong to one of the 30 engineers rather than to one of the 70 lawyers. In nearly all previous studies, subjects nevertheless judged the stereotypical description to belong almost certainly to an engineer and expressed apparent perplexity over the neutral description by judging both outcomes equally likely.

In base rate studies that use both stereotypical descriptions and "neutral" descriptions devoid of diagnostic information about the criterion (e.g., information about the individual's profession), subjects' probability estimates for the neutral description provide a clearer measure of the attention given to base rate information. That is, the weight prior probabilities should normatively have in a judgment is partly a function of the perceived diagnosticity of the individual description; if the individual description leaves no doubt that a particular person or event belongs to the minority class, base rate information should not be considered at all, no matter how disproportionate the prior probabilities of both classes are. At the extreme, if the description in effect indicates that the person *is* an engineer, base rates do not matter, even if there were only one engineer and 29 laywers in the sample. Conversely, the *less* that is known about an individual, the more people should rely on base rate information. Thus, it is possible that subjects in a base rate experiment might consider the stereotypical descriptions highly diagnostic and therefore underutilize base rate information. For the neutral description, however, subjects in effect indicate by judgments of equiprobability that they consider the description uninformative about the outcome. With no good information about the particular case, subjects who are appropriately sensitive to the base rate information could be expected to give estimates closer to the specified composition of the sample (i.e., 30% engineers).

In the Zukier and Pepitone (1984) study, then, the manipulation of the alleged sponsorship of the study and of role assignment should have little effect if the base rate fallacy results from a fairly general insensitivity to certain kinds of "statistical" information. However, if the base rate fallacy reflects subjects' adoption of a narrative orientation to the task, a change in orientation should affect the kinds of information being considered. In the study, the judgmental orientation had a substantial effect on subjects' probability estimates ($p < .005$). Description also had an effect ($p < .001$), as expected, and there were no interaction effects. Specifically, subjects in the narrative orientation replicated previous findings, with a mean estimate of .42 and a median of .5 for the neutral description and a high average estimate (.76) for the stereotypical description. By contrast, in the paradigmatic orientation, the neutral description produced an average estimate of .31, which was not significantly different from the specified base rate of .3. The stereotypical description also produced lower estimates (mean = .64) than it did in the narrative orientation, presumably under the influence of the low base rate information. Clearly, then, for both the stereotypical and the neutral description, subjects in a paradigmatic orientation fully incorporate prior probabilities in their judgments; by contrast, subjects in the narrative orientation focus primarily on the specific description and on the story that it does (or does not, in the neutral description) tell about the individual.

Problem Formulation, Narrative Embeddedness, and the Use of Base Rate Information

In the first experiment, judgmental mode was directly and explicitly manipulated by having the instructional set provide for differential role assignment. A second experiment (Zukier & Pepitone, 1984) examined whether slight variations in the formulation of the problems would be sufficient to evoke contrasting modes and would produce different answers on formally equivalent problems. Each subject made probability estimates for three problems in a within-subjects design. One problem, the classic "engineers–lawyers" problem, was expected to evoke a narrative orientation; two other problems, a "divorce" problem and a "burglary" problem, were designed to evoke a paradigmatic orientation and hence to lead subjects to fully utilize base rate information, even if they neglected it in the "engineer–lawyer" problem. For each problem, subjects read two descriptions of individuals, a stereotypical description and a neutral description, and were then asked to estimate the likelihood of a given outcome.

In the control problem, subjects received the standard "engineer–lawyer" instructions and descriptions and estimated the likelihood that the individual who was described was one of the 30 engineers.

In the "divorce" problem, subjects were told that "a recent survey in the New York area has shown that within 3 years of getting married, 27% of the couples are divorced and 73% are still married." Subjects then read the description of an individual that was designed to evoke the stereotype of somebody likely to get divorced (e.g., "an airline pilot . . . away from home for a total of 2 weeks each month . . . considered attractive and adventurous by his friends and co-workers") and a neutral vignette that conveyed no information about this issue. Subjects indicated, after each vignette, the probability that the individual was one of the 27% who get divorced.

In the "burglary" problem, subjects were told that "the crime statistics of a certain New York City block show that 68% of the apartments have been broken into at least once during the last ten years." Subjects then read about two apartments. The stereotypical description described a couple whose lifestyle (e.g., at home a great deal) would make a break-in less likely; the neutral description was uninformative in this regard.

The results of this experiment fully confirmed the role of orientation in the use of base rate information. In the classic "engineer–lawyer" problem, the results replicated earlier findings: with a specified base rate of .3, subjects estimated the probability that the stereotypical description belonged to an engineer at .79 and that the neutral description belonged to an engineer at .5. The same subjects, however, gave very different responses to the two other problems. In the "divorce" problem, with a base rate of .27, subjects assigned a probability of .30 to the uninformative description; in the "burglary" problem, with a specified rate of .32, subjects assigned a probability of .26 to the uninformative description.

These estimates were not significantly different from their respective base rates and resemble the predictions of subjects in the scientific role/paradigmatic mode of the first experiment.

Together, the results of the two experiments suggest that people can readily adopt either the paradigmatic or the narrative orientation, depending on the context of the judgment as it is made salient by assumed roles or by the formulation of the problem. Thus, equivalent problems may produce quite different answers if people approach them with different orientations. This high context sensitivity of inference and susceptibility to variations in orientation is also reflected, in a different domain, in the vulnerability of memory to slight changes in the phrasing of questions (e.g., Loftus, 1975; Loftus, Miller, & Burns, 1978) and to other subtle reformulations (Hayes & Simon, 1977; Kahneman & Tversky, 1984).

The effects of variations in the formulation of the base rate problems also suggest that the context sensitivity and flexibility of judgments may have considerable educational implications. In the Zukier and Pepitone (1984) experiment, the alternative formulations of the problems readily evoked stories about the base rates (e.g., stories about unsafe neighborhoods or negligent tenants). The use of base rates under these conditions suggests that paradigmatic concepts (for example, many statistical notions) might be made easily intelligible and available, even when people operate in a narrative mode, by embedding the concepts in an appropriate narrative.

Learning Goals and Strategy Selection

The paradigmatic and narrative modes constitute very general processing orientations that entail different strategies and forms of output. Other research that has considered goal-guided processing typically has been concerned with various specific goals, dictated by the particular situation or by the experimenter. In general, however, little systematic research is available on goal orientation in inference, and no comprehensive taxonomies of "middle-level" or concrete goals have emerged from these studies. Nor is this preliminary research extensive enough to elucidate the organizing processes that are evoked by particular goal orientations and that presumably underlie the clear inferential differences resulting from the various orientations.

In some studies, the goal orientation is associated with the features of a specific context. For example, in one study (Anderson & Pichert, 1978), subjects were given a story about two boys playing at one of the boys' home. Subjects were asked to read the story from the perspective of either a burglar or a person interested in buying a home. The story contained some information that would be of particular interest to a burglar (e.g., location of the color TV, the china, the jewelry) and other information that would be distinctively relevant for a real estate prospect (e.g., damp basement, leak in the roof, condition of the plumbing). After recalling the story once, subjects were asked to shift perspective and then recall the story again. On the second recall, subjects remembered significantly more information relevant to the newly adopted perspective than they had remembered initially, and they also recalled less information than before that was important for the first perspective but not for the second one. For instance, the newly appointed burglar now recalled the location of the china instead of the condition of the plumbing. Other research on witness testimony or jury decisions indicates that witness testimony elicited by a lawyer in an adversary role will be considerably more biased than testimony under nonadversary role conditions (Sheppard & Vidmar, 1980). At a different level, experimental procedures designed to prevent demand characteristics (e.g., Orne, 1962; Rosenthal, 1966) also reflect concern about the effects of the great variety of subject expectations and goal orientations that may be inadvertently evoked, even in the highly stylized conditions of the laboratory.

Several investigators have explored the role of specific learning goals on inference and recall, and their findings also are important for the more general paradigmatic and narrative orientations. In these studies, the goals were explicitly given in the instructions, and they often corresponded to the tasks employed in the laboratory: impression formation, recall, prediction.

One extensive program of research (Hoffman, Mischel, & Baer, 1984; Hoffman, Mischel, & Mazze, 1981; Jeffery & Mischel, 1979) has examined the inferential effects of various goal orientations and how these effects may be mediated by the information structuring associated with the goals. In one study (Hoffman et al., 1981), subjects read several vignettes describing the behavior of a college student in a variety of situations. The descriptions were all potentially classifiable in terms of the personality characteristics the student displayed or in terms of the goals her behaviors served. Subjects were asked to sort the descriptions into groups under one of four goal orientations: recall, impression, prediction, or empathy. The goal orientations substantially affected the ways in which subjects organized the information. Subjects who were asked to remember the behaviors or to understand them from the character's point of view organized the information around the character's goals; subjects who were asked to form an impression of the student or to predict her future behavior used trait dimensions to organize that same information. Hoffman et al. (1981) have suggested that trait dimensions are particularly useful for impression formation because they are well established in memory, contain an implicit evaluative component, and allow for easy interindividual comparisons because of their nomothetic nature. Trait information also may facilitate prediction, because it generally has broad implications for the person's likely behavior in different contexts—from the perspective of the naive perceiver, if not from that of the psychologist (Mischel, 1968). By contrast, goal categories reflect the character's viewpoint and what he or she is trying to do. Thus, they may be more appropriate for an empathy orientation. Also, goal concepts provide a coherent summary of diverse samples of behavior linked by a common goal and therefore may serve as good recall cues for related behaviors.

Hoffman *et al.* (1981) also found evidence that the differential organization of the information affected its later recall. Material that had been categorized by subjects in a recall condition was better remembered by a new group of subjects than the same material previously categorized by subjects in an impression-formation or no-purpose condition. Specifically, recall was facilitated by the organization of the behavioral information in goal categories rather than trait categories. A similar versatility in the structuring of information as a function of goal requirements was evident in a communication study (Hoffman *et al.*, 1984). In a series of experiments, subjects received behavioral information about an individual and were asked to indicate their impression of the person. Subjects who expected at the beginning of the task to later engage in verbal communication about the person (whether as speaker or as listener) described the person in more global, dispositional terms than subjects who expected to convey their impression in nonverbal form or who did not expect to communicate it at all. Hoffman *et al.* (1984) have suggested that people's apparent preference for dispositional accounts of other people's behavior (Nisbett & Ross, 1980) may reflect, in part, the requirements of the communication system and of the linguistic code, and hence that dispositional accounts are particularly prominent in interpersonal verbal communication.

These results are consistent with indications from research by Cohen and her colleagues (Cohen, 1981; Cohen & Ebbesen, 1979), who identified three broad categories of goal orientation. In an "information-seeking orientation," the actor's behavior serves as a source of information about the observer's social and nonsocial environment. For example, an individual may watch his or her friend play tennis in order to learn something about the game. In a "personality analysis" orientation, the observer seeks to understand the actor, his or her attributes and attitudes. And in a "judgment" orientation, the observer evaluates the actor's behavior along some specific dimension—for example, his or her likability or ability in a given domain.

In a series of studies, Cohen and Ebbesen (1979) explored the effects of these different orientations on inference. Subjects watched brief videotaped sequences of a woman performing various ordinary tasks. The experimenter primed one of two goal orientations by instructing subjects either to form an impression of the actor or to learn the tasks that she performed. Subjects also were asked to "unitize" the actor's behavior (Newston, 1976) by pressing a button each time they saw a discrete behavioral unit on the screen. After viewing the videotapes, subjects either rated the actor or were asked to recall her task-related behavior. Goal orientation considerably affected subjects' performance: the "unitizing" measure suggested that subjects with different goals actually attended to different behavioral features, and subjects with a task-learning orientation were more accurate in subsequent recall than subjects with an impression-formation orientation.

These results are also consistent with findings by Spiro (1977). Subjects read a story about an engaged couple in what was presented either as a memory experiment or as a study on "reactions to situations involving interpersonal relations." Subjects in the memory condition later recalled the material significantly better than the "interpersonal relations" subjects.

The findings of these studies converge to indicate the superiority of memory goals over impression-formation goals for the recall of information. These results contrast with indications from several other lines of research that suggest that an impression-formation orientation in fact facilitates recall significantly more than a memory orientation. This provocative pattern first emerged in a series of studies by Hamilton and his associates (Hamilton, Katz, & Leirer, 1980a, 1980b). In their experiments, subjects read several behavioral descriptions of an individual. Some subjects were asked to form an impression of the person, and others were asked to try to remember as much information as they could. On subsequent free-recall tasks, subjects with an impression-formation orientation typically recalled more information than subjects with a memory orientation. Similar results were also obtained by Srull and Wyer (e.g., Srull, 1981, 1983; Wyer & Gordon, 1982; Wyer, Srull, Gordon, & Hartwick, 1982; see also Hartwick, 1979; Reber, Kassin, Lewis, & Cantor, 1980). Indeed, Wyer and Srull have developed a processing model that explicitly incorporates goal-orientations. Since their program of research is presented elsewhere in this volume, it will not be discussed in the present context.

Thus, all these studies agree that different kinds of orientations (e.g., an impression-formation or a memory orientation) substantially affect inference, recall, or recognition. The evidence conflicts, however, on which orientation does in fact facilitate recall. In some accounts, the results are particularly intriguing because they reveal orientation effects quite different from the specified and presumably intended purpose. The studies provide little evidence about the factors that underlie the orientation effects. Hamilton *et al.* (1980b) suggested that the differences in recall are due to the nature of information integration and organization in each orientation, rather than to differences in the mere amount of integrative activity. Evidence from the Hoffman *et al.* (1981) study suggests that different goal orientations may lead not only to different structuring of information but also to the selection and use of different kinds of information. For example, goal categories may be more useful than trait categories for the recall of information, and trait concepts may be more useful for predictions and other speculative inferences.

The patterns of findings that emerge from these studies also may be specifically related to the operation of the paradigmatic and narrative orientations. The impression-formation, personality analysis, and empathy goals activated in the studies all appear to evoke a narrative orientation. By contrast, the standard memory goals used in these studies are consistent with a more paradigmatic orientation. Indeed, the impression-formation goal entails incorporating the information "sequentially over time" (Hamilton *et al.*, 1980b, p. 126) and requires people "to develop . . . [a] coherent . . . representation of the person" in a process where "isolated descriptive facts . . . [become] integrated into an overall impression," into "an interlocking network of associative relationships among the various items of information" (Hamilton *et al.*, 1980b, pp. 126–127). This description, with its emphasis on an integrative organization structured sequentially over time into an interlocking network, is characteristic of the narrative mode. Memory goals do not call for such a complex integrative elaboration and are more related to a paradigmatic mode. Evaluative judgments, which ask the observer to assess a person's behavior on a particular dimension—such as the person's likability (Cohen & Ebbesen, 1979)—are most clearly paradigmatic, since they involve the assignment of an individual to a superordinate (e.g., evaluative) category. Thus, the fundamental differences in information integration that are assumed to characterize the narrative and paradigmatic orientations also may lead to the inferential differences that result from various instructional sets.

ENDURING DETERMINANTS OF JUDGMENTAL MODE

The studies reviewed so far explored the contingent determinants of goal orientation: how inference is affected by the specific objectives evoked by external, temporary factors; instructional sets, problem formulation, and representation; and orientations associated with role assignment. These studies also suggested that the various goals are not equally prevalent in everyday judgments. In many conditions, the narrative orientation appears to dominate "spontaneously," just as in person perception studies the "impression-formation" orientation, rather than the "prediction" or "recall" orientations, seems prevalent.

This raises the possibility that a particular orientation, and even specific judgmental objectives, may at times come to constitute a more enduring feature of people's inferences. For example, there may be individual differences in preferences, or in inclination to adopt a particular judgmental orientation, because this orientation is more readily available or better understood or otherwise salient. Judgmental orientation may be related to cognitive style, which produces consistent individual differences despite the generally low cross-situational consistency found in trait studies (Mischel, 1968). Enduring differences in general orientation or in specific objectives also may be associated with structural features of the immediate context. For example, an interpersonal communication context is likely to impose constraints on both speaker and listener if they want to communicate clearly and effectively with each other. Enduring differences in orientation also may be related to the broader sociocultural context, such as social class or sex differences.

Individual Differences in Judgmental Orientation: A Doctors' Case

In a follow-up on the experiment showing the effects of experimentally induced orientations on the use of base rate information, Zukier and Pepitone (1984) explored the stability and generality of orientation effects in a natural context. In this experiment, a group of first-year medical students and a group of surgery residents estimated the likelihood that the classic stereotypical "engineer" descriptions and the "neutral" description belonged to an engineer. Zukier and Pepitone hypothesized that a medical education, with its emphasis on diagnostic procedures and the differential likelihood of various etiologies, might sensitize people to a paradigmatic orientation and that this orientation would also dominate in other, unrelated tasks.

Some additional data were collected to tentatively rule out some alternative factors that might cause group differences. For instance, residents might differ from first-year medical students on motivational or cognitive dimensions, and some self-selection might occur in the course of studies, which might then produce differences in performance. An examination of the registration data for the previous 5 years at the medical school where the study was conducted revealed a drop-out rate of 4% between the beginning of studies and residency. Thus, the two groups were essentially similar in composition. Zukier and Pepitone also asked another group of first-year students and residents to evaluate the diagnosticity of the descriptions, to see whether residents perhaps discarded the diagnosticity of any individuating information. However, there were no differences between the groups in the perceived diagnosticity of either description.

Would residents, then, use base rate information differently than first-year students in estimating the probability of category membership? The results strongly suggest that they do. There was a main effect for educational level ($p < .0001$) as well as the expected main effect for description ($p < .001$), with no interaction effects.

For both the stereotypical and the neutral conditions, residents relied much more on the specified base rate of .3 than the first-year students did. The pattern of estimates suggests that many residents in surgery approached the task quite differently than first-year students.

In the neutral condition, where the description was uninformative about category membership, 18 out of 20 residents gave a probability of .3 (for an overall mean of .31), while 9 out of 20 medical students assigned a probability of .5 to the description (for an overall mean of .47). Thus, when the description was not helpful for the prediction, nearly half of the medical students judged both outcomes equiprobable, and nearly all residents relied entirely on base rate information.

A similar pattern was evident for the stereotypical description. Residents gave a mean estimate of .51, and first-year medical students gave a mean estimate of .69. The distribution of the residents' responses was bimodal: residents assigned either a probability of .3 to the description or probabilities higher than .7. In side comments, most residents who assigned a high "engineer" probability to the stereotypical description also indicated that they realized that the overall probability was .3 but considered that the stereotypical description was diagnostic enough to suggest the higher estimates in this particular case.

The results suggest that base rate information, and presumably the corresponding paradigmatic orientation, dominated the residents' responses. Their judgments did not combine the prior probabilities and the specific information about the individual. Rather, most residents apparently neglected case-specific information entirely, even in the stereotypical condition, where the specific information was considered relevant to the outcome. In effect, the residents' judgment strategy was the mirror image of the medical students' approach. On all normative accounts, the residents consistently and considerably *overutilized* the base rate rule. They showed a reversal of the base rate fallacy seemingly as extensive as the first-year medical students' traditional tendency to underutilize that same base rate information. Presumably, the paradigmatic and narrative orientation, respectively, were underlying the different judgmental strategies of both groups.

Structural Context Determinants of Orientation in the Communication Process

An extensive program of research on interpersonal communication, by Higgins and his colleagues (e.g., Higgins, 1981; Higgins & McCann, 1985) has explored enduring, role- and motivation-related factors in the selection of communicative objectives. The studies have examined primarily the inferential components of communication concerned with encoding, organization, and recall of information. The studies used a "communication game" approach, which focused on the social relations dimensions of interpersonal communication. This perspective differs from the traditional "information-transmission" models of communication, which emphasize the factors involved in accurate and efficient transmission of information and the adherence, by speakers and listeners, to a common set of general communication rules. In contrast, the "communication game" paradigm studies the process of communication in terms of the interdependent social roles of speaker and listener, which require co-orientation between the participants and may be concerned, in addition to information-transmission, with the creation or maintenance of a social relationship between speaker and listener. In that view, different rules, or Gricean-like maxims (Grice, 1971) are associated with the roles of speaker and listener. For example, the speaker should take the audience's characteristics into account, should be coherent and comprehensible, should be relevant, and should produce a message that is appropriate to the context. The listener should determine the speaker's intent or purpose and should provide feedback to the speaker about his understanding of the message. Thus, the various rules, in effect, require the speaker to modify his or her message as a function of the listener's characteristics.

Higgins and his colleagues examined the conditions and consequences of such message modification. For example, in one study (Higgins & McCann, 1985), subjects read a vignette, purportedly of a fellow student whom they were then asked to describe for an audience that was said to either like or dislike the student. Subjects, who were either high or low authoritarians, were also told that the message recipient had either equal status or higher status than they did. Two weeks later, subjects were asked to reproduce the original description, to give their own impression of the person, and to indicate their attitude toward him. The results indicated that the social relationship between the communicator and the audience considerably affected the transmission of information. Both high and low authoritarians modified their description of the fellow student in the direction of the audience's attitude toward that student when the audience had equal status. When the audience had higher status, high authoritarians were much more likely than low authoritarians to distort their description to suit the audience's attitude. The message modification also affected the speakers' memory, impression, and evaluation of the individual they had described. Subjects' subsequent judgments and recall were more positive if their description had been designed for an audience that liked the individual than if it had been designed for an audience that disliked him. This memory effect increased over time for the high authoritarian subjects. Higgins and his colleagues suggested that these results, and similar ones from earlier studies, indicate that people tend to use their audience-tailored description of the individual as a basis for subsequent judgments and recall, without sufficiently taking into account the "context-driven" nature of the description.

The Higgins and McCann study pitted an information-processing goal (referential accuracy) against a personal, social-relationship goal (consideration of the audience's attitudes, such as the high authoritarians' wish to defer to a high-status partner). Research on cognitive tuning (Zajonc, 1960) has also examined the interplay of the speaker's and the listener's processing goals in interpersonal communication. The research and subsequent elaborations of Zajonc's formulation showed, for instance, that transmitters of a communication organize the information in a more rigid, unitary, and polarized way than recipients who are expecting the message.

Sociocultural Context Determinants of Orientation

The base rate study among medical doctors (Zukier & Pepitone, 1984) suggested that medical education may produce lasting changes in orientation. Similarly, enduring differences in orientation, or in goals, may be associated with socialization practices and with such factors as social class or sex. Such an association is most vividly articulated in Bernstein's sociolinguistic work (e.g., Bernstein, 1972; see also Cazden, 1970; Scribner & Cole, 1982). Bernstein is concerned with language as a process of socialization, through which individuals come to learn their social roles. According to Bernstein, children who have access to different speech systems or "codes" will adopt very different social and intellectual orientations and procedures, despite a common potential. He distinguishes two fundamental types of communication codes: an "elaborated" code, in which the speaker selects from a wide range of syntactic alternatives that are flexibly organized; and a "restricted" code, in which the syntax is much simplified and more rigidly organized.

The elaborated code, but not the restricted one, facilitates the expression of the speaker's intent. The different codes are generated by and express different forms of social relations. Specifically, the restricted code is associated with the working class, whereas the elaborated code is characteristic of the middle class. In Bernstein's (1972) analysis, the codes differ essentially in the "social-relations" goals they embody for their speakers. The restricted code creates social solidarity with the group at the expense of verbal elaboration of individual experience. This form of communication reinforces social relations oriented toward identification with the community and widely shared assumptions and refers to other people in terms of a common group or status membership. By contrast, the elaborated code encourages the speaker to consider the experience of others as different from his or her own and therefore forces the speaker to explicate and specify his or her own intentions and to convey only universalistic meanings that also are intelligible to the listener. Thus, both the restricted and the elaborated codes articulate and enforce, from early childhood on, a different set of social-relations goals, which in turn influence the cognitive processing of the speakers.

Different "social-relations" goals also may underlie sex differences in communication (for reviews, see Deaux, 1985; Philips, 1980). In one suggestive example, Lakoff (1975, 1979) has emphasized differences in speech style between men and women. Cultural norms lead women to use less assertive and more tentative language and more polite, deferential, and proper forms of speech. For instance, women tend to use more tag questions (e.g., "It's really nice weather today, isn't it?") and hedges (e.g., "perhaps," "I guess") than men do. These differences in speech patterns may be related, in part, to the social structure context that modulates behavior by implicitly articulating different expectations and goals for the participants in an interaction (Berger, Rosenholtz, & Zelditch, 1980).

THE ACTION FORMAT OF NARRATIVE STRUCTURING

The body of communication studies indicates most vividly how forms of communication, and of judgment in general, are linked to the intended uses of the inferential act and to the behavior of the individual. Narrative thinking, however, is also action-linked in a more structural way. In contrast to paradigmatic thinking, narrative thinking is assumed to be structured around various combinations of the arguments of action (Burke, 1969): the action itself, the agent, the scene or context of the action, the agency or instrumentalities of the action, and the agent's goals and intentions. Studies by Asch and Zukier (1984) and by Zukier (1985) provided a preliminary description of the format of narrative structuring. The Asch and Zukier (1984) study was not directly concerned with narrative thinking, but it nevertheless provided very suggestive evidence. In that study, subjects received brief descriptions of individuals in the form of two disposition terms (cf.

Asch, 1946). Each pair of terms consisted of either two congruent or two discordant traits. For example, the individual was alternatively described as "intelligent and witty," "envious and critical," "sociable and lonely," or "generous and vindictive." Subjects were asked to try to imagine a person with these qualities and to describe briefly what the person might be like. Each subject interpreted six pairs, which were shown in succession. These stripped-down materials and procedures produced lively, rich, and realistic narratives about people, which incorporated the information that was given and then "filled in" the overall picture. Asch and Zukier's analysis was concerned primarily with the organizing and unifying operations that underlie impression formation. They identified several rules to "pull together" the information (particularly the incongruent items) into a unitary impression and a number of "rules of dominance" in a pair. Nevertheless, the organizing principles that emerged from that analysis correspond quite closely to the structuring elements of the narrative mode. Several examples will illustrate this.

The first mode of reconciling incongruent dispositions described by Asch and Zukier (1984) is "segregation." In a prototypical example, "brilliant–foolish": "A brilliant person in a particular field may be lacking in common sense, skills or social graces that people who are not brilliant possess." Or for "generous–vindictive": "He never forgets the smallest favor or slight. Is generous to those who treated him benevolently, and vindictive to those who have done him the slightest harm." In Asch and Zukier's formulation, segregation entails assigning each of the clashing dispositions to a different sphere of the person's life space. Segregation eliminates the spatiotemporal simultaneity of incongruence by locating disparities in different regions, times, and circumstances, resulting in a reinterpretation of the scope and meaning of the respective dispositions. Clearly, in terms of the narrative framework, segregation involves relating the clashing dispositions or actions to different scenes. The evocation of a single scene could also serve to resolve the conflict. For example, "sociable–lonely" produced accounts of sociable people who had to travel for professional reasons and were feeling lonely because they were temporarily among strangers.

Another mode of resolution is "means–end," which corresponds, in its two forms, to a description of agency and instrumentalities or to an articulation of goals and intentions. Some accounts of "generous–vindictive" captured these dimensions well: "Is generous for ulterior motives; not altruistic but selfish—a scheming, plotting individual." In this type of example, the full sense of one term or disposition is denied by subordinating it and considering it as a deliberate means to the more significant component. As Asch and Zukier (1984) noted: "*Generous* lost its altruistic character and became destructive in intent, a means to unsavory aims" (p. 1235). The "means–end" category is primarily coordinated to the intentions of the actor. By contrast, the "enabling" category does not relate directly to intentionality but describes exclusively an agency/instrumentalities category. The other categories identified by Asch and Zukier also correspond closely and provide suggestive evidence for the action-linked elements of narrative structuring.

NARRATIVE AND CONFLICT

The paradigmatic and narrative orientations are complementary but fundamentally irreducible modes of thinking. In different contexts, one or the other mode will tend to dominate. Indeed, it is a general feature of goal-guided processing that the inference process typically involves multiple simultaneous goals (e.g., "task-oriented" goals and "social-relationship" goals). Inevitably, then, an individual's goals in a particular situation will be incompatible at times, and goal conflicts will develop. Many studies bypass this issue by explicating one specific goal of the particular experimental situation (e.g., impression formation, evaluation, recall).

The studies by Asch and Zukier (1984) and by Zukier (1985) also provide indications about the conditions in which the narrative orientation will be prevalent. Narrative structuring is oriented toward intensive and rich accounts that seek to encompass as many features of the particular case as possible. Narrative structuring thus trades generality for comprehensiveness and articulates the multiple facts in an overall pattern that derives its persuasiveness from its verisimilitude. This sequential, "horizontal" pattern is considerably more flexible than the "vertical" paradigmatic structure. It involves no prototypical attributes or other sharp criteria of "belongingness" and relevance to a particular argument. Thus, narrative structuring can more easily accommodate and make sense of diverse or inconsistent information. This flexibility makes narrative structuring particularly appropriate, and more likely to be invoked, for the processing of information or in situations involving conflicts, tensions, contradictions, or exceptions. This flexibility, however, also makes narrative structuring more resistant to disconfirming evidence, not because of any inherent rigidity, but because conflicting information often can be plausibly reinterpreted or accommodated within the original argument.

This pattern indeed emerges from the experimental evidence. In the Asch and Zukier (1984) study, subjects received both incongruent and harmonious pairs. Although the harmonious pairs (e.g., "warm and humorous," "intelligent and ambitious") were less problematic and required no reconciliation, they often produced accounts of lesser "quality" than the incongruent pairs. The accounts had a "rather forced quality," and "harmonious relations were generally less interesting, less focused, less articulated, more difficult to categorize—all of these perhaps a consequence of absence of tension between their components" (Asch & Zukier, 1984, p. 1237).

The study by Zukier (1985) further documented the narrative structuring of complexity. In a variant of the impression-formation paradigm, subjects were asked to describe individuals who were successively characterized by an increasing number of trait descriptions. For example, after subjects had described an individual who was "ambitious," they were told: "Now, if you also know the individual is 'hostile,'" and so on, up to five terms. The descriptions also included harmonious and incongruent terms, generating tension at the beginning and, as the number of terms and contradictions increased, producing both conflict and overload. For congruent and easy pairs, subjects' accounts were paradigmatic, treating the character as a type or member of a category. As the number of trait descriptors increased and the information became complex and diversified, subjects shifted to more narrative accounts. A similar trend already appears at early developmental levels (Wells & Higgins, 1985).

NARRATIVE AND PARADIGMATIC ORIENTATIONS IN SOCIAL COGNITION

In addition to the experimental evidence reviewed so far, current research in social cognition also provides some indirect support for the notion of two basic orientations, particularly for the operation of the narrative mode.

The Fundamental Attribution Error and the Agency Bias

One of the most pervasive and best documented phenomena in social inference is what has been termed the "fundamental attribution error" (Jones & Nisbett, 1971; Ross, 1977). Actors and observers often give "divergent" explanations for the causes of an individual's behavior. Observers tend to adopt a "dispositional" view, attributing another person's behavior to enduring personal characteristics and traits that manifested themselves in a particular situation. By contrast, the actor typically explains his or her own behavior in terms of situational contingencies and personal objectives. Jones and Nisbett (1971) suggested that this attributional divergence or bias stems from differences in the kinds of information to which actors and observers have access and which is salient to them. They also suggested that the divergence indicates that actors and observers differ fundamentally in the processing of available data. Their argument primarily pertains to the kinds of information being utilized, but it can be broadened to suggest that the fundamental attribution error illustrates the divergence in judgmental orientation between actors and observers. The observer tends to adopt a paradigmatic perspective and to take the actor's behavior as evidence that he or she is a certain "type" of person. By contrast, the actor adopts a narrative orientation and tells an elaborate story about the complex situational factors, about his or her intentions and purposes, that demanded this particular response. In other circumstances, he or she would have responded differently, and there would have been a different story.

   This account can be further elaborated. Indeed, there is a remarkable asymmetry between the power and pervasiveness of the fundamental attribution error and the reasons that are invoked to account for it: at the empirical level, various forms of salience, such as the actor perceived as figure or as ground; the greater linguistic availability of personality categories; and at the inferential level, representativeness effects, such as similarity links between the behavior and the actor. Despite this abundance of factors (or perhaps because of it), the phenomenon still appears underdetermined. The narrative framework suggests that the appeal of dispositional explanations of behavior may derive, in part, from the articulation of an agentive causality to which action-linked thinking has particular affinity.

From this perspective, the fundamental attribution error is but one manifestation of a very general predilection for agentive explanations or agency bias. This bias also underlies, for example, the young child's animism or attribution of agency consciousness or will to inanimate physical objects or events (Piaget, 1972). It is illustrated in the work of Michotte (1963) and in that of Heider and Simmel (1944), in which simple patterns of movement of geometrical figures compellingly lead observers to make causal attributions. For instance, a movement of two rectangles is constructed as follows: "It is as if *A*, in touching *B*, produced an electric current that set *B* going." In history, the agency bias characterizes teleological and conspiratorial conceptions of history and society (Popper, 1962), in which institutions are depicted as the result of conscious design, and in which social collectives (such as nations or social groups) are viewed as conspiring agents. As a consequence, whatever happens in society—including such things as unemployment or poverty—is considered to be the direct design of some powerful individuals or groups. More generally, "great men" theories of literature (cf Bloom, 1973; Eagleton, 1983), or of history, consistently related major accomplishments or events to the near-exclusive influence of a few outstanding figures. Carlyle (1942), for example, noted that, "Universal History, the history of what man has accomplished in this world, is at bottom the History of the Great Men who have worked here." These "great men" theories were most vehemently and elaborately denounced by L. Tolstoy, in the Epilogue of *War and Peace* (1869), as an invidious residue of ancient beliefs and superstitions.

Clinical Intervention

Clinical theory and treatment typically also are structured in the narrative or the paradigmatic mode. Freud (1893–95/1953) captured this tension in his "Studies on Hysteria": "It still strikes me myself as strange that the case histories I write should read like short stories and that, as one might say, they lack the serious stamp of science" (p. 160). Psychoanalytic theory, indeed, has the quality of narrative construction (Zukier, 1985), as is reflected in recent arguments (e.g., Schafer, 1976; Spence, 1982) that suggest that the therapeutic efficacy of psychoanalytic interpretations does not depend so much on the degree to which it captures the *historical* truth of the patient's experience and past as it depends on the *clinical* truth—on the interpretation's "rhetorical appeal" and believable narrative pattern for the patients. By contrast, the classic psychiatric diagnosis model is a paradigmatic model, in which knowledge is structured in terms of psychiatric syndromes, their associated clinical features, and decision rules for assigning a patient to a diagnostic category (see Cantor, 1982). Cognitive-behavior therapy and symptom reattribution strategies exemplify paradigmatic approaches to treatment. Clinical interpretation is also centered on agentive arguments, whether an "unconscious" agency is imputed to the patient despite the patient's denials or whether agency is denied by the patient through the use of self-handicapping strategies (Jones & Berglas, 1978) to protect his or her self-esteem and to justify anticipated failure.

The Dilution Effect and the Reduction of Stereotypes

Narrative structuring also affects the dynamics of stereotyping. Much research has documented the intractability of stereotypes and their resistance to change, through "expectancy-confirmation" cycles (Darley & Gross, 1983), perseverance effects (Ross, Lepper, & Hubbard, 1975), and other persistence processes (Hamilton, 1981; Rosenthal & Jacobson, 1968; Snyder, Tanke, & Berscheid, 1977). Attempts to reduce stereotyping have mostly involved exposing the prejudiced person to multiple disconfirmations or stereotype-inconsistent information (Rothbart, 1981; Weber & Crocker, 1983). Often, however, this disconfirmation fails because of the selective perception underlying the perseverance process.

A series of studies on the "dilution effect" (Nisbett, Zukier, & Lemley, 1981; Zukier, 1982; Zukier & Jennings, 1983) has explored an alternative way of stereotype change, by exposure to irrelevant information. These studies have indicated that irrelevant information may weaken or "dilute" the impact of a stereotype or of extreme predictions based on diagnostic information. For instance, in one study (Nisbett et al., 1981), subjects predicted that an engineer was likely to tolerate a considerable amount of electric shock in a psychological experiment. These predictions were significantly moderated when subjects also learned some irrelevant background information about the engineer (e.g., he reads science fiction for pleasure, his religious background is Catholic). The dilution effect also seems related to the effects of a narrative orientation. Stereotypes about other people are fairly simple categorical beliefs about the stereotyped individual or group. Nondiagnostic information, although it is not inconsistent with the stereotype, introduces greater complexity which is handled by a more differentiated narrative, producing more moderate judgments. Since narrative structuring seeks to encompass most aspects of a person and has more loosely articulated criteria of relevance, it forces a shift away from a highly selective paradigmatic conception. In stereotyping, extremity is of a piece and is expected to characterize most aspects of the stereotyped person. Irrelevant or nondiagnostic information provokes no "resistances" and is not filtered out. Hence, it adds a touch of ordinariness to the stereotyped individual, "normalizes" him or her ("can't believe it—a professor who plays pinball!"), and produces more conservative, "regressive" judgments. Research on intergroup perception suggests a similar link between the complexity of the representation of a group and the extremity of evaluative judgments about members of the group. Thus, out-group members, because less is known (or processed) about them, are often more harshly evaluated (Linville & Jones, 1980; Quattrone & Jones, 1980; Zukier, 1985).

Moral Judgment

As a final example, the moral development of the child, as described by Piaget (1932/1965; see also Kohlberg, 1963) also seems to involve a shift in judgmental orientation. According to Piaget (1932/1965), the young child is characterized by a "heteronomous" morality, which evaluates any act as "good" or "bad" depending on whether or not adults approve it. At this stage of "moral realism," the child considers all rules, even the rules of children's games such as marbles, as given in nature, immutable, and inherent in the universe, like physical laws. By contrast, in the "autonomous" stage, the child understands that rules are the products of negotiation and agreement between people and that they serve to promote justice or simple pragmatic utility. In terms of the orientation framework, moral development involves a shift from an entirely paradigmatic orientation (an act sanctioned or not by adults) to a mixed, paradigmatic–narrative orientation. The narrative orientation would be particularly central in considerations of more complex issues, such as qualifications to principles, moral excuses, and the like.

CONCLUDING REMARKS

Goal-Guided Processing

Most observers of human behavior have insisted that one essential, distinctive feature of social behaviors—and, one might add, of inferential acts—is their purposefulness and their orientation to the context. At the beginning of his major treatise, the sociologist M. Weber (1968) defined the object of his science—social action: "We shall speak of 'action' insofar as the acting individual attaches a subjective meaning to his behavior . . . action is 'social' insofar as it is . . . oriented in its course" (p. 4). This is echoed by the philosopher R. Nozick (1981), who remarks in the concluding pages of his *Philosophical Explanations* that "unlike physics and chemistry, the social sciences are studying subjects who have a view of what they are doing which affects their action." Hence, he emphasizes the "purposeful nature of human action within a network of intentions and goals" (p. 636). Social-psychological research to date also has acknowledged the importance but taken little account of a perspective that considers the deliberative and goal-oriented aspects of the inference process. Social inference is linked to the future and is influenced by the individual's future behavior at the same time that it affects that behavior. Experimental studies have clearly demonstrated that a person will structure and process information quite differently, depending on the future use he or she intends to make of it. Information integration clearly is preceded by future-oriented decision-making processes, which guide data selection and the choice of an appropriate strategy or mode from among the several that are available.

Local Knowledge

The processing goals are evoked, in part, by the immediate and larger context of the inferential act. Such context sensitivity is necessarily part of any discriminative and adaptive system of inference or of behavior. Studies of judgmental heuristics often have defined rationality in terms of invariance and consistency of responses to formally similar problems framed in different contexts. Thus, experimental results that have demonstrated people's "susceptibility to framing" have led to the conclusion that "the moral of these results is disturbing: invariance is normatively essential, intuitively compelling, and psychologically unfeasible" (Kahneman & Tversky, 1984, p. 344).

The research on goal-guided processing suggests, however, that the variability is an indication of flexibility and deliberate sensitivity, rather than helpless susceptibility. If one does take account of "subjects' view of what they are doing," an image emerges of inferential processes consisting of differentiated and diversified procedures and strategies. This diversity is rooted in both people and contexts. For example, the evidence indicates that in a wide variety of domains of skilled problem solving, experts differ from nonexperts not merely on quantitative measures but also in the qualitatively different representations and strategies they use (e.g., Adelson, 1984; Chase & Simon, 1973; Chi, Glaser, & Rees, 1981). It has also been argued that there exist two fundamental, irreducible modes of thinking. The multiplicity of strategic repertoires and contexts strongly suggests that rational invariance is discriminative and flexible, hence that its particular expression will be different across contexts.

Such is indeed the emerging focus of personality theory. The search for the elusive locus of personal consistency has recently turned to "context-bound consistencies" by "linking the behavior of interest to a circumscribed set of contexts, thus pursuing consistency on a more local and specific (rather than global) level" (Mischel, 1984, p. 359). Similarly, in anthropology, Geertz (1983) noted that "it [anthropology] has always had a keen sense of the dependence of what is seen upon where it is seen from and what it is seen with . . . [and] the shapes of knowledge are always ineluctably local" (p. 4). Philosophers have also argued for "complex" or context-bound conceptions of equality and spheres of justice, in contrast to universal, simple equality (Walzer, 1983). Social cognition research, too, must transcend the limitations of universality to discover the local complexities and the diversity of cognition.

Acknowledgment

I would like to thank the editors for their helpful comments on an earlier version of this chapter.

References

Abelson, R. P. (1981). Psychological status of the script concept. *American Psychologist, 36*, 715–729.

Abramson, L. Y., Seligman, M. E. P., & Teasdale, J. D. (1978). Learned helplessness in humans: Critique and reformulation. *Journal of Abnormal Psychology, 87*, 49–74.

Adelson, B. (1984). When novices surpass experts: The difficulty of a task may increase with expertise. *Journal of Experimental Psychology: Learning, Memory and Cognition, 10*, 483–495.

Ajzen, I. (1977). Intuitive theories of events and the effects of base rate information on prediction. *Journal of Personality and Social Psychology, 35*, 303–314.

Allport, G. W. (1961). *Pattern and growth in personality.* New York: Holt.

Anderson, R. C., & Pichert, J. W. (1978). Recall of previously unrecallable information following a shift in perspective. *Journal of Verbal Learning and Verbal Memory, 17*, 1–12.

Aristotle. (1973). Poetics. In R. McKeon (Ed.) *Introduction to Aristotle*. Chicago: University of Chicago Press.

Asch, S. E. (1946). Forming impressions of personality. *Journal of Abnormal Social Psychology, 41,* 258–290.

Asch, S. E., & Zukier, H. (1984). Thinking about persons. *Journal of Personality and Social Psychology, 46,* 1230–1240.

Bar-Hillel, M. (1980). The base rate fallacy in probability judgements. *Acta Psychologica, 44,* 211–233.

Barthes, R. (1975). Introduction to the structural analysis of narrative. *New Literary History, 6,* 237–272.

Bartlett, F. C. (1932). *Remembering: A study in experimental and social psychology.* Cambridge: Cambridge University Press.

Berger, J., Rosenholtz, S. J., & Zelditch, M., Jr. (1980). Status organizing processes. *Annual Review of Sociology, 6,* 479–508.

Bernstein, B. (1972). A sociolinguistic approach to socialization, with some reference to educability. In J. J. Gumperz & D. Hymes (Eds.), *Directions in sociolinguistics* (pp. 465–497). New York: Holt, Rinehart and Winston.

Bloom, H. (1973). *The anxiety of influence: A theory of poetry.* New York: Oxford Univeristy Press.

Borgida, E., & Brekke, N. (1981). The base rate fallacy in attribution and prediction. In J. H. Harvey, W. Ickes, & R. F. Kidd (Eds.), *New directions in attribution research* (pp. 63–96). Hillsdale, NJ: Erlbaum.

Brown, A. L. (1977). Development, schooling and the acquisition of knowledge about knowledge. In R. C. Anderson, R. J. Spiro, & W. E. Montague (Eds.), *Schooling and the acquisition of knowledge.* Hillsdale, NJ: Erlbaum.

Burke, K. (1969). *A grammar of motives.* Berkeley: University of California Press.

Cantor, N. (1982). Everyday versus normative models of clinical and social judgment. In G. Weary & H. L. Mirels (Eds.), *Integrations of clinical and social psychology* (pp. 27–47). New York: Oxford University Press.

Cantor, N., & Mischel, W. (1979). Prototypes in person perception. In L. Berkowitz (Ed.), *Advances in experimental social psychology* (Vol. 12, pp. 3–52). New York: Academic Press.

Carlyle, T. (1942). *Heroes and hero-worship.* New York: Greystone Press.

Cazden, C. B. (1970). The situation: A neglected source of social class differences in language use. *Journal of Social Issues, 26,* 35–60.

Chase, W. C., & Simon, H. A. (1973). Perception in chess. *Cognitive Psychology, 4,* 55–81.

Chi, M., Glaser, R., & Reese, E. (1981). Expertise in problem-solving. In *Advances in the psychology of human intelligence* (Vol. 1, pp. 7–75). Hillsdale, NJ: Erlbaum.

Cohen, C. E. (1981). Goals and schemata in person perception: Making sense from the stream of behavior. In N. Cantor & J. F. Kihlstrom (Eds.), *Personality, cognition, and social interaction* (pp. 45–68). Hillsdale, NJ: Erlbaum.

Cohen, C. E., & Ebbesen, E. B. (1979). Observational goals and schema activation: A theoretical framework for behavior perception. *Journal of Experimental Social Psychology, 15,* 305–39.

Cole, M., & Scribner, S. (1974). *Culture and thought.* New York: Wiley.

Darley, J. M., & Gross, P. H. (1983). A hypothesis confirming bias in labeling effects. *Journal of Personality and Social Psychology, 44,* 20–33.

Deaux, K. (1985). Sex and gender. *Annual Review of Psychology, 36,* 49–81.

Duncker, K. (1945). On problem solving. *Psychological Monographs, 58* (5, Whole No. 270).

Eagleton, T. (1983). *Literary theory.* Minneapolis: University of Minnesota Press.

Erber, R., & Fiske, S. T. (1984). Outcome dependency and attention to inconsistent information. *Journal of Personality and Social Psychology, 47,* 709–726.

Fiske, S. T., Kenny, D. A., & Taylor, S. E. (1982). Structural models for the mediation of salience effects on attribution. *Journal of Experimental Social Psychology, 18,* 105–127.

Fiske, S. T., & Taylor, S. E. (1984). *Social cognition.* Reading, MA: Addison-Wesley.

Freud, S. (1953). Studies on hysteria. In J. Strachey (Ed.), *The standard edition of the complete psychological works of Sigmund Freud* (Vol. 2). London: Hogarth Press. (Original work published 1893–95)

Garfinkel, H. (1967). *Studies in ethnomethodology*. Englewood Cliffs, NJ: Prentice-Hall.

Geertz, C. (1983). *Local knowledge: Further essays in interpretive anthropology*. New York: Basic Books.

Goffman, E. (1959). *The presentation of self in everyday life*. Garden City, NY: Doubleday.

Greimas, A. J. (1966). *Sémantique structurale*. Paris.

Grice, H. P. (1975). Logic and conversation. In P. Cole & J. L. Morgan (Eds.), *Syntax and semantics* (Vol. 3). New York: Academic Press.

Hamilton, D. L. (Ed.). (1981). *Cognitive processes in stereotyping and intergroup behavior*. Hillsdale, NJ: Erlbaum.

Hamilton, D. L., Katz, L. B., & Leirer, V. O. (1980a). Cognitive representation of personality impressions: Organizational processes in first impression formation. *Journal of Personality and Social Psychology, 39*, 1050–1063.

Hamilton, D. L., Katz, L. B., & Leirer, V. O. (1980b). Organizational processes in impression formation. In R. Hastie, T. Ostrom, E. Ebbesen, R. Wyer, D. Hamilton, & D. Carlston (Eds.), *Person memory: The cognitive basis of social perception* (pp. 121–153). Hillsdale, NJ: Erlbaum.

Hartwick, J. (1979). Memory for trait information: A signal detection analysis. *Journal of Experimental Social Psychology, 15f,* 533–552.

Hastie, R., Ostrom, T., Ebbesen, E., Wyer, R., Hamilton, D., & Carlston, D. (Eds.). (1980). *Person memory: The cognitive basis of social perception*. Hillsdale, NJ: Erlbaum.

Hayes, J. R., & Simon, H. A. (1977). Psychological differences among problem isomorphs. In N. J. Castellan, D. B. Pisoni, & G. R. Potts (Eds.), *Cognitive theory*. Hillsdale, NJ: Erlbaum.

Heider, F., & Simmel, M. (1944). An experimental study of apparent behavior. *American Journal of Psychology, 57*, 243–259.

Higgins, E. T. (1981). The "communication game": Implications for social cognition and persuasion. In E. T. Higgins, C. P. Herman, & M. P. Zanna (Eds.), *Social cognition: The Ontario Symposium* (Vol. 1, pp. 343–392). Hillsdale, NJ: Erlbaum.

Higgins, E. T., King, G. A., & Mavin, G. H. (1982). Individual construct accessibility and subjective impressions and recall. *Journal of Personalit y and Social Psychology, 43*, 35–47.

Higgins, E. T., Rholes, W. S., & Jones, C. R. (1977). Category accessibility and impression formation. *Journal of Experimental Social Psychology, 13*, 141–154.

Hoffman, C., Mischel, W., & Baer, J. S. (1984). Language and person cognition: Effects of communicative set on trait attribution. *Journal of Personality and Social Psychology, 46*, 1029–1043.

Hoffman, C., Mischel, W., & Mazze, K. (1981). The role of purpose in the organization of information about behavior: Trait-based versus goal-based categories in person cognition. *Journal of Personality and Social Psychology, 39*, 211–255.

Jeffery, K. M., & Mischel, W. (1979). Effects of purpose on organization and recall of information in person perception. *Journal of Personality, 47*, 397–419.

Johnson-Laird, P. N., & Wason, P. C. (Eds.). (1977). *Thinking*. Cambridge: Cambridge University Press.

Jones, E. E., & Berglas, S. (1978). Control of attributions about the self through self-handicapping strategies: The appeal of alcohol and the role of underachievement. *Personality and Social Psychology Bulletin, 4*, 200–206.

Jones, E. E., & Nisbett, R. E. (1971). The actor and the observer: Divergent perceptions of the causes of behavior. In E. E. Jones, D. E. Kanouse, H. H. Kelley, R. E. Nisbett, S. Valins, & B. Weiner (Eds.), *Attribution: Perceiving causes of behavior*. Morristown, NJ: General Learning Press.

Kahneman, D., Slovic, P., & Tversky, A. (Eds.). (1982). *Judgment under uncertainty: Heuristics and biases*. New York: Cambridge University Press.

Kahneman, D., & Tversky, A. (1973). On the psychology of prediction. *Psychologial Review, 80*, 237–251.

Kahneman, D., & Tversky, A. (1984). Choices, values and frames. *American Psychologist, 39*, 341–350.

Kohlberg, L. (1963). Development of children's orientations toward a moral order. *Vita Humana, 6*, 11–36.

Köhler, W. (1925). *The mentality of apes*. New York: Harcourt, Brace and World.

Lakoff, R. T. (1975). *Language and woman's place.* New York: Harper & Row.

Lakoff, R. T. (1979). Stylistic strategies within a grammar of style. In J. Orasanu, M. K. Slater, & L. L. Adler (Eds.), Lanugage, sex and gender: Does a difference make a difference? *Annals of the New York Academy of Science, 327*, 53–80.

Langer, E. J. (1975). The illusion of control. *Journal of Personality and Social Psychology, 32*, 311–328.

Linville, P. W., & Jones, E. E. (1980). Polarized appraisals of out-group members. *Journal of Personality and Social Psychology, 38*, 689–763.

Loftus, E. (1975). Leading questions and the eyewitness reprot. *Cognitive Psychology, 7*, 560–572.

Loftus, E., Miller, D., & Burns, H. (1978). Semantic integration of verbal information into a visual memory. *Journal of Experimental Psychology: Human Learning and Memory, 4*, 19–31.

Lyons, J. (1969). *Introduction to theoretical linguistics.* Cambridge: Cambridge University Press.

Maier, N. R. F. (1931). Reasoning in humans II: The solution of a problem and its appearance in consciousness. *Journal of Comparative Psychology, 12*, 181–194.

Mandler, J. M. (1979). Categorical and schematic organization in memory. In C. R. Puff (Ed.), *Memory organization and structure.* New York: Academic Press.

Mandler, J. M. (1983). Representation. In P. H. Mussen (Ed.), *Handbook of child psychology* (pp. 420–494). New York: Wiley.

Markus, H. (1977). Self-schemas and processing information about the self. *Journal of Personality and Social Psychology, 35*, 63–78.

McArthur, L. Z. (1981). What grabs you: The role of attention in impression formation and causal attribution. In E. T. Higgins, C. P. Herman, & M. P. Zanna (Eds.), *Social cognition: The Ontario Symposium* (Vol. 1, pp. 201–246). Hillsdale, NJ: Erlbaum.

Mead, G. H. (1934). *Mind, self and society.* Chicago: University of Chicago Press.

Michotte, A. (1963). *The perception of causality.* New York: Basic Books.

Minsky, M. (1975). A framework for representing knowledge. In P. H. Winston (Ed.), *The psychology of computer vision.* New York: McGraw-Hill.

Mischel, W. (1968). *Personality and assessment.* New York: Wiley.

Mischel, W. (1984). Convergences and challenges in the search for consistency. *American Psychologist, 39*, 351–364.

Nelson, K. (1977). Cognitive development and the acquisition of concepts. In R. C. Anderson, R. J. Spiro, & W. F. Montague (Eds.), *Schooling and the acquisition of knowledge* (pp. 215–239). Hillsdale, NJ: Erlbaum.

Nelson, K., & Gruendel, J. M. (1981). Generalized event representations: Basic building blocks of cognitive development. In M. E. Lamb & A. L. Brown (Eds.), *Advances in developmental psychology* (Vol. 1, pp. 131–158). Hillsdale, NJ: Erlbaum.

Newell, A., & Simon, H. A. (1972). *Human problem solving.* Englewood Cliffs, NJ: Prenctice-Hall.

Newston, D. (1976). The foundations of attribution: The unit of perception of ongoing behavior. In J. H. Harvey, W. J. Ickes, & R. F. Kidd (Eds.), *New directions in attribution research* (Vol. 1, pp. 223–247). Hillsdale, NJ: Erlbaum.

Nisbett, R. E., & Borgida, E. (1975). Attribution and the psychology of prediction. *Journal of Personality and Social Psychology, 32*, 932–943.

Nisbett, R. E., & Ross, L. (1980). *Human inference: Strategies and shortcomings of social judgment.* Englewood Cliffs, NJ: Prentice-Hall.

Nisbett, R. E., Zukier, H., & Lemley, R. (1981). The dilution effect: Nondiagnostic information weakens the effect of diagnostic information. *Cognitive Psychology, 13*, 248–277.

Nozick, R. (1981). *Philosophical explanations.* Cambridge, MA: Harvard University Press.

Orne, M. T. (1962). On the social psychology of the psychological experiment. *American Psychologist, 17*, 776–783.

Ostrom, T. S. (1984). The sovereignty of social cognition. In R. S. Wyer & T. K. Srull (Eds.), *Handbook of social cognition* (Vol. 1, pp. 3–38). Hillsdale, NJ: Erlbaum.

Ostrom, T., Lingle, J. Pryor, J., & Geva, N. (1980). Cognitive organization of person impressions. In R. Hastie, T. Ostrom, E. Ebbesen, R. Wyer, D. Hamilton, & D. Carlston (Eds.), *Person memory: The cognitive basis of social perception* (pp. 55–88). Hillsdale, NJ: Erlbaum.

Philips, S. V. (1980). Sex differences and language. *Annual Review of Anthropology, 9*, 523–544.

Piaget, J. (1932). *The moral judgment of the child.* London: Kegan Paul.

Piaget, J. (1965). *The moral judgement of the child.* New York: Free Press. (Original work published 1932)

Piaget, J. (1970). Piaget's theory. In P. H. Mussen (Ed.), *Carmichael's Manual of child psychology* (pp. 703–733). New York: Wiley.

Piaget, J. (1972). *The child's conception of the world.* Totowa, NJ: Littlefield, Adams.

Popper, K. (1962). *Conjectures and refutations: The growth of scientific knowledge.* New York: Basic Books.

Popper, K. (1968). *The logic of scientific discovery.* New York: Harper & Row.

Quattrone, G. A., & Jones, E. E. (1980). The perception of variability within in-groups and out-groups: Implications for the law of small numbers. *Journal of Personality and Social Psychology, 38,* 141–152.

Rawls, J. (1971). *A theory of justice.* Cambridge, MA: Harvard University Press.

Reber, A. S., Kassin, S. M., Lewis, S., & Cantor, G. (1980). On the relationship between implicit and explicit modes in the learning of a complex rule structure. *Journal of Experimental Psychology: Human Learning and Memory, 6,* 492–502.

Rosch, E. (1978). Principles of categorization. In E. Rosch & B. B. Lloyd (Eds.), *Cognition and categorization* (pp. 27–48). Hillsdale, NJ: Erlbaum.

Rosenthal, R. (1966). *Experimental effects on behavioral research.* New York: Appleton-Century-Crofts.

Rosenthal, R., & Jacobson, L. (1968). *Pygmalion in the classroom.* New York: Holt, Rinehart and Winston.

Ross, L. (1977). The intuitive psychologist and his shortcomings: Distortions in the attribution process. In L. Berkowitz (Ed.), *Advances in experimental social psychology* (Vol. 10, pp. 173–220). New York: Academic Press.

Rothbart, M. (1981). Memory processes and social beliefs. In P. Hamilton (Ed.), *Cognitive processes in stereotyping and intergroup behavior.* Hillsdale, NJ: Erlbaum.

Rumelhart, D. E. (1984). Schemata and the cognitive system. In R. S. Wyer, Jr., & T. K. Srull (Eds.), *Handbook of social cognition* (Vol. 1, pp 161–189). Hillsdale, NJ: Erlbaum.

Rumelhart, D. E., & Ortony, A. (1977). The representation of knowledge in memory. In R. C. Anderson, R. J. Spiro, & W. E. Montague (Eds.), *Schooling and the acquisition of knowledge* (pp. 99–135). Hillsdale, NJ: Erlbaum.

Schafer, R. (1976). *A new language for psychoanalysis.* New Haven: Yale University Press.

Schank, R. C., & Abelson, R. P. (1977). *Scripts, plans, goals and understanding.* Hillsdale, NJ: Erlbaum.

Scribner, S., & Cole, M. (1982). Literacy without schooling: Testing for intellectual effects. *Harvard Educational Review.*

Searle, J. R. (1979). *Expression and meaning.* Cambridge: Cambridge University Press.

Sheppard, B., & Vidmar, N. (1980). Adversary pretrial procedures and testimonial evidence: Effects of lawyer's role and Machiavellianism. *Journal of Personality and Social Psychology, 39,* 320–332.

Simon, H. A., & Hayes, J. R. (1976). The understanding process: Problem isomorphs. *Cognitive Psychology, 8,* 165–190.

Slovic, P., Fischhoff, B., & Lichtenstein, S. (1976). Cognitive processes and societal risk taking. In J. S. Carroll & J. W. Payne (Eds.), *Cognition and social behavior.* Hillsdale, NJ: Erlbaum.

Smith, E. E., & Medin, D. L. (1981). *Categories and concepts.* Cambridge, MA: Harvard University Press.

Snyder, M., Tanke, F. D., & Berscheid, E. (1977). Social perception and interpersonal behavior: On the self-fulfilling nature of social stereotypes. *Journal of Personality and Social Psychology, 35,* 656–666.

Spence, D. S. (1982). *Narrative truth and historical truth.* New York: Norton.

Spiro, R. J. (1977). Remembering information from text: The "state of schema" approach. In R. C. Anderson, R. J. Spiro, & W. E. Montague (Eds.), *Schooling and the acquisition of knowledge* (pp. 137–165). Hillsdale, NJ: Erlbaum.

Srull, T. K. (1981). Person memory: Some tests of associative storage and retrieval models. *Journal of Experimental Social Psychology, 7*, 440–463.

Srull, T. K. (1983). Organizational and retrieval processes in person memory: An examination of processing objectives, presentation format, and the possible role of self-generated retrieval cues. *Journal of Personality and Social Psychology, 44*, 1157–1170.

Srull, T. K., & Brand, J. F. (1983). Memory for information about persons: The effect of encoding operations on subsequent retrieval. *Journal of Verbal Learning and Verbal Behavior, 22*, 219–230.

Srull, T. K., & Wyer, R. S., Jr. (1979). The role of category accessibility in the interpretation of information about persons: Some determinants and implications. *Journal of Personality and Social Psychology, 37*, 1660–1672.

Srull, T. K., & Wyer, R. S., Jr. (1980). Category accessibility and social perception: Some implications for the study of person memory and interpersonal judgments. *Journal of Personality and Social Psychology, 38*, 841–856.

Taylor, S. E. (1982). The availability bias in social perception and interaction. In D. Kahneman, P. Slovic, & A. Tversky (Eds.), *Judgment under uncertainty: Heuristics and biases* (pp. 190–200). New York: Cambridge University Press.

Taylor, S. E., & Fiske, S. T. (1978). Salience, attention and attribution: Top of the head phenomena. In L. Berkowitz (Ed.), *Advances in experimental social psychology* (Vol. 11, pp. 249–288). New York: Academic Press.

Thorndike, E. L. (1911). *Animal intelligence: Experimental studies.* New York: Macmillan.

Todorov, T. (1977). *The poetics of prose.* Ithaca: Cornell University Press.

Tolstoy, L. N. (1869/1984). *War and peace.* Harmondsworth: Penguin.

Tversky, A., & Kahneman, D. (1974). Judgment under uncertainty: Heuristics and biases. *Science, 185*, 1124–1131.

Tversky, A., & Kahneman, D. (1980). Causal schemata in judgments under uncertainty. In M. Fishbein (Ed.), *Progress in social psychology* (pp. 117–128). Hillsdale, NJ: Erlbaum.

Tversky, A., & Kahneman, D. (1981). The framing of decisions and the rationality of choice. *Science, 211*, 453–458.

Tversky, A., & Kahneman, D. (1983). Extensional versus intuitive reasoning: The conjunction fallacy in probability judgment. *Psychological Review, 90*, 293–315.

Walzer, M. (1983). *Spheres of justice: A defense of pluralism and equality.* New York: Basic Books.

Weber, M. (1968). *Economy and society.* New York: Bedminster Press.

Weber, R., & Crocker, J. (1983). Cognitive processes in the revision of stereotypic beliefs. *Journal of Personality and Social Psychology, 45*, 961–977.

Wells, R. S., & Higgins, E. T. (1985). *Children's integration of social cues in interpreting emotions: Developmental similarities and differences.* Unpublished manuscript, New York University.

Wittgenstein, L. (1958). *Philosophical investigations.* New York: Macmillan.

Wyer, R. S., & Gordon, S. G. (1982). The recall of information about persons and groups. *Journal of Experimental Social Psychology, 18*, 128–169.

Wyer, R. S., Jr., & Srull, T. K. (1981). Category accessibility: Some theoretical and empirical issues concerning the processing of social stimulus information. In E. T. Higgins, C. P. Herman, & M. P. Zanna (Eds.), *Social cognition: The Ontario Symposium* (Vol. 1, pp. 161–197). Hillsdale, NJ: Erlbaum.

Wyer, R. S., & Srull, T. S. (Eds.). (1984). *Handbook of social cognition.* Hillsdale, NJ: Erlbaum.

Wyer, R. S., Jr., Srull, T. K., Gordon, S. E., & Hartwick, J. (1982). Effects of processing objectives on the recall of prose material. *Journal of Personality and Social Psychology, 43*, 674–688.

Zajonc, R. B. (1960). The process of cognitive tuning and communication. *Journal of Abnormal and Social Psychology, 61*, 159–167.

Zajonc, R. B. (1980). Feeling and thinking: Preferences need no inferences. *American Psychologist, 35*, 151–175.

Zukier, H. (1982). The dilution effect: The role of the correlation and the dispersion of predictor variables in the use of nondiagnostic information. *Journal of Personality and Social Psychology, 49*, 1163–1174.

Zukier, H. (1983). Situational determinants of behavior. *Social Research, 49*, 1163–1172.

Zukier, H. (1985). Stereotyping and minority group identity. In: C. F. Graumann and S. Moscovici (Eds) *Conceptions of conspiracy*. London: Cambridge University Press.

Zukier, H. (1985). Freud and development: The developmental dimensions of psychoanalytic theory. *Social Research, 52*, 211–252.

Zukier, H. (1985). *The narrative mode in impression formation*. Unpublished manuscript, New School for Social Research.

Zukier, H., & Hagen, J. (1978). The development of selective attention under distracting conditions. *Child Development, 49*, 870–873.

Zukier, H., & Jennings, D. L. (1983). Nondiagnosticity and typicality effects in prediction, *Social Cognition, 2*, 187–198.

Zukier, H., & Pepitone, A. (1984). Social roles and strategies in prediction: Some determinants of the use of base rate information. *Journal of Personality and Social Psychology, 47*, 349–360.

CHAPTER 17

The Role of Chronic and Temporary Goals in Social Information Processing

THOMAS K. SRULL
ROBERT S. WYER, JR.
University of Illinois at Urbana-Champaign

Few would doubt that human behavior is goal-directed. Through the years, behavioral scientists have told us, in one form or another, that people have needs, purposes, wants, desires, ergs, predispositions, motives, and so on. The human being, in other words, is an *intentional system*. It is this assumption—that human behavior is purposive, intentional, and goal-directed—that largely separates the orientation of the psychologist from that of the physical or biologial scientist (Staddon, 1983). It is important to note that the intentions and goals that govern overt behavior also have an influence on the cognitive system that mediates the generation of this behavior. This chapter reviews the empirical evidence that bears on the nature of this influence. Specifically, it is concerned with how cognitive processes are influenced by both the immediate and the long-term goals of the processor.

Although it is now obvious that cognition and motivation are two sides of the same coin, attempts to analyze their relationship have a short history. The most extensive writings on the topic were actually done by the psychoanalytic theorists around the turn of the century. Freud and others constructed entire theoretical systems that focused not only on the goal-directed nature of behavior but also on the delicate interplay between cognitive and motivational factors (see Fenichel, 1945; Freud, 1899/1956, 1900/1965a, 1901/1965b, 1915/1967, 1917/1977; Henle, 1984).

Unfortunately, this work was largely conducted within a clinical setting. Although the ideas were perceived to be important by many research psychologists, they were not subjected to experimental examination until the 1940s and 1950s. At that time, Jerome Bruner and his colleagues began to report an impressive set of experiments (Bruner, 1948, 1951, 1957; Bruner & Goodman, 1947; Bruner & Klein, 1960; Bruner & Postman, 1948, 1949) that continue to have an important influence on the field today. Their importance lies in the fact that the focus of mental activity was taken out of the physical apparatus and placed squarely in the psychological nature of the situation and the way in which it is constructed by the perceiver. Rather than relying on clinical interviews, Bruner and his associates used experimentation to demonstrate that many of the "mechanical" acts of perception are, in fact, strongly influenced by psychological processes related to prior expectancies, values, attitudes, psychodynamic defenses, and so on. The phenomena discovered by Bruner and his colleagues, as well as their theoretical orientation, soon became known as the "New Look" in perception. It is worth noting that Bruner and his colleagues concentrated on cognitive processes that were attentional and perceptual in nature. However, more recent developments in cognitive psychology have made us realize that the influence of goals on cognition extends far beyond that of pure perceptual processes.

One of the most important concepts to come out of recent work is the distinction between declarative and procedural knowledge. This distinction has been useful in constructing theories of such diverse phenomena as semantic memory, person memory, knowledge representation, prose comprehension, artificial intelligence, and human problem solving. Declarative knowledge refers to specific facts we know about the world, or *knowing that* something is true. Procedural knowledge, on the other hand, refers to *knowing how* to do one thing or another. Procedural knowledge is a set of mental routines that, when activated, allow us to generate an appropriate response. For example, most people *know that* George Washington was the first president of the United States (declarative knowledge) but only *know how* to determine who was the 22nd president (procedural knowledge). Similarly, most people have stored away in memory procedures or mental routines for how to ride a bicycle, or take someone's temperature, or fix a flat tire, or tie a shoelace.

Many of the most important goals of social interaction are also part of our procedural knowledge base. Although cognitive psychologists traditionally have studied relatively simple mental routines, such as knowing how to add up digits, people also *know how* to form impressions, to go about changing opinions, to make causal attributions, and to do many other things that are of interest to those working in the area of social cognition. (For a further discussion of some of these issues, see Kihlstrom & Cantor, 1984.)

The mental routines involved in attaining many important goals of social interaction can exert an influence on: (1) attentional and perceptual processes, (2) encoding and organizational processes, (3) storage and retrieval processes, (4) higher order integration and judgment processes, (5) response selection processes, and (6) affective and emotional reactions. We will discuss each of these stages in this chapter. In organizing the discussion around such stages, we are by no means suggesting that each stage is distinct and independent of the rest. On the contrary, they are highly interactive. Nonetheless, a complete understanding of social interaction requires a thorough analysis of each stage. As we will attempt to show, research efforts related to each of these stages has contributed substantially, but in unique ways, to our general understanding of the relationship between the motivational and cognitive systems.

EFFECTS OF GOALS ON ATTENTION AND PERCEPTION

It was once thought that information from the physical environment was picked up in more or less veridical form. The human who was seeing or hearing, or generally "processing information," was little different from a computer reading ones and zeros. Thus, when psychologists studied perception, they tended to examine either characteristics of the physical stimulus (hue, saturation, brightness, pitch, and so on) or characteristics of the biological apparatus (rods, cones, cochleae, and so on). Intrapsychic factors were thought to be irrelevant and thus were ignored almost entirely.

The psychological world is now seen quite differently. Intrapsychic factors are currently recognized as a critical component not only of social perception but also of object perception. We are now reminded periodically that "perception, by most accounts, involves an interaction between the environmental stimuli that are currently present *and the individual's readiness to perceive some over others*" (Bargh, 1984, p. 15, emphasis added).

Motivation and Category Accessibility

One of the most forceful contributions of work emanating from the New Look in perception is the general concept of *category accessibility*. Bruner (1957) originally suggested that the relative accessibility of a category is a function of "the expectancies of the person with regard to the likelihood of events to be encountered in the environment, and the search requirements imposed on the organism by his needs and ongoing enterprises" (p. 133). We now know that the determinants of category accessibility can be either chronic states of the person, as in the case of traits, motives, or various characteristics of one's cognitive structure (cf. Higgins, King, & Mavin, 1982; Klinger, 1971), or transitory factors associated with temporary need states or immediately prior cognitive activity (for reviews, see Bargh, 1984; Higgins & King, 1981; Wyer & Srull, 1981).

When a category becomes relatively more accessible in memory, it has a sensitizing effect on both attentional and perceptual processes. For example, it may direct attention toward inputs that can be accommodated in terms of the category. Similarly, category-related stimuli will tend to capture a disproportional amount of the attentional resources available to the person (Bargh, 1984).

At the perceptual level, increasing a category's accessibility has three independent effects, each of which was originally postulated by Bruner (1957). First, it decreases the threshold of the physical stimulus (in terms of duration intensity, clarity, and so on) necessary for perceptual recognition to occur (see Bargh, 1982, Bargh & Pietromonaco, 1982). Second, it leads a wider range of stimulus inputs to be perceived as belonging to the category in question (see Johnston & Chesney, 1974). Third, other categories that provide an equally good match to the stimulus are more likely to be masked (see Higgins, Rholes, & Jones, 1977; Srull & Wyer, 1979, 1980). As we will see, all of these effects are at least partly determined by the goals and processing objectives of the individual.

The Effects of Current Concerns on Perception and Attention

In an insightful and provocative analysis of motivational phenomena, Klinger (1975) has introduced the concept of "current concerns." The concept is defined in terms of the interaction of the person's needs, values, with so on, and incentives in the environment. Although some of these current concerns are short-lived, others can be quite long-lasting. Current concerns can guide both thought and behavior. A person who suddenly loses his or her job will begin to think about virtually everything in terms of its implications for his or her financial status. Such a current concern could last for years if the person's employment status did not change. A more transitory current concern is exemplified by a new Ph.D. recipient on a job visit who tends to think of everything (a dropped fork at dinner, a limp handshake at the airport, etc.) in terms of how it reflects on his or her chances of being offered the position. Klinger (1971) has shown that current concerns not only preoccupy thought content but also tend to enter dream material. In general, they appear to involve material that breaks into consciousness forcefully, frequently, and in response to minimal cues from the environment.

Both anecdotal and experimental evidence suggests that people can become exceptionally sensitized to goal-related stimuli that are relevant to their current concerns. For example, sleeping mothers develop a specific sensitivity to only the cries of their newborn infants (Klinger, 1975). Similarly, subjects who are instructed before going to sleep to clench their fists whenever they hear a randomly selected name while sleeping have been found to do this fairly frequently, although they virtually never clench their fists in response to similar control names (Oswald, Taylor, & Treisman, 1960).

In a well-known experiment, Corteen and Wood (1972) demonstrated that subjects show physiological reactions to words that were previously paired with electric shock, even when the words cannot be consciously recognized. In an equally provocative but less well known experiment, Luria and Vinogradova (1959) told subjects that they would be read a long list of words. They were told to respond as soon as they heard a particular word (e.g., *doktor*). Subjects showed physiological orienting reactions (an increase in finger and scalp blood volume) not only when they heard the critical word but also when they were presented with synonyms (e.g., *vrach*, which also means "doctor"). In contrast, there were no unusual physiological reactions to phonologically similar words (e.g., *diktor*, which means "announcer"). As Klinger (1975) has noted: "The results thus provide evidence that subjects who are set to achieve a goal are sensitized to various goal-related stimuli" (p. 5). As we have seen, this is true at the perceptual level, the attentional level, and the physiological level.

Personal Values and Category Accessibility

Values are more generalized orientations and therefore are relevant to a wider range of activities than current concerns. Moreover, their role in goal-directed behavior is more passive and indirect. Nevertheless, there is evidence that values affect perceptual processes in much the same way. Although the early work in this area typically used ambiguous stimuli in investigating these effects, more recent evidence indicates that value-related categories, like categories activated experimentally, influence the perception and recognition of unambiguous stimuli as well. Although such effects are invariably larger when ambiguous stimuli are used, the fact that any differences at all are found with unambiguous stimuli indicates just how important the perceiver's contribution to the perceptual act can be (cf. Bruner, 1983).

The effects of values on the perception of ambiguous stimuli were first demonstrated by Bruner (1951). The stimuli were pictures that could be interpreted in two ways, each of which required the use of concepts related to a different one of the six Spranger values: religious, economic, theoretical, social, political, and aesthetic. For example, one of the pictures could be seen as either a man bending over at work or a man bending over to pray. Subjects with different value orientations (as measured by the Allport-Vernon Study of Values test) were shown the pictures tachistoscopically and were asked to describe what they saw. The results were quite powerful. For example, subjects with strong religious values tended to see the picture as a man praying, those with strong values related to the work ethic tended to see the picture as depicting a man working, and those who were not characterized by either of these values showed no consensus in how they perceived the picture (indicating that it was truly ambiguous). Comparable results were found with each of the other pictures.

Another study (reported in Bruner, 1983) showed conceptually similar effects on perceptions of unambiguous stimuli. In this experiment, six words representing each of six key values assessed by the Allport-Vernon scale (36 words in all) were presented to subjects, and the time required to recognize each word was determined. The stimuli were clearly printed and were placed on a contrasting background to make them as easily readable as possible. On average, it took about 75 ms of exposure time for subjects to recognize words associated with their strongest values, about 85–90 ms to recognize words associated with moderate values, and about 100 ms to recognize words associated with their weakest values.

There is also evidence that values will often automatically direct attention to environmental stimuli that are relevant to them. As a consequence, they may interfere with the processing of auxiliary information. It is interesting that this is true even if the auxiliary information is necessary to obtain a specific but more temporary goal. Consider an experiment reported by Erdelyi and Appelbaum (1973) in which members of a Jewish organization were shown stimulus arrays for 200 ms and then were asked to recall the stimuli portrayed. The stimulus objects that subjects were told to consider were all neutral in emotional tone and were presented in a circular array. In the center of each array, however, was an ostensibly task-irrelevant object, the nature of which varied over conditions. Specifically, it was either a swastika, a Star of David, or a window. Relative to the window (control) condition, presenting the Star of David interfered with performance substantially, and the swastika interfered with performance to a still greater degree.

The Erdelyi and Appelbaum (1973) study is interesting for several reasons. First, it demonstrates how emotionally charged material can *automatically* capture the attentional resources one has available, so that less concurrent cognitive activity is possible. In other words, even though the specific goal of the subject was to ignore the center item and concentrate on the stimuli along the perimeter of the circle, this was not possible because of the automatic funneling of attention to the center item. This was true for both positively and negatively valenced stimuli. More generally, the experiment demonstrates how long-term personal values can often interfere with explicit, consciously directed processing objectives.

The Influence of Chronic Personality Dispositions on Perceptual Processes

The study of general value orientations has decreased dramatically over the years, and much more attention is now being paid to the influence of stable personality traits on the processing of information. Following the widely cited paper by Markus (1977), researchers have hypothesized that individuals who are "schematic" with respect to some trait dimension will process information that is interpretable in terms of this dimension more quickly and will remember it better later on. Support has generally been found for both of these hypotheses (Bargh, 1982; Markus, 1977; Markus, Crane, Bernstein, & Siladi, 1982). The most analytic conceptualizations of this work suggest that such chronic states of category accessibility also have motivational consequences. For example, people who are "schematic" with respect to a given trait are more likely than aschematics to resist information that is inconsistent with their own self-image (Markus, 1977). In addition, these chronic states seem to gain their advantage through some type of automatic attentional process (cf. Bargh & Pietromonaco, 1982; Geller & Shaver, 1976). It seems reasonable to suppose that for people who are schematic with respect to a given trait, this trait functions very much like a personal value or, for that matter, a current concern. Therefore, it influences information processing in much the same fashion (see also Higgins, King, & Mavin, 1982).

ENCODING AND ORGANIZATIONAL PROCESSES

The effects of general goals and processing objectives on the encoding and organization of information in memory have been the subject of much research in recent years. Several qualitatively different types of phenomena have been identified, and a good understanding of them in terms of the underlying mechanisms that are responsible has been obtained. These mechanisms have generally been evaluated on the basis of recall data collected under different instructional conditions. For example, subjects are given information about one or more persons under instructions that establish different processing objectives (e.g., to remember the information, to form an impression of the persons described, to make a particular judgment, etc). Later, they are asked to recall the information they have received. It is often possible to draw conclusions concerning the manner in which the information is encoded and organized in memory by (1) varying the type and amount of information presented and (2) measuring the type, amount, and order in which the information is subsequently recalled.

Goals as Determinants of the Amount of Information Recalled

Much of the interest in processing objectives in social cognition research can be traced to what has now become a classic and very influential experiment in person memory by Hamilton and Katz (1975; Hamilton, Katz, & Lierer, 1980a). In this study, subjects were asked to read a set of behavior statements that exemplified four separate conceptual categories (interpersonal, intellectual, sports, and religious activities). In some conditions, the subjects were given a "memory set"; that is, they were explicitly told to remember as much of the information as possible. Other subjects were given a general "impression set"; that is, they were told to form a general impression of what a person who manifested the behaviors would be like, and they were given no indication that they should try to remember them. After receiving the information, all subjects were given a free-recall test.

The results of this experiment, in the context of knowledge existing at the time it was conducted, were very counterintuitive. Specifically, even though impression-set subjects had not expected to be given a memory test at the time they received the information, they nevertheless recalled much more of it than memory-set subjects did. This general finding of greater recall under impression-set than under memory-set conditions has proved to be an extremely robust one, and it has been found with both recall tasks (Hamilton, Katz, & Leirer, 1980a, 1980b; Srull, 1981, 1983; Srull, Lichtenstein, & Rothbart, 1985; Wyer, Bodenhausen, & Srull, 1984; Wyer & Gordon, 1982) and recognition tasks (Hartwick, 1979; Srull, 1981; Wyer et al., 1984). Thus, the effects not only provide a dramatic demonstration of the influence of processing objectives on recall but also raise the more fundamental question of what it is about the cognitive apparatus that produces the effect.

The Effects of Goals on Memory for Information About Single Persons

The first clue to understanding the way in which processing objectives affect encoding and organizational processes was found in a subsequent series of studies by Hamilton and his colleagues (Hamilton *et al.*, 1980a, 1980b). These studies showed that when subjects have read a list of a person's behaviors under a memory-set condition, the order in which they recall them tends to resemble the order in which the behaviors were presented. In contrast, when they read the behaviors with an impression set, the ones they recall tend to be clustered in terms of the categories (religious, social, etc.) the behaviors exemplify. In other words, subjects with the goal of remembering the information appear to use some type of rote rehearsal strategy in which the individual items are linked to one another in a manner resembling the temporal order in which they are received (for further evidence of this, see Srull, 1983). In contrast, subjects with an impression-formation objective seem to impose their own organization on the information by linking each item to other items in the same conceptual class, and they do this regardless of where in the temporal string the items occur. This greater organization of the information apparently leads to better recall (cf. Cohen & Ebbesen, 1979).

Is such an explanation of the different effects obtained under memory-set and impression-set conditions adequate? In one sense it is, but in another sense it is not. It is true that the processing objectives of the subject have a dramatic effect on encoding and organizational processes. This is seen in the raw amount of information recalled, in the order in which it is recalled, and in several other findings (see Hamilton *et al.*, 1980b). On the other hand, it is not entirely clear what "more organization" means or why it should produce any of the effects described. In other words, using the term "more organization" to explain any of these effects is, at least in some sense, simply offering a descriptive label for basic phenomena that still need to be explained.

A series of subsequent studies helps provide this explanation. In one study (Wyer & Gordon, 1982) subjects were first presented trait adjective descriptions of a person, followed by behaviors that varied in their consistency with these traits. This was done under either memory-set or impression-set conditions, similar to those constructed by Hamilton. Later, subjects recalled the information they had read. Two findings are particularly relevant to the issues of concern here. First, although subjects with an impression objective recalled more behaviors than did subjects with a memory objective, they did *not* recall more trait adjectives. Second, subjects with an impression set recalled more behaviors that exemplified a given trait if an adjective describing the trait was also recalled than if such an adjective was not recalled. In other words, the recall of a trait adjective appeared to facilitate the recall of behaviors that exemplified the trait. In contrast, memory-set subjects' recall of behaviors did *not* depend on their recall of the trait adjectives. In combination, these findings suggest that subjects with an impression set encoded the target's behaviors in terms of trait concepts activated by the adjectives used to describe the person. This established trait–behavior associations that led the trait concepts to serve as retrieval cues for those behaviors that were encoded in terms of them. In contrast, subjects with a memory objective did not perform these higher level encodings of the behavior. Therefore, their recall of the trait concepts, although just as good as that of impression-set subjects, did not facilitate their memory for the behavioral information. Subsequent research (Gordon, 1981; see also Wyer & Gordon, 1984) suggests that unlike memory-set subjects, those with an impression set also tend to *spontaneously* encode a target's behavior in terms of various personality trait concepts.

Organization of Information Around an Evaluative Theme

In addition to encoding behaviors in terms of the traits they exemplify, people with the goal of forming an impression of someone (unlike those with a memory objective) may attempt to extract an evaluative theme from the information they receive that will allow them to decide if the person is likable or dislikable. Once this theme is identified, it may also (like trait concepts) provide a basis for organizing subsequent information about the person. Evidence that the evaluative implications of information play a role in organization independently of its descriptive features was obtained by Hartwick (1979). He found that the introduction of impression objectives increased errors in responding to recognition items that were evaluatively consistent with previous information about a target person but did not increase errors in response to descriptively consistent lures.

The objective of forming a consistent evaluative impression of a person may have another important effect on subjects' organization of information. Specifically, it may stimulate subjects to try to reconcile behaviors of a person that are evaluatively inconsistent with the impression they have formed. One consequence of this cognitive activity is that inconsistent behaviors are thought about in relation to other behaviors of the person, leading to the establishment of associations among them. Because this cognitive activity occurs only when inconsistent behaviors are presented, more associative pathways are formed between those behaviors than between consistent ones, and thus the inconsistent behaviors enjoy a recall advantage later on. This has been demonstrated empirically in several studies (Hastie, 1980; Srull, 1981; Srull et al., 1985; Wyer et al., 1984; Wyer & Gordon, 1982). The fact that the critical variable accounting for these effects is evaluative inconsistency, not descriptive inconsistency, has also been established (Wyer & Gordon, 1982). A more formal theoretical statement of the organization of behaviors under an impression-formation condition is provided elsewhere (Srull, 1981; Srull et al., 1985; Wyer et al., 1984; Wyer & Gordon, 1984) and will not be reiterated here. However, the research cited provides a further indication of the role of processing objectives on the organization of social information.

The Organization of Information Around Several Different Persons

The aforecited series of studies establishes the fact that impression-formation objectives, unlike memory objectives, lead subjects to encode and organize information about a person in terms of higher order trait concepts and that the trait–behavior linkages resulting from this encoding facilitate the recall of information later on. Conceptually similar processes may also occur when subjects receive information about several *different* persons or objects.

A series of studies by Srull (1983; Srull & Brand, 1983) obtained evidence of this and, in addition, provided further insight into the effects of goals on encoding and organizational phenomena. In one experiment (Srull, 1983), subjects were presented with 128 behavior statements, with instructions either to remember them or to form impressions of the persons described by them. The number of persons described, and the number of behaviors per person, were systematically varied. Specifically, subjects received (1) 8 behaviors manifested by each of 16 different target persons, (2) 16 behaviors by each of 8 targets, (3) 32 behaviors by each of 4 targets, or (4) 64 behaviors by each of 2 targets. In some cases, this information was "blocked" by target person, so that all items pertaining to the same target were in adjacent positions. In other cases, however, the 128 statements were presented in a random order.

The results explicate several different ways in which the ultimate organization of the information depends on the initial processing. For example, if subjects simply organized the behaviors in memory in the order they were presented, the amount of clustering by target would be low in the random-presentation condition and high in the blocked condition. This was in fact true in the case of memory-set subjects. However, impression-set subjects showed a high degree of clustering around persons, regardless of how the information was presented.

In conceptualizing the implications of these findings, it is useful to note that one variable under consideration (processing objectives) is internal to the organism, whereas the other (information presentation order) is external. That is, the random versus blocked presentation manipulation creates environmental constraints on how the information is acquired, whereas the impression set versus memory set manipulation presumably determines how the subject attempts to impose a meaningful organization on what is acquired. Viewed in this way, the results indicate that under impression-set conditions, the effect of the internally imposed organization of the information completely overrode the effects of external constraints. This provides a vivid demonstration of how important the perceiver's contribution to the mental representation of information can be.

Another way of addressing the organizational question is to examine exactly which items are recalled. This can be done by breaking down the total number of behaviors recalled (R_B) into two components, one pertaining to the number of persons about whom at least one behavior was recalled (R_P) and the other pertaining to the average number of behaviors recalled per person ($R_{B/P}$). (Thus, $R_B = R_P R_{B/P}$.) Using this type of analysis, Srull (1983) found that when a blocked-presentation format was used, impression-set subjects did not recall any more target persons than memory-set subjects did; that is, R_P was similar in both conditions. However, impression-set subjects *did* recall a much larger number of behaviors per person ($R_{B/P}$) than memory-set subjects did. In other words, the impression set did not lead subjects to access any more target persons. However, once a particular target was accessed, many more individual behaviors could be retrieved.

In the random-presentation format condition of Srull's (1983) experiment, subjects with an impression set accessed more individual targets as well as more behaviors per target person. In accounting for these effects, Srull postulated that both intraindividual and interindividual organizational processes are induced when subjects must form separate mental representations of multiple targets. Both of these processes can be conceptualized in terms of interitem linkages that ultimately provide additional retrieval routes—to the higher order person categories in the case of interindividual organization and to the behaviors within a person category in the case of intraindividual organization (see Srull, 1983, for details).

The possibility that processing objectives can affect both intracategory and intercategory organization was examined further by Srull and Brand (1983). In a series of experiments, they demonstrated that both types of organization are largely a function of the encoding operations used at the time of information acquisition. These, in turn, are primarily determined by the processing objectives activated at the time.

Subjects in one study were given either 0, 10, or 20 behaviors about one target (Sam) and either 0, 10, or 20 behaviors about another target (Peter). All of the behaviors were presented in a random order. Some subjects (memory set) were told to remember the information as well as possible. Other subjects were given an anticipated interaction set. Specifically, they were told to form an impression of what the individuals would be like, because they would later meet them (or one of them) and would be asked to try to change their opinion on a controversial social issue. (Subjects who received information about two separate targets were not told in advance which target they would meet.) After receiving the information, subjects in both conditions were asked to recall as much of the information as possible.

In general, the probability of recalling any given item from a category decreases as the total number of items in the category increases (Raaijmakers & Shiffrin, 1980, 1981; Roberts, 1972; Rundus, 1971). Because of this "set-size" effect, Srull and Brand (1983) were able to diagnose the organizational structure of the mental representation that subjects formed of the information in each instructional condition.

Figure 17.1 presents the probability of recalling any given behavior about Sam or Peter as a function of the number of items presented about both the same target and the other (filler) target. In the memory-set condition (shown in the left-hand panel), there were both within-person and between-person set size effects. Within-person set-size effects can be seen by looking down any of the three vertical columns of points. These effects are present for both targets and at each set size condition associated with the filler target. Between-person set-size effects can be seen by looking at any three points connected by a single line. Again, these effects are present for both targets and for each set-size condition. Within-person

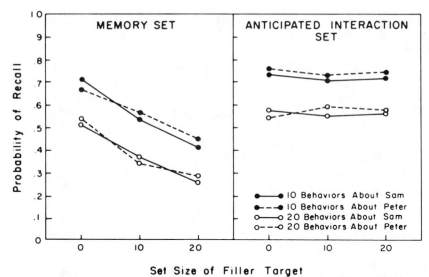

Set Size of Filler Target

FIGURE 17.1   Probability of recalling behavior statements about two people as a function of various set-size combinations.

set-size effects also occurred in the anticipated-interaction condition (shown in the right-hand panel). However, there was no evidence whatsoever of between-person set-size effects in this condition.

In sum, memory-set subjects appear to have treated the behaviors presented as belonging to a single category (list), and thus the likelihood of their recalling a given behavior in the category decreased with its size (i.e., with the total number of behaviors presented about each target person). In contrast, subjects with an impression set formed separate categorical representations of each target person. Consequently, the recall of a given behavior was a function only of the number of behaviors presented in the same-person category but was not a function of the number presented in the other category.

A second experiment by Srull and Brand (1983) indicated that the organizational effects just described are a direct function of the subject's processing objectives and are not due to simply organizing the information into different semantic categories. In this study, subjects learned various numbers of nouns and adjectives pertaining to a single target person. The nouns were said to be personal possessions of the target (e.g., a baseball autographed by Mickey Mantle, an antique player piano, etc.), and the adjectives were said to be personality traits that have been used to describe the persons's behavior. Note that both of these are relevant classes of information if one's objective is to form a coherent impression of the person. However, mentally compartmentalizing the information into these different categories is inconsistent with the overall objective of forming a coherent impression based on all the information. The results of the experiment were consistent with this reasoning. That is, both between-category and within-category set-size effects were obtained in both the impression-set and memory-set conditions.

It might be noted in passing that results such as these bear on a current controversy in the person memory literature. It has generally been assumed that people organize their social world around individual people (i.e., the number of individuals present and who those people are). However, Pryor and Ostrom (1981) recently presented evidence that this is only true when those people are already highly familiar individuals. Considered in the context of the studies we have described, however, it is important to acknowledge the role of the initial processing objectives. Specifically, Pryor and Ostrom considered only situations in which subjects received an initial memory set. As we have seen, however, such a situation serves to minimize the strength of person category cues relative to more general context cues, and little evidence of categorical organization is likely to be found in such situations. However, other processing objectives, such as attempting to form a coherent impression of each of the individual target persons, will greatly enhance the strength of person category cues. Thus, one would expect, and indeed it has been found (Srull, 1983; Srull & Brand, 1983), that there is an important degree of organization around persons under these conditions.

Summary

The research reviewed in this section demonstrates the important role that one's goals and intentions play in the encoding and organization of information and therefore on how well it is recalled. In this review, we have restricted our consideration to a particular content domain—namely, the organization of information about persons. However, it is clear that analogous effects are likely to occur in other domains as well. The particular encoding and organization that occurs may, of course, depend in part on the type of information presented and also on its modality (visual, verbal, etc.). However, the fundamental influence of processing goals on the memorial representation of the information, and therefore its likely influence on judgments of the persons and objects to which it is relevant, seems incontrovertible.[1]

STORAGE AND RETRIEVAL PROCESSES

Few studies have been specifically designed to examine the way in which processing objectives mediate the storage and retrieval of information. Part of this is because of the way in which both storage and retrieval processes are inexorably intertwined with encoding and organizational processes. For example, Srull's (1983) finding that when given information about a group of individuals, impression-set subjects recall more behaviors per person than memory-set subjects is, in some sense, due to a retrieval advantage. However, this is only true because the retrieval process is operating on a more organized and interrelated mental structure.

In general, one simply cannot talk about the nature of mental organization without (implicitly or explicitly) postulating a specific type of retrieval process. Similarly, it is impossible to discuss retrieval without making detailed assumptions concerning the underlying mental representation.

Each of these issues comes to the foreground when considering the mediating role of goals or processing objectives. For example, in a series of studies (Hastie, 1980, 1984; Srull, 1981; Srull *et al*, 1985; Wyer *et al.*, 1984; Wyer & Gordon, 1982), it has been found (1) that items that are incongruent with a general impression are better recalled than congruent items, (2) that this difference is much more pronounced under impression-set conditions than under memory-set conditions, and (3) that regardless of the initial orienting task, the difference between the proportion of congruent and incongruent items recalled remains fairly constant across time, indicating that there are no differential rates of forgetting. Although, in the preceding section, we attributed the recall advantage of incongruent items to encoding mechanisms, could it not just as easily be due to some type of retrieval difference?

The answer is that both encoding differences *and* retrieval differences are probably involved. In the first regard, we know that the initial encoding operations have a dramatic effect on what is recalled (Srull, 1981; Wyer & Gordon, 1982). We also know that the recall advantage typically observed disappears if only limited capacity to encode the information is available to the subject at the time of input (Srull, 1981; Srull *et al.*, 1985) or if certain types of causal attributions for the behaviors are not made (Crocker, Hannah, & Weber, 1983; Hastie, 1984). On the other hand, there is also evidence that the retrieval process changes following the recall of a congruent or incongruent item in terms of both the speed with which it proceeds and the subsequent likelihood of accessing different types of items (Srull, 1981; Srull *et al.*, 1985). We also know that different results are often found as a function of whether free-recall or recognition tasks are employed (Srull, 1981; Wyer *et al.*, 1984) and that different processing objectives often result in different types of retrieval cueing (Wyer & Gordon, 1982). Both of these latter results directly implicate some type of retrieval mechanism. However, the important point is that the initial processing objectives of the subject can determine characteristics of the retrieval process *because of* the way in which the information is initially encoded and organized.

Despite the inherent difficulties of separating encoding and retrieval processes, several bodies of literature pertain directly to the effects of processing objectives on retrieval. It is to these that we now turn.

The Effects of Post-Information-Acquisition Objectives on Retrieval

One way to examine the effects of processing objectives on storage and retrieval processes *per se* is to create a situation in which the objectives are not established until *after* the relevant information has been received. The effects that occur under these conditions are of obvious practical as well as theoretical importance. That is, people are often required to use information to attain a goal that was not apparent at the time the information was first received. Because of their importance, it is surprising that so little is known about these effects. However, the available evidence suggests that whereas post-information-processing goals will affect which aspects of previously acquired information a person will use to make a judgment or decision, they have little effect on one's ability to recall information that was received before these objectives were introduced.

Snyder and Cantor (1979), for example, reported a study in which, after receiving information about a target person, subjects were asked to evaluate the target's suitability for a job that required either introverted or extraverted personality characteristics. Before making this judgment, they were asked to write down everything they could remember that they considered relevant to the judgment they were asked to make. Subjects reported more information that confirmed the hypothesis they were asked to "test" (e.g., that the person was suited for an extraverted job) than information that disconfirmed this hypothesis. Moreover, their subsequent judgments reflected the implications of this bias. Although these results are provocative, the failure to obtain an indication of exactly how much information subjects were capable of recalling prevents one from drawing firm conclusions about the effects of post-information-processing objectives on retrieval processes *per se.* For example, subjects may have been able to recall all aspects of the information presented equally well but may have reported only those aspects that they believed to be relevant to the judgment they were asked to make.

It is nevertheless interesting that the information subjects chose as relevant confirmed the hypothesis they were asked to test. Presumably, subjects with the objective of deciding if a person is suitable for a job activate a set of concepts about attributes of a prototypical person who is successful in the position and then search for specific information that exemplifies these concepts. Thus, the processes involved here may be similar to what occurs when goal-relevant concepts are activated before information is received. The only difference is that the information being processed in this case is retrieved from long-term memory, rather than entering the system from an external source.

In a second study, R. C. Anderson and Pichert (1978) investigated both prestorage and poststorage processing objectives on recall. Subjects read a story describing a house and its surroundings. Before doing so, however, they were told to consider the information from the perspective of either someone who was considering buying the house or someone who was considering burglarizing it. They were then asked to reconsider the information from a different perspective and were told that this might improve their memory. These subjects not only recalled a greater proportion of the information relevant to the second perspective than they had at first, but they also recalled a lower proportion of information relevant to their original perspective than they had initially. Although small in magnitude, these effects appear to parallel the effects of a prestorage processing objective.

Unfortunately, implications of the Anderson and Pichert (1978) study for the processing of social information are difficult to determine for two reasons. First, in situations outside of the laboratory (and perhaps the classroom), people very seldom receive information with the explicit objective of trying to recall it later on. Second, the procedure of the study may have produced a response bias similar to that in the Snyder and Cantor (1979) study. Specifically, explicitly telling subjects to use the perspectives they were given as devices for recalling the information may have led them to infer that the investigator was more interested in their recall of perspective-relevant features than their recall of irrelevant ones, and this may have created a bias in their reports.

Wyer, Srull, Gordon, and Hartwick (1982) conducted a similar study that avoided these problems. They used exactly the same materials as Anderson and Pichert. However, in this case, subjects read the passage with either a very general objective (to form an impression of the situation described) or with one of two more specific goals in mind (to consider the information with the objective of either a burglar or a home buyer). Then, after reading the passage, they reconsidered the information with either the same objective, a different specific objective, or a more general goal in mind. Finally, they were unexpectedly asked to recall the information they had read. Wyer *et al.* found that considering the information with a specific objective in mind at the time it was presented increased the recall of goal-relevant material and decreased the recall of goal-irrelevant material. However, reconsidering the information with a specific goal in mind *after* it had been received did not have these effects. Instead, subjects' recall of *both* goal-relevant and goal-irrelevant material was slightly but significantly increased by reconsidering the information for a specific purpose, regardless of whether this purpose was the same as or different from the one they had had when initially reading it. In other words, there was no evidence that considering information from a new point of view after it had been presented increased the recall of information that was uniquely relevant to this point of view. Nor did it decrease the recall of material that was not relevant to this viewpoint.

The results of Wyer *et al.* (1982) suggest that the conditions under which information is initially encoded place important constraints on how it can be retrieved. Research by Baker (1978) provides direct support for this principle. Subjects read short episodes in either a normal chronological order or a "flashback" sequence (e.g., "Dan did X. Before that, he had done Y."). She explicitly told subjects that they would be tested on their recall of the chronological order of the events in each episode, rather than of the order in which they were described. After reading the episodes, subjects were presented pairs of events from each episode and were asked to indicate as quickly as possible whether their order as presented corresponded to the chronological order of their occurrence. Decisions were faster when the events had originally appeared in chronological order than when they had been presented in flashback order. A second experiment indicated that when the items had been presented in a flashback sequence, it was easier to verify the order in which they were presented than to verify their chronological order. Taken together, these results indicate that event information is not stored in a reorganized form that reflects the temporal order of the events described. However, it is tagged in such a way that this order can be computed if necessary.

The Influence of Pre- and Post-Information-Acquisition Goals on Control Processes

The studies by R. C. Anderson and Pichert (1978) and by Wyer *et al.* (1982) exemplify abundant evidence that a processing objective may lead features that are irrelevant to it to be "filtered out," thus making them unlikely to be retrieved later on. However, even goal-relevant information may not be fully encoded into long-term memory at the time it is received, and therefore it also may not be recalled completely in all of its original detail. The question then arises as to whether people generally have conscious control over the processes that govern the storage of relevant information. In addition, what precisely are the cognitive mechanisms involved in exercising such control?

The nature of these processes is postulated in a more general theoretical model of social information processing developed by Wyer and Srull (1980, 1984). In this model, processing objectives are assumed to be critical in activating a variety of "control processes" or routines for processing information that are under direct volitional control. However, the model also takes into account a number of structural constraints on the cognitive system. That is, there are limits to what the person can do, and these are limits that generally cannot be overcome by any conscious strategy. An implication of this is that immediate goals or processing objectives can have a dramatic impact on cognitive processing, so long as one is working within the limits of the system. However, once these limits are reached, short-term processing objectives will have little or no influence.

The Wyer and Srull (1980, 1984) model is complex and detailed, and an exposition of it is far beyond the scope of this chapter. However, there is one aspect of the model in which goals have a dramatic mediating influence on various types of cognitive processing. One of the central theoretical constructs introduced by Wyer and Srull is that of a "work space." The construct is somewhat analogous to that of working memory, but its role in the model is guided by four fundamental assumptions that, in combination, render it unique.

The first assumption is that the "work space" is a temporary repository devoted primarily to the current information activities of the person. During the period that a person engages in information processing (during virtually the entire waking state), the "work space" may contain several different types of information units. In a typical laboratory experiment, these would include such things as (1) the original stimulus information (e.g., a set of behavior statements or a stream of interpersonal activity displayed on a videotape), (2) the processing objectives or "goals" of the person, (3) previously existing concepts or knowledge structures that are used to interpret or organize the new information, and (4) any higher order encoded representations of the stimulus information (e.g., the formation of person "schemata").

The second assumption is that the "work space" has some limited capacity. Consequently, as more and more information begins to be processed and/or more complex information processing objectives are adopted, the "work space" will need to be cleared. This means that during the course of a normal day, an almost constant influx of new information and clearing of old information to long-term memory will take place.

Third, although the person is often "forced" to clear the "work space" in order to pursue additional processing objectives, a variety of control processes (see Atkinson & Shiffrin, 1968) are also involved. That is, the person is assumed to have some volitional control over when the "work space" is cleared; specific theoretical predictions have been made concerning the factors that govern this (Srull & Wyer, 1983; Wyer & Srull, 1980, 1984).

The final assumption is that no exact "copy" of the information presented is transmitted to long-term memory; rather, only a more integrated representation of the new stimulus information with what is already known is transferred to long-term memory. Any specific details that are not integrated into the encoded representation will no longer be available for recall or for use in making judgments once the "work space" is cleared. As Wyer and Srull (1980) noted, the encoded representation may, under various conditions, be characterized by additions to, transformations of, or deletions from the original information. Consequently, the implications of the material retrieved and used as a basis for judgments may depend substantially on whether the "work space" has or has not been cleared at the time recall and/or judgments take place.

A series of experiments by Srull and Wyer (1983) specifically tested the implications of this formulation and explored, more generally, the role of control processes in both memory and judgment. These experiments produced several important findings. First, subjects have considerable control over their own encoding operations. In one study, for example (Srull & Wyer, 1983, Exp. 1), subjects were told before they received information about a target person that there would be either a long (45 min) or a short (5 min) delay before they would be asked to recall it. The former subjects were subsequently able to recall more of the information than the latter, and this was true regardless of whether the actual delay interval was long or short. Subjects who anticipated a long delay presumably encoded the information more elaborately at the time it was received, and this facilitated the recall of it later on. Thus, subjects have strong control over the encoding mechanisms they use at the time they receive information.

More relevant to the present considerations, however, is evidence that subjects also have a large degree of control over when the "work space" is cleared. In general, the probability of recalling any given item is much greater if the item is still in the "work space" than if it is not. Srull and Wyer (1983) were able to use this principle to determine how temporary goal states will influence recall. For example, consider a situation in which subjects are given information about a target person and only *afterward* are told to expect either a 5-min or a 45-min delay before recalling it. Moreover, suppose that—independently of the expected delay—the actual delay interval is also manipulated. Because these variables are introduced after the information has been encoded, their effects are presumably due primarily to whether the information is retained in the "work space." Theoretically, the "work space" is more likely to be cleared automatically when the actual delay is long than when it is short. This is because of the processing demands that are placed on the system during the interim. However, it should also be cleared *volitionally* when subjects *anticipate* a long delay and wish to prepare for the next, intervening task. In contrast, when both the anticipated and the actual delay are short, subjects may attempt to retain information in the "work space" and, moreover, are capable of doing so. Consequently, their recall of the information should be greater in this condition than when either the actual *or* the anticipated delay is long. This is exactly what was found.

In another experiment, Srull and Wyer (1983) held the actual length of the delay before recall constant and varied the nature of the intervening cognitive activity. They found that a difficult syllogism task performed for 5 min led to a much lower level of recall than a relatively easy proofreading task performed for 5 min. This suggests that *when* the "work space" is cleared is a function of the complexity of the intervening cognitive activity as well as the length of the actual temporal delay.

An important feature of the Wyer and Srull (1980, 1984) model is that it has direct implications for both memory and judgment. For example, both Higgins *et al.* (1977) and Srull and Wyer (1980) found that the effects of priming manipulations on judgments of a person described by stimulus information increase over the time interval between the presentation (and encoding) of the stimulus information and the reporting of judgments based on it. Conceptually similar effects have been obtained in quite different experimental paradigms by Carlston (1980) and by Moore, Sherrod, Liu, and Underwood (1979). According to the Wyer and Srull model, the explanation of this increase is straightforward. When only a short time interval has elapsed between presentation of stimulus information and judgments, both this information and the encoded representation of it are available in the "work space," and judgments may be based on a random sample of the implications of each. Therefore, because features of the information that are not captured by the encoded representation of it are likely to have relatively neutral implications for judgments, the judgments made before the "work space" is cleared may be only moderately extreme. However, after a period of time has elapsed, the original information presented is cleared from the "work space," and only the encoded representation of it, retrieved from "permanent storage," is available. Therefore, judgments must be based on this representation alone and consequently are more polarized.

If this is the case, however, other experimental manipulations that theoretically affect the likelihood that the "work space" is cleared should also influence the extremity of judgments. Srull and Wyer (1983) demonstrated that this is true in a series of studies paralleling the recall experiments described earlier. In one study, both the actual and the anticipated delay between presenting stimulus information about a person and reporting judgments of the person were manipulated. Judgments were more extreme when either the anticipated or the actual delay was long than when they were short. A second study showed that the extremity of judgments based on a set of stimulus information increased with the complexity of the task performed in the interval between presenting this information and reporting the judgments. In other words, judgments in both studies were more polarized in precisely those conditions in which recall was poorest.

These experiments thus provide consistent support for the model's assumptions concerning the role of the "work space" in information processing, as reflected in both the recall of information and the judgments. More generally, they indicate that both the actual and the anticipated processing objectives can influence the retention of information and the judgments based on it.

Goals as a Moderator of the Relationship Between Recall and Judgment

There have been numerous demonstrations of independent variables that have similar effects on both the recall of information and the judgments to which this information is relevant. However, when the relationship between recall and judgment has been examined at the level of the individual subject, it has historically been found to be extremely weak. In the attitude domain, for example, a long line of studies have found only weak relationships between memory for information in a persuasive communication and attitude formation and attitude change (Greenwald, 1968; Insko, 1964; N. E. Miller & Campbell, 1959; Watts & McGuire, 1964). In fact, it was precisely this type of "problem" that led to the "cognitive response" approach to the study of persuasion that is so dominant today. (See Greenwald [1968] for an early demonstration of the importance of examining cognitive responses and Petty, Ostrom, & Brock [1981] for a recent review of the existing literature.)

The same type of weak relationship between memory and judgment has also been found in other domains. For example, in a classic impression-formation study, N. H. Anderson and Hubert (1963) provided subjects with trait adjectives. Their essential finding was that there are strong primacy effects in impression formation (cf. Asch, 1946) but reasonably large *recency* effects in recall. They concluded from this that the impression judgments and memory for the trait adjectives are independently stored and accessed in memory. Dreben, Fiske, and Hastie (1979) reported a conceptually similar study in which they replicated these effects. These investigators also found that temporal delays had a large effect on recall but produced very modest changes in impression ratings. They also concluded from this that there is some independence between episodic memory and evaluative impression (see also Riskey, 1979). A similar lack of correspondence between memory and attributional judgments has been reported by S. T. Fiske and her colleagues (Fiske, 1981, 1982; Fiske, Kenny, & Taylor, 1982; Fiske, Taylor, Etcoff, & Laufer, 1979; Taylor & Fiske, 1975, 1978, 1981).

Although this is an extremely complicated issue, there have been recent indications in the literature that a person's goals at the time of information acquisition are an important mediating variable in determining the relationship between memory and judgment. One of the most important conceptual distinctions in contemporary cognitive psychology is that between "retrieval" and "computational" processes (see Lachman, Lachman, & Butterfield, 1979; Shoben, 1980). Suppose that a person is asked, "Is Gore Vidal an intelligent person?" A retrieval model would suggest that, at least for most people, the answer to such a question has already been determined and stored in memory. Thus, one simply needs to "retrieve" it from memory to answer such a question.

In contrast, a computational model would suggest, at least for most of us, that the answer to such a question has *not* already been determined. Rather, to answer such a question, we would need to retrieve whatever information we can about Gore Vidal, compare it to our referents for "intelligent person," and then "compute" or figure out an answer on the spot. Of course, if we were asked the same question again, we would not need to recompute an answer but could simply retrieve our previous judgment.

Lichtenstein and Srull (1985) have recently proposed a model that suggests that the subject's information-processing objectives or "goals" are a critical mediating variable that determines the nature of the relationship between recall and judgment. The reason for this, according to the model, is that prior processing objectives often determine whether such judgments have been prestored or need to be computed on the spot.

In particular, the theory postulates that when a person acquires information about a target with the (implicit or explicit) objective of making an evaluation of that person, the global evaluative judgment will be made at the time of information acquisition and will be stored in memory separately and independently from the specific behavioral information that is learned. If the person is later asked to make a specific judgment, the evaluation already will have been "computed" and will simply be accessed at the time. Thus, under these conditions, there is no reason to expect any strong relationship between the specific facts that are recalled at any given time and the global evaluation that is made. One can see that this is a very straightforward retrieval model, in which the previous judgment and the specific episodic facts on which it is based are independently stored and accessed. It is a process that is consistent with the conceptualizations outlined by N. H. Anderson and Hubert (1963) and by Dreben *et al.* (1979).

At least one alternative process might also occur. For example, when a person acquires information about a target with no specific objective in mind or with a very general one, such as to comprehend the information being presented, a global evaluation of the target may not be made at the time of information acquisition. If the person is later asked to make a specific evaluation of the target, he or she will be forced to retrieve the previously acquired information, or some subset of it, and use it as a basis for his or her evaluative judgment of the target. In other words, a judgment will have to be computed on the spot. Therefore, under these conditions, a strong relationship between the judgment and the evaluative implications of the information that is recalled would be expected.

As noted by Hastie, Park, and Weber (1984), these latter conditions have rarely been investigated. In the few studies that have included such conditions, however, a strong correspondence between memory and judgment has indeed been found. For example, Sherman, Zehner, Johnson, and Hirt (1983) provided subjects with current information about two historically rival football teams. In one case, the goal was to remember the information as well as possible. In another case, the goal was to form an impression of the potential outcome of an upcoming game between the two teams. Sherman *et al.* found a very weak relationship between memory for the information and subjects' judgments of the outcome when they had formed their impression at the time of information acquisition. However, this relationship was quite strong among those subjects who had initially been given a memory set. The authors suggest that the "availability" of information in memory will affect judgments only when those judgments are initially unanticipated. A similar finding has been reported by Reyes, Thompson, and Bower (1980).

Lichtenstein and Srull (1985) have also reported several experiments based on the foregoing theoretical analysis. In one, subjects received information about an unfamiliar product (e.g., a computer-based instrument that was said to translate English prose into five foreign languages while maintaining correct syntactic structure). The information was presented in the form of a complex "informational ad" that resembled a *Consumer Reports* article. Subjects either formed impressions of the product "on-line" or did not form an integrated impression of the product until afterward. These processing objectives had no effect on either the number of product attributes recalled or the extremity of product evaluations. However, they substantially influenced the degree to which these variables were related. In fact, in each of 12 independent comparisons, the correlation between recall and judgment was higher in the impression-after condition than in the on-line condition. As in the study by Sherman *et al.* (1983), this same effect was found regardless of whether subjects were tested after a short or a long delay and regardless of whether recall was assessed before or after the judgments were made.

A second experiment indicated that interpolated judgments have the same effects as interpolated retrieval attempts for impression-after subjects but *not* for on-line subjects. Lichtenstein and Srull (1985) interpreted this as direct evidence that making a global evaluation requires the retreival of specific episodic facts—or in this case, product attributes—for impression-after subjects. However, on-line subjects, who theoretically have already made their evaluations, can simply access them independently of the episodic facts on which they are based. This experiment shows quite clearly the mediating role that processing objectives can play, and the data appear to be uninterpretable in terms of any (reasonably simple) competing model of the judgment process.

It is worth noting that these studies have still left many questions unanswered (cf. Higgins, McCann, & Fondacaro, 1982). For example, none of them have investigated the evaluation of individuals on the basis of specific behavioral acts, the types of order effects that we know are often important in impression formation, and the conditions under which people will spontaneously form a global evaluation of a target in the absence of explicit instructions to do so. Nevertheless, taken as a whole, they have gone a long way toward explaining when and why a weak or strong correspondence between recall and judgment is likely to be obtained. Regardless of the theoretical interpretation that one might want to place on these studies, it is clear that the initial goal of the subject should occupy a central place in any explanatory scheme.

EFFECTS OF PROCESSING GOALS ON HIGHER ORDER JUDGMENT PROCESSES

Most psychologists, and particularly those with a cognitive orientation, like to break complex chunks of behavior into their more elementary components. A tremendous amount of research has therefore been directed toward relatively simple perceptual processes, the principles of mental organization, and even the types of search and retrieval processes discussed in the preceding section. As a result, we know a good deal more about each of these processes than we did even 20 years ago.

However, a person does not passively perceive and remember isolated bits of information; rather, the goal-directed nature of behavior will result in an active search for relationships and interdependencies in what is seen. The person will attempt to integrate isolated bits into more meaningful units. In the process, the person will make judgments and categorizations that require consideration of many individual pieces of information in conjunction with one another. Despite the importance of these processes, however, they have never received a substantial amount of research effort, and they still are not well understood.[2]

Let us consider a concrete example of the type of process that is involved here. It is quite common for us to meet and interact with a person for a few minutes or a few hours, perhaps observe the person's behavior with others, and finally come away with some categorization, such as "That is an honest person." It turns out, however, that this type of categorization process is enormously important for virtually all subsequent cognitive activity. This is partly because, in general, there is very little opportunity to discover that our initial categorization is inappropriate. As Bruner (1957) stated: "There is either a delay or an absence of opportunity for additional cue checking. Moreover, there is also the likelihood, since cues themselves are so equivocal in such a case, that available equivocal signs will be distorted in such a manner as to confirm the first impression" (p. 148). It is quite possible that this difficulty in checking the validity of one's categorizations, which is somewhat unique to the domain of *social* perception, is primarily responsible for the fact that inappropriate category systems (based on first impressions, group stereotypes, etc.) are so resistant to change.

General Ego-Defensive and Ego-Sensitive Mechanisms

It is clear, even at first glance, that higher order judgment processes entail many degrees of freedom. Different pieces of information can be entered into the judgment, and they can be weighted differentially. Moreover, there may be motivational reasons that predispose one to keep the judgment consistent with separate judgments of the same person or (as in the case of balance) with similar judgments of other people.

Bruner (1957) once suggested: "Perhaps the most noticeable perceptual unreadiness comes from interference with good probability learning by wishes and fears" (p. 128). What he meant was that such judgments have a strong hedonic tone associated with them. In fact, there is experimental evidence that both the learning process and the judgment process are influenced by the hedonic implications of the situation. For example, probability learning proceeds much more quickly when what is learned has positive rather than negative implications for the subject (Irwin, 1953; Marks, 1951).

These hedonic influences also affect higher order judgments. Consider, for example, a very simple study by Weinstein (1980). He had subjects rate a series of events in terms of (1) how likely they were to occur to the subject himself or herself and (2) how likely they were to occur to the average student at the subject's university. The events were either positive or negative. In nearly every case, subjects reported positive events as more likely to occur to them than to other students but reported negative events as less likely to occur to them than to others. Some of the judgments, such as whether one's home doubles in value within 5 years, might be "rationalized" by the conviction that one is particularly perceptive or hardworking. However, others in the list (e.g., being sterile) are clearly due to the luck of the draw. Thus, it is difficult to imagine that the pattern of judgments obtained in this study is the result of any purely rational judgment process.

Results such as these are by no means unique. In a classic study by Hastorf and Cantril (1954), for example, Princeton and Dartmouth students viewed films of an important, and particularly rough, Princeton–Dartmouth football game. Princeton students thought that most of the rough play and most of the legitimate infractions were by Dartmouth players. They also thought that when the referees made a mistake, it tended to involve a call going against Princeton. As one might expect, however, the judgments of Dartmouth students showed exactly the opposite pattern.

The role of hedonic relevance in higher order judgments can also have an important protective aspect associated with it. For example, clinically depressed subjects often see themselves in more negative terms than nondepressed controls. However, at least one study has found that depressives are more accurate than nondepressed control subjects in judging how others see them. This appears to be due primarily to the fact that most normals, unlike depressives, assume that others see them in a more positive light than is actually the case (Lewinsohn, Mischel,

Chaplin, & Barton, 1980). In other words, normals' judgments are systematically distorted so that a positive self-image can be maintained despite the feedback they receive from others.

Goals as a Guide to Comprehension and Causal Reasoning

Not only are people goal-directed organisms, but their cognitive apparatus gives them the flexibility that is needed to pursue whatever goals are activated at any given time. In other words, information can be processed in many different ways, and the strategy one selects is crucial in determining what the perceiver will "bring to" the situation.

Consider a very simple experiment reported by Smith, Adams, and Schorr (1978). They gave subjects a small set of sentences, each of which described the behavior of a single target. In some cases, the sentences were unrelated. In others, they could all be related to the same underlying theme (e.g., "Jim broke the bottle," "Jim christened the ship").

Smith *et al.* (1978) instructed some subjects to commit the sentences to memory. In a later speeded-recognition task, they found a typical "fan effect." In other words, the more sentences that were presented about the same target, the longer it took subjects to recognize any one of them.

In another condition, Smith *et al.* (1978) instructed subjects at the time they learned the sentences to consider whether they could be related to one another. In this case, there was no fan effect whatsoever. Thus, by using a different strategy, these subjects were able to eliminate the interfering effects of learning new information about the same target.

Such studies raise the question of what type of strategy people normally use in processing new information. Although the selection of a strategy obviously depends on the goals of the subject, the predominant goal in any social situation is simple comprehension. For the most part, people are not exposed to isolated actions. Rather, they tend to encounter complicated action sequences that contain inherent relationships and interdependencies. To comprehend the nature of such events, it is important to understand the relationships between the individual elements. Sometimes, people are told these relationships explicitly. More often, however, the relationships must be inferred through some type of causal reasoning process.

One of the major tasks in comprehending complex action sequences is to infer the goals of the major participants. The goals of the participants provide a context for making causal inferences about the relationships of the individual acts. Consider a thought experiment based on materials developed by Stephen Read (1983). One group of subjects is given a story that contains five sentences:

1. John gave Mary the money.
2. They walked out the door of the apartment.

3. Later, John picked Mary up on the corner near the drugstore.
4. They drove back to the apartment.
5. They made love.

Another group of subjects is given a story that contains the same five sentences but in a different order:

1. John picked Mary up on the corner near the drugstore.
2. They drove back to the apartment.
3. John gave Mary the money.
4. They made love.
5. They walked out the door of the apartment.

It seems reasonable to conclude that subjects will comprehend these two stories quite differently. The meaning attached to them will be different; the internal referents for some of the words (e.g., "love") will be different; the inferences that subjects make will be different; and the intrusions and substitutions they make in recalling them will be different. Yet the only difference is in the order in which the sentences are presented.

In comprehending complex action sequences, people most often try to identify the goals of the character by drawing some causal connection between actions in the sequence. When this is done successfully, memory for the information is enhanced (Black & Bern, 1981). When events that are inconsistent with the presumed goal structure are encountered, they are read more slowly and tend to be reviewed to determine whether some "hidden meaning" was missed. When two or more of these inconsistent acts are encountered, subjects also attempt to draw some causal connection between them (Mio & Black, 1979). In general, comprehension involves an active search for the relationships and interdependencies that exist among the individual elements.

There are also situations in which causal connections cannot be drawn among the individual actions unless each of them is also linked to some more general goal or intention of the actor. For example, Brewer and his colleagues (Brewer & Dupree, 1983; Lichtenstein & Brewer, 1980) have presented subjects with a series of behavioral actions on videotape. In one short episode, for example, a person took a card from her pocket, looked at it for a moment, replaced it in her pocket, picked up a telephone, dialed the telephone, and then talked. Brewer and his colleagues have consistently found that events (e.g., the person's taking the card from her pocket) are better recalled when the actor's superordinate goal (e.g., trying to figure out a recipe) is known than when it is not.

Abbott and Black (1982) have obtained conceptually similar results with written materials. They presented subjects with "triples" in a story format. The three sentences were linked either by the presence of several common objects or by obvious goal-related inferences. Abbott and Black found that the goal-related triples tended to be recalled in an all-or-none fashion. That is, if one of the elements was recalled, there was an extremely high probability that all three would be recalled. In contrast, when the triples were linked by the presence of the same object, retrieval of any one of them was independent of the rest.

Causal inferences about a character's goals and intentions not only allow us to see relationships between two or more behaviors; they also help us understand the person's thoughts and feelings. This is particularly true when two or more goals conflict with one another. Moreover, the nature of these conflicts can be either intrapersonal or interpersonal. For example, consider a person who religiously adheres to a very strict diet and yet ends up eating a large piece of cake at a birthday party. It is likely that a knowledgeable observer will be able to infer quite a bit about the person's internal state at the time. This is because two salient goals (celebrating the friend's birthday and adhering to the diet) are diametrically opposed to one another, and one who is aware of the two goals will immediately recognize the conflict. Similar conflicts often occur on the interpersonal level, such as when two people bid against one another at an auction, compete with one another for the same job, or wish to spend the evening together and yet prefer to see a different movie.

It is important to realize that these types of inferences and causal reasoning processes not only can occur but *do* occur when the overriding objective is to comprehend the significance of any (even reasonably) complicated action sequence. A great deal of research is currently being conducted in this area, the bulk of which has been masterfully reviewed in two monographs by Black, Galambos, and Read (1984) and Read (1983).

Effects of Goals on Response Selection Strategies

Among the higher level processes a person must engage in is that of selecting an overt response. This response may be a verbal utterance, a rating along a scale, a behavioral decision, or some motor act. The selection of these responses presumably depends, in part, on all of the cognitive factors we have discussed earlier in this chapter—perception, encoding, and organization; storage and retrieval; and higher level comprehension and integration processes. In considering response selection strategies in social situations, however, some additional considerations arise. This is because the response made in such situations is often a communication to another. In such circumstances, the respondent not only must retrieve information from memory but must also take into account the knowledge, expectancies, and desires of the person to whom the communication is directed.

The rules that govern response selection strategies and their relationship to the goals of the respondent have been the subject of much research and theory in cognitive as well as social psychology. In the cognitive domain, this concern is typified by the work of Grice (1975). Grice postulated several axioms or rules of communication that are implicitly assumed by both the communicator and the listener. Although several of these axioms appear self-evident at first glance, their implications are far-reaching. For example, one rule is simply that a communication should be informative. In other words, a person who communicates to another presumably attempts to convey information that the other does not already know but also information that the other will understand. In doing so, the communicator typically must make assumptions about the other's prior knowledge. Thus, suppose that a man is asked where he is from by a person he meets during a visit to New York. He is likely to respond "Chicago" rather than "America" or "Hyde Park." This is because he assumes that the questioner already knows he is an American but is unlikely to know Chicago well enough to make much sense out of information as specific as "Hyde Park." Presumably, if the man were asked this same question by a German during his vacation abroad or by someone he meets on the streets of Chicago, his response would be quite different. One application of this communication axiom may underlie some of the "distinctiveness" effects identified by McGuire in his work on the spontaneous self-concept (see McGuire, McGuire, Child, & Fujioka, 1978; McGuire & Padawar-Singer, 1976). Specifically, McGuire found that persons spontaneously describe themselves in ways that render them distinctive in their past or immediate social environment. To the extent that communicators believe that distinctive features are more informative than nondistinctive ones, this tendency would be partially explained in terms of such an axiom.

It has been recognized in most social psychological research that people's responses are governed, in part, by their attempts to generate responses that are considered acceptable, if not desirable, by the people to whom they are communicating. This concern has manifested itself in two general research areas. The most obvious is conformity. Beginning with the work of Asch (1956), it has been clear that many subjects in a social situation attempt to respond in a way that they believe will elicit social approval from others, and that in doing so, they may often have to sacrifice competing goals (e.g., to respond accurately or to convey their true beliefs and opinions). The situational and individual difference factors that determine the relative strengths of these competing communication objectives have been the subject of considerable research and theory (for but a few examples, see Harvey & Consalvi, 1960; Hollander, 1958; Wyer, 1966).

A concern with response selection strategies has also manifested itself in a very different area—namely, the social psychology of the psychology experiment. The specific conceptualizations bearing on this matter vary, as evidenced by postulated variables such as experimenter bias (Rosenthal, 1966), compliance with experimental demand characteristics (Orne, 1962), evaluation apprehension (Rosenberg, 1965), and impression management (Schlenker, 1980). However, all formulations make the assumption that one implicit goal of subjects in a psychology experiment is to respond in a way they believe is expected or desired by the person to whom they are communicating.

Effects of Response Selection on Subjects' Own Beliefs and Attitudes

Although a detailed consideration of the role of processing objectives on response selection is beyond the scope of this chapter, one interesting facet of response selection phenomena deserves mention. That is, the goal of communicating to another in a way that is consistent with the other's expectancies may sometimes affect the communicator's *own* representation of the person or object being communicated about and, therefore, his or her own judgments of this referent. Suppose that a subject wants to communicate information about a person to someone who likes this person. The subject is apt to convey the information in words that the recipient will approve of. In the course of doing so, however, the subject may form a representation of the person whose features are encoded in terms of the concepts used to generate the communication. This representation, which is stored in memory, may then provide a basis for the subject's own judgments of the target later on, for reasons similar to those noted earlier in this chapter (cf. Carlston, 1980; Wyer, Srull, & Gordon, 1984).

Two studies by Higgins and his colleagues tested this hypothesis. In one (Higgins & Rholes, 1978), subjects read a paragraph about a target person who was either liked or disliked by another. Then they were given the goal of conveying this information to the other in a way that would permit the recipient to identify the target. The paragraph contained several behavioral descriptions (e.g., "wanted to cross the Atlantic in a sailboat," "was well aware of his ability to do things well," etc.) that could alternatively be interpreted in terms of favorable trait concepts (adventurous, self-confident, etc.) or unfavorable ones (reckless, conceited, etc.). As expected, subjects applied concepts in describing the referent that were evaluatively consistent with the recipient's ostensible attitude. More important, subjects later reported greater liking for the target of whom they had communicated a favorable description than for the target of whom they had communicated an unfavorable one. Moreover, their recall of the original information was evaluatively biased in the direction of the communication they had written.

A later study (Higgins & McCann, 1984) demonstrated that the aforementioned phenomena depended, in part, on individual differences in subjects' motivation to communicate a favorable or unfavorable description. This study was similar to the earlier one, with the addition of two variables. First, the recipient was ostensibly either of higher status or lower status than the subject. Second, subjects were either high or low in authoritarianism. High authoritarian subjects, but not low authoritarians, tailored their description of the referent to coincide with the ostensible attitudes of the high-status recipient, and this description eventually became represented in memory in a form that could not be distinguished from the original information. Thus, the two factors appear to interact. First, as suggested by Grice (1975), there may be a general tendency to take an audience's perspective or prior knowledge into account in constructing a communication. However, idiosyncratic factors associated with personal characteristics of the communicator may determine the extent to which this tendency is actually manifested.

GOAL SEEKING AND AFFECTIVE REACTIONS

Thus far, we have considered the effects of processing objectives on "cold" cognitive processing. Moreover, the specific processing objectives we have considered have typically been void of affect or emotional content. However, it is obvious that emotion and affect are important ingredients of goal-directed information processing. On the one hand, affective and emotional reactions may be an important consequence of goal-directed activity. On the other hand, these reactions may also be a *stimulant* to goal-directed cognitive functioning. In this section, we will consider both possibilities in turn. First, we will consider factors that underlie the influence of goal-directed activity on both the intensity and the type of affect that people experience. Our conceptualization is based on earlier work by Mandler (1975) and by Ortony, Clore, and Collins (1983). We will then turn briefly to a discussion of the possibility that affect and emotion can be a determinant, as well as an effect, of particular types of cognitive activity.

The Interruption and Completion of Plans

To the extent that behavior is goal-directed, positive affect may result from the attainment of various goals. Correspondingly, negative affect may result from a blocking of a goal or an interruption of the activities required to attain it. This may seem self-evident as a general principle. However, when it is applied in the context of a more precise specification of the nature of goal-directed activity and its cognitive mediators, some interesting implications evolve. The pursuit of a goal often requires a series of steps, each of which is preceded by a conscious decision. The type and amount of negative affect that results from an interruption of this goal-seeking activity may depend on where in the sequence this interruption occurs as well as on the circumstances that surrounded its occurrence. Similarly, the positive affect that results from attaining the goal may depend on the number and difficulty of the steps required to attain it. To understand these contingencies, a more precise statement of the nature of goal-directed behavior and its cognitive mediators is required.

Goal-directed activity can often be conceptualized as mediated by a *plan* (G. A. Miller, Galanter, & Pribram, 1960; see also Bower, 1975; Schank & Abelson, 1977). A plan, as we will use the term, is a cognitively based routine for attaining a specified objective. This routine may consist of a series of steps, each of which may be thought of as a subgoal that must be attained to reach the superordinate goal. Thus, a plan may be conceptualized as a hierarchically organized set of goals and subgoals, along with a specification of the temporal order in which they must be attained.

The general structure of a plan may be seen in Figure 17.2, and an instantiation of this plan, pertaining to "going to the theater," is provided in Figure 17.3. In this example, the superordinate goal, "going to the theater," is broken down at the first level of the hierarchy as a routine consisting of two subgoals, "arrange for tickets" and "get to the theater on time." The attainment of each subgoal, in turn, involves a subroutine defined in terms of a sequence of more specific subgoals at the next level of the hierarchy. These subgoals could presumably be broken down still further. Note that as one goes further down the hierarchy, the goals (e.g., "look up phone number") become more closely

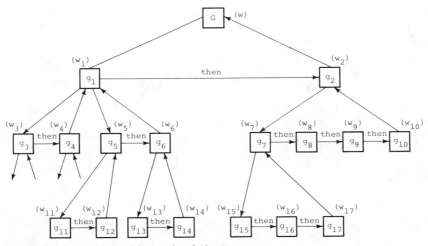

FIGURE 17.2 A hypothetical hierarchical plan structure.

associated with specific well-learned behavioral acts or routines that, once initiated, are carried out with a minimum of effort or cognitive activity. At higher levels, however, the goals are more abstract and require conscious decisions. Moreover, several alternative subroutines may be available for attaining them. (For example, the subgoal "arrange for tickets" may be attained either by calling up the theater and making reservations or by driving to the theater and purchasing them at the box office.)

The general conceptualization of plans outlined here provides a mechanism for conceptualizing the affective consequences of interruptions in goal-directed activity (cf. Mandler, 1975) and the factors that may affect their intensity. The intensity of the affect experienced by interrupting a given routine seems likely to depend on three factors: (1) the *importance* of the goal, (2) the *psychological distance* of the interruption from the attainment of the superordinate goal, and (3) the degree of *investment* of time and energy that is expended in vain as a consequence of the interruption. The last factor is partly a function of how much of the interrupted routine has been completed and partly a function of the availability of alternative routines for attaining the goal that is being pursued at the time the interruption takes place. For example, in the plan shown in Figure 17.3, the goal seeker is likely to experience less negative affect as a result of not finding the theater's number in the telephone directory if the alternative routine "call directory assistance" is available than if it is not. Moreover, he or she is less likely to be upset if "drive to ticket office" is available as an alternative subroutine for "arrange for tickets." However, suppose that the person had chosen the latter routine, had driven to the box office, and had found it closed. He or she would be more upset in this case than if he or she had simply been thwarted in the attempt to find the telephone number. This is because the person's investment of time, at the point of interruption, is

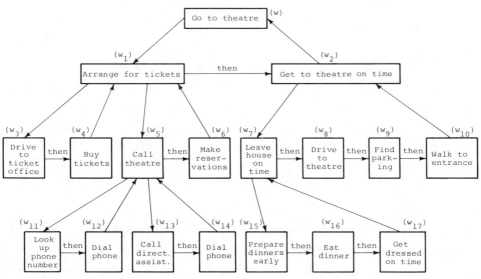

FIGURE 17.3   A concrete hierarchical plan structure.

greater in the former subroutine than it is in the latter. The greatest negative affect is experienced from an interruption that occurs close to the attainment of the goal and when no alternative subroutine is available for attaining it. For example, if a couple, having driven to the theater, find that they have forgotten to bring the tickets and that they have no money to purchase additional ones, the negative affect experienced is likely to be considerable.

Although the foregoing analysis involved a relatively mundane goal, a similar approach can be taken in conceptualizing the consequences of interruptions in the pursuit of more general life goals that take place over a long period of time. For example, consider an undergraduate who has a plan of becoming a clinical psychologist. Subgoals involved in this plan include (1) taking a psychopathology course from the great Professor X, (2) getting high scores on the GRE, (3) going to Harvard for graduate training, and (4) getting a job at a major university. If the student attempts to enroll in Professor X's psychopathology course and finds it is closed, the negative affect experienced may be relatively low, particularly if there are other psychopathology courses available, or if X will offer the course again. On the other hand, if the student is rejected by Harvard, the negative affect will be greater because (1) the interruption is closer to the superordinate goal, and (2) there is a greater commitment to the plan for attaining it. Even in this case, however, an alternative routine may be available (e.g., the student may have been admitted to other universities). In contrast, if the student is convicted of a felony during his or her first year of graduate work, such an interruption would presumably eliminate all alternative pathways to the attainment of the superordinate goal. In this case, the affective reaction may be extremely intense, perhaps even leading to some type of clinical depression.

An Attempt at Formalization

If the preceding analysis is correct, it can potentially be formalized in a way that allows specific predictions to be made of the intensity of negative affect experienced as the result of an interruption. This requires, of course, that the plan structure be specified *a priori* and that the time and effort associated with the attainment of goals comprising the various subroutines can be estimated. However, assume that the plan conveyed in Figures 17.2 and 17.3 is essentially complete and that the relative magnitudes of the time and effort required to attain each subgoal in the hierarchy are estimated by the weights shown in Figure 17.2. Note that the weight attached to a particular subgoal is equal to the sum of the weights of the subgoals comprising the subroutine required to attain it (or, if two or more alternative subroutines are available, the *minimum* of the summed weights computed for each subroutine). Thus, for example:

$$W \text{ (total time and effort required to attain } G) = w_1 + w_2$$

$$w_1 = \min(w_3 + w_4, \ w_5 + w_6), \text{ etc.}$$

Given these assumptions, the factors assumed to determine the amount of affect generated by an interruption can be quantified. For example, the distance of an interruption from a goal (D) is simply the difference between W and the sum of the weights associated with the subgoals attained prior to the interruption. Thus, suppose that an interruption occurred between g_8 and g_9 (i.e., between "drive to theater" and "find parking"). Then,

$$D = W - (w_1 + w_7 + w_8).$$

Investment in the interrupted subroutine (I) can be defined as the sum of the weights of the subgoals that would have to be retraced to reinitiate a new subroutine that would permit the superordinate goal to be attained. Note that this is determined, in part, by the existence of alternative subroutines to the one that has been interrupted. Thus, for example, should an interruption occur between g_{11} ("look up phone number") and g_{12} ("dialing phone"), $I = w_{11}$, since only g_{11} would have to be retraced to initiate an alternative subroutine that would attain the subgoal being sought (g_5, or "calling theater"). However, suppose that the interruption occurred between g_8 and g_9. Then the investment is much greater ($I = w_1 + w_7 + w_8$), since no alternative path for attaining the superordinate goal is available.

It seems reasonable to suppose that the negative affect resulting from an interruption may be a positive function of investment and a negative function of distance to the goal. However, these effects should be systematically greater when the importance or value of the goal (V) is high than when it is low. Therefore,

$$\text{Negative affect} = V(k_1 I - k_2 D). \tag{17.1}$$

The application of this conceptualization may often require *a priori* assumptions about the alternative subroutines available for attaining goals at different levels of the plan hierarchy and about the relative amounts of time and energy involved in negotiating them. However, these problems do not seem insurmountable, at least in a controlled experimental setting.

The Loss of Goals Already Attained

We have restricted the foregoing analysis to interruptions in the pursuit of goals that have not already been attained. However, it may also apply to the effects of a disruption in a desirable state of affairs that already exists. Ortony *et al.* (1983) recognized the existence of *preservation* goals (e.g., keeping one's job, preserving the life and health of one's family, or maintaining one's personal property) that do not typically require conscious, goal-directed activity unless an event occurs that makes them salient (one gets fired, one's mother dies, or one's home is burglarized). When such an event occurs, however, the negative affect experienced may be considerable.

The effects of a disruption of a preservation goal may potentially be conceptualized in terms of Equation 17.1. In this case, the distance of the disruption or interruption from the goal (D) is of course zero, since the goal has already been obtained at the time of the disruption. Therefore, the negative affect experienced is likely to be substantial for this reason alone. However, according to Equation 17.1, this affect should also be a function of (1) the importance of the goal (V) and (2) the investment in the goal (I). In this context, investment is presumably a function, in part, of the availability of alternative subroutines for regaining the disrupted goal state. Thus, losing one's job may be traumatic if one is financially dependent on it and there is no alternative subroutine for regaining it or an equivalent goal state. However, it may be relatively less devastating if one is independently wealthy or if one has several alternative job opportunities. In contrast, the death of one's mother is likely to be extremely debilitating because the disrupted goal state is impossible to reestablish.

Positive Affect

Whereas negative affect is assumed to result from the interruption of goal-directed activity, positive affect presumably results from its successful completion. Although this seems self-evident, few cognitive theories of purposive behavior have adequately addressed this possibility. For example, Mandler's (1975) assumption that affect is generated by the interruption of a plan seems inapplicable to the generation of positive affect; it is difficult to imagine any interruption of plan that would lead to a positive affective state. Other conceptualizations of the dynamics of positive affective states (e.g., Berlyne, 1967, 1971; Csikszenthmihalyi, 1975; Csikszenthmihalyi & Bennet, 1971; Deci, 1975; D. W. Fiske & Maddi, 1961; Klinger, 1975, 1977; Solomon & Corbit, 1974) have provided important theoretical insights into these phenomena, but a general conceptualization of the determinants of positive affect in goal-directed activity remains elusive.

With some auxiliary assumptions, however, the general analysis we have proposed could be applied, in principle, to positive affective states as well. That is, the positive affect one experiences from attaining a goal, like the negative affect resulting from failure to attain it, is presumably a function of the subjective importance of the goal. In addition, it seems reasonable to suppose that reactions such as "pride," "satisfaction," and "joy" resulting from successful completion of a plan will be (1) a positive function of the time and effort expended and (2) a negative function of the subjective likelihood (i.e., expectancy) that the goal will actually be attained. Thus, the positive affect experienced at any point along the path to a goal is given by

$$\text{Positive affect} = V(1 - P)D_b, \tag{17.2}$$

where V is the subjective value of the goal, P is the subjective likelihood of attaining it, and D_b is the subjective distance from the *beginning* of the plan at which the affect is being assessed. Thus, if the main goal is completed, D_b is simply the sum of the weights of the various subgoals involved in attaining it. On the other hand, the equation may also be applicable in predicting the positive affect experienced in attaining various subgoals themselves.

The formulation outlined here is attractive because it potentially predicts both the negative affect resulting from failure to attain a goal and the positive affect resulting from attaining it in terms of an overlapping set of parameters. However, note that Equations 17.1 and 17.2 predict only the *intensity* of affect experienced, not the *type* of affect that is likely to be elicited by different combinations of events. We now turn to a consideration of this matter.

Types of Affective Reactions Resulting from Goal-Directed Behavior

To understand the particular type of affective reaction that is likely to be elicited by goal-directed activity, one must consider the specific circumstances that surround the attainment of a goal or, alternatively, its interruption. In particular, one must conceptualized more precisely the relationship between a given behavioral event and the reason it either did or did not result in goal attainment. Two provocative conceptualizations of this relationship have been proposed by Roseman (1979) and, more recently, by Abelson (1983). In these formulations (which are conceptually related though differing in detail), the type of emotional reaction to an event is assumed to be a function of variables such as (1) the recipient of the event's outcome (self or other), (2) the value of the *imagined* outcome (positive, negative, or neutral), (3) the value of the *actual* outcome, (4) the causal agent of the outcome (self, other, or situation), and (5) whether the factors assumed to produce the imagined and actual events were the same or different. Table 17.1 shows the possible reactions resulting from certain combinations of these variables. For example, "gratitude" arises when one receives an unexpected positive outcome as the result of another person's actions, whereas "anger" arises when a negative event occurs as a result of one set of circumstances when a positive

TABLE 17.1   Predicted Emotional Reactions as a Function of Social and Perceptual Factors

| Predicted Emotion | Recipient | Perceptual Factor | | | | Cause of Actual and Imagined Outcomes |
| | | Imagined Outcome | | Actual Outcome | | |
		Agent	Value	Agent	Value	
Gratitude	Self	?	Negative	Other	Positive	?
Pride	Self	Self	Negative	Self	Positive	Different
Joy	Self	?	Neutral	?	Positive	?
Anger	Self	Self	Positive	Other/self	Negative	Different
Disappointment	Self	Self	Positive	Self	Negative	Same
Sorrow	?	?	Neutral	?	Negative	?

outcome was expected as a result of a different set of circumstances. (This anger may be directed toward either self or other, depending on the causal agent.)

Although Abelson's (1983) and Roseman's (1979) specific formulations differ in detail—and both postulate variables in addition to those shown in Table 17.1 that influence emotions—the general approach they have taken seems fruitful. Moreover, to the extent that the type of affective reactions can be conceptualized in this manner and the *intensity* of emotional reactions can be predicted on the basis of the sort of hierarchical plan–goal analysis suggested earlier, the seeds may exist for developing a comprehensive formulation of the effects of goal seeking on affective reactions.

Affective Reactions to Goal Conflicts

The foregoing analysis has been limited to the affective consequences of behaviors directed toward the pursuit of a single goal. To this extent, it is grossly oversimplified. It is obvious that people typically have several different goals, of varying importance, that they pursue more or less simultaneously. A recognition of this fact raises an additional consideration in understanding the effects of this goal-seeking activity on affect and emotion. That is, situations may frequently arise in which the behavior that facilitates the attainment of one goal may interfere with the attainment of another. Under these conditions, conflict arises that may itself be a source of affect. The clearest and best-known analysis of the nature of these conflicts and their effects was provided by N. E. Miller (1959). The three basic types of conflicts Miller identified will be reviewed in the present context as a preface to considering the effects of conflicts in more complex goal-directed activity of the sort than often arises in social decision making.

Approach-Approach Conflicts
These conflicts arise when two equally attractive goals cannot both be pursued simultaneously. Such conflicts, which occur frequently in everyday life,

may involve goals that are either of little consequence (e.g., "Should I read *Psychological Review* or the *New Yorker*?") or of extreme importance (e.g., "Should I sign a pro football contract or accept admission to Harvard Law School?"). As the absolute value of the two alternative goals increases, the amount of negative affective experienced will also increase. However, relative to other types of conflicts (to be noted), the persistence of this affect is low. This is because the conflict is usually resolved as soon as one begins to lean in favor of, or even think about, one of the alternatives rather than the other. Moreover, the negative affect generated by the conflict itself is rarely of sufficient magnitude to override the positive affect experienced by anticipation of the goals themselves.

Avoidance-Avoidance Conflicts

These conflicts arise when one is confronted with two equally unattractive situations and the avoidance of one requires experiencing the other. For example, a woman who is unhappily pregnant may be morally opposed to having an abortion, or a person with a toothache may be terrified of going to the dentist. Such conflicts are intense and difficult to resolve. They produce considerable stress, not only because they are unavoidable but because their resolution necessarily requires exposure to an aversive situation.

Approach-Avoidance Conflicts

These conflicts arise when a single object or outcome has both attractive and unattractive features. Therefore, exposure to the positive features requires exposure to the aversive ones as well, and avoidance of the undesirable aspects requires giving up the positive ones. A child who is forced to finish his spinach to have dessert, a teenager who is sexually curious but morally inhibited, and a coauthor who objects to certain statements in a paper but does not want to offend her colleague all experience such conflicts. N. E. Miller (1959) pointed out that as one approaches the object or situation, the unpleasant aspects of it become more prominent. The ultimate result is a vacillation between approach and avoidance. Such a conflict is difficult to resolve and consequently generates considerable negative affect.

Multiple-Conflict Situations

Although it is useful to analyze the dynamics of conflict situations into the three types identified by N. E. Miller (1959), many conflicts that one encounters in the real world do not have the "pure" forms we have described. For example, a person who must choose between taking a job at University *A* or remaining at University *B* may see both attractive and unattractive features of each alternative. Such a situation is actually a composite of all three types of conflict, and which type a person experiences at any given time may depend on which aspects of the choice alternatives he or she happens to think about. For example, attention to only the attractive features of the two alternatives may elicit an approach-approach conflict. However, a comparison of only the unattractive features of the two alternatives may elicit an avoidance-avoidance conflict. Finally, a consideration of each alternative in isolation, taking into account both its attractive and its unattractive features, may elicit an approach-avoidance conflict.

It is interesting to speculate about the implications of this analysis for conflict resolution. Recall from our previous discussion that approach-avoidance conflicts are the most difficult to resolve and that avoidance-avoidance conflicts are the most aversive. Thus, to the extent that a decision maker wishes to eliminate the conflict and to minimize the negative affect associated with it, he or she may ultimately conceptualize the choice situation in a way that produces an approach-approach conflict rather than one of the other types, thereby facilitating its resolution and maximizing the resulting positive affect. It would also be interesting to investigate the extent to which people who are confronted with a given choice situation will experience different amounts of affect, and will resolve the conflict more or less easily, if they are led via various experimental (e.g., priming) manipulations to conceptualize the situation in one of the alternative ways.

A complication in resolving such conflict situations arises from the fact that the attractive (or unattractive) features of choice situations cannot always be compared along the same dimensions. For example, how much is high salary (available at University A) worth in terms of the quality of students (available at University B)? In resolving such conflicts, one is often forced to use a weighting scheme that is difficult to justify on purely rational grounds and the validity of which may be questioned by the decision maker, even after the choice is made. Because of these ambiguities, the affect generated in the course of resolving a conflict may linger for some time after the resolution. Indeed, the manner in which this affect is eliminated following a decision has been the focus of much research and theory, notably in the area of cognitive dissonance (Festinger, 1957; Wicklung & Brehm, 1976).

Motivational Consequences of Affective States

Affective states may sometimes be a determinant as well as an effect of behavior. This is most obvious in the case of negative affect. That is, when a person experiences an unpleasant emotional state, this experience may instigate cognitive or motor activity designed to determine the reason for this aversive state and, if possible, to decrease or eliminate it. This possibility is well known, and the pursuit of its empirical implications has provided substantial insight into cognitive functioning. This has been particularly evident in research on cognitive dissonance phenomena by Zanna and Cooper and their colleagues (for a review, see Zanna & Cooper, 1976).

In general, research has suggested that people who experience positive affect are likely to take responsibility for its occurrence and use it as a basis for their self-judgments without seeking alternative explanations that might also account for it. However, when people experience negative affect, they search for explanations that do not reflect adversely on themselves, and they attribute it to themselves only if no alternative explanation is apparent. This possible asymmetry in the effects of positive and negative affect (or the conditions that produce it) has been detected in several different research paradigms. In a study by Arkin, Gleason, and Johnston (1976), subjects were led to believe that they had either succeeded or failed on a task under conditions in which (1) they either did or did not have a choice as to how to perform the task and (2) other people had typically succeeded or typically failed on it. Those who failed attributed responsibility to themselves only under conditions in which it could not be externally attributed. In contrast, subjects who succeeded took responsibility for this outcome regardless of the availability of alternative explanations.

In a study bearing more directly on the effects of affect *per se*, Schwarz and Clore (1983) induced a positive or negative mood in subjects by having them write an essay describing either a happy or sad past experience. Subjects wrote their essays in a soundproof booth that, they were told, would make them either feel elated or feel depressed or would have no affect on them. Subsequently, they were asked to judge their satisfaction with their life in general. Subjects who were put in a sad mood reported themselves to be less satisfied with their life when they had been in a booth that would ostensibly make them feel elated than when they were told that the booth would make them feel depressed. Thus, they apparently attributed their affect to the booth in the latter condition. In contrast, subjects who were put in a happy mood reported themselves to be satisfied with their life as a whole regardless of whether the booth provided an alternative explanation for their affective state. In other words, they used their mood as a basis for self-judgments regardless of whether there were alternative reasons for its occurrence.

Finally, Wyer and Frey (1983) gave subjects either positive or negative feedback about their performance on an intelligence test and then asked them to read a communication containing both arguments that supported the validity of such tests and arguments that disparaged them. Later, subjects recalled the information in the communication. Negative feedback tended to increase subjects' recall of information that supported intelligence tests, suggesting that they actively tried to refute these arguments and that this cognitive activity led them to recall them better later on. In contrast, positive feedback did *not* increase the recall of anti-intelligence test information.

These studies suggest that the experience of negative affect as a result of an experience stimulates cognitive activity intended to account for it and perhaps to eliminate it. This activity may involve either a search for explanations of the affect that do not bear negatively on oneself or an active attempt to discredit the source of the affect. In contrast, positive affect is simply enjoyed and the responsibility for it self-attributed, without engaging in any cognitive work to explain its occurrence.

CONCLUSIONS

In this chapter, we have attempted to compile evidence of the wide range of influences that subjective goal states have on information processing. Goals often determine what we attend to, how we perceive objects and events, how we use reasoning processes to make inferences about causal connections, how these events are organized and represented in memory, how they affect both long-term storage and retrieval of relevant information, how they influence the integration of information (or lack thereof) to make higher order judgments, and how they enter into possible affective reactions.

It is clear that goals have a wide range of influences on infomation-processing activities. It is equally clear, however, that many classic theories have not completely taken their influence into account. Attribution theory, for example, has been highly developed and has generated an enormous archive of empirical findings. From the current perspective, however, the utility of attribution theory rests on specifying those conditions under which people are likely to engage spontaneously in the type of computational activity dictated by the theory. This would seem to us to be a central issue, yet it has been ignored almost entirely. Similarly, considerable effort has been directed toward understanding the effects of salient stimuli in the environment (Nisbett & Ross, 1980; Taylor & Fiske, 1978). However, salience has almost always been defined in terms of physical variables. The current framework would suggest that salience must ultimately be defined in terms of psychological characteristics and that those stimuli that are "salient" or "vivid" at any given time are likely to be determined through an interaction of the physical properties of the stimulus with the current psychological state of the perceiver. As we noted earlier, the person is generally "prepared" to pick up some things from the environment while simultaneously ignoring many others. At one level, this is self-evident. However, it has not yet been translated into most of our empirical investigations.

These things are not unique to social information processing. In fact, they are central to all of cognitive psychology—and the guidelines are the same. As Broadbent (1973) has reminded us, theorists should think in terms of optional rather than obligatory strategies. Two people may use different strategies when put in the same situation, and the same person may use different strategies on different occasions. A recognition of this fact lends a fresh perspective to the question of whether the task of the psychologist is to search for general laws or to search for individual differences. It may very well turn out, at least within the social domain, that a search for general laws will proceed most quickly at the level of investigating the *capabilities* of the subject. In contrast, reliable individual differences may become most apparent at the level of investigating those determinants that systematically govern the choice of one strategy over another.

It should also be noted that the same performance level can be produced, in different ways, by several different strategies. Researchers should remember that averaging over subjects who are using different strategies will conceal, rather than reveal, the nature of the underlying processes that are activated.

It is hoped that this chapter will provide useful guidelines for how current theories of cognition and motivation can become more integrated. Similarly, it is hoped that researchers will be able to identify ways to track the development and operation of many of the goal-based strategies that have not been discussed here. It is certainly true that the goals and processing objectives of the subject are a major determinant of his or her performance on any given task and that they complicate the job of the psychologist considerably—but they surely make it more interesting, challenging, and important as well.

Acknowledgments

The preparation of this chapter, and much of the research reported herein, was supported by National Science Foundation grants BNS76-24001 and BNS83-02105 and by National Institute of Mental Health grant R01 MH38585-01, BSR.

The authors are indebted to Galen Bodenhausen, Tory Higgins, Norbert Schwarz, and Richard Sorrentino for very helpful comments on an earlier draft of the chapter.

Notes

1. We have also intentionally avoided discussing the work of Mischel and his colleagues in this section (e.g., Hoffman, Mischel, & Mazze, 1981; Jeffery & Mischel, 1979). These researchers have also conducted several experiments related to the effects of goals in social memory. The typical procedure is to present one group of subjects with a list of behaviors and ask them to sort them into different categories under either a memory-set or an impression-set condition. A second group of subjects is then given the information as sorted by a yoked subject from the first group. They are first asked to infer what categories had been used to sort the behaviors and are then asked to recall them as well as possible. The typical finding is that subjects recall more of the information when it was originally sorted under a memory set than under an impression set. This suggests that whereas the criteria for sorting items under a memory set are fairly consensual, the criteria for sorting under an impression set are more abstract and idiosyncratic and therefore do not transfer well from one subject to the next. At any rate, the work is not discussed in detail because it is impossible to draw any conclusions about the way in which a single person encodes, organizes, and retrieves social information.

2. The substantial work by N. H. Anderson (1981) and others on information integration processes should be noted in this context. This research has provided substantial support for an algebraic model of the way in which individual pieces of information combine to affect judgments. However, as Wyer and Carlston (1979) pointed out, this research has been conducted in rather artificial research paradigms that may predispose subjects to use an integration procedure that would not occur in the course of making everyday judgments or decisions (see also Abelson, 1976, for a discussion of this matter). The issues of concern in this section pertain primarily to these latter types of judgments.

References

Abbott, V., & Black, J. B. (1982, October). *A comparison of the memory strength of alternative text relations.* Paper presented at the annual meeting of the American Education Research Association, New York.

Abelson, R. P. (1976). Script processing in attitude formation and decision making. In J. S. Carroll & J. W. Payne (Eds.), *Cognition and social behavior* (pp. 33–45). Hillsdale, NJ: Erlbaum.

Abelson, R. P. (1983). Whatever became of consistency theory? *Personality and Social Psychology Bulletin, 9*, 37–54.

Anderson, N. H. (1981). *Foundations of information integration theory.* New York: Academic Press, 1981.

Anderson, N. H., & Hubert, S. (1963). Effects of concomitant verbal recall on order effects in personality impression formation. *Journal of Verbal Learning and Verbal Behavior, 2*, 379–391.

Anderson, R. C., & Pichert, J. W. (1978). Recall of previously unrecallable information following a shift in perspective. *Journal of Verbal Learning and Verbal Behavior, 17,* 1–12.

Arkin, R. M., Gleason, J. M., & Johnston, S. (1976). Effect of perceived choice, expected outcome, and observed outcome of an action on the causal attributions of actors. *Journal of Experimental Social Psychology, 12,* 151–158.

Asch, S. E. (1946). Forming impressions of personality. *Journal of Abnormal and Social Psychology, 41,* 258–290.

Asch, S. E. (1956). Studies of independence and conformity: I. A minority of one against a unanimous majority. *Psychological Monographs, 70*(9).

Atkinson, R. C., & Shiffrin, R. M. (1968). Human memory: A proposed system and its control processes. In K. Spence (Ed.), *The psychology of learning and motivation* (Vol. 2, pp. 89–195). New York: Academic Press.

Baker, L. (1978). Processing temporal relationships in simple stories: Effects of input sequence. *Journal of Verbal Learning and Verbal Behavior, 17,* 559–572.

Bargh, J. A. (1982). Attention and automaticity in the processing of self-relevant information. *Journal of Personality and Social Psychology, 43,* 425–436.

Bargh, J. A. (1984). Automatic and conscious processing of social information. In R. S. Wyer & T. K. Srull (Eds.), *Handbook of social cognition* (Vol. 3, pp. 1–43). Hillsdale, NJ: Erlbaum.

Bargh, J. A., & Pietromonaco, P. (1982). Automatic information processing and social perception: The influence of trait information presented outside of conscious awareness on impression formation. *Journal of Personality and Social Psychology, 43,* 437–449.

Berlyne, D. E. (1967). Arousal and reinforcement. In W. J. Arnold (Ed.), *Nebraska Symposium on Motivation* (Vol. 15, pp. 92–116). Lincoln: University of Nebraska Press.

Berlyne, D. E. (1971). *Aesthetics and psychology.* New York: Appleton.

Black, J. B., & Bern, H. (1981). Causal coherence and memory for events in narratives. *Journal of Verbal Learning and Verbal Behavior, 20,* 267–275.

Black, J. B., Galambos, J. A., & Read, S. J. (1984). Comprehending stories and social situations. In R. S. Wyer & T. K. Srull (Eds.), *Handbook of social cognition* (Vol. 3, pp. 45–86). Hillsdale, NJ: Erlbaum.

Bower, G. H. (1975). Cognitive psychology: An introduction. In W. K. Estes (Ed.), *Handbook of learning and cognitive process* (Vol. 1, pp. 25–80). Hillsdale, NJ: Erlbaum.

Brewer, W. F., & Dupree, D. A. (1983). use of plan schemata in the recall and recognition of goal-directed actions. *Journal of Experimental Psychology: Learning, Memory, and Cognition, 9,* 117–129.

Broadbent, D. E. (1973). *In defence of empirical psychology.* London: Methuen.

Bruner, J. S. (1948). Perceptual theory and the Rorschach test. *Journal of Personality, 17,* 157–168.

Bruner, J. S. (1951). Personality dynamics and the process of perceiving. In R. R. Blake & G. V. Ramsey (Eds.), *Perception: An approach to personality* (pp. 121–147). New York: Ronald Press.

Bruner, J. S. (1957). On perceptual readiness. *Psychological Review, 64,* 123–152.

Bruner, J. S. (1983). *In search of mind.* New York: Harper & Row.

Bruner, J. S., & Goodman, C. C. (1947). Value and need as organizing factors in perception. *Journal of Abnormal and Social Psychology, 42,* 33–44.

Bruner, J. S., & Klein, G. S. (1960). The functions of perceiving: New look retrospect. In B. Kaplan & S. Wapner (Eds.), *Perspectives in psychological theory: Essays in honor of Heinz Werner* (pp. 121–138). New York: International Universities Press.

Bruner, J. S., & Postman, L. (1948). Symbolic value as an organizing factor in perception. *Journal of Social Psychology, 27,* 203–208.

Bruner, J. S., & Postman, L. (1949). On the perception of incongruity: A paradigm. *Journal of Personality, 18,* 206–223.

Carlston, D. E. (1980). The recall and use of observed behavioral episodes and inferred traits in social inference processes. *Journal of Experimental Social Psychology, 16,* 779–804.

Cohen, C. E., & Ebbesen, E. B. (1979). Observational goals and schema activation: A theoretical framework for behavior perception. *Journal of Experimental Social Psychology, 15,* 305–329.

Corteen, R. S., & Wood, B. (1972). Autonomic responses to shock-associated words in an unattended channel. *Journal of Experimental Psychology, 94*, 308–313.

Crocker, J., Hannah, D. B., & Weber, R. (1983). Person memory and causal attributions. *Journal of Personality and Social Psychology, 44*, 55–66.

Csikszentmihalyi, M. (1975). *Beyond boredom and anxiety.* San Francisco: Jossey-Bass.

Csikszentmihalyi, M., & Bennet, S. (1971). An exploratory model of play. *American Anthropologist, 73*, 45–58.

Deci, E. L. (1975). *Intrinsic motivation.* New York: Plenum.

Dreben, E. K., Fiske, S. T., & Hastie, R. (1979). The independence of item and evaluation information: Impression and recall order effects in behavior-based impression formation. *Journal of Personality and Social Psychology, 37*, 1758–1768.

Erdelyi, M. H., & Appelbaum, G. A. (1973). Cognitive masking: The disruptive effect of an emotional stimulus upon the perception of contiguous neutral items. *Bulletin of the Psychonomic Society, 1*, 56–61.

Fenichel, O. (1945). *The psychoanalytic theory of neuroses.* New York: Norton.

Festinger, L. (1957). *A theory of cognitive dissonance.* Stanford, CA: Stanford University Press.

Fiske, D. W., & Maddi, S. R. (1961). *Functions of varied experience.* Homewood, IL: Dorsey Press.

Fiske, S. T. (1981). Social cognition and affect. In J. H. Harvey (Ed.), *Cognition, social behavior, and the environment* (pp. 175–202). Hillsdale, NJ: Erlbaum.

Fiske, S. T. (1982). Schema-triggered affect: Applications to social perception. In M. S. Clark & S. T. Fiske (Eds.), *Affect and cognition* (pp. 55–78). Hillsdale, NJ: Erlbaum.

Fiske, S. T., Kenny, D. A., & Taylor, S. E. (1982). Structural models for the mediation of salience effects on attribution. *Journal of Experimental Social Psychology, 18*, 105–127.

Fiske, S. T., Taylor, S. E., Etcoff, N. L., & Laufer, J. K. (1979). Imaging, empathy, and causal attribution. *Journal of Experimental Social Psychology, 15*, 356–377.

Freud, S. (1956). Screen memories. In J. Strachey (Ed.), *The standard edition of the complete psychological works of Sigmund Freud* (Vol. 3, pp. 128–146). London: Hogarth Press. (Original work published 1899)

Freud, S. (1965a). *The interpretation of dreams.* New York: Avon. (Original work published 1900)

Freud, S. (1965b). *The psychopathology of everyday life.* New York: Norton. (Original work published 1901)

Freud, S. (1967). The unconscious. In J. Strachey (Ed.), *The standard edition of the complete psychological works of Sigmund Freud* (Vol. 14, pp. 1–116). London: Hogarth Press. (Original work published 1915)

Freud, S. (1977). *Introductory lectures on psychoanalysis.* New York: Norton. (Original work published 1917)

Geller, V., & Shaver, P. (1976). Cognitive consequences of self-awareness. *Journal of Experimental Social Psychology, 12*, 99–108.

Gordon, S. E. (1982). *Alternative organizations in memory for trait-relevant behaviors.* Unpublished doctoral dissertation, University of Illinois.

Greenwald, A. G. (1968). Cognitive learning, cognitive response to persuasion, and attitude change. In A. G. Greenwald, T. C. Brock, & T. M. Ostrom (Eds.), *Psychological foundations of attitudes* (pp. 147–170). New York: Academic press.

Grice, H. P. (1975). Logic in conversation. In P. Cole & J. L. Morgan (Eds.), *Syntax and semantics: Vol. 3. Speech acts* (pp. 68–134). New York: Academic Press.

Hamilton, D. L., & Katz, L. B. (1975, August). *A process-oriented approach to the study of impressions.* Paper presented at the annual meeting of the American Psychological Association, Chicago.

Hamilton, D. L., Katz, L. B., & Leirer, V. O. (1980a). Cognitive representation of personality impressions: Organizational processes in first impression formation. *Journal of Personality and Social Psychology, 39*, 1050–1063.

Hamilton, D. L., Katz, L. B., & Leirer, V. O. (1980b). Organizational processes in impression formation. In R. Hastie, T. M. Ostrom, E. B. Ebbesen, R. S. Wyer, D. L. Hamilton, & D. E. Carlston (Eds.), *Person memory: The cognitive basis of social perception* (pp. 121–153). Hillsdale, NJ: Erlbaum.

Hartwick, J. (1979). Memory for trait information: A signal detection analysis. *Journal of Experimental Social Psychology, 15,* 533–552.

Harvey, O. J., & Consalvi, C. (1960). Status and conformity to pressure in informal groups. *Journal of Abnormal and Social Psychology, 60,* 182–187.

Hastie, R. (1980). Memory for information which confirms or contradicts a general impression. In R. Hastie, T. M. Ostrom, E. B. Ebbesen, R. S. Wyer, D. L. Hamilton, & D. E. Carlston (Eds.), *Person memory: The cognitive basis of social perception* (pp. 155–177). Hillsdale, NJ: Erlbaum.

Hastie, R. (1984). Causes and effects of causal attribution. *Journal of Personality and Social Psychology, 46,* 44–56.

Hastie, R., Park, B., & Weber, R. (1984). Social memory. In R. S. Wyer & T. K. Srull (Eds.), *Handbook of social cognition* (Vol. 2, pp. 151–212). Hillsdale, NJ: Erlbaum.

Hastorf, A. H., & Cantril, H. (1954). They saw a game: A case study. *Journal of Abnormal and Social Psychology, 49,* 129–234.

Henle, M. (1984). Fredu's secret cognitive theories. In J. R. Royce & L. P. Mos (Eds.), *Annals of theoretical psychology* (Vol. 1, pp. 111–134). New York: Plenum.

Higgins, E. T., & King, G. (1981). Accessibility of social constructs: Information processing consequences of individual and contextual variability. In N. Cantor & J. F. Kihlstrom (Eds.), *Personality, cognition, and social interaction* (pp. 69–121). Hillsdale, NJ: Erlbaum.

Higgins, E. T., King, G. A., & Mavin, G. H. (1982). Individual construct accessibility and subjective impressions and recall. *Journal of Personality and Social Psychology, 43,* 35–47.

Higgins, E. T., & McCann, C. D. (1984). Social encoding and subsequent attitudes, impressions, and memory: "Context-driven" and motivational aspects of processing. *Journal of Personality and Social Psychology, 47,* 26–39.

Higgins, E. T.. McCann, C. D., & Fondacaro, R. (1982). The "communication game": Goal-directed encoding and cognitive consequences. *Social Cognition, 1,* 21–37.

Higgins, E. T., & Rholes, W. S. (1978). "Saying is believing": Effects of message modification on memory and liking for the person described. *Journal of Experimental Social Psychology, 14,* 363–378.

Higgins, E. T., Rholes, W. S., & Jones, C. R. (1977). Category accessibility and impression formation. *Journal of Experimental Social Psychology, 13,* 141–154.

Hoffman, C., Mischel, W., & Mazze, K. (1981). The role of purpose in the organization of information about behavior: Trait-based versus goal-based categories in person cognition. *Journal of Personality and Social Psychology, 40,* 211–225.

Hollander, E. P. (1958). Conformity, status, and idiosyncrasy credit. *Psychological Review, 65,* 117–127.

Insko, C. A. (1964). Primacy versus recency in persuasion as a function of the timing of arguments and measures. *Journal of Abnormal and Social Psychology, 69,* 381–391.

Irwin, F. W. (1953). Stated expectations as functions of probability and desirability of outcomes. *Journal of Personality, 21,* 329–335.

Jeffery, K. M., & Mischel, W. (1979). Effects of purpose on the organization and recall of information in person perception. *Journal of Personality, 47,* 397–419.

Johnston, V. S., & Chesney, C. L. (1974). Electrophysiological correlates of meaning. *Science, 186,* 944–946.

Kihlstrom, J. F., & Cantor, N. (1984). Mental representations of the self. In L. Berkowitz (Ed.), *Advances in experimental social psychology* (Vol. 15, pp. 1–47). New York: Academic Press.

Klinger, E. (1971). *Structure and functions of fantasy.* New York: Wiley.

Klinger, E. (1975). Consequences of commitment to and disengagement from incentives. *Psychological Review, 82,* 1–25.

Klinger, E. (1977). *Meaning and void: Inner experience and the incentives in people's lives.* Minneapolis: University of Minnesota Press.

Lachman, R., Lachman, J. L., & Butterfield, E. C. (1979). *Cognitive psychology and information processing: An introduction.* Hillsdale, NJ: Erlbaum.

Lewinsohn, P. M., Mischel, W., Chaplin, W., & Barton, R. (1980). Social competence and depression: The role of illusory self-perceptions? *Journal of Abnormal Psychology, 89*, 203–212.

Lichtenstein, E. H., & Brewer, W. F. (1980). Memory for goal-directed events. *Cognitive Psychology, 12*, 412–445.

Lichtenstein, M., & Srull, T. K. (1985). Conceptual and methodological issues in examining the relationship between consumer memory and judgment. In L. F. Alwitt & A. A. Mitchell (Eds.), *Psychological processes and advertising effects: Theory, research, and application* (pp. 113–128). Hillsdale, NJ: Erlbaum.

Luria, A. R., & Vinogradova, O. S. (1959). An objective investigation of the dynamics of semantic systems. *British Journal of Psychology, 50*, 89–105.

Mandler, G. (1975). *Mind and emotion.* New York: Wiley.

Marks, R. W. (1951). The effect of probability, desirability, and "privilege" on the state of expectations of children. *Journal of Personality, 19*, 332–351.

Markus, H. (1977). Self-schemas and processing information about the self. *Journal of Personality and Social Psychology, 35*, 63–78.

Markus, H., Crane, M., Bernstein, S., & Siladi, M. (1982). Self-schemas and gender. *Journal of Personality and Social Psychology, 42*, 38–50.

McGuire, W. J., McGuire, C. V., Child, P., & Fujioka, T. (1978). Salience of ethnicity in the spontaneous self-concept as a function of one's distinctiveness in the social environment. *Journal of Personality and Social Psychology, 36*, 511–520.

McGuire, W. J., & Padawer-Singer, A. (1976). Trait salience in the spontaneous self-concept. *Journal of Personality and Social Psychology, 33*, 743–754.

Miller, G. A., Galanter, E., Pribram, K. (1960). *Plans and the structure of behavior.* New York: Holt, Rinehart and Winston.

Miller, N. E. (1959). Liberalization of basic S-R concepts: Extensions to conflict behavior, motivation, and social learning. In S. Kock (Ed.), *Psychology: A study of science* (Vol. 2, pp. 196–292). New York: McGraw-Hill.

Miller, N. E., & Campbell, D. T. (1959). Recency and primacy in persuasion as a function of the timing of speeches and measurements. *Journal of Abnormal and Social Psychology, 59*, 1–9.

Mio, J. S., & Black, J. B. (1979). *Attribution inferences in story comprehension.* Unpublished manuscript, University of Illinois at Chicago.

Moore, B. S., Sherrod, D. R., Liu, T. S., & Underwood, B. (1979). The dispositional shift in attribution over time. *Journal of Experimental Social Psychology, 15*, 553–559.

Nisbett, R., & Ross, L. (1980). *Human inference: Strategies and shortcomings of social judgment.* Englewood Cliffs, NJ: Prentice-Hall.

Orne, M. T. (1962). On the social psychology of the psychological experiment: With particular reference to demand characteristics and their implications. *American Psychologist, 17*, 776–783.

Ortony, A., Clore, G. L., & Collins, A. M. (1983). *Principia mathematica.* Unpublished manuscript, University of Illinois.

Oswald, I., Taylor, A. M., & Treisman, M. (1960). Discriminative responses to stimulation during human sleep. *Brain, 83*, 440–453.

Petty, R. E., Ostrom, T. M., & Brock, T. C. (Eds.). (1981). *Cognitive responses in persuasion.* Hillsdale, NJ: Erlbaum.

Pryor, J. B., & Ostrom, T. M. (1981). The cognitive organization of social information: A converging-operations approach. *Journal of Personality and Social Psychology, 41*, 628–641.

Raaijmakers, J. G. W., & Shiffrin, R. M. (1980). SAM: A theory of probabilistic search of associative memory. In G. H. Bower (Ed.), *The psychology of learning and motivation* (Vol. 14, pp. 207–262). New York: Academic Press.

Raaijmakers, J. G. W., & Shiffrin, R. M. (1981). Search of associative memory. *Psychological Review, 88*, 93–134.

Read, S. J. (1983). *Constructing causal scenarios: A knowledge structure approach to causal reasoning.* Unpublished manuscript, Northwestern University.

Reyes, R. M., Thompson, W. C., & Bower, G. H. (1980). Judgmental biases resulting from differing availabilities of arguments. *Journal of Personality and Social Psychology, 39*, 2–12.

Riskey, D. R. (1979). Verbal memory processes in impression formation. *Journal of Experimental Psychology: Human Learning and Memory, 5*, 271–281.

Roberts, W. A. (1972). Free recall of word lists varying in length and rate of presentation: A test of total-time hypotheses. *Journal of Experimental Psychology, 92*, 365–372.

Roseman, I. (1979, August). *Cognitive aspects of emotion and emotional behavior.* Paper presented at the annual meeting of the American Psychological Association, New York.

Rosenberg, M. J. (1965). When dissonance fails: On eliminating evaluation. *Social Psychology, 1*, 28–42.

Rosenthal, R. (1966). *Experimenter effects in behavioral research.* New York: Appleton-Crofts.

Rundus, D. (1971). Analysis of rehearsal processes in free recall. *Journal of Experimental Psychology, 89*, 63–77.

Schank, R. C., & Abelson, R. P. (1977). *Scripts, plans, goals, and understanding.* Hillsdale, NJ: Erlbaum.

Schlenker, B. R. (1980). *Impression management.* Monterey, CA: Brooks/Cole.

Scharz, N., & Clore, G. L. (1983). Mood, misattribution, and judgments of well-being: Informative and directive functions of affective states. *Journal of Personality and Social Psychology, 45*, 513–523.

Sherman, S. J., Zehner, K. S., Johnson, J., & Hirt, E. R. (1983). Social explanation: The role of timing, set, and recall on subjective likelihood estimates. *Journal of Personality and Social Psychology, 44*, 1127–1143.

Shoben, E. J. (1980). Theories of semantic memory: Approaches to knowledge and sentence comprehension. In R. S. Spiro, B. C. Bruce, & W. F. Brewer (Eds.), *Theoretical issues in reading comprehension* (pp. 309–330). Hillsdale, NJ: Erlbaum.

Smith, E. E., Adams, N., & Schorr, D. (1978). Fact retrieval and the paradox of interference. *Cognitive Psychology, 10*, 438–464.

Snyder, M., & Cantor, N. (1979). Testing hypotheses about other people. *Journal of Experimental Social Psychology, 15*, 330–342.

Solomon, R. L., & Corbit, J. D. (1974). An opponent-process theory of motivation: I. Temporal dynamics of affect. *Psychological Review, 81*, 119–145.

Srull, T. K. (1981). Person memory: Some tests of associative storage and retrieval models. *Journal of Experimental Psychology: Human Learning and Memory, 7*, 440–463.

Srull, T. K. (1983). Organizational and retrieval processes in person memory: An examination of processing objectives, presentation format, and the possible role of self-generated retrieval cues. *Journal of Personality and Social Psychology, 44*, 1157–1170.

Srull, T. K., & Brand, J. F. (1983). Memory for information about persons: The effect of encoding operations on subsequent retrieval. *Journal of Verbal Learning and Verbal Behavior, 22*, 219–230.

Srull, T. K., Lichtenstein, M., & Rothbart, M. (1985). Associative storage and retrieval processes in person memory. *Journal of Experimental Psychology, 11*, 316–345.

Srull, T. K., & Wyer, R. S. (1979). The role of category accessibility in the interpretation of information about persons: Some determinants and implications. *Journal of Personality and Social Psychology, 37*, 1660–1672.

Srull, T. K., & Wyer, R. S. (1980). Category accessibility and social perception: Some implications for the study of person memory and interpersonal judgment. *Journal of Personality and Social Psychology, 38*, 841–856.

Srull, T. K., & Wyer, R. S. (1983). The role of control processes and structural constraints in models in memory and social judgment. *Journal of Experimental Social Psychology, 19*, 497–521.

Staddon, J. E. R. (1983). *Adaptive behavior and learning.* Cambridge: Cambridge University Press.

Taylor, S. E., & Fiske, S. T. (1975). Point-of-view and perceptions of causality. *Journal of Personality and Social Psychology, 32*, 439–445.

Taylor, S. E., & Fiske, S. T. (1978). Salience, attention, and attribution: Top of the head phenomena. In L. Berkowitz (Ed.), *Advances in experimental social psychology* (Vol. 11, pp. 249–288). New York: Academic Press.

Taylor, S. E., & Fiske, S. T. (1981). Getting inside the head: Methodologies for process analysis in attribution and social cognition. In J. H. Harvey, W. Ickes, & R. F. Kidd (Eds.), *New directions in attribution research* (Vol. 3, pp. 459–524). Hillsdale, NJ: Erlbaum.

Watts, W. A., & McGuire, W. J. (1964). Persistency of induced opinion change and retention of the inducing mesasge contents. *Journal of Abnormal and Social Psychology, 68*, 233–241.

Weinstein, N. D. (1980). Unrealistic optimism about future life events. *Journal of Personality and Social Psychology, 39*, 806–820.

Wicklund, R. A., & Brehm, J. W. (1976). *Perspectives on cognitive dissonance.* Hillsdale, NJ: Erlbaum.

Wyer, R. S. (1966). Effects of incentive to perform well, group attraction and group acceptance on conformity in a judgmental task. *Journal of Personality and Social Psychology, 4*, 21–26.

Wyer, R. S., Bodenhausen, G. V., & Srull, T. K. (1984). The cognitive representation of persons and groups and its effect on recall and recognition memory. *Journal of Experimental Social Psychology, 20*, 445–469.

Wyer, R. S., & Carlston, D. E. (1979). *Social cognition, inference, and attribution.* Hillsdale, NJ: Erlbaum.

Wyer, R. S., & Frey, D. (1983). The effects of feedback about self and others on the recall and judgments of feedback-relevant information. *Journal of Experimental Social Psychology, 19*, 540–559.

Wyer, R. S., & Gordon, S. E. (1982). The recall of information about persons and groups. *Journal of Experimental Social Psychology, 18*, 128–164.

Wyer, R. S., & Gordon, S. E. (1984). The cognitive representation of social information. In R. S. Wyer & T. K. Srull (Eds.), *Handbook of social cognition* (Vol. 2, pp. 73–150). Hillsdale, NJ: Erlbaum.

Wyer, R. S., & Srull, T. K. (1980). The processing of social stimulus information: A conceptual integration. In R. Hastie, T. M. Ostrom, E. B. Ebbesen, R. S. Wyer, D. L. Hamilton, & D. E. Carlston (Eds.), *Person memory: The cognitive basis of social perception* (pp. 227–300). Hillsdale, NJ: Erlbaum.

Wyer, R. S., & Srull, T. K. (1981). Category accessibility: Some theoretical and empirical issues concerning the processing of social stimulus information. In E. T. Higgins, C. P. Herman, & M. P. Zanna (Eds.), *Social cognition: The Ontario Symposium* (Vol. 1, pp. 161–197). Hillsdale, NJ: Erlbaum.

Wyer, R. S., & Srull, T. K. (1984). *Human cognition in its social context.* Unpublished manuscript, University of Illinois.

Wyer, R. S., Srull, T. K., & Gordon, S. E. (1984). The effects of predicting a person's behavior on subsequent trait judgments. *Journal of Experimental Social Psychology, 20*, 29–46.

Wyer, R. S., Srull, T. K., Gordon, S. E., & Hartwick, J. (1982). Effects of processing objectives on the recall of prose material. *Journal of Personality and Social Psychology, 43*, 674–688.

Zanna, M. P., & Cooper, J. (1976). Dissonance and the attribution process. In J. Harvey, W. J. Ickes, & R. F. Kidd (Eds.), *New directions in attribution research* (Vol. 1, pp. 199–217). Hillsdale, NJ: Erlbaum.

CHAPTER 18

Action Identification

DANIEL M. WEGNER
Trinity University

ROBIN R. VALLACHER
Florida Atlantic University

People do what they think they are doing. Ordinarily, they would prefer to think about their acts in the most encompassing way possible. But when they cannot perform an act so broadly conceptualized, they concern themselves with thinking of a detail of the act. These three statements capture the essence of the theory of action identification (Vallacher & Wegner, 1985). Through them, it is possible to envision how people "intend" to act, how they are "motivated," how they act "on impulse," how they "regulate" their action, how they appear to respond to "unconscious drives," how they "learn," and how they "create" new courses of action. All of these implications are not immediately apparent of course. The purpose of this chapter is to show how these various human tendencies, long documented and studied by psychologists, can be understood within a unified system prescribed by the three principles of the theory.

THE REIFICATION OF ACTION

Psychologists, like people in general, regularly assume that actions are real. After all, an act such as "throwing a brick through a window" seems real enough. Like an umbrella or a Buick, it seems to be a "thing." It has qualities that can be described (e.g., "nice arch, good follow-through"); people can distinguish it from other things (i.e., no one thinks it is "graduating from barber college"); and it can have very real consequences for the actor (e.g., a stay in jail). Any action seems to be real in these senses. Thus, it is hard to grasp, at first, that this action, like all others, is a reification—a mental construction that imposes a presumed reality on experience. The theory trades on the idea, however, that actions have a certain unreality in that their nature depends on how they are identified.

Fallible Distinctions

Psychologists have often noted that people may identify one thing in different ways (Brown, 1958; Rosch, 1973). The *identities* of things, therefore, do not inhere in the things themselves but rather are the products of human thought. This observation makes sense, also, when it is applied to action. As philosophers have long recognized (e.g., Anscombe, 1957; Austin, 1961; Danto, 1963; Goldman, 1970; Wittgenstein, 1953) and psychologists have more recently discovered (e.g., Kruglanski, 1975; Newtson, 1976), any action can be identified in multiple ways. "Throwing a brick through a window," for instance, might also be identified as "creating a nuisance," "scaring people in the building," "moving one's arm," "getting rid of a brick," "breaking glass," and so on. These identifications are not simple synonyms, so the person who performs this act would seem to be doing many different things. Any one action identification, in this light, is a seemingly arbitrary choice from numerous possibilities. And every action, in turn, is less than exactly real, for it is only an act *under one identity*—one that is chosen somehow from many.

This realization seems damaging to many of the typical assumptions psychologists make about human behavior. It makes some commentators wonder, for instance, whether textbook chapters on "aggressive behavior," "cooperation," "obedience," and so on, might represent nothing but senseless fabrications (cf. Gergen, 1982). If the action of a participant in a psychological experiment can be identified in more than one way, who is to say that the psychologist has discovered the right identity to use as the basis for classification? Perhaps Milgram's (1963) subjects weren't "obeying" but were merely "pushing buttons." All psychologists can say about the behaviors they classify as instances of "obedience"—or any other grouping—is that at least one identity of each act is classifiable. Even when psychologists take pains to establish operational definitions of actions, all they really do is define an act by pointing to its reified identity—and then note a few other identities as well. An operational definition of "aggression," for instance, may include mention of "giving another person an electric shock," "pushing buttons," or the like. It is unclear that just because one or a few identities of an act are classified for study, all the other identities of the act should be understood as unreal accompaniments of the real act.

Nevertheless, this leap is commonly made. On assuming that one identification of an action is the correct one, it is common practice to suggest that the other, unreal identifications are not action names but something else entirely. Once the reified identity is accorded status as the *act*, some other identities may be called *means* or *subacts* (when they indicate how the act is achieved). Still others may be called *intentions, purposes, goals, consequences, reasons,* or *side effects* of the act (when they indicate why or with what effect the act is done). Should these consequences seem more moving or important than the reified act itself, they may then be accorded the label of *motives*. And when such identities are unknown to the actor, they may be given positions as *unconscious drives*. Finally, when act identities signify states of being of the actor (e.g., "being aggressive"), they may be taken as indicants of the actor's *personality traits*. In short, once an act is reified in terms of one identity, many of its other identities fall into place as relevant adjuncts to the action. Each of these other identities is thus reified in its own position as a member of the constellation of psychological baggage that comes with the reified action.

All of these labels are jarred loose, perhaps permanently, when we recognize that the reified identity of the act is no more real than any other. It is conceivable, for example, that one might perform an action that could be variously identified as "drinking coffee," "becoming alert," "bringing a cup to one's lips," "moving one's arm and mouth," "satisfying a caffeine habit," "getting nervous," and "quenching one's thirst." If "bringing a cup to one's lips" were reified as the *act*, then "moving one's arm and mouth" might be a *means*, "drinking coffee" a *goal*, "getting nervous" an unintended *side effect*, and perhaps "becoming alert" a *conscious motive* and "satisfying a caffeine habit" an *unconscious drive*. Perhaps, however, the real act is "getting nervous"—as one might well attest after too many cups. If this is the case, one must soak the labels off the various identities and redistribute them— noting now that "bringing a cup to one's lips," "moving one's arm and mouth," and "drinking coffee" all serve as *means*, "satisfying a caffeine habit" might be the *motive*, and so on—in a juggling act that profoundly disturbs one's theoretical sensibilities. Because all these terms are defined in relation to the identity that is assumed to mark the real act, they represent but fallible distinctions, subject to chaotic reordering whenever a different reification is imposed. In the end, all are just different ways of identifying what was done.

Action identification theory thus has no room for these terms. Instead, it supposes only two "kinds" of action identification. First, the theory assumes that a person who is asked "What are you doing?" will have an immediate answer. This identification of action, which is the one most accessible to the person at the time, is termed the person's *prepotent identity*. Second, the theory assumes that the person, on probing, could very well identify the act in many other ways. These additional identifications are components of the person's organized knowledge about the action—the person's *act identity structure*. In a way, then, the theory appreciates the reification tendency we have noted in both laypersons and psychologists; it assumes that people will hold one identity of an action, the prepotent one, to be the real act, and that they will view other identities as lesser claimants to this status. However, the theory makes a more crucial suggestion: It holds that since actions are *not* real, but instead are only identified parcels of behavior, the prepotent identity of an act is a psychological matter. Quite simply, the person's preferred understanding of an act could change, moving at different times and settings to any of the identities in the person's act identity structure.

The principles of the theory that were iterated at the outset now can begin to make sense. The first principle—that people do what they think they are doing— says that people *do* the act that is described by their prepotent act identity. The second and third principles, in turn, indicate how that prepotent identity may change, moving about the act identity structure to settle in sequence on more "encompassing" or more "detailed" understandings of the act. To grasp more clearly how this movement occurs, it is important to consider how act identities may be related in a person's structure of knowledge about action.

Act Identity Structures

When people talk about act identities, they commonly reveal an implicit *ordering* of identities. They may say that one "prevents cavities" *by* "brushing one's teeth," for example, or that one "brushes" *by* "moving one's hand." This ordering is not seen as reversible: One does not "brush" *by* "preventing cavities" or "move one's hand" *by* "brushing." Psychologists and philosophers who have observed this phenomenon (Danto, 1963; Goldman, 1970; Lichtenstein & Brewer, 1980; G. A. Miller, Galanter, & Pribram, 1960; Schank & Abelson, 1977) have suggested that the structure of act descriptions corresponds to the structure of action itself and that relational terms such as *by* prescribe a simple hierarchy of action, subaction, subsubaction, and so on. In this view, "preventing cavities" might be accorded the highest position in an act hierarchy, with "brushing one's teeth" and other subacts (e.g., "visiting the dentist," "avoiding sweets") taking up subordinate positions. One "prevents cavities" *by* doing each of these subacts. Each of the subacts, it follows, may have its own array of components.

This interpretation makes good sense, and it has served as the basis for a wide range of research on the "script" as the fundamental organizational unit of action understanding (Abelson, 1981). A script is typically represented as a simple hierarchy with one overarching act identity at the top and subordinate identities arranged hierarchically below it (Bower, Black, & Turner, 1979). When people are asked to indicate the alternative identities for an action, however, they seldom produce just the names of subacts. On describing what one does in "robbing a store," for example, subjects in one study (Vallacher, Wegner, Bordieri, & Wenzlaff, 1981) went beyond the specification of details (e.g., "holding a gun") to recount multiple consequences of the action (e.g., "getting the police after you," "obtaining money," "breaking the law"). They indicated what one does *by* "robbing a store" in five of the nine most frequently mentioned identities of the act. Thus, instead of seeing the act in terms of a simple hierarchy of identities, they portrayed it in terms of multiple, overlapping hierarchies. Such an act identity structure for nine identities of "robbing a store" is shown in Figure 18.1. This structure was mapped by having subjects judge the sensibleness of each possible *by* relation and its inverse (e.g., would one "rob a store" *by* "obtaining money" or "obtain money" *by* "robbing a store?") and then representing the most clearly asymmetric relations as arrows from the lower level identity to the higher level identity (e.g., from "robbing a store" to "obtaining money.").

Such observations suggest that the person's cognitive representation of action is considerably more complex than a "script." People seem to think not only about *how* to do an act—by means of lower level identities; they also conceptualize *why* or *with what effect* the act is done, volunteering higher level identifications. These higher level identities are the "encompassing" ways of understanding action that

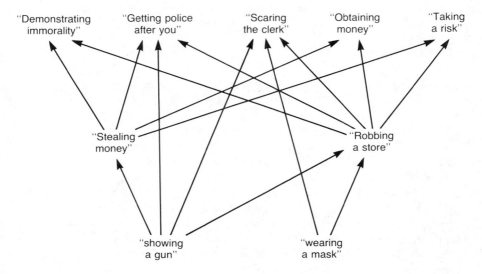

FIGURE 18.1   "Robbing a store" act identity structure.

are noted in the second principle of the theory. And according to that principle, they are very attractive. To say someone is "moving a finger," for instance, identifies the act at a relatively low level and thus presents what seems to be an impoverished conceptualization of what is done—especially if there are cues available to suggest higher level meanings of the act. If we learn that the person's finger is posed on the *h* key of a typewriter, we are prone to infer immediately that the person is "typing an *h*" (*by* "moving a finger"). Should we learn that the paper in the typewriter is a page of prose about dog breeding, the act may become "writing about dogs." And if there are many pages next to the typewriter and a book contract in the file cabinet nearby, we may quickly assume that the person is "writing a book," "earning a living," or even "helping to improve the dog breeds of the world."

Many features of the context surrounding an act provide potential cues for inferring higher level meanings of the act. Given the observation of body movement alone, we can identify only what Danto (1963) has called a "basic act" (e.g., "moving a finger"). However, certain features of the act's context will allow us to identify the act at a higher level (cf. Goldman, 1970). These "identity conditions"—contextual features that must be present for a given basic act to generate a higher level identification—must be counted as important but implicit features of the person's act identity structure. For the person to know of a possible higher level identification of an act, he or she must know that a particular array of identity conditions is present in the setting of the act. These identity conditions may be potential causal effects; for example, "moving an arm" while holding a cue stick in the presence of a particular configuration of billiard balls generates the higher level identity of "putting the 8 ball in the pocket." Identity conditions may be potential conventional interpretations; for instance, "winking" in certain circles may generate, by convention, the higher level identity of "flirting shamelessly." Identity conditions may be environmental circumstances (as when "talking" generates the higher level identity of "talking to a crowd"). Identity conditions may also arise in other potential actions with which the current action is compared (as when "running" generates the higher level identity of "running faster than one did earlier"). In short, causation, convention, circumstance, and comparison each provide a variety of identity conditions that allow the person to know that a particular body movement will be interpretable as a particular higher level act (cf. Goldman, 1970).

Higher level action identifications allow the identity structures surrounding particular acts to become connected. The seemingly disparate acts of "reading a magazine" and "drinking a beer," for example, could both be understood by a particular person to have "relaxing" as a higher level identity. "Walking to work" and "eating at McDonald's," in turn, might both generate the higher level identity of "saving money." The higher level identities of "relaxing" and "saving money," however, might be linked at an even higher level in terms of the overarching identity of "doing the right thing." Still other connections might be made among all the different higher level identities the person knows for many different actions. Thus, although it is often theoretically convenient to speak only of particular domains of the person's identity structure—those surrounding identities of special interest—the "encompassing" nature of high-level identities reminds us that these domains may very well be linked in a yet higher order structure that the person uses to understand all action.

Identification as Personal Reification

The principles of the theory of action identification indicate how people go about referring to their act identity structures in the course of determining what they will do. The first principle, as we have already noted, says that people will perform the prepotent identity in the structure. This means that the other identities in a particular structural domain will *not* be consciously entertained—although they may very well be done anyway because they are a part of, or a result of, the prepotent identity. The prepotent identity *will* be consciously considered, however, and it will stand as the person's own reification of the action, characterizing exactly, at that time, what the person thinks the act really is.

The second and third principles of the theory propose how the prepotent identity for an action is determined. In a sense, they suggest an algorithm by which the person moves from one prepotent identity to another in the act identity structure. The second principle indicates that people will always be ready to appreciate higher level identities of their actions. People search for meaning in action, and they find it by identifying the action at higher and higher levels. The third principle indicates, however, that there is a critical limitation on this tendency—the person's own ability. If the person cannot perform an act that is understood at a particular level of identification, this principle suggests that the person will move to think about the act at a lower level of identification. For example, if one has difficulty "driving a golf ball to the green," one will become consciously concerned with some detail of this act, perhaps then worrying about "keeping one's eye on the ball," "getting a good grip on the club," and so forth. This tendency thus provides a constant and stringent ceiling on the level of identification that may become prepotent for a person in any particular action domain. Quite simply, the person will not long identify an action at a level that is higher than the one at which he or she can perform the action successfully.

This specification suggests that there *is* a criterion—other than the identification—for determining the "reality" of an act. This other criterion is the person's skill in acting. In any particular setting, at any particular time, a certain person will either be able to perform the act specified by an identity or not. The different factors that may promote or inhibit a person's capacity to act, of course, might well comprise an interminable list; we could start with genetic predispositions and the person's history of experience and eventually speak of the person's diet, the lighting, the presence of high winds, and a host of other factors. The point, however, is that all these factors come together each time a person acts, and they determine whether the person will be able to do the act as identified. The person's own capacity to act thus determines whether an identified act can become a reality.

When a person can do an act as indicated by a prepotent identity, the theory proposes that there will be an immediate tendency for the person to move to a higher level of prepotent identification. This means that a person who successfully "butters the toast," for example, can now think of "making breakfast." At this higher level position, however, the person may not have sufficient skill to complete the act as identified. The person may not have the training in cooking, perhaps, to be able to complete the preparation of breakfast in a completely automatic, unthinking way. Thus, the theory argues that the person will move to thinking about the act again at a lower level, now considering something like "frying eggs" or "sectioning grapefruit." Both of these acts are parts of "making breakfast" that, at least for this person at this time, must be conceptualized separately for their completion to ensue. A particularly inexperienced cook might have to descend to even lower levels, thinking about "getting the eggs out of the fridge," or some such, for the action to continue. In sum, the person thinks of how to continue when an act cannot be done and thinks of what effect it has when it can be done. In this way, the person's current action is guided through his or her identity structures to keep him or her acting all the time.

The principles of the theory describe a system that makes people identify acts at the level at which they can do them. Therefore, although the theory proposes that people are always prepared to accept higher level identifications, it suggests that their personal capacity to do an act—upon only thinking about it in terms of the prepotent identity—will bring them back from the ephemeral reaches of high-level identification. Over time, then, people will move in these cycles toward an optimal, personal reification of any action. This personal reification will tend to be at the level at which, given no special disruptions or complications, they can perform the act only by thinking of it in terms of a single identity.

Our empirical investigations of the theory have centered on two major sets of implications of these ideas. First, we have examined how identification affects the performance of action; this is the study of *action maintenance*. This line of inquiry is focused on the ways in which the prior identification of an action influences the subsequent nature and quality of the action. Thus, it is relevant to questions of how people "intend" to act, "regulate" their action, and are "motivated" to act. Second, we have examined how action identification may change, thereby leading action on a new course; this is the study of *action emergence*. Our concern here is with the ways in which people may come to understand their acts differently—and as a result, may come to behave differently. This research thus offers insight on how people "learn," how they act "on impulse," how they "create" new actions, and even on how they seem to respond to "unconscious drives." In the remainder of the chapter, we take up the topics of maintenance and emergence in turn.

ACTION MAINTENANCE

It is not unusual to encounter a psychological theory that suggests a role for mind in action. William James (1890) suggested something much like the first principle of action identification theory when he developed the notion of "ideomotor action." By his analysis, people get ideas of what they will do, and an act is the immediate result of such an idea coming to consciousness. Many theorists have since echoed this notion, making it a part of theories of cybernetics (Carver & Scheier, 1981; G. A. Miller *et al.*, 1960), private speech (Luria, 1961; Vygotsky, 1962), motor learning (Schmidt, 1975), action hermeneutics (Gauld & Shotter, 1977; Harré & Secord, 1972), artificial intelligence (Abelson, 1973), and others. In this sense, the present analysis can be portrayed as "one of those theories that says people know what they are doing."

The Optimal Identification Level

There are limits on how people may know their actions and still do them successfully. Some identifications of action may be effective ones, allowing the person to perform the act as identified. Other identities may not be effective, resulting in a failure to maintain the act. Certainly, it is easy to see that an identity might be ineffective because it is too high-level for the person to do. There are very few baseball players, for instance, who could step up to bat and follow a coach's injunction to "triple to left field." Although this might very well be a desirable state of affairs, and although the player might know exactly the identity conditions that would be necessary for this act to occur (e.g., the ball falling far from a fielder), the player's capacity to produce such an act may simply be lacking. Thus, the act will not be done.

An identification might also be ineffective by being too low-level. The player who is capable of hitting the ball squarely each time at bat, for example, might be admonished at some point to "keep your forward arm straight." This identity consists of only a part of what is usually a fluid, well-integrated action. In trying to perform this identity, however, the skilled player might produce a disintegrated action, one that fails even to meet the criterion of "hitting the ball." Many everyday actions can be disrupted in just this way. Most people can remember a point at which their "driving a car" was disrupted by a backseat driver who reminded them to "stay in the lane" or "use the turn signal." Thus, it is not surprising that psychologists discovered fairly early that attention to a skilled action can disturb its course (Bryan & Harter, 1899). In terms of our theory, the point is that thinking about lower level identities can be ineffective when one can ordinarily perform the act at a higher level of identification.

This line of reasoning suggests that there is an optimal level of identification for any person performing a particular action. Identifying the act at levels higher or lower than this would be ineffective. This optimal point would be determined by the person's skill level in doing the act in the particular setting. However, people do not always identify their acts optimally. Although the principles of the theory suggest that people would tend to move toward optimal identification levels, this movement may often be incomplete. People may not have performed an action before, for example, and therefore may have to make an essentially random start at identifying it at some level. Or they may have made a "lucky shot," performing an act identified at high level when their true skill would not allow them to perform it well at that level on a subsequent occasion. Perhaps they have even been swayed by what others say about the act, and so try to perform it at a consensual level of identification that does not match their personal level of skill.

These departures from optimal identification levels should have observable effects. Our studies of the action maintenance process have centered on this possibility. In general, our plan has been to determine whether deviations from optimal identification levels have the expected ill effects on action performance. To determine what level of identification is likely to be optimal for a given action, we have depended on subjects' judgments of several maintenance indicators—qualities of actions that indicate how difficult the actions are to maintain. Wegner and Vallacher (1983) asked 50 subjects to rate 25 different actions (e.g., "eating," "talking to a child," "climbing a tree") on the following characteristics:

1. *Difficulty*: How difficult is the action?
2. *Familiarity*: How familiar are you with the action?
3. *Complexity*: How many ways are there to do the action?
4. *Duration*: How long does it take to do the action?
5. *Learning time*: How long does it take to learn to do the action well?

These indices were all significantly correlated across the 25 acts, so ratings on them were summed (with familiarity ratings reversed) to yield an overall index of the degree to which the actions were easy versus difficult to maintain.

The notion of optimal identification level suggests that, generally, people would identify the more difficult actions at lower levels and the easier actions at higher levels. Thus, it is worth noting that this study called for a second sample of subjects ($N = 272$) to indicate their preferred identification level for each act. This was done by having each subject consider the act identity (e.g., "eating") and judge which of two other identities for the act was a better descriptor of the act. One of these other identities was always lower in level (e.g., "chewing"), whereas the other was higher in level (e.g., "getting nutrition"). Such choices were offered subjects for each of the 25 initial act identities, and the proportion of low-level choices was calculated across subjects for each. This score was significantly correlated across actions with the maintainability index, $r(25) = .39$, $p < .02$. Multiple regression analyses carried out with the individual maintenance indicators revealed significant prediction of identification level as well. In sum, as the theory suggests, people generally identify difficult actions at lower levels than easy actions.

The notion of an optimal identification level implies that for each individual, a notable departure from the usual level of identification will portend poor act performance. This means that for easy actions (which are usually identified by most people at high levels), low-level identification should predict poor performance. In contrast, for difficult actions, low-level identification should be optimal, and thus high-level identification should predict poor performance. To present some of the data we have accumulated on these possibilities, we will concern ourselves first with a study of the maintenance of an easy action—one rated as easy to maintain by subjects in the aforementioned study. We will focus on the identification and performance of "drinking alcoholic beverages," an act considered easier than 21 of the 25 actions rated. Then we will turn to research on the most difficult of the 25 acts—"rearing a child."

Maintaining Easy Actions

An action that is easy to maintain can be carried out without much conscious thought. Seldom do adults have to remind themselves to "step out of the car" when they have reached their destination; seldom, also, do they think about "bending the left knee" as they are walking. Yet they do these things, and when they are asked, they can identify them quite clearly. Our idea is that for many of the simple and frequently performed actions of everyday life, people only find it necessary to think about what they are doing in relatively large action segments. They can identify easily maintainable actions at high levels because, as a result of practice or the inherent simplicity of the act, they have it in their grasp to perform all the details of the act only by thinking of a high-level identity. This allows people the freedom to gloss over the mechanics, even if they were once painful to learn, and intend their actions in the largest units of which they are capable. There is thus an elegant economy in the way people identify action.

For many of the easy actions one performs in a day, economy of identification is a definite advantage. Yet there are some easy actions that might be more adaptively performed if they were *not* quite so economical to intend. "Drinking an alcoholic beverage" is one of these. The theoretical ideas that have been advanced to this point would lead us to believe that people who perform this easy act frequently and proficiently should identify it at high levels. In so doing, however, these people might also tend to lose conscious contact with the details of "drinking." For instance, they might not notice just how many drinks they are having, how deeply they are quaffing the drink they have in hand, or even whether they have had enough. Their high-level identification of the act could prevent them from prepotent identification of the act at lower levels and thus perhaps even hinder their attempts to control their drinking behavior. This reasoning suggests that drinkers' identifications of the act of drinking could be an important topic of study—one that might offer a test of the theory and might suggest potentially beneficial lines of intervention for alcohol abuse as well.

Wegner, Vallacher, and Dizadji (1983) examined the relationship between alcohol consumption and the identification of "drinking alcoholic beverages." First, an action identification questionnaire was constructed by having 15 subjects (with widely varying degrees of drinking experience) each give multiple answers to the question "What do you do in drinking alcoholic beverages?" The 50 most common responses were isolated, translated into a common form (the gerund phrase), and used for the questionnaire. To complete the questionnaire, each subject was instructed to rate each identity on a 1–7 scale according to how well it described the act of "drinking alcoholic beverages."

Two samples of subjects completed this questionnaire: a group of 94 undergraduates from Trinity University and a group of 87 inpatients from the Chicago Alcohol Treatment Center (CATC). We trusted that the CATC subjects would be relatively uniform in their high level of alcohol experience. All had been admitted to the center only after (1) their attempts to stop drinking had failed, (2) alcohol use had affected a significant area of their lives, (3) blackouts had been experienced, (4) a loss of control during alcohol use was reported, and (5) they had lost their jobs as the result of alcohol problems. The Trinity sample, however, was expected to vary somewhat in alcohol experience. Thus, these subjects completed an additional questionnaire on alcohol use. This measure, derived from the factor analysis of a larger questionnaire, exhibited satisfactory reliability in this sample ($\alpha = .78$). It contained six items: (1) number of different kinds of alcoholic beverages used (of 12 categories provided); (2) number of days in which alcohol is consumed in a typical week; (3) number of drinks likely to be consumed at a party; (4) whether drinking had ever been continued to the point of illness; (5) self-rated drinking experience; and (6) self-rated enjoyment of the taste of alcohol. Standardized scores on these items were summed to yield an overall alcohol use index for each undergraduate.

TABLE 18.1 "Drinking Alcoholic Beverages" Identity Factors

Factor	Loading	Identity
1. Low level	.81	lifting a glass
	.77	touching a glass to my lips
	.71	swallowing liquid
	.71	holding a liquid in my mouth
	.64	drinking from a glass
	.61	drinking by swallowing liquid
	.57	experiencing wetness in my mouth
	.48	holding a glass in my hand
	.39	experiencing a taste
2. Hurting myself	.76	letting myself down
	.61	demonstrating a lack of self-control
	.59	letting myself down by drinking
	.53	experiencing shame
	.51	causing damage to my health
	.44	disappointing my friends
	.42	acting out of habit
	.39	making myself withdrawn
3. Relieving tension	.88	relieving tension by drinking
	.61	relieving tension
	.43	getting my mind off my problems
4. Overcoming boredom	.57	overcoming boredom by drinking
	.48	satisfying my needs
	.42	passing time
	.40	following my impulses
5. Getting drunk	.70	getting drunk
	.56	drinking too much
	.43	joining in with others who are drinking
	.36	getting in a good mood
6. Rewarding myself	.80	rewarding myself
	.69	rewarding myself by drinking
	.51	demonstrating my good taste
	.40	getting myself energized
	.36	clearing my mind
	.36	enjoying myself

The act identity ratings made by all subjects were submitted to a principal axis factor analysis with varimax rotation. This procedure yielded six factors with eigenvalues greater than 1.0 that together accounted for 59% of the rating variance. A .35 loading criterion used to assign items to factors resulted in the factor structure shown in Table 18.1. As we have found in other such analyses (cf. Vallacher & Wegner, 1985), a low-level identification factor arose along with several high-level factors tapping different general interpretations of the act. The high-level factors in this case could be interpreted as "hurting myself," "relieving tension," "overcoming boredom," "getting drunk," and "rewarding myself." The mean reliability for factor indices formed by summing the ratings of the identities loaded on each factor was .81.

To determine the relationship between alcohol use and action identification, subjects were assigned to four groups monotonically increasing in alcohol use: low-, middle-, and high-use undergraduates (as partitioned by scores on the alcohol use questionnaire), and CATC clients. Then a complete multiple regression was performed using subject age, sex, and scores on each of the six identification factor indices to predict alcohol use. This regression yielded a significant overall equation accounting for 63% of the criterion variance, $F(8, 175) = 37.49, p < .01$. Given that the Trinity sample was younger than the CATC sample, it is not surprising that age was the strongest predictor of alcohol use, $\beta = .31, F(1, 175) = 28.13, p < .05$. However, as we would expect, low-level identification was a significant *negative* predictor, $\beta = -.12, F(1,175) = 3.94, p < .05$. All of the high-level indices, in turn, were positive predictors, with betas ranging from .06 to .22. Of these, "hurting myself" was significant, $F(1, 175) = 8.89, p < .01$, as was "relieving tension," $F(1, 175) = 10.74, p < .01$.

These findings indicate that identification of the act of "drinking alcoholic beverages" indeed varies with alcohol use. People who use alcohol a great deal tend to identify their act at higher levels, noting that they are behaving reprehensibly or relieving tension. People who do not perform the act so frequently or proficiently describe it in terms of its details. Thus, even though the act is a relatively easy one to perform, some people can remain teetotalers, never seeing the act as much more than "raising a glass to one's lips." Others, however, have become so proficient at the act that they skim over these details in a headlong rush to perform more encompassing and distant identities. We suspect that this high-level conceptualization of the act may serve as a barrier to the act's suppression. This is because, rather than monitoring the act in steps as it occurs, a person who understands an act in a high-level way is likely not to think about the act at all once it is initiated. Rather, this person will monitor only whether the high-level identity of the act has been achieved.

A similar analysis can be made of a variety of other habitual or addictive behaviors. In the case of "eating," for example, it appears that undereaters (e.g., anorexics) identify the act at low levels, whereas overeaters (e.g., the overweight) identify it at high levels (Wegner, Vallacher, Ewert, & Reno, 1983). Eating, like drinking alcohol, is relatively easy to do, and thinking about the details of the act is thus a sign of poor performance. Thinking about the consequences of the act, however, seems to do little to help when the act is performed to excess. Although overweight people often identify "eating" as "gaining weight," their recognition of this unwanted feature of the act does not seem to be sufficient to slow them down. In our view, this very concentration on a high-level identity is the problem. As self-regulation theorists have noted (Kanfer, 1970; Kirschenbaum & Tomarken, 1982), the successful control of habitual behaviors may require something like an "obsessive-compulsive" mindset—a detailed monitoring of ongoing habitual behavior. This seems to entail the identification of action in terms of the low-level identities that precede the completion of the action, rather than the high-level identities that follow it.

In drawing lessons about self-control from these studies, we should not forget the theoretical message of the findings. Quite simply, as the optimal identification level hypothesis would have it, easy actions appear to be performed most proficiently by people who have come to identify them at relatively high levels. It is most fortunate that people have the capacity to "unitize" the chains of movement that go into an easy action, for this allows them the luxury of not thinking about each movement as the act is performed. If they do report thinking about these pieces of action, it seems that the integration and fluidity of the action itself is called into question. Thinking about act details is only useful when one must build the action from its parts each time it is undertaken.

Maintaining Difficult Actions

Some actions are so difficult to maintain that they can never be completed merely by reference to a high-level identity. For most people, "playing jazz piano" might be such an action. Years of practice are required before one can go beyond "putting fingers on keys" to the level of "playing a pleasant pattern of notes," and even then, one may still fall short of "going for the jazz" (cf. Sudnow, 1978). Eventually, however, even this act could conceivably be mastered; a fine jazz stylist can simply intend jazz and have it happen. However, there are many actions one is called on to perform in daily life that are even more complex or time-consuming and that are complicated still further by the absence of any chance to practice. Imagine, for example, trying to "go to college" by merely setting out to do it and then noting when it is done. "Earning a living," "making a home," "rearing a child," and the like, are even more difficult to maintain. Such acts can take a lifetime, and without multiple lifetimes in which to learn them, it is quite clear that one cannot maintain them only at high levels of identification.

The successful performance of difficult actions depends on lower level identification. A focus on the details of action is optimal in these cases, because it is simply impossible for the human information processor to conceptualize in one identity, and then enact automatically, such extended and intricate action. The "maintenance indicators" assessed in the research by Wegner and Vallacher (1983), give some sense of the dimensions of actions that give rise to this necessary concern with detail. As actions become more difficult, less familiar, more complex in their possible patterns of lower level acts, more lengthy, and more time-consuming to learn, they become more likely to be enacted in pieces. The person must think of each piece separately, and little can be done if the identities of the pieces do not become prepotent at their appropriate points of enactment.

Wegner, Richard, and Vallacher (1982) tested the hypothesis that "rearing a child" would be done most successfully by people who identify the act in terms of its details. Working with the Girl Scout and Boy Scout organizations of San Antonio, we arranged for 202 parents to complete a series of questionnaires. One

TABLE 18.2 "Rearing a Child" Identity Factors

Factor	Loading	Identity
1. Teaching and training	.72	encouraging the child to do well in school
	.70	helping the child with homework
	.69	helping the child make good decisions
	.66	teaching the child about sex
	.63	teaching the child to handle money
	.62	encouraging the child to participate in activities outside school
	.58	disciplining the child for misbehaving
2. Caretaking	.78	getting the child clothes to wear
	.67	teaching the child how to get dressed
	.60	providing the child's meals
	.51	driving the child to school or activities
	.47	taking the child to the dentist or doctor
	.36	protecting the child from danger
	.36	talking with the child's friends
	.19	giving the child money
3. Experiencing costs	.70	getting too little appreciation
	.66	making myself feel bad for not being a perfect parent
	.63	missing out on being with people my own age
	.51	getting extra worries
	.49	getting exhausted
	.40	getting less money to spend on other things
	.37	increasing family tension and arguments
	.14	getting embarrassed from time to time
4. Experiencing rewards	.65	arranging for someone to take care of me when I am older
	.62	raising someone to take my place in the world
	.62	raising someone to do the things I couldn't
	.60	getting a companion
	.59	being admired and imitated by the child
	.51	getting praise from friends and family about the child
5. Fulfilling a duty	.71	taking time away from more interesting things
	.61	doing what I have a duty to do
	.55	risking my personal property
	.42	raising someone to help around the house

was an action identification questionnaire for "rearing a child"; the 40 identities on this form were generated by 30 people in the free-response format noted earlier for the "drinking alcoholic beverages" questionnaire. The other questionnaires asked parents for detailed demographic information, for estimates of the amount of time per day they typically devote to each of 20 activities (including child care, child-centered activities, and children's organized activities), and for an array of indicators of child-rearing effectiveness. This latter form called for the parent to report certain objective indices (e.g., whether the child had received awards, had been in trouble with neighbors or the police, had received special treatment for emotional or learning problems) and also asked for more subjective reports (e.g., whether the child was easy to get along with, well-behaved, doing well in school).

A factor analysis with varimax rotation performed on the action identification ratings revealed a solution of five factors, which are shown in Table 18.2 along with their associated identities. It should be noted that a .40 item-loading criterion was relaxed somewhat in specific cases when identities appeared to be meaningfully associated with only one factor. The low-level identities clustered in two factors, one dealing with the lower levels of "teaching and training," the other capturing the lower levels of "caretaking." Higher level identifications were revealed in the remaining factors: "experiencing costs," "experiencing rewards," and "fulfilling a duty."

The results of this investigation bore out our hypothesis. Correlational and multiple regression analyses revealed that lower level identification was predictive of child-rearing success as measured by multiple criteria. Parents who concerned themselves with the details of the act reported that their children got into trouble less frequently and had not as often required therapeutic intervention for emotional or learning problems. Parents who were low-level identifiers also reported spending more time with the child and having better relations with the child. Several of the high-level factors also evinced significant relations with the child-rearing success indices. Most notably, the view of child-rearing as "experiencing costs" and as "fulfilling a duty" seemed to accompany child difficulties (e.g., poor school performance, a lack of awards or honors for the child). These general relationships were found to exist even after demographic predictors had been entered into the prediction equations of hierarchical multiple regression analyses.

These findings should be generalizable to many of the more difficult actions people perform. For example, the person who dwells on "becoming famous" as an identity of "writing a book" would seem by this analysis to be in a position to "write a book" only poorly. By the same token, the person who presses toward "inventing a revolutionary new computer" will meet certain failure. Although people might very well *begin* acts with these identities, and might even have these identities come to mind from time to time during the actions, they cannot use these identities alone as guides to action performance. High-level identities do not convey how difficult actions are to be done and, for this reason, are not sufficient for the cognitive control of difficult actions. It is only when relevant low-level identities come to mind that the action can be carried on, perhaps eventually to meet the high-level identity with which it was initiated.

This analysis is relevant to a number of important problems of action performance. Phenomena such as "choking under pressure" (cf. Baumeister, 1984) or other performance deficits that arise from overmotivation (e.g., Atkinson & Birch, 1978; Zajonc, 1965) can be understood as action identification errors. People may often fail to perform optimally because, as a result of their personal dispositions or the identity conditions made salient by the specific performance setting, they have it in mind to do too much. A basketball player, for example, might feel great pressure to perform a high-level identity such as "winning the game" or "pleasing the crowd." If the player's skill were sufficient, these are things that might in fact be done. However, without the skill to do these acts merely by intending them, the player who attempts action identified at these levels may fail to remember to "hold on to the ball" or "put it through the hoop." Thus, failure will often be the consequence.

This sort of performance handicap should also arise when a person underestimates the difficulty of maintaining an action. Suppose, for example, that one visits a physician and is told that one is likely to suffer blindness as a result of glaucoma later in life. The physician prescribes a medical regimen whereby one must take eyedrops four times a day for the rest of one's life if this condition is to be prevented. Because most people have taken eyedrops at some point, the action appears to be easy. Thus, one identifies what one is doing as "preventing blindness." This high-level identity, however, does little to convey the series of lower level actions that must be done regularly for successful performance. Actually, although "taking eyedrops" may be easy, doing anything four times a day for the balance of one's life is difficult indeed. Thus, one's identification fails to promote the maintenance of the action.

Research by Wegner, Kyser, and Vallacher (1983) provides empirical support for this account. This study called for 87 people receiving glaucoma treatment in San Antonio and Little Rock, Arkansas, to complete an action identification questionnaire for "using glaucoma medication." In addition, their self-reports of compliance with their prescribed medical regimens were assessed in a detailed questionnaire. The factor analysis of their action identifications yielded three low-level factors ("remembering the medication," "going to the doctor," and "taking the medication") and two that were higher level ("experiencing unpleasant consequences" and "preventing blindness"). Correlational and regression analyses revealed that "remembering the medication" and "going to the doctor" were associated with enhanced compliance, whereas "experiencing unpleasant consequences" was predictive of noncompliance. Apparently, thinking about the act in such a way as to make its details part of one's daily routine is an important path to proper self-medication. Thinking about it only in a high-level way is insufficient to bring about this integration.

People often fail to self-medicate for glaucoma; studies have suggested that only about 60% of patients follow this self-care regimen correctly (Norrell, 1981). The action identification approach to this problem suggests, however, that there is a useful avenue of intervention. Patients are regularly given some counseling by the physician or assistant when they begin such a regimen. We suspect, however, that this counseling may not emphasize clearly enough the difficulty of the act nor make salient the critical components of the act that must be prepotent for its proper performance. An emphasis on techniques of "remembering" and stress on the importance of "going to the doctor" could serve, in this context, to alert people to the low-level identities of the act that would enhance their self-care effectiveness.

Identification as a Cause of Action

We have now seen how identification level is related to the performance of several acts—drinking, eating, rearing a child, and taking medication; and the relationships we have reviewed appear to support the optimal identification level hypothesis. Whether lower level identities enhance or retard performance seems to be a matter of the maintainability of the act; lower level identification improves the performance of acts that are hard to maintain, but impairs the performance of acts that are easy to maintain. The soundness of this analysis rests, however, on an assumption we have made in conducting this research—that identification differences can cause action differences.

Although this assumption helps us forge the theoretical links among all these varied findings, it was not tested explicitly in the correlational research we have reported to this point. Thus, one could approach any of the results of these studies and propose an alternative path of causation. It could be argued that performing an easy or difficult act poorly or well is the cause of the observed level of identification. People may merely observe their completed actions and describe them in accord with what they believe they have done. Alternatively, one could even argue that neither action nor identification is the cause of the other, but that some unobserved third variable is in fact the cause of both. In the case of alcohol drinking, for example, it might be said that a physiological addiction to alcohol drives the act and simultaneously leads people who drink a lot to think about the act only in high-level terms.

We have not concerned ourselves with attempting to rule out such possibilities in this research, for a simple reason. Such reversed or circuitous causal paths, like the direct causal link between identification and action, are often perfectly reasonable to the theory. Although the theoretical principles certainly do not embrace all possible causal paths—especially those including third variables—they do prescribe a *system* of sequential interrelationships among acts and identities. The principles suggest that successes and failures in action provoke identification changes; such identification changes, in turn, produce different kinds of actions. These actions, then, are again susceptible to success or failure and thus can promote yet further identification changes. Jumping into such an ongoing system to proclaim one component the "cause" of the other is an oversimplification of the dynamic interplay of the components (cf. von Bertalanffy, 1968). We suspect that path-analytic or time-series investigations designed to establish the causal priorities of action and identification in the domains we have studied would partition the causality all around.

To examine the causal links between identification and action, we have undertaken a more fine-grained analysis of the processes by which actions and identifications change. In particular, we have conducted a series of experimental studies of the stepwise action change process that is implied by the theory—one we have taken to calling the process of "action emergence." Both the impact of action on identification and the influence of identification on action are parts of this process. More important, however, it is through the process of action emergence that both identifications and actions can change, leading people to do new things and understand differently what they are doing.

ACTION EMERGENCE

It has always been fashionable in certain psychological circles to suggest that people do not know what they are doing. Freud (1914/1960) held that the motives underlying most human actions are so obscure that people are lucky to find them out even after years of psychoanalysis. Outside the realm of psychoanalytic thought, similarly dour views of the rationality of human action have often arisen (Hampshire, 1959; Mead, 1938; Merton, 1968; Ryle, 1949), culminating most recently in theories that rest largely on the idea that people try to discern what they have done only after the action is over (Bem, 1972; Nisbett & Wilson, 1977). By such analyses, actions are typically seen as caused by nonconscious mechanisms (arising from psychoanalytic, cybernetic, behavioristic, or other causes), and are thus merely data to be interpreted once they have become available for inspection. The identification of action, in this view, is always a *post hoc* affair.

Action in Prospect and Retrospect

The idea that people understand their acts only in retrospect is, of course, at odds with action identification theory. We have proposed that people always know what they are doing—that is, that there is always a prepotent identity for any time of action. How, then, could people sometimes come to learn the identity for their action only *after* it has occurred? We believe that there is room for such reflective understanding of action in the theory and, moreover, that the process by which people come to such *emergent* identifications of their acts is the central mechanism whereby action identification can promote behavior change. In incorporating the notion of retrospective identification into the theory, however, we do not simultaneously accept the idea that actions are *not* known beforehand. Because an action can be identified in many ways, there is nothing to stop us from suggesting that a person may identify an act in one way before it occurs and then come to identify it in another way after it has happened. In this manner, people can understand actions in advance and yet "discover" what they have done after the fact. Their initial and later identifications of the act simply differ.

An empirical example may help illustrate this point. Wegner, Vallacher, and Kelly (1983) asked people to identify what they were doing in "getting married." Telephone interviews were conducted with people who, according to newspaper announcements in San Antonio or the campus grapevine at Trinity University, were en route to the altar. The usual free-response array of act identities was assembled for this study, and we simply asked respondents to indicate what one does in "getting married" by rating how well each of the identities described the act. Respondents we questioned over a month before their wedding day endorsed most strongly a relatively high-level identity of the act—"expressing my love." Those questioned a day or two before the wedding, however, endorsed a low-level factor containing identities such as "getting a special outfit," "saying vows," "hiring a photographer," and so on. Subjects questioned a month or two following their wedding no longer saw the act in such low-level terms and more strongly advocated a high-level factor of "getting problems" as the identity of the act. It seems the honeymoon was over.

Most people seem to know that "getting married" can change in this way. What they seldom recognize is that because actions are not real, *all* actions are, in principle, open to such reidentification. Everyday experience does not seem to bear this out, however; the tendency to reify an action in terms of its prepotent identity often seems to keep people from accepting alternative identifications. For example, if we tell an avid butterfly collector that he is not "collecting butterflies," but rather "wasting his time," we are likely to be singularly unsuccessful in convincing him. Likewise, if we inform someone who is "lobbying for a larger national defense budget" that she is actually "promoting nuclear war," she will not readily adopt our conception of her act. Different high-level identities often convey very different evaluations of an act, and people seem unusually resistant to accepting one high-level conception of what they are doing when they already have another. Why is it, then, that subjects in the "getting married" study could change their conception of what they were doing?

According to the theory, the period of low-level identification that occurred near the wedding day was the critical condition for the change in identification. The theory holds that people can move from higher to lower levels of identification; this is the message of the third principle. It also holds that people can move from lower to higher levels of identification; this is conveyed by the second principle. However, simple lateral movement in an identity structure is not allowed. Thus, to move from one high-level conception of the act ("expressing love") to another ("getting problems"), individuals must necessarily pass through a transitional state in which they consider the details of the action. This, then, is what keeps people from accepting, willy-nilly, any high-level identification that is offered for an act they already know at high level. It is only when an initial comprehensive understanding of the action is dissipated—by a consideration of low-level identities—that a new comprehensive understanding can be instituted in its place.

We believe that this sequence is characteristic of each instance in which an act is viewed in different high-level ways in prospect and retrospect. The initial and later identifications of the act can differ because the low-level identification that occurs during the act erases the initial identification, making way for a later identification that makes sense of the person's later circumstances. This general statement can be generalized yet further when we note that the low-level period does not necessarily have to be induced by performance of the act. It could occur at some other time and thus make an emergent understanding possible. The newness and difficulty of an act that is ongoing, of course, may often make people descend to lower levels to maintain it. But what if people were asked, for instance, to consider the details of their wedding plans some years before or after engaging in the act? By our analysis, their movement to lower levels even at this time could pave the way for an emergent high-level understanding. Any suggestion of a high-level conception of "getting married," whether it is the person's original conception or something quite different, will be attractive. Thus, identification changes should be open to manipulation at any time, provided that some stimulus to lower level identification is available.

We should note that low-level identification promotes a readiness for a new understanding of action but does not require it. Often, a person will come to think of the details of an action and then will encounter information from memory or experience that suggests the same high-level identification with which the action was initiated. The person who does not experience any problems when the honeymoon is over, for example, may emerge from the low levels of the wedding experience to adopt a renewed appreciation of the act as "expressing love." Such a return to the initial high-level identification of the act will be particularly likely if the person is reminded of that act meaning by some current experience. A special candlelight dinner, for instance, could lead both partners back to their romantic interpretation of their union. A period of low-level identification seems to make people sensitive to any cues about the larger meaning of what they have done, whether they knew that meaning of the act in prospect or only in retrospect.

The Emergence Process

The remarkable aspect of action identification change is that it may produce action change. The person who comes to identify "getting married" as "getting problems," for instance, would seem to be less inclined to get married the next time the chance arises. Indeed, it is conceivable that an emergent understanding of an action could center on an identity that would give the action an entirely new direction, one that would capture little if any of the originally intended character of the act. The examination of this possibility has been the focus of several of our studies. In each case, we have engaged research participants in a series of events designed to move them from their initial understanding of an act to a relatively low level of identification. Then we have provided them with a suggestion about a new high-level understanding. The measures of interest in these studies indicate the degree to which the subjects adopt such emergent identifications and proceed to act on them.

Emergent identification of the act of "drinking coffee" was the topic of research by Wegner, Vallacher, Macomber, Wood, and Arps (1984, Exp. 2). Participants in this study were asked to drink coffee in the laboratory. (They were not so informed, but the coffee was decaffeinated.) One group received their coffee in normal coffee cups; another group was given coffee in disruptive cups designed to move their identification of the act to lower levels. These disruptive cups were fastened securely atop tin cans that had been weighted with rocks; thus, they were heavy, tall, and unwieldy. In a separate study designed to check this manipulation of identification level, it was found that subjects with disruptive cups came to identify "coffee drinking" more in terms of details (e.g., "moving my arm," "bringing a cup to my lips") than did subjects using normal cups.

Both the normal and disruptive-cup groups were subsequently exposed to potential higher level identifications of the act. They completed a questionnaire on the "effects of coffee" that was arranged to suggest to them that coffee drinking can be identified either as "making myself seek stimulation" or as "making myself avoid stimulation." The subjects in the "seeking stimulation" group were asked to rate their certainty that coffee drinking makes them "go out and do things," "look for excitement," "enjoy loud, exciting music," and so on. The subjects in the "avoiding stimulation" group, in contrast, rated their certainty that coffee drinking makes them "avoid going out and doing things," "do things that are calming and soothing," "prefer soft, restful music," and the like. Our expectation was that the subjects who had used the disruptive cups, and who were consequently at a lower level of identification of the act, would emerge with the potential high-level identification suggested by this questionnaire.

We arranged to test this by having all subjects spend some time listening to music. They were told that their physiological reactions to the music would be measured and that they could adjust their headphone volume level by means of a control knob within easy reach. Their preferred volume level over the course of 8 min of music was used to assess the degree of emergence in the various conditions of the experiment. As it happened, subjects with disruptive cups were very sensitive to the new meaning of their action conveyed by the "effects of coffee" questionnaire. Those in the "seeking stimulation" condition proceeded to seek stimulation by turning up the music volume; those in the "avoiding stimulation" condition proceeded to avoid stimulation by turning down the volume. Subjects who had been served their coffee in normal cups, however, showed no such evidence of emergence. Instead, they showed a slight (nonsignificant) tendency to react against the suggestions offered in the questionnaire by turning their volume level in the direction opposite the one suggested.

This research illustrates what we believe to be the common course of action emergence. People undertake an act and, as a result of some error or disruption, find they cannot maintain it in terms of its initial identification. They move toward lower levels of understanding in service of continuing the act. However, from this lower level position, any high-level identity that is suggested by their memory or current circumstances becomes appealing and thus is adopted. If they have sufficient skill to maintain this new, emergent identity, their subsequent action will be guided by it—and they will thus perform an emergent action. In this way, people come to do things they did not envision before they began to act. As we shall see, such emergent action can be considerably more important than the simple adjustment of music volume.

Several broad categories of social behavior studied by psychologists appear to be amenable to an emergence analysis. Research by Wegner, Vallacher, Kiersted, and Dizadji (in press), for example, showed emergence effects in the genesis of altruism versus egoism and cooperation versus competition. In the altruism/egoism experiment, we set out to determine whether subjects' conceptions of what they had done in a psychological experiment could be directed toward an altruistic or egoistic identification. After subjects had participated in a memory study, we measured their identifications of the act of "participating in an experiment." Because this act contained elements of both helpfulness (to the experimenters) and selfishness (in that subjects received extra course credit for participating), subjects' conceptions of what they had done were potentially manipulable in either direction. Those subjects who understood their participation primarily at low levels (e.g., "making marks in a booklet"), we believed, would be ripe for emergence, whereas those who understood their participation at higher levels (e.g., "testing my memory") would be resistant to emergent identification.

The identification level variable that was measured in this way was then crossed with a second variable—the high-level identity suggested to subjects as the meaning of their act of "participation." We arranged to expose subjects to either an altruistic or an egoistic interpretation of their action by filling the last portion of their action identification questionnaires with items pointing toward one or the other interpretation. For subjects in the altruism condition, the last seven act identities rated included "helping people study psychology," "aiding the experimenter," and the like. For subjects in the egoism condition, these items included "getting extra credit in my psychology class," "getting a better grade in psychology," and the like.

Following completion of the questionnaires, subjects were told that the memory study was over. They were asked to stay in the laboratory for a few minutes, though, and at this point were given an opportunity to volunteer for additional participation in future experiments. They were given a sheet describing ten upcoming studies and were asked to rank their preferences and then sign the sheet. One of these studies called for egoistic participation; it promised an inordinate amount of extra credit for the amount of participation time. Another study called for altruistic participation; its description promised no extra credit but expressed a great need for help.

The results showed that volunteering for participation in these studies was indeed predictable as a function of action emergence. Subjects who identified their earlier participation at low levels differed significantly in their choices. Those exposed to the altruistic identity of their earlier participation opted for the upcoming "helpful" study, whereas those exposed to the egoistic identity of their earlier participation more often chose the upcoming "extra credit" study. However, subjects who had not identified their earlier participation at low levels did not emerge with a new identification and thus did not strongly prefer either helping or extra credit. Their initial high-level identifications of the act had taken quite different forms, and they were therefore no more likely to help or to be selfish. In sum, although altruism and egoism can represent opposing forces in everyday social life, the findings of this study indicate that they may have similar beginnings in the process of action emergence.

A second study conducted by Wegner, Vallacher, Kiersted, and Dizadji (in press) extended this analysis to cooperative and competitive action. Subjects in this study were asked to describe a recent interaction they had. They were to enter descriptions of what they did into a computer console. Some were prompted to describe their actions at lower levels (i.e., "Try to provide as much detail as you can; indicate the particular comments you made, questions you asked, or behaviors you performed"), and others were led to describe their actions at higher levels (i.e., "Be somewhat general in your answers; indicate what opinions and values you communicated, or perhaps what personality traits you demonstrated"). Subsequent coding of their responses by trained judges revealed that this manipulation of identity level was successful.

The computer then delivered an ostensible "personality analysis," telling subjects either that they were very cooperative or very competitive. The subjects in the low-level condition reported greater belief in this feedback—either cooperative or competitive—than did subjects in the high-level condition. Subjects in the low-level condition also rated themselves on an adjective self-description form in ways consistent with the feedback. Those who received competitiveness feedback rated themselves as more competitive, whereas those who received cooperativeness feedback rated themselves as more cooperative. Moreover, when all subjects were later given choices to participate in future experimental tasks that required cooperative or competitive behavior, those who had initially been led to describe their acts at low levels chose to participate in tasks consistent with the bogus personality feedback they had been given. Low-level subjects who received cooperative feedback opted for cooperative tasks, whereas low-level subjects who received competitive feedback preferred to perform competitive tasks. In contrast, the subjects who were prompted to describe their acts initially at high levels were not significantly swayed to participate in tasks that would be consistent with their feedback.

The results of both of these studies should be evocative to readers familiar with the social psychology of self. The altruism/egoism study mirrors in some ways a common paradigm initiated in social research by Freedman and Fraser (1966). Their "foot in the door" paradigm has been used to show that when people are induced to perform some small helpful act, they later become more likely to perform a larger helpful act (cf. Wegner, 1980). Bem's (1972) self-perception theory is often used to explain this phenomenon. In essence, it is reasoned that people who perform the small helpful act come to see themselves as helpful people and thus continue to behave as self-perceived. Our cooperation/competition study, in turn, seems reminiscent of the many studies of the effects of social feedback on self-conceptions (e.g., R. L. Miller, Brickman, & Bolen, 1975). This line of research follows from the symbolic interactionist proposition that people's self-concepts are the result of the appraisals of themselves that they receive from others (Cooley, 1902; Mead, 1934).

The results of our studies of emergence provide a new theoretical understanding of the bases of self-perception and social feedback processes. These findings suggest that people "discover" what they have done, and thus learn what sorts of people they are, principally when they have entered a period of low-level action identification. During such a period, the self is the author of only relatively drab and concrete low-level actions. When these are put together in terms of an emergent high-level act identity, the self becomes newly understood as the source of an encompassing and meaningful action. The self becomes "helpful" or "selfish," "cooperative" or "competitive," or the agent characterized by many other action-producing qualities. In this light, people who understand their actions at high levels have stable self-views. People who, for whatever reason, come to identify their actions at lower levels, in turn, are momentarily robbed of a stable and meaningful self. It is in such moments of low-level identification that emergence can happen and can lend people a new basis for self-understanding.

Emergence and Impulse

Action emergence creates new actions. Instead of following the track laid down by a prior high-level identification, the person who experiences an episode of emergence can adopt a new, perhaps untried action direction. Such emergence only has *immediate* consequences for action, however, when the identity conditions for the emergent identity are available as the initial action is ongoing. For instance, one might be "working on a project at one's desk" one day and find it necessary to begin the lower level act of "searching for paper in the top drawer." While surveying the contents of the drawer, one encounters the address of an old friend and, in short order, finds onself "writing a letter to an old friend." By our account, this would not have happened had one kept "working on the project" in mind all along. The descent to lower levels in search of the paper served to disrupt this line of action, and because the identity conditions for a different higher level act were available at the time, the act could emerge on the spot with a new character and a new result. We believe such a sequence can do much to explain the nature of impulsive action.

Let us take as an empirical example a study performed by Wegner and Vallacher (1982). We arranged for a group of subjects to observe a videotape of a research participant performing a cold pressor task—a standard laboratory induction of pain. Subjects observed as an experimenter explained that the participant was to perform a series of manual tasks (putting together nuts and bolts, putting metal rings on an upright rod, etc.) while his hands were submerged in an aquarium full of icewater. The participant was then instructed to carry out this task, trying to keep his hands in the icewater for as long as possible up to a limit of 2 min. The participant did so, and subjects were then asked to identify the action that had been performed. Their identifications were made in response to a 40-item questionnaire that had been constructed by means of the free-response technique.

Each subject was then called on to perform the icewater task. Measures were taken of three different indices of pain: duration of hand immersion, manual task performance, and the subject's posttask self-report of pain. By all three measures, we found that subjects who understood the task at a low level in advance experienced greater pain. They removed their hands from the icewater more quickly, performed fewer of the nuts-and-bolts tasks, and reported feeling more pain. This experience of pain is understandable as an emergence phenomenon. The subjects who began the task at a higher level of identification knew what they were doing in a durable and long-term way. They concerned themselves with "learning about psychology," "helping the experimenters," or some other high-level identification of the act, and therefore monitored their environments primarily with the identity conditions for these larger acts in mind. The subjects at low level, in contrast, had an unsatisfactory understanding of their action. They knew they were "moving fingers," and the like, but they were not considering the act's larger meaning. Thus, when a very clear meaning became available—"I am exposing myself to pain"—they emerged with this understanding of what they were doing.

The state of low-level action identification is likely to make people sensitive to their experiences. Because people in this state are understanding their acts in only a mechanical and relatively meaningless fashion, they are likely to remain alert to the variety of stimuli in their environments that could serve as identity conditions for the higher level understanding of their action. In one sense, this means that people in this state are often going to be surprised; their low-level identification prevents foresight regarding the consequences of their actions. In another sense, though, this means that low-level identification will portend a special flexibility of action, a capacity to reformulate the action in response to new stimulation. A person at high level in "working," for example, might well work straight through lunch. A person at low level in the same job, however, might "move toward the office door" and, at the same time, feel a hunger pang. The hunger stimulation would be processed for its possible relevance to the meaning of the ongoing action, and the person might well emerge with "going to lunch."

This seemingly impulsive quality of emergent action has led us to investigate the connection between low-level identification and impulse. In a study by Wegner, Myers, and Vallacher (1982), we arranged for subjects to encounter a hypothetical opportunity for impulsive action—a theft. Subjects were asked to imagine that they were walking down a hallway in a campus building. To aid in this exercise, they were shown a videotape made by walking a camera down a hall. The tape simulated a crime opportunity. At the end of the hall, it showed a couch with a jacket and some notebooks on it. On the floor in front of the couch was a $20 bill. The camera zoomed in on the money and then zoomed back to pan the empty hallway in both directions. The tape ended at this point, and subjects were asked to identify what they would be doing if they had taken the money. They were also asked to indicate whether they would have taken the money under these circumstances and whether they would have been *tempted* to take the money.

Although only 10% of the sample of 40 subjects indicated that they would have taken the money, over 40% said they would have been tempted. The interesting feature of the results of this experiment, though, was the relationship between action identifications and self-predictions. By the usual factor-analytic technique, identifications of the act were found to cluster around four main meanings: a low-level factor (e.g., "looking around," "clasping the bill in my hand"); a high-level factor signifying the "criminal" quality of the act (i.e., "committing a crime"); a high-level factor euphemizing the action (i.e., "borrowing"); and a high-level factor conveying enjoyment of the action (i.e., "getting in a better mood"). Simple correlations between these identification factors and the self-predictions revealed that two of the high-level meanings were most predictive of self-reported theft likelihood. Identifying the act as "committing a crime" was negatively correlated with self-predicted theft, $r(40) = -.29$, $p < .05$, whereas identifying the act as "borrowing" was positively correlated with this self-report, $r(40) = .37$, $p < .01$. Low-level identification, however, was the only factor correlated with self-reports of being tempted, $r(40) = .43$, $p < .01$. Apparently, although thinking about the details of this action does not lead people to report that they would do it, it does lead them to report a strong feeling of temptation.

These data lead us to wonder whether people may predict their future actions primarily on the basis of their high-level identities for action. Thinking of this act in a positive light ("borrowing") is associated with predicting that one will do it, whereas thinking of the act in a negative light ("committing a crime") inclines one to predict that one will not do it. What is intriguing about these findings, though, is that the admission of temptation to act is so strongly associated with low-level identification. It could be that in the heat of the moment, those individuals who lose their initial high-level identification—for whatever reason—become especially compelled by the current circumstance. The opportunity to get money emerges on the spot as the meaning of the low-level identities, and the person takes the money "on impulse." Further research in nonhypothetical settings will be necessary to assess the validity of this reasoning.

There is yet another line of evidence linking low-level identification with impulsive action. Wegner, Gould, and Vallacher (1983), gave 42 Trinity University undergraduates a general individual difference measure of action identification level. This Behavior Identification Form (BIF) consisted of 25 forced-choice items; for each, the subject was given one act identity (e.g., "eating") and was asked to choose whether this was better described by a lower level identity ("chewing") or a higher level identity ("getting nutrition"). This measure, developed by Vallacher, Wegner, and Cook (1982), was the one used in the maintenance research by Wegner and Vallacher (1983) mentioned earlier. It exhibits substantial internal consistency (Cronbach's $\alpha = .84$; $N = 272$) and repeat reliability over two weeks (.96; $N = 42$) and indicates to us that despite the considerable variability in identification level that is accounted for by differences in situations and in action domains, there are also general individual differences in level of identification. Such differences are of course interesting in their own right, and we have discussed them in depth elsewhere (Vallacher & Wegner, 1985). For present purposes, however, suffice it to say that the undergraduates who completed the BIF in this study were also asked to complete a self-report scale of impulsiveness and to describe in detail the course of their activities in the past week. Two weeks later, they returned and again described their activities over the past week.

High-level identification scores on the BIF were negatively correlated with self-reported impulsiveness, $r(42) = -.31$, $p < .05$. Thus, people who generally identify their actions at higher levels are less likely to report that they do things on impulse. Evidence corroborating this relationship was derived from a comparison of the activity schedules the subjects reported. A measure of action instability was calculated by determining the difference between the amounts of time allocated to each of 20 action classes in the two time periods. The correlation between BIF scores and this measure of action instability was significantly negative, $r(42) = -.26$, $p < .05$. This means that, in this sample, individuals who typically identified action at higher levels were also more consistent in their action over a two-week period. Those who identified action at lower levels reported allocating their time to different acts in the two time periods. These data suggest that high-level identifiers have a broadly conceived plan of action that keeps them doing the same things from one week to the next. Low-level identifiers have no such plan and so emerge moment by moment in diverse action directions.

Taken together, the results of these various studies of emergent action provide some insight into the nature of impulse. Whether a person removes a hand from icewater on impulse, is tempted to take a $20 bill on impulse, or generally does different things from one week to the next on impulse, the common thread that underlies this sort of behavior is a tendency toward lower level action identification. Such lower level identification may be chronic in the person—leading to a life of repeated emergence with new action directions; or it may be chronic with regard to only a specific domain of action—leading the person to emerge in a new direction whenever that domain of action is approached. Perhaps most generally, though, lower levels of action identification may arise whenever a person cannot do an action according to a higher level identity alone. Environmental events that produce disruption, confusion, and error should make anyone—regardless of personal proclivities—identify action at lower levels and so become prey to impulsive action tendencies. The emergence process portrays impulsive action as a standard human response to the lack of high-level action understanding.

Impulse has more traditionally been understood in psychology by means of the Freudian notion of unconscious motivation. Psychoanalysts maintain that remarkable meanings can usually be found in slips of the tongue, memory lapses, spontaneous emotional expressions, and impromptu actions, and that these meanings must be orchestrated by unconscious motives. Thus, actions have very different meanings than the one known consciously by the actor (Schafer, 1976). The emergence analysis of impulsive action suggests a different interpretation: Impulsive or unplanned action occurs when a person is identifying ongoing acts at a low level. The person is performing what Heider (1983) has called an "existential walk"—an aimless journey marked by incessant small decisions of what to do next. In this state, the person suddenly finds something more substantial to do; a low-level act can be identified at higher level, and the high-level path is thus followed. Far from being a consequence of unconscious motives, then, the person's impulsive act is simply a rapid reidentification and redirection of ongoing action.

Later, such spontaneous emergence of action can certainly *seem* to have come from the unconscious. A good psychoanalyst could offer several interpretations of the act that are high enough in level to provide an impressive advance in meaning. Usually, this high-level meaning will be one that the actor cannot remember having entertained prior to the action, for the actor was at a low level at that time. The actor may thus be likely to accept this interpretation as a psychoanalytic insight—even though the analyst's identification of the action may characterize only by chance what the person was really doing. The person was actually committing a low-level act, which, with the proper identity conditions, could emerge into impulse. It is informative, of course, regarding the person's knowledge structures, that the person could appreciate those identity conditions and so perform that act. But such knowledge is far from "unconscious" in the Freudian sense, and our theory thus departs significantly from the psychoanalytic formulation. It suggests, instead, that people will often seem to do things motivated by the unconscious when they are consciously concerned with *how* to act rather than with *why* they are acting.

INTELLIGENT ACTION

The principles of action identification theory prescribe a system that allows people to act intelligently. All the acts that people think about, from the most mundane to the most complicated and far-reaching, are performable because people can, indeed, think about them. The theory indicates that thinking plays a relatively simple role in easy actions: thought gets the action started, and motor systems that do not require conscious thought move the body to play the action to its conclusion. Because such easy actions can usually be done without thinking about action details, emergence need not take place, and these acts thus stand as a stable array of things the person can do.

The theory suggests that thought plays a more critical and remarkable role in difficult actions. People can do these acts only because they can think about details of action. In performing difficult actions in such tiny steps, however, people will often lose sight of their initial action directions. The theory holds that thought about action will make the most intricate and difficult human actions susceptible to almost constant reshaping through emergence. Different identifications will be "tried on for size"—such that at any particular time, the one will be adopted that is most descriptive of what the person's motor systems can do in the given circumstance. Thoughts of actions that are entirely beyond human abilities will thus be dissipated whenever such actions are attempted. Therefore, people will be able to behave intelligently, doing what they can do and remaining continually open to what they might do.

Obviously, the kind of intelligent action described by the theory is not available to organisms that do not symbolize their actions. Therefore, raccoons are out, no matter how much it looks like they are "washing their food." Human infants are also beyond the scope of the theory. Certainly, they may represent their actions to themselves by means of motor or sensory memories (cf. Bruner, 1964), and their systems of action representation and performance could bear a structural resemblance to the system we have proposed. However, until infants develop the capacity to symbolize their actions to themselves (Luria, 1961), their behavior is organized by processes that are opaque to our theoretical analyses. Oddly enough, though, certain *computer* action, like adult human action, may be understandable in terms of the theory.

Artificially intelligent computer programs that guide action—such as the one that guides the robot SHAKEY through the halls of a building (Fikes, Hart, & Nilsson, 1972)—are often run by systems that appear to be "action identifiers." They perform acts that are characterized in advance by plans; they move to consider acts in greater detail when the plans are thwarted; and they move back to continuing their more general plans when the obstructions have been removed. It is in this way, for example, that Winograd's (1972) SHRDLU describes picking up a box and knows, first, to remove another box that is sitting on top of it. Each of these steps is usually carried out by a separate subroutine that is called by a higher level program. Thus, just as a person might need to think of the name of a lower level action (e.g., "removing the box on top") as a part of a higher level act (e.g., "retrieving the lower box"), programs identify levels of action in terms of separately named subroutines that perform each action level.

The system described by action identification theory suggests that humans have action production capacities that are more "intelligent" than any artificially intelligent systems yet developed. The human ability to move to higher levels of identification as the actions described at lower levels are mastered and made automatic, for example, is one that is implemented only in a very rudimentary way in even the best computer programs (Boden, 1977). This capacity for integrating actions entails a kind of *self-modification* that allows humans to perform some of the most complex actions with but a single conscious intent. The gap between human and machine intelligence in action is even wider, however, in yet another domain. Action identification theory indicates that people are remarkably facile in reorienting themselves to different higher level meanings of their action. Computer programs seldom contain more than one high-level identification; they have an impoverished understanding of the variety of different purposes that might be served by their acts (Dreyfus, 1979). Such flexibility and potential creativity is difficult to build into a machine for the simple reason that each higher level identity brings with it a myriad of information—in the form of new lower level identities, connections to these and to previously existing lower level identities, and connections to yet other higher level identities.

Just as artificial intelligence analysts have found it difficult to implement the multiplicity of high-level act meanings in their machines, psychologists have found this feature of humans hard to understand. At best, psychologists have contented themselves with composing lists of human needs and motives or with tracking down all the various lower level actions that can be ascribed to one such motive. With the action identification approach, these "motives" are seen as actions themselves and thus are embraced in a single system that allows the continuity from the lowest level minutia of action to the highest level goal to be understood. It is within such a framework that we can begin to understand how people may do things that last a lifetime or may do things that change in their very doing to become something entirely new.

Acknowledgments

The research reported in this chapter was supported in part by NSF Grant BNS 78-26380. We wish to thank Toni Giuliano for helpful comments on an earlier draft.

References

Abelson, R. P. (1973). The structure of belief systems. In R. C. Schank & K. M. Colby (Eds.), *Computer models of thought and language* (pp. 287–340). San Francisco: Freeman.

Abelson, R. P. (1981). Psychological status of the script concept. *American Psychologist, 36*, 715–729.

Anscombe, G. E. M. (1957). *Intention*. Oxford: Blackwell.

Atkinson, J. W., & Birch, D. (1978). *An introduction to motivation*. New York: Van Nostrand.

Austin, J. L. (1961). *Philosophical papers*. London: Oxford University Press.

Baumeister, R. (1984). Choking under pressure: Self-consciousness and paradoxical effects of incentives on skillful performance. *Journal of Personality and Social Psychology, 46*, 610–620.

Bem, D. (1972). Self-perception theory. In L. Berkowitz (Ed.), *Advances in experimental social psychology* (Vol. 6, pp. 1–62). New York: Academic Press.

Boden, M. (1977). *Artificial intelligence and natural man*. New York: Basic Books.

Bower, G., Black, J., & Turner, T. (1979). Scripts in text comprehension and memory. *Cognitive Psychology, 11*, 177–220.

Brown, R. W. (1958). How shall a thing be called? *Psychological Review, 65*, 14–21.

Bruner, J. S. (1964). The course of cognitive growth. *American Psychologist, 19*, 1–15.

Bryan, W. L., & Harter, L. (1899). Studies on the telegraphic language: The acquisition of a hierarchy of habits. *Psychological Review, 6*, 345–378.

Carver, C. S., & Scheier, M. F. (1981). *Attention and self-regulation: A control-theory approach to human behavior*. New York: Springer-Verlag.

Cooley, C. H. (1902). *Human nature and the social order*. New York: Scribners.

Danto, A. (1963). What we can do. *Journal of Philosophy, 40*, 435–445.

Dreyfus, H. L. (1979). *What computers can't do: The limits of artificial intelligence*. New York: Harper & Row.

Fikes, R. E., Hart, P. E., & Nilsson, N. J. (1972). Learning and executing generalized robot plans. *Artificial Intelligence, 3*, 251–288.

Freedman, J. L., & Fraser, S. C. (1966). Compliance without pressure: The foot in the door technique. *Journal of Personality and Social Psychology, 4*, 195–202.

Freud, S. (1960). *The psychopathology of everyday life*. New York: Norton. (Original work published 1914)

Gauld, A., & Shotter, J. (1977). *Human action and its psychological investigation*. London: Routledge and Kegan Paul.

Gergen, K. J. (1982). From self to science: What is there to know? In J. Suls (Ed.), *Psychological perspectives on the self* (Vol. 1, pp. 129–150). Hillsdale, NJ: Erlbaum.

Goldman, A. I. (1970). *A theory of human action*. Princeton, NJ: Princeton University Press.

Hampshire, S. (1959). *Thought and action*. London: Chatto and Windus.

Harré, R., & Secord, P. F. (1972). *The explanation of social behaviour*. Oxford: Blackwell.

Heider, F. (1983). *The life of a psychologist: An autobiography*. Lawrence: University of Kansas Press.

James, W. (1890). *Principles of psychology*. New York: Holt.

Kanfer, F. H. (1970). Self-monitoring: Methodological limitations and clinical applications. *Journal of Consulting and Clinical Psychology, 35*, 148–152.

Kirschenbaum, D. S., & Tomarken, A. J. (1982). On facing the generalization problem: The study of self-regulatory failure. In P. C. Kendall (Ed.), *Advances in cognitive-behavioral research and therapy* (Vol. 1). New York: Academic Press.

Kruglanski, A. W. (1975). The endogenous-exogenous partition in attribution theory. *Psychological Review, 82*, 387–406.

Lichtenstein, E. H., & Brewer, W. F. (1980). Memory for goal-directed events. *Cognitive Psychology, 12*, 412–445.

Luria, A. R. (1961). *The role of speech in the regulation of normal and abnormal behavior* (J. Tizard, Trans.). New York: Liveright.

Mead, G. H. (1934). *Mind, self, and society*. Chicago: University of Chicago Press.

Mead, G. H. (1938). *The philosophy of the act*. Chicago: University of Chicago Press.

Merton, R. S. (1968). *Social theory and social structure*. New York: Free Press.

Milgram, S. (1963). Behavioral study of obedience. *Journal of Abnormal and Social Psychology, 67*, 371–378.

Miller, G. A., Galanter, E., & Pribram, K. H. (1960). *Plans and the structure of behavior*. New York: Holt.

Miller, R. L., Brickman, P., & Bolen, D. (1975). Attribution versus persuasion as a means of modifying behavior. *Journal of Personality and Social Psychology, 31*, 430–441.

Newtson, D. (1976). Foundations of attribution: The perception of ongoing behavior. In J. H. Harvey, W. J. Ickes, & R. F. Kidd (Eds.), *New directions in attribution research* (Vol. 1, pp. 223–247). Hillsdale, NJ: Erlbaum.

Nisbett, R. E., & Wilson, T. D. (1977). Telling more than we can know: Verbal reports on mental processes. *Psychological Review, 84*, 231–259.

Norrell, S. (1981). Monitoring compliance with pilocarpine therapy. *American Journal of Ophthalmology, 92*, 727–731.

Rosch, E. H. (1973). Natural categories. *Cognitive Psychology, 4*, 328–350.

Ryle, G. (1949). *The concept of mind*. London: Hutchinson.

Schafer, R. (1976). *A new language for psychoanalysis*. New Haven: Yale University Press.

Schank, R. C., & Abelson, R. P. (1977). *Scripts, plans, goals, and understanding*. Hillsdale, NJ: Erlbaum.

Schmidt, R. (1975). A schema theory of discrete motor learning. *Psychological Review, 82*, 225–260.

Sudnow, D. (1978). *Ways of the hand*. New York: Harper & Row.

Vallacher, R. R., & Wegner, D. M. (1985). *A theory of action identification*. Hillsdale, NJ: Erlbaum.

Vallacher, R. R., Wegner, D. M., Bordieri, J., & Wenzlaff, R. (1981). Models of act identity structures. Unpublished research data.

Vallacher, R. R., Wegner, D. M., & Cook, C. (1982). Construction of the Behavior Identification Form. Unpublished research data.

von Bertalanffy, L. (1968). *General system theory*. New York: Braziller.

Vygotsky, L. S. (1962). *Thought and language*. Cambridge, MA: MIT Press.

Wegner, D. M. (1980). The self in prosocial action. In D. M. Wegner & R. R. Vallacher (Eds.), *The self in social psychology* (pp. 131–157). New York: Oxford University Press.

Wegner, D. M., Gould, J., & Vallacher, R. R. (1983). Action identification level and behavior consistency. Unpublished research data.

Wegner, D. M., Kyser, G., & Vallacher, R. R. (1983). Identification of the act of using glaucoma medication. Unpublished research data.

Wegner, D. M., Myers, R., & Vallacher, R. R. (1982). Identification of the act of taking $20. Unpublished research data.

Wegner, D. M., Richard, M., & Vallacher, R. R. (1982). Identification of the act of rearing a child. Unpublished research data.

Wegner, D. M., & Vallacher, R. R. (1982). Identification of the act of performing a cold pressor task. Unpublished research data.

Wegner, D. M., & Vallacher, R. R. (1983). Action identification level and maintenance indicator ratings. Unpublished research data.

Wegner, D. M., Vallacher, R. R., & Dizadji, D. (1983). Identification of the act of drinking alcohol. Unpublished research data.

Wegner, D. M., Vallacher, R. R., Ewert, J., & Reno, L. (1983). *Knowing what one is doing: Action identification and self-control*. Unpublished manuscript, Trinity University.

Wegner, D. M., Vallacher, R. R., & Kelly, M. (1983). Identification of the act of getting married. Unpublished research data.

Wegner, D. M., Vallacher, R. R., Kiersted, G., & Dizadji, D. (in press). Action identification and the emergence of social behavior. *Social Cognition*.

Wegner, D. M., Vallacher, R. R., Macomber, G., Wood, R., & Arps, K. (1984). The emergence of action. *Journal of Personality and Social Psychology, 46*, 269–279.

Winograd, T. (1972). *Understanding natural language*. New York: Academic Press.

Wittgenstein, L. (1953). *Philosophical investigations*. Oxford: Blackwell.

Zajonc, R. B. (1965). Social facilitation. *Science, 149*, 269–274.

Author Index

Abbott, V., 528
Abelson, R., 101, 107
Abelson, R. P., 67, 455, 471, 475, 532, 537, 538, 553, 557
Abramson, L. Y., 44, 45, 354, 356, 437, 472
Ach, N., 415
Adams, N., 527
Adelson, B., 496
Adler, A., 23, 31, 98-99
Adler, J. M., 423
Adorno, T. W., 46, 47
Ahlm, K., 55
Ajzen, I., 127, 169, 175, 192, 206, 236, 238, 350, 411, 477
Allen, L., 150
Allen, R. B., 177
Alloy, L. B., 437
Allport, G., 285
Allport, G. H., 101, 320, 326
Allport, G. W., 30, 31, 145, 160, 170, 192, 205, 209, 214, 475
Alper, T. G., 67, 85
Amabile, T. M., 71
Amsel, A., 283
Anastasi, A., 64, 68
Anderson, A. H., 309
Anderson, C. C., 6
Anderson, J. R., 4, 5, 6-7, 171, 190, 406, 407, 410, 411, 413, 414 , 415, 424, 427
Anderson, N. H., 169, 175, 195, 522, 523
Anderson, R. C., 481, 517, 518, 519
Anscombe, G. E. M., 551
Applebaum, G. A., 508
Appleman, A. J., 157
Appelman, R. J., 360
Archibald, W. P., 332
Arieti, S., 46
Aristotle, 468
Arkin, R. M., 157, 360, 541
Armstrong, G. W., 29
Arnold, M. B., 295, 296
Aronson, E., 137, 159, 447, 451
Arps, K., 570
Asch, S. E., 152, 153, 168, 169, 172, 174, 175, 186, 489, 490, 491, 530

Ashmore, R. D., 191, 192
Astington, J. W., 408, 413
Atkinson, J. W., 3, 8, 23, 48, 49, 87, 88, 96, 97, 111, 146, 283, 285, 286, 287, 288, 309, 315, 319, 325, 329, 344, 351, 352, 361, 365, 367, 380, 384, 386, 387, 394, 395, 396, 406, 407, 409, 415, 417, 418, 419, 421, 565
Atkinson, R. L., 5, 520
Austin, J. L., 551
Austin, W., 38
Averill, J. R., 295, 303, 304

Bacharach, V. R., 415, 427
Backman, C. W., 6
Baer, J. S., 466
Bailey, D. E., 27
Bailey, S., 206
Baker, L., 518
Baldwin, L. M., 71
Baldwin, M. W., 133
Bandura, A., 25, 30, 46, 50, 51, 100, 111, 415
Barbour, J. S., 406
Barclay, A. M., 455
Barden, R. C., 260
Bargh, J., 178, 251, 268
Bargh, J. A., 505, 506, 508
Bar-Hillel, M., 477
Bartlett, F., 170
Bartlett, F. C., 123, 261, 471
Bartlett, J., 261
Barton, R., 527
Baumann, D. J., 150
Baumeister, R., 565
Baumeister, R. F., 97, 114, 157, 332, 333, 460
Baumgardner, M. H., 177
Beaman, A. L., 51
Beattie, A. E., 181, 183, 185, 188
Beck, A. T., 45, 46, 57, 140
Becker, C., 122
Beckmann, J., 428
Bem, D., 568, 573

Bem, D. J., 42, 70, 89, 91, 126, 127, 132, 133, 204, 221, 223, 414
Bem, S. L., 399
Bemporad, J., 46
Ben-Itzhak, S., 461
Bennet, S., 536
Bensenberg, M., 236
Bentler, P. M., 236
Berger, J., 489
Berger, P. L., 123, 124, 139
Berglas, S., 111, 112, 332, 354, 366, 367, 493
Berkowitz, L., 6
Berlyne, D., 288, 374
Berlyne, D. E., 536
Berman, L., 55
Bern, H., 528
Bernstein, B., 488, 489
Bernstein, M., 27
Bernstein, S., 508
Berscheid, E., 92, 208, 332, 438, 455, 494
Bialystok, E., 410, 422
Birch, D., 111, 285, 315, 352, 353, 407, 409, 417, 419, 421, 565
Birenbaum, G., 424
Bisanz, J., 266
Black, J., 553
Black, J. B., 528, 529
Blankenship, V., 366, 419, 420
Blascovich, J., 111, 160, 328, 331, 332, 333, 337, 436
Blum, G. S., 7, 266, 269, 270, 406
Boden, M., 579
Bodenhausen, G. V., 509
Boggiano, A. K., 254, 362
Bolen, D., 573
Bongort, K., 417
Bonoma, T. V., 132
Bordieri, J., 553
Borgida, E., 213, 236, 477
Bottenberg, E. H., 297
Bower, G., 553
Bower, G. H., 13, 134, 139, 140, 174, 179, 244, 261, 262, 270, 406, 410, 411, 414, 415, 524, 532
Bradley, G. W., 131, 350, 360
Braly, K. W., 191
Brand, J. F., 512, 513, 514, 515
Breckler, S. J., 12, 147, 157
Brehm, J. W., 67, 368, 540
Brekke, N., 477
Brendal, A., 71
Brewer, M. R., 171
Brewer, W. F., 528, 553
Brickman, P., 27, 28, 332, 346, 354, 358, 359, 362, 369, 384, 573
Brickner, M. A., 154
Bridger, W. H., 249
Brigham, J. C., 191
Broadbent, A. E., 5

Broadbent, D. E., 261, 542
Brock, T. C., 522
Brody, N., 423
Bromley, D. B., 80
Bronson, G., 248
Brooks, L., 172
Brower, A., 98, 106
Brown, A. L., 469
Brown, E. T., 326
Brown, J., 301
Brown, J. S., 285
Brown, M., 347
Brown, R., 191
Brown, R. H., 359
Brown, R. W., 551
Brown, T., 194
Bruner, J., 5-6, 503, 505
Bruner, J. S., 7, 170, 209, 406, 504, 507, 525, 526, 579
Brunstein, J. C., 415, 426
Bryan, W. L., 558
Bryant, F. B., 299
Buckert, U., 358, 359, 369
Bulman, R. V., 139
Burger, J. M., 157, 360
Burke, K., 469, 472, 476, 489
Burke, P., 114
Burleson, G., 261
Burns, H., 481
Burnstein, G., 177, 184, 196, 372
Burton, M., 71
Burton, R. V., 135
Buss, A. H., 145, 154, 155
Butterfield, E. C., 523
Byers, J. J., 309
Byrne, D., 47

Cal, A. V., 128
Calder, B. J., 127
Cameron, N., 30
Campbell, B., 213, 236
Campbell, B. H., 156
Campbell, D. T., 330, 359, 522
Campbell, J., 102, 315, 333, 334, 335, 440, 441, 442, 449, 451, 452, 458, 459
Campbell, J. D., 135, 438
Campbell, S., 450
Campos, J., 246, 248
Campos, J. J., 247
Canter, G., 484
Cantor, N., 7, 11, 12, 96, 98, 102, 106, 109, 110, 112, 114, 170, 172, 234, 323, 325, 470, 471, 493, 504, 516, 518
Cantril, H., 145, 146, 209, 526
Carlsmith, J. M., 159, 447, 451
Carlston, D. E., 177, 178, 521, 531
Carlyle, T., 493
Carr, T. H., 415, 427
Cartwright, D., 417

Carver, C. S., 36, 44, 45, 109, 145, 154, 155, 254, 255, 414, 557
Cazden, C. B., 488
Chaiken, S., 133, 204
Chandler, C., 304
Chaplin, W., 527
Charlesworth, W. R., 249
Charters, W. W., 51
Chase, W. C., 496
Chase, W. G., 190
Chassin, L., 114, 117, 236
Chen, J., 214
Chesney, C. L., 506
Chew, B., 115
Chi, M., 496
Chi, M. T. H., 190
Chibnall, B., 136
Child, P., 172, 530
Chomsky, N., 5
Christensen, C. M., 6
Cialdini, R. B., 150, 154, 334, 437
Citrin, J. C., 194
Clark, K. B., 52
Clark, M., 117, 261
Clark, M. P., 52
Clark, M. S., 13, 168, 174, 179, 244, 267
Clark, R. A., 87, 146, 380
Clark, R. D., 246
Clark, R. W., 351
Clayton, J. P., 399
Clore, G. L., 532, 541
Coates, D., 27, 28
Cohen, A. R., 337, 338
Cohen, B. D., 29
Cohen, C. E., 483, 485, 510
Cohen, J. L., 410
Colby, K. M., 30
Cole, M., 468, 488
Coleman, J. M., 52
Collins, A. M., 532
Combs, A. W., 101, 320, 326, 331, 336
Consalvi, C., 530
Conway, F., 138
Conway, M., 127, 128, 132, 134, 136, 154
Cook, B. P., 206
Cook, C., 576
Cook, R. E., 368
Cook, T. D., 129, 159
Cooley, C. H., 23, 30, 31, 124, 573
Cooper, J., 136, 137, 207, 208, 222, 540
Cooper, L. A., 410
Coopersmith, S., 327
Corbit, J. D., 536
Corey, S. M., 205, 232
Corteen, R. S., 506
Corty, E., 114, 236
Coven, S., 6
Coyne, J. C., 38
Craik, F. I. M., 266, 423
Crane, M., 508

Crano, W. D., 206
Crary, W. G., 338
Crowne, D., 146, 156
Critchfield, L. L., 332
Crocker, J., 123, 170, 176, 494, 516
Crosby, F., 27
Croyle, R. T., 207
Csikszeutmihalyi, M., 65, 66, 73, 77, 536

D'Andrade, R. G., 72
Danto, A., 551, 553, 554
Darley, J. M., 25, 27, 42, 67, 208, 210, 235, 350, 354, 356, 494
Darwin, C., 4
Davies, R., 303
Davis, F. D., 72
Davis, J. H., 196
Davis, K. E., 350
Davitz, J. R., 297
Dawes, R. M., 7
Dawson, M. E., 406
Deaux, K., 489
de Beauvoir, Simone, 141
de Charms, R., 415
Deci, E. L., 283, 536
De Fleur, M. L., 206, 211
Del Boca, F. K., 191, 192
Dember, W. N., 6, 7
Dembo, T., 101, 319, 365, 394
De Rivera, J., 299
Dermer, M., 92
Derry, P. A., 45
Dickman, S., 268
Diener, C. I., 83, 92
Diener, E., 51, 151
Dillehay, R., 381
Dineen, J., 51
Dipboye, R. L., 101, 151, 331, 337
Dittes, J. E., 332
Dizadji, D., 560, 572, 573
Dodson, J. D., 87
Doob, L. W., 205, 214
Dreben, E. K., 178, 522, 523
Dreyfuss, H. L., 579
Duncker, K., 472
Dupree, D. A., 528
Dural, S., 31, 46, 52, 82, 145, 154, 255
Dweck, C. S., 28, 83, 92, 368
Dyer, L., 190

Eagleton, T., 493
Eagly, A. H., 204
Earle, W. B., 299
Easterbrook, J. A., 260
Ebbesen, E. B., 134, 177, 338, 483, 485, 510
Ebbeson, E., 270, 427
Eckblad, G., 66
Effrein, E. A., 220
Eiser, J. R., 26

Ekman, P., 266
Elliot, E. S., 28
Ellis, A., 295
Ellis, R. A., 328
Ellsworth, P. C., 159, 168
Emde, R., 246, 248
Endler, N. S., 146
Endresen, K., 51
English, L. D., 329
Entin, E. C., 387
Entin, E. E., 315, 319, 321, 344
Epstein, S., 96, 97, 101, 102, 219, 320, 331, 336
Erber, R., 191, 466
Erdelyi, M. H., 260, 268, 406, 508
Erickson, E., 106
Erickson, E. H., 31
Eteoff, N. L., 522
Ewert, J., 562

Feather, N. T., 43, 45, 96, 97, 315, 319, 332, 344, 387, 409, 417
Fazio, R. H., 29, 90, 205, 206, 207, 210, 214, 215, 216, 218, 219, 220, 221, 222, 223, 224, 225, 227, 230, 234, 235, 236, 398
Feldman, N. S., 254
Feldman-Rotman, S., 450
Felipe, A. I., 186
Fenichel, O., 503
Fenigstein, A., 155, 158
Ferris, C. B., 52
Festinger, L., 27, 129, 131, 204, 319, 325, 336, 362, 365, 394, 395, 439, 540
Festinger, L. A., 97, 101
Field, P., 327, 328
Fikes, R. E., 579
Fischer, M., 85
Fischhoff, B., 122, 195, 470
Fischler, G. L., 359
Fishbein, M., 127, 169, 175, 192, 206, 214, 236, 238, 350, 411
Fisher, J., 461
Fiske, D. W., 330, 536
Fiske, S. T., 11, 13, 168, 169, 170, 171, 180, 183, 185, 187, 188, 190, 191, 192, 193, 195, 214, 234, 244, 251, 391, 392, 465, 471, 522, 542
Flacks, R., 160
Flapan, D., 80
Flavell, H. H., 375
Flay, B. R., 129
Fletcher, G. J. O., 128, 131, 140
Foa, E., 455
Foa, N. G., 455
Fodor, J. A., 407, 423
Fogarty, S. J., 260, 262
Folkes, V. S., 292, 293, 301, 302, 362
Fondacaro, R., 468, 524

Fong, K. K., 399
Ford, M., 260
Forsterling, F., 359
Fox, G. A., 359
Fraser, S. C., 51, 573
Freedman, J. L., 573
Frenkel-Brunswik, E., 46
Freud, S., 4, 23, 25, 30, 31, 251, 260, 261, 281, 283, 285, 286, 291, 407, 436, 493, 503, 568
Frey, D., 157, 541
Frieze, T. H., 353
Froming, W. J., 150, 155
Fujioka, T., 172, 530

Gaensbauer, T. J., 248
Galambos, J. A., 529
Galanter, E., 532, 553
Gallie, W. B., 122
Galton, F., 4
Ganellen, R. J., 44, 45
Garfinkel, H., 469, 472
Gati, I., 36
Gauld, A., 557
Geertz, C., 496
Geiger, E., 384, 419, 420, 426
Geller, V., 508
Gerard, H. B., 214, 374
Gergen, K. J., 28, 51, 52, 97, 102, 551
Geva, N., 169, 177, 471
Gibbons, F. X., 90
Gibbs, G., 136
Gibson, J. J., 246, 415
Gilligan, S. G., 261, 262, 270
Gitomer, A., 266
Giuliano, T., 196
Gjesme, T., 409
Glaser, R., 496
Gleason, J. M., 541
Glucksberg, S., 29, 172
Goethals, G. R., 25, 27, 42, 124, 131, 132, 350, 354, 356, 395
Goffman, E., 124, 148, 156, 157, 467, 469, 472
Goldman, A. I., 551, 553, 554, 555
Golin, S., 44, 45
Gollwitzer, P. M., 67, 299, 418, 461
Goodman, C. C., 7, 209, 406, 504
Gordon, C., 102
Gordon, S. E., 186, 484, 509, 510, 511, 516, 518, 531
Gottfried, A. W., 249
Gough, H. G., 71
Gould, J., 576
Gould, R., 332
Graen, G., 409
Graesser, C. C., 196
Graham, S., 254, 303, 304
Graziano, W., 92

Green, P., 192
Greenberg, G., 157
Greene, D., 85, 283
Greenwald, A. G., 12, 96, 97, 101, 102,
    109, 114, 139, 145, 147, 151, 157,
    214, 315, 350, 415, 522
Grice, H. P., 487, 529, 531
Gross, P. H., 494
Gruendel, J. M., 262, 469
Guthrie, E. R., 11, 405

Hackman, J. R., 409
Halal, M., 261
Hallam, J. R., 157
Halverson, R. R., 222
Hamilton, D. L., 7, 10, 169, 175, 176, 427,
    484, 485, 494, 509, 510
Hamilton, V., 407
Hampshire, S., 568
Hancock, R. D., 398, 399
Handel, S., 301, 305
Hannah, D. B., 516
Hantas, M., 262
Harkins, S. G., 154
Harkness, S., 71
Harper, R. J. C., 6
Harré, R., 557
Harris, M. B., 256
Harrison, A. A., 249
Hart, P. E., 579
Harter, L., 558
Hartwick, J., 186, 484, 509, 511, 518
Harvey, J. H., 157, 300
Harvey, O. J., 160, 530
Hastie, R., 170, 171, 178, 196, 469, 511,
    516, 522, 524
Hasturf, A. H., 168, 209, 526
Hayes, J. R., 473, 481
Hayes-Roth, B., 190
Heckhausen, H., 82, 83, 96, 358, 368, 414
Hegel, G. W. F., 4
Heider, F., 37, 42, 45, 101, 253, 292, 293,
    336, 436, 438, 442, 493, 577
Helle, P., 416
Helmreich, R., 328
Helson, H., 26, 359
Hembree, L. M., 246
Henderson, C., 246, 248
Henle, M., 6
Henmon, V. A. C., 84
Hensler, C. P., 194
Herman, C. P., 135, 154, 204, 260
Herr, P. M., 29, 207, 221, 230, 234
Hertel, P. T., 196
Hervitz, F. E., 111
Hewitt, E. E., 341, 342, 344, 371, 379,
    385, 392, 393, 394, 395, 397
Hiatt, S., 246
Higgins, E. T., 3, 10, 11, 25, 27, 28, 29,
    30, 31, 32, 36, 39, 43, 44, 46, 47, 51,
    52, 53, 54, 58, 97, 99, 102, 104, 109,
    117, 170, 172, 174, 175, 186, 204,
    225, 233, 251, 256, 258, 260, 299,
    380, 391, 427, 468, 471, 487, 488,
    492, 505, 506, 508, 521, 524, 531
Higgins, R. L., 157
Higgins, T., 391
Hill, C. A., 338
Hills, P. J., 136
Hirt, E. R., 524
Hoffman, C., 466, 482, 483, 484
Hoffman, M. L., 10, 13, 43, 246, 247, 252,
    253, 254, 255, 256, 261, 269, 272
Hofstedter, D. R., 8
Hogarth, R. M., 196
Hollander, E. P., 530
Holmes, J. G., 400
Hood, R., 90
Hood, W. R., 160
Hormuth, S. E., 105
Horner, M. S., 387
Horney, K., 23, 31
Hovland, C. I., 116, 158, 160
Hubert, S., 522, 523
Huddy, L., 194
Hull, C. L., 4, 5, 281, 285, 287
Hunka, S. M., 6
Hunt, J. McV., 67
Hunt, W. A., 266
Huttenlocher, J., 28
Hyman, H. H., 25, 26, 32

Ickes, W. J., 52
Ilgen, D., 332
Insko, C. A., 522
Irwin, F. W., 526
Isen, A. M., 111, 117, 134, 174, 261, 262,
    264, 268, 270
Izard, C. E., 246, 406, 427

Jacobs, L., 332
Jacobson, L., 494
James, W., 4, 23, 25, 30, 31, 123, 124,
    127, 148, 320, 326, 557
Janis, I., 158, 160, 327, 328
Janis, I. L., 323, 325
Janis, J. L., 195
Janoff-Bulman, R., 27, 28, 359, 362
Jeffery, K. M., 482
Jennings, D. L., 494
Jensen, R., 150
Johnson, J., 524
Johnson, M. M. S., 261
Johnson, M. P., 204, 205
Johnson, V. E., 324
Johnson-Laird, P. N., 472
Johnston, S., 541
Johnston, V. S., 506
Jones, C. R., 51, 174, 225, 471, 506

Jones, E. E., 73, 74, 102, 109, 111, 112, 114, 157, 214, 331, 332, 333, 350, 354, 360, 366, 367, 374, 492, 493, 494
Jones, S. C., 329

Kagan, J., 101, 249, 381
Kahneman, D., 25, 107, 110, 260, 472, 476, 477, 478, 481, 496
Kanfer, F. H., 562
Kant, I., 290, 300
Kaplan, H. B., 46
Karabenick, S. A., 36
Karniol, R., 374
Karp, L., 134, 261
Karsten, A., 420
Kassin, S. M., 484
Katz, D., 191, 209
Katz, L., 266
Katz, L. B., 169, 484, 509
Kauff, D. M., 423
Kelley, H. H., 25, 30, 32, 37, 42, 45, 92, 208, 292, 295, 299, 331, 350, 355, 362
Kelley, K., 47
Kelley, S., 205
Kelly, G. A., 320
Kelly, M., 206, 568
Kelly, R., 338
Kelman, H. C., 150, 159, 160
Kendzierski, D., 114, 213, 236
Kenny, D. A., 471, 522
Kenrick, D. T., 150
Kerr, N. L., 157, 196
Kiersted, G., 572, 573
Kiesler, C. A., 129, 206, 247
Kiewiet, D. R., 194
Kihlstrom, J. F., 96, 102, 114, 504
Kinder, D. R., 190, 193, 194, 214
King, G., 27, 29, 51, 52, 251, 380, 391, 393
King, G. A., 3, 471, 505, 508
King, R. A., 253
Kingdon, J. W., 293
Kintsch, W., 410
Kirk, L., 71
Kirker, W. S., 157, 263, 391
Kirschebaum, D. S., 562
Kirscht, J., 381
Kitt. A. S., 25, 26, 27, 32, 359
Klar, Y., 410
Klein, G. S., 84, 85, 86, 88, 504
Klein, R., 10, 11, 31, 46, 99, 299
Klinger, E., 98, 106, 505, 506, 536
Klos, D. S., 107
Kluegel, J. R., 299
Koch, B., 419
Koenig, K. E., 160
Koeske, R., 190
Kohlberg, L., 381, 399, 494

Kohler, W., 468
Korman, A., 336
Kosslyn, S. M., 410
Kothandapani, V., 204
Kozlowski, L. T., 154
Krauss, H. H., 332
Krauss, R. M., 29
Kremer, J. F., 253
Kruglanski, A. W., 350, 410, 551
Kuhl, J., 11, 13, 14, 50, 101, 111, 366, 384, 405, 407, 409, 410, 411, 412, 413, 415, 416, 417, 418, 419, 420, 422, 425, 426, 427, 428
Kuiper, N. A., 43, 45, 57, 157, 170, 233, 263, 391
Kukla, A., 48, 309, 351, 353, 354, 358, 359, 361, 362, 366, 367, 409, 415
Kunst-Wilson, W. R., 268, 423
Kyser, G., 566

La Berge, D., 427
Lachman, J. L., 523
Lachman, R., 523
Lader, M., 35
Laird, J. D., 247, 261, 262
Lakoff, R. T., 489
Lambel, A. K., 175
Lambert, W. W., 209
Landis, C., 266
Langer, E. J., 471
La Piere, R. T., 205, 232
Larter, W. M., 190, 193
Latané, B., 67, 154, 160, 196, 208
Lathin, D. R., 359
Lau, R. R., 194, 292, 293
Laufer, J. K., 522
Lawler, E. E., 409
Lawson, M. E., 303
Lazarus, R. S., 38, 41, 244, 245, 269, 274, 295, 296, 406
Lecky, P., 101, 320, 326, 336
Leippe, M. R., 177
Leirer, V. O., 484
Lemley, R., 494
Lenauer, M., 70, 89, 91, 92
Lenn, T. M., 220
Leonard, S., 332
Lepper, M. R., 85, 86, 209, 235, 283, 494
Lerman, D., 33, 297, 354
Lerner, M. J., 399, 400
Leventhal, H., 405
Levi, A., 131, 350
Levine, J. M., 197
Levine, M. V., 6
Levinson, D. J., 46, 98
Levy, A., 154
Lewin, K., 5, 9, 23, 24, 30, 31, 69, 101, 283, 285, 287, 309, 319, 365, 394, 407, 412, 417, 424
Lewinsohn, P. M., 526

Lewis, H. B., 31
Lewis, S., 484
Licht, B., 328
Lichtenstein, E. H., 528, 553
Lichtenstein, M., 509, 523, 524
Lichtenstein, S., 470
Lierer, V. O., 509
Lindsay, P. H., 123
Lindskold, S., 101
Lingle, J., 471
Lingle, J. H., 169, 177, 209
Linville, P. W., 170, 254, 494
Lippmann, W., 170
Lipps, T., 247
Little, B., 106
Litwin, G. H., 396
Liu, T. S., 521
Livesley, W. J., 80
Lockhart, R. S., 423
Locksley, A., 70, 89, 91, 92
Loebl, J. H., 254
Loevinger, J., 149
Loftus, E., 481
Loomis, J. W., 107
Lopes, L., 169
Lord, C., 114
Lord, C. G., 209, 235
Lowell, E., 380
Lowell, E. L., 146, 351
Lui, L., 171
Lund, A., 338
Luria, A. R., 506, 557, 579
Lurie, L., 27, 29, 53, 54, 172
Lustig, D. A., 423
Lydon, J., 129
Lynch, J. G., 410
Lynn, S., 55
Lyons, J., 28, 475

MacDonald, M. R., 45
Mackie, D., 114, 235
Macomber, G., 570
Maddi, S. R., 536
Magnusson, D., 146
Mahoney, H. J., 428
Maier, N. R. F., 468
Main, A., 136
Mandler, G., 178-179, 244, 274, 406, 408,
   423, 532, 533, 536
Mandler, J., 170
Mandler, J. M., 469
Manis, J. G., 207
Manis, M. 29
Marcel, A. J., 266, 268, 421 ,422, 423
Marks, I., 35
Marks, R. W., 526
Markus, H., 7, 11, 12, 25, 58, 70, 71, 89,
   91, 96, 101, 102, 108, 109, 111, 116,
   141, 157, 170, 215, 323, 326, 380,
   391, 471, 508

Marlowe, D., 146, 156
Marquis, R. E., 450
Martin, D. J., 45
Martin, G. B., 246
Martin, R. M., 273
Martindale, C., 101
Maslow, A. H., 320
Masters, J., 260
Mavin, G. H., 3, 104, 471, 505, 508
Mayer, D., 262
Mazze, K., 482
McArthur, L. A., 206
McArthur, L. Z., 471
McCall, R., 250
McCann, C. D., 51, 468, 487, 488, 524,
   531
McCarthy, B., 337
McCaul, K. D., 34, 42, 43
McCleary, R. A., 269
McClelland, D. C., 49, 87, 88, 97, 146,
   148, 156, 351, 380, 406
McClelland, J. L., 171
McCloskey, M., 172
McConnell, H. K., 126, 127, 132
McCown, N. E., 157
McDonel, E. C., 214
McDougall, W., 4
McFarland, C., 128, 130, 154
McFarlin, D. B., 11, 12-13, 14, 57, 103,
   109, 114, 160, 328, 331, 332, 333,
   337, 342, 435, 436
McFarlin, R., 382, 385, 391, 393, 399
McGinn, N. C., 38
McGinnies, E., 269
McGinnis, E., 7
McGrath, J. E., 196
McGuire, C. V., 172, 530
McGuire, W. J., 52, 97, 102, 172, 214, 530
McKoon, G., 415
Mead, G. H., 25, 123, 124, 320, 469, 568,
   573
Means, B., 111, 264
Medin, D. L., 172, 186, 234
Mehlhorn, G., 71
Mehlhorn, H. G., 71
Meier, N. C., 441
Melburg, B., 157
Melloy-Carminer, P., 249
Meltzer, B. N., 207
Meltzoff, A. N., 248
Merton, R. K., 25, 26, 27, 32, 160, 359
Merton, R. S., 568
Messe, L. A., 157
Meyer, J. P., 307
Meyer, W. U., 358, 362, 368, 409
Michotte, A., 493
Milbers, S. J., 181, 183, 185, 188
Milgram, S., 211, 551
Miller, A. G., 192
Miller, A. T., 7

Miller, D., 481
Miller, D. T., 45, 131, 350, 372, 374, 400
Miller, G. A., 532, 553, 557
Miller, J. G., 80
Miller, N. E., 522, 538, 539
Miller, R. L., 362, 573
Minesian, A. J., 359
Minsky, M., 471
Mio, J. S., 528
Mirer, T. W., 205
Mischel, H. N., 427
Mischel, W., 7, 114, 127, 134, 170, 172,
    234, 256, 270, 338, 374, 375, 427,
    466, 470, 471, 482, 485, 496, 526
Monson, T., 92
Monteiro, K. P., 261
Moore, B., 256
Moore, B. S., 521
Moore, M. K., 248
Moreland, R. L., 326
Morse, S. J., 28, 51, 52
Moscovici, S., 197
Mueller, J. H., 261
Mulherin, A., 307
Mullen, B., 27, 46
Murray, H. A., 66-67, 87, 88, 106
Myers, R., 575

Nadler, A., 461, 462
Nasby, W., 261, 262
Natale, M., 262
Navon, D., 249
Nebergall, R., 145
Neely, J. H., 227
Neissers, U., 5
Nelson, D. G. K., 178
Nelson, K., 262, 469
Neubers, S. L., 183, 185, 188
Newcomb, T. M., 25, 26, 51, 101, 160,
    336
Newell, A., 5, 467
Newston, D., 483, 551
Nicholls, J. G., 328, 341, 354, 358, 373
Niedenthal, P. M., 11, 12, 114, 115, 323
Nilsson, N. J., 579
Nisbett, R., 3, 7, 10, 458, 542
Nisbett, R. E., 27, 73, 74, 86, 124, 131,
    268, 283, 350, 466, 477, 483, 492,
    494, 568
Nochajski, T., 340, 341 342
Norman, D. A., 13, 123, 244, 406, 410,
    423
Norman, R., 207
Norrell, S., 566
Novem, J., 110, 112
Nowell-Smith, P. H., 122
Nowicki, G., 264
Nurius, P., 11, 12, 25, 102, 108, 109, 111,
    141, 293
Nuttin, J. R., 97, 101, 103, 110
Nygard, R., 409, 417

Olbrich, E., 415, 426
Olney, T., 221
Olshan, K., 186
Olshavsky, R. W., 114, 236
Olson, C. T., 157
Olson, D. R., 29, 43, 408, 410, 413, 422
Olson, J. M., 128, 138, 170, 206, 219, 233
Orne, M. T., 482, 530
Ornstein, R. E., 411
Ortony, A., 170, 532, 536
Osborne, D., 338
Osgood, C. E., 101, 336, 438
Ostrom, T., 465, 471
Ostrom, T. M., 26, 55, 154, 169, 177, 204,
    209, 515, 522
Oswald, I., 506
Ovsiankina, M., 406, 417
Owens, W. A., 446, 450

Padawer-Singer, A., 52, 530
Page, W., 338
Pallak, M. S., 222
Papousek, H., 247
Parducci, A., 26
Park, B., 524
Parsons, J. E., 46, 51
Passer, M. W., 293
Pastore, N., 303
Patrick, R., 264
Patterson, M. B., 58
Paulhus, D., 158, 333, 450, 451, 460
Pavelchak, M. A., 11, 13, 195, 197, 391,
    392
Pazer, S., 253, 254
Peake, P. K., 127
Pearl, R., 328
Peevers, B., 80
Pellegrino, H., 266
Penrod, S., 196, 197
Pepitone, A., 474, 475, 477, 478, 479, 480,
    481, 485, 486, 488
Perloff, R., 157
Peters, M. D., 214
Pettigrew, T. F., 6
Pettit, P., 293
Petty, R. E., 154, 522
Philips, S. V., 489
Piaget, J., 13, 149, 150, 244, 249, 260,
    408, 413, 468, 493, 494
Pichert, J. W., 481, 517, 518, 519
Pidgeon, N., 195
Pietromonaco, P., 110, 178, 251, 268, 506,
    508
Pilkonis, P. A., 247
Pittman, N. L., 92
Pittman, T., 360
Pittman, T. S., 92, 157
Pittman, X. X., 102, 109, 111, 114
Platt, J. J., 107
Pleban, R., 438, 445, 446, 447, 448
Plutchick, R., 406

Polivy, J., 135
Popper, K., 476, 493
Porac, C., 6
Porter, L. W., 409, 410
Posher, M. I., 427
Posse, N., 384, 386
Postman, L., 7, 504
Potter, F. W., 136
Potter, M., 266
Powell, M. C., 207, 216, 220, 227
Pratkanis, A. R., 96, 101, 102, 147, 315
Pratto, F., 195
Prawat, R. S., 308
Prentice, W. C. H., 6
Presson, C. C., 114, 236
Pribam, K., 425, 532, 553
Price, L. H., 417
Pritchard, R. D., 410
Pritchard, S., 157
Proshansky, H. M., 209
Pryor, J., 471
Pryor, J. B., 90, 515
Pylyshyn, Z. W., 410
Pyszczynski, T., 157

Quattrone, G. A., 494

Raaijmakers J. G. W., 513
Radke-Yarrow, M., 253
Ramey, C. T., 246
Ramsay, D., 246
Ratcliff, R., 415
Rawls, J., 467
Raynor, J. O., 3, 8, 11, 12-13, 14, 57, 103,
    109, 315, 319, 321, 325, 326, 329,
    330, 340, 341, 342, 344, 351, 352,
    365, 367, 371, 379, 380, 382, 384,
    385, 386, 387, 388, 391, 393, 394,
    395, 396, 399, 409, 435
Razran, G., 258
Read, S. J., 338, 339, 527, 529
Reber, A. S., 484
Rechman, R. F., 126, 131, 132
Reed, L., 353
Reese, E., 496
Regan, D. T., 210, 218
Reitzes, D. C., 114
Rempel, J. K., 214
Reno, L., 562
Reppucci, N. D., 368
Rest, S., 353
Reyes, R. M., 524
Rholes, W. S., 5, 174, 175, 186, 206, 225,
    258, 471, 506, 531
Richard, M., 563
Richardson, K. D., 437
Riess, M., 157
Rips, L. J., 172
Riskey, D. R., 178, 522
Roberts, W. A., 513
Robinson, G. F., 261

Robinson, J. P., 327
Roby, T. B., 87
Rochberg-Halton, E., 65
Rodgers, H. L., 206
Rodin, J., 461
Roger, C. R., 25, 30, 31
Rogers, C., 101, 320, 331, 336
Rogers, C. M., 52
Rogers, T. B., 157, 263, 266, 391
Rokeach, M., 380, 381, 382, 398, 400
Roney, C., 390, 393
Rosch, E., 36, 58, 172, 474, 551
Rose, A. M., 207
Rose, S. A., 249
Roseman, I., 537
Rosenbaum, R. M., 293, 353
Rosenberg, M. J., 52, 146, 158, 204, 327,
    455, 530
Rosenberg, S., 29, 186
Rosenfeld, P., 157
Rosenfield, D. A., 350
Rosenholtz, S. J., 489
Rosenthal, R., 482, 494, 530
Ross, D. L., 423
Ross, L., 3, 7, 10, 27, 58, 131, 209, 350,
    458, 466, 483, 492, 494, 542
Ross, M., 7, 11, 12, 45, 126, 127, 128, 129,
    130, 131, 132, 134, 136, 138, 139,
    140, 154, 350, 372
Rothbart, M., 494, 509
Rothbaum, F., 140
Rotter, J. B., 283, 285, 288, 309, 415
Routtenberg, A., 406
Rubin, I. S., 387, 388
Ruble, D. N., 27, 28, 46, 52, 254, 351,
    354, 358, 362
Ruhrold, R. E., 107
Rumelhart, D. E., 170, 171, 410, 471
Rundus, D., 513
Russell, D., 33, 292, 293, 297
Rychlak, J. F., 293
Ryle, G., 568

Sagi, A., 246
Salancik, G. R., 127, 132, 236
Salovey, P., 461
Sample, J., 206
Sanders, M. S., 410
Sanford, R. N., 46
Santrock, J., 261
Sarason, S. B., 367
Sarbin, T. R., 27
Sarup, G., 206
Schachter, S., 6, 138, 244, 296
Schacter, F. F., 450
Schafer, R., 493, 577
Schaffer, L. G., 194
Schaffer, M. M., 172
Schank, R., 101, 107
Schank, R. C., 471, 475, 532, 553

Scheier, M. F., 36, 109, 145, 155, 254, 255, 414, 557
Schell, A. M., 406
Schriffrin, R. M., 5
Schlenker, B. R., 132, 148, 156, 157, 337, 360, 460, 530
Schmalt, H. D., 96, 358
Schmidt, F. L., 410
Schmidt, R., 557
Schneider, D. J., 124, 168, 172, 191
Schneider, K., 96, 384, 386, 409
Schneider, W., 398
Schoenfeld, N., 84, 85, 86, 88
Schoenfeldt, L. F., 446, 450
Schofield, J. W., 206
Schorr, D., 527
Schul, Y., 177, 184
Schuman, H., 204, 205
Schutz, A., 103
Schwartz, J., 114
Schwarz, N., 541
Schwartz, S. H., 206
Schwieger, P., 157
Scribner, S., 468, 488
Seamon, J. J., 423
Searle, J., 407, 424
Searle, J. R., 467
Sears, D. O., 194
Sears, P. S., 101, 319, 365, 394
Secord, P., 80
Secord, P. F., 6, 557
Seeleman, V., 209
Seligman, M. E. P., 44, 354, 472
Semmel, A., 44
Sentis, K., 96, 196
Shaeffer, D., 45
Shalker, T. E., 134, 261
Shannon, C. E., 362
Shantz, C. U., 27
Shaver, P., 508
Shaver, P. R., 327
Shavit, H., 332
Sheehy, G., 256
Shefner, J. M., 6
Shepard, R. N., 410
Sheppard, B., 482
Sherif, C. W., 145, 148, 160, 206
Sherif, M., 24, 25, 33, 116, 145, 146, 148, 160
Sherman, S. J., 29, 55, 90, 111, 114, 214, 234, 236, 524
Sherrod, D. R., 521
Shevrin, H., 268, 269
Shiffrin, R. M., 398, 513, 520
Shoben, E. J., 172, 523
Shocker, A. D., 192
Shore, E., 450
Short, J. C., 3, 11, 12, 13, 14, 48, 341, 344, 371, 379, 380, 387
Shotter, J., 557
Shouval, R., 332

Showers, C., 109, 110, 112
Shrauger, J. S., 58, 101, 160, 331, 332, 337, 338, 343, 436
Shulman, R. F., 126, 127
Shure, M. B., 107
Shweder, R. A., 73
Siebel, C. E., 256
Siegelman, J., 138
Sigall, H., 332
Siladi, M., 508
Silverman, L. H., 423
Simmel, M., 493
Simmons, C. H., 399
Simon, H. A., 467, 473, 481, 496
Simner, M. L., 246
Simon, J. G., 43, 45
Simon, H. A., 5, 13, 190, 244
Singer, J., 244, 256
Singer, J. E., 6, 296
Silverman, I., 338
Sivacek, J., 206
Skinner, B. F., 5
Skov, R. B., 111
Slackman, E., 253
Slovic, P., 470
Smith, E. E., 172, 186, 234, 299, 527
Smith, J., 58, 326, 333, 444, 459
Smith, J. D., 178
Smith, M., 266, 442, 458
Smith, M. B., 209, 210
Smith, M. D., 52
Snyder, C. R., 157
Snyder, C. R. R., 427
Snyder, M., 46, 114, 117, 134, 156, 206, 208, 212, 213, 230, 233, 236, 455, 494, 517, 518
Snyder, M. J., 350
Snygg, D., 101, 320, 331, 336
Solomon, R., L., 209, 536
Solomon, S., 157
Soraci, S., 337
Sorman, P. B., 160
Sorrentino, R. M., 3, 11, 12, 13, 14, 48, 341, 342, 344, 371, 372, 379, 380, 385, 386, 387, 388, 390, 392, 393, 394, 395, 396, 397, 398, 399, 400
Speckart, G., 236
Speer, L. K., 194
Spence, D. S., 493
Spence, K. W., 287, 310
Sperry, R. W., 406
Spiro, R. J., 483
Spitz, R. A., 248, 249
Spivak, G., 107
Spizzini, C. C., 246
Srinivasan, V., 192
Srull, T. K., 10, 29, 51, 171, 174, 225, 469, 471, 484, 505, 506, 509, 510, 511, 512, 513, 514, 515, 516, 518, 519, 520, 521, 523, 524, 531
Staats, A. W., 247

Staats, C. K., 247
Staddon, J. E. R., 503
Stamm, J. S., 425
Stapp, J., 328
Stasser, G., 196
Stein, F., 85
Stenberg, C., 246
Stephan, E., 85, 89
Stephan, W. G., 299
Stephen, W. G., 350
Stephens, L., 253
Stern, P., 303
Stock, C. B., 111
Sturms, M. D., 34, 42, 43
Stotland, E., 256, 338
Strauman, T., 10, 11, 31, 46, 99, 299
Straus, E., 210
Strickland, B. R., 156
Stroebe, W., 26
Stucky, R. J., 157
Stults, D. M., 157
Suci, G. J., 438
Sudnow, D., 563
Svejda, M., 246
Suinn, R. M., 338
Sujan, M., 176, 193
Sullivan, H. S., 23, 31, 102
Suls, J., 27, 46
Suls, J. M., 362
Sumner, W. G., 160
Super, C. M., 71
Susmilch, C., 38
Swann, W. B., 206, 208, 212, 230, 338, 339
Sweeney, P. D., 45, 57
Szegda, M., 261

Taft, R., 27
Tagiuri, R., 58
Tanford, S., 196, 197
Tanke, E. D., 208, 494
Tannenbaum, P. H., 101, 336, 438
Taylor, A. M., 506
Taylor, M. S., 328
Taylor, R., 262
Tayler, S. E., 123, 139, 168, 170, 172, 176, 183, 187, 284, 465, 471, 522, 542
Teasdale, J. D., 260, 262, 354, 472
Tedeschi, J. T., 101, 132, 157, 360
Terbovic, M. L., 338
Terrell, F., 44
Tesser, A., 11, 12, 102, 158, 315, 333, 334, 335, 336, 438, 440, 441, 442, 444, 445, 446, 447, 448, 449, 450, 451, 452, 455, 458, 459, 460
Tetlock, P. E., 131, 350
Thibaut, J. W., 331
Thomas, E., 338
Thomas, W. I., 207
Thompson, W. C., 524

Thordike, E. L., 468
Thoreson, C. E., 428
Thorley, S., 338
Thurstone, L. L., 214
Titchener, E. B., 4
Tittler, B. I., 206
Tolman, E. C., 4, 5, 97, 285, 319
Tomarken, A. J., 562
Tomkins, S. S., 282, 307
Treisman, M., 506
Trope, Y., 8, 14, 325, 340, 354, 355, 358, 359, 365, 369, 370, 371, 372, 373, 380, 382, 384, 385, 387, 393, 396, 397
Tucker, D. M., 406
Tulving, E., 266
Turner, R. H., 31
Turner, T., 553
Tversky, A., 25, 36, 107, 110, 470, 472, 476, 477, 478, 481, 496
Tyler, T. R., 194

Underwood, B., 521
Ungar, S., 360
Upshaw, H. S., 26

Vallacher, R. R., 10, 550, 553, 558, 560, 561, 562, 563, 566, 568, 570, 572, 573, 574, 575, 576, 577
Veroff, J., 27, 46, 97, 105, 299
Vidmar, N., 482
Vinogradova, O. S., 506
Volkmann, J., 26
Von Baeyer, C., 44
Von Bertalanffy, L., 567
Vygotsky, L. S., 557

Wagener, J. J., 261
Walster, E., 332, 455
Walzer, M., 496
Ward, L. M., 6
Warland, R., 206
Warner, L. G., 206, 211
Warshaw, P. R., 72
Warwick, D. P., 160
Wason, P. C., 472
Watson, J. B., 4
Watson, J. S., 246
Watson, P. D., 209
Watts, W. H., 224, 522
Weary, C., 300
Weary, G., 157
Weaver, D., 332
Weaver, W., 362
Weber, M., 495
Weber, R., 176, 494, 516, 524
Weber, S. J., 159
Wegner, D. M., 10, 196, 550, 553, 558, 560, 561, 562, 563, 566, 568, 570, 572, 573, 574, 575, 576, 577

Weiner, B., 8, 9, 10, 14, 23, 33, 34, 37, 42, 43, 48, 49, 111, 253, 254, 288, 292, 293, 297, 299, 300, 301, 303, 304, 305, 306, 307-308, 309, 351, 353, 354, 359, 361, 362, 365, 367, 368, 380, 384, 386, 387, 394, 397, 409, 418
Weiner, Y., 332
Weinstein, M. S., 3, 396
Weinstein, N. D., 526
Weiss, M., 415, 426
Weitz, J., 332
Wells, R. S., 492
Wenzlaff, R., 553
White, B. J., 160
White, G. M., 69, 72-73
White, P., 134
White, R. W., 209
Wickelgren, W. A., 171
Wickens, D. D., 266, 268
Wicker, A. W., 127, 204, 205, 232
Wicklund, R. A., 10, 12, 31, 36, 46, 52, 67, 82, 90, 145, 236, 255, 414, 418, 461, 540
Williams, K., 154
Wills, T. A., 160
Wilson, T. D., 124, 268, 568
Wind, Y., 192
Wine, J., 83
Winograd, T., 579
Wittgenstein, L., 469, 551
Wong, P. T. P., 292
Wood, B., 506
Wood, R., 570

Wortman, C. B., 139, 368
Wright, J., 134
Wurb, E., 116
Wyer, R. S., 10, 29, 51, 174, 178, 186, 225, 469, 471, 484, 505, 506, 509, 510, 511, 516, 518, 519, 520, 521, 530, 531, 541
Wylie, R. C., 106, 315, 326, 327, 328

Yando, R., 261, 262
Yarrow, M., 135
Yerkes, R. M., 87

Zahn-Waxler, C., 253
Zajonc, R. B., 40, 170, 178, 244, 245, 249, 268, 274, 405, 406, 423, 468, 488, 575
Zander, A., 338
Zanna, M. P., 128, 129, 175, 176, 204, 205, 206, 208, 214, 218, 219, 222, 247, 260, 540
Zehner, K. S., 524
Zeigarnick, B., 159, 406, 417
Zelditch, M., Jr., 489
Zubeck, J. M., 399
Zuckerman, M., 350, 359, 369, 372
Zeiss, A., 270
Zeiss, A. M., 134
Zeiss, A. R., 338, 427
Zukier, H., 10, 467, 469, 474, 475, 477, 478, 479, 480, 481, 485, 486, 488, 489, 490, 491, 493, 494
Zurcher, L. A., 101

Subject Index

Ability
  and affective value of outcomes, 354
  vs. certainty, 382-383
  esteem associated with, 356-357, 359-360
  and outcome diagnosticity, 355-356
  prior uncertainty regarding, 363, 370-371
  self-assessment of, 362-365
  as source of value, 317
Abnormal motivation, 324
Accessibility
  attitude, 211-215
  category, 6, 505-508
  construct, 3, 391, 392, 393
  of standards in self-evaluation, 51-53
Achievement failure, perceived causes of, 294
Achievement motivation
  as affective disposition, 361-362
  as affective value, 379, 380, 384-385
  collective, 148
  as dominant pursuit, 291
  effect of possible self selection on, 110-114
  effect of previous outcomes on, 367-368
  effect of standard utilization on, 48-50
  ego-task orientation of, 156
  and esteemed abilities, 356-358, 359-360
  general theory of, 387
  individual differences in, 361-362
  and internal attribution, 352-354
  and internal standards, 146, 148, 149
  and life tasks, 98
  n-achievement, 3, 15-17
  perceived causes of failure, 294
  and risk taking, 396-397
  role of emotions in, 286
  self-assessment, 362-365
  self-enhancement, 352-362
  and task choice, 358-359, 365
  vs. task orientation, 87-88
  and uncertainty orientation, 381, 386-390
Achievement tasks, esteem-related
  utility of, 357-358
Acquired guides, in evaluation process, 30-32
  and achievement motivation, 48-50
  changes in, 50-51
  effect of contextual variability on, 50-55

in general appraisal stage, 38
individual differences in use of, 45-48
in interpretation stage, 38, 44-45
and self-esteem, 44-45, 52
use of multiple, 39
  See also Standard utilization
Act identity structures, 552, 553-555
Action
  effect of values on, 317
  and expectancy of goal attainment, 309
  role of emotion in, 306-309
Actional propositions, 413
Action control, 405, 424-425
  and difficulty of enactment, 425-426
  self-regulatory abilities, 426-428
Action emergence, 557, 568-570
  and impulse, 574-578
  process of, 570-574
Action identification
  in alcohol consumption, 560-562
  causal link with action, 567-568
  in child rearing, 563-565
  fallible distinctions in, 551-552
  higher level, 554-555
  and impulse, 574-578
  and intelligent action, 578-580
  as personal reification, 555-557
  prospective and retrospective, 568-570
  structure of, 553-555
Action-linked inference, 468-469, 489-490
Action maintenance, 557
  and causal link between identification and action, 567-568
  for difficult actions, 563-566
  for easy actions, 559-563
  and optimal level of identification, 557-559
Action orientation, 425-426
Action-related knowledge, in memory, 409, 410-414
Action tendencies, 417
  conscious vs. subconscious processing, 421-424
  cumulative instigation of, 419-420
  perseverance of unconsummated, 418-419

Active attentional selectivity, in action control, 427
Actors, dispositional terms employed by, 73-74
Actual/own vs. ideal/own discrepancies, 44-45
Actual self, 30-32
Adaptive behavior, 316
Addictive behaviors, action identification in, 562
Affect
  and formation of emotionally charged categories, 263
  impact on information processing, 260
  interaction with cognition in complex situations, 271-273
  and recall, 133-135, 261-262
  relationship with cognition, 244-246
  role in decision making and problem solving, 264
  and selective processing, 260-261
  and social cognition, 263-264
  and static orientation, 78
  See also Emotion
Affect-generation stage, in social judgment, *See* Evaluative impressions
Affective components, of attitudes, 204
Affective disposition, achievement motive as, 361-362
Affective responses
  autonomic-arousal component of, 267-268
  basic model of, 170-175
  to evaluation and self-enhancement perspective, 331-332
  to goal conflicts, 538-540
  to imagined stimulus, 256-257
  to interruption or completion of plans, 532-537
  to matches between stimulus and representation, 248-250
  to meaning of stimulus, 250-255
  to physical features of stimulus, 246-248
  resulting from goal-directed behavior, 537-538
  role taking, 255-256
  and semantic interpretations, 257-259
  to transformed stimulus, 255-259
  from unconscious processing, 268-270
  See also Emotional consequences; Evaluative impressions; Inference, goal-guided
Affective states, motivational consequences of, 540-541
Affective tags, in social categorization, 171-175
Affective values, 318
  achievement motive as, 380, 384-385
  vs. information value in achievement behavior, 386-390
  negative, 323-324
  in self system, 322

and uncertainty orientation, 384-385
  See also Values
Affiliative motivation, 96-97
  decision strategies in, 114-117
  importance of, 291
  and life tasks, 98
  perceived causes of failure, 294
Agency bias, 492-493
Aggressive behavior, and context, 51
Ahistorical approach, of motivation theories, 289-290
Algebraic processing, in evaluative impressions, 176
Altruism
  and action identification, 572-574
  in ego development, 150
Anger, and causal controllability, 302-306
Anxiety, 260
Appraisal, of stimulus, 252-255
Approach-approach conflict, 538-539
Approach-avoidance conflict, 539
Approach behaviors, 213
Approval motivation
  and ego involvement, 146, 156
  and ego-task orientation, 156
Aristotelian mode, of thinking, 69
Artificial intelligence, vs. human intelligence, 579-580
Aspiration
  and self evaluation, 25, 30-32
  shift in level of, 365-366, 394
Assessing consequences, of stimulus, 252-253, 254
Associative learning, and attitude-behavior consistency, 215
Attentional processes
  effect of category accessibility on, 505-506
  effects of current concerns on, 506-507
  effects of values on, 507-508
  See also Information processing
Attitude activation, automatic upon observing attitude object, 224-227
  and response latency to attitudinal inquiry, 227-230
Attitude accessibility, 211-215
  and manner of attitude formation, 220-224
  measuring, 215
  and strength of object-evaluation association, 215-218
Attitude-behavior consistency, 204
  and automatic attitude activation, 224-230
  automatic vs. controlled processing models of, 236-238
  benefits of present model of, 233
  and definition of situation and event, 207-208
  effect of attitude formation on, 218-224
  effect of norms on, 210-211
  effect of prior related behavior on, 218-220

historical overview of, 205-206
and object-evaluation consistency, 215-218
other factors effecting, 223-224
and perceptions, 208-210
process model of, 207-215
role of attitude accessibility in, 211-218, 220-224
role of selective perceptions, 230-232
and successful categorization, 234-235
Attitude formation, and attitude-behavior consistency, 218-220, 226-227
Attitudes
and behavior recall, 127-129, 132-133
changes in, 125, 126-131
effect of attitude scales on, 220
effects on perception, 208-210
factors effecting anticipatory changes in, 154
false perceptions of temporal consistency of, 128-129
as object-evaluation associations, 218
tricomponent view of, 204
Attitudinal expression, effect on attitude accessibility, 216-217, 222, 224-227
Attributes
in categorization process, 171-175
and self-evaluation, 23-24
as source of value, 317
Attributional theory, of motivation, 292-294
and attribute-linked affect, 300-306
and outcome-dependent affects, 297-299
Audience. *See* Evaluative audience
Authoritarians
personality traits of, 380, 381, 382, 400-401
and self-concept discrepancies, 47-48
and standard utilization, 46
Autobiographical reference points, 27-28, 46
Autochthonous generators, of affect, 246
Autonomic-arousal component, of affective response, 267-268
Availability heuristic, in inference, 470
Avoidance-avoidance conflicts, 539
Avoidance behaviors, 213
Awareness, and information processing, 268-270
Awareness issue, in self evaluation maintenance, 459-460

Base rate information, and judgmental modes, 477-481, 485-487
Beck Depression Inventory, 31
Behavioral consummation, of action tendencies, 417, 418-420
Behavioral differences, and dispositional names, 65
Behavioral intention component, of attitudes, 204
Behavioral reactions, to evaluation and self enhancement perspective, 331-332

Behavioral system, value in, 321. *See also* Self system
Behaviorism
attitude toward mental processes, 284
historical perspective on, 4-5
Behavior recall, relationship with attitudes, 127-129, 132-133. *See also* Recall
Best-case outcomes, and possible self selection, 110-111, 112-114
Bias
in information processing, 270
self-serving, 350-351
Blatt Depressive Experiences Questionnaire, 31, 44, 53

Catastatic mode of action control, 425
Categorization
as communication function, 70, 71
of individual differences, 68-69 (*see also* Dispositional names)
and meaning of stimulus, 250-255
and paradigmatic orientation, 474-475
role of affect in, 263
of stimulus, 250-255
Categorization processes, social, 168
and attitude-behavior consistency, 234-235
basic model, 170-175
and complexity, 189-190
and configural processing, 175-176
defined, 170
descriptive vs. evaluation consistency in, 185-186
in group decision-making, 195-197
in other social judgment models, 177-179
subtyping in, 176
successful, and category-based affect, 180-181
validity of, 525
Category accessibility, 6
and motivation, 505-506
and personal values, 507-508
Category-based interpersonal responses, 174-175
and complexity of stimulus, 189-190
effect of knowledge on, 190-191
effect of set size on, 184-185
efficiency of, 181-183
and modality and reciprocity, 187-188
vs. noncategorical configural processing, 175-176
in other social judgment models, 177-179
overlap with piecemeal processes, 177
and significance of outcome, 191
and successful categorization, 180-181
and time pressure, 190
See also Evaluative impressions
Category label, in categorization, 171-175
Causal attribution, in self evaluation, 33-34
and interpretation stage, 37
interrelationship with other stages, 41-44

Causal dimensions, in attributional theory, 293-294, 296
 and anger and pity, 302-306
 and happiness, 299-300
 and pride, 300-302
Causal reasoning, in high order judgment, 527-529
Causal thinking
 vs. certainty orientation, 379-380
 function of, 292-293
Certainty of orientation, 380
 and achievement behavior, 386-390
 as information value, 382
 and self-assessment, 394
 and self-concept discrepancies, 395-396
 and social comparison, 394-395
 See also Uncertainty orientation
Certainty-oriented person, 400-401
Change
 in action identification, 568-570 (see also Action emergence)
 in self-system, 322-323
 See also Dynamic change; Personal change
Chicago Alcohol Treatment Center, 560
Child rearing, and action identification, 563-565
Children
 mental development of, 149
 self-evaluation orientation for, 27
Choice. See Decision-making
Clarity, and attitude accessibility, 223
Close-minded person, 380
Closeness of others
 and comparison process, 438-439
 impact of, on affecting their performance, 441-444, 453
 impact on measures of self-definition, 448-452, 456-457
 impact of quality and relevance of performance on, 444-448, 454
 and reflection process, 437-439
Cognition
 historical perspective on, 4-5
 hot and cold, 5-8
 impact of affect on, 259-264
 interaction with affect in complex situations, 271-273
 social dimensions of, 465-469 (see also Inference, goal-guided)
 and theories of motivation, 284-285
 See also Categorization; Information processes
Cognition-emotion process, 296-297
Cognitive component, of attitudes, 204
Cognitive consistency theory, 325
Cognitive goals, 466-467
Cognitive mastery, as motive force, 284
Cognitive processes, compared with other processes, 405-409
Cognitive Psychology (Neisser), 5

Cognitive Psychology and Its Implications (Andersen), 6-7
Cognitive simulations, in goal setting process, 110
Collective achievement, 148
 importance of, 160
 situational determinants of, 153-154
 See also Achievement motivation
Collective self
 and deindividualization, 151
 ego tasks of, 147, 148, 149-150, 151
 and identification, 150, 159, 160
 situational determinants engaging, 153-154
 and social accreditation, 152
 varying predispositions for engaging, 155-156
Collective self-esteem, 158
Communication axioms, 529-530
Communication process
 effect on beliefs and attitudes, 530-531
 structural context determinants of orientation in, 487-488
Communicative function, of dispositional names, 70, 71, 73
Comparison, in self-evaluation maintenance, 334-335, 438-439
Comparison reference groups, 30
Comparison with standard, of stimulus, 154-155
Compensatory self-enhancement, 333
Competitive action, and emergent identification, 573
Completion of plan, affective response to, 532-537
Complexity
 as action maintenance indicator, 558
 affective response to, 189-190
Compliance, in social influence, 150, 159-160
Comprehension, as social goal, 527-529
Conditioned response
 and environmental press, 67
 in information processing, 247
Confidence
 and attitude accessibility, 223
 in attributes, 327
Confidence ratings, study of, 84-85
Configural model, of interpersonal response, 168-169
 non-categorical, 175-176
Conflict-based information processing, 269
Conflicts, affective reactions to goal, 538-540
Conformity
 in ego development, 149
 in ego-task orientation, 152-153
Congruent items, recall of, 516
Conscience, 30
Conscientious stage, of ego development, 149
Conscious experience, and motivation theories, 285
Conscious motive, in action identification, 552

Consciousness, motivational significance of, 421-424
Consistency
attitude-behavior, 204-206 (*see also* Attitude-behavior consistency)
in attitude recall, 127-133
and Bem's self-perception theory, 132-133
descriptive vs. evaluative, in categorization, 185-186
and dissonance theory, 131-132
and ego-task orientation, 155-156
implicit theories on, and recall, 124-126
and impression management, 132
Consistency view, of self-evaluation, 436
Construct accessibility, individual differences in, 3, 391, 392, 393
Consumer preferences, 192-194
Consummatory tendencies. *See* Behavioral consummation
Context
and activation of moral standards, 255
in attitude-behavior consistency, 208
effect on affective responses, 175-176
effect on evaluation process, 29
effect on inference, 467-468
effect on recruitment of positive selves, 108-111, 117
and higher level action identification, 554
Context component, of action-related memory structures, 416
Context sensitivity, in inference, 467-468, 481
and narrative orientation, 474
Contextual cues, and category accessibility, 251
Contextual variability, in standard utilization, 50-55
Controllability, as causal dimension, 293-294
and anger and pity, 302-306
Controlled attitude activation, vs. automatic processes, 236-238
Cooperative action, and emergent identification, 573
Credibility, and consistency, 132
Cues
in attitude activation, 213
and category accessibility, 251
selective processing of, 260-261
Cultural value, 319
Cumulative instigation, of action tendencies, 417, 418-420
Curiosity motive, in achievement behavior, 384
Current concerns, 506
Current self-concept, 103-104

Decision-making, 405
expectancy-value models in, 409-410
group, 195-197
and propositional network model of action-related knowledge, 410-417

rational, 421
role of affect in, 264
Declarative knowledge structures, 412-413, 504
Defense, and information processing, 269
Defensive pessimist, achievement strategies of, 112-114
Deindividualization, 151
Deliberativeness, of inference, 466-467
Dependency motive, and uncertainty, 381
Depressed individuals
action-related memory structures of, 416-417
aspiration levels of, 44
self-concepts of, 102-103, 110
and self-evaluation maintenance, 436-437, 526
Descriptive consistency, in successful categorization, 185-186
Diagnostic tasks
and ability, 355-356, 358-359, 364-365
and reduction of uncertainty, 365
and success-oriented people, 384
Difficulty, as action maintenance indicator, 558
Difficulty value, 319
Diffuse self
and deindividualization, 151
ego tasks of, 147-148, 149
situational determinants engaging, 153
Dilution effect, in stereotyping, 494
Direction, of source of value, 317
Discrepant selves. *See* Self-discrepancy
Dispositional terms
actors vs. observers use of, 73-74
assumptions about, 70-73
as behavioral referents, 70-71, 89
as communication function, 70, 71, 73
and self-knowledge, 70, 71, 72
and self-perception theory in ascribing, 89-93
societal origins of, 64-70
and static orientation, 74-76
See also Static orientation
Dispositions
effect on attitude accessibility, 221
effect of, on perceptual processes, 508
and ego-task orientation, 155-156
recalling changes in, 125
Dissonance theory
of attitude consistency, 131-132
and self-improvement programs, 137-138
Distortion
nondepressive, 437
in self-evaluation maintenance, 458-459
Domains of self, 30-32
Dreams, and current concerns, 506
Duration, as action maintenance indicator, 558
Drive theory, precision of, 287

Dynamic change, 405, 417-418
  and cumulation effects, 418-420
  moderating role of consciousness in, 421-424
  and perseverance, 418-420
Dynamic fit, 65
Dynamic orientation, 65-66, 68
  aspects involved in, 69-70, 79
  developmental variables in, 80-81
  and dispositional terms, 68-69, 70-73
  and environmental press, 66-68, 74
  factors effecting, 86-87
  psychological characteristics of, 76-77
  and variations in press, 83-85
  See also Static orientation
Dynamics of Action, The (Atkinson, Birch), 285
Dynamics-of-action theory, 366
Dynamic self-concept, 323

Effort. *See* Action control
Effort expenditure
  and affective value of outcome, 354
  and self-serving biases, 351
Ego-defensive mechanisms, 526-527
Ego-ideal, 25, 30
Ego-involvement
  in confidence testing, 84-85
  and performance context, 67
  three conceptions of, 145-146
Egoistic drift, 256
Ego-task analysis, 145-147
Ego-task goals, 145-147
  collective achievement, 160
  and conformity, 152-153
  and facets of social influence, 150-151
  individual differences in, 155-156
  and motivational facets of self, 147-151
  and self-esteem, 158
  self-presentation, 156-157
  situational determinants of, 153-154
  strategies for achieving, 151-156
Ego-task orientation, 152-156
Egotistical identification, and action emergence, 572-574
Elemental model, of interpersonal responses, 168-169
Emotion
  attributional approach to, 294-297
  attribution linked, 300-306
  -cognition process, 296-297
  defined, 295
  and goal expectancy, 309-310
  impact on recall, 133-135
  importance of, in motivation theories, 286
  as motivator, 306-309
  outcome dependent, 297-299
  pleasure-pain principle of, 283-284
  role of, in action, 306-309
  See also Affect; Affective responses

Emotional consequences, in self-evaluation, 32-34, 56
  and causal attributes, 42-44
  of contextual variability of standard utilization, 50-55
  in general appraisal stage, 38-39
  in identification stage, 35-36
  in interpretation stage, 36-38
  and multiple acquired guides, 39
  self-discrepancies, 23, 31-32
  in stimulus representation stage, 34-35
  and tolerance for self-discrepancies, 47-48
Emotional processes, comparison with other processes, 405-409
Emotion control, in action control, 427
Emotions Questionnaire, 31
Empathetic affective responses, 255-256
Empathy orientation, 482-484
Enactment, of action tendencies, 425-426
Encoding control, in action control, 427
Encoding and organization processes
  about single persons, 510-511
  around several people, 511-515
  conscious control in, 520
  and effect of goals on recall, 509
  evaluative themes in, 511
  and retrieval processes, 516, 518
  trait-behavior associations, 510-511
  See also Information processes
Environmental control, in action control, 428
Environmental orientation. *See* Dynamic orientation; Static orientation
Environmental press, 66-68
  effects of variations in, 83-85
  and static orientation, 75-76, 79
  See also Dynamic orientation
Episodic decision-making, 421
Erhard Seminar Training, 135
Esteem income, 328, 329. *See also* Affective value
Esteem-related affect
  and achievement behavior, 354-355
  and internal attribution, 353-354
  and probability of success, 352-353
  See also Self-esteem
Esteem-related utility, of achievement tasks, 357-358
Evaluation. *See* Self-evaluation
Evaluation apprehension, and ego-involvement, 145-146
Evaluation-object associations, and attitude accessibility, 215-218
Evaluative audiences, 145
  effect on ego-task orientation, 152-153
  other classes of, 161
  in self-presentations, 156-157
  See also Collective self; Diffuse self; Private self; Public self
Evaluative consistency, and successful categorization, 185-186

Evaluative impressions, 168
  basic model of, 170-175
  category-based vs. piecemeal mode of,
    174-175, 177
  and category cuing, 187
  configural vs. elemental model of, 168-169
  consumer preferences, 192-194
  and evaluative consistency, 185-186
  and group decision-making, 195-197
  noncategorical configural processing in,
    175-176
  and political cognitions, 194-195
  stereotyping, 191-192
  types of piecemeal, 176
  See also Affective responses; Category-
    based interpersonal responses
Evaluative standards. *See* Standards
Evaluative themes, in information processing,
  511
Event, definition of, and attitude-behavior
  consistency, 207-208
Examination, in determining behavior, 107-
  108
Expectancy-value theory, 309, 319, 325
  limitations of, 409-410, 412
Expectational structures, in action-related
  memory, 414
Experience, and attitude-behavior consistency,
  219, 220-221, 224-227, 233
Experimental realism, 159
Explanation, in attributional analyses, 293
Expressive goals, 466, 467
Extralinguistic contexts, as reference point in
  evaluation, 28-29
Extrinsic value, 319

Facial expression, affective responses to,
  247-248
Factual points of reference, in self-evaluation
  25-29
  effect of contextual variability on, 50-55
  in general appraisal stage, 38
  individual differences in use of, 45-48
  in interpretation stage, 36-37, 39
  and self-esteem, 45
  See also Standard utilization
Failure
  diagnostic value of, to task attractiveness,
    368-369
  internal and external attributions, 350-354
  perceived cause of achievement, 294
  subjective asymmetries between success and,
    372-373
Failure anxiety, and static orientation, 83
Failure-threatened people
  and diagnosticity, 384-385
  and task difficulty, 386
Familiarity, as action maintenance indicator,
  558
Faulty computer perspective, 6-8

Fear-of-failure motives, 112
Flexibility
  in life tasks, 99
  of working self-concept, 104
Flow experience, 65. *See also* Dynamic
  orientation
Force of resistance, 418
Forgetting, and dissonance, 131, 132. *See also*
  Memory; Recall
Function, and categorization, 250
Fundamental attribution error, 466
  in social inference, 492-493
Future goal orientation, 388
  in inferential selectivity, 472
Future self-image, 327
Future selves, 103. *See also* Possible selves

Galileian mode, of thinking, 69
General appraisal, in self-evaluation, 35,
  38-39, 41
  interrelationship with other stages, 41-44
Gestalt principles, in evaluative impressions,
  168
Gestalt type people, 380, 381, 382, 400
Global motives, 97, 100, 117
  effect of possible selves on, 99, 107
Goal attainment
  and causal search, 293
  expectancy of, 309
Goal-directed behavior
  affective reactions to conflicts in, 538-540
  and affective reactions to interruption or
    completion of plans, 532-537
  consequences of affective states on, 540-541
  effect on attention and perception, 505-508
  effect on encoding and organization
    processes, 509-515
  effect on high order judgment, 525-529
  effect on response selection, 529-531
  effect on storage and retrieval processes,
    515-525
  effect of values on, 507-508
  types of affective reactions resulting from,
    537-538
Goal-guided inference. *See* Inference, goal-
  guided
Goal orientations
  effects on inference and recall, 481-485
  narrative and paradigmatic, 473-477
Goal-oriented instrumental behavior, and
  motivation, 283
Goal-relevance, of standards, 51-52
Goals, ego-task. *See* Ego-task goals
Group composition, effect on self-evaluation, 52
Group decision-making, 195-197
Group pressure. *See* Reference group pressure.

Happiness, as outcome dependent, 297-299
Hedonism
  and diffuse self, 147-148, 149

Hedonism *(cont.)*
and high order judgment, 526
in motivational theories, 283-284
Heuristic judgments, 470
High achiever, acquired guides of, 49-50
High order judgment processes. *See* Judgment processes
High self-esteem individuals
and compensatory self-enhancement, 333
standard utilization of, 44-48
See also Self-esteem
Historical approach, of motivation theory, 289-290
Homeostatic principle, in motivation theory, 281-283
Hopkins Symptom Checklist, 31
Human potential. *See* Possible selves
Human potential orientation. *See* Static orientation

Ideal guides, for behavior, 30-32
Ideal/other guide, and achievement motivation, 49
Ideal/own guide, 31
and achievement motivation, 49-50
Ideal/peers guide, 51
Ideal self, 30, 327
Ideal social self, 25, 30
Identification
in evaluation process, 35-36, 41
interrelationship with other evaluative stages, 41-42
in social influence, 150, 159-160
Identity, and deindividualization, 151
Identity assumption, in information processing, 421
Identity crisis, 325
Ideomotor action, 557
Idiographic approach, to social behavior, 475
Illusion of control, 471
Imagined possibilities, 25, 26, 36-37
in general appraisal stage, 38
Imagined stimulus, affective responses to, 256-257
Impression formation, 466
inferential effects of, 482-484
and irrelevant experience bias, 471
and recall, 509-515
and salience, 471
and trait-behavior associations, 510-511
See also Evaluative impressions
Impression management
and attitude consistency, 132, 155
and ego-task orientation, 155, 156, 158
Impulsive action, 574-578
Incongruent items, recall of, 516
Independence. *See* Individual achievement
Individual achievement
in ego-task orientation, 152-153, 156
and private self-esteem, 158

situational determinants of, 153-154
See also Achievement orientation
Individual differences
in achievement motivation, 361-362, 371-372, 397
in action-related knowledge, 414
in construct accessibility, 391, 392, 393
and resolving uncertainty, 381
Individualistic approach, to judgment determination, 472-473
Individuality, and self-knowledge, 97
Inference, goal-guided, 469-473
action-linked, 468-469, 489-490
conflicts in, 491-492
context-embeddedness of, 467-468
and contingent situation determinants of judgment mode, 477-485
effects of goal orientations on, 481-485
and enduring determinants of judgment mode, 485-489
fundamental attribution error in, 492-493
goal-guided selectivity in, 472-473
narrative and paradigmatic orientations in, 473-477
purposive and deliberate nature of, 466-467
reactive selectivity in, 469-472
sociocultural context determinants in, 488-489
Inferential processing, in self-evaluation, 35
in identification stage, 36
Inferring causality, of stimulus, 253-254
Informational processes
and dynamic principles, 421-424
vs. self-serving biases, 350-351
See also Encoding and organization processes; Judgment processes; Storage and retrieval processes
Information-processing approach, to motivation, 404-405
conscious vs. unconscious, 421-424
expectancy-value models, 409-410
maintenance and enactment of intentions, 424-428
propositional network model of action-related knowledge, 410-417
self-regulatory abilities, 426-428
Information processing modes
imagined stimulus, 256-257
impact of affect on, 259-264
interplay among, 264-271
match between stimulus and schema, 248-250
meaning of stimulus, 250-255
positive bias of, 270-271
role taking, 255-256
selective, 260-261
semantic interpretation of stimulus, 257-259
sequential operation of, 265-267

stimulus event, 246-248
unconscious, 268-270
Information seeking, as achievement motive, 384
Information-seeking orientation, inferential effects of, 483
Information values, 318
vs. affective values in achievement motivation, 14-15, 386-390
in self-confirmation, 339-340
in self-system, 322
uncertainty orientation as, 382-383
See also Values
Inhibitory tendencies, 418, 419
Instigating force, in action tendencies, 417
Instinct, as motivational force, 4
Instrumental value, 319
Intelligent action, 578-580
Intentional propositions, in action-related memory structures, 412-413, 427
Intentional states, maintenance and enactment of, 424-428
Interindividual organizational processes, 513
Internal attribution, and esteemed-related success, 352-353
Internalization
vs. deindividualization, 151
in social influence, 150, 159-160
Interpersonal affect, 168. *See also* Evaluative impressions
Interpersonal closeness. *See* Closeness of others
Interpersonal information processing, 465, 466. *See also* Goal-directed behavior; Inference, goal-guided
Interpersonally significant standards, in self-evaluation, 46-47, 48
Interpretation, in attitude-behavior process, 208-210
Interpretation, in self-evaluation, 35, 36-38, 41
interrelationship with other stages, 41-43
and self-esteem, 44-45, 50
Interruption of plan, affective responses to, 532-537
Intraindividual organizational processes, 513
Intrapsychic factors, in perception, 505
Intrinsic value, 319
Irrational actions, 290

Judgmental stages, in self-evaluation, 33-34
causal attribution, 34
general appraisal, 38-39
identification, 35-36
interpretation, 36-38
interrelation among different, 41-44
stimulus representation, 34-35
See also Self-evaluation
Judgment process, high order, 525

comprehension and causal reasoning, 527-529
response selection strategies, 529-531
role of hedonic relevance in, 526-527
See also Information processing
Judgment orientation
contingent situational determinants of, 477-485
enduring determinants of, 485-489
See also Inference, goal-guided
Judgments
correlation between recall and, 522-525
role of "work space" in, 521-522

Knowledge
declarative vs. procedural, 504
effect on affective response, 190-191
self-, and dynamic orientation, 70, 71, 72

Learned helplessness, 472
Learning goals, role in inference and recall, 481-485
Learning time, as action maintenance indicator, 558
Lifestyle choices, decision strategies in, 114-117. *See also* Affiliative motivation
Life tasks, 97-101
during transition periods, 105-107
individual strategies for approaching, 109-117
Linguistic contexts, as reference point in evaluation, 28-29
Locus, as causal dimension, 293-294
and pride, 300-302
Logical statement analysis, in expectancy-value models, 410
Long-term memory, 520
and active reconstruction, 123
See also Memory; Recall
Low achievers, acquired guides of, 49-50
Low self-esteem individuals
and self-handicapping, 333
standard utilization of, 44-48
See also Self-esteem

Machine intelligence, vs. human intelligence, 579-580
Material self, recalling changes in, 124
Meaningfulness, in evaluation process, 56
Meaningful other, and possible selves, 99
Meaningful other reference points, in self-evaluation, 27, 32, 50
and self-esteem, 52
Means, in action identification, 552
Meier Art Judgment Test, 441
Memory
action-related, 410-414
affectively charged, 244
attitude activation, 212-214

Memory *(cont.)*
  object-evaluation association and
    accessibility of, 215-218
  propositional structures, 410-414
Memory retrieval, 168
  basic model of, 170-175
  in other social judgment models, 177-179
  See also Recall
Memory-set conditions, and informational
    recall, 509-515
Mere exposure effects, 249-250
Metastatic mode, of action control, 425
Mimicry, 247-248
Mirrors, and individual-achievement tasks,
    154
Moderates, behavior of, 381
Mood-congruent information, 262, 270-271
Moods, impact on recall, 133-135
Moral judgment, orientation of, 494-495
Moral standards, 254-255
Motivation
  and attribution-linked affect, 300-306
  attributional theory of, 292-294
  and cognition-emotion process, 296-297
  effect of possible self selection on, 109-111
  historical perspective on, 4-5
  impact of values on, 316-317
  and life tasks, 97-101
  as multiplicative function, 319-320
  and nonattributional thoughts, 309-310
  and outcome-dependent affects, 297-299
  role of emotion in, 306-309
  and self-system, 322, 326
  and time-linked sources of value, 103
  See also Achievement motivation
Motivational bias, in information processing,
    270
Motivational standards, in self-evaluation, 25
Motivation of Behavior, The (Brown), 285
Motivation control, in action control, 427-
    428
Motivation and Emotion, 286
Motivation processes
  action control, 424-428
  comparison with other processes, 405-409
  decision-making, 409-417
  dynamic change, 417-424
  information-processing approach to, 404-
    405
  subconscious vs. conscious, 421-424
Motivation theories, 291-292
  attributional, 292-294
  based on general laws, 288-289
  breadth and precision in, 287
  and concept of self, 285-286
  concern for conscious experience, 285
  hedonistic principle in, 283-284
  homeostatic principle in, 281-283
  and importance of achievement strivings
    and affiliative goals, 291
  importance of cognitive processes in,
    284-285
  importance of emotions in, 286
  need for empirically reliable, 287-288
  and rational and irrational actions, 290-291
  sequential causal relationships in, 289-290
Multiple acquired guides, 39
Multiple-conflict situations, 539-540
Multiple selves, 102-103
Multiplicative function, of motivation, 319-
    320

n-achievement, 3, 15-17
Narrative mode, of goal-guided inference
  action format of, 489-490
  and conflict, 491-492
  description of, 473-477
  and fundamental attribution error, 492-493
  and moral judgment, 494-495
  and reduction of stereotypes, 494
  and specific learning goals, 481-485
  and use of base rate information, 477-481,
    485-487
Need, biasing effect of, 350
Negative affects, to self-evaluation
    maintenance, 461-462
Negative evaluation, 436
Negative self-image, 323-324
Nomothetic approach, to social behavior, 475
Noncategorical configural processing, 175-
    176
Normative standards, in self-evaluation, 30
Norms
  effect on attitude-behavior consistency,
    210-211
  and self-evaluation, 25
Novelty, preference for, 249
n-uncertainty, 382

Object appraisal, and attitude, 209-210
Object-evaluation association
  and attitude accessibility, 215-218, 223-
    224
  and attitude activation, 226-227
Objective self-awareness, and standard
    utilization, 46
Object permanence, and affective responses,
    248-250
Observers, dispositional terms employed by,
    73-74
Open and Closed Mind, The (Rokeach), 380
Open-minded person, 380
Optimist, achievement strategies of, 112-114
Organizational processes. *See* Encoding and
    organization processes
Others. *See* Closeness of others; Meaningful
    others; Significant others
Other standpoint acquired guide, 30-32, 33
  and changes in context, 53

Ought/boss guide, 51
Ought guides, for behavior, 30-32
Ought/other guide, and achievement motivation, 49-50
Ought selves, and possible selves, 99
Ought/teacher guides, 51
Outcome of action, and value in behavioral systems, 321
Outcome diagnosticity
  and ability, 355-356, 364
  and prior uncertainty regarding abilities, 370-371
  and probability of success and failure, 368-370
  in self-assessment, 363-364, 366
  subjective asymmetries between success and failure, 372-373
Outcome, situational
  and causal search, 292-293
  and happiness, 297-299
  and uncertainty orientation, 381
  and values, 317
  See also Performance outcomes
Own standpoint acquired guides, 30-32
  and changes in context, 53

Paradigmatic mode, of goal-guided inference
  description of, 473-477
  and fundamental attribution error, 492-493
  and moral judgment, 494-495
  and specific learning goals, 482-485
  and use of base rate information, 477-479, 485-487
Paralinguistic features, of verbal messages, 247
Parsimony of information processing, in action control, 428
Past, factors effecting recall of, 122-126. See also Recall
Past performance, and self-evaluation, 25, 27-28
Past selves, 103, 108. See also Possible selves
People, types of, 380-381
Perceived competence
  and self-confidence, 328
  and task choice, 366
Perceived difficulty, and achievement motive, 380
Perceived possession, of attribute, 327
Perceptions, in attitude-behavior process
  immediate, 208-210
  selective, 230-232
  of situation and event, 207-208
Perceptual defense, 269
Perceptual processes, 504
  effect of category accessibility on, 505, 506
  effect of current concerns on, 506-507
  effects of values on, 507-508

influence of chronic personality dispositions on, 508
Perceptual readiness, 6
Perceptual standards, in self-evaluation, 25
Perceptual tuning, 427
Performance
  vs. achievement motivation, 87-88
  and dynamic orientation, 70
  effect of previous outcome on, 367-368
  effect of self-concern on, 83
  and self-evaluation, 23-24
Performance deficits, and action identification errors, 565-566
Performance of others
  and comparison process, 438-439
  impact of closeness and relevance on affecting, 441-444, 453
  impact of, on interpersonal closeness, 444-448, 454
  impact on measure of self-definition, 448-452, 456-457
  and reflection process, 437-439
Performance outcomes
  and assessment of ability, 363
  diagnostic value of, 355-356
  effect on persistence and future performance, 367-368
  and esteem-related affects, 352-353
  and inferences about ability, 354-355
  and uncertainty orientation, 379, 381, 391
  See also Outcomes
Performance strategies
  in achievement tasks, 111-114
  in affiliative life tasks, 114-117
Perseverance, of action tendencies, 418-420
Persistence
  as aspect of motivation, 407, 417
  effect of previous outcome on, 367-368
  and esteem-related affect, 353
  and self-presentation, 360-361
  and self-serving biases, 351
  See also Dynamic change
Personal change
  and attitude recall, 126-131
  and ego-task orientation, 155-156
  implicit theories of, and recall, 124-126, 135-139
  and life tasks, 98
  potential, 99
  recalling, 123
  relationship with self-concept, 101, 116
  and self-improvement programs, 135-139
Personal goals, 469
Personal identity, and temporal consistency, 122-123
Personal importance, and ego-task orientation, 154
Personality, basic function of, 316, 324
Personality-analysis orientation, inferential effects of, 483

Personal standards. *See* Self-standards
Person perception, research on, 167-169. *See also* Evaluative impressions
Pessimist, achievement strategies of, 112-114
Phenomenal self-identity, 324-325, 326
Physical features
  affective responses to, 246-248
  and categorization, 250
Physical needs, and motivation, 281-282
Piecemeal interpersonal responses, 174-175,181
  algebraic and thoughtful processing, 176
  effect of set size on, 184-185
  and evaluative inconsistency, 185-186
  inefficiency of, 181-183
  in other social judgment models, 177-179
  overlap with configural processing, 177
  See also Category-based interpersonal responses; Evaluative impressions
Pity, and causal controllability, 302-306
Plans, affective responses to interruption and completion of, 532-537
Pleasure-pain principle, 283-284, 292
Political cognitions, 194-195
Positive bias, in information processing, 270-271
Possible selves, 97-101
  current, 103-104
  effect on achievement strategies, 111-114
  feared and desired, 107-109
  and individual differences in motivated behavior, 109-111
  and strategies for affiliative goals, 116-117
Post-information acquisition objectives, 516-519
  influence on control processes, 519-522
Poststorage processing objectives, and recall, 517
Potential, human. *See* Static orientation
Power motives, 96-97
  and life tasks, 98
Pragmatic goals, 466, 467
Predominant life tasks, 98, 106
Pre-information-acquisition objectives, influence on control processes, 519-522
Prepotent act identity, 552
Press, environmental, 66-68
Prestorage processing objectives, and recall, 517
Pride, and causal locus, 300-302
Primary appraisal, in self-evaluation, 38
Priming studies, and context effects, 29
Primitive self, in ego-task analysis, 147-148
Principles of Behavior (Hull), 285
Private responding, and ego-task orientation, 154
Private self
  ego tasks of, 147, 148, 149, 151
  and individual-achievement tasks, 152-153
  and internalization, 150, 159-160
  and self-presentations, 157

  and self-esteem, 158
  situational determinants engaging, 153-154
  varying predispositions for engaging, 155-156
Private self-consciousness, and ego-task orientation, 155
Probability judgments, 470
  and base rate information, 477-479
Problem solving, role of affect in, 264
Procedural knowledge structures, 412, 504
Processing objectives. *See* Goal-directed behavior
Propositional memory structures, 410-414
Prospective identification, of action, 568-570
Psychoanalytical type people, 380, 381, 382, 399
Psychoanalytic theory, generalizability of, 287
Psychological career
  defined, 324-325
  as source of value, 317
Psychological defensiveness, 268-270
  and negative affective value, 323-324
Psychological distance, of source of value, 317-318
Psychological press, 67
Public image management, vs. self-esteem management, 460-461
Public responding, and ego-task orientation, 154
Public self
  and compliance, 150, 159, 160
  ego tasks of, 147, 148-149, 150
  and self-esteem, 158
  and self-presentations, 156-157
  situational determinants engaging, 153-154
  and social accreditation, 152-153
  varying predispositions for engaging, 155-156
Public self-consciousness, and ego-task orientation, 155
Purposiveness, of inference, 466-467

Rational actions, 290
Rational decision-making, 421
Reactance, theory of psychological, 67
Reactive selectivity, in inference, 469-472
Reasoned action theory, of attitude-behavior process, 238
Recall, 122-123
  and Bem's theory of self-perception, 132-133
  correlations between judgment and, 522-525
  effect of goal orientation on, 482-484, 488
  effects of post-information-processing objectives on, 517-519
  efficiency of category-based, 183
  and false perceptions of temporal consistency, 128-129
  impact of affect on, 261-262

impact of attitude changes on, 126-131
impact of emotions on, 133-135
and implicit theories on change and
  stability, 124-126, 135-139
and impression management, 132
influence of processing objectives on, 509
of information around several people,
  511-515
of information about single persons,
  510-511
nature of, 139
and positive bias of processing, 270-271
role of "work space" in, 519-522
and self-improvement programs, 135-139
and theory of dissonance, 131-132
trait-behavior associations, 510-511
See also Memory
Reconstructive memory. *See* Recall
Reference group pressure
and collective achievement, 153-154
and collective self, 148, 149-150, 151-152
and deindividualization, 151
and self-esteem, 158
and self-presentations, 157
Reference group theory, in self-evaluation,
  32-33
Reflection
in action identification, 568
in self-evaluation maintenance, 334-335,
  437-439
Regression model, of attitude-behavior
  consistency, 236
Reified identity, of action, 550-557. *See also*
  Action identification
Rejection, in static orientation, 78
Relevance, in self-evaluation maintenance, 439
impact of, on affecting another's
  performance, 441-444, 453
impact of, on interpersonal closeness,
  444-448, 454
impact of performance and closeness of
  others on, 448-452, 456-457
Relevant other reference points, 27
Representativeness heuristic, in inference, 470
Research paradigms, 330
Resistance, 418
Response selection processes
effect of, on belief and attitude, 530-531
effect of goals on, 529-530
Responsibility, in ego development, 149
Resultant action tendency, 418
Resultant motivation, 338
Retrieval processes. *See* Storage and retrieval
  processes
Retrospective identification, of action, 568-
  570
Risk taking, and uncertainty orientation,
  396-397
Role assignment, effect on judgmental mode,
  477-479

Role-taking, and affective response, 255-
  256

Salience, in impression formation, 471
Schemata
defined, 170
and inference process, 471-472
matching stimulus with affected, 248-250
and memory retrieval, 171-175
role of affect in formation of, 263
self-, 326
See also Categorization processes
Schema-triggered affect. *See* Category-based
  interpersonal responses
Scientology, 135
Script, in act identity structures, 553
Script categories, social, 475
Scripted behavior, 67
Selective processing, 260-261
Self-assessment, 351
of abilities, 362-365
effects of diagnosticity and probability of
  success and failure on, 368-370
and effects of previous outcomes on
  achievement behavior, 367-368
and individual differences, 371-372
instrumental cost and value of, 373-374
and perceived ability of task choice, 366
and prior uncertainty regarding abilities,
  363, 370-371
regulation of, 374-375
and self-handicapping behavior, 366-367
and shifts in level of aspiration, 365-366
and subjective asymmetries between success
  and failure, 372-373
and task choice, 365
theory and research on, 340-343
and uncertainty orientation, 394
Self-awareness, effect on action-related
  structures, 414-415
Self-awareness theory, of attitude-behavior
  consistency, 236-237
Self-concept, 96-97
and affiliative life-task strategies, 114-117
during transition periods, 105-109
dynamic nature of, 101-104
effect on choice of behavioral strategies,
  109-117
and life tasks, 97-101
and motivation, 285-286, 326
multiplicity of, 101-103
and possible selves, 97-101
as process, 326-327
and self-consistency, 336
in self-evaluation, 25 (*see also*
  Autobiographical reference points)
and temporal consistency, 131-132,
  139-140
Self-confirmation, theory and research on,
  338-340, 342-343

Self-consciousness, of public and private facets of self, 155
Self-consistency
    vs. self-enhancement, 331
    of self-structures, 101
    theory and research on, 336-338, 342-343
Self-deception, 158
Self-definition
    action-related measures of, 451-452
    cognitive changes in, 449-451
    See also Relevance, in self-evaluation maintenance
Self-discrepancy, 30-32, 39
    and accessibility of acquired guides, 52
    and achievement motivation, 48-50
    and low self-esteem, 44-45
    relationship with authoritarianism, 47-48
    and uncertainty orientation, 395-396
Self-enhancement, 351
    and ability attribution, 354-358
    and achievement behavior, 352-362
    and causal attribution, 352-354
    effect of diagnosticity and probability of success and failure on, 368-370
    and effect of previous outcomes on achievement behavior, 367-368
    and esteem-related affect, 352-354
    and individual differences, 361-362
    and perceived ability of task choice, 366
    and prior uncertainty regarding abilities, 370-371
    and self-handicapping behavior, 366-367
    self-presentation approach to, 360-361
    subjective asymmetries between success and failure, 372-373
    and task choice, 365
    theory and research on, 331-333, 342-343
Self-esteem
    ability related, 356-357, 359-360
    assessing, 327-328
    effect of meaningful other on, 52
    and ego involvement, 146
    and expected success at ego tasks, 158, 160
    as independent and dependent variable, 328-330
    and locus of causality, 300-302
    measures of, 160
    public vs. private, 158
    and reconstructing past, 140
    standard utilization and, 44-48
Self-esteem maintenance. *See* Self-evaluation maintenance
Self-evaluation, 23-24
    acquired guides for, 30-32
    effect of contextual variability on, 50-55
    effect of individual differences in standard utilization on, 44-48
    and ego involvement, 145
    and ego-task goals, 150
    emotional consequences of, 32-44

factual points of reference for, 25-29
    interrelationship of stages in, 41-44
    judgmental stages in process of, 34-39
    model of, 24
    vs. social evaluation, 57-58
    standards for, 24-25, 32, 145
    See also Evaluative audiences
Self-evaluation maintenance, 435
    awareness issue in, 459-460
    core assumptions of, 435-437
    and distortion, 458-459
    dynamics of, 439-441
    impact of closeness and relevance on affecting another's performance, 441-444, 453
    impact of performance and closeness of others on relevance, 448-452, 456-457
    impact of quality and relevance of performance on interpersonal closeness, 444-448, 454
    and measures of self-definition, 448-452
    vs. public image management, 460-461
    reflection and comparison processes in, 437-439
    systematic nature of, 452-458
    theory and research on, 333-336, 342-343
    threats to, 461-462
Self-focus, vs. static orientation, 81-82, 83
Self-focused awareness theory, and activation of moral standards, 255
Self-fulfilling prophecy, of attitudes, 129, 235
Self-handicapper, achievement strategies of, 112-114
Self-handicapping, 333, 366-377
Self-image
    negative, 323-324
    as source of value, 317
Self-improvement programs, effectiveness of, 135-139
Self-knowledge, and dynamic orientation, 70, 71-72
Self-monitors
    and attitude accessibility, 223
    effect of standard utilization on, 46
    ego-task orientation of, 155-156
Self-perceptions
    and action emergence, 574
    and implicit theories, 124
Self-perception theory, 132-133
    in ascribing dispositions, 89-91
    in attitude accessibility, 221
    on attitude consistency, 132-133
Self-presentation, 156-157
    believability of favorable, 157
    and public self, 148
Self-presentation approach, to achievement behavior, 360-361
Self-regulatory efficiency, 425
    and difficulty of enactment, 425-426
    and self-regulatory abilities, 426-428

Self-serving bias, 350-351
Self-standards
    discrepancies in, 30-32
    effects of using for self-evaluation, 44-48
Self-system, 315, 342
    defining, 320
    evaluative aspect of, 327-330
    information vs. affective value in, 322
    and negative affective value, 323-324
    and psychological career, 324-325
    reevaluating conceptual variables in, 326-327
    stability vs. change in, 322-323
    structure vs. process approach to, 326-327
    value in, 321-322
Selves Questionnaire, 31
Semantic interpretation, of stimulus, 257-259
    unconscious, 268-269
Semantic memory, as propositional structure, 410-414
Short-term memory, 519-522
Side effect, in action identification, 552
Significant other reference points, 27, 46
    changes in, 50-51, 53
    of public self, 148
Situation, definition of, and attitude-behavior consistency, 207-208
Skinnerian psychology, popularity of, 287
Social acceptability, and public self, 149
Social acceptance, as dominant motivation, 291
Social accreditation
    and ego-task orientation, 153
    and public self, 148, 156
    and self-esteem, 158
Social affect. *See* Affective responses
Social approval, effect on communication, 530
Social categories, 167. *See also* Categorization processes
Social category reference points, 26-27, 33
    vs. social context reference points, 29
Social comparison
    in self-evaluation, 32, 50
    and uncertainty orientation, 394-395
    See also Meaningful other reference points
Social comparison jealousy, 461
Social context reference points, 28-29
    and contextual variations, 53-54
    of high self-monitors, 46
Social Desirability Scale, 156
Social evaluation
    basic model of, 170-175
    vs. self-evaluation, 57-68
    See also Evaluative impressions; Self-evaluation
Social influence, facets of self in, 150-151, 159-160
Socialization, in ego development, 148, 149-150

Social loafing effect, and ego-task orientation, 154
Social rejection, perceived causes of, 294
Social-relations goals, 488-489
Social relationships, effect on self-evaluation, 333-336
"Sociation," 151
Sociocultural context determinants, of goal-guided inference, 488-489
Sociocultural goals, 469
Spiritual self, 25, 30
    recalling changes in, 124, 125
Stability
    as causal dimension, 293-294
    in self-system, 322-323
    See also Consistency
Standard, comparison of stimulus with, 254-255
Standards, in self-evaluation, 24-25
    acquired guides, 30-32
    factual points of reference, 25-29
    interpersonal significance of, 46-47
    See also Acquired guides; Factual points of reference
Standard utilization, in self-evaluation, 34, 57
    and achievement motivation, 48-50
    and causal attribution, 43
    contextual variability in, 50-55
    during general appraisal stage, 38-39
    during interpretation stage, 36-38, 39
    individual differences in, 44-48
Standpoints on self, 30-32
State orientation, 425-426
Static orientation
    achievement motivation as, 87-88
    developmental variables in, 80-81
    factors effecting, 86-87
    and frequency of self-related thoughts, 82-83
    psychological characteristics of, 78-79
    psychological origins of, 74-76
    vs. self-focused attention, 81-82, 83
    and theory of self-perception, 89-93
    variations in press, 83-85
    See also Dynamic orientation
Stereotyping
    and dilution effect, 494
    study of, in social psychology, 191-192
Stimulus representation, 34-35, 41
    interrelationship with other evaluative stages, 41
Storage and retrieval processes
    correlations between recall and judgment, 522-525
    effect of post-information-acquisition objectives on, 516-519
    and encoding processes, 516-518
    "work space," 519-522
    See also Information processing
Stranger anxiety, 248-249

Strategic propositions, in action-related memory structures, 413-414
Stream of behavior, 417
Subception, 269
Subconscious information processing, vs. conscious, 421-424
Subjective expected utility (SEU) principle, 352-353
  and task outcome, 357
Subjective success
  and achievement motives, 380
  and happiness, 306
Success
  diagnostic value of, to task attractiveness, 368-369
  internal and external attributions. 350-354
  subjective asymmetry between failure and, 372-373
Success-oriented people
  and diagnosticity, 384-385
  and task difficulty, 386
Superego, 25, 30
Symbolic interactionism, 207
Symbolic self-completion, 418

Task attractiveness, and diagnostic values of success and failure, 368-370
Task choice
  and achievement behavior, 358-359
  and assessing ability, 364
  effects of diagnosticity and difficulty on, 365
  and esteem-related affect, 353
  perceived ability and, 366
  and possession of low-probability abilities, 359-360
  and self-presentation, 360-361
  and self-serving biases, 351
  and shifts in levels of aspiration, 365-366
Task difficulty
  and achievement motive differences, 386
  effect on task choice, 365
  and uncertainty orientation, 386-387
Task orientation
  vs. achievement motivation, 87-88
  and dynamic orientation, 65-66, 82-83
  See also Life tasks
Thematic Apperception Test, 15
Thoughtful processing, in evaluative impressions, 176
Time-linked sources of value, in self-concept, 103
Time pressure, affective response to, 190
Trait-behavior associations, in recall, 510-511
Trait names. *See* Dispositional names
Trait-related judgments, ambiguity of, 37

Transference, 273
Transformation, of stimulus, 255-259
Transition periods, 105-109. *See also* Self-concept

Uncertainty orientation
  and achievement behavior, 386-390
  and affective values, 384-385
  cognitive dynamics of, 390-393
  general assumptions regarding, 397-398
  as information value, 382-384
  and risk taking, 396-397
  and self-assessment, 394
  and social comparison, 394-395
  theory of, 380-382
Uncertainty-oriented person, 399-400
Unconditioned response, 246-247
Unconscious drive, in action identification, 552
Unconscious information processing, 268-270
Unconsummated action tendencies, perseverance of, 418
Unexpected outcomes, and causal search, 292
Unitary theory, of cognition, 407

Values
  in behavioral system, 321
  and category accessibility, 507-508
  functional role of, 316-317
  general types of, 318
  and multiplicative function of motivation, 319-320
  and psychological careers, 324-325
  and self-evaluation, 25
  in self-system, 321-324
  sources of, 317
  sunstantive types of, 318-319
  See also Affective values; Information values
Verbal communication, semantic components of, 257-258
Viewpoint, self vs. others, 31
Vigilance, and information processing, 269
Viscerogenic needs, and motivation, 281-283

Wish-related structures, in action-related memory, 414
Words, affective response to, 247
Working self-concept, 103-104
  best- or worst-case focus of, 110-111, 112-114
  effect of context on, 108-109
  See also Self-concept
"Work space," in information processing, 519-522
Worst-case outcomes, and possible self selection, 110-111, 112-114